Readings in Canadian History
Post-Confederation

Readings in Canadian History
Post-Confederation

Sixth Edition

R. Douglas Francis
Donald B. Smith
University of Calgary

NELSON

THOMSON LEARNING

Australia • Canada • Mexico • Singapore • Spain • United Kingdom • United States

NELSON

THOMSON LEARNING

Readings in Canadian History:
Post-Confederation, Sixth Edition
by R. Douglas Francis and Donald B. Smith

Editorial Director and Publisher:
Evelyn Veitch

Acquisitions Editor:
Brad Lambertus

Marketing Manager:
Cara Yarzab

Developmental Editor:
Eliza Marciniak

Production Editor:
Emily Ferguson

Production Coordinator:
Helen Jager Locsin

Creative Director:
Angela Cluer

Interior Design:
Sonya V. Thursby,
Opus House Incorporated

Cover Design:
Peter Papayanakis

Copy Editor:
James Leahy

Composition:
Carolyn Hutchings Sebestyen

Printer:
Transcontinental Printing, Inc.

Canadian Cataloguing in Publication Data

Main entry under title : Readings in Canadian history

6th ed.
Includes bibliographical references and index.
Contents: [v. 1] Pre-Confederation—[v. 2] Post-Confederation.
ISBN 0-7747-3746-8 (v. 1)—
ISBN 0-7747-3747-6 (v. 2).

1. Canada — History. I. Francis, R.D. (R. Douglas), 1944–   II. Smith, Donald B., 1946–

FC164.R42 2001   971
C2001-900611-X   F1026.R42 2001

Permission has been requested and granted to Canadianize, metricate, and impose house style for the articles reproduced in this text.

For more information on the photographs featured on the cover, see pages 113, 471, 321, 43, 281, 377, 19, 257, 345, and 217, or contact the institution or individual listed in the Photo Credits (page 501).

Preface

IN THIS sixth edition of our two-volume *Readings in Canadian History*, as in previous editions, our concern has been to provide a collection of articles suitable for introductory Canadian history tutorials. This has meant selecting topics related to the major issues that are explored in such history courses, and providing valuable readings of a general nature. We have included articles that deal with the various regions of the country and, whenever possible, ones that reflect new research interests among Canadian historians. Consequently, we have changed some of the readings. Unfortunately, because of space limitations, the addition of new articles meant that several worthwhile readings in the fifth edition had to be dropped. This new edition, however, will better meet the needs of introductory students in Canadian history today.

This volume includes two or three selections on each of fifteen topics, thereby affording instructors flexibility in choosing readings. Short introductions to each topic set the readings in a historical context and offer suggestions for further reading. It is our hope that this reader will contribute to increased discussion in tutorials, as well as complement course lectures and, where applicable, textbooks. In particular, *Readings in Canadian History* can be used effectively in conjunction with the textbooks *Origins: Canadian History to Confederation*, 4th ed. (Toronto: Harcourt, 2000), and *Destinies: Canadian History since Confederation*, 4th ed. (Toronto: Harcourt, 2000), both by R. Douglas Francis, Richard Jones, and Donald B. Smith.

Important reference works for students preparing essays and reports on different aspects of Canadian history include: *Dictionary of Canadian Biography*, vols. 1–14, with additional volumes in preparation (Toronto: University of Toronto Press, 1966–   ); *Historical Atlas of Canada*, vols. 1–3 (Toronto: University of Toronto Press, 1987–1993); and the annotated bibliographical guides by M. Brook Taylor, ed., *Canadian History: A Reader's Guide*, vol. 1, *Beginnings to Confederation* (Toronto: University of Toronto Press, 1994); and Doug Owram, ed., *Canadian History: A Reader's Guide*, vol. 2, *Confederation to the Present* (Toronto: University of Toronto Press, 1994).

Acknowledgements

In preparing past editions of the readers, we and the publisher sought advice from a number of Canadian historians. Their comments were generously given and greatly improved the original outlines of the collections. We would like to thank, in particular, Douglas Baldwin, of Acadia University; Robert A. Campbell, of Capilano College; Roger Hall, of the University of Western Ontario; and Brent McIntosh, of the North Island College for their valuable reviews of the fifth edition. Thanks, too, for comments on earlier editions to

Douglas Baldwin, of Acadia University; Olive Dickason, of the University of Alberta; Carol Wilton-Siegel, of York University; John Eagle, of the University of Alberta; Roger Hall, of the University of Western Ontario; Hugh Johnston, of Simon Fraser University; and Wendy Wallace and Paul Whyte, of North Island College. Many other individuals made valuable suggestions; we are indebted to John Belshaw, of the University of the Cariboo; Margaret Conrad, of Acadia University; Beatrice Craig, of the University of Ottawa; Chad Gaffield, of the University of Ottawa; Marcel Martel, of Glendon College, York University; Thomas Socknat, of the University of Toronto; Robert Sweeny, of Memorial University; Duncan McDowell, of Carleton University; and Peter Ward, of the University of British Columbia.

Heartfelt thanks also go to Brad Lambertus, Eliza Marciniak, and Emily Ferguson of Nelson Thomson Learning, for their help and constant encouragement toward the completion of this sixth edition, and to James Leahy, who copy edited the book. Finally, we wish to thank those Canadian historians who consented to let their writings be included in this reader. Their ideas and viewpoints will greatly enrich the study and appreciation of Canadian history among first- and second-year students.

Douglas Francis
Donald Smith
Department of History
University of Calgary

Contents

Topic One

A "National Policy"?

William Cornelius Van Horne's party at Stoney Creek Bridge in May

1894. Van Horne was hired to oversee the construction of the

Canadian Pacific Railway.

IN 1879, John A. Macdonald's Conservative government implemented the National Policy, a policy of tariff protection. It imposed a tariff of more than 17.5 percent on many manufactured goods coming into the country from the United States. The policy, which aimed at stimulating the growth of Canadian industries, seemed to Conservative politicians a logical solution to the problem of a depressed Canadian economy in the mid-1870s. Britain had abandoned the mercantile system of trade with its colonies in the late 1840s in favour of free trade, while the United States had adopted its own highly protectionist policy toward Canada after the abrogation of the Reciprocity Treaty in 1866. Certain Canadian leaders, forced to look within for a solution to their problems, believed that a policy of high protection would foster Canadian industrial growth.

Supporters of the National Policy of tariff protection at the time and since have seen it as part of a broader policy of nation building that included, along with the high tariff, the building of a transcontinental railway and large-scale immigration to the West. The logic went as follows: the railway would promote east–west trade, while the growing population of the West would provide the necessary markets for Canadian manufactured goods and a ready source of raw materials for the growing industries of central Canada. The high tariff would force Canadians to buy Canadian products, thus encouraging industrial growth within the nation. From 1879 to the implementation of the new free trade agreement with the United States in 1989, our economic policy was largely protectionist.

Still, not all Canadians have been advocates of the National Policy. Some have questioned why it was implemented: Was it designed to benefit certain classes or regions at the expense of others? To what extent was the policy truly national? Did Canada survive for more than a century because or in spite of the National Policy?

Historian Craig Brown and economist John Dales take two opposing viewpoints concerning the National Policy. In "The Nationalism of the National Policy," Brown explains the policy's popularity at its inception by showing it in a larger historical and international context. Dales questions the logic of the National Policy in terms of its long-range benefits for Canadians in "Canada's National Policies."

Craig Brown presents his argument in greater detail in *Canada's National Policy, 1883–1900: A Study in Canadian–American Relations* (Princeton: Princeton University Press, 1964). John Dales elaborates on his position in *The Protective Tariff in Canada's Development* (Toronto: University of Toronto Press, 1966). Donald Creighton's works contain the traditional defence of the National Policy; see, for example, *Canada's First Century* (Toronto: Macmillan, 1970). Ben Forster analyzes the events leading up to the adoption of the National Policy in *A Conjunction of Interests: Business, Politics, and Tariffs, 1825–1879* (Toronto: University of Toronto Press, 1986). The negative impact of the National Policy on developments in the hinterlands of the Maritimes and the West can be found in *Canada and the Burden of Unity*, ed. D. Bercuson (Toronto: Macmillan, 1977). T.W. Acheson's "The National Policy and the Industrialization of the Maritimes, 1880–1910," *Acadiensis* 1, 2 (Spring 1972): 3–28, is also of interest. Kenneth Norrie's "The National Policy and Prairie Economic Discrimination, 1870–1930," in *Canadian Papers in Rural History*, ed. Donald Akenson (Gananoque, ON: Langdale Press, 1978), pp. 13–33, questions whether Western farmers had legitimate grievances against the National Policy. Michael Bliss looks at the connection between the National Policy and the spread of American branch plants in

Canada in "Canadianizing American Business: The Roots of the Branch Plant," in *Close to the 49th Parallel etc.: The Americanization of Canada*, ed. I. Lumsden (Toronto: University of Toronto Press, 1970), pp. 26–42. The Fall 1979 issue of the *Journal of Canadian Studies* (vol. 14) is devoted to "The National Policy, 1879–1979."

Article One

The Nationalism of the National Policy

Craig Brown

Debating nationalism is the great Canadian national pastime. Since Confederation it has been the preeminent preoccupation of politicians, journalists, scholars, and plain ordinary citizens. All have wrestled diligently with the problem that Canadian nationalism — if such there be — does not fit any of the classic definitions of nationalism. Common language, religion, and ethnic origin must obviously be rejected. Except for the disciples of Harold Adams Innis, geography provided few satisfactory clues to the Canadian identity. And a common historical tradition, in the words of Mill, "the possession of a national history and consequent community of recollections, collective pride and humiliation, pleasure and regret, connected with the same incidents in the past," raises more questions about a Canadian "nationality" than it answers. There is no great national hero who cut down a maple tree, threw a silver dollar across the St. Lawrence, and then proceeded to lead a revolution and govern the victorious nation wisely and judiciously. There are no great Canadian charters of freedom or independence expressing the collective will of the people. But the search goes on. Historians and retired Governors General laboriously attempt to define "the Canadian identity" or "being Canadian." Many nations have manifested their nationalism through great public acts; Canada has asserted its nationalism by looking for it.

Yet there is abundant evidence that Canadians have both thought and acted like contemporary nationalists in other countries. Much, though by no means all, of the evidence is provided by the politicians.[1] The evidence is mundane, for seldom have Canadian politicians been political theorists or philosophers. Rather, their concerns have been with everyday problems of government. But within this framework their thoughts and acts have been decidedly nationalist in character. A brief look at the men who implemented and carried out the National Policy may serve to illustrate the point.

Writing to a Conservative editor in 1872, Sir John A. Macdonald noted in a postscript that "the paper must go in for a National policy in Tariff matters, and while avoiding the word 'protection' must advocate a readjustment of the tariff in such a manner as incidentally to aid our manufacturing and industrial interest."[2] In this obvious afterthought at the conclusion of a letter devoted to the necessity for finding an appropriate label for Macdonald's party, is the origin of the National Policy. The context is significant. Macdonald was looking for a policy that would attract, at one and the same time, voters and dollars to his party, and the National Policy would do both. The manufacturers would

Source: *Nationalism in Canada*, ed. Peter Russell (Toronto: McGraw-Hill Ryerson, 1966), pp. 155–63. Reprinted by permission of the University League for Social Reform.

contribute to the party war chest and the simplicity of the title and concept of the National Policy would appeal to an electorate looking to fulfill the promise of Confederation. Moreover, as a transcontinental railway, immigration, and opening of the Northwest were added to the tariff as items in the National Policy, it took on a strikingly familiar complexion that added to its political attractiveness. It was in most respects a duplication of a similar "national policy" designed for continental expansion in the United States. It was "a materialistic policy of Bigness"[3] in an age when expansionism appealed to nationalist sentiment. Canadians could take pride in their ability to compete with their neighbours in the conquest of the continent.

The National Policy was equally attractive because a policy of tariff protection meant another step in the long path from colony to nation within the Empire. As early as 1859, Galt argued for protection less on its economic merits than on the grounds that tariff autonomy was implicit in responsible government. Referring to Imperial objections to the Cayley-Galt tariff of that year, the crux of Galt's argument was that "self-government would be utterly annihilated if the views of the Imperial Government were to be preferred to those of the people of Canada."[4] With tariff autonomy not only achieved but emphasized by protection, in 1911 the ardent nationalist John S. Ewart proudly summed up the elements of "Canadian Independence" by pointing first to the fact that "we are fiscally independent." "By that I mean that we make our own tariffs; that we frame them as we wish; that we tax British and other goods as we please; and that neither the Colonial Office nor the British Parliament has any right whatever to interfere."[5]

That the National Policy was politically attractive, is, then, evident. By 1886 the Liberal party had been driven so far into a "me too" position that Blake in essence declared his party's policy to be, to borrow a phrase, the National Policy if necessary, but not necessarily the National Policy. It is true that in 1891, with a new leader and the new policy of Unrestricted Reciprocity with the United States, the Liberals came closer to victory than they had at any time since 1874. But within two years the Liberals had again revised their policy to "freer trade" and in 1897 the Liberal government admitted the futility of attempting to destroy Macdonald's brainchild. "I not only would not retire from the Government because they refused to eliminate the principle of protection from the tariff, but I would not remain in the Government if they did eliminate the principle of protection entirely from the tariff," wrote Clifford Sifton. He added that "the introduction of a tariff from which the principle of protection would be entirely eliminated would be fraught with results that would be most disastrous to the whole Canadian people."[6] In 1911, Sifton and 17 other "revolting" Liberals issued their manifesto against reciprocity, "believing as we do that Canadian nationality is now threatened with a more serious blow than any it has heretofore met with."[7] Robert Borden simply added that "we must decide whether the spirit of Canadianism or of Continentalism shall prevail on the northern half of this continent."[8]

In short, the idea of protection embodied in the tariff became equated with the Canadian nation itself. The National Policy, by stressing that Canadians should no longer be "hewers of wood and drawers of water" for the United States, as Tilley put it, recalled and reinforced that basic impulse of survival as a separate entity on this continent that had been born of the American Revolution, made explicit in Confederation, and remained the primary objective of Canadian nationalists. Protection and the National Policy, then, took on a much larger meaning than mere tinkering with customs schedules.

The same idea was evident in the building of the Canadian Pacific Railway and the opening of the Northwest. The Northwest was the key to the future of both the National Policy and the nation, and an expensive and partially unproductive railway through Canadian territory was the price Canada had to pay to "protect" it from American penetration and absorption. It was to be the great market for Canadian industry and the foundation of a "Canadian economy." Emphasizing that building the railway was "a great national question," Sir Charles Tupper remarked that "under the National Policy that Canada has adopted we must look forward not only to building up thriving centres of industry and enterprises all over this portion of the country, but to obtaining a market for these industries after they have been established; and I say where is there a greater market than that magnificent granary of the North-west?"9 He added that upon the success of the venture "the rapid progress and prosperity of our common country depends."

The United States played an interesting role in the National Policy that emphasized its nationalistic assumptions. Fundamental to the thinking of the framers of the policy was the idea that the United States was much less a friendly neighbour than an aggressive competitor power waiting for a suitable opportunity to fulfill its destiny of the complete conquest of North America. The National Policy was intended to be the first line of defence against American ambitions. And this, I think, is the reason any Canadian alternative to it was unsuccessful. It was the "national" implications of the National Policy that hindered the Liberals in their attempt to formulate an opposition policy before 1896. They could not accept Commercial Union because it meant the total surrender of tariff autonomy. Unrestricted Reciprocity was adopted as a compromise that retained autonomy. But its distinction from Commercial Union was too subtle for much of the electorate to grasp and left the party open to skillful exploitation by Macdonald's "loyalty" cry. More important, the very indefiniteness of what the Liberals meant by Unrestricted Reciprocity caused confusion and disruption in party ranks and eventually led to the revelation that Unrestricted Reciprocity did not mean the complete free interchange of all Canadian and American products after all. Rather, most Liberals simply wanted a more extensive reciprocity agreement with the United States than the Conservatives. Or, to put it another way, the Liberals were only interested in somewhat less protection from American competition than their opponents. W.S. Fielding's budget speech in 1897 had a very familiar ring to Canadian ears: "If our American friends wish to make a treaty with us, we are willing to meet them and treat on fair and equitable terms. If it shall not please them to do that, we shall in one way regret the fact but shall nevertheless go on our way rejoicing, and find other markets to build up the prosperity of Canada independent of the American people."10

Other problems in Canadian–American relations in the latter part of the nineteenth century were related to the nationalism of the National Policy. With the abrogation of the fishery articles of the Treaty of Washington by the United States, Canada was forced to adopt what can properly be called a "protectionist" policy for her inshore fisheries. The fisheries and the commercial privileges extended to Americans by the treaty were considered a national asset by Canadians. The object of their government was to use that asset for the benefit of the whole of Canada, not simply the Maritime provinces. It was for this reason that from 1871 on the fishery question was always related to reciprocity. On each occasion when Canada participated in negotiations the policy was always the same: Canada's exclusive and undoubted rights in the inshore fisheries would be bargained for the free exchange of natural products.

A different and more complex problem was presented by the Bering Sea dispute arising out of the seizure of Canadian pelagic sealers by United States revenue cruisers. The central problem was one of international law involving the doctrines of freedom of the seas and *mare clausum*. And because the Canadian vessels were of British registry, the British government assumed a much more active negotiating role than was the case in some other disputes. But Canadian participation was far from negligible, and Sir Charles Hibbert Tupper and Sir Louis Davies made a point of protecting Canadian interests.

Significantly, they argued that despite the legal technicalities, it was a Canadian industry that was threatened with destruction by the illegal acts of the United States government and that the Mother Country had a clear duty to protect that industry.

The Alaska Boundary question also illustrated the relationship between the National Policy and Canada's relations with the United States. All of the evidence available suggests that the Canadian case was hopelessly weak and members of the Canadian government (Laurier and Sifton) as much as admitted it both privately and in public. Why, then, was the case pressed with such vigour? Part of the answer, it seems to me, is that when the Alaska Boundary question became important for Canadians after the Yukon gold rush began, those responsible for Canadian policy, led by Clifford Sifton, regarded the question less as one of boundary definition than of commercial competition with the United States. Definition of the boundary was important because it was related to control of the growing Yukon trade. The intricate legal details of the boundary dispute were generally ignored by the Canadian government. Writing during the meetings of the joint High Commission in 1898, Lord Herschell complained to Lord Salisbury that "I found that the question had not been thoroughly studied or thought out by any Canadian official."[11] The urgent and ill-considered introduction of the Yukon Railway Bill of 1898 providing for a "Canadian" route to the Yukon—a route which was dependent upon trans-shipment privileges at the American customs port at Fort Wrangel and on navigation rights on the American portion of the Stikine River—illustrates the same point. The "imperative reason for immediate action" was that the Yukon trade was at stake, as the Minister of Railways and Canals explained to the House of Commons: "The importance of securing that trade and preserving it to Canada becomes a national question of the greatest interest. . . . It is ours, it is within our own borders and of right belongs to us, if, by any legitimate or proper means, we can secure it for the people of our own country."[12]

Again, in the negotiations at the joint High Commission of 1898–99 the Canadians insisted that if the boundary question went to arbitration, Pyramid Harbour should be reserved for Canada to match American insistence that Dyea and Skagway be reserved for the United States. While both sides thus rejected an unqualified and impartial arbitration, it must be admitted that Dyea and Skagway were established and settled communities under American control; Canada could make no such claim regarding Pyramid Harbour. Pyramid Harbour, as a Canadian outlet to the sea with a corresponding Canadian land corridor to the interior, had not arisen in negotiations until the meetings of the joint High Commission and, as before, the Canadian claim was based primarily on the desire to secure control of the Yukon trade.

Ultimately, of course, Canadian indignation knew no bounds when Lord Alverstone reportedly suddenly changed his mind and awarded Pearse and Wales Islands to the United States in 1903. The settlement of 1903 was unquestionably diplomatic rather than "judicial." Theodore Roosevelt's pressure tactics before and during the meeting of the so-called "judicial tribunal" were certainly deplorable and these factors, combined with the apparent sacrifice of Canadian interests by Great Britain, have supplied grist for the mills of Canadian nationalists ever since. But too often the emphasis in Canadian historiography on this point has been misplaced by concentrating solely on the alleged British sellout. The more interesting point in all the clamour surrounding the Alaska Boundary decision is that, once again, National Policy interests were considered to be threatened by the decision. Alverstone's agreement with Lodge and Root, that Pearse and Wales Islands belonged to the United States, threatened the Laurier Government's first venture in transcontinental railway building. The projected terminus of the Grand Trunk Pacific, chartered just a few short months before, was Port Simpson on Observatory Inlet; Pearse and Wales Islands, which the Canadians believed could be armed by the United States, commanded the shipping lanes into Port Simpson. Thus, though the Yukon trade had drastically declined in value by 1903, from first serious consideration of the problem to final settlement, the National Policy — an "all Canadian" trade route to the Yukon or a secure terminus for a new Pacific railway — dominated Canadian consideration of the Alaska Boundary dispute.

I have tried to suggest that the National Policy was a manifestation of Canadian national sentiment. Its basic assumptions — protection against the United States, the need for a "Canadian economy" with a strong industrial base and secure markets, and the implicit assumption of achieving greater autonomy within the Empire — all crystallized that ill-defined, but deeply felt, sense of difference that set Canadians apart from both their neighbours to the south and the mother country. But why did this desire to proclaim a national identity take its form in economic terms?

Perhaps a part of the answer rests in the dilemma posed at the beginning of this paper. Appeals to a common language, a common cultural tradition, or a common religion were simply impossible for Canadians, and when they were attempted they were rightly regarded by French Canadians as a violation of their understanding of Confederation. Most Canadians, especially those who built or paid for the building of the transcontinental railways, argued that the Canadian nation would have to be built in spite of its geography and regarded their efforts as "the price of being Canadian." Appeals to national history could also be a divisive rather than a unifying factor for, as often as not, the two ethnic groups disagreed as to what, in their historical tradition, was a matter of pride or of humiliation. What was necessary, then, as Cartier put it in the Confederation debates, was to "form a political nationality." And it is not at all surprising that the political nationalism of the early decades of Confederation was expressed in terms of railways and tariffs.

It is a commonplace to equate the politics of North America in the latter part of the nineteenth century with self-seeking capitalism. But we might remind ourselves that the age of Darwinism and of industrialism was also a great age of nationalism. The nationalism of the large assertive states of the age — the United States, Germany, and Great Britain — was assuredly economic in its emphasis. In the United States, in particular, nationalism was equated with the problems of industrialism and industrial expansion. In keeping with Darwinian assumptions, bigness was a virtue for a nation state, and industrialism was the key to bigness. At the very time their own nation was being born, Canadians reasoned that industrialism was the determining factor in the victory of the North in the Civil War and in the apparent reunification of the United States. Industrialism meant power; power to withstand the pressures from the south and power to expand and consolidate the Canadian nation. And a political programme that emphasized expansion and industrialism had the added advantage of ignoring the potentially divisive issues that would disrupt a "political nationality."

In sum, then, the National Policy, a policy for a "Canadian economy" and a "Big Canada," a materialistic policy for a materialistic age, was the obvious policy to give expression to Canadian national sentiment. That policy was adopted in 1878 and accepted by the Liberal party in 1896. Three years later J.I. Tarte urged Laurier to do more than simply accept the National Policy, to expand upon it with more railways, canals, and harbour improvements (and presumably with higher tariffs). "Voilà," he observed, "le programme le plus national et le plus populaire que nous puissons offrir au pays."[13]

NOTES

1. Carl Berger, "The True North Strong and Free," in *Nationalism in Canada* (Toronto, 1966), 3ff.
2. *Macdonald Papers* (P.A.C.), Macdonald to T.C. Patteson, February 27, 1872.
3. John Dales, "Protection, Immigration and Canadian Nationalism," in *Nationalism in Canada*, 167–70.
4. A.B. Keith, *Selected Speeches and Documents on British Colonial Policy, 1763–1917* (London, 1953), 60.
5. J.S. Ewart, *The Kingdom Papers*, vol. 1 (Ottawa, 1912), 3.
6. *Sifton Papers* (P.A.C.), Sifton to James Fleming, March 13, 1897.
7. *Manifesto of Eighteen Toronto Liberals on Reciprocity*, February 20, 1911; cited, *Canadian Annual Review* (Toronto, 1911), 49.
8. Henry Borden, ed., *Robert Laird Borden: His Memoirs*, vol. 1 (Toronto, 1938), 327.
9. *House of Commons Debates*, April 15, 1880, pp. 1424–25.
10. *House of Commons Debates*, April 22, 1897.
11. Cited in R.C. Brown, *Canada's National Policy, 1883–1900* (Princeton, 1964), 379.
12. *House of Commons Debates*, February 8, 1898, pp. 191–92.
13. *Laurier Papers* (P.A.C.), Tarte to Laurier, April 3, 1899.

Article Two

Canada's National Policies

John Dales

I

To the infant industry argument for protectionism Canadians have added an infant nation argument. Among Canadian academic historians, journalists, and citizens at large there seems to be a dangerous unanimity of opinion that Canada is a transparently artificial entity whose very existence has always depended on something called a national policy. Canada, in this view, is a denial of geography and a travesty of economics that stands as living proof of the primacy of politics in the affairs of men. Critical comment to the effect that most Canadian manufacturers still depend on protective tariffs is very apt to be greeted first by astonishment that anyone would think the comment worth making, and then by patient explanation that of course many parts of the Canadian economy — not only manufacturing — have always depended on government bounty in one form or another, and that Canada simply would not exist as a nation if public support were not continuously made available to key sectors of the economy. Such a policy is necessary, the explanation continues, both in order to overcome the outrageous geography of the country and in order to defend the nation's economy against the formidable efficiency, and thus the natural expansionism, of the American economy. In Canada infant industries are not *expected* to grow up.

Source: The Protective Tariff in Canada's Development (Toronto: University of Toronto Press, 1966), pp. 143–58. Reprinted by permission of University of Toronto Press Incorporated.

I reject this view of Canada. It seems to me to be subversive not only of the nation's wealth but also of the nation's pride. National pride and economic performance I believe to be positively, not negatively, correlated; both efficiency and honour, as the parable of the talents teaches, come from making the most of what one has, not from having the most. And yet Canadian economic policy—and, what is more important, the economic policy of so many developing nations today—aims consistently at maximizing the purse, gross national product, rather than the performance, gross national product per citizen.

Sir John A. Macdonald gave us our first national policy, and our first lessons in the irrelevance of economics. Western lands, he argued, must be controlled by the Dominion because provincial land policies "might be obstructive to immigration," i.e., provinces might actually try to sell land rather than give it away. Canadian railways, in Macdonald's view, were not to be thought of primarily as business enterprises; they were instruments of national development and served this end by providing both attractive objects of government expenditure and reliable sources of party support. As for the tariff, Macdonald rang all the changes on the protectionist fallacies and promised that *his* tariff would benefit everyone, the teachings of the dismal science notwithstanding. Macdonald was the first great Canadian non-economist.

It is hard to believe, though, that Macdonald deserves the whole credit for the low esteem in which economics and economists are held in Canada today. Macdonald has in any event had powerful support from Canadian historians, of both the political and economic persuasions, who have rationalized his national policy and have encouraged Canadians to believe that by disregarding economics they could build a nation that would represent a victory over mere materialism. The national policy originally consisted of government support for three main ventures: railway building, Western settlement, and manufacturing development. (We adopt the original convention of using "national policy" for the famous trinity of Canadian nation-building policies, and of reserving "National Policy" for the protective tariff policy.) The mutual consistency of Western settlement and railway building was perhaps fairly obvious; land grants helped to finance railways, and railway companies encouraged settlement. From an economist's point of view, however, the rationalization has been carried a little far. The government has been praised for using valuable lands as a loss-leader, while the CPR has been praised for selling land to immigrants at prices considerably below those charged by other land owners, and for showing great initiative in developing uneconomic irrigation projects.

What was at first difficult for historians to discover was the consistency between Macdonald's tariff policy and the other two prongs of his national policy. The late Professor H.A. Innis seems to have provided the connecting argument. The role of the tariff in the Canadian economy, he taught, was to inhibit Canadian–American trade, to promote east–west trade in Canada, and in this way to provide revenue for Canadian transcontinental railways. Though I cannot resist a long footnote on the subject, I do not want to make a full textual analysis of Innis's writings in order to try to find out whether he believed that his tariff–railway link was (a) the *ex post* result of the two policies—the way things worked out—or (b) the *ex-ante* design—the way things were intended to work out—or (c) either or both of these combined with the opinion that the link was felicitous.[1] I wish only to suggest that once the Innis link was forged the way was wide open for a full-scale rationalization of the national policy. Thus D.G. Creighton:

> [The tariff] was intimately and vitally related to the other national policies. By means of the tariff, the settlement of the west would provide a national market; and this national market would supply east–west traffic for Canadian transcontinental railways and areas of exploitation for eastern Canadian industry.[2]

And J.B. Brebner:

Looking backward from the present, it is easy to see that the very existence of both the Province and the later Dominion of Canada as entities separate from the United States has depended on such expensive transportation services that a large proportion of their cost has had to be met from the public purse. . . . it was [in the exuberant 1850s] that Canadians . . . began systematically to adopt the *only* procedure by which they could surmount this handicap, that is, the imposition of quite high tariffs on manufactured goods.[3]

W.T. Easterbrook and H.G. Aitken:

[The detailed program of Canadian nation building] appeared slowly and in piecemeal fashion but by 1879 . . . the parts of the comprehensive and more or less complete pattern had fallen into place: a transcontinental railway, protective tariffs, land settlement policy, the promotion of immigration.[4]

And the present author, who providentially has written very little on the subject:

The Dominion immediately proceeded to fulfil its purposes. A transcontinental railway system was constructed, an energetic settlement policy was adapted to the needs of the West, and the tariff was designed to develop Canadian industry and stimulate Canadian trade. These policies proved effective in the period of prosperity which began towards the end of the nineteenth century.[5]

Two features of the historians' stereotype of the national policy should be noted. First, much emphasis is placed on the consistency of the three pillars of the program, while inconsistencies are either ignored or glossed over. Among the authors I have consulted, several mention the regional inconsistency inherent in the policy. V.C. Fowke, in particular, interpreted the national policy as a program designed by and for central Canadians. The national policy is therefore seen not as national at all but rather as a policy of central Canadian imperialism. Fowke comes dangerously close to shattering the whole myth of the national policy, yet in the end he refuses to be an iconoclast. Thus his glosses that the national policy was "prerequisite to western development" and that "the groundwork [for western development] . . . was laid . . . by the institution of the 'National Policy' or tariff protection"[6] seem wildly inconsistent with his main position, particularly in view of his insistence that Macdonald's railway policy was not prerequisite to western development: "As far as the western provinces are concerned . . . Canadian railways are expensive alternatives to American railways rather than to no railways at all."[7] Brebner and Careless both hint at the logical inconsistency inherent in protectionism, namely, the attempt to build a wealthy nation by lowering the standard of living of its population. Thus Careless notes that "A protective tariff plainly meant that goods would cost more to buy in Canada," yet after a token flirtation with this line of reasoning he surrenders to the stereotype on the following page and concludes that "as far as Canada is concerned the protective tariff system that was adopted under Macdonald . . . did much in the long run to develop the wealth and encourage the industry of the Dominion."[8] He then goes on to paint the usual picture of the wonderful consistency among Canada's railway, settlement, and tariff policies.

None of the authors I have examined has flatly challenged the national stereotype of the beneficence of the national policy. W.A. Mackintosh, however, writes very cautiously about this subject. He outlines the "Basic National Decisions" and their interrelations in chapter 2 of his *The Economic Background of Dominion–Provincial Relations*,[9] but adds at the end of the chapter (p. 21): "It is not suggested that these national decisions were taken by governments, or still less by electorates, in full consciousness of their implications, nor that the interrelations among them were fully appreciated. They were in large measure the outcome of conflicts of interest and, to some extent, of political expediency." Later (p. 37) he notes the regional conflicts occasioned by the national policies, and the tendency of these policies to rigidify the economy by creating "vested interests, regional and sectional, which would resist readjustment." Also two other authors, both political historians, have distinguished themselves by refusing to have anything to do with the standard patter. Chester Martin disdains even to mention the tariff in his *Foundations of Canadian Nationhood*;[10] A.R.M. Lower bluntly refers to the National Policy as being a "frank creation of vested manufacturing interests living on the bounty of government," and in exasperation writes that "Macdonald's way of imposing the new tariff was simple: he just invited anyone who wanted a duty to come to Ottawa and ask for it."[11]

The stereotype of the national policy is powerful enough not only to bridge logical inconsistencies but also to abridge time. To its defenders the national policy was both a well-designed and a powerful engine of nation building. Yet it refused to function for some twenty or 30 years. Many authors simply ignore this awkward gap in timing, as I did myself in the quotation above. Others mention it and then ignore it, as for example Easterbrook and Aitken: "The three decades following Confederation seemed to many a prolonged period of marking time. . . . Not until the turn of the century did the program of nation-building begin to pay off" (p. 381). After a long account of the Time of Troubles in both its economic and political aspects, Careless finds himself concluding that "conservative nationalism was played out," and thus in imminent danger of rending the stereotype beyond repair. But he draws back at the very brink of the abyss, and proclaims in strident tones that "Macdonald nationalism had not failed. It was the age that had failed" (p. 295).

Why can we not bring ourselves to say quite simply that the national policy was a dismal failure? Everyone admits, for example, that the land settlement policy was a failure before 1900. After 1900 the demand for western land was so brisk, and the CPR and various land companies so zealous in attracting settlers to the region, that it is hard to believe that the homestead policy was in any sense necessary as a means of settling the West. It was, indeed, probably undesirable. After writing of the efficiency and enterprise of the private land companies, Martin notes that "The general opening of 'Dominion lands,' even- and odd-numbered sections alike, to homestead entry after 1908 brought a deluge of less selective migration to Western Canada. In vain the government had sought to reserve vast areas with marginal rainfall in 'Palliser's triangle' for grazing and other purposes. In the queues which formed up at the land offices prospective settlers, as one observer records, 'held their place in the line day and night for two or three weeks to enable them to file on certain lands,' and places in the queue were frequently bought and sold for 'substantial sums of money.'" Uneconomically low prices inevitably produce queues. No one, I suggest, really believes that without the homestead policy in particular, and the settlement policy in general, the West would not have been settled. These policies were powerless to promote settlement before 1900; after 1900 their chief effect was to promote not settlement but *rapid* settlement, and there is much evidence to suggest that the rapidity of settlement did much short-term and long-term harm in Western Canada. Martin's trenchant criticism of the homestead system certainly permits one to believe that Canada would have been better off without this member of the national policy trilogy.

As with land settlement policy so with tariff policy; the burden of the argument suggests that we would have been much better off still if we had never tangled with the National Policy. Historically, it need only be noted that manufacturing was developing in Canada well before the tariff of 1879; Mackintosh notes that the "Census of 1871 reveals that Canada had made some progress along the path of industrialization," and that "The new protectionist policy intensified, broadly speaking, industrial trends already visible."[12] Moreover, Canadian manufacturing grew less rapidly than American manufacturing both before and after the tariff, and net emigration from Canada was a feature of the decades both before and after 1879. To the extent that the National Policy was intended to reverse, or even to reduce, the disparity in Canadian and American growth rates, it was clearly a failure. After 1900 the Canadian economy, including Canadian manufacturing, grew more rapidly than the American economy for a dozen years, and Canadian historians have not hesitated to attribute this surge to the beneficial, if somewhat delayed, effects of the National Policy. As Careless wrote,[13] it was the "age that had failed" before 1900 and the rise of a prosperous age after 1900 that "spelt success at long last for the National Policy." In Canadian history it is heads the National Policy wins, and tails the age loses.

There remains the curious case of the CPR. While a Canadian transcontinental railway, as Fowke argues, was not prerequisite to western development, economists and political scientists can agree that as a matter of political economy such a railway was an essential adjunct of nationhood for the new Dominion. The railway had to be built for political reasons, whatever the subsidy involved; sensible economic policy required only that the subsidy be kept as low as possible. The CPR was in fact heavily subsidized. Still, given the lacklustre performance of Canadian settlement and tariff policies before the middle 1890s one might have expected, on the basis of the national policy stereotype in general and the Innis link in particular, that the CPR would have been unable to survive its first bleak decade. Surely no one would wish to argue that the population of Western Canada in 1895 (perhaps a third of a million people, an increase of something over 100 000 since the completion of the CPR) was able to supply either enough wheat or a large enough market for manufactured goods to make a paying proposition out of even so heavily subsidized a transcontinental railway as the CPR. Yet the CPR was profitable from the minute it was completed and began to pay dividends on its common stock in 1889. The Wheat Boom that began in the closing years of the century was only the frosting on the cake that allowed the Company to raise dividends from 4 percent in 1897 to 10 percent in 1911, despite large decreases in railway rates around the turn of the century. The chronology of CPR earnings thus raises a nagging doubt about whether the CPR ever *needed* to be subsidized indirectly by the tariff as well as directly by grants of money and a kingdom in land. Professor Fogel's conclusion that the Union Pacific Railway would have been profitable *without* subsidies, despite unanimous opinion, before the fact, that it would not be,[14] suggests a need for testing the hypothesis that the CPR would have been profitable with direct subsidies alone, or even, subversive thought, without *any* subsidy! Careful analysis of this matter seems to be an urgent necessity. The core of the national policy has always been the protective tariff, and although today the tariff is more and more often brazenly defended simply on the grounds that we must protect the vested interests we have built up, the argument of last resort is still that the tariff is the defender of the railways, and thus of the east–west economy. The defence retains its appeal since the railways still carry a great deal of freight, if not many passengers, and the Innis link remains persuasive. If it were possible to deny the validity of the Innis argument that without the tariff there would be no CPR, it would be much more difficult for present-day nationalists to argue that if there were no tariff there would be no Canada.

There are, therefore, reasonable grounds for questioning the validity of the historians' stereotype of the national policy. To stress the consistency of the national policy as an interrelated whole is to ignore all too cavalierly its inconsistencies. And to write as if the wisdom and power of a nation-building program that is ineffective for two or three decades is somehow "proved" or "demonstrated" by a subsequent period of great prosperity is to mislead the public with a monstrous example of the *post hoc ergo propter hoc* fallacy. Moreover, the whole tortuous exercise is so unnecessary, for a much more reasonable, and very much simpler, explanation of the Great Canadian Boom is also standard fare in our textbooks. This explanation runs in terms of a number of world events and developments in the last decade of the nineteenth century, all of which reacted favourably on the Canadian economy — the "closing" of the American frontier, rising world prices, falling shipping rates, the development of the gradual reduction process for milling wheat, and the development of the technique of making paper from wood pulp are perhaps the principal items in the list. None of these factors owed anything to the national policy.

Why, then, do historians insist on overdetermining their explanation of the Great Boom by trying to fit a perfectly straightforward argument into the national policy stereotype, as Fowke, for example, does when he writes that "This conjuncture of world circumstances created the opportunity for Canadian expansion, but a half-century of foundation work along the lines of the national policy had prepared Canada for the opportunity."[15] Economic man does not need to be prepared by government policy before he reacts to opportunities for making profits. Is it crude hero worship, or an unconscious human predisposition to human explanations of history that leads Canadians to believe that what success they have enjoyed "must" reflect Macdonald's wise nation-building policies? Or are we all of us merely prisoners of our own history — as it has been written? It is very odd that, enjoying one of the highest standards of living in the world, Canadians in all walks of life should nevertheless believe that their economy is a frail, hothouse creation, whose very survival depends on the constant vigilance of a government gardener well provided with props and plant food. Who but historians could have created this chasm between reality and belief? It is high time that someone should write the history of Canada since Confederation as a triumph of the forces of economic and political development over the national policies of Macdonald and his successors.

II

Our national policies were laid down when Canada was young, both politically and economically. The country looked forward to a long period of what I shall call *extensive* economic growth — a combination of geographical expansion, immigration, the exploitation of new resources, railway building, and the extension of manufacturing and service industries to keep pace with the growth of the national economy. The national policies were adopted to facilitate this "natural" growth process; they were designed to increase natural resources through political expansion, human resources through immigration, social capital by railway building, and private capital by means of the tariff. This "vision" of growth was surely not unreasonable in 1870, even though, as things turned out, it failed to materialize during the next generation. In retrospect it is easy enough to see why the expectation was premature: world demand for wheat had not yet grown to the point where, even with rail transportation, wheat could be profitably exported from the Canadian prairies; technology had not yet released the wealth of the Canadian Shield in terms of base metals, pulpwood, and waterpower; and the absence of cheap coal and iron ore hampered manufacturing development. It was only with the "conjuncture" around 1900 that natural economic expansion gave the national policies something to facilitate. For a generation thereafter, extensive growth was the stuff of Canadian economic development.

Extensive growth, which is essentially a process of increasing the quantity of resources, provides the sort of massive economic development that fascinates economic historians. Yet from an economic point of view it is such a simple type of growth that it holds almost no interest for economic theorists, who concern themselves primarily with the efficient use of *a given quantity* of resources, and who therefore tend to think of economic progress not in terms of amassing resources but in terms of making better use of existing resources. Fortunately, however, economic historians and economic theorists *do* have a common interest in an improvement of resource *quality* as a third path to the wealth of nations. Historians have long manifested an interest in technological change, which may be considered as a means of improving the quality of capital resources, and in such things as health, diet, training, and a wide range of institutional factors that affect the quality of human resources. Only recently have economic theorists invaded in force the fields of technology, health, education, recreation, and governmental activities, but already the power of economic analysis is beginning to make itself felt in public policies relating to these matters.

Both better resource allocation and resource improvement, but especially the latter, result in what I shall call *intensive* economic growth, a type of growth that has little to do with the mere multiplying of resources that is the basic characteristic of extensive economic growth. Intensive growth, as against extensive growth, involves better job opportunities rather than more job opportunities, more highly trained people rather than more people, better use of capital and land rather than more capital and land — in brief, a better performance rather than a larger one. Extensive growth implies primary concern with the GNP growth rate; intensive growth implies primary concern with the GNP per capita growth rate. What must now be asked is whether the rough-hewn concepts of extensive and intensive growth have any operational significance, and if so whether national policies designed for extensive growth have any place in an age of intensive growth.

It is, of course, true that it would be hard to find historical examples of either pure intensive or pure extensive growth. The important question is whether it is legitimate to characterize certain periods as periods of *predominantly* intensive or extensive growth. Both traditional history and Professor Gallman's quantitative work suggest that for the United States it is meaningful to distinguish between the extensive growth of the last half of the nineteenth century and the intensive growth of the first half of the twentieth. Thus Gallman found that "the rate of increase of commodity output over the first fifty years of the twentieth century was very far below the rate for the last 60 years of the nineteenth," but "the average rate of change of commodity output per capita was about the same in the twentieth as in the nineteenth century."[16] That twentieth-century economic growth in the United States has been mainly of the *intensive* variety is made clear by Gallman's findings that "the twentieth century average decade rate of increase of gainful workers in commodity production was only . . . slightly more than one-fifth as large as that of the nineteenth. The twentieth-century increases in commodity output were largely productivity increases. . . . Productivity advance in commodity production was sufficiently high to maintain a high rate of growth of commodity output per member of the population, despite the fact that a sharply declining share of the population was engaged in commodity production."[17]

In Canada we have only the beginnings of a statistical history of our economic growth before 1926 and we cannot with confidence argue from the statistical record. Nevertheless the Canadian GNP data, based on Firestone's figures for the pre-1926 period, fail to show any evidence of retardation in the growth of GNP since 1900, or even since 1880, and clearly suggest some modest acceleration of GNP growth in the period since the Second World War. Taken at face value—and I find it hard to believe that the general trends of the data are misleading—the suggestion is that Canada has remained in a period of extensive economic growth for the past 60 or 70 years. Qualitative evidence, however, is clearly at odds with this hypothesis. Most economic historians would agree with Fowke's suggestion that 1930 marked "the end of the establishment phase of the wheat economy and the completion of the first national policy"[18] and would even go farther by using 1930 to mark the end of the period of extensive growth that started in Canada in the mid-1890s. By this time the West had been settled, the railways built, and the pulp and paper, hydroelectric, and mining industries established.[19] It is true that since the Second World War there have been some dramatic new mining developments in Canada—petroleum, iron ore, uranium, and potash—but the industries built on these new resources have been neither land-intensive nor labour-intensive and they have had a much smaller impact on the postwar economy than the earlier "staple industries" had on the pre-1930 economy. In retrospect, there seems as much reason to have expected some retardation in the growth of GNP in Canada after 1930 as there was to expect a slowing down of the GNP growth rate in the United States after 1900, that is to say, for a replacement of predominantly extensive growth by predominantly intensive growth.

Yet our growth statistics are still those of a period of extensive growth. In part, the statistics reflect the postwar resource discoveries mentioned above, and in part, I think, the likelihood that the expansion in manufacturing in Canada after 1940 was unusually large not only because of the war but also because normal growth had been suspended in the 1930s. In a sense, those technological trends that were differentially favourable to Canadian manufacturing had just begun to take hold in the 1920s, were submerged by the depression of the 1930s, and became fully apparent only in the 1940s and 1950s. But when this has been said, there still remains a strong suspicion that Canadian *policy* has had much to do with the perpetuation of very high GNP growth rates characteristic of a period of extensive growth long after our period of extensive growth apparently came to an end.

The change in "national policies" after 1930 was not, perhaps, as sharp as Fowke suggested.[20] Indeed two out of three of the main pillars of the old national policy—tariff protection and the promotion of immigration—are as much a feature of present-day Canadian policy as they were of Canadian policy 60 years ago. As has been argued throughout, the Canadian tariff and Canadian immigration policy operate jointly to "force the pace" of manufacturing growth and, more generally, of growth in population and GNP. The danger is that in a period of intensive growth, when the growth in natural resources is slower than the growth in population, part of the growth in GNP will be at the expense of growth in GNP per person. American adjustments to the "closing" of their "frontier" included, one might suggest, a rapid extension of birth control practices, severe limitations on immigration, land conservation policies, and, more recently, growing concern for the wise use of air and water. Some of these adjustments have also been in evidence in Canada. But our *national* economic policies today are substantially those of 1900—more factories, more people, more cities, more GNP. Is it not time to consider whether these are appropriate policies for a country whose "frontier" was "closed" a generation ago?

NOTES

1. The Innis link was derived from Galt's argument, made in reply to protests from British manufacturers against his raising of the Canadian tariff in the late 1850s, that increased tariff revenue
was necessary to help pay for Canadian canals and railways that could not be profitably built by
private concerns, and that British manufacturers ought to be pleased with the arrangement
because the cheaper cost of transportation would lower the price of British manufactured goods
in Canada and thus increase the market for them. (Innis accepted as profound this economic
doubletalk of a suave politician, though with a certain amount of incredulity about its source:
"whether or not [Galt's] explanation was one of rationalization after the fact, or of original theoretical analysis, reliance on the customs was undoubtedly the only solution.") Surely it was
not the only solution; if the canals had been paid for by domestic taxation, or by import duties
that were no heavier than domestic excise duties, the British manufacturers would have been
at least as well off, and Canadians would have been better off. A subsidy is always to be preferred to a tariff on both economic grounds and political grounds; on economic grounds
because direct payments distort resource allocation less than indirect payments, and on political
grounds because direct payments involve less deception than indirect payments.

   Galt was talking *mainly* of revenue tariffs. Innis extended the Galt argument to tariffs that
were mainly protective, and thereby compounded Galt's error. "The National Policy was
designed not only to increase revenue from customs [as in Galt's argument] but also to increase
revenue from traffic from the standpoint of the railways. The increasing importance of railways
has tended to emphasize the position of protection rather than revenue." As economic theory
this is absurd, not only because the railways, like the canals, could have been financed more
efficiently by subsidy than by tariff, but also because a tariff cannot at the same time maximize
both protection and revenue; the greater the protective effect of a tariff the less the revenue it
will provide. The charitable interpretation of this passage is that Innis was indulging in "rationalization after the fact." In the article in which these passages occurred, Innis at any rate doubt-
ed the *future* application of his argument: "Dependence on the application of mature technique,
especially in transport, to virgin natural resources must steadily recede in importance as a basis
for the tariff. It will become increasingly difficult to wield the tariff as the crude but effective
weapon by which we have been able to obtain a share of our natural resources."

   All of the above quotations are taken from an article by Innis published in 1931, and reprinted in H.A. Innis, *Essays in Canadian Economic History* (Toronto, 1956), 76–77. Two years later
Innis was in a deep quandary about the effect of the Canadian tariff. "Inflexibility of the tariff
downward contributed to the difficulties during the period of prosperity which began . . . in
1896" (p. 91). On the following page he wrote that "During a period of prosperity the tariff
should be raised to act as a brake. . . . If railroad rates are lowered at the beginning of a period
of prosperity tariff rates should be raised accordingly. . . . Lowering the tariff during the period
of a depression and raising the tariff during a period of prosperity might do much to alleviate
the problem of a staple-producing area" (pp. 92–93). The only way I can see of resolving the
contradiction between these two quotations is to suppose that in the first Innis was thinking of
the combined effect on CPR revenues of the wheat boom and the continued support of the tariff, and the consequent effect of swollen railway revenues in promoting a new, and uneconomically large, railway-building program in Canada: had the tariff been lowered, and the CPR's
profits thereby dampened, the incentive to build *two* new transcontinental railways in Canada
would have been reduced; and that in the second he was thinking of the Western farmer: the
wheat boom might have been dampened by raising farm costs by means of *increased* tariff rates
in order to offset the advantages that farmers gained by lowered railway rates. Since the final
part of the second quotation recommends a counter-cyclical tariff policy (Innis must have
known how politically impracticable *this* was!), with no qualification about how railway rates
should be changed, one can only make sense out of this passage by supposing that by 1933
Innis was willing to sacrifice the railways to the farmers during depression and the farmers to
the railways during prosperity; his recommended policy would be counter-cyclical for farmers

and pro-cyclical for railways! Perhaps the subtlety, or the confusion, was covering a retreat. Realizing that a high tariff may "become inadequate" during depressions (p. 91), and suggesting that the period of resource expansion in Canada had ended, Innis in fact repudiated his linking of the National Policy and railways by reverting to the lesser economic confusions of Galt's position: "Assuming relative stability in the production of raw materials as a result of exhaustion of natural resources the tariff must assume to an increasing extent the position of a toll, as Galt originally planned, and should approximate the deficit on transportation finance" (p. 93). Unfortunately the damage had been done, for textbook writers cannot spare the time to assess qualifications to, or second thoughts on, powerful generalizations.

2. D.G. Creighton, *Dominion of the North* (Toronto, 1944), 346.
3. J.B. Brebner, *North Atlantic Triangle* (New Haven and Toronto, 1945), 158. My italics.
4. W.T. Easterbrook and H.G. Aitken, *Canadian Economic History* (Toronto, 1956), 383.
5. J.H. Dales, *Engineering and Society*, pt. 2 (Toronto, 1946), 246.
6. V.C. Fowke, *Canadian Agricultural Policy* (Toronto, 1946), 8. Fowke may mean that the national policy was a prerequisite from central Canadians' point of view, i.e., that central Canada would not have "invested" in the West without it. At the same time he would not argue that eastern investment was a *sine qua non* of western development; see note 7.
7. V.C. Fowke, *The National Policy and the Wheat Economy* (Toronto, 1957), 69.
8. J.M.S. Careless, *Canada* (Toronto, 1953), 277–78.
9. W.A. Mackintosh, *The Economic Background of Dominion–Provincial Relations* (Ottawa, 1939).
10. Chester Martin, *Foundations of Canadian Nationhood* (Toronto, 1956).
11. A.R.M. Lower, *Colony to Nation* (Toronto, 1946), 373–74.
12. Mackintosh, *Economic Background*, 17 and 20.
13. Careless, *Canada*, 295 and 312.
14. R.W. Fogel, *The Union Pacific Railroad* (Baltimore, 1960), *passim*.
15. Fowke, *The National Policy and the Wheat Economy*, 70.
16. R.E. Gallman, "Commodity Output, 1839–1899," in *Trends in the American Economy in the Nineteenth Century* (Princeton, 1960), 18 and 20.
17. Gallman, "Commodity Output," 20.
18. V.C. Fowke, "The National Policy—Old and New," in *Canadian Journal of Economics and Political Science* (August 1952), 277–78.
19. See J.H. Dales, *Hydroelectricity and Industrial Development* (Cambridge, MA, 1957), ch. 8, esp. p. 166.
20. Fowke, "The National Policy—Old and New."

Topic Two

Regional and National Conflict in
the Late Nineteenth Century

Attendees at the first interprovincial conference, called by Honoré

Mercier in 1887.

20

IN THE late nineteenth century, social, political, cultural, and regional issues arose that challenged Canadian unity. Politically, provincial governments questioned and attacked John A. Macdonald's vision of a strong and dominant central government, while culturally, an emerging English-Canadian nationalism clashed with an equally powerful French-Canadian nationalism, chiefly over the question of language rights for French-speaking Canadians outside the province of Quebec.

Ontario led the opposition to Macdonald's centralist perspective. During the Confederation debates, the tension between the two levels of government was not so evident since George Brown and his Clear Grits (later known as the Liberals) had strongly supported Confederation and the idea of a highly centralized federation. They had done so, however, on the assumption that local interests would be maintained in the new federal union.

By the 1880s, a series of contentious issues brought the two governments into opposition. In "Provincial Rights," political scientist Peter H. Russell shows how Macdonald's original conception of a highly centralized federation was altered in favour of a "classical federalism" of an equal division of federal and provincial powers. This change came about as a result of challenges to federal powers by Oliver Mowat, premier of Ontario from 1872 to 1896, and the chief political advocate of provincial rights; the decisions of the highest court of appeal, the Judicial Committee of the Privy Council, to uphold Ontario's position; and an emerging belief in "the myth of Confederation as a compact entered into by sovereign provincial communities." Russell reveals the impact of these late-nineteenth-century political and constitutional developments on Canada today.

Conflict also arose between English- and French-speaking Canadians in the late nineteenth century over the question of the educational and linguistic rights of French-speaking Canadians outside of Quebec. This issue undermined the country's already fragile political unity, achieved through Macdonald's scheme of territorial expansion, a national policy, and regional integration. In "Unity/Diversity: The Canadian Experience; From Confederation to the First World War," J.R. Miller explains the shift from the concept of "unity in diversity" to "diversity into unity," and the resulting political alienation of French-speaking Quebec from English-speaking Canada.

On the provincial-rights movement in Ontario, see Margaret Evans's biography, *Sir Oliver Mowat* (Toronto: University of Toronto Press, 1992); J.C. Morrison, "Oliver Mowat and the Development of Provincial Rights in Ontario: A Study in Dominion–Provincial Relations, 1867–1896," in *Three History Theses* (Toronto: Ontario Department of Public Records and Archives, 1961); and Garth Stevenson, *Ex Uno Plures: Federal–Provincial Relations in Canada, 1867–1896* (Montreal/Kingston: McGill-Queen's University Press, 1993). Christopher Armstrong discusses the evolution of relations between Ontario and the federal government in *The Politics of Federalism: Ontario's Relations with the Federal Government, 1867–1942* (Toronto: University of Toronto Press, 1981).

The literature on the question of Canadian duality is extensive. Perhaps the most complete overview of relations between French and English Canadians in the late nineteenth century is to be found in Volume 1 of Mason Wade's *The French Canadians*, 2 vols. (Toronto: Macmillan, 1977). A short, lively summary of the issue is presented in Susan Mann Trofimenkoff's *The Dream of Nation: A Social and Intellectual History of Quebec* (Toronto: Gage,

1982), and a more detailed account can be found in P.B. Waite's *Canada, 1874–1896: Arduous Destiny* (Toronto: McClelland and Stewart, 1971). The rise of a militant Anglo-Canadian Protestant movement agitating to make Canada a unilingual country, and the French-Canadian response to it, is described in J.R. Miller, *Equal Rights: The Jesuits' Estate Act Controversy* (Montreal/Kingston: McGill-Queen's University Press, 1979). Miller reviews the ideas and the activities of D'Alton McCarthy, regarded as the leading advocate for the assimilation of the French Canadians, in "D'Alton McCarthy, Equal Rights, and the Origins of the Manitoba School Question," *Canadian Historical Review* 54 (December 1973): 369–92, and " 'As a Politician He Is a Great Enigma': The Social and Political Ideas of D'Alton McCarthy," *Canadian Historical Review* 58 (December 1977): 399–422. The French Canadians' changing attitude toward Confederation is explored by A.I. Silver in *The French-Canadian Idea of Confederation, 1864–1900*, 2nd ed. (Toronto: University of Toronto Press, 1997). Ramsay Cook reviews the idea of Confederation as a compact of provinces or cultures in *Provincial Autonomy: Minority Rights and the Compact Theory, 1867–1921* (Ottawa: Queen's Printer, 1969). Ronald Rudin's *The Forgotten Quebecers* (Québec: Institut québécois de recherche sur la culture, 1985) provides a history of the English-speaking population of Quebec from 1759 to 1980.

Article Three

Provincial Rights

Peter H. Russell

The great conceit of constitution makers is to believe that the words they put in the constitution can with certainty and precision control a country's future. The great conceit of those who apply a written constitution is to believe that their interpretation captures perfectly the founders' intentions. Those who write constitutions are rarely single-minded in their long-term aspirations. They harbour conflicting hopes and fears about the constitution's evolution. The language of the constitution is inescapably general and latent with ambiguous possibilities. Written constitutions can establish the broad grooves in which a nation-state develops. But what happens within those grooves — the constitutional tilt favoured by history — is determined not by the constitutional text but by the political forces and events that shape the country's subsequent history.

Canada's constitutional development in the decades immediately following Confederation is a monument to the truth of these propositions. Although a majority of the Fathers of Confederation favoured a highly centralized federation, it soon became apparent that their aspirations would not be fulfilled. Instead, the most effective constitutional force in the new federation was the provincial rights movement. Far from moving toward a unitary state, Canada, by the end of the nineteenth century, had become a thoroughly federal country.

One might have expected the stiffest challenge to Macdonald's centralism to have come from Nova Scotia or Quebec. Nova Scotians voted against Confederation in the provincial

Source: *Constitutional Odyssey: Can Canadians Become a Sovereign People?* (Toronto: University of Toronto Press, 1993), pp. 35–52. Reprinted by permission of University of Toronto Press Incorporated.

and federal elections of 1867. Immediately following Confederation a significant secessionist movement was developing in the province.[1] In 1868 Joseph Howe led a delegation
to London seeking a repeal of the union. Nova Scotian opposition to Confederation, however, was not based on a desire for stronger provincial powers. In the end, Nova Scotian
separatism was quelled by persuading Howe to join the federal cabinet and by offering
Nova Scotia better terms, not through a constitutional amendment but by bringing its debt
allowance into line with New Brunswick's.

From the very beginning, the province of Quebec, in the words of A.I. Silver, "was seen
as the geographical and political expression of the French-Canadian homeland."[2] It was
not just the *rouge* opponents of Confederation who championed the cause of provincial
autonomy and resisted federal interference in provincial affairs. The *Bleus* had promoted
Confederation in Quebec largely on the grounds that it would give the French majority in
Quebec exclusive control over matters basic to their culture. A *bleu* paper in 1872, for
example, claimed that "as Conservatives we must be in favour of provincial rights and
against centralization."[3]

It was not Quebec but Ontario that spearheaded the provincial rights movement.
Ontario would seem the least likely province to play this role. After all, support for
Confederation had been stronger in Ontario than in any other province. With the largest
and fastest-growing population, Ontario was expected to be able to dominate national politics. Why at this formative stage in the federation's history should its provincial government be in the vanguard of the provincial rights movement?

The answer is to be found in the pattern of partisan politics that developed soon after
Confederation and has endured ever since. Even before Confederation, the Great Coalition of
Conservatives and Reformers had broken up. The first federal government after Confederation was headed by the Conservative leader John A. Macdonald. As Ontario Reformers and
Quebec Liberals began to organize a competing national party, they naturally took up the
provincial cause. In the words of Christopher Armstrong, "If Macdonald's Conservatives
were the party of centralism, then its opponents would become the party of localism and
provincialism, recruiting the anti-Confederates of the Maritimes to the Reform cause."[4]

The Conservatives dominated the first 30 years of federal politics, holding office in
Ottawa for all but four of those years. During that same period the Liberals were having
their greatest success at the provincial level. Nowhere was this more true than in Ontario,
where Oliver Mowat's Liberals won six successive elections between 1875 and 1896.
While Mowat found Liberal allies in other provincial capitals, notably Quebec's Honoré
Mercier, he was in office the longest and built the strongest record of provincial rights
advocacy. Mowat's championing of this cause is remarkable in that he began his professional career as a junior in John A. Macdonald's law office, was a Father of Confederation,
and had moved the Quebec Resolutions setting forth the division of powers between the
two levels of government.[5]

The pattern of politics in which one party dominates at the federal level while its main
opposition gathers strength in the provincial capitals has been repeated several times in
Canadian history. For a long stretch of the twentieth century the Liberals dominated the
federal scene while the Conservatives and other opposition parties won in the provinces.
The reverse has been developing since the Mulroney Conservatives came to power in
Ottawa in 1984. The fact that the largest national parties have gone through long periods
in which their experience in government has been concentrated at the provincial level has
done much to make provincial rights a cause that transcends partisan politics.

Although this phenomenon is one that stems from the fluctuating fortunes of partisan
politics, it is closely tied to the Canadian system of parliamentary government. Responsible

government tends to concentrate power in the hands of the prime minister and the Cabinet. After Confederation it soon became apparent that this concentration of power would occur in the provincial capitals as well as in Ottawa. In Canada, provincial premiers emerged as the strongest political opponents to the federal prime minister. State governors in the United States, hemmed in by an elaborate system of checks and balances, are political pygmies compared with provincial premiers who perform as political giants on the national stage. Canadians, without any conscious design, found their liberal check and balance not *within* the national or provincial capitals but in the rivalry and tensions *between* those capitals.

The success of the provincial rights movement cannot be attributed to weak governments at the national level in Canada's formative years. Quite to the contrary, federal administrations presided over by John A. Macdonald, who was prime minister of Canada for nineteen of the country's first 24 years, were strong nation-building governments not at all shy about asserting federal power. Under Macdonald's leadership, Canada's "manifest destiny" of becoming a continental nation-state was quickly fulfilled. In 1869 the Hudson's Bay Company's territories covering the prairies and the far north were purchased and added to Canada. A year later, following military suppression of the Métis led by Louis Riel, the Province of Manitoba was carved out of the Northwest Territories. In 1871 Canada was extended to the Pacific, when British Columbia became a province on terms agreeable to its colonial government. Prince Edward Island became the seventh province, agreeing to join Confederation in 1873. To this expanding national territory Macdonald's Conservatives applied a National Policy, completing the transcontinental rail link, erecting tariff walls to protect manufacturing, and stimulating immigration to populate the west and provide a market for the protected industries.[6]

Important as the achievements of Macdonald's governments were in building the material conditions of nationhood, they contributed little to a Canadian sense of political community. Nor did they translate into constitutional gains for the federal government. The Conservatives' economic nationalism, as Reg Whitaker has observed, relied "on elites and on their exclusively economic motives."[7] It did not have much emotional appeal at the mass level. Government in far-away Ottawa had difficulty competing with provincial governments for the allegiance of citizens in the new provinces. During these years it was the provinces, not Ottawa, that seized and held the initiative in constitutional politics.

The first objective of the provincial rights movement was to resist and overcome a hierarchical version of Canadian federalism in which the provinces were to be treated as a subordinate or junior level of government. An early focal point of resistance was the office of provincial lieutenant-governor. From a Macdonald centralist perspective, the lieutenant-governors were essentially agents of the federal government in provincial capitals. In the 1870s, however, Ontario, under Mowat's leadership, began to insist that lieutenant-governors had full Crown powers in matters of provincial jurisdiction and that they exercised these powers on the advice of provincial ministers. Not surprisingly, the issue first arose over a question of patronage—the power to make lawyers queen's counsels.[8] Implicit in the provincial claim was an assertion of the provinces' constitutional equality with the federal government.

No element of the Constitution was potentially more threatening to provincial autonomy than the federal powers of reservation and disallowance. These powers derived from an imperial rather than a federal structure. Under the reservation power, the lieutenant-governor of a province could refuse to sign a bill that had passed through the provincial legislature and could reserve it for consideration by the federal Cabinet. If, within a year, the lieutenant-governor was not instructed to give royal assent, the bill would die.

Disallowance was simply a veto power under which the federal government could render null and void any provincial law within a year of its passage by the provincial legislature. These federal powers mirrored powers of reservation and disallowance over federal legislation that the imperial government retained and that were also written into the *BNA Act*.[9] The only difference was that the British government had two years rather than one to decide whether to block Canadian legislation.

The powers of reservation and disallowance are classic examples of how a shift in political sentiment and principle can render formal legal powers unusable. Well before Confederation, the British government had greatly reduced the use of its imperial powers of control over the British North American legislatures. Soon after Confederation these powers fell into desuetude. In the first decade a few Canadian bills were reserved, but royal assent was always granted and there were no reservations after 1878. Only one Canadian act was disallowed, in 1873, and the act in question was clearly unconstitutional.[10] At imperial conferences in the late 1920s declarations were made that these imperial powers would never be used and that steps would be taken to remove them from Canada's Constitution. Although the latter step was never taken, no one really cares that the powers remain formally in the Constitution because there is a clear political understanding — a constitutional convention — on both the British and Canadian sides that the powers are completely inoperative.[11] This convention of desuetude was established because use of the imperial powers was incompatible with the principle of Canadian self-government, a principle which, at least in matters of domestic policy, was so firmly in place by the 1870s that breach of it would have had the gravest political consequences.

A similar process occurred with respect to the federal government's powers of reservation and disallowance. Over time, the principle of provincial autonomy — self-government in those areas constitutionally assigned to the provincial legislatures — became so strongly held in the Canadian political system that the federal powers of reservation and disallowance, though remaining in the Constitution, became politically unusable. This did not happen all at once. It occurred only because the idea that the provinces are not subordinate to but coordinate with the federal government became the politically dominant conception of Canadian federalism.

At first federal governments — not only Macdonald's but the Liberals too when they were in power in the 1870s — made extensive use of the powers of reservation and disallowance.[12] Macdonald's first administration withheld assent on 16 of 24 provincial bills reserved by lieutenant-governors. Between 1867 and 1896, 65 provincial acts were disallowed by the federal government. Although the powers continued to be used, they came under increasing attack from the provinces, and from no province more than Ontario. Even when, as was most often the case, the rationale for using these powers was the federal government's view that the legislation was outside the province's jurisdiction, provincial rights advocates were inclined to argue that questions concerning the division of powers should be settled in the courts, not by the federal cabinet. When the Macdonald government in 1881 disallowed Ontario's *Rivers and Streams Act* primarily to protect the interests of a prominent Conservative, Mowat decided to fight back. He promptly had the legislation reenacted. After being disallowed and reenacted three more times, the legislation was allowed to stand. The courts had the final say when the Judicial Committee of the Privy Council upheld the provincial law in 1884.[13]

Abolition of the federal disallowance power topped the list of constitutional proposals emanating from the Interprovincial Conference in 1887. The conference was called by Honoré Mercier, premier of Quebec, who had come to power largely on the strength of Quebec's resentment of the use of federal power in the hanging of Louis Riel. Macdonald and the Conservative premiers of British Columbia and Prince Edward Island declined Mercier's invitation. Delegates from the Liberal governments of the four original provinces and from Manitoba's Conservative administration, "angered by repeated disallowances of their railway legislation,"[14] met for a week under Mowat's chairmanship behind closed doors. The 22 resolutions that they unanimously endorsed amounted to a frontal attack on the centralist conception of Confederation. Besides calling for the abolition of federal disallowance and an increase in federal subsidies, the conference proposed that half of the federal Senate be chosen by the provinces. Once these proposals had been approved by the provincial legislatures, they were to be submitted to London for enactment as constitutional amendments by the imperial Parliament.

In the end, nothing concrete came of these proposals. Only the lower houses of New Brunswick and Nova Scotia sent them on to London. The imperial authorities refused to act without having heard from the federal government or the other provinces.[15] Nonetheless, the 1887 conference is a significant landmark in Canada's constitutional politics, for it clearly demonstrated that the constitutional initiative had passed to the provinces. Strong centralist voices could still be heard, not least John A. Macdonald's, but the centralist view was losing its ascendancy in both French and English Canada.

During the first 30 years of Confederation, the provinces made their most tangible constitutional gains not through the process of formal constitutional amendment but through litigation in the courts. Their judicial victories were achieved in London before the Judicial Committee of the Privy Council. The Supreme Court of Canada had been created by the federal Parliament in 1875, but it was supreme in name only. Although the Liberal government which had sponsored the *Supreme Court Act* aimed at making the court Canada's highest tribunal, the Conservative opposition and the Colonial Office were able to thwart this objective.[16] The right of appeal to the highest court in the British Empire, the Judicial Committee of the Privy Council, was retained in Canada until 1949.

Retaining the Judicial Committee as Canada's highest court had significant consequences for the development of the Canadian Constitution. In the 1870s when the practice of bringing constitutional challenges against legislation in the courts was just beginning, the newly created Supreme Court of Canada decided a few cases very much in the federal government's favour. In *Severn v. The Queen*, decided in 1878, the Supreme Court found an Ontario law licensing brewers unconstitutional or *ultra vires*, outside the powers of the provincial legislature.[17] The Supreme Court judges gave the widest possible interpretation of the federal Parliament's exclusive power to make laws in relation to "the Regulation of Trade and Commerce," and supported this judgement by arguing that the Constitution's framers wished to avoid the "evils" of states rights that had plagued the American federation. A year later in *Lenoir v. Ritchie*, the Supreme Court firmly rejected provincial pretensions to Crown prerogative by denying provincial governments the power to appoint queen's counsel.[18]

It did not take long for the English law lords who manned the Judicial Committee of the Privy Council to reverse the Supreme Court's approach to the Constitution. By the 1880s a steady stream of constitutional cases was being taken on appeal to London. The fact that so many constitutional questions were coming before the courts gives the lie to the pretension of the Fathers of Confederation to have settled all questions of jurisdiction.

One of the Judicial Committee's earliest decision, *Citizens Insurance Co. v. Parsons*,[19] is a good example of the kind of issue that arose and the kind of outcome that obtained in the Judicial Committee. Section 91(2) of the *BNA Act* gave the federal Parliament exclusive jurisdiction over "the Regulation of Trade and Commerce." Section 92(13) gave the provincial legislatures exclusive jurisdiction over "Property and Civil Rights in the

Province." At issue in the *Parsons* case was whether an Ontario statute regulating fire insurance contracts was within provincial powers. Such a law would seem clearly to be a regulation of trade and commerce and a regulation affecting property and civil rights in Ontario. Under which power did the Ontario legislation fall? The Judicial Committee reasoned that unless some limits were attached to trade and commerce and to property and civil rights, such broadly phrased powers would contradict each other. In this case they chose to put limits on the federal trade and commerce power, ruling that it applied to interprovincial and international commerce and to trade "affecting the whole Dominion," but not to the regulation of an industry within a province. Thus the Ontario act was upheld as a law relating to property and civil rights.

Between 1880 and 1896 the Judicial Committee decided eighteen cases involving twenty issues relating to the division of powers. Fifteen of these issues (75 percent) it decided in favour of the provinces. What is even more important, as Murray Greenwood has observed, is that in these decisions the committee reversed "every major centralist doctrine of the [Supreme] Court."[20] No area of policymaking was as hotly contested as the consumption of alcohol. At first, the Judicial Committee appeared to favour federal power by upholding the *Canada Temperance Act*, a federal law providing a nationwide system whereby towns and cities could opt for local prohibition.[21] However, in subsequent decisions it ruled that only the provinces could provide for the licensing of taverns and retail liquor outlets in areas that did not opt for prohibition.[22] Finally, in 1896, the Judicial Committee upheld an Ontario local prohibition scheme. It was in this case that the imperial court called for a restrained interpretation of the federal Parliament's general or residual power to make laws for the "Peace, Order, and good Government of Canada." That power should be confined "to such matters as are unquestionably of Canadian interest and importance," and must not encroach on any of the subjects assigned exclusively to the provinces. "To attach any other construction of the general power which, in supplement of its enumerated powers, is conferred upon the Parliament of Canada, would," wrote Lord Watson, "not only be contrary to the intendment of the Act, but would practically destroy the autonomy of the provinces."[23]

The Judicial Committee went beyond the details of the division of powers to articulate a conception of federalism which would have been anathema to John A. Macdonald. The key judgement came in 1892 in the *Maritime Bank* case and involved that touchiest of constitutional questions—sovereign Crown powers.[24] At issue was New Brunswick's use of the Crown's prerogative to claim priority over other creditors seeking to recover funds from the liquidators of an insolvent bank. In upholding the province's right to use this power, Lord Watson set down the following thesis about the purpose of the *BNA Act*:

> The object of the Act was neither to weld the provinces into one, nor to subordinate provincial governments to a central authority, but to create a federal government in which they should all be represented, entrusted with the exclusive administration of affairs in which they had a common interest, each province retaining its independence and autonomy.

So much for John A. Macdonald's view that "the true principle of a Confederation lay in giving to the General Government all the principles and powers of sovereignty."[25] For the tribunal which had the final say in interpreting the Canadian Constitution, the provinces were not a subordinate level of government. The federal and provincial governments were coordinate levels of government, each autonomous within the spheres allotted to them by the Constitution.

The theory espoused by the Judicial Committee of the Privy Council is often called the theory of "classical federalism."[26] There can be no doubt that Macdonald and many of Canada's constitutional founders did not think of the country they were building as a classic federation. Some of the Fathers of Confederation, however, especially Quebec leaders like Cartier and Taché, were apprehensive of the centralist view and hoped that the provinces would be autonomous in the areas of law making reserved for them. The Quebec supporters of Confederation realized they could not retain their political support if they portrayed Confederation publicly in centralist terms. The political coalition that put Confederation together never came to a clear and explicit accord on federal theory.[27] What the Judicial Committee did was to give official legal sanction to a theory of federalism congenial to those who, at the time of Confederation and afterwards, could not accept centralism.

The impact of the Judicial Committee's constitutional decisions demonstrates a fundamental feature of constitutional development which is still, at most, only dimly understood by the Canadian public. In countries with written constitutions stipulating the powers of government and the rights of citizens, and in which the constitution is taken seriously, judges will play an important role in enforcing the constitution. The process through which judges play that role is called "judicial review." In performing the function of judicial review, judges review the acts of the executive and legislature and rule null and void those that do not conform with the constitution. Through these determinations, especially those of the highest court, the meaning of the constitution's general terms is fleshed out. This process of judicial review has been so important in the United States that it is said that "the constitution is what the judges say it is."[28]

The Fathers of Confederation did not discuss judicial review. Although some of them were aware of the important role the Supreme Court was playing in the United States, they did not see that there would be an immediate need for a Canadian Supreme Court.[29] Their constitutionalism was much more British than American, and hence more attuned to an unwritten constitution. They were accustomed to having the Judicial Committee of the Privy Council, as the highest imperial court, review colonial laws for their conformity with imperial law. Since the Canadian Constitution took the form of an act of the imperial Parliament, it was logical that this mechanism of imperial judicial control would apply to the *BNA Act*. For enforcing the rules of federalism internally, within Canada, it is evident that the Fathers of Confederation looked more to the federal executive using its powers of reservation and disallowance than to the judiciary. Also, it was to the federal executive, not the judiciary, that the *BNA Act* directed minorities to appeal if they believed a province had infringed their constitutional right to denominational schools.[30]

Federal government enforcement of the Constitution made sense, of course, so long as Canadian federalism was viewed primarily as a hierarchical, quasi-imperial structure in which the provinces were a junior level of government. From this perspective, the objective of constitutional enforcement was to keep the provinces from exceeding their powers. John A. Macdonald never contemplated that Canadian courts would find federal laws unconstitutional.[31] Once, however, the hierarchical view of federalism began to be eclipsed by the theory of classical federalism and dual sovereignty, it was much more logical for a judicial tribunal independent of both levels of government to exercise the primary responsibility for applying the Constitution.

Judicial review in Canada could not be justified in the same way as it was in the United States. There it was possible to justify judicial review on the grounds that in vetoing laws passed by popular majorities, the judiciary was giving effect to the enduring will of the American people as expressed in the Constitution.[32] Given the imperial and undemocratic foundations of the Canadian Constitution, this justification could hardly be advanced in

Canada. Nonetheless, the Judicial Committee's constitutional interpretation could not have made the impact it did had it not coincided with powerful political forces in Canada. By the late nineteenth century, Canada had moved too far away from colonialism toward self-government to have complied with the rulings of an imperial tribunal that were out of line with political opinion in the country. The federal election of 1896 demonstrated that in Canada's national politics, the tide was running in favour of provincial rights and a balanced view of Canadian federalism.

The 1896 election was won by the Liberals led by Wilfrid Laurier. The Liberals and Laurier were to remain in power for the next fifteen years. Laurier's political success stemmed in part from his championing of provincial rights. This support occurred in a most ironic setting — the Manitoba Schools crisis.[33] In the 1896 election, Laurier, a French Catholic from Quebec, opposed the Conservative government's threat to force Manitoba to restore the denominational schools of that province's Roman Catholic minority.

In 1890, Manitoba, which by that time had developed into a largely English Protestant province, passed legislation reducing the rights of the French Catholic minority.[34] One law made English Manitoba's official language, ignoring the clause in Manitoba's terms of union guaranteeing the use of English and French in the province's courts and legislature.[35] Nearly a century would pass before this statute would be effectively challenged in the courts.[36] The other statute replaced a dual system of Roman Catholic and Protestant schools in existence since 1871 with a system of secular public schools to be supported by all taxpayers, including parents of children attending the Roman Catholic schools. This legislation was immediately challenged on the grounds that it violated another clause in Manitoba's terms of union guaranteeing denominational school rights held "by law or practice" at the time of union.[37] Although the challenge was initially successful in the Supreme Court of Canada, it failed in the Judicial Committee of the Privy Council.[38] Nevertheless, in a subsequent decision, the Judicial Committee ruled that Manitoba's Catholics could, under another section of the constitutional guarantee, appeal to the federal cabinet to introduce remedial legislation forcing Manitoba to restore their school rights.[39] A few months before the 1896 election, the Conservatives, now led by Charles Tupper, agreed to submit a remedial bill to Parliament. This was the bill that Laurier successfully opposed in the ensuing election campaign.

It was not the substance of that bill which Laurier and the Liberals opposed. They were strongly committed to the restoration of Catholic school rights in Manitoba. In national politics the Laurier Liberals provided the main resistance to a growing movement within English Canada led by D'Alton McCarthy, president of the Ontario Conservative Association, calling for a Canada free of papism and rejecting "the *nationaliste* thesis that the French were a permanent and equal element in Canada."[40] Still, Laurier, who drew his strongest political support from Quebec, remained as committed to provincial rights as to minority cultural rights. Instead of federal coercion of a province, Laurier proposed the "sunnier ways" of negotiating an accommodation with the provincial government. In the end, it was Laurier's "sunnier ways" and his respect for provincial rights that prevailed politically.[41]

The success of the provincial rights movement did not mean that in terms either of governmental power or of citizens' allegiance the provincial political realm had come to surpass the federal. Laurier, after all, was a national leader whose government would pursue important initiatives in domestic and international politics. Indeed, Laurier and other Quebec leaders, by supporting the rights of French Catholics outside Quebec, were encouraging Quebeckers, in the words of A.I. Silver, to look beyond "the still-special home of Quebec" and see that "all Canada should yet be a country for French-Canadians."[42] Since the 1890s there have been shifts back and forth in the balance of power between the two levels of government, but there has always been a balance; neither level has been able to dominate the other. Canada's citizens have been thoroughly schizophrenic in their loyalties, maintaining strong associations with their provincial governments as well as the federal government. In this sense Canada, despite the ambiguities and contradictions in its Constitution, became, as Donald Smiley put it, "in the most elemental way a federal country."[43]

One measure of how ingrained the balanced view of federalism has become is the fate of those imperial powers of reservation and disallowance which the federal government held over the provinces. They are still in the Constitution, but they are simply not used any more. Disallowance has not been used since 1943. The last time a lieutenant-governor reserved a provincial bill was 1961, and then his action was totally repudiated by the federal prime minister, John Diefenbaker, as violating the basic principles of Canadian federalism.[44] When the Parti Québecois came to power in Quebec in the 1970s and enacted Bill 101, the Charter of the French Language, the Trudeau government in Ottawa, which bitterly opposed this legislation, did not ever indicate that it would disallow it. And again in 1988, when Quebec adopted Bill 178 to overcome a Supreme Court ruling and restore a unilingual French sign policy, although Prime Minister Mulroney and opinion leaders throughout English Canada denounced the legislation, neither government nor opposition leaders called for disallowance of the legislation. By the 1980s political parties and leaders of all persuasions, like Laurier and the Liberals a century earlier, would not protect minority rights at the cost of violating provincial rights.

The sovereignty at issue in the struggle for provincial rights was not the sovereignty of the people but the sovereignty of governments and legislatures. The sovereignty claimed and won for provincial legislatures and governments within their allotted sphere of jurisdiction was primarily a top-down kind of sovereignty.[45] Canadian constitutional politics continued to be highly elitist, with federal and provincial leaders contending against each other in intergovernmental meetings and the courts. Still, traces of a more democratic constitutionalism were beginning to appear in the rhetoric, if not the reality, of the constitutional process.

Robert Vipond has shown how exponents of provincial rights defended the sovereignty of provincial "parliaments" against federal intrusions by emphasizing the right to self-government of local electorates. Provincial leaders attacking federal intervention in provincial affairs appealed to the same principles of self-government as earlier colonial politicians had invoked in objecting to imperial intervention in internal colonial affairs. The exercise of the federal powers of disallowance and reservation was portrayed as "autocratic and tyrannical" whereas, according to Liberal leader Edward Blake, to support provincial autonomy was to sustain "the educating and glorious attributes which belong to self-government, to a government of the people, by the people, for the people."[46] Although the provincial leaders were still too British, too wedded to the notion of parliamentary sovereignty, to talk about the people as sovereign in the constituent American sense, they were edging closer to this conception of popular sovereignty when they referred to the rights of provincial legislatures as powers entrusted to them by the people.[47]

Out of this rhetoric and the political success of its authors was born the myth of Confederation as a compact entered into by sovereign provincial communities. According to the compact theory, the provinces as the founding, constituent units of the federation retained the right to alter the terms of their original union.[48] This was the theory promulgated by Honoré Mercier and the other provincial premiers who attended the 1887 Interprovincial Conference: "the conference represented all of the original parties to the compact of 1864, and the partners should now assess the state of their joint enterprise."[49] Not surprisingly, the theory found its most articulate spokesmen in Quebec, where the notion of the province as a founding community could be infused with a sense of ethnic nationalism.

What is meant in referring to the compact theory as a "myth" is that its validity depends not on its historical accuracy but on its capacity to serve as a set of "beliefs and notions that men hold, that they live by or live for."[50] Confederation, as we have seen, did involve a two-stage agreement, first between English- and French-Canadian politicians and then between Canadian and Maritime politicians. Leading participants in the agreement, including John A. Macdonald and George-Étienne Cartier, as well as some of the imperial authorities, frequently referred to the Quebec Resolutions as a treaty or pact. But it is not clear that when they used this terminology they had the same thing in mind. It is most unlikely that when John A. Macdonald talked of a treaty he meant that the parties to the agreement exercised and retained sovereign political authority.

From a strictly legal point of view, the founding colonies in 1867, as colonies, did not have sovereign powers to retain. They did not formally sign or give legal authority to the Constitution. Further, given the elitist quality of the process and the failure, indeed the disinclination, to seek a clear popular mandate for the Confederation deal, it is a total fabrication to maintain that the peoples of the founding provinces had covenanted together to produce the Canadian federal union. This fabrication flies in the face of the top-down process whereby new provinces were added — especially the two provinces carved out of the Northwest Territories in 1905. As Arthur Lower observed, "there was not the slightest vestige of a 'compact' in the Acts of Parliament that created the provinces of Alberta and Saskatchewan in 1905."[51]

Nor was the compact theory strictly followed in constitutional practice. If the Canadian Constitution was a compact or treaty among the provinces, then no changes should have been made to it without the consent of all the provinces. Formally constitutional changes, as amendments to the *BNA Act*, were enacted by the British Parliament, but that body would act only on a request from Canada. During the period that the compact theory was gathering force, however, several amendments were made to the *BNA Act* at the request of the federal government and Parliament without consulting the provinces or seeking their consent. While none of these amendments directly affected the powers of the provinces, two of them related to the structure of the federation: one empowered the federal Parliament to create new provinces and the other provided for the representation of territories in the federal Parliament.[52] Prior to the 1907 amendment,[53] which revised the subsidies paid to the provinces, Laurier did hold a federal–provincial conference and eight of the nine provinces (British Columbia held out for better terms) agreed to the federal proposal. But the provinces were not consulted on the 1915 amendment that redefined the divisions of the Senate, forming a new section out of the four western provinces.[54]

Even though the compact theory was not consistently observed in the constitutional amendment process, it had become a powerful constitutional ideal by the turn of the century. Provincial rights and the compact theory had, as Ramsay Cook put it, "attained a position close to motherhood in the scale of Canadian political values. It would be difficult to find a prominent politician who was not willing to pay lip-service to the principle of provincial rights and its theoretical underpinning, the compact theory."[55] As a constitutional doctrine, the compact theory may have contained ambiguities and lacked precision, but its strength as a political value in Canada meant that the Canadian political community that was forming would be complex and deeply pluralist. Canada would take its place in the world as an interventionist state and its nationwide activities would take on increasing significance in the lives of its citizens, but the provinces would nonetheless endure as strong constituent elements of the Canadian community.

The ambiguities of the compact theory were intensified by the coexistence of two competing versions of the compact: a compact of founding provinces and a compact of founding peoples.[56] The latter contended that Canada was founded on the basis of a covenant between English Canadians and French Canadians. In the final analysis, the making of Canada in 1867 was "the free association of two peoples, enjoying equal rights in all matters."[57] These were the words of Henri Bourassa, the theory's most eloquent spokesman and founder of the great Montreal newspaper *Le Devoir* in 1910. Again, the significance of this theory in Canada's constitutional politics rests not on its historical accuracy but on its potency as a political myth. It is easy to show that neither in law nor in politics was the *BNA Act* a formal agreement between the French and English people of British North America. Nonetheless, that constitutional settlement depended, as we have seen, on English- and French-Canadian leaders agreeing to a federal structure with a province in which the French Canadians would remain a majority. For many English Canadians, assent to this agreement was only grudgingly given; for French Canadians it represented liberation from Lord Durham's scheme to assimilate them into a unicultural English political community, the triumph of their cultural survival — and, indeed for many, of national survival. The expectations on the French side flowing from that agreement gave rise to the theory that Confederation was based on a compact between two founding peoples.[58]

As originally espoused by Bourassa and other French Canadians, the two founding peoples theory was applied to all of Canada. Indeed, it was advanced as the theoretical underpinning for a pan-Canadian nationalism that viewed all Canada in dualist terms. Its exponents defended the rights of the French minorities outside Quebec and of the English minority in Quebec. In this sense, it may have provided "moral support for minimizing the consequences of the compact of provinces" and of provincial rights.[59] At the same time, this dualist view of Canada always retained a special place for the province of Quebec. As the homeland of one of the founding peoples, it had the right to be secure against intrusions into its culture by the general government answerable to an English-speaking majority.

Lurking within these rival compact theories were deep-seated differences on the nature of Canada as a political community. The idea that Quebec has a special place in Confederation as the only province in which one of the founding peoples forms the majority would collide with the doctrine of provincial equality. More fundamentally, the idea of a Canada based on the English and the French as its two founding peoples would be challenged at the end of the twentieth century by Canadians who were neither British nor French in their cultural background and by the Aboriginal peoples.

So long as Canadians were not interested in taking custody of their Constitution into their own hands, this conflict over the nature of Canada as a political community was of no great political importance. It was bound, however, to become salient once that condition changed. The time arrived in 1926, when the Balfour Declaration declared Canada and the other self-governing dominions to be "autonomous Communities" within the British Commonwealth.[60] Canada's political leaders then faced the challenge of arranging for Canada to become constitutionally self-governing.

NOTES

1. For an account see W.P.M. Kennedy, *The Constitution of Canada, 1534–1937: An Introduction to Its Development, Law and Custom,* 2nd ed. (London: Oxford University Press, 1938), 318–20.
2. A.I. Silver, *The French-Canadian Idea of Confederation, 1864–1900* (Toronto: University of Toronto Press, 1982), 111.

3. Ibid., 121.

4. Christopher Armstrong, *The Politics of Federalism: Ontario's Relations with the Federal Government, 1867–1942* (Toronto: University of Toronto Press, 1981), 14.

5. A. Margaret Evans, *Sir Oliver Mowat* (Toronto: University of Toronto Press for The Ontario Historical Studies Series, 1992).

6. For a succinct account of the National Policy see Craig Brown, "The Nationalism of the National Policy," in *Nationalism in Canada*, ed. Peter H. Russell (Toronto: McGraw-Hill, 1966), 155–63.

7. Reginald Whitaker, "Democracy and the Canadian Constitution," in Keith Banting and Richard Simeon, eds., *And No One Cheered: Federalism, Democracy and the Constitution Act* (Toronto: Methuen, 1983), 250.

8. For a full account see Paul Romney, *Mr. Attorney: The Attorney General for Ontario in Court, Cabinet and Legislature, 1791–1899* (Toronto: University of Toronto Press, 1986), chap. 6.

9. Sections 55–7.

10. R. MacGregor Dawson, *The Government of Canada*, 4th ed., revised by Norman Ward (Toronto: University of Toronto Press, 1966), 142.

11. For a contemporary statement on this point see Peter W. Hogg, *Constitutional Law of Canada*, 2nd ed. (Toronto: Carswell, 1985), 38.

12. For a full account of the use of these powers see Gerard V. LaForest, *Disallowance and Reservation of Provincial Legislation* (Ottawa: Department of Justice, 1965).

13. For a detailed account see Romney, *Mr. Attorney*, 255–56.

14. Armstrong, *Politics of Federalism*, 29.

15. See Paul Gérin-Lajoie, *Constitutional Amendment in Canada* (Toronto: University of Toronto Press, 1950), 142–43.

16. For a full account see Frank MacKinnon, "The Establishment of the Supreme Court of Canada," *Canadian Historical Review* 27 (1946): 258–74.

17. [1878] 2 S.C.R. 70. For a compendium of Supreme Court and Judicial Committee decisions on the constitution see Peter H. Russell, Rainer Knopff, and Ted Morton, *Federalism and the Charter: Leading Constitutional Decisions* (Ottawa: Carleton University Press, 1989).

18. [1979] 3 S.C.R. 575.

19. [1881] 7 App. Cas. 96.

20. F. Murray Greenwood, "Lord Watson, Institutional Self-Interest and the Decentralization of Canadian Federalism in the 1890's," *University of British Columbia Law Review* 9 (1974): 267.

21. *Russell v. The Queen* (1882), 7 App. Cas. 829.

22. *Hodge v. The Queen* (1883), 9 App. Cas. 177 (upholding provincial power), and the *McCarthy Act Reference* (not reported). For a discussion see Russell et al., *Federalism and the Charter*, 53.

23. *Attorney General for Ontario v. Attorney General for Canada*, [1896] A.C. 348.

24. *Liquidators of the Maritime Bank of Canada v. Receiver General of New Brunswick*, [1992] A.C. 437.

25. P.B. Waite, ed., *The Confederation Debates in the Province of Canada, 1865* (Toronto: McClelland and Stewart, 1963), 156.

26. For a classical statement of the theory see K.C. Wheare, *Federal Government*, 4th ed. (London: Oxford University Press, 1963). On the basis of the centralizing elements in the constitutional text, Wheare concluded that Canada was not a true federation but a "quasi-federation."

27. On the absence of a theoretical understanding or agreement on federalism at the time of Confederation see P.B. Waite, *The Life and Times of Confederation, 1864–1867: Politics, Newspapers, and the Union of British North America*, 2nd ed. (Toronto: University of Toronto Press, 1962), chap. 8.

28. The saying is attributed to Charles Evans Hughes, later chief justice of the United States. See A.T. Mason and W.M. Beaney, *American Constitutional Law* (Englewood Cliffs, NJ: Prentice-Hall, 1959), 3.

29. For a discussion of the views of the Fathers of Confederation on this subject see Jennifer Smith, "The Origins of Judicial Review in Canada," *Canadian Journal of Political Science* 16 (1983): 115–34.

30. Section 93(4).

31. For the evidence see Peter H. Russell, *The Supreme Court of Canada as a Bilingual and Bicultural Institution* (Ottawa: Queen's Printer, 1969), chap. 1.

32. See Alexander Hamilton, "The Federalist No. 78," *The Federalist Papers* (New York: Modern Library, 1937).

33. For an account see W.L. Morton, *The Kingdom of Canada: A General History from Earliest Times*, 2nd ed. (Toronto: McClelland and Stewart, 1969), chap. 19.

34. On the demographic changes see Janice Staples, "Consociationalism at Provincial Level: The Erosion of Dualism in Manitoba, 1870–1890," in Kenneth McRae, ed., *Consociational Democracy: Political Accomodation in Segmented Societies* (Toronto: McClelland and Stewart, 1974), 288–99.

35. Section 23 of the *Manitoba Act, 1870*.

36. *Attorney General for Manitoba v. Forest*, [1979] 2 S.C.R. 1032. Earlier challenges that were successful in the local courts were simply ignored.

37. Section 22 of the *Manitoba Act, 1870*.

38. *City of Winnipeg v. Barrett*, [1892] A.C. 445.

39. *Brophy v. Attorney General for Manitoba*, [1895] A.C. 445.

40. Morton, *Kingdom of Canada*, 379.

41. After the election, Laurier worked out a compromise with Manitoba premier Greenway that allowed periods of minority language and religious instruction where numbers warranted.

42. Silver, *French-Canadian Idea of Confederation*, 243.

43. D.V. Smiley, *Canada in Question: Federalism in the Eighties*, 3rd ed. (Toronto: McGraw-Hill Ryerson, 1980), 1.

44. See Edwin Black, *Divided Loyalites: Canadian Concepts of Federalism* (Montreal and London: McGill-Queen's University Press, 1975), 132–35.

45. For a fuller elaboration see Whittaker, "Democracy and the Canadian Constitution."

46. Quoted in Robert Vipond, *Liberty and Community: Canadian Federalism and the Failure of the Constitution* (Albany: State University of New York Press, 1991), 79.

47. Ibid., especially chap. 3.

48. For a full account of the theory see Ramsay Cook, *Provincial Autonomy, Minority Rights and the Compact Theory, 1867–1921* (Ottawa: Queen's Printer, 1969).

49. Black, *Divided Loyalties*, 154.

50. This is the definition of myth given by R.M. MacIver in *The Web of Government* (New York: Macmillan, 1947), 4. For the application of this sense of myth to the compact theory see Donald V. Smiley, *The Canadian Political Nationality* (Toronto: Methuen, 1967), 30.

51. Arthur R.M. Lower, *Colony to Nation: A History of Canada*, 4th ed. (Toronto: Longmans, 1964), 32.

52. The *British North America Act* of 1871 and the *British North America Act* of 1886. The third, the *Parliament of Canada Act, 1875*, concerned the privileges and immunities of the House of Commons. For a brief account of all constitutional amendments up until 1964 and how they were obtained see the Honourable Guy Favreau, *The Amendment of the Constitution of Canada* (Ottawa: Queen's Printer, 1965).

53. The *British North America Act* of 1907.

54. The *British North America Act* of 1915.

55. Cook, *Provincial Autonomy*, 44.

56. For an analysis of the relationship between the two compact theories see Filippo Sabetti, "The Historical Context of Constitutional Change in Canada," *Law and Contemporary Problems* 45 (1982): 11–32.

57. Quoted ibid., 21.

58. For an analysis of this tendency for French-speaking Canadians to view the Constitution as a compact between two peoples while the English-speaking population view the Constitution as an organic development see Daniel J. Elazar, "Constitution-Making: The Pre-eminently Political Act," in Keith G. Banting and Richard Sineon, eds., *Redesigning the State: The Politics of Constitutional Change in Industrial Nations* (Toronto: University of Toronto Press, 1985), 245–46.

59. Sabetti, "Historical Context of Constitutional Changes in Canada," 20.

60. Dawson, *Government of Canada*, 63.

Article Four

Unity/Diversity: The Canadian Experience; From Confederation to the First World War

J.R. Miller

I

While everyone conceded in the 1860s that the object of the Fathers of Confederation was to produce the bases of one political entity, no one anticipated that this task would be performed by imposing uniformity on the diverse peoples and regions of British North America. Indeed, had such a goal been sought, it would have proved impossible of attainment. The various colonies, with their unique historical development, their different religious denominations, and their distinct nationalities, could not have been homogenized culturally as they were joined politically. The peculiarities of language, creed, and regional identity had to be maintained, for several good and compelling reasons.

Diversity was both desirable and unavoidable, first, because the existing differences were simply too strong to be dismissed. This was true not just in the case of the French Canadians, but even with the local autonomists of Ontario, the Grits, and, most especially, in the Maritimes. The *Acadian Recorder* lamented: "We don't know each other. We have no trade with each other. We have no facilities or resources or incentives to mingle with each other. We are shut off from each other by a wilderness, geographically, commercially, politically and socially. We always cross the United States to shake hands." Joseph Howe, as usual, put it more pungently: "Take a Nova Scotian to Ottawa, away above tidewater, freeze him up for five months, where he cannot view the Atlantic, smell salt water, or see the sail of a ship, and the man will pine and die."[1] Diversity was a force too powerful to be exorcised.

Even were it possible to assimilate all British North Americans, to what would you assimilate them? Unlike the United States, a community created by revolution and compact, the proposed Canada was to be produced as the result of an evolutionary process by an act of an external authority, the United Kingdom. Rather than a society of revolution and consensus, Canada was to be a community of evolution and allegiance. The society of allegiance did not require conformity to any one model; the Canadians had no object of assimilation.[2] If they copied anything at all, it was the British pattern, which, since the days of imperial expansion and Catholic Emancipation, meant not something monolithic, Protestant, and Anglo-Saxon, but a number of things more diversified. Canadians could not, at Quebec and Charlottetown, have sought unity at the expense of diversity because there was nothing to which they could conform, and no imperative of revolution to force them to make such a compact.

Finally, Canadian unity was not purchased at the price of homogenization because the colonial politicians who produced it had no intention of creating problems for themselves

Source: "Unity/Diversity: The Canadian Experience; From Confederation to the First World War," *Dalhousie Review* 55, 1 (Spring 1975): 63–82. Reprinted by permission.

by debating something as abstract and theoretical as the cultural basis of the new state. These were practical politicians with painfully real problems. Their attention was devoted to solving the difficulties created by deadlock, acquisition of the Northwest, inadequate defences, and promotion of intercolonial commerce, not to searching for new ones. They were, as Donald Creighton has observed, "as far away from the dogmas of the eighteenth-century Enlightenment as they were from twentieth-century obsession with race, and with racial and cultural separatism." These men "saw no merit in setting out on a highly unreal voyage of discovery for first principles."[3] In short, the delegates at Quebec were not about to open a new can of worms by debating the place of various cultural and religious groups in Canada. Such a discussion was as undesirable as it was unnecessary.

These were the reasons why the British North American colonies, as Arthur Lower pointed out, "were carpentered together, not smelted."[4] Or, as G.F.G. Stanley observed: "The Canadian Confederation came into being not to crush but to reconcile regional diversities. . . . Union, not unity, was the result."[5] As one might expect, it was the French-Canadian leader, George-Étienne Cartier, who expressed the idea of unity in diversity most clearly:

> In our own Federation we should have Catholic and Protestant, English, French, Irish and Scotch, and each by his efforts and his success would increase the prosperity and glory of the new Confederacy. . . . They were placed like great families beside each other, and their contact produced a healthy spirit of emulation. It was a benefit rather than otherwise that we had a diversity of races. . . .
>
> Now, when we were united together, . . . we would form a political nationality with which neither the national origin, nor the religion of any individual, would interfere. It was lamented by some that we had this diversity of races, and hopes were expressed that this distinctive feature would cease. The idea of unity of races was utopian—it was impossible. Distinctions of this kind would always exist. Dissimilarity, in fact, appeared to be the order of the physical world and of the moral world, as well as of the political world.[6]

The key words were "a political nationality": the unity that Confederation was to produce union at the political level, not cultural. While "carpentering" political unity, British North Americans would retain regional, religious, and cultural diversity; Canada was founded on unity in diversity. And, in passing, one might note the type of diversity intended—"Catholic and Protestant, English, French, Irish and Scotch." This was a very Britannic mosaic.

II

Of course, the formula "Unity in diversity" raised as many questions as it answered. What did the concept mean? How did you hold a diverse country together? Specifically, what were the rights and privileges of the most distinctive minority, the French Canadians? More specifically still, what was to become of the principle of cultural and political *duality* that had evolved in the Province of Canada (the future Ontario and Quebec) between 1841 and 1867? It would take a decade and more to work out the first set of answers to these riddles; and, then, the first essay at a resolution of them would come under attack and be modified substantially.

The first question dealt with was the fate of the duality of the Canadian union. Here the answer was starkly simple: duality would be eliminated. This did not mean any tampering with the official status of the French language that was protected by Section 133 of the *British North America Act* in the courts and Parliament of Canada, as well as in the courts and Legislature of Quebec. However, in succeeding years it was evident that Canadians were not prepared to foster the expansion of this limited, pragmatic recognition of French into a great principle of *duality* throughout the land. Although French was officially countenanced in Manitoba and the Northwest Territories, under special and pressing circumstances, it was not enshrined in the other new provinces of British Columbia and Prince Edward Island. Indeed, in New Brunswick, the Acadian minority suffered the loss of an important cultural bulwark in the 1870s, when their legislature deprived them of public support for their denominational schools. In short, the first generation of Canadian politicians was prepared to grant French culture official status where temporary exigencies and local pressures made it politically expedient to do so, and nowhere else. They certainly were not about to erect linguistic duality into a great principle of the federation.

Moreover, other aspects of dualism, the double political and administrative institutions that had developed in the United Province, were deliberately removed. Governor General Monck's invitation to John A. Macdonald to form the first Dominion Cabinet explicitly forbade the continuation of the dual premiership. Sectional equality in the Cabinet was replaced by a careful balancing of regional, economic, religious, and cultural interests in Macdonald's first ministry, and in almost all that have succeeded. Duality of administrative posts was also abolished, essentially because the unsatisfactory quasi-federalism of the Union was replaced by a real federation and division of powers between levels of government. There were, for example, no longer two Superintendents of Education because the schools were now the responsibility of the provinces. Similarly, two attorneys-general were not needed because French Canada's peculiar civil law was to be controlled by Quebec. And so it went. Institutional duality, whether at the political or civil service level, was eradicated because it was unnecessary and unwanted.

Whatever else the first decade demonstrated, it proved that unity in diversity did not mean the retention of any more duality than was essential. There still remained the more difficult question: if unity in diversity did not mean duality, what did it mean? How was it to be formalized, embodied, made concrete? How did you tack together "a political nationality" out of diverse elements?

The first indication of the means that would be used to hold the country together came in 1868, in Minister of Justice Macdonald's memorandum on the federal power of disallowance. Macdonald laid down guidelines for the federal veto of provincial legislation that were sweeping. They were so general as almost to be unqualified, as was suggested by the provision that provincial statutes "as affecting the interests of the Dominion generally" could be struck down if Ottawa wished.[7] This was Macdonald's instinctive reversion to the eighteenth-century Tory tradition of centralized governmental power. Under his leadership, the first government after Confederation followed a highly centralist policy, one suspects because he regarded such centralization as being as essential to the well-being of the fragile union as it was congenial to his Conservative temperament.

Gradually during the 1870s the rest of the apparatus for ensuring the unity of the state was put into place. The policy of pushing the Indians out of the arable lands of the prairie West and replacing them with white, agricultural settlers was one such project. The gargantuan task of binding the newly acquired and sparsely populated West to the rest of the country with a transcontinental railroad was another. And the policy of forcing economic diversification and regional specialization of economic function through the imposition of the protective tariff was the final means chosen to produce enduring unity out of diversity and distance. The objective of these national policies of expansion and development was to provide an economic *raison d'être* for the political state; or, if you prefer, it was the means of putting the flesh of economic self-interest on the bare bones of the constitutional skeleton. The West, once filled, would produce agricultural products for export and would serve as a captive market for Canadian manufacturers. Central Canada would manufacture goods, protected and encouraged by the tariff; would fuel her industries with Nova Scotian coal; and would sell her products to Maritimers and Westerners alike. The whole scheme would be facilitated by the network of railways that was so essential to the Canadian federation: the Grand Trunk, Intercolonial, and Canadian Pacific. And, finally, the scheme of economic nationalism — the encouragement of a transcontinental economy of diverse, but integrated economic regions — would be supervised and protected by a powerful central government.

Now, the formulation of these policies was undoubtedly much more accidental than the foregoing sketch suggests. The steps toward adoption of the various pieces were often hesitant, taken out of a sense of constitutional obligation (the promise of a railway to BC), and motivated more by partisan political calculations than nation-building ambitions. And, yet, what seems striking is the fact that the pieces fit, that they made up a coherent, compelling, and politically appealing program of national self-defence through economic expansion and integration. Furthermore, when the pieces are put together, they provide an answer to the question of how unity could be maintained amidst diversity. The answer was that diverse regions, religious groups, and nationalities could stay united politically while remaining different culturally because they had a program of economic development from which they could all benefit. And, moreover, these policies meant that the focus of political life at the federal level would not be on sensitive issues of religion and nationality, but on economic issues that cut across regional, religious, and cultural lines. Macdonald's nationalism would make unity in diversity possible by concentrating on those things that united Canadians, or, at least, did not divide them according to religion and language. The recipe was: diversity locally, but political unity in pursuit of common economic objectives.

Not the least significant feature of this concoction is the fact that, to a large extent, it succeeded. The French Canadians participated in the scheme as enthusiastically as anyone else. There were no more fervent protectionists than Quebec's leaders, who saw the industrialization of the Townships as the alternative to the continuing hemorrhage of French-Canadian youth to the detested United States. Ontario was satisfied, for the key to Macdonald's scheme was the realization of Ontario's traditional dream of opening and developing the West in Ontario's image and for Toronto's pecuniary benefit. The national policies embodied Ontario imperialism. And the Maritimes benefited too, although the advantages were offset by the general deterioration of the Atlantic economy in the waning years of wind and wood transportation. There was substantial growth in the Nova Scotian coal industry, as the industrialization encouraged by the tariff created markets for the fuel in urban Quebec.[8] The only region that did not benefit very much from the scheme was the West. There the response to centralization and the national policies was protest: formation of the Manitoba and Northwest Farmers' Union, Riel's second Rebellion, the provincial autonomy campaign in Manitoba, and the steady intonation of the litany of grievances (freight rates, elevators, and tariffs) that was to become so familiar. But, frankly, no one worried much about western complaints, for colonies were only supposed to produce wealth, not be happy. Western grievances aside, however, the Tory scheme of unity through economic expansion was quite successful.

III

This unity based on pursuit of common economic goals under the direction of a strong central government began to erode in the 1880s as the result of three corrosive influences. Political opportunism inspired an attack on centralization by the Liberal parties at the federal and provincial levels. The economic stagnation that returned after 1883 destroyed the rosy dreams of prosperity and unity. As is normally the case in difficult times, economic discontent led to internal bickering: the provinces versus Ottawa; and Ontario against the rest, especially Quebec, when the provinces succeeded in extorting "better terms" from the Conservative federal government. Finally, the desired unity within the country was eroded by the influence in Canada of radically new theories of national unity that focused upon language and culture, rather than economic cooperation, as essential criteria for unification.

The new theories which sought unity at the expense of cultural diversity were represented in the 1880s and 1890s by such men as D'Alton McCarthy and Goldwin Smith. McCarthy, an Anglo-Saxon supremacist, imperialist, and tariff reformer, was worried about the lack of cohesion in Canada and anxious about the declining power of the central government. To him the villain of the piece seemed to be the French Canadian who insisted on having his own way, thereby preventing fusion:

> My own conviction is that it is not religion which is at the bottom of the matter but that it is a race feeling. There is no feeling so strong—no feeling which all history proves so strong— as the feeling of race. Don't we find the French today in the province of Quebec more French than when they were conquered by Wolfe upon the plains of Abraham? Do they mix with us, assimilate with us, intermarry with us? Do they read our literature or learn our laws? No, everything with them is conducted on a French model; and while we may admire members of that race as individuals, yet as members of the body politic I say that they are the great danger to the Confederacy.[9]

In McCarthy's view, "It was the language of a people that moulded its nationality."[10] The "science of language" demonstrated "that there is no factor equal to language to band people together, and . . . as is demonstrated in our own case, that nothing is more calculated to keep people asunder."[11] If McCarthy's analysis was correct, then it followed that Canadian unity could be achieved only through the imposition on Canada of one language: unity was to be achieved, not through diversity, but through cultural uniformity brought about by assimilation. His program for national unity was summarized in his resolution calling for the abolition of the official use of French in the Northwest Territories: that it was "expedient in the interest of national unity that there should be community of language among the people of Canada."[12]

Goldwin Smith, free trader, continentalist, and Anglo-Saxon racist, advocated a slightly different program to achieve the same end. He believed that French Canada was an obstacle to unity not just because of its language, but also because of its obscurantism and economic backwardness, both of which were the results of clerical domination:

> Quebec is a theocracy. While Rome has been losing her hold on Old France and on all the European nations, she has retained, nay tightened, it here. The people are the sheep of the priest. He is their political as well as their spiritual chief and nominates the politician, who serves the interest of the Church at Quebec or at Ottawa. . . . Not only have the clergy been the spiritual guides and masters of the French Canadians, they have been the preservers and

champions of his nationality, and they have thus combined the influence of the tribune with that of the priest.[13]

The French province, the people of which live on the produce of their own farms and clothe themselves with the produce of their spinning, is uncommercial, and lies a non-conductor between the more commercial members of the Confederation.[14]

Unlike McCarthy, Smith did not seek a solution to this problem in Canada, because he believed the political parties were totally and irrevocably the tools of the Quebec clergy. To Smith it was "perfectly clear that the forces of Canada alone are not sufficient to assimilate the French element or even to prevent the indefinite consolidation and growth of a French nation."[15] The answer, then, was obvious: "French Canada may be ultimately absorbed in the English-speaking population of a vast Continent; amalgamate with British Canada so as to form a united nation it apparently never can."[16] Canada should join the Americans to form an Anglo-Saxon republic of North America in which the French Canadians would drown.

There is a two-fold significance in the emergence of such advocates of Anglo-Saxon cultural uniformity as McCarthy and Smith. The first is that they are evidence that in English Canada, for a variety of reasons, many people had by the 1890s rejected the pursuit of unity in diversity. The second is that the country as a whole rejected the extreme prescriptions put forward by continentalists and cultural assimilationists alike for coercive uniformity. Parliament's response to McCarthy's call for linguistic uniformity was a compromise resolution that said that nothing had happened since Confederation to justify taking from the French Canadians the guarantees they received at the time of union, while allowing the populace of the Northwest Territories itself to decide the fate of the official use of French on the prairies.[17] And in the 1890s such annexationist schemes as Smith's Continental Union Association were rejected by the electorate.

Though McCarthy and Smith failed, they were not without lingering influence. French Canadians, seeing assimilationist movements such as the Equal Rights Association, Equal Rights League, Protestant Protective Association, and Continental Union Association, found renewed cause for anxiety about their future as a distinct cultural entity within the Canadian "political nationality." This disquiet was aggravated by a new phenomenon of the late 1890s and early 1900s, massive European immigration to the Canadian West. As French-Canadian leaders quickly perceived, this demographic change made Cartier's doctrine of diversity a source of danger.

IV

The problem arose because of English-Canadian reaction to the immigration of the Laurier period. As thousands of Poles, Russians, Germans, Italians, Scandinavians, and Ukrainians flooded the West, middle-class, Anglo-Saxon Canadians began to join working-class critics of extensive immigration. Whereas the old trade union criticism of immigration was essentially economic in character,[18] the new critique was fundamentally concerned with the cultural effects of immigration. Stephen Leacock observed disapprovingly that the new immigration was "from the Slavonic and Mediterranean peoples of a lower industrial and moral status," and consisted of "herds of the proletariat of Europe, the lowest class of industrial society."[19] Principal Sparling of Wesley College, Winnipeg, warned that Canadians "must see to it that the civilization and ideals of Southeastern Europe are not transplanted to and perpetuated on our virgin soil."[20]

While Ralph Connor fictionalized Sparling's injunction in *The Foreigner*,[21] a poet, of sorts, expressed similar ideas in verse:

> They are haggard, huddled, homeless, frightened at—they know not what:
> With a few unique exceptions they're a disappointing lot;
> But I take 'em as I get 'em, soldier, sailor, saint and clown
> And I turn 'em out Canadians—all but the yellow and brown.[22]

In the era of the Laurier Boom many Canadians recoiled from the tidal wave of immigration, sorrowfully concluding that they could "not make a nation by holding a basket at the hopper of an immigration chute."[23]

The English-Canadian answer to these cultural dangers was a drive to assimilate the "foreigner" by inculcating in him the values of British-Canadian civilization. What precisely that meant, and the danger it portended, manifested itself in the prescriptions critics of immigration put forward for the solution of the problem. "One of the best ways of Canadianizing, nationalizing, and turning all into intelligent citizens," said one Protestant clergyman in 1913, "is by means of a good English education."[24] When J.S. Woodsworth asked himself how "are we to break down the walls which separate these foreigners from us?" his conclusion was that first and foremost was "the Public School. Too great emphasis cannot be placed upon the work that has been accomplished and may—yes, must—be accomplished by our National Schools."[25] Linguistic uniformity imposed by the schools was the answer:

> If Canada is to become in any real sense a nation, if our people are to become one, we must have one language. . . . Hence the necessity of national schools where the teaching of English —our national language—is compulsory.

The public school system was "the most important factor in transforming the foreigners into Canadians."[26]

French Canada, not unnaturally, took alarm at such programs, which drew no distinction between the worthy French Canadian and the despised "Galician." The emerging champion of French-Canadian nationalism, Henri Bourassa, protested that the Fathers of Confederation had never intended "to change a providential condition of our partly French and partly English country to make it a land of refuge for the scum of all nations."[27] Bourassa's complaint was that diversity, by which Canadians had meant a mixture of English, French, and Scot, now seemed to mean Ukrainian, German, and Italian; and that English Canadians, in reacting to this new form of diversity, attacked French-Canadian rights as well as the pretensions of the European "scum." Bourassa knew whereof he spoke, for, in the early years of the twentieth century, Woodsworth's prescription (and Bourassa's nightmare) was realized. In 1901 and 1905 on the prairies, and in 1912 in Ontario, unilingual education was imposed in an effort to assimilate all minorities, including the French Canadians. In the era of massive European immigration, Cartier's "multicultural argument could only accelerate, not retard the unilingual process."[28]

Bourassa's, and French Canada's, response to this danger was to work out a new theory of Canadian unity that protected rather than jeopardized French-Canadian cultural rights. The new spokesman of French Canada found his justification of his culture in Providence and History. God, he argued, had placed the Latin culture of French Canada in North America as a spiritual beacon in the materialistic, Anglo-Saxon darkness. And what God planted, not even the Canadian Parliament ought to root out. Furthermore, he insisted,

Canadian history was the record of the preservation of cultural duality. The *Royal Proclamation of 1763* and *Quebec Act of 1774* had ensured the survival of the primary agency of French Canada, the Roman Catholic Church. A political process stretching from the *Constitutional Act of 1791* to the struggle over responsible government of the 1840s had expanded the limited eighteenth-century guarantees into semi-official recognition of duality. Confederation, in Bourassa's historical recitation, became the adoption by the new Dominion of Canada of biculturalism and bilingualism. Hence, French Canada should be respected because it was a coordinate partner with a special providential mission to perform. Not even the infringements of the Confederation compact in the West and Ontario between 1890 and 1912 could alter that fact. "The Canadian nation," Bourassa argued, "will attain its ultimate destiny, indeed it will exist, only on the condition of being biethnic and bilingual, and by remaining faithful to the concept of the Fathers of Confederation: the free and voluntary association of two peoples, enjoying equal rights in all matters."[29] In other words, in flight from the vulnerability of diversity, Bourassa had erected duality as a new line of defence. Bourassa and biculturalism had replaced Cartier and diversity as the theoretical justification of French Canada's right to exist.

In the first half-century of Confederation, then, Canadians' concept of their political community as a unity in diversity had come under attack on two fronts. English assimilationists had argued for cultural homogenization as an answer to disunity, and French-Canadian nationalists had responded with a messianic and historical defence of cultural duality. The two conflicting viewpoints were the subject of much public discussion in the early years of the twentieth century, as each struggled for mastery. As it turned out, with the coming of the Great War the English-Canadian assimilationist model triumphed. Several provinces terminated the official use of French; Ontario refused to soften the assimilationist thrust of its 1912 policy; and Quebec, as a result of the language issue and the conscription crisis, was politically isolated and alienated.

NOTES

1. *Acadian Recorder*, quoted in John Ricker, John Saywell, and Ramsay Cook, *Canada: A Modern Study* (Toronto, 1963), 101; J. Howe, quoted in J.M. Beck, *Joseph Howe: Anti-Confederate* (Ottawa, 1956), 15.
2. W.L. Morton, *The Canadian Identity* (Madison and Toronto, 1961), 100–107, 110–12.
3. D.G. Creighton, *The Road to Confederation* (Toronto, 1964), 141–42.
4. A.R.M. Lower, *Canadians in the Making* (Don Mills, 1958), 289.
5. G.F.G. Stanley, "Regionalism in Canadian History," *Ontario History* 51 (1959): 167.
6. P.B. Waite, ed., *Confederation Debates in the Province of Canada/1865* (Carleton Library edition, Toronto, 1963), 51 and 50.
7. Quoted in J.M. Beck, ed., *The Shaping of Canadian Federalism* (Toronto, 1971), 159.
8. P.B. Waite, *Canada, 1874–1896: Arduous Destiny* (Toronto, 1971), 184.
9. Quoted in F. Landon, "D'Alton McCarthy and the Politics of the Later Eighties," Canadian Historical Association, *Report of the Annual Meeting, 1932*, 46.
10. Stayner Speech, 12 July 1889, *Toronto Daily Mail*, 13 July 1889.
11. *Speech of Mr. D'Alton McCarthy delivered on Thursday, 12 December 1889 at Ottawa* (n.p., n.d.).
12. *Debates of the House of Commons*, Fourth Session, Sixth Parliament, vol. 29 (1890), columns 674–75.
13. G. Smith, *Canada and the Canadian Question* (Toronto, 1891), 5–6.
14. Smith, *Canada and the Canadian Question*, 206–207.
15. Smith, *Canada and the Canadian Question*, 275.
16. Smith, *Canada and the Canadian Question*, 215.
17. *Debates of the House of Commons* (1890), columns 881–82 and 1017–18.

18. With the exception, of course, of British Columbia, where the objections had been based on both economic and racial arguments. See J.A. Munro, "British Columbia and the 'Chinese Evil': Canada's First Anti-Asiatic Immigration Law," *Journal of Canadian Studies* 6 (1971): 42–49.

19. S. Leacock, "Canada and the Immigration Problem," *The National Review* 52 (1911): 317 and 323.

20. Principal Sparling, "Introduction" to J.S. Woodsworth, *Strangers within Our Gates, or Coming Canadians* (Toronto, 1909).

21. R. Connor [C.W. Gordon], *The Foreigner: A Tale of Saskatchewan* (Toronto, 1909), especially 23–25 and 37–41. This theme in Connor's work has been analyzed carefully in J.L. Thompson and J.H. Thompson, "Ralph Connor and the Canadian Identity," *Queen's Quarterly* 79 (1972): 166–69.

22. R.J.C. Stead, "The Mixer" (1905), quoted in R.C. Brown and R. Cook, *Canada, 1896–1921: A Nation Transformed* (Toronto, 1974), 73.

23. Leacock, "Canada and the Immigration Problem," 318.

24. Rev. W.D. Reid, in R.C. Brown and M.E. Prang, eds., *Confederation to 1949* (Scarborough, 1966), 84.

25. J.S. Woodsworth, *Strangers within Our Gates*, 281.

26. J.S. Woodsworth (1905), quoted in Brown and Cook, *Canada, 1896–1921*, 73.

27. H. Bourassa (1904), quoted in Brown and Cook, *Canada, 1896–1921*, 74.

28. A. Smith, "Metaphor and Nationality in North America," *Canadian Historical Review* 51 (1970): 268. This paper owes far more than this isolated quotation to Professor Smith's stimulating analysis, as students of the topic will realize.

29. H. Bourassa (1917), quoted in R. Cook, *Canada and the French-Canadian Question* (Toronto, 1966), 51.

Topic Three

The North-West Rebellion of 1885

Prominent South Branch Métis in irons in front of the Regina land titles office. The government prosecutors persuaded these men to plead guilty to charges of treason-felony by threatening them with high treason, which carried the death penalty. They were sentenced to various prison terms.

FEW ISSUES in Canadian history have generated more heated debate than the North-West Rebellion of 1885. For a long time, the debate centred on the main protagonist, Louis Riel, the ill-fated leader of both the Métis resistance of 1869/70 and the rebellion of 1885. To what extent was he alone responsible for the North-West Rebellion of 1885? Should he be seen as a rebel leader or as a mere victim of circumstances? Did he represent cultural, linguistic, or regional interests?

More recently, Canadian historians have shifted their focus from Riel to his followers. Moving away from the "Great Man Theory of History," these historians have been more interested in ascertaining why certain Métis, Natives, and white settlers in the North-West followed Riel while others did not than in explaining why Riel led them into rebellion. They also try to discover whether Riel's followers represented particular interest groups in their respective communities.

The following three articles reflect this new historiographical trend. In "The Métis Militant Rebels of 1885," David Lee examines the cultural background of the most radical of the Métis participants in the rebellion. He shows that a correlation existed between the militancy of these individuals and their livelihood, language, age, and social outlook. A. Blair Stonechild examines the other main participants in the rebellion—Native people —in "The Indian View of the 1885 Uprising." The difficulty in reconstructing their perspective on the uprising, as Stonechild notes, is the lack of traditional written sources. What the author uses instead are oral histories and stories to present a refreshingly new, Native-oriented explanation for why some of the First Nations communities joined the rebellion. He notes that to a great extent they were forced into the conflict as a result of misunderstanding, prejudice, and sinister intent on the part of influential government and Métis leaders in the region.

Stonechild's article presents a First Nations' view of the rebellion. In "'Captured Women': A Re-examination of the Stories of Theresa Delaney and Theresa Gowanlock," historian Sarah Carter constructs the white settlers' quite different perspective of the rebellion through an analysis of Delaney and Gowanlock's account of their captivity during the rebellion in *Two Months in the Camp of Big Bear*, and the reaction at the time among non-Natives to their story. Carter shows how issues of gender and race played a defining role in the settlers' perspective of the rebellion, and in the strained relations between Native people as the "foreign element" and newcomers, including non-Native women, as "bearers of civilization" and agents of control and power in the North-West.

The literature on Riel and the Métis is extensive. For a concise overview of the history and culture of the Métis, see D.B. Sealey and A.S. Lussier's *The Métis: Canada's Forgotten People* (Winnipeg: Métis Federation Press, 1975). A growing literature exists on Louis Riel and the Métis in 1869–70 and 1885. The five-volume *Collected Writings of Louis Riel/Les Écrits complets de Louis Riel* (Edmonton: University of Alberta Press, 1985), under the general editorship of George F.G. Stanley, is currently available. Secondary studies include G.F.G. Stanley's *The Birth of Western Canada: A History of the Riel Rebellion* (Toronto: University of Toronto Press, 1961 [1936]); Thomas Flanagan's *Louis "David" Riel: "Prophet of the New World,"* rev. ed. (Toronto: University of Toronto Press, 1996); H. Bowsfield's *Louis Riel: The Rebel and the Hero* (Toronto: Oxford University Press, 1971) and his edited collection, *Louis Riel: Selected Readings* (Toronto: Copp Clark, 1987); Joseph Kinsey

Howard's *Strange Empire* (New York: William Morrow, 1952); and, for the uprising of 1885, B. Beal and R. Macleod's *Prairie Fire: A History of the 1885 Rebellion* (Edmonton: Hurtig, 1984). Hugh Dempsey presents one First Nations leader's response in his *Big Bear* (Vancouver: Douglas and McIntyre, 1984). For a critical view of the Métis position, see T. Flanagan, *Riel and the Rebellion: 1885 Reconsidered* (Saskatoon: Western Producer Books, 1983). The opposite viewpoint is presented in D.N. Sprague, *Canada and the Métis, 1869–1885* (Waterloo: Wilfrid Laurier University Press, 1988).

George F.G. Stanley reviews the various interpretations of Riel in "The Last Word on Louis Riel—The Man of Several Faces," in *1885 and After*, ed. F. Laurie Barron and James B. Waldram (Regina: Canadian Plains Research Centre, 1986), pp. 3–22. A good historiographical article is J.R. Miller's "From Riel to the Métis," *Canadian Historical Review* 69 (March 1988): 1–20. Diane Payment's *"The Free People—Otipemiswak": Batoche, Saskatchewan, 1870–1930* (Ottawa: Canadian Parks Service/National Historic Parks and Sites, 1990) is an in-depth study of the important Métis community of Batoche. In *Views from Fort Battleford: Constructed Visions of an Anglo-Canadian West* (Regina: Canadian Plains Research Centre, University of Regina, 1994), Walter Hildebrandt discusses aspects of the conflict between the First Nations and the Anglo-Canadians on the Prairies. His *The Battle of Batoche: British Small Warfare and the Entrenched Métis* (Ottawa: National Historic Parks and Sites, Parks Canada, 1985) discusses the military engagement at Batoche. Ramon Hathorn and Patrick Holland have compiled an interesting anthology entitled *Images of Louis Riel in Canadian Culture* (Lewiston, NY: E. Mellen Press, 1992). George Melnyk's *Radical Regionalism* (Edmonton: NeWest Press, 1981) and his edited collection *Riel to Reform: A History of Protest in Western Canada* (Saskatoon: Fifth House Publishers, 1992) examine the roots of Western protest, and its relationship to regional identity.

An important study of the Native involvement in the North-West Rebellion is Blair Stonechild and Bill Waiser, *Loyal till Death: Indians and the North-West Rebellion* (Calgary: Fifth House, 1997). For a fuller discussion on the Delaney-Gowanlock captivity, see Sarah Carter, *Capturing Women: The Manipulation of Cultural Imagery in Canada's Prairie West* (Montreal/Kingston: McGill-Queen's University Press, 1997). Hugh Dempsey explains the participation of Big Bear's band in the North-West Rebellion in *Big Bear: The End of Freedom* (Vancouver: Douglas and McIntyre, 1984), as does J.R. Miller in *Big Bear (Mistahimusqua)* (Toronto: ECW Press, 1996).

Article Five

The Métis Militant Rebels of 1885

David Lee

A great avalanche of writing on the North-West Rebellion or "resistance" of 1885 appeared in the decade preceding the centenary of that dramatic event.[1] These studies pursue a variety of themes, theories, and preoccupations, some conflicting with others. Still, the writers generally agreed on the larger picture. They viewed the rebellion of 1885 as a response

Source: "The Métis Militant Rebels of 1885," *Canadian Ethnic Studies* 21, 3 (1989): 1–19. Reprinted by permission.

by the Métis of the Northwest Territories to the trauma of an abrupt and perceivedly bane-ful change in circumstances. These people, of mixed Indian and French ancestry, futilely attempted (with the assistance of a few Indians) to resist the notion of change by taking up arms. The indicators of change were numerous and inescapable: the disappearance of the buffalo; decline of the fur trade; the supplanting of cart and canoe freighting by rail and steamboat; the prospect of having to live a sedentary, agricultural life; an increasingly interventionist yet dilatory government bureaucracy, slow to act on land entitlements and surveys; and the influx of aggressive immigrants who knew how to use government authority to serve their own interest. Feeling that they were about to lose control over their destiny, the Métis reacted by establishing their own provisional government on the South Saskatchewan River and by taking violent action against agents of the Canadian government.

However, despite the depth and breadth of the avalanche, some parts of the story still remain relatively unexamined. Little has been done, for example, to examine the range of opinion in the Métis community regarding the notion of rebellion, to gauge the degree of support for that course of action, to identify those Métis most militantly committed to tak-ing up arms, or to inquire into their backgrounds.

Thomas Flanagan has written that "probably a strong majority" of the community "accepted" the notion of insurrection.[2] Walter Hildebrandt lists Gabriel Dumont and ten others as the "hardcore" of Louis Riel's followers.[3] However, Louis Schmidt, a Métis who was present during the uprising but did not fight, put the number of highly committed combatants much higher. In his memoirs, he estimated that one-quarter to one-third of the Métis fought "vaillamment" (ardently); the remainder, he recalled, participated only "mollement" (lukewarmly) or not at all, either due to a lack of ammunition or because the idea of "révolte . . . les rend timides."[4] George Woodcock has opined that it was "the wilder" of the Métis who were the most "discontented" and committed to armed insur-rection; he estimated the militants to number "at most a few dozen men."[5] Discussion of commitment among the rebels, then, has been rather limited.

The study which follows will examine the people of mixed Indian and European ances-try living on the South Saskatchewan River in 1885 and, more specifically, the men who fought in the battles of Duck Lake, Fish Creek, and Batoche in the spring of that year. The study will show that there was a fairly wide spectrum of both political opinion and cultural background within the Métis community. More significantly, it will be seen that the two spectra were almost congruent with one another. It will also show that, while the most militant men in the community were chiefly older and less acculturated, the insurrec-tionary movement was quite deeply based.

Métis Community

As might be expected, the South Saskatchewan Métis were not a fully homogeneous group but rather a community with a variety of internal divisions and tensions, both polit-ical and cultural. At one end of the cultural spectrum were a small number of Métis who, through education or perhaps solely ambition, were well on their way to acculturation; that is, they were adjusting their lifestyles to meet the demands of an increasingly intru-sive Euro-Canadian society. Some of these people were active in commerce while a few held salaried, government positions. At the other end of this spectrum were Métis who (though they considered themselves distinct from, and sometimes even superior to, Indians) were, in many ways, close to the Plains Cree and Saulteaux in culture; these peo-ple were not receptive to the ways of the powerful newcomers. They were unable or unwilling to abruptly take up such new endeavours as agriculture, animal husbandry, technical crafts, or retail trade, for example. The reasons could have been lack of confidence, incentive, capital, aptitude, or education, but may also have included satisfaction and pride in their traditional lifeways. These more conservative, or "more Indian," Métis would, for example, have been far more at ease in a tent on the Plains than in a house at Prince Albert or Saskatoon. As will be seen, they were often not much different from many so-called "Treaty Indians" living on nearby reserves. With regard to the community's political attitudes, i.e., its feelings regarding the notion of insurrection, the spectrum ranged from militancy through moderation to opposition. More significantly, it will be seen that the most militant proponents of rebellion can be largely characterized as conservatives while opponents were among the most acculturated in the community.

The evidence presented in this study involves a consideration of the background, age, livelihood, religion, social structure, and language of the South Saskatchewan River Métis. The evidence is scattered, fragmented, and usually nonquantifiable, but it is nevertheless revealing in the aggregate. Before proceeding any further, two questions, both of definition, must be resolved.

The most obvious question is, if the Métis exhibited such a wide diversity of culture, how can they be identified? The problem is readily resolved, however, if (as Joe Sawchuk has suggested) one employs a concept of ethnicity (rather than of culture or biology), especially the ascriptive approach advanced by the anthropologist Fredrik Barth.[6] By ascription, anyone could be a member of the Métis ethnic group who identified himself as such and who was considered as such by others, both inside and outside the group. By this means, then, the word Métis can encompass wide variations in culture, such as language, degree of acculturation, and expectations for the future. It even allows for "ethnic boundaries" (as Barth calls them) to be crossed; as will be seen, in the 1880s it was not uncommon on the South Saskatchewan for people to move back and forth between Indian and Métis groups (though there was little or no interchange with the European group). Indeed, there were people in each group who were culturally quite similar, sharing, for example, the same language, the same territorial claims, historical experiences, expectations for the future, and often even religion and a common, mixed ancestry. Marcel Giraud has observed that some Métis felt inferior in the presence of whites,[7] but, nevertheless, there is no doubt that they took pride in their ethnic identification. They were especially proud of their record of individualism, self-regulating independence, equestrianism, and survival as a group. Developing in the relative isolation of the northwest, this ethnic pride had grown into a feeling of separate nationhood.

A second question which must be answered involves the meaning of the word "Indian." As will be seen later, many residents of the northwest who were considered Métis spoke only native languages while, on the other hand, many who were considered Indian were themselves of mixed ancestry and had already undergone some acculturation, for example, conversion to Christianity. For the purposes of this study, an Indian will be anyone who in the 1870s and 1880s sought official Indian status and was granted that status by the Canadian government. This is an artificial, administrative identification but it was consciously taken. These people chose to "take treaty," an act which entitled them to an annuity and other benefits from the Department of Indian Affairs; most of them lived on reserves set aside for their bands.

The territory under consideration in this study embraced two distinct Métis settlements on the South Saskatchewan River, one small, one larger. The first was the tiny community of Prairie-Ronde, located near Dundurn, a little south of Saskatoon. Initially used as a wintering camp for buffalo hunters in the 1850s, Prairie-Ronde had become a year-round Métis settlement by 1885. The population was probably less than 100, most of them members of one extended family — the Trottiers. The people of Prairie-Ronde had recently established links with White Cap's band of Sioux Indians, who had recently moved onto a reserve nearby. The community had no church or resident priest but missionaries visited frequently from Batoche, 100 kilometres to the north (downstream).[8]

48

The second, larger settlement consisted of a triangle of land, encompassing both sides of the South Saskatchewan River, stretching from St-Louis-de-Langevin in the north to Duck Lake on the west and Fish Creek on the south; the missions of St-Laurent-de-Grandin, Sacré-Coeur (Duck Lake), and St-Antoine-de-Padoue (Batoche) lay within this ambit. In the 1880s this triangle, 50 kilometres long at most, was often generally referred to as the South Branch settlement. Some observers have viewed the triangle as the home territory and even the final refuge of the Northwest Métis.[9] However, even this circumscribed area was not exclusively theirs; by 1885 a number of Europeans had moved in and more were expected. Living within the area were at least fifteen Anglo-Canadian families, a half-dozen or so French-Canadian households, as well as three or four French Oblate Catholic priests.[10] Just outside the triangle lay several Cree Indian reserves, including those of Beardy and Okemasis near Duck Lake, and that of One Arrow, which abutted the village of Batoche. And only 30 kilometres north of St-Louis was the fast-growing town of Prince Albert. The majority of the inhabitants in this area were Anglo-Canadian but it also included a strong component of people of mixed British and Indian ancestry, usually identified as "Halfbreeds" rather than Métis; most of this group was English-speaking and Protestant.

It was in the early 1870s that a number of Métis first decided to build permanent homes on the South Branch; many of these original settlers were people who had lived most of their lives on the Plains. Although they intended to plant gardens, good soil was not a major consideration in their choice of land; they were more interested in a spot close to productive haylands, good wood lots, and reliable supplies of water. In succeeding years, the area attracted two further migrations of Métis (1877–78 and 1882–83). Most of these later migrants came from Manitoba, where their most recent experience was in small-scale farming and stock raising, practices which they hoped to continue on the South Branch.[11]

For those who were serious about pursuing an agricultural life, the early years on the Saskatchewan were disappointing. Seed and equipment were expensive, local demand for their produce was weak, and, in the two years before the rebellion, unseasonable weather curtailed production. A few Métis (such as the Tourond family) did enjoy some success in agriculture, but they were not numerous. More than one outside observer felt that the Métis were not fully committed to farming as a livelihood. In 1884 Lawrence Clarke, Chief Factor for the Hudson's Bay Co. at Prince Albert, claimed that "these men are not farmers [but] merely cultivating small patches of land little larger than kitchen gardens. They live by hunting and freighting." These pursuits, he said, were in decline, so the Métis were "getting poorer by the year."[12] The Dominion Lands Agent at Prince Albert felt similarly; he concluded that most of the Métis who were pressing land claims before him were more interested in hunting than farming.[13] Many of those who applied for land in 1884 called themselves farmers but, as Diane Payment has noted: "Poussés à se déclarer agriculteurs, il est probable que plusieurs hesitent, ou négligent de dire qu'il font encore la chasse."[14] At Prairie-Ronde the population was even less involved in agriculture, as the story of Charles Trottier indicates. Although the settlement was dispersed after the rebellion, the people returned to the area in the early years of the twentieth century; Trottier, leader of the settlement (almost an Indian band chief, in fact) applied for land there on his return in 1903. In his application, he swore that "I took up this land as far back as 1855 when I was with my parents hunting the buffaloes in the plains." He said that on the eve of the rebellion he had a house and stable there and had broken fifteen acres of soil; but he admitted that he had not got around to sowing it before fleeing to the United States "on account of the rebellion."[15]

In effect most Métis on the South Saskatchewan in the mid-1880s sought their livelihood as hunters, gatherers, freighters, trappers, and farmers in varying degrees of precedence. Hunting remained important. For example, when applying for land in the years following the rebellion, some men who had taken part in that conflict still listed their occupation as "Hunter, freighter & farmer"—in that order.[16] The days of the great buffalo hunts were over, however. The last organized hunt from the Saskatchewan, led by Gabriel Dumont in 1880, had ridden as far south as the Cypress Hills and even into the United States in search of buffalo.[17] With the disappearance of the buffalo there was hunger on the Plains, it is true. But there was still other game around, even in later decades. One of the people whose family later returned to Prairie-Ronde has recalled that, while the Métis who resettled there "weren't no farmers," they were still able to hunt deer (and this was the twentieth century).[18] Augustin Laframboise, one of the fighters killed at the Battle of Duck Lake, is known to have been in the Cypress Hills—undoubtedly hunting—as late as 1882,[19] and there must have been others from the South Branch also hunting there in the years immediately preceding the rebellion. Small game, such as prairie chickens and ducks, were also still fairly plentiful on the Plains. Gathering, as a pursuit, included the traditional Métis and Cree practices of collecting duck eggs, picking berries, and digging roots —particularly Indian turnips (*Psoralea lanceolata*)—as dietary supplements. Wood was also cut and hauled for sale in Prince Albert and Saskatoon.[20]

Freighting had long been important, especially as payment was made in cash and as it provided the Métis the chance to satisfy their love of travelling the Plains. The use of Red River carts to transport freight declined with the arrival of regular steamboat service on the Saskatchewan River and the building of the Canadian Pacific Railway across the southern Plains in the 1880s. Demand for freighters rose again for awhile, however, when Fort Carlton was made a distribution point for the Hudson's Bay Co. in 1884.[21] Lastly, some Métis found they were able to shift from hunting buffalo to trapping fur-bearing animals in the parklands and woodlands north of the Saskatchewan River. Again, in addition to the economic inducement, it may have been their traditional love of travel which drew the Métis to trapping. In any case, there seems no doubt that, because they pursued other means of livelihood—hunting, gathering, freighting, and trapping—the Métis were absent for long periods from whatever crops or livestock they may have been trying to raise, and their agricultural effectiveness suffered significantly.

By mid-1884 the Métis population of the South Branch was estimated to be 1300 people. Adding the 100 or so at Prairie-Ronde, the South Saskatchewan Métis numbered no more than 1400 men, women, and children. About 1100 were originally from Manitoba.[22] The remaining 300 had been born in what, in 1870, had become the Northwest Territories. As will be seen, it was from this small group, combined with a number of men who had been born in Manitoba but had lived most of their lives on the Plains, that most of the militantly committed rebels of 1885 came.

In their fight with the Canadian authorities, the Métis had to rely almost exclusively on this small population base. Few outsiders came to join the fighting. Messages were sent to solicit assistance from Prince Albert, as well as from Métis communities at Qu'Appelle and Battleford, but the response was disappointing. A Militia Roll, drawn up after the Battle of Duck Lake, shows a fighting force of 18.5 companies, each consisting of a captain and ten soldiers—over 200 names in all.[23] This number is incomplete, however. A list provided by Philippe Garnot to Bishop Taché after the rebellion notes the names of about 280 men who were present (though not necessarily active combatants) at the Battle of Batoche.[24] The Militia Roll and the Garnot list cover the adult male population of the two South

Saskatchewan communities involved and, as such, include a handful of people of mixed British and Indian ancestry who lived in the area. (A significant number of reserve Indians also joined in the fighting; their participation will be examined later.) The number of men who could take an active part in the actual fighting was limited by the supply of arms available. One report notes an initial stock of 253 guns, of which 48 were inoperative.[25] By the end of the hostilities this stock had been reduced — through loss, damage, and lack of ammunition — to only 60 or 70 guns.[26] The best estimate of the number of Métis who had any involvement in the hostilities of March, April, and May 1885 would be about 250. Not all were combatants; many served auxiliary roles — guarding prisoners, carrying messages, caring for livestock and horses, scrounging for supplies, performing reconnaissance.

Militant Métis

An estimate of those Métis who could be considered the most militantly committed to the notion of rebellion is also difficult to compute. Upon first consideration one might think that membership in the "Exovedate" would help identify the militants. This body was the council or provisional government which Louis Riel set up to handle the administrative and military (and even theological) affairs of the community during the insurrection. Over twenty men were appointed to the council but two — J-B. Boyer and C. Nolin — were unsympathetic to the rebellion and left town. The council also included three non-Métis — White Cap, the Sioux chief from Saskatoon, and two French Canadians, conscripted for their literacy, who served for short periods as secretary. A second indicator of militancy might be appointment as captain of one of the nineteen militia companies.[27] Among these men, however, was one — W. Boyer — who refused to take up arms and quietly left town. The exceptions show that mere appointment to these two bodies is not necessarily an accurate guide to insurrectionary ardour; some men were evidently appointed in ignorance of their opinions. A third consideration in determining militancy might be the secret oath drawn up by Louis Riel on 5 March 1885, to which ten Métis affixed their marks; in it, the men swore to take up arms, if necessary, to save their country from a wicked government.[28] As will be seen, however, it would be too restrictive to limit militancy to only ten men.

Instead, this study will use two other criteria to identify the most ardent rebels. First, it will include all those who fled to the United States after the Battle of Batoche. In effect, these men identified themselves as highly implicated in rebellion. After all, removing themselves from the heartland of the Métis nation and (often) their families was a serious step; their flight will be taken as evidence that their involvement in the insurrection was so deep that they expected particularly severe treatment from the victorious Canadian authorities. Flight cannot be considered mere cowardice, for the fugitives included many men of undoubted courage. Most of the participants chose not to flee, however, and these included some of the most ardent proponents of rebellion. Canadian authorities charged many of them with the crime of treason felony. Eighteen were found guilty and sentenced to prison terms of one, three, or seven years. The second indicator of militancy, then, will be those whose involvement in rebellion was judged by the courts to deserve the severest sentence.[29] As Table 5.1 shows, at least 28 Métis rebels are known to have fled to the United States and nine more were sentenced to seven-year prison terms. The table includes most, but not all, of those who signed the secret oath and of those appointed to the Exovedate and as militia captains. Louis Riel is covered by none of the criteria, nor was he a member of the Exovedate or a combatant; in some ways he was an outsider and not

Table 5.1 Fugitive and Imprisoned Militants

Name	Age	Fug./Sentence	Years in NWT	Remarks
J-Bte. Boucher Sr.	47	fugitive	since 1882	Exovede
Josué Breland		fugitive		
Ambroise Champagne		fugitive	Plains Métis*	militia captain
Norbert Delorme	48	fugitive	since 1874	Exovede
Maxime Dubois	36	7 years		
Michel Dumas	36	fugitive	since 1880	Public Servant
Edouard Dumont	45	fugitive	born in NWT	militia captain
Elie Dumont	39	fugitive	Plains Métis*	
Gabriel Dumont	47	fugitive	Plains Métis*	Exovede/took oath
Jean Dumont	52	fugitive	Plains Métis*	cousin of above three
Philippe Gariépy	48	7 years	since 1872	militia captain/oath
Pierre Henry	40	7 years	since 1882	Exovede
Antoine Lafontaine	36	fugitive		militia captain
Calixte Lafontaine	39	fugitive		militia captain/oath
Louis Lafontaine		fugitive	by at least 1876	
Pierre Laverdure	66	fugitive	by at least 1870	
Maxime Lépine	49	7 years	since 1882	Exovede/took oath
William Letendre		fugitive	Plains Métis*	
Albert Monkman	29	7 years		Protestant Halfbreed
Abraham Montour Sr.	53	fugitive	born in NWT	took secret oath
Jonas Moreau		fugitive		militia captain
Napoléon Nault	27	fugitive	since 1878	took secret oath
Julien Ouellette	36	fugitive	since 1868	
J-Bte. Parenteau	55	fugitive	since 1858	
Pierre Parenteau	72	7 years	since 1882	Exovedate Pres./oath/ famed buffalo hunter
John Ross Jr.	28	fugitive	born in NWT	took secret oath
Pierre Sansregret	44	fugitive	by at least 1866	
James Short	50	7 years	born in NWT	
André Trottier	25	fugitive	Plains Métis*	nephew of Charles Sr.
Charles Trottier Sr.	49	fugitive	Plains Métis*	Exovede
Isidore Trottier	22	fugitive	Plains Métis*	son of Charles Sr.
J-Bte. Trottier	20	fugitive	Plains Métis*	son of Charles Sr.
Johny Trottier	22	fugitive	Plains Métis*	nephew of Charles Sr.
Rémi Trottier	24	fugitive	Plains Métis*	son of Charles Sr.
J-Bte. Vandal	54	7 years	born in NWT	militia captain
Pierre Vandal	39	7 years	since 1872	sent to seek Big Bear's support
James Ward	34	fugitive	born in NWT	

*Plains Métis: Permanent, long-time resident of what became the Northwest Territories (1870), even though perhaps born in what became the province of Manitoba (1870) and occasionally trading there.

Sources: Census, Prince Albert, Wood Mountain, and Cypress Hills, 1881, NAC, MG31, Microfilm C 13285. (Unfortunately, the pages are often illegible so the census data are not fully available.) Clarence Kipling Collection, NAC, MG 25, G 62. Dumont family genealogy in NAC, MG 17, A 17, no. 88, pp. 724–29. G.F.G. Stanley et al. (eds.), *The Collected Writings of Louis Riel* (Edmonton, 1985), vol. 5, Biographical Index. Affidavit of Père André, Canada, Parlement, *Documents de la Session*, 1886, no. 52, pp. 389–94. William Pearce Report, Canada, Parlement, *Documents de la Session*, 1886, no. 86, pp. 1–18. Diane Payment, "Monsieur Batoche," *Saskatchewan History*. (Autumn 1979): 81–103. For references regarding fugitives, see note 29.

part of the South Branch community. For these reasons, he and men such as William H. Jackson will be excluded from those considered in this study as militants.

Some weaknesses are apparent in employing the above criteria to identify the most militantly committed rebels. First, there quite possibly may have been more than 28 men who fled the country in May 1885; this figure is simply the total so far uncovered in various documentary sources. Second, there were doubtless some Métis among the nineteen killed at Duck Lake, Fish Creek, and Batoche who were as deeply committed to the uprising as those noted in Table 5.1. Death in battle is no certain indication of ardour but, undoubtedly, a number of the men, had they lived, would either have felt compelled to flee the country or have received long prison sentences for their activities during the rebellion. For example, three of the dead had signed the secret oath to take up arms if necessary. For this reason, Table 5.2, noting the men who died in the fighting, has been drawn up. Inclusion on this list can be considered as at least a secondary indicator of militancy.

A third weakness of the criteria is that the courts may have erred in determining which men were the most deeply implicated rebels. Albert Monkman, for example, was undoubtedly one of the most militant rebels throughout most of the uprising (he was accused of forcing others to fight) and received a seven-year court sentence. By the end, however, he had aroused Riel's suspicions (perhaps for not delivering the support of the Protestant Halfbreeds of Prince Albert) and Riel had him arrested before the Battle of Batoche.[30]

Table 5.2 Men Killed in Battle

Name	Age	Battle	Years in NWT	Remarks
François Boyer	28	Fish Cr.		
Isidore Boyer	60	Batoche		
Damase Carrière	34	Batoche		Exovede
Michel Desjarlais	30	Fish Cr.		
Isidore Dumont Jr.	55	Duck L.	born in NWT	militia captain; took secret oath
Ambroise Jobin	35		born in NWT	Exovede; died of wounds, 23 May
Augustin Laframboise	46	Duck L.	Plains Métis	militia captain; took secret oath
André Letendre	48	Batoche	Plains Métis	bro. of F-X. Letendre
J-Bte. Montour		Duck L.	Plains Métis	
Joseph Montour		Duck L.		
Joseph Ouellette Sr.	93	Batoche	Plains Métis	took secret oath
St. Pierre Parenteau	25	Fish Cr.	since 1882	
Donald Ross	63	Batoche		Exovede
John Swan (Swain)	56	Batoche		
Calixte Tourond		Batoche	since 1882	
Elzéar Tourond		Batoche	since 1882	
Michel Trottier Sr.	64	Batoche	Plains Métis	uncle of Charles Trottier Sr.
Joseph Vandal	75	Batoche		
Joseph Vermette	56	Fish Cr.		

Sources: Census, Prince Albert, Wood Mountain, and Cypress Hills, 1881, NAC, MG 31. Stanley et al., *Collected Writings*, vol. 5, Biographical Index. Registre de la paroisse St-Antoine-de-Padoue (Batoche, Sask.), sépultures. A. Ouimet, B.A.T. de Montigny (eds.), *La vérité sur la question Métisse au Nord-Ouest* (Montréal, 1889), p. 138. William Pearce Report, Canada, Parlement, *Documents de la Session*, 1886, no. 8, pp. 1–18. Payment, "Monsieur Batoche." NAC, RG 15, D II, 1, Commission on Rebellion Losses, vol. 914, f. 892,789, no. 21.

Sixteen trials were held at Battleford and Regina in the summer of 1885 for crimes arising out of the rebellion. The accused were generally grouped by ethnicity and locality. The largest group was the 30 residents of the South Saskatchewan who, after pleading guilty to treason felony, received their sentences at Regina on 14 August. One witness complained that, through negligence, some important rebels had never been arrested but he gave no names. All members of the Exovedate who were not dead or had not fled were charged; one received a suspended sentence, two were given three years in prison, while five received seven-year terms. Appointment as a militia captain was not considered important — seven captains were not even charged, though the three who were, received seven-year sentences. Still, the court's conclusions were not manifestly capricious. The deciding factors by which it assessed the degree of involvement in rebellion was the testimony given in affidavits by anglophone settlers whom the rebels had held as prisoners, by local priests, and by a few Métis who had taken no part in the uprising. Thus, although not foolproof, a seven-year sentence is, on the whole, not an unreasonable guide to the degree of insurrectionary involvement.[31]

At the other end of the political spectrum from the most militant rebels were a smaller number of men who opposed taking up arms. Their feelings may not have been known at the beginning of the uprising and, as a result, some of them were named to positions in the militia or the Exovedate. For several reasons, the support of these men would have brought important benefits to the insurrectionary cause. They were generally younger than the militants. Some were educated and had useful skills to offer; others were merchants with valuable stocks of provisions and ammunition. Their nomination may also have been made in a (vain) hope of uniting all sectors of the community. Table 5.3 lists ten Métis now known to have opposed the notion of rebellion and who made sure they were absent from the scene of action. When hostilities began, the merchants F-X. Letendre (also known as Batoche), for whom the village was named, and Salomon Venne were away and refused to return; Letendre's store was looted for its supplies. The other eight men fled the

Table 5.3 Métis Who Opposed Rebellion

Name	Age	Occupation	Remarks
C-E. Boucher	20	store clerk	father a fugitive in the U.S.
J-Bte. Boucher	23	store clerk	father a fugitive in the U.S.; initially named a militia captain
J-Bte. Boyer	40	merchant	initially named to Exovedate
William Boyer	34		initially named a militia captain
Georges Fisher		merchant	
Roger Goulet		farmer	initially named a militia soldier
F-X. Letendre	44	merchant	wealthiest Métis on South Branch
Louis Marion		Pub. Servant	instructor at Beardy Indian reserve
Charles Nolin	48	entrepreneur	member of Manitoba Assembly, 1874/79; initially named to Exovedate
Salomon Venne	48	merchant	

Sources: RG 15, D II, 1, Commission on Rebellion Losses, claim of J-Bte. Boucher, vol. 915, f. 892,789, no. 64. D. Payment, "Monsieur Batoche." D. Payment, *Batoche, 1870–1910*, p. 103. MG 26, G, (Laurier Papers), vol. 2, A. Fisher to Laurier, 14 Mar. 1888, pp. 676–91. Stanley et al., *Collected Writings*, vol. 5, Biographical Index. Walter Hildebrandt, *The Battle of Batoche* (Ottawa, 1985), p. 20.

South Branch, taking refuge at either Prince Albert or Qu'Appelle. Louis Marion was threatened with death for treason before escaping. Charles Nolin initially supported the insurrection but, for reasons which remain unclear, reversed his position; arrested by the rebels, he feigned submission and then fled. Of course, besides these known examples, there may have been other men who left quietly to avoid enlistment into the cause.[32]

The vast majority of Métis on the South Saskatchewan can probably be said to have occupied neither end of the political spectrum—they were neither militantly committed to rebellion nor opposed to it. Some of them, initially indifferent or undecided, were undoubtedly coerced into participating. At the treason felony trial of August 1885, a number of witnesses testified that some Métis had been threatened with destruction of property and even death if they did not show proper devotion to the insurrectionary cause. The enforcers singled out were, of course, the militants; care was taken, however, to implicate only those who could not be hurt further—men such as Joseph Vandal and Damase Carrière (both killed at Batoche), or Napoléon Nault, Norbert Delorme, and Gabriel and Jean Dumont (all safely in the United States).[33] Despite the intimidation, however, morale was not a problem among the less committed, even after the first men were killed in action at Duck Lake. When Mrs. Louis Marion arrived in Prince Albert to join her husband, who had fled there, she reported on the situation at Batoche; though obviously not sympathetic to the rebel cause, she insisted that there had been no tears shed at the funerals and that the people were as determined as ever to resist.[34]

It is evident that the Métis who were on the end of the political spectrum which opposed rebellion (Table 5.3) were those who had found some success in adapting to the new circumstances of life in the Northwest Territories. They all seem to have had some formal education; seven of them were involved in trade while one held a government position. Most were related to one another.[35] These men comprised nearly all the incipient acculturates among the South Saskatchewan Métis. The only known exceptions—the only men with similar backgrounds who supported the notion of rebellion—were Emmanuel Champagne, Michel Dumas, and Maxime Lépine. The first was a successful farmer and fur trader who was charged with treason felony but received a suspended sentence (probably for age and health reasons). Dumas, although a farm instructor at the One Arrow Indian reserve, was a militant proponent of rebellion who fled to the United States. Lépine, a small-scale businessman and farmer, was also a militant rebel; he received a seven-year prison sentence.

The militants, for their part, were almost entirely made up of long-time freighters and buffalo hunters; they were middle-aged men who had found it difficult to adjust to a sedentary, agricultural life. Thus, it can be seen that the political and cultural spectra of the community closely corresponded. As Table 5.1 shows, seventeen were what will be referred to hereafter as Plains Métis (Marcel Giraud called them "métis de l'Ouest");[36] that is, they were men who had spent much of their lives in what, in 1870, had become the Northwest Territories, or had been born there. Some, it is true, had been born in American territory or in what had become the province of Manitoba; many traded in Manitoba regularly and a few had even received the land or scrip to which they were entitled by the Manitoba Act. Many of the Dumonts and Trottiers had this background, but there can be no doubt that they were Métis of the Plains. Another example is Jean-Baptiste Parenteau, rebel and fugitive in 1885, who was born at Red River about 1830; in 1900, in an affidavit supporting his son's application for land, he swore that

> I was married at Winnipeg 42 years ago (1858) to Pélagie Dumont [sister of Gabriel] and since that time I have always lived in the North-west Territories & until about twenty five years ago

I was a Buffalo hunter and at the time of the Red River Rebellion [1869] I was living . . . near Fish Creek where the Traders & Hunters used to winter. I never had a house in . . . Manitoba since I was married and I only went there in the Spring of each year to sell furs, returning in the fall. When I was out hunting the whole family used to follow me. My son Alexandre was born on the third day after we arrived in Winnipeg in the spring twenty five years ago and about fifteen days after his birth we started out on our journey back.[37]

Most of the militants seem to have been among the original Métis settlers of the South Saskatchewan, i.e., those who had arrived in the early 1870s; few were among the more agriculture-oriented settlers who had come after 1877. Of the militants whose age is known (Table 5.1), the average was 41 years old. A few of the militants were young, but it is revealing to learn that at least four children of fugitive militants, though living in the area and old enough to fight, took no part at all in the insurrection.[38] The evidence in Table 5.2 listing the Métis killed in action also supports a conclusion that the militants were largely made up of older (average age 51) Plains Métis, representatives of the Plains buffalo-hunting tradition. And, as will be seen, many of these men were, in various ways, close to the Plains Indians in culture.

Many Métis undoubtedly considered themselves distinct from, and superior to, Indians. Others, however, though they called themselves Métis, were not reluctant to point out the similarities between the two groups, especially the Plains Métis, who had long followed lifeways similar to their kin the Plains Cree and Saulteaux—a migratory life based on the hunt. In 1877 a number of Plains Métis petitioned the government for relaxation of the game laws and for assistance in establishing themselves on farms. They described themselves as leading "an entirely nomadic life, as the Indians on the plains."[39] Among the petitioners were at least three Métis who participated in the rebellion on the South Saskatchewan, and one, James Ward, is classified as a militant in Table 5.1. Another interesting document is a recently discovered petition forwarded by Inspector James Walsh of the North-West Mounted Police from the Cypress Hills in 1876.[40] The petitioners describe themselves as "half-breeds of the Cree and Saulteaux Tribes" who "have lived from childhood upon the prairies and adopted the customs of the Indians." They ask to be admitted into Treaty No. 4 as a group and elect their own chief. Again, among those affixing their marks to the petition were two or three Métis who later participated in the South Saskatchewan conflict. Two years later, another petition was circulated in the Cypress Hills among Métis who described themselves as having been long "in the habit of roaming over the prairies of the North-West for the purposes of hunting." They asked for a "special reserve" of land "to the exclusion of all whites" except government officials. Signing the petition were fourteen men who are listed among the militants or the dead in Tables 5.1 and 5.2.[41]

While some of those petitioners who, in the 1870s, called themselves Métis or Halfbreeds continued to identify with that group, many others ended up on reserves as Treaty Indians. Government officials early recognized that it was difficult to determine an Indian by ancestry alone;[42] people of mixed Indian and European ancestry who wished to identify themselves as Indians were permitted to "take Treaty." Many did so to take advantage of Treaty benefits—an annuity, land on a reserve, agricultural assistance and instruction, and so forth. By the mid-1880s, however, many Treaty Indians had become dissatisfied with reserve life and some of those with mixed ancestry then decided to withdraw from Treaty. Withdrawals accelerated when the government finally acted on the demand of the Northwest Métis that they, like their kin in Manitoba, should be compensated for the extinguishment of their territorial claims. The land question had long rankled the Métis, and government inaction culminated in rebellion in March 1885. The North-West Half Breed Commission established later offered the Métis compensation in the form of land or scrip.[43] This concession prompted a large number of people, who for a decade had identified themselves as Indians, to leave the reserves. In 1886 over half the Métis who were granted scrip by the Commission were mixed bloods who had withdrawn from Treaty.[44] Within a few years, some, however, were asking to be readmitted to Treaty.[45]

Thus, in the 1870s and 1880s, many people moved back and forth across the ethnic boundaries between Indian and Métis groups, for not only did the Métis retain many elements of their Indian heritage, but Indians were assimilating European traits at the same time as well. To cross the Métis ethnic boundary, it appears one had only to have mixed ancestry, profess Christianity, and identify oneself as Métis. With these characteristics, it seems that one was readily accepted as Métis and, as well, was acknowledged by outsiders as such. Mixed ancestry was essential, however; no whites are known to have been considered as Métis. One Indian, Kitwayo or Alexandre Cadieux — "une sauvage pur sang," as he was described — did live among the South Branch Métis; but, despite the French name, he was always identified as an Indian because of his unmixed parentage.[46]

Inter-ethnic movements were particularly easy on the South Saskatchewan River. In the Duck Lake area, for example, even those people who had chosen to live on reserves as Indians were almost entirely of mixed ancestry.[47] In addition, a large number of the reserve Indians had been baptized and regarded themselves Christian.[48] Indeed, the first person killed in the 1885 uprising was a Christian Cree (from the Beardy reserve) shot at the Battle of Duck Lake.[49] The Métis group may have been more orthodoxly and homogeneously Christian but still the Christianity which some of them practised included elements of Indian origin such as healing rituals, precognition, and seeing at a distance.[50]

While the Plains Métis retained traces of Indian religion, their social structures also remained remarkably similar to those of the Cree. Following the individualistic traditions of their Indian ancestors, each Métis was a generalist; that is, there was little specialization of work beyond age or sex — although there was considerable sharing within the community, each family made its own cart, dwelling, clothing and so on. On the South Saskatchewan the only exceptions were a few Métis merchants and traders. (The handful of priests and teachers living in the area were all outsiders.) Also, like the Cree, the Métis had no strong social or political hierarchy; strict obedience to leaders was common only in the buffalo hunt and in war.[51] Indeed, the organization of the Métis militia in 1885 strongly resembled Indian custom. Commanding the militia was Gabriel Dumont, whose authority was, in many ways, similar to that of a Plains Indian chief. Louis Riel wrote Sir John A. Macdonald, pointing out that, while the government had recognized even the "most insignificant" chiefs in treaties, "Gabriel Dumont was altogether ignored." This indignity, Riel claimed, "has always been rankling in his mind."[52]

When the time came for armed action, Dumont naturally expected assistance from Indians throughout the northwest. He was only partly successful. Big Bear, Poundmaker, and other Cree chiefs living up the North Saskatchewan River also rose in rebellion in the spring of 1885; Dumont sent messengers requesting their help on the South Branch but none arrived before the final defeat at Batoche on 12 May.[53] Aid was also requested from reserves to the south but the only Indians who came from that direction were White Cap and about twenty of his men from Moose Woods near Saskatoon. Surprisingly, these were Sioux with whom the Métis traditionally had few ties; there is some reason to believe that the aggressive Trottier family of nearby Prairie-Ronde coerced them to travel to Batoche. Four Sioux died in the fighting. The most important support came from Indians in the South Branch area. Scores of men arrived from the One Arrow, Beardy, Okemasis,

Chakastapaysin, and Petaquakey reserves; only one was killed in the fighting, but a chief, One Arrow, was subsequently sentenced to three years in prison.[54]

Dumont and the other militants had every reason to count on support from neighbouring reserves because of the strong ties between the Métis and those Indians. Indeed, at least six Métis who participated in the rebellion had themselves been on the paylists (i.e., for annuities) of neighbouring reserves as recently as 1884.[55] Another combatant, Charles Trottier Jr., was still a Treaty Indian (Beardy's reserve) at the time of the uprising. A nephew of Charles Trottier Sr., leader of the Prairie-Ronde clan, he was married to the daughter of Okemasis, chief of a South Branch band. He fought at Duck Lake and seems to have fled the country; but, as he was a Treaty Indian, he is excluded from Table 5.1.[56]

It is not surprising that there was frequent inter-marriage between South Branch Métis and reserve Indians; Diane Payment affirms that there are numerous cases mentioned in local church registers.[57] Although the couples may not have resided full-time on the reserves, the spouse was able to collect an annuity. Several combatants of 1885 had Treaty Indian wives. One was Augustin Laframboise, Métis militia captain killed at Duck Lake; his wife was on the paylist of Petaquakey reserve.[58] Another was Michel Trottier, a Métis killed at Batoche; married to an Indian of Duck Lake Agency, he was the brother of Charles Trottier Sr.[59]

Gabriel Dumont himself had close kin on reserves, including that of One Arrow, which was only a short distance from his residence. There, his first cousin, Vital Dumont (also known as Cayol), son of his uncle Jean-Baptiste, had chosen to live as a Treaty Indian (even though both his parents were of mixed ancestry). In 1885 Vital Dumont and his two adult sons, Louis and Francis, answered Gabriel's call to arms. The three of them subsequently felt so deeply implicated in the rebellion that they fled to the United States.[60] As Treaty Indians, however, they too will be excluded from Table 5.1.

Language was another cultural trait which many Métis shared with the Plains Indians. Because most Métis had French ancestors and bore French names, they were labelled as French. Many, however, also had Indian names and, perhaps not surprisingly (given their strong kinship ties with local Indians), many of them were, in fact, unilingual Cree-speakers. This linguistic persistence was particularly evident among the Plains Métis and, indeed, among the militant supporters of the 1885 rebellion. For years Roman Catholic missionaries on the South Saskatchewan had lamented their parishioners' preference for Cree. It is known that, at religious services in the 1880s, hymns were sometimes sung in Cree. In education, however, the policy of the Church was to try to downgrade native language and encourage the use of European languages, especially French. The efforts were not always successful. As late as 1897 it was reported that most Métis school children at Batoche could understand neither French nor English![61] For many years the use of Cree remained vigorous among people of mixed ancestry living in scattered parts of the northwest. By the twentieth century, certainly, some groups had incorporated elements of European languages into their speech, thus developing a tongue known popularly as "Michif." Linguists studying Michif have discovered that, while its noun phrases are usually French in origin, syntax and verb structures are mainly Cree. As one linguist has said, "Michif is best viewed as a dialect of Cree."[62]

In August 1885 the 30 South Saskatchewan Métis charged with the crime of treason felony went on trial at Regina. At the outset, all but one requested that the court proceedings be translated into Cree and the judge complied with their wish. Even so, the lawyer for the accused remarked that his clients were still not clear about the meaning of their charge, "the interpreter not being able to translate into their language the words of the law."[63] In the end, the only Métis who did not understand Cree was given a conditional discharge while, of those who preferred Cree, eighteen were sentenced to prison, including, of course, the eleven militants listed in Table 5.1 who received seven-year terms. It can be said, then, that of all the Métis whose linguistic preference is known, the most militant proponents of insurrection in 1885 were men who were most at ease speaking the language of the Plains Indians.

Less is known of the language spoken by the other Métis listed in Tables 5.1 and 5.2. However, some impression can be gained by examining the preferences of their children. In the months after the rebellion, the Half Breed Commission visited the South Branch area offering scrip to the Métis. Few people accepted the offer in 1885, though many did in ensuing years. Naturally, those who had participated in the uprising were reluctant to apply, but two adult children whose fathers were fugitives and two whose fathers had been killed in the fighting did dare to request scrip. The Commission's procedure that year provided for an explanation of one's rights in a choice of languages. Of the four, all of whose fathers appear in Tables 5.1 and 5.2, one requested an explanation in French, two in Cree, and one in both languages.[64] This number, though small, would again suggest that, in the houses of the most militant rebels, it was the language of the Plains Cree which was spoken.

It is quite possible that the language spoken by the Métis accused of treason felony and those whose children applied for scrip after the rebellion included a degree of French in addition to Cree; that is, they probably spoke a form of incipient Michif. Even so, however, their stated preference for Cree once again indicates that most of the militant supporters of insurrection in 1885 were culturally close to Plains Indians.

From the foregoing examination of their background, age, livelihood, religion, social structure, and language, it can be seen that the Métis who were the most militantly involved in the 1885 rebellion were the most conservative, most Indian-like in the community. The militants were, with only a few exceptions, men of an older generation, former buffalo hunters and freighters only marginally involved in agriculture; they were Métis of the Plains tradition who were unable or unwilling to adjust their lives to the rapidly changing conditions of the new northwest. In contrast, the Métis who opposed taking up arms were, with no apparent exceptions, younger men who had enjoyed some success in fields which held promise in the new order of things. While there was a fair measure of diversity in both the political spectrum and the cultural spectrum of the South Saskatchewan community, the two spectra were almost congruent.

Conclusion

A number of implications may be seen to arise from these conclusions. For example, although both contemporaries and more recent observers commonly speak of French Métis, Scottish mixed bloods, and English Halfbreeds, this is a labelling often based only on their names. However, it is evident that in the 1880s (and even later) there was a substantial group of people of mixed ancestry outside Manitoba who spoke only native languages or whose best facility was in a native language. (Not only Cree was used; Métis beyond the Saskatchewan even today speak a number of Dene tongues.) For these people, a linguistic characterization is meaningless. Thus, insofar as one is concerned with their European traits, it may be more useful to categorize them as either Roman Catholic or Protestant mixed bloods, for they were virtually all one or the other.

The persistence of Plains hunting traditions among many Métis can have other implications — for example, in their decision in 1885 to take up arms. It should not be surprising that these people should have reacted violently when confronted with a faceless, seemingly immovable government bureaucracy which appeared to be totally indifferent to their customs, anxieties, and needs. Numerous petitions had been sent to the government, whose response was usually long in coming, if it came at all. The complicated statutes and regulations of the Department of the Interior were unfathomable to this non-literate people, and the length of time it took to obtain a decision from Ottawa became intolerable.

The Plains Métis were men of action, unaccustomed to standing passively by as their situation deteriorated. They had much honour to lose if they did not take action; and, also, as the least acculturated in the community, generally had the least property to lose if they did. The missionaries tried to talk them out of insurrection but, again as the least acculturated, their respect for the authority of the Church was perhaps not as strong as, for example, that of the men listed in Table 5.3. And when it came to military planning, the leading insurrectionists totally miscalculated the power behind the government's authority. Accustomed only to fighting Indians, the Plains Métis did not expect the soldiers to come in such great numbers; nor were they aware that, unlike Indians, the new enemy, after suffering losses at Duck Lake and Fish Creek, would be more determined to fight, not less.

The sizable number of militants which has been identified above indicates that, apart from the few, more acculturated people in the community, the insurrectionary movement on the South Saskatchewan was quite deeply based. This finding would contradict the views of some contemporary observers as well as more recent commentators. At the treason felony trial of August 1885 the missionary fathers, André and Fourmond, testified that the militant proponents of rebellion were very few—essentially just Riel and three others: Gabriel Dumont and Napoléon Nault (both fugitives in the United States) and Damase Carrière (killed at Batoche). Using tricks, threats, and lies, this handful of men were said to have seduced a large but weakly committed group of gullible Métis into taking up arms.[65] However, by resting the blame entirely on Riel and those who were conveniently beyond reach of the law, it is likely that the priests were seeking to minimize their parishioners' role in the uprising and thus mitigate the court's punishment. Similarly, the arguments of two recent historians have also diminished the importance of free will in the actions of the rebels: Thomas Flanagan and Donald McLean contend that the Métis were manipulated into rebellion either by Louis Riel, or by Sir John A. Macdonald and Lawrence Clarke, each for his own purpose.[66] By the findings of this study, however, it would appear that the rebellion was a popular movement. The militants may have tricked or coerced some Métis into participating, but those militants were a sizable group in themselves.

NOTES

1. See, for example, F.L. Barron, J.B. Waldram (eds.), *1885 and After: Native Society in Transition* (Regina, 1986); Bob Beal, Roderick Macleod, *Prairie Fire: The 1885 North-West Rebellion* (Edmonton, 1984); Thomas Flanagan, *Louis "David" Riel: "Prophet of the New World"* (Toronto, 1979); Thomas Flanagan, *Riel and the Rebellion: 1885 Reconsidered* (Saskatoon, 1983); Julia Harrison, *Métis: People between Two Worlds* (Vancouver, Toronto, 1985); Walter Hildebrandt, *The Battle of Batoche: British Small Warfare and the Entrenched Métis* (Ottawa, 1985); A.S. Lussier (ed.), *Riel and the Métis: Riel Mini-Conference Papers* (Winnipeg, 1979); Gilles Martel, *Le messianisme de Louis Riel* (Waterloo, 1984); Donald McLean, 1885: *Métis Rebellion or Government Conspiracy?* (Winnipeg, 1985); Diane Payment, *Batoche (1870–1910)* (St-Boniface, 1983); J. Peterson, J.S.H.

Brown (eds.), *The New Peoples: Being and Becoming Métis in North America* (Winnipeg, 1985); G.F.G. Stanley et al. (eds.), *The Collected Writings of Louis Riel*, 5 vols. (Edmonton, 1985); George Woodcock, *Gabriel Dumont: The Métis Chief and His Lost World* (Edmonton, 1975).

2. Flanagan, *Louis "David" Riel*, p. 148.

3. Hildebrandt, *Battle of Batoche*, p. 21. The ten men were D. Carrière, I. Dumont, D. Ross, N. Delorme, N. Nault, M. Dumas, M. Lépine, Ph. Cariépy, P. Garnot, and J-B. Boucher.

4. Journal of Louis Schmidt, National Archives of Canada (NAC), MG 17, A 17, no. 37.

5. Woodcock, *Gabriel Dumont*, pp. 120, 156.

6. Fredrik Barth, *Ethnic Groups and Boundaries* (Boston, 1969), pp. 9–15. See also Joe Sawchuk, The *Métis of Manitoba* (Toronto, 1978), pp. 8–10, 39.

7. Marcel Giraud, *Le Métis Canadien* (Paris, 1945; St-Boniface, 1984), p. 1190.

8. Rita Schilling, *Gabriel's Children* (Saskatoon, 1983). Norbert Walsh, *The Last Buffalo Hunter* (Mary Weekes, ed.), (Toronto, 1945), passim.

9. Beal, Macleod, *Prairie Fire*, p. 228. Diane Payment, "The Métis Homeland: Batoche in 1885," *NeWest Review* 10 (May 1985): 11, 12.

10. Report of William Pearce on South Branch land claimants, Canada, Parlement, *Documents de la Session*, 1886, no. 8b, pp. 10–18.

11. Diane Payment, "Batoche after 1885: A Society in Transition," in Barron, Waldram, *1885 and After*, pp. 174, 182. P.R. Mailhot, D.N. Sprague, "Persistent Settlers: The Dispersal and Resettlement of the Red River Métis, 1870–1885," *Canadian Ethnic Studies* 17, 2 (1985): 8.

12. NAC, MG 26A, Sir John A. Macdonald Papers, Clarke to J.A. Grahame, 20 May 1884, vol. 105, pp. 42244–50.

13. E.A. Mitchener, "The North Saskatchewan River Settlement Claims, 1883–84," in Lewis Thomas (ed.), *Essays in Western History* (Edmonton, 1976), pp. 134–35.

14. Payment, *Batoche (1870–1910)*, pp. 14–15, 34 (n. 24).

15. Saskatchewan Archives Board, homestead records, Charles Trottier affidavit, 17 December 1903.

16. NAC, RG 15, D II, 8(b), North West Half Breed land applications, A. Letendre, vol. 1329, no. 1301, and J-B. Parenteau fils, vol. 1362, no. 953.

17. Giraud, *Le Métis Canadien*, p. 1164.

18. Schilling, *Gabriel's Children*, p. 115.

19. NAC, RG 15, D II, 8(c), land applications, vol. 1353, no. 319.

20. Diane Payment, "Structural and Settlement History of Batoche Village," Parks Canada, *Manuscript Report Series*, no. 248 (1977), pp. 73–75. D.M. Loveridge, B. Potyondi, "From Wood Mountain to the Whitemud," ibid., no. 237 (1977), p. 95.

21. G.F.G. Stanley, *The Birth of Western Canada* (Toronto, 1936), p. 185. Mailhot, Sprague, "Persistent Settlers," p. 8. Giraud, *Le Métis Canadien*, p. 1171.

22. Mailhot, Sprague, "Persistent Settlers," p. 12.

23. Canada, Parliament, *Sessional Papers*, 1886, no. 43h, pp. 16–18.

24. Archives de l'Archévêché de St-Boniface (Manitoba), T, fonds Taché, lettres reçues, Garnot to Taché, 28 juillet 1885.

25. NAC, MG 17, A 17, no. 38, Cloutier report, "Effectifs."

26. Hildebrandt, *Battle of Batoche*, p. 74. NAC, MG 17, A 17, journal of Père Végreville, 16 mai 1885.

27. Listed in Canada, Parliament, *Sessional Papers*, 1886, no. 43h, pp. 16–18.

28. See text in Stanley, *Birth of Western Canada*, pp. 442–43 (n. 67).

29. For sentencing, see Canada, Parlement, *Documents de la Session*, 1886, no. 52, p. 308. References to fugitives are numerous; all are at NAC. RG 10, Dept. of Indian Affairs, Report of Sgt. Paterson, NWMP, 3 Oct. 1885, vol. 3722, file 24, 125; Insp. A.R. Cuthbert to Supt. A.B. Perry, 20 Jan. 1886, vol. 3585, file 1130-8. MG 27, I C4, Edgar Dewdney Papers, Report of J. Anderson, 29 Nov. 1885, 8 Dec. and 18 Dec. 1885, pp. 1524–26, 1531, 1536: McKay Report, 8 Jan. 1886, p. 1263; Report of O. Pichette, 1 Feb. 1886, pp. 1274–79; Report on half-breeds, 30 Mar. 1886, pp. 611–12; Nichol Report, May 1886, pp. 1290–97; Report of Cpl. Bossange, 22 April 1888, pp. 1337–39. RG 13, Dept. of Justice, B2, North-West Rebellion records, vol. 816, pp. 2398-2404, 2409-12; vol. 818, pp. 2780–86; vol. 821, pp. 3474–3518.

30. Jackson and Sanderson affidavits, Canada, Parlement, *Documents de la Session*, 1886, no. 52, pp. 399, 416. William Pearce Report, ibid., 1886, no. 8b, p. 12.
31. Affidavits and proceedings of the trial published in Canada, Parlement, *Documents de la Session*, 1886, no. 52, pp. 375–416.
32. Diane Payment, "Monsieur Batoche," *Saskatchewan History* (Autumn 1979): 95–96, 102 (n. 60). NAC, RG 13, Dept. of Justice, vol. 817, Marion testimony, pp. 2787–90. Hildebrandt, Battle of Batoche, p. 20.
33. Canada, Parlement, *Documents de la Session*, 1886, no. 52, pp. 389–416. NAC, RG 15, Dept. of the Interior, vol. 914, file 892,789, rebellion losses claim of Josephte Tourond, no. 21. NAC, RG 13, Dept. of Justice, B2, vol. 817, C. Nolin statement, pp. 2780–86.
34. NAC, MG 17, A 17, no. 37, André to Grandin, 31 mars 1885.
35. Payment, "The Métis Homeland," pp. 11, 12.
36. Giraud, *Le Métis Canadien*, p. 1148 *et passim*.
37. NAC, RG 15, vol. 1362, no. 667.
38. In addition to J-B. Boucher's sons cited in Table 5.3, the sons of Ambroise Champagne and Pierre Sansregret also avoided any involvement in the uprising. NAC, RG 15, Dept. of the Interior, vol. 1326, scrip claim no. 1555, and vol. 1331, claim no. 1504; vol. 915, rebellion losses claim, file 892,789, no. 64.
39. Canada, Parliament, *Sessional Papers*, 1886, no. 45a, pp. 4–5.
40. NAC, RG 10, vol. 3637, file 7089, petition 6 Sept. 1876.
41. N. Delorme, A. Lafontaine, L. Lafontaine, P. Laverdure, Jul. Ouellette, A. Trottier, C. Trottier, I. Trottier, J-B. Trottier, J. Trottier, I. Dumont, A. Laframboise, Jos. Ouellette, M. Trottier in Canada, Parliament, *Sessional Papers*, 1886, no. 45, pp. 10-16.
42. Alexander Morris, *The Indian Treaties of Canada* (Toronto, 1880), pp. 293–95. John L. Taylor, "The Development of an Indian Policy for the Canadian North-West, 1869–1879," Ph.D. thesis, Queen's University, 1975, pp. 228–31.
43. Ken Hatt, "The North-West Rebellion Scrip Commissions, 1885–1889," in Barron, Waldram, *1885 and After*, pp. 189–204.
44. Dept. of Interior, Annual Report, 1886, in Canada, Parliament, *Sessional Papers*, 1887, no. 7, Part I, p. 76.
45. Giraud, *Le Métis Canadien*, pp. 1217–18.
46. Canada, Parlement, *Documents de la Session*, 1886, no. 52a, p. 393.
47. David Mandelbaum, *The Plains Cree* (Regina, 1979), p. 10.
48. Canada, Indian Affairs Branch, *Annual Report*, 1892, pp. 318–19.
49. NAC, MG 17, A 17, no. 37, André to Grandin, 31 mars 1885.
50. Payment, "The Métis Homeland," p. 12. Guillaume Charette, *Vanishing Spaces: Memoirs of Louis Goulet* (Winnipeg, 1980), p. 146.
51. Mandelbaum, *Plains Cree*, p. 115.
52. NAC, MG 26, A, p. 42529, Riel to Macdonald, 17 July 1885.
53. Adolphe Ouimet, B-A-T. de Montigny (eds.), *La Vérité sur la question Métisse au Nord-Ouest* (Montréal, 1889), p. 130.
54. Canada, Parliament, *Sessional Papers*, 1886, no. 52, pp. 22, 49–50. NAC, RG 10, vol. 3584, file 1130, list of reserves, 1885.
55. RC 10, Paylists, vol. 9417, pp. 70, 85: J. Parisien, B. Deschamps, J. Vandal; vol. 9419, p. 137: J. Trottier, J. Flammant. RG 15, vol. 1369, scrip no. 1124: A. Trottier. Canada, Parliament, *Sessional Papers*, 1886, no. 43h, pp. 16–18, 44.
56. RG 10, Paylists, vol. 9421, p. 155. RG 15, vol. 1369, no. 1722 & no. 2108.
57. Payment, *Batoche (1870–1910)*, p. 121.
58. RG 10, vol. 9419, pp. 115–18.
59. RG 15, vol. 1369, no. 73.
60. RG 10, Paylists, vol. 9423, p. 304. RG 15, vol. 1345, no. 1251; vol. 1346, no. 148. Dumont genealogy in MG 17, A 17, no. 88, p. 727.
61. J. Brian Dawson, "The Relationship of the Catholic Clergy to Métis Society in the Canadian North-West, 1845–1885, With Particular Reference to the South Saskatchewan District," Parks

Canada, *Manuscript Report Series*, no. 376 (1979), p. 255. Payment, *Batoche (1870–1910)*, pp. 44, 55, 63 (n. 6). Giraud, *Le Métis Canadien*, p. 1042. J.E. Foster, "The Métis: The People and the Term," in Lussier, *Riel and the Métis*, p. 90. Among the militants known to have Indian names were N. Delorme, C. Lafontaine, and C. Trottier Sr.

62. John C. Crawford, "What Is Michif?" in Peterson, Brown, *The New Peoples*, p. 238.
63. Canada, Parlement, *Documents de la Session*, 1886, no. 52, pp. 374, 377–78.
64. RG 15, vol. 1326, no. 1555: N. Champagne; vol. 1327, no. 1292: J. Dumont; vol. 1329, no. 1301: A. Letendre; vol. 1331, no. 1504: P. Sansregret.
65. Canada, Parlement, *Documents de la Session*, 1886, no. 52, pp. 389–94, 403–05.
66. Flanagan, *Riel and the Rebellion*; McLean, *1885: Métis Rebellion or Government Conspiracy?*

Article Six

The Indian View of the 1885 Uprising

A. Blair Stonechild

The Indian Version of the Rebellion: An Untold Story

Although there is no shortage of written material on the North-West Rebellion of 1885, Indian Elders have said that the full story of the Indian involvement has yet to be told.

As one Elder put it, "This story was told only at night and at bedtime. And not the whole story. No way. They did not want to tell on anyone who were [*sic*] involved. It is like when something is covered with a blanket and held down on the ground on all four sides. They talked about it in parts only. And they got nervous telling it. They were afraid of another uprising and more trouble. And they were also afraid of getting the young people into trouble."[1]

Some Elders did not like to tell the stories simply because it made them sad. Other Elders did not tell their stories to any white person, even priests, as they were afraid that these stories would be used for the profit of others.

Most historians have used only written documents and official interpretations in their research. After the rebellion the Indian people did not have the freedom or luxury of doing their own research and putting forward their own views. As a result, contemporary interpretations of the Indian role have remained very biased.

How the Rebellion Started

The first Indian involvement in the rebellion is said to have been at the Duck Lake fight on 26 March 1885. A few Indians were among Gabriel Dumont's group of about 30 men; but then, considering that the fight itself occurred on Beardy's Reserve, it should not be so

Source: "The Indian View of the 1885 Uprising," in *1885 and After: Native Society in Transition*, ed. F. Laurie Barron and James B. Waldram (Regina: University of Regina, 1986), pp. 155–70. Reprinted by permission of the author.

surprising that Indians were present at all. One of the least understood aspects of the Duck Lake fight is why one of Chief Beardy's Headmen (Assiyiwin) was shot during the purported parley preceding the fight. How did an old, half-blind, unarmed Headman of the Band become involved in the fracas?

What does Indian oral history have to say about this? The following story is told by Harry Michael of Beardy's Reserve. Harry Michael's grandfather was the nephew of Assiyiwin:

Assiyiwin had gone to town, to Duck Lake to visit a friend, a half-breed by the name of Wolfe. Over there he heard that there was going to be some trouble. Something very bad was going to happen. He had gone to town on horseback and he bought some goods from the store in Duck Lake which he tied on his saddle. He then started walking home. The town of Duck Lake was not too far from the camp.

The old man had very poor eyesight—he was almost blind. And as he was approaching the reserve and the camp he noticed something. He heard a lot of voices, a lot of talking. But he could not see anything until he came near the people.

It was then a half-breed spoke to him—called in Cree and said, "Stop! Don't you know what is going to happen?"

Assiyiwin said, "I am blind. Exactly what is it?"

The half-breed answered, "There is going to be a battle. Didn't you hear about it?"

Assiyiwin answered, "Yes, I heard about it."

The half-breed replied, "You have walked right into it. Turn back where you came from."

Assiyiwin answered, "Ha! I cannot turn back. I'm going home. This is my reserve land. If you are going to have a battle, if you are going to spill blood, you cannot do it on our reserve land." And he remained standing there with his horse.

The half-breed said, "Go back where you came from."

Assiyiwin replied, "No, I am going home."

This half-breed threw his coat to Assiyiwin. His name was Joe McKay. He said, "Step over my coat . . . I'll shoot you."

That was the time when Assiyiwin heard someone saying while he was standing there, "Don't shoot each other. Don't shoot." It was said in Cree. It was a half-breed. He must have been very brave, coming into the centre of the two sides of the people on horseback, half-breeds and Indians on one side and the Northwest [sic] Mounted Police on the other side. He was trying to tell the people not to shoot each other. He came running from the half-breed side. He did not know the name of this man. He was waving his hands shouting, "Don't shoot each other! People are trying to find a way on how they can get along better. Don't try and kill each other." He got as far as their location.

It was then Assiyiwin stepped over and passed the coat of McKay and said, "I am going home."

Assiyiwin witnessed the days of intertribal [sic] battles with the Blackfeet. Assiyiwin performed some brave acts when he had the strength and power in his legs. He had some scalps in a wooden box. He had fought and killed in battles and scalped. This was a brave man. That is why he did not back out from Joe McKay's orders. He refused Joe McKay and stepped over past the coat and said he was going to go on home. He was not about to get frightened. His bravery must have returned to him in spite [of the fact] that he was an old man.

The gun went off and fired. McKay shot the old man Assiyiwin down, hitting him in the stomach. Then there were blasts of gunfire coming from all directions.

They came later after the old man. He didn't die right away that night. He died at sunrise the following morning. He was the first Cree Indian killed. That's how my grandfather told this story.[2]

The official interpretation of the event at Duck Lake was that Beardy's Band had joined the rebellion. The story of Assiyiwin, however, presents an entirely different view. An older man, with poor eyesight, Assiyiwin was hardly likely to be associating with young fighters. Moreover, as one of Beardy's Headmen, he probably shared Beardy's disassociation from Riel's activities, and Beardy's dislike of intruders on their Indian reserve land.

It appears that Assiyiwin's mistake was being in the wrong place at the wrong time, and being too bold in asserting his indignation at what was occurring. Gabriel Dumont did not see his brother Isidore or Assiyiwin approach Crozier and McKay. What was probably not so much a parley as an effort to defuse a tense situation turned into a senseless slaughter when Joe McKay pulled his trigger.

It later became clear that Chief Beardy had not ordered his men to support the rebellion, yet through the incident at Duck Lake the Indian people were fully implicated.

Indian Treaties Were a Commitment to Peace

In order to more clearly understand the Indian attitude at the time of the rebellion, one has to look back to the period prior to the signing of the treaties. Indian Nations waged tremendous battles against each other as a result of inter-tribal conflicts created by the expansion of the fur trade. In some battles between the Cree and the Blackfoot, such as that on the Oldman River in 1870, several hundred warriors were killed. An even greater killer — the epidemics — wiped out over half of the tribes in some outbreaks. The result of all this was the drastic depopulation of the Indian Nations, and an increasing awareness among Indian leaders that their Nations had to come to grips with a very fundamental and real issue — that of survival.

Because of these experiences a strong peace movement began to develop among the Indian Nations. One famous peacemaker was the Cree Chief Maskipitoon, who strove to mend relations between the Cree and the Blackfoot during the 1860s. He eventually fell victim to a misguided warrior's bullet. The adoption of the Cree Poundmaker by the Blackfoot Chief Crowfoot was another important development in the cementing of peaceful relations between the two Nations.

It was because of this sentiment for peace that Indian leaders were receptive to the signing of treaties in the 1870s. Not only had Indians never been at war with whites in the northwest, but they also sought to prevent such a thing from ever happening. Treaty Six stated, "they will maintain peace and good order between each other, and also between themselves and others of Her Majesty's subjects."[3] To Indian Nations, that was one of the most important principles of the treaty.

For Indians, the signing of treaties was far more than a political act — it was also a sacred act. By the ceremony of smoking the Sacred Pipe, the Indian people pledged before the Creator that they would uphold the treaties. As Senator John Tootoosis puts it, "We signed an agreement with the Crown, with the Queen not to fight any more. We were to live in peace. We had to live up to this Treaty. We promised in the name of the Creator to keep the Treaty. The Indian people feared offending the Creator."[4] If the treaty was ever broken, it would not be the Indian people who broke it first.

Around the time of the rebellion, white people did not fully appreciate the commitment of the Indian people. They had the perception that Indian people were no more than hunters and warriors. When the Marquis of Lorne, Queen Victoria's son-in-law, met Poundmaker in 1881, he expected to hear many war stories, and was surprised that instead he heard mainly about the spiritual and political ideas of the Indian people.

The Solutions to Treaty Problems Would Be Political

The Indian leadership was aware that there were serious shortcomings in the implementation of the treaties. In the councils of the political leaders the focus of attention was on the dissatisfaction being experienced by those Indians settling on reserves. During those days of "The Time of the Great Hunger," Indians were seeing few of the benefits promised them under the treaty. The meager rations provided to them did little to stop the loss of life. Between 1880 and 1885 the Indian population dropped from 32 549 to 20 170—a death rate of nearly 10 percent per year.[5]

At the Duck Lake Council, held in early August of 1884, Indian leaders presented a list of eighteen specific treaty grievances including complaints about untamed horses and cows, inadequate rations, poor implements, lack of schools and medical assistance and general dissatisfaction with government measures. The report on their presentation stated "that requests for redress of their grievances have been again and again made without effect. They are glad that the young men have not resorted to violent measures to gain it. That it is almost too hard for them to bear the treatment received at the hands of the government after its 'sweet promises' made in order to get their country from them. They now fear that they are going to be cheated. They will wait until next summer to see if this council has the desired effect, failing which they will take measures to get what they desire. (The proposed 'measures' could not be elicited, but a suggestion of the idea of war was repudiated.)"[6]

One measure being proposed by the Chiefs was a meeting of the Grand Council to be held on Little Pine's Reserve in 1885. The Blackfoot would be invited to attend. Once a united position was agreed upon, a delegation of Chiefs would travel to Ottawa where it was believed someone with sufficient authority could make some changes.

Thus, the Indian people were charting their own course of action to deal with Indian problems. It was a plan which called for concerted political action, and under it any outbreak of violence would be viewed as an undesirable course of events.

The Spread of the Rebellion Tests Indian Loyalties

Following the outbreak of hostilities at Duck Lake, Riel, attempting to spark a Territory-wide insurrection, sent messengers to many reserves urging the Indians to join him. The response of most Indian leaders was to send messages to government authorities reaffirming their loyalty.

On 28 March 1885, a delegation of Touchwood Chiefs sent a message expressing "to his Excellency the Lieutenant-Governor and through him to the Governor-General, their loyalty to their Great Mother the Queen, and further wish to express their disapproval of the course of action pursued by those at the head of the present struggle."[7]

At a meeting called by Riel's messengers at the Crooked Lakes Reserves, the Indians decided to remain loyal. Chief Kahkewistahaw made the following statement: "Agent, you remember the time I promised I would go to my reserve. I also said that I and my young men's fighting days were over. I stick to those words no matter what may be done up north, we will remain on our reserves and attend to our work."[8]

Chief Piapot, the main Cree leader in the South, wrote: "It is eleven years since I gave up fighting. When I took the government Treaty I touched the pen not to interfere with the whiteman and the whiteman not to interfere with me."[9]

Also on 28 March, Indian Agent Rae visited old Chief Mosquito on his reserve a few miles south of Battleford and received the Chief's assurances that the band would remain loyal. At about the same time, Riel's messengers were visiting both Mosquito's and Red Pheasant's Reserves.

On Mosquito's Reserve a band member named Itka had been grieving over the death of his daughter, which he blamed on Farm Instructor Payne. A few days before her death, Payne had physically thrown the frail girl out of his house. Itka decided the time was opportune for revenge, went to the Farm Instructor's home and shot him dead. Relatives of Itka, convinced that Canadian authorities would conduct an American-style retaliation against them, decided that their best alternative would be to seek refuge. They went to the house of Barney Tremont, a local farmer, demanding horses. When Tremont refused, he was shot and killed.

While these events were occurring on the Mosquito Reserve, Chiefs Poundmaker and Little Pine, concerned about the outbreak at Duck Lake, decided to travel to Battleford to express their loyalty to the Queen. Poundmaker also decided that at the same time he would take the opportunity to attempt to gain government concessions for food and other treaty provisions. Hearing this, most of the band members decided to accompany their Chiefs in the hope that they would be present for the distributions.

The two Chiefs and their followers met with Chief Young Sweetgrass on 28 March at the Sweetgrass Reserve, about ten miles west of Battleford. Farm Instructors Jefferson and Craig debated whether or not they should accompany the Indians to Battleford, but decided against it for fear of disapproval by their superiors, who wanted Indians to remain on their reserves.

Also present was Peter Ballantyne, who was operating as a spy for Edgar Dewdney. He checked on the Indians' plans and came to the conclusion that their intentions were peaceful.

Meanwhile in Battleford, rumours were rampant that Poundmaker was approaching to attack the town.

Battleford — The Siege That Never Occurred

When Poundmaker and his followers reached Battleford on the morning of 30 March, they were surprised to find the town deserted. The residents had taken refuge in the North-West Mounted Police Barracks on the other side of the river.

Poundmaker sent a message to the fort stating his peaceful intentions and requesting a meeting with Indian Agent Rae. Rae refused to leave the fort, but Peter Ballantyne and Hudson's Bay Company Factor McKay came out to meet Poundmaker. McKay agreed to release food to the Indians from the Hudson's Bay Company store.

Governor Dewdney was sent a telegram stating, "Indians willing to go back to reserves tomorrow if their demands for clothing are met. Strongly urge you to deal with them as we are not in a position at present to begin an Indian war."[10] Dewdney later replied, although too late, that he would meet with Poundmaker.

There were other groups who had arrived at Battleford — some of the Stoneys from Mosquito's Reserve, and Riel's agitators from Duck Lake. As Ballantyne and McKay were returning to the fort after failing to arrange talks with Rae, some of the Métis took shots at them. Later that day, some of the Stoneys began to break into stores and loot. Poundmaker and Little Pine tried to restrain their followers from looting, but with only limited success.

By the next morning, Poundmaker and most of his followers were on their way home. The strain of the troubles was too great for Little Pine, who had been suffering from temporary blindness and other symptoms of starvation. He died on 31 March 1885, a few miles before reaching his reserve. Little Pine's death, and that of old Chief Red Pheasant a few days earlier, meant that Poundmaker had become the main Indian leader in the Battleford area.

Accounts of the siege were blown well out of proportion. The telegraph line had not been tampered with, allowing the Battleford residents to send out daily messages of alarm. During the 25 days before relief troops arrived, the 500 settlers barricaded in the fort were even able to obtain water safely from their only source a mile outside of the barracks. According to one observer, "one solitary individual—the cook—had the temerity to continue in residence at the old government house. He had many visitors that day, gave them to eat, when they departed without harming him."[11]

Interestingly enough, another observer reported, "They [the Indians] had been too hurried to take much; the principal looting was the work of white men. As soon as the coast was clear in the morning they came over in detachments and finished what the Indians had begun. They made a clean sweep."[12]

Not the least of these raiders was Farm Instructor Craig, who "devoted his time and attention to looting the stores and houses that had been broken into by the Indians, but his enterprise was frustrated by persistent robbing of his tent whenever he left it."[13]

Several observers were of the opinion that looting would never have taken place had the townspeople not deserted their houses and stores. By and large, the "siege" was a fabricated event.

Big Bear's Misfortune Peaks at Frog Lake

Big Bear had become the principal leader of the northern Plains Cree in 1877, following the death of Chief Sweetgrass. Unfortunately, he had a poor relationship with the government. One of the tactics used by the government during treaty negotiations had been to fail to send notification of the meetings to Indian leaders who were considered difficult to deal with. Such was the reason for Big Bear's arrival at Fort Pitt a day after Treaty Six had been signed.

During a speech objecting to the lack of consultation with the several bands he was representing, Big Bear said:

> I have come off to speak for the different bands that are out on the Plains. It is no small matter we were to consult about. I expected the Chiefs here would have waited until I arrived. . . .
> I heard the Governor was to come and I said I shall see him; when I see him I will request that he will save me from that which I most dread, that is: the rope to be about my neck, it was not given to us by the Great Spirit that the red man or the white man should shed each other's blood.[14]

The official treaty interpreter had already left and Reverend McKay, whose mastery of Cree was far from perfect, misinterpreted Big Bear's words to mean a fear of hanging (*ayhahkotit*). Big Bear was actually saying that he did not wish to lose his freedom, like an animal with a rope around its neck (*aysakapaykinit*).[15] Nevertheless, the impression created of Big Bear was that he was evil and cowardly, an image which would haunt him up to his final days.

68

Steadfast in his belief that he could get a revision of Treaty Six, similar to those of Treaties One and Two, Big Bear held out from signing Treaty Six longer than any other Chief. He was forced to sign six years later, when it became clear that his Band members would starve unless they obtained government rations.

In 1884, after years of urging, Big Bear agreed to choose a reserve next to Pound-maker's. Deputy Superintendent-General of Indian Affairs Lawrence Vankoughnet, a man who disliked Big Bear, vetoed the plan, suggesting that it would not be a good idea to have too many "idle Indians" in one area. Instead, Vankoughnet warned Big Bear to take a reserve already set aside near Fort Pitt — a location which Big Bear had already rejected — or face a cut-off of rations during the winter of 1884–85. Big Bear refused to comply.

An unhealthy blend of ingredients was being mixed. Many members of Big Bear's band, including his son Imases and the War Chief Wandering Spirit, were becoming frustrated with the state of affairs. Compounding the problem was the presence of Indian Agent Quinn, a man known to have been abusive to Indians, and Farm Instructor Delaney, who had been accused of violating Indian women. The government was aware of the unpopu-larity of these men with the Indians, and had been planning to relocate them.

News of the Duck Lake fight did not reach Agent Quinn until late on 31 March 1885. The next day, 1 April or "Big Lie Day," as the Indians called it, Quinn summoned Big Bear's band members to inform them of the incident. Imases, speaking on behalf of Big Bear, who was out hunting for food for the band, replied:

> They have already risen; we knew about it before you. They have beaten the soldiers in the first fight, killing many. We do not wish to join the half-breeds, but we are afraid. We wish to stay here and prove ourselves the friends of the white man.[16]

Imases then asked Quinn to provide rations to the band. Quinn refused, saying he would have to speak to Big Bear first.

Later that day Big Bear returned empty-handed from hunting and led a delegation to request rations from Quinn. Big Bear was upset at his refusal. Imases, hoping to win a compromise, suggested that Quinn give the Indians food for a feast as a gift to the band, and he would not then have to call it rations. Quinn, however, had decided to give them nothing.

That night, unknown to Big Bear, Wandering Spirit and several members of the Rattler's Warrior Society held a dance in secret. As dawn broke some twenty armed war-riors came to the Frog Lake community, waking up the residents and herding them to Quinn's house.

That morning, when asked for food and other supplies, Quinn was willing to comply, and various Indians were allowed to have goods from the stores.

That day was Holy Thursday, and two priests who had come for the occasion asked per-mission to hold church services. The hostages were all allowed to attend church. By this time Big Bear had learned of the trouble and had joined the whites in the church to ensure that nothing worse occurred.

As the church service progressed, the noise outside increased. The warriors had broken into the stores and had found wine, spirits, and painkillers. As these were consumed the shouting and yelling of the warriors grew louder, and they eventually began to enter the church and disrupt the service.[17]

Big Bear decided to leave the church and begin warning the other residents of the com-munity, who were in their houses, to leave in case trouble broke out. He was at Mrs. Simpson's house when he heard shots. The church service had been cut short.

Wandering Spirit, the War Chief, ordered the whites to go to the Indian camp, a short distance away. Quinn refused to move, and after repeated warnings Wandering Spirit shot him dead.

Big Bear ran outside, yelling at the warriors to stop it, but it was too late. Urged on by the prompting of Wandering Spirit, the warriors soon killed eight white men.

Perhaps the violence would have been averted had Quinn simply given food to the starving band the day before. It did not appear that the band was thinking seriously of any sort of insurrection at that time. Even on the following day, had Quinn been liberal with Indian requests for food and simply complied with the warriors' orders, it is possible that bloodshed could have been averted entirely. The presence of alcohol and painkillers can be the only explanation for the gruesomeness of the murders. In Indian thinking, it was considered dishonourable and cowardly to kill an unarmed man for no reason at all.

Big Bear's hopes of peaceful dealings with government had all but vanished, yet he distinguished himself by protecting the lives of the remaining white captives, and by preventing greater bloodshed at Fort Pitt.

The warriors moved to seize the provisions at Fort Pitt on 14 April. Big Bear, no longer in control of the band, argued for an attempt to arrange a peaceful surrender of the Fort. He held the warriors back for one night, and the next day persuaded 44 civilians to surrender to the band. With this achieved, the North West Mounted Police detachment had little reason to stay, and was allowed to escape down the river by boat. Big Bear's vigilance was an important factor in preventing any deaths among them.

The Unprovoked Attack on Cutknife Hill

Although Poundmaker had been forced to relinquish power to the warrior society, he was influential in maintaining calm among the Indians camped at Cutknife Hill following the so-called siege of Battleford.

Lieutenant-Colonel Otter arrived at Battleford on 24 April 1885 with close to 550 troops. Also, part of his arsenal was a Gatling gun sent for demonstration by the United States Army.

Otter's troops were sorely disappointed at not seeing action on arrival at Battleford. Otter had been ordered by Middleton to stay at Battleford and guard the townspeople. Sensing the unrest of his troops, and seeing the opportunity to gain personal glory, Otter wired Dewdney, "I proposed taking part of my force at once to punish Poundmaker leaving 100 men to garrison Battleford. Great depredations committed. Immediate decisive action necessary. Do you approve?"[18]

Dewdney, probably after consulting the Prime Minister, wired Otter with approval.

Otter planned to surprise Poundmaker and force him to surrender. On the evening of 28 April, he left Battleford for Cutknife Hill. Otter's timing was good, and he arrived at the foot of Cutknife Hill at 5:15 the following morning. Fortunately for Poundmaker's camp, an old man, Jacob With the Long Hair, was awake and heard the sounds of the approaching soldiers. He ran through the camp shouting warnings.

At that point Otter ordered his guns to open fire on the sleeping camp. The barrage knocked over some tipis, but all of the occupants managed to scramble to safety.

Some of the Indian warriors ran out to confront the troops while others began shooting from nearby coulees. According to Robert Jefferson, an eyewitness, "Not more than 50 [Indians] altogether, had taken part in the battle. This was excusable since few were armed."[19] As the battle continued throughout the morning, Otter realized that his troops were in a vulnerable position and were slowly being surrounded. Just before noon, he ordered his men to retreat.

The warriors wanted to pursue Otter. Knowing the land like the backs of their hands and gaining the advantage of nightfall, the warriors could have inflicted heavy casualties on the tiring soldiers. Poundmaker refused to agree, maintaining that while the Indians were right in defending themselves on their land, it would be wrong to go on the offensive.

There had been a split among the people at Cutknife Hill. On the one side was the pro-Riel faction consisting of the Métis agitators and the Stoney warriors. On the other side were those led by Poundmaker who wanted to have as little as possible to do with the rebellion. Poundmaker had tried to lead his followers west toward the hilly country around Devil's Lake, with plans to eventually take refuge near Crowfoot, but the warriors and Métis prevented them from leaving.

Poundmaker was essentially being used as a spokesman by the belligerent faction. An example of this was a letter to Riel dictated by Riel's sympathizers but bearing the "signatures" of Poundmaker and several other Indians. Poundmaker's lack of verbal or written knowledge of either French or English put him at a great disadvantage. The fact was that Poundmaker was not in control, and the insinuation of support for Riel contained in the letter was out of character with his actions. That letter later became the main piece of evidence used in convicting Poundmaker.

Following the Battle of Cutknife Hill, it was decided that it was no longer safe to remain on the reserve. When the pro-Riel faction decided to join Riel at Batoche, Poundmaker attempted to lead his followers west, away from trouble. The dispute nearly led to bloodshed, but Poundmaker's poorly armed followers relented. Poundmaker's lack of cooperation and additional efforts to break away from the camp slowed the Indians' progress to Batoche by several days.

Poundmaker's stalling tactics saved many Indian lives, for as they neared Batoche on 14 May, they received news that Middleton's army had just defeated the Métis. After some discussion, Poundmaker sought terms of surrender from Middleton; when refused, he surrendered unconditionally at Battleford on 26 May 1885.

Poundmaker's plan to abandon his reserve and seek refuge by moving to an isolated area was not unique. A significant number of band members, from reserves such as Mosquito's, Red Pheasant's, One Arrow's and Thunderchild's, went north to avoid any involvement in the troubles.

During this period, Sir John A. Macdonald was attempting to exploit tribal differences by inquiring about sending Indian patrols against Poundmaker and Big Bear. He wrote Dewdney on 29 March 1885, "I understand that the Crees dread the Blackfeet like the devil. Now a corps of scouts under Crowfoot might be formed."[20] Because of the relationship between Crowfoot and Poundmaker this plan never succeeded, despite repeated requests from the Prime Minister.

At Batoche against Their Will

Part of the strategy of Riel's provisional government was based on the belief that they held influence over the Indians. In a note to the English half-breeds on 22 March 1885, they wrote, "We are sure that if the English and French half-breeds unite well in this time of crisis, not only can we control the Indians, but we will also have their weight on our side."[21] With Indians outnumbering both Métis and whites in the northwest, their support in a conflict could be critical, but the presumption of Indian involvement was made without consultation with any of the Indian leaders.

On 18 March 1885, one day before Riel's proclamation of his provisional government, that process of "controlling" Indians began. About 40 Riel supporters arrived at One Arrow's Reserve, approximately two miles east of Batoche, taking the Indian agent and farm instructor prisoner. The next day, One Arrow and fifteen of his men came to Batoche. As One Arrow testified at his trial,

> I am an old man now. . . . I was taken to the place, Batoche's, to join Riel by Gabriel. I did not take myself to the place. They took me there. I could not say how many there were of them that took me there, but there was quite a number of them. . . . so when I went there and got there I was taken prisoner.[22]

Witnesses testified that One Arrow was seen in the area during both the Duck Lake fight and the Battle of Batoche. In his defence, One Arrow testified that,

> All that was said against me was thrown upon me falsely. I did not take up my gun with the intention to shoot at any man. I was on the brink of the hill the whole day, and I had my gun there, but, of course, not with the intention to use the gun against any man, and when I saw the whitemen coming down, I ran down the hill too, and ran off.[23]

On 10 April 1885, around twenty Riel supporters arrived at Whitecap's Reserve, a few miles south of Saskatoon. Whitecap, the Chief of a band of refugee American Dakota, had resisted Riel's overtures two weeks previous. Before the Métis began forcing Whitecap and twenty of his men toward Batoche, Whitecap managed to send a message to a white friend in Saskatoon, Gerald Willoughby, asking him for assistance. When the group reached Saskatoon, a group of nine citizens tried to persuade the Métis to allow Whitecap to return to his reserve. Outnumbered, they were unsuccessful.

When Whitecap arrived at Batoche, he was appointed the only Indian member of Riel's council on internal matters, but because he understood neither French nor Cree, he attended only one meeting.

Whitecap's men were seen at the battles of Fish Creek and Batoche. Testimony provided by the main prosecution witnesses showed that Whitecap could not be positively identified as having been among the several old Indian men at Batoche, but it was mainly because of the evidence showing that Whitecap had been coerced to fight that all charges against him were dropped.[24]

The Indian Trials: Unwarranted Punishment

Poundmaker, despite evidence of his efforts to maintain peace, was convicted of treason-felony on the basis of the letter to Riel bearing his name. Speaking after hearing the guilty verdict, Poundmaker categorically denied any wrongdoing, saying, "Everything that is bad has been laid against me this summer, there is nothing of it true."[25] On hearing that he was sentenced to three years at Stony Mountain, Poundmaker declared, "I would prefer to be hung at once than to be in that place."[26] Poundmaker was released in the spring of 1886, largely because of public sympathy, but he died in June after making a trek on foot to visit his adoptive father, Crowfoot.

Although the evidence was strongly in favour of Big Bear, it appeared that the outcome of his trial was predetermined, and he was sentenced to the same three-year term as Poundmaker. There was less public sympathy for Big Bear, and he was not released until 3 February 1887, after a medical report confirmed his badly deteriorating health. He had no band to return to, as it had been dispersed by the government. Most of his family he would never see, as they were fugitives in the United States. With his heart broken and no cause to live for, he died on 18 January 1888.

When Chief One Arrow heard the charges of treason-felony translated to him, it came out in Cree as "knocking off the Queen's bonnet and stabbing her in the behind with a sword."[27] This moved One Arrow to ask the interpreter if he was drunk. The conviction of One Arrow was based on his presence at the battle sites, and his account of how he came to be there was ignored.

One Arrow was not so fortunate as to make it back to his own reserve. He was released from Stony Mountain Prison on 21 April 1886, and died four days later at Archbishop Taché's residence in St. Boniface. He was baptized just before his death and lies in St. Boniface cemetery in an unmarked grave.

In order to save money, a decision was made not to hold all of the rebellion trials at Regina. Several of them were held in Battleford instead. The atmosphere in Battleford was not hospitable toward Indians, as an editorial in the *Saskatchewan Herald* on 23 April 1885 shows:

> The petted Indians are the bad ones. The Stonies have been treated as being of a superior race, and are the first to shed the blood of their benefactors. Poundmaker has been petted and feted, and stands in the front rank as a raider. Little Pine, bribed to come north and kept in comfort, hastens to the carnage. Big Bear, who has for years enjoyed the privilege of eating of the bread of idleness, shows his gratitude by killing his priests and his best friends in cold blood. Little Poplar, a non-treaty Indian, has been liberally supplied with provisions and other necessaries and thus enabled to spend all his time in travelling up and down the land plotting mischief and preparing for this season's carnival of ruin. The petted Indians have proved the bad ones, and this gives weight to the old adage that the only good Indians are the dead ones.[28]

Judge Rouleau, who would pass the judgements, had narrowly missed being murdered along with Farm Instructor Payne, and was also bitter about the burning of his mansion at Battleford. He was known before the trials to advocate harsh punishment as a deterrent to future rebellious acts by Indians.

The eight Indians eventually hanged were at a disadvantage. They knew nothing of the legal system and had no legal counsel or other advice. No effective defence of any sort was mounted which might have created sympathy for the defendants — for example, the reality of their starvation under Indian Affairs administration, or the excesses brought on by alcohol and drugs at the Frog Lake massacre.

Several Indian Elders are certain that at least one of the Indians, Man-Without-Blood, was wrongly hanged for the shooting of Farm Instructor Payne. They claim it was done by the other Stoney, Man-With-a-Black-Blanket. According to one story,

> The two of the Stoney young men were arrested also. They were accused of killing the farm instructor and they were both arrested. And at that time people were very respectable. There was a lot of respect for the older people. Now the one who did not kill the Indian Agent, he was the one who was accused by his partner. So the one who was accused of killing the farm instructor, when he went to trial, the officer asked him, "Is it true what you did? Or is it not true?" He replied, "Maybe it is true, and maybe it is not." And he really had nothing to do

with it, he didn't shoot the Indian Agent. So when he said, "Maybe they are telling the truth," that was accepted as his plea, as telling the truth. So he got the blame for the death of the farm instructor. So he was one of them that got hanged. They weren't going to sympathize with him or feel sorry for him.[29]

According to another story, "It's him who killed the ration feeder. And the one who followed him shot the dog. He was the one who got hung instead, said my father, the one who shot the dog. He did not want to report his partner."[30]

No clear evidence of committing murder was shown against Iron Body and Little Bear, two of the six Indians tried for their role in the Frog Lake massacre. They were hanged on the basis that, by aiding and abetting the others, they were equally guilty.

Four Sky Thunder received a sentence of fourteen years for burning down the Frog Lake church. Another Indian, whose only wrongdoing was having been seen with Big Bear, was sentenced to six years in prison.[31]

Several Indians were never brought to justice. Among them was Man-Who-Speaks-Our-Language, who nearly caused the outbreak of fighting with the North West Mounted Police on Poundmaker's Reserve in 1884, and was responsible for some of the killings at Frog Lake.

The hangings at Battleford took place on 27 November 1885. Indians from several reserves were there to witness the event.

A new section was built at Stony Mountain Penitentiary to accommodate the 25 Indians and eighteen Métis sentenced to prison. Several of the Indians never returned to their reserves, and are buried in the St. Boniface cemetery.

The Aftermath: Suppression of Indians

The government saw the rebellion as an opportunity to achieve a goal which had eluded it since 1870, that of gaining total control over Indians. In July of 1885, Assistant Commissioner Hayter Reed drew up a list of fifteen recommendations on actions to be taken following the rebellion. Among these were the following:

The leaders of the Teton Sioux who fought against the troops should be hanged and the rest be sent out of the country;

Big Bear's band should either be broken up and scattered among other bands or be given a reserve adjacent to that at Onion Lake;

One Arrow's band should be joined with that of Beardy and Okemasis and their reserve surrendered;

No annuity money should be now paid any bands that rebelled, or to any individuals that joined the insurgents;

The tribal system should be abolished in so far as is compatible with the Treaty;

All half-breeds, members of rebel bands, although not shown to have taken any active part in the rebellion, should have their names erased from the paysheets;

No rebel Indians should be allowed off the Reserves without a pass signed by an Indian Department official; and

All Indians who have not during the late troubles been disloyal or troublesome should be treated as heretofore.[32]

Reed had also prepared a list of every Indian band in the northwest and had identified 28 disloyal bands. In his enthusiasm he erroneously included several reserves, such as Sweetgrass and Thunderchild, which had been very loyal. Most of the others had actually been loyal, with only the odd individual implicated in the rebellion. Of all the bands identified as disloyal in the rebellion, it is clear that none of the Chiefs, whether Big Bear, Poundmaker, Mosquito, Red Pheasant, Little Pine, Beardy, One Arrow or Whitecap, politically supported the rebellion. All were drawn into the conflict by circumstances beyond their personal control. In all, less than five percent of the Indian population of the northwest was involved.

The original proposal to disallow rebel Indians from leaving their reserves without a pass soon became a measure to be applied to all Indians. In approving this plan, Sir John A. Macdonald was aware that he was contravening the treaties. He noted:

> Mr. Dewdney thinks that the pass system can be generally introduced in July. If so, it is in the highest degree desirable. As to the disloyal Bands, this should be carried out as the consequence of their disloyalty. The system should be introduced in the loyal Bands as well and the advantage of the change pressed upon them. But no punishment for breaking bounds could be inflicted and in the case of resistance on the grounds of Treaty rights should not be insisted on.[33]

The measures taken against Indians, in particular those restricting them to reserves, were measures which would have a profound effect on subsequent Indian developments. What little influence Indian people had over their own lives was removed, and Indian people became vulnerable to government whim, manipulation and mismanagement.

It was regrettable that Sir John A. Macdonald, who was Superintendent General of Indian Affairs and Prime Minister, never once bothered to visit the people over whom he had charge during the eight critical years he held office, from 1879 to 1887.

Had the Indian people been able to retain their freedom of movement, things might have turned out much differently. Big Bear and other Indian leaders might have met Sir John A. Macdonald in 1885. Nationally, efforts to form the League of Indians of Canada in the 1920s and the North American Indian Brotherhood in the 1940s would have been more successful and probably would have received the bulk of their strength from the prairies. Indian political development in Canada was probably put back by two generations.

The rebellion has left a legacy of a century of suspicions about Indian political abilities and loyalties, and misconceptions about the validity of Indian treaties.

In concluding, I would say that a clear understanding of the Indian view of the 1885 Uprising is the least that can be done to right the blunders of the past.

NOTES

1. Florence Paul, interview by Wilfred Tootoosis, One Arrow Indian Reserve, 15 March 1985.
2. Harry Michael, interview by Wilfred Tootoosis, Beardy's Indian Reserve, 14 March 1985.
3. Canada, *Treaty Number Six Between Her Majesty the Queen and the Plain and Wood Cree Indians and other Tribes of Indians* (Ottawa: Queen's Printer, 1964), 5.
4. John B. Tootoosis, interview by Wilfred Tootoosis, Poundmaker Indian Reserve, 30 November 1984.
5. Canada, *Sessional Papers*, 1886, No. 36, 2.
6. Public Archives of Canada (hereafter PAC), RG 10, Vol. 3697, File 15,423, MacRae to Dewdney, 25 August 1884.

7. PAC, RG 10, Vol. 3584, File 1130, Pt. 3A, McBeath to Macdonald, 28 March 1885.
8. PAC, RG 10, Vol. 3584, File 1130, Pt. 3A, Macdonald to Indian Commissioner, 8 April 1885.
9. PAC, RG 10, Vol. 3584, File 1130, Pt. 3A, Piapot to Macdonald, 30 April 1885.
10. Dewdney Papers, Vol. 5, 1879–1880, Rae to Dewdney, 30 March 1885.
11. Robert Jefferson, *Fifty Years on the Saskatchewan* (Battleford: Canadian Northwest Historical Society, 1929), 127.
12. Ibid., 128.
13. Ibid., 126.
14. Alexander Morris, *Treaties of Canada With the Indians of Manitoba and the North-West Territories* (Toronto: Coles Publishing Limited, 1971), 239.
15. Hugh Dempsey, *Big Bear — The End of Freedom* (Vancouver: Douglas and McIntyre, 1984), 74.
16. W.B. Cameron, *Blood Red the Sun* (Edmonton: Hurtig Publishers, 1977), 33.
17. Dempsey, *Big Bear*, 155.
18. Dewdney Papers, Vol. 5, p. 1806, Otter to Dewdney, 26 April 1885.
19. Jefferson, *Fifty Years*, 146.
20. PAC, MG 26A, Vol. 526, p. 1404, Macdonald to Dewdney, 29 March 1885.
21. Bob Beal and Rod Macleod, *Prairie Fire: The 1885 North-West Rebellion* (Edmonton: Hurtig Publishers, 1984), 148.
22. Canada, *Sessional Papers*, 1886, No. 52, 33.
23. Ibid., 32.
24. Ibid., 13.
25. Ibid., 336.
26. Ibid., 337.
27. Beal and Macleod, *Prairie Fire*, 309.
28. *Saskatchewan Herald* (Battleford), 23 April 1885.
29. Lawrence Lonesinger, interview by Wilfred Tootoosis, Sweetgrass Indian Reserve, 13 March 1985.
30. Alex Sapp, interview by Wilfred Tootoosis, Little Pine Indian Reserve, date not available.
31. S.E. Bingaman, "The North-West Rebellion Trials, 1885" (Master's thesis, University of Regina, 1971), 133.
32. PAC, RG 10, Vol. 3710, File 19, 550–3, Reed to Dewdney, 20 July 1885.
33. PAC, RG 10, Vol. 3710, File 19, 550–3, Vankoughnet to Superintendent General, 17 August 1885.

75

Article Seven

Two Months in Big Bear's Camp, 1885: Narratives of "Indian Captivity" and the Articulation of "Race" and Gender Hierarchies in Western Canada

Sarah Carter

Theresa Gowanlock and Theresa Delaney are not familiar names in Canadian history today, but they were among the greatest celebrities of the tumultuous events of 1885 in Western Canada.[1] Visitors to the cemetery at the site of the Frog Lake settlement (in present-day Alberta) will find inscribed on a stone cairn the words "They Took Prisoners Mrs.

Source: Adapted from the introduction to *Two Months in the Camp of Big Bear* (Regina: Canadian Plains Rersearch Centre, 1999), vii–xxxviii. Reprinted by permission of the author.

Theresa Delaney, Mrs. Theresa Gowanlock," beneath the names of nine men, including their husbands. The men were killed on April 2, 1885 by "rebel Indians under Big Bear," the plaque declares. The settlement of Frog Lake that adjoined the Woods Cree reserves was abandoned in the spring of 1885, but for many years Theresa Delaney's flowers, and the hedge around her garden continued to grow untended. The cellar depression of the Delaney home can still be found even though the shrubs, stunted poplars, and grasses of the parkland belt have largely reclaimed this site, and two miles away some remnants of the Gowanlock home and mill on Frog Creek are discernible. The site of Frog Lake today conveys a sense of the shattered lives of these women, but visitors learn little about them beyond the words found on the stone cairn.

For two months after the deaths of their husbands, Mrs. Delaney and Mrs. Gowanlock were among a large group that some Plains Cree harboured while they attempted to evade the North-West Field Force. During this time, as Canada mobilized over 5000 men to suppress what was interpreted then as a Métis and Indian "rebellion," a frenzy of media attention came to focus on the two white women captives, or "fair daughters of Ontario." Following the defeat of the Métis at Batoche on May 12, the final task of the North-West Field Force was to pursue this group of Cree. Even though the Cree camp included a large number of women, men, and children of diverse ancestries, the two Theresas became the focus of the campaign, which took on the appearance of a crusade to save the two white women. When they emerged at Fort Pitt early in June, telegraphs announcing the glad tidings were read in the House of Commons, and it was stated in one Ontario newspaper that "A thrill of pleasure will influence every Canadian man and woman on learning that Mrs. Delaney and Mrs. Gowanlock have escaped from the Indians safe and uninjured. The news will give as much genuine cause of congratulation as that of the success at Batoche."[2] It is curious that these women who were so central to the drama of that momentous year are scarcely mentioned in the many histories of 1885, although their book *Two Months in the Camp of Big Bear: The Life and Adventures of Theresa Gowanlock and Theresa Delaney* is often drawn on as an "eyewitness" account of Frog Lake.

Yet there is a great challenge involved in any attempt to restore the two women to a place in history, as it is difficult to know with any certainty what actually happened to them. From the beginning of their ordeal, and even months after, different versions of the experiences of Mrs. Gowanlock and Mrs. Delaney were proposed, and their two months with the Cree came to constitute another battleground of 1885. These two women, who emerged so suddenly from obscurity that spring, found their experiences, or their imagined experiences, twisted, turned, and altered to suit a variety of purposes. They were at the centre of a debate over critical issues of the age, including the purposes and quality of government administration of Indian affairs, and whether Aboriginal males and white women should be granted the franchise. At the heart of these debates was the issue of the kind of nation Canada was to be — whether Canada was prepared at this time in its newly acquired territories to embrace cultural diversity and to extend the privileges of citizenship. Those who wished to warn against the potential dangers of a pluralistic and more egalitarian nation, and wanted to defend and protect "race"[3] and gender divisions and hierarchies, cast Delaney and Gowanlock as helpless and vulnerable victims of Aboriginal savagery. It was this script that emerged triumphant through the publication of the separate narratives of the two women in one book entitled *Two Months in the Camp of Big Bear*. The women present themselves as vulnerable females, torn from the paternalistic order and thrown into a chaotic world at the hands of brutal captors. As the accounts of the women themselves, surely these texts can be understood to represent their unvarnished testimony. Yet as this article will show, the version of events presented in *Two Months* differed from the accounts the women gave when they first emerged from their ordeal, and there may have been pressures and constraints that account for the nature of their published presentation of events. Certain stories were selected for emphasis in *Two Months* while others were neglected or excluded. Their accounts conform to conventions, expectations, and representations typical of the "Indian captivity" narrative. As widows they were anxious to secure government pensions, and this may have compelled them to place events in a certain light—to convey some impressions while suppressing others. To enhance our thinking and understanding of 1885 we need to appreciate that sources such as *Two Months* are problematic and selective, and we need to pay attention to the perspectives of many others involved in order to portray a more varied and complicated past.

The events of 1885 are almost always presented from a purely masculine perspective, but women, Aboriginal and non-Aboriginal, were at the centre and not the periphery of these events. A focus on the experiences of Delaney and Gowanlock, and consideration of their book *Two Months*, provides insight into the ways in which women of different ancestries, or "races," were categorized in the dominant society of non-Aboriginal Canada. Racially specific ideas of womanhood and femininity were devised and manipulated at this time in Canada's West.[4] To be white and female in 1885 meant something quite different from being Aboriginal and female. While great sympathy was extended to the two white women who were understood to have endured "the severest trials of any concerned in the whole of the rebellion in the North-West," little concern was voiced about the several Cree women who died in 1885, or the Métis women and children who were left homeless and destitute.[5] No white women were killed or injured in 1885. But the two Theresas came to signify vulnerable, threatened, frail, white womanhood in need of rescue and protection. An emphasis on the horrors of their ordeal justified the righteous vengeance that was taken, such as the mass hanging of eight men at Fort Battleford in November 1885. Aboriginal women were cast as the opposite of white women, as the antithesis of frailty and purity, as harried beasts of burden who were treated brutally in their own society. They were powerful symbols of the shortcomings of Aboriginal society just as white women represented all that was noble and virtuous about non-Aboriginal Canada.

The Authors

Beyond the sparse biographical detail provided in *Two Months*, little is known about the lives of these two women before and after 1885. Theresa (Johnson) Gowanlock was born in 1863 at Tintern in Lincoln County, Ontario. Her parents, Martha (Upper) and Henry Johnson, were both from pioneering families of that district, and their house on the Johnson farm, where Theresa and her eight brothers and sisters were born, remained standing until very recently on the outskirts of Tintern.[6] They were a Presbyterian family. Theresa Johnson married John A. Gowanlock (1861–1885) in October 1884. He was from Stratford, Ontario, and worked as a farmer, speculator, surveyor, and storekeeper in the Battleford district before securing a a federal government contract to build and operate a grist mill on Frog Creek with his partner Richard Laurie.[7]

In the Battleford newspaper, the *Saskatchewan Herald*, it was noted on October 31, 1884, that while on a trip down east John Gowanlock had taken "unto himself one of Ontario's fair daughters and brought her out west to grow up with the country." They were married in Tintern, then visited Parkdale (today part of Toronto), where two of Gowanlock's brothers owned the Parkdale *Times* newspaper, book, and publishing office. They immediately left for the west, travelling by boat and by rail, then overland from Swift Current. Theresa

Gowanlock spent six weeks in Battleford, and only arrived at Frog Creek mill in mid-December 1884. Following her brief few months in Western Canada, Theresa Gowanlock returned to her parents' home at Tintern, and she died there at age 36 in 1899.[8]

Although she was often cast as a "fair daughter of Ontario" during the events of 1885, Theresa (Fulford) Delaney was from the province of Quebec, as she was born and raised on the Aylmer Road, Hull Township, near Ottawa. Marshall and Bridget (Ryan) Fulford's eldest daughter Theresa was born in 1849, and there were at least three other sisters and four brothers in this Roman Catholic family.[9] It was the lumbering business that first brought John Delaney, originally from Nepean, Ontario, to the Aylmer Road, where he worked as a foreman. But in 1879 he headed west, chosen as one of the first contingent of farm instructors to the residents of the new Indian reserves.[10] At Frog Lake his job was to assist the Woods Cree to farm, and he was also often the person in charge of the stores and rations. As was the case with some other of the early government instructors and agents, Delaney had relationships with Cree women, and this may have been the cause of the resentment some felt toward him. After three years as a farm instructor, Delaney returned to the Aylmer Road, married Theresa Fulford, and together they left for Frog Lake in August 1882. Theresa Delaney, therefore, had a much longer stay at Frog Lake than Theresa Gowanlock before the upheaval of 1885. As mentioned in her narrative, Mrs. Delaney worked as "farm instructress" to the Woods Cree women, giving lessons in baking, milking, churning, making butter, knitting, and dressmaking. Theresa Delaney returned to the Aylmer Road in 1885, and there she taught school and was supported by her government pension until her death in Ottawa in 1913.[11]

Canada and the Indigenous People of the Northwest

It was not until the early 1880s that non-Aboriginal women such as the two Theresas began to arrive in prairie Canada west of Manitoba, and they did not appear in large numbers until the completion of the Canadian Pacific Railway (CPR) in 1885. The railroad was a critical component in the plan to consolidate Canada's control over the northwest. This plan also necessitated control over the area's Aboriginal population. Mrs. Gowanlock and Mrs. Delaney were brief visitors to the ancient homeland of a great diversity of Aboriginal people, who sought, through treaties of the 1870s, to enter into an equal partnership with the nation of Canada in order to secure their physical and cultural survival, to gain assistance in the transition to new economies based on agriculture and husbandry, and to establish peaceful, equitable relations.[12] These developments were not unique to Western Canada at this time, as there was a global pattern of European powers moving to consolidate control over territories and the indigenous inhabitants in Africa, Asia, and Latin America, while in North America governments incorporated land that became part of the nation-states. As in other colonial settings, this process of empire building generally involved the extension of the power of the central government, a dwindling land base for indigenous populations, the attempted domination of the colonizers over the colonized, and measures to facilitate the commercial enterprise of the colonizers. Also as in other colonial settings, the resistance of indigenous people was met with force, and in some cases overwhelming force.

In the Canadian west, a first resistance of Aboriginal people took place in 1869–70 at the Red River Settlement (Winnipeg), when the Métis, led by Louis Riel, objected to the transfer of their territory to the Dominion of Canada without their knowledge or consent. By 1884 another crisis in colonial authority was brewing in the northwest, where the

Aboriginal population greatly outnumbered the Euro-Canadians.[13] Since the mid-1870s the Métis of the South Saskatchewan settlements expressed a desire that their land rights be recognized. As surveys proceeded and new settlers began to surround them, the Métis remained without recognized title to their land. In 1884, frustrated by the lack of federal action, the Métis, led once again by Louis Riel, began to talk of the use of force. They seized arms and ammunition and on March 19, 1885 elected a provisional government. Several days later, Major-General Frederick Middleton, commanding the Canadian military, received orders to put the militia into alert. The first confrontation broke out at Duck Lake, where the Métis encountered a government force commanded by the North-West Mounted Police (NWMP). The strategy of the North-West Field Force was to proceed north in three columns from three points along the CPR. The column commanded by Middleton headed from Qu'Appelle station (Troy) toward Batoche, while Lieutenant-Colonel William Otter led his men from Swift Current to Battleford, where the non-Aboriginal residents had barricaded themselves in the NWMP post. Major-General Thomas Bland Strange took his column from Calgary toward Edmonton, and it was primarily his men who were engaged in the pursuit of Big Bear's camp.

Government officials projected 1885 as a concerted uprising of both Métis and First Nations in Western Canada, and while this notion has been effectively challenged, it must be kept in mind that by the mid-1880s there was considerable discontent, especially among the Plains Cree, and this discontent was gaining momentum.[14] Big Bear, a Plains Cree chief of the Fort Pitt district, was a central leader in the Cree campaign for autonomy and consolidation. He had refused to agree to Treaty 6 in 1876, and had since that time pursued a strategy aimed at securing better treaty terms and preserving the independence of the Cree within the treaty relationship. As the buffalo diminished, however, so did Big Bear's ability to remain independent. In 1882, faced with the anger and impatience of some of his own followers who were not permitted the rations given to treaty people, Big Bear agreed to adhere to Treaty 6. He remained active, however, in organizing councils of prominent Cree chiefs to press for better treaty terms. Discontent was widespread in the face of a food crisis, and inadequate, substandard implements and livestock that crippled efforts at agriculture. Government officials were extremely concerned about Big Bear's efforts to organize and concentrate the Cree. A major council of the Plains Cree was to be held in the summer of 1885. The top government official in Western Canada, Indian Commissioner and later Lieutenant-Governor Edgar Dewdney, was prepared to arrest and depose Cree leaders as he was convinced that these steps were necessary to assure Canadian control over the Cree. As historian John Tobias has argued, the soldiers sent in 1885 provided Dewdney with a new instrument to make his coercive policy effective and to end the Cree political movement. The events at Frog Lake on the morning of April 2 and the subsequent flight of the Plains Cree with captives provided Dewdney with the excuse he needed "virtually to declare war on the bands and leaders who had led the Cree movement for treaty revision."[15]

Frog Lake

Frog Lake was in the parkland or transition belt that divides the open grasslands from the forested northern regions of Western Canada. It had long been the home of the Woods Cree, whose economy took advantage of the resources of both the plains and the parkland. In 1879 two reserves were surveyed on Frog Lake: that of Chief Onepohayo and that of Chief Pus-kee-ah-kee-he-win. Onepohayo was head chief of the Woods Cree in 1885.

Despite the efforts of the Woods Cree, a viable farming economy had not been established on these reserves, and there was inadequate food, shelter, clothing, and footwear.

In the fall of 1884 the resources of the Frog Lake district were strained even further by the arrival of Big Bear and his Plains Cree followers, who numbered just over 500, almost equalling the combined population of the reserves at Frog Lake, Onion Lake, and Long Lake. A reserve site for Big Bear and his people was under negotiation in the fall of 1884, but as these negotiations proceeded, permission was sought from Onepohayo to allow Big Bear to camp on his reserve. This is where they spent the winter of 1884–85, which was one of great hardship. The Frog Lake district was almost entirely devoid of game that year, and it was an extremely cold winter with deep snow. Confidence in Big Bear's leadership was diminishing among some of his own followers during this desperate winter.

The settlement of Métis and non-Aboriginal people at Frog Lake in 1885 consisted of a Hudson's Bay Company (HBC) post, the buildings of the Indian agency, a Roman Catholic mission, a store operated by George Dill, and a six-man NWMP detachment. Thomas Quinn was the Indian subagent at Frog Lake. He was of part Dakota ancestry, and was married to a Cree woman named Owl Sitting (also known as Jane Quinn after her marriage). Just before the violent outbreak of April 2, and for reasons that remain obscure, the NWMP evacuated Frog Lake and went to Fort Pitt. Among the residents of Frog Lake who were later to be part of Big Bear's camp were John Pritchard, his wife Rose (Delorme), and their eight children. Pritchard, a Métis, was the interpreter for the government Indian agency. Interpreters were vital at these agencies, as most employees, such as John Delaney, were unable to speak the languages of the people they worked among.[16]

"April is the cruellest month," wrote T.S. Eliot, and he could certainly have been describing the parkland belt of Western Canada.[17] April of 1885 was particularly cruel because it had been a winter of great hardship and there were few signs that winter was over. Yet the earliest non-Aboriginal accounts of the events at Frog Lake stressed that there were no indications of unrest or difficulties in the entire district; it was a happy, placid settlement where a benevolent little group laboured long and zealously to better the lives of their Indian neighbours.[18] The outbreak of violence was unpredictable, and was due to the fierce, savage temperament of Aboriginal people. In these non-Aboriginal accounts, blame was also laid on the nefarious influence of Riel, on the sinister Métis of the Frog Lake settlement, on the notorious Big Bear and his malign influence, and on the perfidy and collusion of the HBC.

Accounts from the perspectives of Aboriginal people stressed the frustrations with government policy and with individual employees, as well as the conditions of poverty and starvation in the district and the multiple tensions that had built up.[19] Mary Dion told her grandson, author Joe Dion, about many instances of the casual cruelty of the white people at Frog Lake, their disdain and contempt, and their merriment at the sight of human misery.[20] In order to receive the meagre rations, Aboriginal people had to perform debilitating work in subzero temepratures, and in threadbare clothing.

On the morning of April 2, and under the leadership not of Big Bear but of Wandering Spirit, and Ayimasis, one of Big Bear's sons, some of the Plains Cree began to remove goods from the stores at Frog Lake and to round up some of the residents, including Quinn and the Gowanlocks, Delaneys, and Pritchards. When Quinn adamantly refused to move with the Cree to a new camp, he was shot by Wandering Spirit. In short order, Charles Gouin (a Métis carpenter employed by the Indian agency), John Delaney, John Gowanlock, Father Adelarde Fafard, Father Felix Marchand (visiting from Onion Lake), John Williscraft (Fafard's lay assistance), George Dill, and William Gilchrist (Gowanlock's clerk) all met the same fate.

With the Cree

The two widowed women were quickly pulled from their husbands, but from this point on it becomes a challenge to discern precisely what happened to them, as competing and conflicting versions were presented. In 1885 and for years afterward, the question of just who "saved" the white women from death or the "fate worse than death," was hotly contested, with many trying to take or assign credit while discrediting others who tried to do so.[21] Although it is not clear just how it was arranged, it is certain that for the next two months the women were billeted with the Pritchard family.

From the beginning of their ordeal, Delaney and Gowanlock were far from the only reluctant adjuncts in the camp of Big Bear, and their numbers were to be greatly augmented over the next weeks, although not all can be aptly described as reluctant. They included a mixture of the many diverse peoples of the northwest. Mrs. Quinn, another widow of the events of Frog Lake, and her daughter, were in the camp. The others included HBC store manager James Simpson (a son of Sir George Simpson and one of his "country-born" wives), his wife Catherine, and her sons, Louis and Benjamin Patenaude.[22] Edward Francois Dufresne, Indian department cook, and his wife Marguerite Mondion were also brought into the camp. Dufresne was from Quebec and had worked for the HBC for over 50 years.[23] Louis Goulet, Adolphus Nolin, Andre Nault, Pierre Blondin, and other Métis were also part of the Plains Cree camp. On April 3 a group of Cree brought two other white men to the camp: John Fitzpatrick, farm instructor for the Chipewyans at Cold Lake, and Henry R. Halpin, HBC clerk at the same place. Big Bear had sent his son-in-law, Lone Man, to retrieve these men, as he was concerned about their safety.[24] A man by the name of John Perry, who arrived at Frog Lake on April 3 to attend Good Friday services, immediately sought the safety of John Pritchard and another Métis, and he remained with Big Bear's camp for the next few months. The Woods Cree were also among the "unhappy campers," although the non-Aboriginal public found this impossible to believe, just as it was questioned whether the Métis could possibly also be prisoners. Musunekwepan recalled that when he located his parents' tipi at the Plains Cree camp, he saw that the Holy Stem was placed just outside. "It was in the centre. They had put it there purposely to show that we were captured."[25]

Fort Pitt Residents Join the Cree

In mid-April the numbers in Big Bear's camp were greatly augmented by the population that had congregated at Fort Pitt. The HBC's Fort Pitt was a small huddle of buildings on the North Saskatchewan under the supervison of Chief Trader W.J. McLean. McLean's wife Helen and their eight children also lived at Fort Pitt and another McLean child was expected that year. The three eldest McLean sisters — Amelia, Eliza, and Kitty — were well educated, having attended school at Red River, but they could also ride, shoot, and were fluent in Cree and Saulteaux. Other employees of the HBC resident at Fort Pitt also found themselves with the Plains Cree camp, including clerk Stanley Simpson, servant Malcolm McDonald, servant Alfred Schmidt and his family of six, and cook Robert Hodson. Hodson, an Englishman, had been a hangman, but as this was not steady work he had served with the HBC for a number of years. (Hodson executed the eight condemned men at Battleford in November 1885, and the following year he was appointed public hangman for the Dominion of Canada.)[26]

The population of Fort Pitt had increased dramatically in the early weeks of April as people from the surrounding districts sought protection there, some with the assistance of Aboriginal friends. Twenty-three NWMP were stationed at the fort under the command of Francis Dickens (the son of the famous novelist Charles Dickens). These included the police who had evacuated Frog Lake. Other recent arrivals included an English couple, Reverend Charles and Mrs. Quinney. He was the Church of England missionary at Onion Lake, and they had been escorted to Fort Pitt on the advice of Woods Cree Chief Seekaskootch and councillors, who wished to ensure their safety.[27] Mrs. Quinney was in the later stages of pregnancy in the spring of 1885, and gave birth to a boy on June 21 at Battleford.[28] The Onion Lake agency farm instructor, George Mann, his wife Sarah (both originally from Bowmanville, Ontario), and their three children also took refuge at Fort Pitt. They, too, had been warned of danger and were escorted to Fort Pitt by people of the Onion Lake reserve, who feared for their safety.[29]

The people of Fort Pitt could have evacuated for Battleford. Chief Seekaskootch initially urged them to construct rafts and leave by the river, but they opted to stay. Steps were taken to barricade the fort, and sentries were posted in front of the five buildings, with the eldest McLean sisters taking their turn at sentry duty. This routine lasted almost two weeks, when on April 14 a Plains Cree party from Frog Lake, including Big Bear, assembled on a ridge overlooking Fort Pitt. Through a messenger they asked to speak to McLean, who met with them for lengthy talks. McLean was on friendly terms with these people and believed that he did not have to fear for himself and his family. The talks lasted into a second day when a violent encounter broke out. In statements made later, McLean never hesitated to lay the blame for this on the poor judgement of Inspector Dickens, who, the day before, had sent out two NWMP and a scout to gather information about the whereabouts of Aboriginal groups.[30] Their sudden appearance led the Cree to believe that they were under attack. One NWMP was killed (Constable David Cowan), another wounded (Constable Clarence Loasby), while the scout (Thomas Quinn, nephew of Thomas Quinn) escaped briefly and was caught later that day. Three Cree were also killed during this confrontation. Following this event, all of the inhabitants of Fort Pitt, except for the NWMP, agreed to evacuate the fort and become part of Big Bear's camp. Under cover of darkness, the NWMP escaped on a scow down the river to Battleford.

W.J. McLean and the other 44 inhabitants of Fort Pitt decided to opt for the protection of Big Bear and also of the Woods Cree. The Quinneys, for example, sought the advice of Chief Seekaskootch, who assured them that they would be well cared for. Amelia and Kitty McLean had shown their bravery but also their confidence in their friendship with the Cree when they walked into the Cree camp unescorted just after the confrontation, and while their mother and sister tended to Loasby's wounds. They wanted to see if their father was safe, and Amelia declared they were not afraid: "We have lived together as brothers and sisters for many years. We speak the same language. Why should we be afraid of you?"[31] The people of Fort Pitt gathered their belongings and left for Big Bear's camp. It was an intensely cold night and a blinding snowstorm soon developed. As the McLeans neared the camp, some of the Cree came out to greet them and, according to Elizabeth McLean, showed her mother the greatest respect: "They gave a hand in setting up the tent which she had sent out ahead of her, and rendered very useful little services in view of the impending snowstorm, which came upon us during the night as expected."[32] Everyone from Fort Pitt was billeted with Woods or Plains Cree families.

The absorption of the people of Fort Pitt into the camp, and of other people gathered from the surrounding countryside, suggests that Big Bear and the Woods Cree leaders saw this as essential in order to protect those whose lives might be in danger. Their goal was to keep them out of harm's way not to do harm to them. The great number of "captives" or "prisoners" had opted for the protection of the Cree camp upon the advice of Aboriginal friends or leaders. This was difficult for the general non-Aboriginal public to comprehend.

This large group began to move toward Frog Lake on April 17 to join up with those left at that camp, which included some of the Woods Cree, Plains Cree women and children, and Mrs. Gowanlock and Mrs. Delaney. Two days later the Fort Pitt group arrived at Frog Lake and remained there for the next two weeks. During this time the numbers in this camp grew further, as a group of Saulteaux, travelling to visit relatives in Edmonton, were detained by the Plains Cree.[33] The Chipewyan from Cold Lake voluntarily joined the group, accompanied by their priest Rev. Laurent Legoff, who held services in the camp.[34]

On May 1 this camp began to move in an easterly direction. They did not go far, remaining for some weeks in the vicinity of Frenchman Butte. During all of April and most of May, there was no evidence of any soldiers in pursuit. Middleton and Otter were engaged elsewhere, and Strange's column took weeks to take shape, as he had difficulties finding staff officers and supplies.[35] Strange's column did not set out from Edmonton until the middle of May.

The Cree and other assorted campers experienced a fairly monotonous routine. One of the out-of-the-ordinary events that took place in the early weeks of May was the murder of an old woman in the camp. She had become very ill, then delirious, and, according to Cree belief, was in danger of becoming a cannibal, or windigo. As one of the McLean sisters (Amelia McLean Paget) explained in a book she wrote in later years, *The People of the Plains* (1909), the people had no asylums or any means of isolating people who were mentally ill, "so that any person showing marked signs of insanity was dispatched."[36]

The Cree were holding a Thirst Dance near Frenchman Butte when they learned that soldiers were approaching. The confrontation was only a minor skirmish but was elevated by the military to the title "Battle of Frenchman's Butte" when medals were issued for the campaign. On the morning of May 28, the soldiers opened fire but did not attempt a direct assault, as they found the Cree position to be strong. A sharp fire was maintained for about three hours, but then, fearing that the Cree were going to encircle them, and with three men wounded, Strange decided to retreat to Fort Pitt. The Cree did not pursue the retreating soldiers but abandoned this site and headed in a northerly direction, toward Loon Lake.

Imagined Experiences of Mrs. Gowanlock and Mrs. Delaney

During April and May the attention of the non-Aboriginal public became increasingly fixated on the widowed white women of Frog Lake. From the time that news of the events at Frog Lake became known to the wider public, hideous tales of their deaths and/or mistreatment circulated. The earliest of the reports included Mrs. Gowanlock among the dead. She was described as having pinioned the arms of the man who had killed her husband as he aimed his rifle at another; the man was said to have shaken her off and fired, killing her instantly.[37] By mid-April the sad fate of the Gowanlocks was lamented across the nation, while there was now greater concern for the fate of Mrs. Delaney. In the Charlottetown *Daily Patriot* on April 14, the story of the Gowanlocks was described as "the most touching of all . . . their death now at the hands of the Indians is unspeakably sad, but not so horrible probably, as the fate of Mrs. Delaney, wife of the murdered farm instructor, who was carried off a prisoner by the blood-thirsty fiends."

It was the NWMP that had escaped from Fort Pitt who first provided the news, learned from Chief Seekaskootch, that both Mrs. Gowanlock and Mrs. Delaney were alive and were billeted with Métis. But during May rumours that they were being treated horribly flourished in the media and among the military. Some newspapers, generally those that supported the Conservative administration, were not as quick to print these rumours. The *Toronto Daily Mail* insisted that there was litle fear that the women would be ill-treated, since "outrages of this sort has never been, and is not now, an Indian habit."[38] Other papers, however, described the brutal treatment given the hapless brides, or "Ontario's fair daughters," and by the later weeks of May these horrifying tales abounded, inflaming public opinion and galvanizing the troops to capture Big Bear and the perpetrators of the Frog Lake murders. There was criticism in some quarters of Strange's delay and hints at his incompetence. The *Toronto Morning News* claimed that it was "scandalous apathy" and a discredit to humanity that so little was being done to release the captives from their "inhuman custodians." This would surely encourage similar atrocities on defenceless women, stated the *News*. The field force must "impress upon Indians that the honour of a white woman is sacred, and that outrage and murder will be promptly avenged, no matter at what cost."[39]

By the end of May it was widely reported in newspapers and circulated throughout the field force that Mrs. Delaney had died, after being repeatedly "outraged."[40] There were various reports about Mrs. Gowanlock, that her body had been found dumped in a well, and that she had been made the wife of an Indian.[41] A surgeon with the Alberta Field Force wrote some years later that the "revolting" stories of the fate of the women wound the "whole force up to a pitch of fury." He added, "Had Big Bear and his band fallen into our hands while these reports were credited, I do not think man, woman, or child would have been spared."[42] From other quarters came calls for a war of extermination against Big Bear's band. After describing how Mrs. Delaney purportedly met her end, the editor of the *Macleod Gazette* asked, "Will you blame us if we kill men, women and children of such an outfit?" and replied, "No but we will never forgive you if you don't."[43]

Rumours of the supposed fate of the white women were used to justify extremely harsh measures against the "enemy," but they also served other purposes. Those who wished to condemn government administration seized upon the tales of the women's mistreatment and death. It was suggested in the *Moosomin Courier* that the government should get an "illuminated copy of the account of Mrs. Delaney and Mrs. Gowanlock's treatment at the hands of Big Bear's band, nicely framed and hung conspicuously in the Legislative Hall in memoriam of the hellish effects of their 'Dishwater Administration' in the North-West Territories."[44]

Mrs. Gowanlock and Mrs. Delaney also found themselves part of a debate about the Macdonald government's 1885 *Electoral Franchise Act*. As initially introduced on March 19, 1885, the act provided that Indian males as well as white widows and unmarried women who met the necessary qualifications would be granted the franchise. The bill was the subject of heated debate in the House of Commons and the press throughout the course of the resistance of 1885, and it was suggested at that time and since that this was a diversionary tactic devised by Macdonald to draw attention away from the events in the West.[45] The bill also helped the prime minister appear enlightened on Indian affairs at a time when his policy was under attack. Although the extension of the franchise to widows and unmarried women was soon dropped from the bill, the question of the "Indian vote" remained before the House during the weeks of military engagement in the West. In the press much scorn was heaped on the notion that the franchise would be granted to those who had been "butchering women and children" (events that did not happen).[46] Sensational fabrications about the fate of Theresa Delaney were used as ammunition against the franchise bill. Readers of the Ottawa *Free Press* were warned that the bill "would confer the ballot upon the wretches who dishonoured Mrs. Delaney, till her death mercifully relieved her of the sense of the ignominy to which she had been compulsorily and brutally subjected."[47] The issues of women's suffrage and the Indian franchise were often linked. This same editorial was critical of a bill that would give the vote to the "savage" who had "violated the unfortunate woman until she died, but refuse it to the intelligent women of Canada, who might use their ballots to avenge their sister's wrongs." The act that was eventually passed gave the federal vote to all adult male Indians in Eastern Canada who met the necessary property qualifications, with Western Canadian Indians excluded entirely. The power of white males of the middle class to claim exclusive rights to full citizenship was upheld and sustained in this case by drawing upon images of the "savages" at the margins of the new nation, and upon images of weak and vulnerable white womanhood.

The frenzy over Mrs. Gowanlock and Mrs. Delaney, and in particular the insistence that they had been subjected to rape or "outrage," has parallels in other colonial settings at times of crisis in colonial authority. Terrifying stories of brutalities to white women took hold of the colonial imagination in the India Rebellion of 1857 and the Jamaican "revolt" of 1865, bearing no resemblance to the actual level of rape or assault.[48] In the case of the India Rebellion it has been argued that this crisis in British authority was managed and British strategies of counterinsurgency introduced through the circulation of stories about the violation of English women.[49] The threat of violence against white women was a rationale for securing greater control, for suppressing indigenous people, and clarifying boundaries between colonizers and colonized. Even when these stories of attacks on white women were shown to be illusory, they remained fixed in memory and on canvas and ink. Some of the tales that circulated about Mrs. Gowanlock and Mrs. Delaney drew on the stockpile of horrors from the British colonial world. Similarly, the idea that they had been subjected to brutal treatment proved resiliant, even after they emerged safely from their ordeal to declare that the rumours were not true. Another feature that 1885 shared with other colonial crises was the image projected of the horrible brutality of indigenous women.[50] All of these were absolute fabrications but they served to further inflame non-Aboriginal public opinion.

Safe and Unharmed

By the end of their two months with the Cree, the idea predominated that two vulnerable and helpless white women had been cruelly mistreated by their captors and had likely died as a result. It came as a great relief, as well as a surprise, to learn early in June that they were alive and well. The women arrived at Fort Pitt on June 5 along with 43 Métis men, women, and children, including the Pritchards. This group had taken leave of the Cree camp some days after the confrontation at Frenchman's Butte. Under cover of heavy fog one morning, they had fallen to the rear and then struck off to the east. It is likely that they were allowed to leave, and that this was not strictly an escape. For three days they had travelled in different directions through the bush until they were located by a party of ten of General Strange's scouts led by William McKay and Peter Ballendine, both Métis. The Quinneys and others, including W.B. Cameron, had escaped some days earlier, with the assistance of Woods Cree. On June 17 a group that included the Manns and the McLeans was allowed to leave the Cree camp.

There were several correspondents on the scene at Fort Pitt, and in their initial statements Mrs. Gowanlock and Mrs. Delaney announced that they had been treated well, had had plenty to eat, and had been subjected to no cruelties or "indignities."[51] There were occasions when the menacing behaviour of certain individuals made them fear for their lives and their "virtue," and both had suffered mental anxiety, but they had been well protected and had met with little suffering. They had cooked and laundered, but had not been forced to do these tasks; they had done them of their own accord because it had given them some occupation. Their principal problem had been loneliness, since neither of them spoke Cree or French. They stressed that they never had to walk, that they had ridden in the Pritchard's wagon. Once or twice they had walked off together when their cart was not ready, but they had never been compelled to walk. In fact, John Pritchard had made his children walk so that the two might ride. Mrs. Delaney stated that "Pritchard and all the Breeds walked always, though by making us walk they could have ridden. His two little boys, aged thirteen and fifteen, walked, though their feet became very sore at times, but they never complained, because they knew their walking enabled us to ride. They were noble little fellows."[52]

The two women reserved their highest praise for John Pritchard, Adolphus Nolin, and Pierre Blondin. They were all credited, especially Pritchard, with having saved them from suffering and hardship as well as from the menacing behaviour of some Plains Cree men. According to the women, Pritchard and Nolin had each paid some Cree males a horse for Mrs. Delaney, and Pierre Blondin had given two horses for Mrs. Gowanlock. From time to time Pritchard and Nolin had also given up other possessions such as blankets and dishes. Mrs. Delaney had some critical words to say about the administration of Indian Affairs. According to one correspondent, she assigned to Lieutenant-Governor and Indian Commissioner Edgar Dewdney "the greatest portion of the blame for the Indians' antipathy to the instructors and . . . a share in the causes that led to the massacre."[53] Theresa Delaney was reported as saying that on his visits to Frog Lake Dewdney made many promises and raised expectations that were unfulfilled.

Changing and Contested Stories of Captivity

After hearing so many stories of the nameless horrors that the women had been subjected to, and having invested so much in the costly military campaign against what was understood to be a Métis and Indian insurrection, it was difficult for many in the non-Aboriginal public to accept the women's initial statements that they had been treated well, and that they were particularly grateful to the Métis men and their families. Much of the later stages of the campaign had been understood as a crusade to save the white women. English as well as French-speaking soldiers had literally "tramped the soles off their boots" to reach the women and avenge their treatment. These were the heroic rescuers, not Métis such as Pritchard, who, after all, were the "enemy." Criticism of government was not entirely welcomed either, as the campaign was about maintaining and consolidating Canada's hold over the West. The womens' accounts contained many shades of grey, rather than the simplistic dichotomy of dark villains and white heroes; this was not what the hour called for.

John Pritchard soon became the focus of media attention, and his reputation was increasingly sullied, his motives questioned. When news of the women's safe return first became public there was some talk of a reward for Pritchard and Blondin, and a campaign was launched to this effect in Toronto's literary magazine *The Week*, which appealed in its June 18 issue to the "sisterhood" of women in Canada to each contribute 25 cents. But there also emerged a strong campaign to impugn Pritchard and to terminate all efforts to reward him or any other Métis. At the forefront of this campaign was a Rev. Dr. Hooper of Kingston, who was strident and vocal in his claim that Pritchard and other Métis men had purchased the women for their own vile purposes, and "were only defeated in their intentions by the resolute conduct of their victims. Foiled in their base plans they made literal slaves of them during their captivity."[54] Pritchard was obliged to defend himself against these and other charges that he had stolen goods, and on August 8, 1885, he published a letter in the *Toronto Daily Mail*. Pritchard also had his defenders. In an editorial in the *Edmonton Bulletin* of August 18 it was stressed that Pritchard had sacrificed a great deal in the cause of humanity, and deserved a reward as well as to have his horses and property returned to him. "Pritchard behaved like a man, in the case, and deserves the title of hero far more than many another who has received it by general acclamation. To their credit may it be said many of the women of Canada desired to recognize in a substantial manner his chivalrous action, but unfortunately were deterred therefrom by some blackguard, said to have reverend prefixed to his name, raising a false report concerning him." Despite his supporters, Pritchard never did receive a reward, compensation, pension, or recognition.

As the debate over Pritchard's motives indicate, the experiences of the two women continued to be a battleground long after, with some interpreting good treatment and others seeing harsh treatment. According to the Regina *Leader*, which congratulated the wisdom of government administration, the fact that all of the prisoners had been restored without being ill-treated "shows that the past policy of kindness to the Indians has not been in vain . . . the way Big Bear's band treated Mrs. Gowanlock and Mrs. Delaney shows the civilizing influence of kindness." On the other hand were editorials such as those of P.G. Laurie of the Battleford *Saskatchewan Herald*. Like the owner of the *Leader*, Laurie was a strong Conservative, so simple party lines do not account for the conflicting opinions. He took great exception to any complimentary statements about the treatment of the women. "Big Bear," he wrote, "had sold the unfortunate women just as he would horses, regardless of what fate might be in store for them," and it was heartless to say "that two months imprisonment of these ladies in the camp of savages is neither injury nor ill treatment."[55] It was this latter highly negative view of the women's two months that began to take centre stage as June gave way to July.

Mrs. Gowanlock and Mrs. Delaney spent two weeks in Battleford, and then left for Eastern Canada. At many of the stops along the route they were greeted by crowds of well-wishers, and the journey was detailed in the press at every stopover. The women took the train to Port Arthur and then went by steamer to Owen Sound. As they walked down the gangway of the steamer, they were met by Andrew Gowanlock, Theresa's brother-in-law, who accompanied them to Toronto, which they reached on July 13. As mentioned earlier, the Gowanlock brothers owned the *Parkdale Times* Newspaper, Book and Publishing Company.

Two Months in the Camp of Big Bear

There could be many possible reasons why the book *Two Months* was produced, and so quickly. There was a high degree of public interest in the two women's story. They were approached by agents, and even church ministers, to take to the lecture platform. The Gowanlock brothers may have hoped to profit from a book that detailed the experiences of the two women who had captivated the nation, and perhaps it was hoped that the book might provide some income for the authors. The women authors likely wished to make it very clear that the rumours of the spring were not true; they had not been made to suffer the "fate worse than death." Such a cloud hanging over them would have made it difficult for them to function socially upon their return to the East. But there may have been other pressures as well. According to some descendants of Mrs. Delaney's family, she was pressured into preparing her account by the Gowanlock family, and both women were reluctant to criticize government actions or policies for fear of jeopardizing their chances of receiving government pensions.[56] Mrs. Delaney received her government pension by order-in-council dated November 14, 1885 (the day before Riel went to the gallows), while Mrs. Gowanlock received a settlement from the Commission on Rebellion Losses as well as a pension, although this was not granted until 1888.[57] It is interesting to compare these pensions with that of Jane Quinn, also a widow of Frog Lake, who had a daughter to support. While Mrs. Delaney received $400 a year, Jane Quinn was granted a mere $12 a month, "upon the understanding that she would lead a moral life." For a time Jane Quinn lived in Montana, and upon her return to southern Alberta in 1912 she applied for her pension. The chief of police at Fort Macleod had to first report on whether she was leading a moral life, and when he found her to be a "hard working woman with a good reputation in the district," her pension was resumed. Cheque no. 4540, the first "resumed" pension cheque, for $12 arrived at Fort Macleod on the day Mrs. Quinn died in January 1913.[58]

The stories presented in *Two Months* differ in significant respects from some of the statements the women made immediately upon their release. Overall the book stresses the "untold suffering and privations" they had to endure at the hands of "savages." The women are prostrated by their bereavement, by fatigue, and by "the constant dread of outrage and death." They endure "physical pains, dangers, colds, heats, sleepless nights, long marches, scant food, poor raiment."[59] They are constantly made to walk, and are worked to death. While Pritchard is praised and thanked by both women, there are also hints throughout that the Pritchards were not entirely trustworthy. Pierre Blondin and Gregory Donaire are especially vilified, despite the fact that the women had initially voiced their appreciation for Blondin in particular. There is also very little that could be interpreted as criticism of government administration. Mrs. Delaney emphasized in her section of *Two Months* that the Indians were treated with generosity and kindness, and had no grievances or complaints. The true villain in her account was the HBC. While the government wished to enlighten and civilize, the company wished to keep Aboriginal people in a state of "savagery," as hunters and trappers rather than peaceful agriculturalists. She claimed that rebellion served the interests of the HBC.

How and why did *Two Months* come to project this particular version of events? As mentioned above, the women's need to acquire pensions probably caused them to downplay any criticism they might have of government administration. It is also possible that *Two Months* represents their reflections on their experiences in a much more sustained way than permitted in their initial statements. Perhaps their original statements reflected the immediacy of their experiences, their need to survive in that world, whereas they began to feel differently looking back after weeks and months. (The "Stockholm syndrome" is the term used today to explain the behaviour of hostages or prisoners who appear to accept and replicate the behaviour of their captors.)[60]

Two Months also conformed to the conventions of the classic Indian captivity narrative, and this form had an influence over the way in which the story was presented. From the seventeenth century Indian captivity narratives were a popular form of literature in North America, particularly in the United States. Today there is an enormous body of literature that analyzes and interprets these narratives.[61] These studies indicate that care must be taken in making broad generalizations about these narratives, as there were many different kinds, and certain themes dominated at certain periods, according to the major preoccupations of the day.[62]

The typical American Indian captivity narrative of the late nineteenth century was essentially a device for anti-Indian propaganda. They functioned to sustain the established hierarchies of "race" and gender. Such narratives shared a reasonably consistent structure, and similar rhetorical devices and illustrations. They generally told the story of an innocent captive who was doing his or her best to establish "civilization" in a bountiful wilderness. They could be about men or women, but captivity narratives were especially useful when the protagonists were women, as they appeared more vulnerable than male captives. By the late nineteenth century, a culture of delicate and frail white femininity prevailed, and the loss of a protective husband supposedly left a woman totally defenceless. The death of the husband was the key event in the narrative, and the survivors were plunged into an alien world, experiencing great suffering until the heroic rescue by white males. Throughout the narrative the white woman's weakness and vulnerablity is stressed, helping to define and highlight white masculine strength and courage. Aboriginal males and females are the reverse or negative images of their white counterparts. Aboriginal women, for example, are inevitably presented as drudges, or beasts of burden, mistreated within their own society. This forms a sharp contrast to the "tenderly reared" and delicate white women captives. Captivity narratives inevitably included an illustration of such mistreatment of Aboriginal women intended to starkly depict this contrast. Aboriginal males were cast as brutal threats to the virtue of white women, and as savage not chivalrous warriors. With the heroic rescue of white women captives, law and order is restored. The captives gratefully return to patriarchal protection. The future of the nation, not of individuals, has been at stake and has been rescued. In the United States, captivity narratives helped to establish and to sustain boundaries between indigenous people and the evolving community of the American nation. The narrators inevitably only reluctantly agreed to write about their experiences; the women especially claimed only an indifferent education and promised a plain and unvarnished tale.

The accounts of Mrs. Gowanlock and Mrs. Delaney were in many ways transformed, embellished, and embroidered in order to conform to the expectations of the nineteenth-century Indian captivity narrative. The authors promise truthful and accurate accounts, making it clear that they do not possess or aspire to literary excellence. This is the story of inexplicable brutality against innocent, virtuous people who "left comfortable homes in the east in order to carry civilization into the remote places of the west."[63] Frog Lake is extolled as a beautiful and enchanting location, and there is great praise for the West as a potential home for industrious white farmers. Yet this tranquil and prosperous settlement is destroyed. The weak and vulnerable women survivors, prostrated by fatigue and exposure, are subjected to untold suffering. There are obligatory passages on Indian customs and manners, particularly in Mrs. Gowanlock's section, containing a sampling of the dominant stereotypes of the day. Just as the darkest hour is that which precedes dawn, the women believe they faced certain death just before their escape and rescue. There are odes to the brave men from Eastern Canada who sacrificed so much to come to their assistance. The women return to the sacred precincts of the paternal hearth. In her conclusion, Mrs. Gowanlock provides a panoramic view of her experiences, emphasizing once again how sinister Blondin was, and how she had to witness numerous heart-rending scenes, such as the desecration of her husband's body (a sight she likely did not see). In her conclusion, Mrs. Delaney makes a direct reference to the great nation that she predicts will grow from these struggles, dangers, and tempests.

Yet there are occasions in *Two Months* when the authors break free of conventions and expectations. Mrs. Gowanlock acknowledges the kindnesses of some Aboriginal people, particularly women. In her description of "Indian boys" she breaks free for a moment from her very negative descriptions to say that they took delight in picking the prettiest flowers for her. She also makes it clear that Big Bear wanted peace, and that he did not have control over some of his men. Mrs. Delaney also at times challenges the conventions of the genre. She insists that Pritchard was "A TRULY GOOD MAN," the only time that such emphasis is given.

Two Months was published in November 1885, the same month that Louis Riel was hanged in Regina (November 15) and eight males were hanged at Battleford (November 27), among whom were those found guilty of the Frog Lake murders. The perspective presented in the two women's narratives would have helped confirm that this public spectacle of repression of indigenous people was the best and most obvious course. Public opinion was divided on the hanging not only of Riel but also of the eight Aboriginal men. In the editorials of several of the eastern newspapers, the wholesale execution of eight people was condemned as unworthy of a civilized nation and as carrying bloodthirstiness too far. The *Montreal Herald* called for the hangings to be postponed indefinitely in favour of life imprisonment, stating that "the proposal to give the public an exhibition of wholesale hanging is terribly repulsive to all humane persons."[64] By being released at this time, and serialized in a paper such as the *Huron Expositor*, *Two Months* kept the issue of Frog Lake, and especially indignities to white women, before the reading public.

After 1885 there was a shift in the attitudes of Euro-Canadians toward Aboriginal people. While there had been limited tolerance and understanding of their situation before, they now were viewed as threats to the property, safety, and prosperity of the white settlers. One Methodist missionary called for the removal of all Indians to a province north and east of Lake Winnipeg, as 1885 had destroyed the confidence of the white settlers, and peace and contentment could never be attained if the reserves remained scattered throughout.[65] A removal policy was not adopted, but as in other colonial settings where acts of resistance were met with extremely harsh retribution, repressive measures were introduced in the Canadian West. Also as in other colonial settings, protecting white women became a pretext for suppressing and controlling the indigenous population. An 1886 government pamphlet stressed that measures were necessary, otherwise white women might once again be dragged into horrible captivity.[66] Whole bands that were declared "disloyal" had their arms, ammunition, horses, and even items such as matches removed. New policies were pursued, such as a pass system, that aimed at rigidly monitoring and controlling the lives of people on reserves.[67] The major goal of Indian Affairs administrators after 1885 was to disband, break up, and assimilate what was seen as a "foreign element" in the midst of the nation.[68] *Two Months* helped to define the indigenous residents as the "foreign element," and to establish white women as the "civilizers" who would create and uphold the moral and cultural environment of the nation still to take shape. Boundaries between Aboriginal people and newcomers had to be clarified and maintained if the West was to be home for white women.

NOTES

1. Sarah Carter, *Capturing Women: The Manipulation of Cultural Imagery in Canada's Prairie West* (Montreal/Kingston: McGill-Queen's University Press, 1997).
2. Canada, House of Commons, *Debates*, 8 June 1885, 2357. *Free Press* (Ottawa), June 8, 1885.

3. "Race" is placed within quotation marks to indicate that it is an imagined concept that refers to nothing that should be recognized as real. See Kwame Anthony Appiah, "Race," in *Critical Terms for Literary Study*, ed. Frank Letricchia and Thomas McLaughlin (Chicago: University of Chicago Press, 1990), 277.

4. On the topic of race-specific ideologies of womanhood, see Vron Ware, *Beyond the Pale: White Women, Racism and History* (London: Verso, 1992); Hazel Carby, *Reconstructing Womanhood: The Emergence of the Afro-American Woman Novelist* (New York: Oxford University Press, 1987); Phylllis Palmer, *Domesticity and Dirt: Housewives and Domestic Servants in the United States, 1920-1945* (Philadelphia: Temple Press, 1989).

5. *Globe* (Toronto), July 13, 1885.

6. For information on Theresa Gowanlock I am grateful to Roy A.C. Johnson of Ridgeville, Ontario, family historian, for sharing his research and providing copies of the *Johnson Reporter*. I would also like to thank Margaret Comfort of Tintern for her assitance and for her article "The Village of Tintern: Tintern Bride," *Niagara Farmers' Monthly* (April 1992), 24. Art Seehagel of Tintern was also very helpful during my visit there in June 1996.

7. George Stanley (Musunekwepan), "An Account of the Frog Lake Massacre," in *The Frog Lake "Massacre": Personal Perspectives on Ethnic Conflict*, ed. Stuart Hughes, Carleton Library no. 97 (Ottawa: McClelland and Stewart, 1976), 160; Keith Davidson, "Ten Acres for Theresa: A Frog Lake History Mystery," *Lloydminster Regional Times* (September 16, 1998), 9a. I am very grateful to Robert and Shirley Hendriks, Heinsburg, Alberta, for sending me the Davidson article.

8. Theresa Johson Gowanlock is buried with her parents in St. Ann's II United Churchyard. On her headstone is inscribed "Theresa M. Johnson, wife of John Gowanlock, who on April 1 1885 was taken prisoner by Big Bear during the massacre of Frog Lake, NWT and after 2 months captivity was rescued by Col. Strange, d. Sept. 12, 1899, age 36 yr, 11 m. 15d."

9. Thanks to Diane Aldred, Aylmer, for her research in locating the tombstone of Theresa Fulford Delaney in St. Paul's Roman Catholic Cemetery on the Aylmer Road. See also Anson A. Gard, *Pioneers of the Upper Ottawa and the Humours of the Valley*, South Hull and Aylmer edn. (Ottawa: Emerson Press, 1906), 23; Robert Fulford, "Big Bear, Frog Lake and My Aunt Theresa," *Saturday Night*, June 1976, 9–10; and Robert Fulford, "How the West Was Lost," *Saturday Night*, July 1985, 5–8.

10. Sarah Carter, *Lost Harvests: Prairie Indian Reserve Farmers and Government Policy* (Montreal/Kingston: McGill-Queen's University Press, 1990), chap. 3, "The Home Farm Experiment," 79–129.

11. On the issue of her government pension, see National Archives of Canada (NA), Record Group 10 (RG 10), Records relating to Indian Affairs, vol. 3719, file 22649, Mrs. M.L. Walsh et al. to minister of the Interior, April 14, 1915.

12. For general background on treaties, see Treaty 7 Elders and Tribal Council, with Walter Hildebrandt, Dorothy First Rider, and Sarah Carter, *The True Spirit and Original Intent of Treaty 7* (Montreal/Kingston: McGill-Queen's University Press, 1996).

13. The population of the northwest in 1885 was as follows:

	Whites	Métis	Indians	Total
Assiniboia	16 574	1 017	4 492	22 083
Saskatchewan	4 486		6 260	10 746
Alberta	4 878	1 237	9 418	15 533
Total	25 938	2 254*	20 170	48 362

*The Saskatchewan figure includes white and Métis. P.B. Waite, *Canada 1874–1896: Arduous Destiny* (Toronto: McClelland and Stewart, 1971), 149.

14. Blair Stonechild and Bill Waiser, *Loyal Till Death: Indians and the North-West Rebellion* (Calgary: Fifth House, 1997).

15. John Tobias, "Canada's Subjugation of the Plains Cree, 1879–1885," in *Out of the Background: Readings on Canadian Native History*, ed. Robin Fisher and Kenneth Coates (Toronto: Copp Clark Pitman, 1988), 205–6.

91

16. C.D. Denney, "In Memory of Mary Rose (Pritchard) Sayers: The Last Witness," *Saskatchewan History* 24, 2 (Spring 1971): 63, 67.
17. T.S. Eliot, *The Waste Land and Other Poems* (London: Faber and Faber, 1985), 27.
18. See, for example, G.M. Adam, *From Savagery to Civilization: The Canadian North-West, Its History and Its Troubles* (Toronto: Rose Publishing, 1885), 301–16. Other accounts, such as William B. Cameron's *Blood Red the Sun*, are contained in Hughes, ed., *The Frog Lake "Massacre."*
19. Norma Sluman and Jean Goodwill, *John Tootoosis: A Biography of a Cree Leader* (Ottawa: Golden Dog Press, 1982). See also George Stanley (Musunekwepan) in Hughes, ed., *The Frog Lake "Massacre"*; Isabelle Little Bear, "My Own Story: Isabelle Little Bear, One of the Last Remaining Links with the Riel Rebellion," in *Reflections: A History of Elk Point and District*, ed. Mary Bennett (Winnipeg: Inter-Collegiate Press, 1977), 197–202; and the accounts contained in *Land of Red and White* (Heinsburg: Frog Lake Community Club, 1977) and *Fort Pitt History Unfolding, 1829–1925* (Frenchman Butte: Fort Pitt Historical Society, 1985). Recent histories that attempt to bring together multiple perspectives are Bob Beal and Rod Macleod, *Prairie Fire: The 1885 North-West Rebellion* (Edmonton: Hurtig Publishers, 1984), 179–204; Blair Stonechild and Bill Waiser, *Loyal Till Death: Indians and the North-West Rebellion* (Calgary: Fifth House, 1997), 106–125.
20. Joe Dion, *My Tribe the Crees* (Calgary: Glenbow-Alberta Institute, 1979), 91–2.
21. Stanley (Musunekwepan), "An Account of the Frog Lake Massacre," in Hughes, ed., *The Frog Lake "Massacre,"* 164–65. See also Dion, *My Tribe the Crees*, and Jimmy Chief's recollections in *Fort Pitt History Unfolding*, 101. Other accounts include William B. Cameron, *Blood Red the Sun*, (1926; rev. ed., Vancouver: The Wrigley Printing Company Ltd., 1950), chap. 10, "The Rescue of the White Women," 67–71; Guillaume Charette, *Vanishing Spaces: Memoirs of a Prairie Métis* (Winnipeg: Éditions Bois-Brulés, 1976), 158–59.
22. Doug Light, *Footprints in the Dust* (North Battleford: Turner-Warwick Publications, 1987), 208.
23. Ibid., 208.
24. Stonechild and Waiser, *Loyal Till Death*, 119.
25. Stanley (Musunekwepan), in Hughes, ed., *The Frog Lake "Massacre,"* 164.
26. Light, *Footprints in the Dust*, 534.
27. *Fort Pitt History Unfolding*, 42.
28. Ibid., 501.
29. Ibid., 42.
30. W.J. McLean, "Tragic Events at Frog Lake and Fort Pitt during the North West Rebellion," in Hughes, ed., *The Frog Lake "Massacre,"* 245–49.
31. Duncan McLean with Eric Wells, published as "The Last Hostage," in Harold Fryer, ed., *Frog Lake Massacre* (Surrey, BC: Frontier Books, 1984), 81–82.
32. Elizabeth McLean, "The Siege of Fort Pitt," *Beaver Outfit*, 277, December 1946, 22.
33. Elizabeth McLean, "Prisoners of the Indians," *Beaver Outfit*, 278, June 1947, 15.
34. See Anonymous, "Fr. Laurent Legoff O.M.I. during the Rebellion," in Hughes, ed., *The Frog Lake "Massacre,"* 298–302.
35. Desmond Morton, "Capturing Big Bear," *The Last War Drum: The North-West Campaign of 1885* (Toronto: Hakkert, 1972), chap. 7, 127–144.
36. Amelia M. Paget, *People of the Plains*, (Toronto: William Briggs, 1909), 56–57.
37. *Toronto Daily Mail*, April 14, 1885.
38. *Toronto Daily Mail*, April 23, 1885.
39. *Toronto Morning News*, May 25, 1885.
40. These rumours may have begun with a letter written by Captain and Quarter-Master R. LaTouche Tupper of the 92nd Winnipeg Light Infantry. He wrote a letter to a friend in Minnedosa that appeared in the *Minnedosa Tribune*, May 22, 1885. See also Charles R. Daoust, *Cent-vingt jours de service actif: Récit historique très complet de la campagne du 65ème au Nord-Ouest* (1886; English translation by Roberta Cummings, Wetaskiwin: City of Wetaskiwin, 1982), 58.
41. *Free Press* (Ottawa), May 29, 1885.
42. John P. Pennefather, *Thirteen Years on the Prairies* (1892), in Fryer, ed., *Frog Lake Massacre*, 61, 71.
43. *Macleod Gazette*, June 6, 1885.

44. Quoted in ibid.
45. D.N. Sprague, *Canada and the Métis, 1869–1885* (Waterloo, ON: Wilfred Laurier Press, 1988), 176. See also Richard H. Bartlett, "Citizens Minus: Indians and the Right to Vote," *Saskatchewan Law Review* 44 (1979–80): 163–94.
46. *London Advertiser*, May 5, 1885.
47. *Free Press* (Ottawa), May 22, 1885.
48. Jenny Sharpe, "The Unspeakable Limits of Rape: Colonial Violence and Counter-Insurgency," *Genders* 10 (Spring 1991); Jenny Sharpe, *Allegories of Empire: The Figure of Woman in the Colonial Text* (Minneapolis: University of Minnesota Press, 1993); Norman Etherington, "Natal's Black Rape Scare of the 1870s," *Journal of Southern African Studies* 15, 1 (1988).
49. See Sharpe, "Unspeakable Limits," and *Allegories of Empire*.
50. Sharpe, "Unspeakable Limits," 33.
51. *Minneapolis Pioneer Press*, June 25, 1885; *Toronto Evening News*, June 9, 1885; *Globe*, June 23, 1885; and *Montreal Daily Star*, June 23, 1885.
52. Part of a deposition given by Mrs. Delaney was quoted at length in C.P. Mulvaney, *The History of the North-West Rebellion of 1885* (Toronto: A.H. Hovey & Co., 1885), 405.
53. *Globe*, July 7, 1885.
54. *Macleod Gazette*, July 21, 1885.
55. *Saskatchewan Herald*, July 6, 1885.
56. Hughes, ed., *The Frog Lake "Massacre,"* 1.
57. NA, RG 10, vol. 3719, file 22-649, L. Vankoughnet to Sir John A. Macdonald, 24 July 1885, and order-in-council, November 14, 1885; and N.O. Cote, controller, to W.W. Cory, deputy Minister of the Interior, May 5, 1915.
58. NA, RG 10, vol. 3831, file 63891, assistant deputy and secretary to W.J. Hyde, 7 October 1912, and E. Foster Brown to Department of Indian Affairs, January 20, 1913.
59. Theresa Gowanlock and Theresa Delaney, *Two Months in the Camp of Big Bear: The Life and Adventures of Theresa Gowanlock and Theresa Delaney* (Parkdale: Times Office, 1885), 119. Reprint, 1999 (Regina: Canadian Plains Research Centre), with introduction by Sarah Carter.
60. Christopher Castiglia, *Bound and Determined: Captivity, Culture-Crossing, and White Womanhood from Mary Rowlandson to Patty Hearst* (Chicago: University of Chicago Press, 1996), 98.
61. The most comprehensive book is June Namias, *White Captives: Gender and Ethnicity on the American Frontier* (Chapel Hill: University of North Carolina Press, 1993).
62. Colin Calloway, ed., *North Country Captives: Selected Narratives of Indian Captivity from Vermont and New Hampshire* (Hanover, NH: University Press of New England, 1992).
63. *Two Months*, 43.
64. *Montreal Herald and Daily Commercial Gazette*, November 19, 1885.
65. E.R. Young, "The Indian Problem," *Canadian Methodist Magazine and Review* (June 1885): 465-69.
66. *The Facts Respecting Indian Administration in the North-West* (Ottawa: Department of Indian Affairs, 1886).
67. See Sarah Carter, *Lost Harvests: Prairie Indian Reserve Farmers and Government Policy* (Montreal/Kingston: McGill-Queen's University Press, 1990), chap. 4, "Assault upon the 'Tribal' System: Government Policy after 1885," 130–58.
68. Ibid., 146.

Imperialism, Continentalism, and Nationalism

MOTHER BRITANNIA.—" *See ! Why, the dear child can stand alone !* "
UNCLE SAM.—" *Of course he can ! Let go of him Granny ; if he falls I'll catch him !* "

"Child Canada Takes Her First Steps." Soon after Confederation, tensions emerged regarding Canada's future. Some advocated stronger ties to Britain, some favoured a closer union with the United States, and some supported Canadian independence.

IN THE late nineteenth and early twentieth centuries, Canadians debated their country's future: Should they seek greater unity with Britain through an imperial federation? Closer union with the United States in a form of continental union? Or independence? All three possibilities were, in their own ways, forms of Canadian nationalism, debated in the light of the advancement of Canadian interests.

The idea of an imperial federation or closer union of Britain and Canada became popular among English Canadians in the economically depressed and ethnically divided Canada of the late nineteenth century. Some twenty years after Confederation, a number of Canadians saw their country as a dismal failure. The National Policy had not stimulated economic growth; the anticipated population explosion had not occurred; and the nation seemed cursed by political, social, and regional dissent. At the same time, the rival German Empire and an expanding American nation challenged Britain's world supremacy. A group of imperial enthusiasts in both Canada and Britain dreamed of a consolidated British Empire that would bring glory to Britain and a "sense of power" to Canada. Carl Berger outlines the ideas of Canadian imperialists in his introduction to *Imperialism and Nationalism, 1884–1914: A Conflict in Canadian Thought*, reprinted here.

While the majority of English-speaking Canadians favoured some form of imperial federation or continental union, a significant group of French-speaking Canadians advocated greater Canadian independence. Henri Bourassa, the grandson of Louis-Joseph Papineau (the leader of the Parti Patriote before the Lower Canadian Rebellions of 1837/38), spoke for those French Canadians who felt Canada should weaken its ties to Britain. From the start of the Boer War in 1899 to the end of the First World War in 1918, Bourassa advanced the cause of Canadian independence and a bilingual Canada. Joseph Levitt summarizes the ideas of this important and influential French-Canadian thinker in his introduction to *Henri Bourassa on Imperialism and Bi-culturalism, 1900–1918*, reprinted here.

Carl Berger analyzes English-Canadian imperial thought in greater detail in *The Sense of Power: Studies in the Idea of Canadian Imperialism, 1867–1914* (Toronto: University of Toronto Press, 1970). For a different perspective on Canadian imperial thought, see Robert Page, "Canada and the Imperial Idea in the Boer War," *Journal of Canadian Studies* 5 (February 1970): 33–49, and his book *Imperialism and Canada, 1895–1903* (Toronto: Holt, Rinehart and Winston, 1972). A more recent study is Carman Miller, *Painting the Map Red: Canada and the South African War, 1899–1902* (Montreal/Kingston: Canadian War Museum, McGill-Queen's University Press, 1992). For British views of Canada in this period, see R.G. Moyles and D. Owram, *Imperial Dreams and Colonial Realities: British Views of Canada, 1880–1914* (Toronto: University of Toronto Press, 1988). Useful collections of essays are Colin M. Coates, ed., *Imperial Canada 1867–1917* (Edinburgh: Centre of Canadian Studies, University of Edinburgh, 1997); and *Imperial Relations in the Age of Laurier*, ed. Carl Berger (Toronto: University of Toronto Press, 1969), as well as Frank H. Underhill's collection of interpretative lectures, *The Image of Confederation* (Toronto: Canadian Broadcasting Corporation, 1964). On literature and the empire, see Barrie Davies, " 'We Hold a Vaster Empire Than Has Been': Canadian Literature and the Canadian Empire," *Studies in Canadian Literature* 14, 1 (1989): 18–29. On the negative side of imperialism, see Sarah Carter, *Capturing Women: The Manipulation of Cultural Imagery in Canada's Prairie West* (Montreal/Kingston: McGill-Queen's University Press, 1997).

Goldwin Smith's continentalist tract, *Canada and the Canadian Question*, first published in 1891, remains relevant today. Elisabeth Wallace's *Goldwin Smith: Victorian Liberal* (Toronto: University of Toronto Press, 1957) is a full-scale study of the life and ideas of this advocate of Canadian and American union.

Henri Bourassa's ideas on national questions are analyzed in M.P. O'Connell's "The Ideas of Henri Bourassa," *Canadian Journal of Economics and Political Science* 19 (1953): 361–76; S.M. Trofimenkoff's *The Dream of Nation: A Social and Intellectual History of Quebec* (Toronto: Gage Publishing, 1983), pp. 167–83; and Mason Wade's *The French Canadians, 1760–1945* (Toronto: Macmillan, 1955), pp. 447–539. See as well Joseph Levitt's brief account in *Henri Bourasssa: Catholic Critic*, Canadian Historical Association, Historical Booklet no. 20 (Ottawa: CHA, 1976).

Article Eight

Imperialism and Nationalism, 1884–1914: A Conflict in Canadian Thought

Carl Berger

Introduction

Imperialism in Canada presented many faces and its story has been told from various perspectives. Its aim was to consolidate the British Empire through military, economic, and constitutional devices. Those Canadians who supported imperial unity, or imperial federation, believed that Canada could attain national status only by maintaining the connection with the Empire and by acquiring an influence within its councils. Their opponents were convinced that imperialism was incompatible with Canada's national interests, internal unity, and self-government. The conflict between these two forces was a major theme in Canadian life in the 30 years before the First World War, and the struggle was bitter and divisive. It was fought out in many arenas, in Parliament, at Colonial and Imperial Conferences, and in polemical literature, and it centred upon several issues — commercial policy, participation in the Boer War, and military and naval preparedness. But it was above all fought out in the minds of Canadians, and it is from this point of view, as a problem in Canadian intellectual history, that it is presented in this book. The questions raised here do not concern, at least not primarily, elections, the formulation of tariff policy, or the problems of military cooperation. These readings are intended rather to bring into sharper focus the guiding ideas and divergent conceptions of the Canadian future that underlay the clash between imperialism and nationalism.

Imperialism and nationalism are vague words which must be defined in terms of their historical context. The organized movement for imperial unity originated in the later

Source: *Imperialism and Nationalism, 1884–1914: A Conflict in Canadian Thought*, ed. Carl Berger (Toronto: Copp Clark, 1969), pp. 1–5. Reprinted by permission of the author.

1880s. The cumulative impact of the long depression, the failure of Macdonald's National Policy to generate prosperity and economic integration, and the cultural crisis that followed the execution of Louis Riel produced a widespread feeling of pessimism about Canada's future. The commitment of the Liberal party to unrestricted reciprocity, or free trade with the United States, climaxed the fears of those who, rightly or wrongly, identified such a policy with continentalism. It was at this point — in 1887 and 1888 — that branches of the Imperial Federation League, an organization founded in England in 1884, were set up in Canada, and they quickly became the centres of a perfervid British Canadian patriotism. As a countermeasure to reciprocity, the supporters of imperial unity advocated the idea of an economic union of the Empire to be secured through preferential tariffs. Imperial preference remained the central plank in the agenda of Canadian imperialism long after unrestricted reciprocity was defeated in the election of 1891, and long after the Liberal party rejected it in 1893. Canadian imperialists were far more emphatic on the commercial aspects of imperial unity than were their counterparts in England. In fact the difference of opinion between those who stressed imperial preference and those who placed their faith in military and naval cooperation was one of the chief reasons why the Imperial Federation League disintegrated in 1893. Its branches in Canada, however, were simply reconstituted as organs of the British Empire League. When in 1897 the new Liberal government of Wilfrid Laurier extended a preference on British manufactured commodities entering Canada, the action was widely hailed as a practical implementation of the imperial ideal.

Imperial unity was as much a state of mind as a political platform, and the appeals of those who underlined the necessity for Canada to maintain and strengthen the British connection customarily transcended commercial and economic arguments. The leading spokesmen of imperial unity — Colonel George T. Denison of Toronto, a police magistrate and military thinker, George R. Parkin, a New Brunswick–born teacher and writer, and Rev. George M. Grant, Principal of Queen's University — all believed that Canada could grow and survive only if it held fast to the imperial connection. They were convinced, or they convinced themselves, partly through their reading of Goldwin Smith's plea for continental union, *Canada and the Canadian Question* (1891), that though unrestricted reciprocity might bring prosperity it would also ultimately end in political extinction. As a consequence, their arguments against a particular trade policy moved away from a discussion of the comparative prices of eggs in Toronto and Pittsburgh to an attempt to awaken an appreciation for, and an attachment to, those traditions and institutions which in their minds made the Canadian nationality worthy of preservation. In this sense imperial unity began as a defence of Canada.

In the later eighties and early nineties imperial unity found its main support in the older section of English Canada and particularly among the descendants of the United Empire Loyalists. Both Denison and Parkin traced their roots back to the Loyalists, who were described, in the mythology of the day, as "Canada's Pilgrim Fathers." Though the Imperial Federation League in 1889 counted one quarter of the members of the Dominion Parliament in its ranks, its most vocal and devoted supporters were drawn from a narrow group of politicians, lawyers, teachers, and Protestant ministers. It received no support from labour or the farming population, and in French Canada its progress was viewed firstly with indifference, then alarm, and finally with massive hostility. This is hardly surprising. Members of the Orange Order, who interpreted imperial federation to mean Protestant supremacy, were often members of the League, and D'Alton McCarthy, the leader of the Equal Rights Movement, which endeavoured to limit French language rights and separate schools to Quebec alone, was prominent among the adherents of imperialism. Not all imperialists, of course, were supporters of Orangeism and Equal Rights. One of the most sympathetic defences of the state-supported separate schools of Manitoba was penned by G.M. Grant, who had been instrumental in deposing McCarthy from his position in the League because he had jeopardized the cause of imperial unity. Yet in general, the obvious racial overtones of the imperial sentiment, and the strange allies with whom the imperialists consorted, were enough to alienate French Canada.

Born in a period of doubt and despair, imperialism by the late 1890s had become more impatient, assertive, and bellicose. The appointment of Joseph Chamberlain to the Colonial Office in 1895 signalized the increasing seriousness of purpose of British imperialism. In 1899, in spite of his own personal predisposition to remain uninvolved, Laurier was forced by public pressure in English Canada to dispatch Canadian soldiers to fight in the Boer War. This action was in itself a testimony to the growing strength of the imperial cause. Fourteen years before, Macdonald had shrugged off similar suggestions that Canada aid Britain in the Soudan and his reaction was endorsed by Denison, one of the most militant of Canadian imperialists, who was never one to miss a war if he could help it. The Boer War was the decisive event in the history of Canadian imperialism. To many English Canadians it was not a matter of aiding England. For them that experience was invested with all the enthusiasm of nationalism. Canada's participation, niggardly though some thought it was, marked the entry of the Dominion into world politics. She had become a force within the Empire and her path forward was straight and clear. Now that Canadians had demonstrated their willingness to support the Empire with more than emotional speeches, was it not only fair that they be accorded some influence over the direction of imperial foreign policy? French Canadians saw the matter very differently. The spectacle of Canadians fighting in so remote a war, one waged against a non-British minority with which they so easily identified themselves, generated an imperialist reaction which grew and gained momentum. Some time before, the nationalist Premier of Quebec, Honoré Mercier, had warned that the imperial federationists wanted "us to assume, in spite of ourselves, the responsibilities and dangers of a sovereign state which will not be ours. They seek to expose us to vicissitudes of peace and war . . . ; to wrest from our arms our sons, . . . and send them off to bloody and distant wars, which we shall not be able to stop or prevent."[1] And the prophecy had come true. In 1899 Henri Bourassa left the Liberal party charging that Laurier had capitulated to pressure from the Colonial Office and had thereby established a precedent, fatal to Canadian self-government, that Canada must fight in all imperial wars. In 1903, in conjunction with a group of young French-Canadian nationalists, Bourassa founded the Ligue Nationaliste to combat the imperial menace. The zest with which imperialists had supported the South African war was proof to them of the essentially colonial-minded character of English Canada.

These two extremes, the one demanding that Canada take up imperial obligations and be accorded a voice in Empire affairs, the other insisting on Canadian neutrality and freedom from such burdens, were not easily reconciled, and for some time Laurier did not try to reconcile them. He turned aside Chamberlain's suggestions at the Colonial Conference of 1902 that cooperation be institutionalized. Though he declared in the same year that Canada must take some steps to ensure her security, and though in 1903, after the unpopular Alaska Boundary decision, he also urged that the Dominion make her own foreign policy, Laurier made no fundamental decisions in either direction, except for taking over the management of the naval bases at Halifax and Esquimalt. The imperial question lay quiescent until the "naval scare" of 1909 made postponement impossible. The threat that the German ship-building program would undermine the supremacy of British seapower set off a wide-ranging and acrimonious debate over what stand Canada should take. The imperialists contended that Canada, now strong and prosperous, should help sustain the force upon which her own security depended; to the anti-imperialists this appeared as the payment of tribute to the motherland whose interests were very different from Canada's. In reality the debate was more complex than this, for even imperialists were in disagreement about the exact extent and nature of Canada's contribution to imperial defence. But Laurier's proposal for the creation of a Canadian navy which in times of crisis would become part of the British fleet angered both extremes and in part accounted for his defeat in 1911. Long before this time Bourassa had come to think of Laurier as the main instrument of the imperialist conspiracy. On July 13, 1911, he wrote in *Le Devoir*: "English and African soldiers fell on the veldt for the glory of Chamberlain; women and children died of shame and misery for the grandeur of Laurier; children's entrails were cut out in the Concentration camps for the honour of the Empire." From the imperialist Stephen Leacock, on the other hand, came this greeting at the news of Laurier's defeat:

> Sir Wilfrid, it may be said, with all the gentleness of speech which is becoming in speaking of such a man on such an occasion, touched in this election upon the one point on which he never fully enjoyed the confidence of the Canadian people—our relations to the British Empire. It has been his fortunate lot to represent us on great occasions. He has ridden for us in coaches of State, to the plaudits of a London multitude. He has coined phrases for us, of summoning us to Imperial councils and the like, grandiloquent in the utterance, but meaning less and less as they recede into retrospect. That he never really understood the feelings of his English-speaking fellow citizens of Canada towards their Mother Country, that he never really designed to advance the cause of permanent Imperial unity—these things may well be doubted. . . . We are . . . groping for something which we desire but still seek in vain. The great problem of our common future is to find an organic basis of lasting union.[2]

Such was the burden of the two extremes which tore apart the man who searched for the fragile consensus.

In the 30 years before 1914, the difference between nationalism and imperialism was much more complicated than the desire for Canadian autonomy on the one hand and a willingness to live under Downing Street rule on the other. Not even the anti-imperialists thought it was that simple. John Ewart, for example, who defined nationalism as the end of subordination of one state to another, remarked that those Canadian imperialists with whom he was acquainted were really Canadian nationalists. And within the terms of his own definition he was right. What divided those who called themselves nationalists from those who preferred to be known as imperialists was not the question of whether Canada should manage her own affairs and have the power to formulate a foreign policy expressive of her interests; what divided them was disagreement over how these powers were to be acquired and for what purposes they were to be employed. The imperialists saw the British Empire as the vehicle in which Canada would attain national status; the anti-imperialists were so convinced of the incompatibility of imperial and Canadian interests that they saw all schemes for cooperation as reactionary and anti-national. In a fundamental sense, therefore, the differences between, say, Stephen Leacock and Henri Bourassa stemmed from their very different ideas about Canada, her history, and place in the world. The only way to understand the conflict between the positions these two men embodied is to understand the divergent conceptions which underlay them.

There are some limitations to the purpose of this volume as well as some particular problems that are raised by such an approach. It is not intended as a self-contained presentation of every facet and ramification of the nationalist–imperialist conflict. Such a project would require several more volumes. Nor does the approach suggest that intellectual history offers some magical key that will unlock all the puzzles and problems raised by the theme. And certainly it is not intended to supersede all other approaches. Someone has said that the practice of intellectual history is like trying to nail jelly to the wall, and indeed the entities that are subject to examination are nebulous and intangible. Any exact and scientific way of measuring the force and impact of ideas, furthermore, has yet to be devised, and the question must always arise as to the connection between ideas and the motives of those active men of power who made the crucial decisions. Yet when all this is said our understanding of Canadian history would be narrow indeed if we left out of account the climate of opinion in which the battle between imperialism and anti-imperialism took place. In the accounts of the Boer War crisis or the naval debate, for example, one invariably encounters allusions to the "imperialist pressure from English Canada" for this or that policy; yet one often comes away with the impression that we are told a good deal more about how extreme positions were accommodated or compromised at the centre than we learn about the extremes themselves. If we want to understand what imperialism and nationalism meant we must look to those who were the exponents and interpreters of these beliefs and try to grasp what these convictions meant to them. Only by doing so can we appreciate why their opposition was so fundamental and why Canadian historians are still divided as to the meaning of imperialism as a factor in Canadian history.

NOTES

1. Quoted in George R. Parkin, *Imperial Federation: The Problem of National Unity* (London, 1892), 85–86.
2. Stephen Leacock, *The Great Victory in Canada* (reprint from *The National Review*, London, 1911), 12.

Article Nine

Henri Bourassa on Imperialism and Biculturalism, 1900–1918

Joseph Levitt

Henri Bourassa had a clear vision of how to bring about Canadian nationhood, and with unbelievable stubbornness he struggled to persuade both French and English Canadians to accept his ideas. Although not an original thinker, he was well read, highly intelligent, and had absorbed the principles of three of the most important ideologies of late-nineteenth-century Western Europe: Catholicism, nationalism, and liberalism. These he integrated into the coherent world outlook which underlay his conception of a Canadian nation.

Bourassa's ideas penetrated the consciousness of his contemporaries because they dealt with the fundamental difficulties that confronted the builders of a Canadian nation: the

Source: *Henri Bourassa on Imperialism and Bi-culturalism, 1900–1918* (Toronto: Copp Clark, 1970). Reprinted by permission of the author.

relations between Canada and Great Britain, the relations between French and English Canadians, and the economic and social relations between rich and poor in an industrial and capitalist society.

The reception that Bourassa's contemporaries gave his ideas was enhanced by Bourassa's formidable forensic talent and massive personality. Many saw Bourassa as a great orator who skillfully articulated the aspirations of his French-Canadian audiences. Bourassa's power as a writer is striking even today. On the one hand, with very few exceptions, he used meticulously documented facts to appeal to reason (see his pamphlets *Great Britain and Canada* and *Que Devons-Nous à l'Angleterre?*); on the other, by always giving his ideas an ethical basis, he aroused moral passion. To Bourassa a policy was always either morally *right* or morally *wrong*.

Bourassa had unusual political gifts: forceful personality, keen intellect, eloquence. When he first entered Parliament, some believed that he would succeed Laurier as the most prominent French Canadian in the Liberal party. But Bourassa possessed characteristics fatal to any politician. In him were combined a dread of forcing a decision on his reluctant supporters and a positive distaste for exercising power. "I am of such a temperament that I never feel like being a whip," he commented. "I have enough trouble in keeping myself in line: I have no desire to keep others in line."[1] He had little or no tolerance for other people's opinions. He was totally unable to compromise. This made him hopeless as a politician but superb as a critic. Because he had no need to cope with political realities, his proposals were straightforward, clear, consistent with one another, and suffused with moral rectitude.

Although Bourassa accepted the parliamentary system, he believed that party leaders, corrupted by their love of power, too often sacrificed principle to keep themselves in office; party policy was dictated by political advantage rather than concern for the good of the country. The only way to offset this weakness in parties was to arouse public opinion to the point where it would compel politicians anxious to win elections to take up patriotic policies. It was as such an educator of public opinion that Bourassa saw himself and indeed acted. Working outside Parliament and through his newspaper, *Le Devoir*, he won the following of enough French Canadians to make the policies he advocated of pivotal importance in the elections of 1911 and 1917. As the feat of an individual, this accomplishment is unmatched in twentieth-century Canadian politics.

Bourassa and Canadian Nationhood

Nationalist, Catholic, and liberal values all went into Bourassa's conception of Canadian nationhood. Accepting the nationalist nineteenth-century idea that each nation had been given a specific task by God, he believed that French Canada's mission was to build the ideal society on Catholic principles and by its example win back to the Church millions of Protestants and free-thinkers in North America. The situation of French Canadians was complicated: not only were they under British rule, but they also lived with Anglo-Canadians, more numerous than they, in the same confederation. But Bourassa was able to reconcile his patriotism to French Canada with a genuine loyalty to Canada, a British Dominion, because he was a cultural nationalist. He wished French Canada to have a culture separate from that of English Canada, but not to be a sovereign state of its own. Thus he was both a French-Canadian nationalist and a Canadian nationalist at the same time.

Bourassa desired amity between English and French Canadians. He wished to see an Anglo–French Canadian nation, one in which each group would keep its own culture but would be united with the other "in a sentiment of brotherhood in a common attachment to a common country."[2] The necessary legal framework for such a bi-cultural country was possible only on the basis of liberal principles: Canada must be free to choose her foreign policies on the sole basis of her own interests, not those of the British Empire, and French Canada must be free to develop her culture everywhere in the Dominion. But Bourassa's aspirations were frustrated by the majority of Canadians who believed that Canada ought to cooperate with Great Britain in imperial defence and by an English Canada that refused to accept cultural duality.

Imperial Defence

The turn of the century saw the heyday of the imperialist movement in England. Of the many causes of this complex phenomenon, we are concerned with only one: the growing vulnerability of the Empire to powerful rivals. Faced with potential threats, Imperial defence planners turned to the Dominions for help. They wished the Dominions to contribute to a system of imperial defence controlled centrally in London. But colonial politicians saw things differently. Previously, a colony had been responsible only for its own defence while Great Britain protected the rest of the Empire. Now a centralized defence would mean that the colonies were contributing large amounts of money to further policies over which they had no control.

Canadian politicians stood firm in defence of their military autonomy. At the Imperial conference of 1902 Laurier rejected any proposals for defence centralization, "not so much from the expense involved," but because it represented "an important departure from the principles of colonial self-government."[3] In 1904 his government placed all Canadian military affairs under the command of a Militia Council which itself was under the direct control of the Canadian Minister of Militia. Then in 1907, Canada helped to persuade the British General Staff to agree that Dominion officers whom it trained would be responsible to their own Cabinet ministers and not to British officials; this implied that the principle in defence relations was to be cooperation and not automatic commitment. Two years later the Laurier government was an important influence in the admiralty's decision to concede the principle of naval decentralization for the Empire. Yet while insisting on defence cooperation, Laurier did not neglect military reform. New training schemes for officers were begun and military institutions in the country were made more efficient. Such was the progress that the government accepted a plan for the dispatch of a Canadian contingent overseas if necessary.

The government's defence policy, however, aroused passionate controversy on two occasions: once in 1899 over the sending of troops to South Africa, and then again in 1910 over its decision to found a Canadian navy. At first Laurier did not believe that Canada should participate in the Boer War. He stated publicly that soldiers could not be legally sent to South Africa because the Boers did not present a threat to Canadian security. Many Anglo-Canadians, including members of his own cabinet, would not accept his decision and compelled him to change his mind; the Cabinet authorized the dispatch of troops to South Africa but emphasized that this action was not to be taken as a precedent. Bourassa, however, because he believed that the government's action was a serious step toward Canada's being automatically committed to take part in every British war, resigned from his seat in the Commons. Laurier, on the other hand, was criticized for not fully supporting the imperial cause since Canadian troops once in South Africa were to be paid by Great Britain.

As a response to the "dreadnought" crisis which had blown up in 1909 over the possibility of the German fleet catching up to the British, Laurier proposed forming a small navy which the Cabinet could turn over to the Admiralty if it thought necessary. Bourassa and his supporters opposed the Naval Bill, arguing that it would commit Canada to every British war. Many Anglo-Canadians, however, objected to Laurier's proposal for exactly the opposite reasons; it gave the Cabinet the alternative of not sending the navy and thus undermined the principle of "One King, One Fleet, One Flag." But in Quebec Bourassa's attack on Laurier's federal naval policy was so popular that candidates whom he supported in the 1911 federal election won sixteen seats from the Liberals. This loss of Quebec support contributed to the defeat of the Laurier government and the election of a Conservative administration headed by Robert Borden.

Although Canada was automatically committed to war in 1914, there was almost unanimous sentiment for participation. This did not, however, end the speculation over imperial relations. It was clear that as a consequence of their taking part in the War, the Dominions would demand a voice in imperial foreign policy; and denial of this claim would result in the shattering of the Empire. This was the thesis of a book by Lionel Curtis, the leader of a group of thoughtful imperialist-minded people devoted to building imperial unity through the exchange of information and propaganda. But it was not only these intellectuals of the Round Table (the name of a quarterly founded by Curtis in which he expounded his ideas) who were concerned with the fate of the Empire. Even while leading the Canadian war effort, Prime Minister Borden found the question important enough to help set up in London an Imperial War Conference, composed of overseas prime ministers and British cabinet ministers, to chart the future of the Empire.

Bourassa and the British Connection

The roots of Bourassa's disagreement with Laurier over imperial defence lay in their differing concepts of the British Empire. To Laurier, the British Empire represented liberty and justice;[4] to Bourassa, all empires, including the British, were "hateful," and stood in the way of "liberty and intellectual and moral progress." Bourassa believed that the Empire imposed serious constraints on the life of nationalities, preventing them from achieving the destiny that God had planned for them; thus it was necessary to choose between "British ideals and British domination."[5]

Bourassa was convinced that the aim of British imperialists was to assure the military, commercial, and intellectual supremacy of the Anglo-Saxon race. Since this could be achieved only by force, the British were led to demand military aid from the Dominions. To ensure that this help was forthcoming, Imperialists like Joseph Chamberlain, the British Colonial Secretary, and Lord Grey, the Governor General of Canada, were plotting to revolutionize imperial defence relations so that Great Britain would continue to control foreign policy but would be able to commit the colonies, including Canada, to her wars — hence the danger of Laurier accepting the premise that when Great Britain was at war Canada was at war.[6] Canada, Bourassa insisted, could go to war only by its own consent and not by some Imperial act. This reaction was anti-imperialist, not pacifist. He was ready to agree to Canada's going to war, but only if she were directly attacked or if her vital interests were in jeopardy.

Laurier's decision to send troops to South Africa had raised in Bourassa's mind the question of Canadian responsibilities in British wars. What made Laurier's action even more reprehensible to Bourassa was that Laurier had knowingly violated the existing law.

Under pressure from London, Laurier had set a precedent which, if followed, would mean that Canadian forces would be automatically put at the disposal of the British in all their future wars. The consequences would be very grave for Canada: "If we send 2000 and spend $2,000,000 to fight two nations, aggregating a population of 250,000 souls, how many men shall we send and how many millions shall we expend to fight a first class power, a coalition of powers?"[7]

Bourassa was going too far to claim that a precedent had been set, even though he offered as proof the fact that Chamberlain regarded the Canadian action as such. Influential Anglo-Canadians believed that although Canada had sent troops to fight the Boers, she had not given up the right to choose whether she would engage in British wars or not. They supported Laurier when he rejected Chamberlain's plea to Canada to accept the principle of centralized defence at the Imperial Conference of 1902.

Laurier's intention to develop a Canadian navy posed the same issue. He believed that British naval supremacy was necessary to protect the Empire and all the values it stood for; if it were threatened, Canada must aid Great Britain with all her force. But he wished the Canadian Cabinet to decide whether or not the navy should be turned over to the Admiralty. Bourassa, though, viewed the question from an entirely different perspective. The fact that the proposed fleet was to include cruisers and destroyers suggested to him that its purpose was not to defend Canadian coastal waters but to form part of the British fleet in time of war. Laurier claimed he would put the Canadian fleet under British control only if he believed the danger to Britain great enough, but Bourassa maintained that he would in fact do this for all wars in which Great Britain became involved. Bourassa did not trust Laurier: the prime minister was bound to cave in under imperial pressure in an emergency, even as he had done in 1899 over the Boer War. To emphasize his point Bourassa implied that at the Imperial Conference of 1909 Laurier had agreed that in time of war the fleet would automatically come under British control and that this commitment had been given the force of law by the Naval Bill of 1910. This was an unfair presentation of Laurier's position.

It was natural that Bourassa would be interested in the discussion on postwar imperial relations. He believed that by their contribution to the imperial war effort the Dominions had left behind their colonial status. They should not put up with less say on British foreign policy than a "single cab driver in London";[8] if the Canadian people insisted on taking part in British wars they ought to have some control over the way in which their men and money were used.

Still, for Bourassa such imperial partnership was even at best a poor alternative to complete Canadian independence. Independence would mean that Anglo-Canadians would acknowledge for once and for all that Canada and not Great Britain was their homeland. This would eliminate the major reason for quarrels between the two Canadian peoples. In foreign affairs Canada's position would be safer, for she would not be exposed to attacks from British enemies. She would have a national personality of her own and would make her decisions about war and peace for her own interests.

Such practical advantage reinforced Bourassa's ideological conviction that it was right for Canada to become independent. He believed that the natural evolution of human societies was toward nationhood. A centralized Empire was ultimately impossible because each part separated from the other by the ocean would develop in its own way according to its geographical situation, its economic needs, and its temperament. Canada, like the other communities in the Empire, was progressing toward nationhood, the achievement of which would be marked by independence — the only status that could satisfy the aspirations of a free people.

In becoming independent, Canada would be also fulfilling God's design. Bourassa believed that God had wished Canada to separate herself from the old world by breaking the imperial tie to fulfill her destiny chosen by Him in North America. That Canada, by taking part in European wars because of imperial membership, was not carrying out this mission was no small reason for Bourassa's ardent desire for her independence.

Bourassa's desire to see Canada a nation was similar to that of English-speaking Liberals like John Dafoe, the editor of the *Winnipeg Free Press*, or of French-speaking ones like Wilfrid Laurier. But Dafoe believed that it was possible for the Empire to be based on the principle of autonomy and that Canada could be a greater nation for being part of it; Bourassa considered Canadian autonomy or freedom and her membership in the Empire to be mutually exclusive. Laurier, too, differed from Bourassa in his conviction that autonomy was not necessarily incompatible with retaining the British connection. To Laurier, imperial sentiment in Canada, whether reasonable or not, was a force which responsible leaders must accommodate. To Bourassa it was precisely this loyalty to the Motherland that was the main barrier to Anglo-Canadians and French Canadians cooperating to build a nation and therefore this loyalty must be opposed.

French Cultural Rights

In the decade before the war, French cultural rights outside of Quebec became a burning issue: non–French-speaking immigration to the West and French-Canadian immigration to Ontario provoked a great public debate on whether one of the functions of the schools in these areas was to further French-Canadian culture.

Responding to the demands of settlers, the Laurier government decided to form two new Western provinces. Written into the Autonomy Bill of 1905 was the legal framework for a school system that many people, including Clifford Sifton, the Minister of the Interior, believed substituted denominational for what should have been public schools. A public uproar arose; some regarded it as an attack on the autonomy of the new provinces; militant Protestants objected to turning over the direction of any schools to the Church; many Westerners favoured the idea of the melting pot and opposed a school system which would further divide a population already fragmented by ethnic origin. To satisfy these critics, Laurier rewrote the offending clause: the schools would be run by the provincial government, not by religious institutions. Catholics were free to set up a separate school in districts where they were a *minority*; however, since they clustered together, they were usually the majority in their district and thus were compelled to attend public schools. In 1905 there were only nine Catholic "separate" schools in the Northwest. French Canadians were granted two other concessions in the new provinces. They were allowed religious instruction for a half-hour after half-past-three, and could have a primary course in the French language if they desired it.

In 1912 the separate school question was briefly revived in the West when the territory of Keewatin was joined to Manitoba. A demand arose that one of the conditions of annexation would be the guarantee of the territory's right to separate schools. But Robert Borden, then prime minister, made no provision for such rights in his annexation bill and public interest soon petered out.

French cultural rights became a burning issue when the movement of French Canadians into eastern Ontario changed the relative positions of French and English in the schools. Although still the legal language of instruction, English became just another subject on the curriculum; French became the real means of communication. Toward the end of 1910 opposition to this arrangement arose in Ontario: Canadian nationalists were convinced that a common Canadian consciousness could not be created unless English were the common language.[9] Orangemen feared that the spread of French would undermine the Anglo-Saxon character of the province and so injure the Empire; Irish Catholics believed that the identification of separate schools with French would prejudice their schools receiving public grants. What these three groups had in common was a conviction that everybody must learn English and a determination to reject any legal status for French. This point of view was accepted by the two major provincial parties, the Conservatives and the Liberals.

In September 1910 at the Eucharistic Congress in Montreal, Archbishop Bourne of Westminister sparked public debate by declaring that if the Catholic Church wished to make progress in Canada, it ought to be English-speaking. Bourassa's rebuttal came in his most celebrated speech, *Religion, Langue, Nationalité*. The excitement aroused by this clash led the French-Canadian press to reveal the details of a well-kept secret: that Bishop Michael Francis Fallon, the Bishop of London, had undertaken to eliminate French in the Catholic schools of his diocese on the grounds that students were learning neither English nor French. The subsequent public furor caused the government to assign Dr. F.W. Merchant, an official of the Ontario Department of Education, to investigate the schools where French was the language of instruction. After the Merchant report found that much was lacking in the teaching of English in these schools, the Conservative provincial government issued Regulation 17 late in 1912. Regulation 17 was to apply only to certain schools, designated each year as English–French schools. In these schools French was permitted as a language of instruction only for the first two years of school. Where French had "hitherto" been a subject of study, instruction in the French language for no more than one hour each day might be provided. (Many French Canadians, including Laurier, took this to mean that French would be prohibited in all future schools.) Any school which did not comply with Regulation 17 would no longer be entitled to public funds.

Although the government claimed to be interested only in improving the quality of the English spoken by Franco-Ontarians, the majority of French Canadians saw Regulation 17 as a prelude to the complete removal of French from Ontario schools. Franco-Ontarian teachers in the Ottawa Valley refused to comply with the Regulation and their students walked out of schools. In 1915 some 150 schools outside of Ottawa refused to accept the Regulation and gave up the provincial grant. In Ottawa itself the majority of the Separate School Board defied the Department of Education. The government responded by appointing a commission to take over its duties. Meanwhile important Quebec personalities, including Church dignitaries, led a campaign to raise funds for "les blessés d'Ontario." The Quebec legislature, asserting that the Ontario government did not understand British principles, authorized local Catholic commissions to contribute officially to the fund.

Outside intervention helped to ease the crisis. In October 1916 Pope Benedict XV issued an encyclical which most Catholics interpreted as supporting the position of Bishop Fallon: the study of French was not to be pushed to the point where it endangered Catholic schools in Ontario. Significantly, Bourassa was silent on the encyclical. A month later, the Privy Council in London established the basis for a compromise by ruling that Regulation 17 was legal, but the commission which had taken over the duties of the Separate School Board was not.

For four years the controversy had raged, becoming especially violent after the Great War began. Many French Canadians believed the majority of Ontarians hypocritical in supporting a war for freedom while repressing French at home. Armand Lavergne, a colleague of Bourassa's, spoke for many of his compatriots when he cried out in the Quebec legislature, "I ask myself if the German regime might not be favourably compared with the Boches of Ontario."[10] On their side, Anglo-Ontarians continued to support Regulation 17 because they wished Ontario to be exclusively English. Many of them believed that the French Canadians were using the question of French in Ontario schools as an excuse for not giving full support to the war and they resented what they regarded as an attempt of French Canada to compel them to change the Regulation by threatening to slow down the war effort. Either Regulation 17 or the war would have strained relations between the English and French; the conjunction of the two exacerbated hostility to a level of bitterness hitherto unknown between the two peoples.

Bourassa and Biculturalism

Bourassa became the most prominent spokesman of French-Canadian resentment. Deeply convinced that Catholics should control the schools their children attended to ensure the teaching of religious values, he also believed God had bestowed on French Canadians a particular genius, character, and temperament which could be fully expressed only through the French language. They were something more than British subjects who happened to speak French. Bourassa exhorted his compatriots to fight for French-Canadian culture. If they meekly accepted that it had no legal rights in English Canada, on what basis would they oppose the application of this false principle to Quebec itself?

For Bourassa, faith and language were inextricably united. He vehemently rejected the contention of English-speaking Catholics that it would be better for the Church to present an English image: it was the natural right of everyone to speak his maternal tongue; to use the Church as an instrument of assimilation would be "odious." There were other practical reasons for the Church to reject the argument: English-speaking Catholics themselves were open to the social influences of Protestant and free-thinking North Americans, while apostasy was rare among French Canadians, whose language served as a barrier to heretical influences.

But such Catholic and racial values, although acceptable to significant segments of French-Canadian opinion, made little impression in English Canada where the majority was Protestant. Yet French-Canadian culture could only survive outside Quebec if Anglo-Canadians accepted cultural duality. To persuade them, Bourassa advanced two main propositions: the Constitution was based on the principle of cultural duality and the Canadian confederation could not survive unless such biculturalism was accepted by English Canada. These arguments were not mere debating tricks with Bourassa; he believed them with total sincerity.

Bourassa viewed Confederation as the result of an agreement between English and French to accept the equal rights of each culture throughout the Dominion. The Fathers of Confederation had envisaged Canada as a bicultural country. If their behests had been followed, then the West, acquired "in the name of and with the money of the whole Canadian people,"[11] would have been French as well as English, Catholic as well as Protestant. It would have been made clear to all immigrants that the West was Anglo-French.

In the first years after Confederation, maintained Bourassa, the federal government affirmed the bicultural nature of the country by the *Manitoba Act of 1870* and the *North West Territories Bill of 1875*, each of which accepted French as one of the official languages and established a denominational school system. But in 1890, Ottawa had permitted the territorial government of the northwest to extinguish the legal status of French. Two years later, the school system began to be modified until in 1901 it was, in fact, a state school system.[12] Because the ordinances of the Territorial Government which had changed the school system violated the spirit and text of the 1875 law passed by the federal government, a government superior in authority to that of the Northwest Territories, Bourassa considered them illegal. By accepting the Sifton amendment in 1905, the government legitimized these illegal school ordinances and ratified the limitations of the rights of Western French Canadians to schools of their own.

The bicultural compact implied the right not only to separate schools but also to instruction in French. By giving both French and English official status in Parliament, the Fathers had made it clear that they wished both languages to coexist everywhere in public life: in church, in court, and in government. These rights would be meaningless if the English provinces prevented French-Canadian children from acquiring a perfect knowledge of their own language.

Bourassa also insisted that cultural duality was necessary if Confederation were to last. The materialist ethos of the United States was penetrating Canada; the unchecked consequence of the invasion of such values would lead to the slow absorption of Canada into the United States. The greatest barrier to "l'américanisme"[13] was French Canada, because being Catholic, it rejected materialism and the American way of life. But if French Canadians continued to be humiliated, they would no longer resist Americanization, for they could see no advantage to remaining British.

Refusal to accept cultural duality threatened Confederation in yet another way. French Canadians would never feel that Canada was their homeland unless their culture was free to develop. Thus national unity was conditioned on cultural duality. The alternative was constant instability and crisis. Confederation, Bourassa maintained, would not survive without the reciprocal respect of the rights of the two races.

Such was Bourassa's general attitude toward cultural duality. He also had a number of specific points to make about each issue. The Autonomy Bill specifically forbade Catholics from organizing separate schools where they were a majority in the district. Yet they would reconcile themselves more easily to sending their children to a government school if it were called "separate" and not "public"; Catholic school boards would hire Catholic teachers and thus all lessons would be infused with a Church spirit. The new bill compelled most Catholic children to attend public schools where they could not be protected should the Minister of Education decide to suppress religious or French teaching. The advantages to Catholics of attending schools that could be called separate even though they were essentially controlled by the government were so important to Bourassa that he declared that if the Catholics were allowed to set up such "separate" schools he would withdraw his opposition to the new bill.

Bourassa denied that instruction in French in Ontario schools would harm national unity. Even if proficient in French, French Canadians had no more intention of becoming attached to France than Americans had of becoming British colonists again. Nor did it mean, if French were granted official status in English Canada that the languages of the immigrants ought to receive similar recognition: the French claim, after all, was based on the bicultural compact. Bourassa also denied that a bilingual people could not form a homogeneous nation, arguing that discord would stem only from the attempts of the majority to force their language on the minority.

Then too there were some practical advantages to French.

Outside the English-speaking world French was useful in commerce and diplomacy. More important, it was the language of cultivated minds. When Canada had developed sufficiently to appreciate art and literature, claimed Bourassa, it would turn to French as an instrument of communication with the best of European civilization.

Bourassa's claim that Confederation was based on a bicultural pact is debatable. True, the Fathers had recognized the separateness of the French Canadians of Lower Canada: the predominately French-Canadian province would still control its French Catholic schools, and French would be an official language in the federal Parliament and courts. Such measures would enable French Canadians in Quebec both to develop their own culture and take part in the public life of the new Dominion. But on the other hand, the Fathers made no provision for the legal status of French in provinces other than Quebec; the Constitution furnished no protection for the Acadians. Professor Donald Creighton has shown that the *Manitoba Act of 1870* and the *Territorial Act of 1875* were not conscious steps in a plan to extend biculturalism to the West; instead, they were passed because of fortuitous circumstances and indeed were then quickly reversed.[14] Thus the Fathers did not object to cultural duality but neither did they determine to make Canada a bicultural country.

However, Bourassa's proposition that Confederation would not survive without cultural duality has been accepted by a large number of English-speaking Canadians. Many feel guilty about the shabby treatment given to French outside of Quebec. More important, many believe such cultural equality necessary if Quebec is to remain in Confederation.

Conscription

As the war went on, it became clear that there was a great difference of opinion between French and English over Canada's responsibility to the Allied side. Great numbers of Anglo-Canadians believed that Canada should be ready to fight to the end of her resources in both men and money. French Canadians, however, indicated by their markedly low rate of enlistment that they thought Canada should play a relatively minor role. This issue came to the fore over the proposal of the Borden government in the spring of 1917 to conscript men for overseas service. Voluntary enlistments, which were falling due to war-weariness, could not fill the gaps left by the high casualty rate suffered by Canadian troops on the Western front since the first of the year.

Borden asked Laurier to join him in a coalition government on a program of introducing conscription. The latter refused for a number of reasons: conscription was repugnant to him personally; if he took part in a coalition he would become responsible for a policy that he had no share in making; he suspected that it was a trick to split the Liberal party. But equally important, as he emphasized to friends, if he accepted conscription, he would be breaking his promise to Quebec and thus would virtually be handing over the province to Bourassa and his friends. Borden, however, succeeded in inducing a number of Liberals to join him in a "union" government which defeated Laurier in the federal election of December 1917. In contrast to the election of 1911, Bourassa now threw his support behind Laurier.

Bourassa had no objection to conscription as such. His attitude to it was conditioned by what he thought about the war. Although in 1914 he had supported Canadian participation, by 1916 he had come to modify his opinion: the war was supposedly being fought for the right of small nations to live, but in fact the great powers were smashing up the small nationalities. He followed the lead of Pope Benedict XV in calling for an end to the war, for a negotiated peace in which neither side would emerge solely victorious. Since he believed that there was no real Canadian interest involved in the war, he was logically consistent to claim that those who opposed conscription were the most patriotic Canadians; and that if French Canadians adopted this stand, it was because they were very clear in their minds that they owed their patriotism to Canada and Canada alone, unlike Anglo-Canadians whose focus of loyalty shifted between Canada and Great Britain.

Bourassa's Achievements

Many Canadian historians have been critical of Bourassa, presenting him as the spokesman for narrow French-Canadian clerical and racial elements that had refused to do their part in building Canadian unity. Yet it would be difficult to find any statement of his in support of Canadian autonomy within the Empire or of French-Canadian rights outside of Quebec that was not logically consistent with his program of achieving Canadian nationhood.

What his critics object to, however, is not Bourassa's program but the consequence of his determination to promote it. In 1911, by attacking Laurier, he helped bring the "more Imperialist of the two national parties"[15] to power. And since many of the Quebec members who had been elected because they had been endorsed by Bourassa gave their support to the Conservative naval program, French Canadians in Borden's Cabinet soon lost popularity in French Canada. Without influence in Quebec, their voices in Ottawa became feeble. Thus the manpower crisis was met by a government that was to all intents and purposes Anglo-Canadian.

Again Bourassa used rhetoric that was so strong about the French language issue during the war that he substantially embittered French–English relations and thereby contributed to the emotional climate out of which came the storm around conscription. In sum, the charge against Bourassa is that he went too far, that he was an extremist.

Yet from his own point of view, Bourassa's tactics made good sense. What he was trying to do in 1911, he said, was to send to Ottawa a block of members (whom he called Nationalists) who would hold the balance of power between the two parties and thus force the new government to revise the Naval Bill. What is more, he would have achieved his purpose if Borden had won a few seats less in Ontario and the Nationalists a few more in Quebec.[16] Even with the number of seats the Nationalists did win, they would have formed an important force within the Conservative government had Bourassa accepted a Cabinet position. But he was not prepared to undertake the tough responsibility of political leadership.

It was only natural for Bourassa to take advantage of the Anglo-Canadians' claim that they were fighting for freedom abroad to demand that they show good faith by granting equal rights to Franco-Ontarians at home. If as a consequence Canada's war effort were to slacken, it would not be too serious since Canada's role was a minor one and the Allies ought to be aiming at negotiating a just peace and not at winning the war.

Bourassa then had some grounds for believing that his tactics would be successful. But even without such hopes he would have acted the same way. He was not pragmatic: that he might not succeed in persuading Anglo-Canadians to do the right thing was no reason for not trying. It was on this point that Laurier differed profoundly from him. Although Laurier agreed with a great deal of Bourassa's program of Canadian nationalism, he did not defy Anglo-Canadian opinion because he wished the Liberal party to be the instrument of building unity between French and English. As an independent critic, Bourassa proclaimed what Anglo-Canadians ought to do; as a politician with responsibilities, Laurier proposed only what they would agree to do.

Many who are sympathetic with Laurier fail to see that even if he was right to contend that satisfactory relations between English and French must be founded on the possible rather than the ideal, it does not mean that left to himself he would have found the right point of compromise. Laurier's most significant action for Canadian unity was to reject conscription and refuse to join the Union coalition. This left the way open for the preservation of the Liberal party as an effective forum for the reconciliation of English and French in the postwar decade in Canada. But, as Professor Ramsay Cook has argued, Laurier's primary motive for these actions was his fear of handing Quebec over to Bourassa.[17] Because Bourassa would not compromise, Laurier was unable to compromise; it was the tension between the critic and the politician that determined the fate of the Liberal party.

Bourassa did a great deal to turn Canadian public opinion against any form of centralization of imperial foreign policy and defence. His greatest accomplishment, however, was to convince succeeding generations of French Canadians that their language ought to have the same rights as the English language. Thus he, more than any other individual, was responsible for making his dictum that Canada could only survive as a bicultural country much truer now than when he first enunciated it at the turn of the century.

NOTES

1. H. Bourassa, *Canada: House of Commons Debates*, Feb. 19, 1900, p. 500.
2. H. Bourassa, "Réponse amicale à la vérité," *La Nationaliste*, April 3, 1904.
3. Quoted in R. Preston, *Canada and Imperial Defense* (Toronto, 1976), 305.
4. H.B. Neatby, "Laurier and Imperialism," Canadian Historical Association, *Report* (1955), 25.
5. H. Bourassa, *Canadian Nationalism and the War* (Montreal, 1916), 14.
6. Bourassa usually ignored Laurier's qualifications. What Laurier said was this: "If England is at war, we are at war and liable to attack. I do not say that we shall always be attacked, neither do I say that we would take part in all the wars of England. That is a matter that we must be guided by the circumstance upon which the Canadian Parliament will have to pronounce, and will have to decide in its own best judgement." O.D. Skelton, *Life and Letters of Sir Wilfrid Laurier* (Toronto, 1965), 11: 125.
7. H. Bourassa, *Canada House of Commons Debates*, March 13, 1900, p. 1802.
8. H. Bourassa, *Independence or Imperial Partnership* (Montreal, 1916), 47.
9. C.B. Sissons quotes a small English boy to a French teacher: "This country does not belong to France and you must all learn English; my grandpa says so." C.B. Sissons, *Bilingual Schools in Canada* (London, 1917), 66.
10. *Canadian Annual Review*, 1916 (Toronto, 1917), 34.
11. H. Bourassa, *Canada, House of Commons*, July 5, 1905, p. 8848.
12. In the same speech Bourassa did not refer to the abolition of the rights of French culture in Manitoba, probably because he had supported Laurier's position on the Manitoba School question in 1896.
13. H. Bourassa, *La langue française et l'avenir de notre race* (Quebec, 1913), 17.
14. D.G. Creighton, "John A. Macdonald, Confederation, and the Canadian West," in C. Brown, *Minorities, Schools and Politics* (Toronto, 1969), 8.
15. H.B. Neatby, *Laurier and a Liberal Quebec: A Study in Political Management* (unpublished Ph.D. thesis, University of Toronto, 1956), 350.
16. J.M. Beck, *Pendulum of Power* (Scarborough, 1968), 133.
17. Ramsay Cook, "Dafoe, Laurier, and the Formation of Union Government," *Canadian Historical Review* 42, 3 (September 1961): 197.

Topic Five

Immigrants, Native Peoples, and Anglo-Conformity

Arrival of immigrants at Union Station in Toronto, ca. 1910.

114

BETWEEN 1896 and 1914, Canada received more than two million immigrants. Many came from Britain and the United States. But, for the first time, significant numbers were also arriving from central and eastern Europe. Those from Britain and the United States assimilated relatively easily into English-speaking Canadian society, since they spoke the same language and observed the same customs. The immigrants from continental Europe faced greater hardships. The difficulties they experienced were attributable, in part, to the attitudes toward foreign immigrants held by the dominant Anglo-Canadian community. In "Reluctant Hosts: Anglo-Canadian Views of Multiculturalism in the Twentieth Century," Howard Palmer sketches these changing attitudes in Canada from 1867 to the post–World War II period, describing the prevailing views in each period and explaining why they changed over time.

Native people also faced pressures to assimilate from the dominant Anglo-Canadian society, as well as from the Canadian government. The government's first step in its effort to assimilate the Plains Indians was to make treaties with them (often negotiated by federal "Indian agents"), then to place them on reserves, where they would be Christianized and trained as farmers. Unfortunately, many First Nations groups had a significantly different understanding of the meaning of the treaties from that of the government negotiators. Consequently, the two sides often talked at cross-purposes.

Christian missionaries reinforced the work of the Indian agents on the reserves. Through a series of stringent measures that included placing First Nations children in residential schools, the missionaries hoped to absorb them into Canadian society. Yet, according to J.R. Miller, in "Owen Glendower, Hotspur, and Canadian Indian Policy," these policies proved largely ineffective. Miller argues that the Indians "resisted, evaded, and defied efforts to control their decision making, limit their traditional rites, and deprive them of their children," and concludes that Canada's Native peoples continued, from the era of fur commerce and military alliance until the twentieth century, to be "active, if lamentably ignored, actors in the country's history."

For an overview of immigration to Western Canada, see the chapter entitled "Opening Up the Land of Opportunity" in R.C. Brown and R. Cook's *Canada, 1896–1921: A Nation Transformed* (Toronto: McClelland and Stewart, 1974), pp. 49–82, and Gerald Friesen's *The Canadian Prairies: A History* (Toronto: University of Toronto Press, 1984). Pierre Berton's *The Promised Land: Settling the West, 1896–1914* (Toronto: McClelland and Stewart, 1984) is a popular treatment of the subject. On Canadian immigration policy, see Reg Whitaker, *Canadian Immigration Policy since Confederation: Canada's Ethnic Groups*, Canadian Historical Association, Historical Booklet no. 15 (Ottawa: CHA, 1991). For cross-border migration, see Randy William Widdis, *With Scarcely a Ripple: Anglo-Canadian Migration into the United States and Western Canada* (Montreal/Kingston: McGill-Queen's University Press, 1999).

Elizabeth B. Mitchell's *In Western Canada before the War* (Saskatoon: Western Producer Prairie Books, 1981 [1915]) is a contemporary look at Western settlement. David Jones recounts the settlers' experience in the dry-belt area of southern Alberta and southern Saskatchewan in the 1920s in *Empire of Dust: Settling and Abandoning the Prairie Dry Belt* (Edmonton: University of Alberta Press, 1987). On attitudes toward immigrants, see Donald Avery, *Reluctant Host: Canada's Response to Immigrant Workers, 1896–1994* (Toronto: McClelland and Stewart, 1995). *Immigration and the Rise of Multiculturalism*, ed. H. Palmer

(Toronto: Copp Clark, 1975), contains a good selection of primary readings on the subject of immigration. An important study is Donald Avery's *Dangerous Foreigners: European Immigrant Workers and Labour Radicalism in Canada, 1896–1932* (Toronto: McClelland and Stewart, 1979). Howard Palmer reviews the Anglo-Albertans' reaction to "foreign" immigrants in *Patterns of Prejudice: A History of Nativism in Alberta* (Toronto: McClelland and Stewart, 1982). The immigrant's viewpoint is portrayed in John Marlyn's novel *Under the Ribs of Death* (Toronto: McClelland and Stewart, 1971), as well as in R.F. Harney and H. Troper's *Immigrants: A Portrait of the Urban Experience, 1890–1930* (Toronto: Van Nostrand Reinhold, 1975) and in Arnold Itwaru's *The Invention of Canada* (Toronto: Tsar Publications, 1990). See also R. Harney, " 'So Great a Heritage as Ours': Immigration and the Survival of the Canadian Polity," *Daedalus* 117, 4 (Fall 1988): pp. 51–98. The Department of the Secretary of State has published individual histories of several ethnic groups in Canada. In the series' introductory volume, *Coming Canadians: An Introduction to a History of Canadian Peoples* (Toronto: McClelland and Stewart, 1988), Jean Burnet and Howard Palmer survey ethnic relations in Canada. On Clifford Sifton's role in promoting immigration to the West, see D.J. Hall's two-volume biography, *Clifford Sifton*, vol. 1, *The Young Napoleon, 1861–1900* (Vancouver: University of British Columbia Press, 1981), vol. 2, *A Lonely Eminence, 1901–1929* (Vancouver: University of British Columbia Press, 1985), and his "Clifford Sifton: Immigration and Settlement Policy, 1896–1905," in *The Settlement of the West*, ed. H. Palmer (Calgary: University of Calgary Comprint Publishing Co., 1977), pp. 60–85. Three articles that provide overviews of work in the area of immigration and ethnic history are H. Palmer, "Canadian Immigration and Ethnic History in the 1970s and 1980s," *Journal of Canadian Studies* 17 (Spring 1982): 35–50; Roberto Perin, "Clio as Ethnic: The Third Force in Canadian Historiography," *Canadian Historical Review* 64 (December 1983): 441–67; and Donald Avery and Bruno Ramirez, "Immigration and Ethnic Studies," in *Interdisciplinary Approaches to Canadian Society*, ed. A.F.J. Artibise (Montreal/Kingston: McGill-Queen's University Press, 1990), pp. 77–111.

Recent valuable studies of the settlement of the Native peoples during and after the treaty period include Sarah Carter, *Aboriginal People and Colonizers of Western Canada to 1900* (Toronto: University of Toronto Press, 1999), and her *Lost Harvests: Prairie Indian Reserve Farmers and Government Policy* (Montreal/Kingston: McGill-Queen's University Press, 1990); J.R. Miller, *Shingwauk's Vision: A History of Native Residential Schools* (Toronto: University of Toronto Press, 1996), and his *Canada and the Aboriginal Peoples 1867–1927*, CHA Historical Booklet no. 57 (Ottawa: CHA, 1997); John S. Milloy, *A National Crime: The Canadian Government and the Residential School System, 1879–1986* (Winnipeg: University of Manitoba Press, 1999); the essays in *1885 and After: Native Society in Transition*, ed. F. Laurie Barron and James B. Waldram (Regina: Canadian Plains Research Centre, 1986); and Helen Buckley, *From Wooden Ploughs to Welfare: Why Indian Policy Failed in the Prairie Provinces* (Montreal/Kingston: McGill-Queen's University Press, 1992). Brian Titley reviews the Canadian government's Indian policy in *A Narrow Vision: Duncan Campbell Scott and the Administration of Indian Affairs in Canada* (Vancouver: University of British Columbia Press, 1986), pp. 1–22. *The Spirit of the Alberta Indian Treaties*, ed. Richard Price (Montreal: Institute for Research on Public Policy, 1979), contains valuable essays and transcripts of interviews with Indian elders conducted in the mid-1970s. Jean Friesen provides a modern view of the treaties in "Magnificent Gifts: The Treaties of the Indians of the North-West, 1869–70," *Transactions of the Royal Society of Canada*, series 5, vol. 1 (1986): 41–51. A good case study of an eastern Canadian Indian reserve in the late nineteenth century is Hélène Bédard's *Les Montagnais et la réserve de Betsiamites: 1850–1900* (Québec: Institut québécois de recherche sur la culture, 1988). Other useful studies include J.R. Miller,

Skyscrapers Hide the Heavens: A History of Indian–White Relations in Canada, 2nd ed. (Toronto: University of Toronto Press, 1991), and Olive Patricia Dickason, Canada's First Nations: A History of Founding Peoples from Earliest Times (Toronto: McClelland and Stewart, 1992).

116

Article Ten

Reluctant Hosts: Anglo-Canadian Views of Multiculturalism in the Twentieth Century

Howard Palmer

Introduction

The way in which Anglo-Canadians have reacted to immigration during the twentieth century has not simply been a function of the numbers of immigrants or the state of the nation's economy. The immigration of significant numbers of non-British and non-French people raised fundamental questions about the type of society which would emerge in English-speaking Canada; hence, considerable public debate has always surrounded the issue of immigration in Canada. The questions which have repeatedly been raised include the following: Were the values and institutions of Anglo-Canadian society modelled exclusively on a British mould and should immigrants be compelled to conform to that mould? Or, would a distinctive identity emerge from the biological and cultural mingling of Anglo-Canadians with new immigrant groups? Would cultural pluralism itself give English-speaking Canada a distinctive identity? These three questions reflect the three theories of assimilation which have dominated the twentieth-century debate over immigrant adjustment.

The assimilation theory which achieved early public acceptance was anglo-conformity. This view demanded that immigrants renounce their ancestral culture and traditions in favor of the behaviour and values of Anglo-Canadians. Although predominant prior to World War II, anglo-conformity fell into disrepute and was replaced in the popular mind by the "melting pot" theory of assimilation. This view envisaged a biological merging of settled communities with new immigrant groups and a blending of their cultures into a new Canadian type. Currently, a third theory of assimilation — "cultural pluralism" or "multiculturalism" — is vying for public acceptance. This view postulates the preservation of some aspects of immigrant culture and communal life within the context of Canadian citizenship and political and economic integration into Canadian society.[1]

There has been a recent burgeoning of historical and sociological research on Anglo-Canadian attitudes toward ethnic minorities. Much of this research contradicts the view which has been advanced by some Anglo-Canadian historians[2] and politicians that Anglo-

Source: Adapted from Multiculturalism as State Policy, 1976 Canadian Consultative Council of Multiculturalism, Department of Canadian Heritage. Reproduced with the permission of Public Works and Government Services Canada, 1997.

Canadians have always adopted the "mosaic" as opposed to the American "melting pot" approach. Much of this rhetoric has simply been wishful thinking. Perhaps immigrant groups did not "melt" as much in Canada as in the United States, but this is not because Anglo-Canadians were more anxious to encourage the cultural survival of ethnic minorities. There has been a long history of racism and discrimination against ethnic minorities in English-speaking Canada, along with strong pressures for conformity to Anglo-Canadian ways.

The "Settlement" Period and the Predominance of Anglo-Conformity: 1867–1920

Among the several objectives of the architects of the Canadian confederation in 1867, none was more important than the effort to accommodate the needs of the two main cultural communities. There was virtually no recognition of ethnic diversity aside from the British–French duality. This is, of course, somewhat understandable since at the time of Confederation, only 8 percent of the population of 3.5 million were of non-British[3] or non-French ethnic origin. There were, however, significant numbers of people of German and Dutch origin, well-established black and Jewish communities, as well as a few adventurers and entrepreneurs from most European ethnic groups now in Canada.

The proportion of people of other than British, French, or Native origin in Canada remained small until nearly the turn of the twentieth century; the United States proved more attractive for most European emigrants. In fact it was attractive for many Canadians as well, and the Dominion barely maintained its population. But with the closing of the American frontier, which coincided with improving economic conditions in Canada and an active immigration promotion campaign by Wilfrid Laurier's Liberal government, many immigrants began to come to the newly opened land of western Canada in the late 1890s.[4] Immigration policy gave preference to farmers, and most non-British immigrants came to farm in western Canada. However, some immigrants ended up working in mines, laying railway track, or drifting into the urban working class.[5] During this first main wave of immigration between 1896 and 1914, three million immigrants, including large numbers of British labourers, American farmers, and eastern European peasants, came to Canada. Within the period of 1901 to 1911, Canada's population rocketed by 43 percent and the percentage of immigrants in the country as a whole topped 22 percent. In 1911, people of non-British and non-French origin formed 34 percent of the population of Manitoba, 40 percent of the population of Saskatchewan, and 33 percent of the population of Alberta.

Throughout the period of this first large influx of non-British, non-French immigrants (indeed up until World War II), anglo-conformity was the predominant ideology of assimilation in English-speaking Canada.[6] For better or for worse, there were few proponents of either the melting pot or cultural pluralism. Proponents of anglo-conformity argued that it was the obligation of new arrivals to conform to the values and institutions of Canadian society—which were already fixed. During this period when scarcely anyone questioned the verities of God, King, and country, there was virtually no thought given to the possibility that "WASP" values might not be the apex of civilization which all men should strive for.

Since at this time the British Empire was at its height, and the belief in "progress" and Anglo-Saxon and white superiority was taken for granted throughout the English-speaking world, a group's desirability as potential immigrants varied almost directly with its members' physical and cultural distance from London (England), and the degree to which their skin pigmentation conformed to Anglo-Saxon white. Anglo-Canadians regarded

British and American immigrants as the most desirable.[7] Next came northern and western Europeans who were regarded as culturally similar and hence assimilable. They were followed by central and eastern Europeans, who in the eyes of Clifford Sifton and immigration agents, had a slight edge on Jews and southern Europeans, because they were more inclined to go to and remain on the land. These groups were followed in the ethnic pecking order by the "strange" religious sects, the Hutterites, Mennonites, and Doukhobors, who were invariably lumped together by public officials and the general public despite significant religious and cultural differences between them. Last, but not least (certainly not least in the eyes of those British Columbians and their sympathizers elsewhere in the country who worried about the "Asiatic" hordes), were the Asian immigrants — the Chinese, Japanese, and East Indians (the latter of whom were dubbed "Hindoos," despite the fact that most were Sikhs). Running somewhere close to last were black immigrants, who did not really arise as an issue because of the lack of aspiring candidates, except in 1911, when American blacks were turned back at the border by immigration officials because they allegedly could not adapt to the cold winters in Canada — a curious about-face for a department which was reassuring other American immigrants that Canadian winters were relatively mild.[8]

As might be expected, prevailing assumptions about the relative assimilability of these different groups were quickly transformed into public debate over whether immigrants whose assimilability was problematic should be allowed into the country. During this first wave of immigration, considerable opposition developed to the entry of central, southern, and eastern European immigrants, Orientals, and to the three pacifist sects. Opposition to these groups came from a variety of sources, for a variety of reasons. But one of the most pervasive fears of opinion leaders was that central, southern, and eastern Europeans, and Orientals would wash away Anglo-Saxon traditions of self-government in a sea of illiteracy and inexperience with "free institutions."[9] Many English-Canadian intellectuals, like many American writers at the time, thought that North America's greatness was ensured so long as its Anglo-Saxon character was preserved. Writers emphasized an Anglo-Saxon tradition of political freedom and self-government and the "white man's" mission to spread Anglo-Saxon blessings.[10] Many intellectuals and some politicians viewed Orientals and central, southern, and eastern European immigrants as a threat to this tradition and concluded that since they could not be assimilated they would have to be excluded. The introduction in Canada of a head tax on Chinese immigrants, a "gentlemen's agreement" with Japan which restricted the number of Japanese immigrants, the passing of orders-in-council which restricted immigration from India, the gradual introduction of restrictive immigration laws in 1906, 1910, and 1919 relative to European immigration, and the tightening of naturalization laws were based in considerable part on the assumptions of anglo-conformity — immigrants who were culturally or racially inferior and incapable of being assimilated either culturally or biologically would have to be excluded.[11] Those who rose to the immigrants' defence argued almost entirely from economic grounds: immigration from non-British sources was needed to aid in economic development, not because it might add anything to Canada's social or cultural life.

Although the trend toward restrictionism during the early 1900s seemed to indicate a government trend toward anglo-conformity in response to public pressure, for the most part between 1867 and 1945, there was no explicit federal government policy with regard to the role of non-British and non-French ethnic groups in Canadian society. It was generally assumed, however, that immigrants would eventually be assimilated into either English-Canadian or French-Canadian society. A recent careful study of Clifford Sifton's attitudes toward immigrant groups in Canadian society concludes Sifton assumed that central and eastern Europeans "would be 'nationalized' in the long run through their experience on the land."[12] The federal government's concern was tied to the economic consequences of immigration, while schools, the primary agents of assimilation, were under provincial jurisdiction. The federal government had encouraged Mennonites and Icelanders to settle in blocks in Manitoba during the 1870s and had given them special concessions (including local autonomy for both and military exemptions for the Mennonites) to entice them to stay in Canada rather than move to the United States.[13] But this was not because of any conscious desire to make Canada a cultural mosaic, nor was it out of any belief in the value of cultural diversity. Block settlements, by providing social and economic stability, were simply a way of getting immigrants to settle in the west and remain there.[14] The government policy was pragmatic and concerned primarily with economic growth and "nation building"; there was little rhetoric in immigration propaganda picturing Canada as a home for oppressed minorities who would be able to pursue their identities in Canada.

Provincial governments were faced with the problems of assimilation more directly than the federal government since the provinces maintained jurisdiction over the educational systems. The whole question of the varying attitudes of provincial authorities toward assimilation is much too complex to outline in this article; suffice it to say that with some notable exceptions (like the bilingual school system in Manitoba between 1896 and 1916, and the school system which was established for Hutterites in Alberta), anglo-conformity was the predominant aim of the public school system and was an underlying theme in the textbooks.

Anglo-conformity was most pronounced during World War I as nationalism precipitated insistent hostility to "hyphenated Canadianism" and demanded an unswerving loyalty. For many Anglo-Canadians during the war, loyalty and cultural and linguistic uniformity were synonymous. During the war, western provincial governments acted to abolish the bilingual schools which had previously been allowed.[15] The formation of the Union government of Conservatives and Liberals during the First World War was an attempt to create an Anglo-Saxon party, dedicated to "unhyphenated Canadianism" and the winning of the war; even if this meant trampling on the rights of immigrants through press censorship and the imposition of the War Time Elections Act, which disfranchised "enemy aliens" who had become Canadian citizens after March 21, 1902.[16] Various voluntary associations like the YMCA, IODE, National Council of Women, Canadian Girls in Training, Girl Guides, Big Brothers and Big Sisters Organizations, and Frontier College, as well as the major Protestant denominations, also intensified their efforts to "Canadianize" the immigrants, particularly at the close of the war when immigrant support for radical organizations brought on anti-radical nativist fears of the "menace of the alien."[17] The pressures for conformity were certainly real, even if English-Canadians could not always agree completely on the exact nature of the norm to which immigrants were to be assimilated.

All the major books on immigration prior to 1920, including J.S. Woodsworth's *Strangers within Our Gates*, J.T.M. Anderson's *The Education of the New Canadian*, Ralph Connor's *The Foreigner*, Alfred Fitzpatrick's *Handbook for New Canadians*, C.A. Magrath's *Canada's Growth and Some Problems Affecting It*, C.B. Sissons' *Bilingual Schools in Canada*, and W.G. Smith's *A Study in Canadian Immigration*, were based on the assumptions of anglo-conformity. To lump all these books together is of course to oversimplify since they approached the question of immigration with varying degrees of nativism (or anti-foreign sentiment) and humanitarianism. Nor were all of the voluntary organizations' attempted "Canadianization" work among immigrants motivated solely by the fear that immigrants would undermine the cultural homogeneity of English-speaking Canada. Many of these writers and organizations saw their work with the immigrants as a means of fighting social problems and helping immigrants achieve a basic level of political, social, and economic integration into Canadian society. But it cannot be denied that their basic assumption was that of anglo-conformity. Cultural diversity was either positively dangerous, or was something that would and should disappear with time, and with the help of Anglo-Canadians.

Perhaps it should be emphasized that the individuals advocating anglo-conformity were not just the reactionaries of their day. Protestant Social Gospellers (including J.S. Woodsworth, later one of the founders of the CCF), who played such a prominent role in virtually all the reform movements of the pre–World War I period (including women's rights, temperance, and labour, farm, and penal reform), believed that immigrants needed to be assimilated to Anglo-Canadian Protestant values as part of the effort to establish a truly Christian society in English-speaking Canada.[18] Women's groups pushing for the franchise argued that certainly they deserved the vote if "ignorant foreigners" had it, and joined in the campaign to Canadianize the immigrants who "must be educated to high standards or our whole national life will be lowered by their presence among us."[19]

But there was a central contradiction in Anglo-Canadian attitudes toward ethnic minorities. Non–Anglo-Saxon immigrants were needed to open the west and to do the heavy jobs of industry. This meant not only the introduction of culturally distinctive groups, but groups which would occupy the lower rungs of the socioeconomic system. The pre-1920 period was the period of the formation of, and the most acute expression of, what was later called the "vertical mosaic." Anglo-Canadians were not used to the idea of cultural diversity, nor the degree of class stratification which developed during this period of rapid settlement and industrialization. The answer to all the problems of social diversity which the immigrants posed was assimilation. The difficulty, however, with achieving this goal of assimilation was not only the large numbers of immigrants, or the fact that not all (or even a majority) of them wanted to be assimilated. One of the major factors preventing assimilation was discrimination by the Anglo-Canadian majority.

The basic contradiction, then, of Anglo-Canadian attitudes as expressed through the "Canadianization" drives was the tension between the twin motives of humanitarianism and nativism — between the desire to include non-British immigrants within a community and eliminate cultural differences and the desire to stay as far away from them as possible because of their presumed "undesirability." This contradiction was graphically revealed at the national conference of the IODE in 1919. The women passed one resolution advocating a "Canadianization campaign" to "propagate British ideals and institutions," to "banish old world points of view, old world prejudices, old world rivalries and suspicion" and to make new Canadians "100 percent British in language, thought, feeling, and impulse." Yet they also passed another resolution protesting "foreigners" taking British names.[20]

It does not appear that this was simply a case of the Anglo-Canadian majority being divided between those who wanted to pursue a strategy of assimilation and those who wanted to pursue a strategy of subordination and segregation. Certainly there was some division along these lines, but as suggested by the IODE resolutions, discrimination and anglo-conformity were often simply two different sides of the same coin — the coin being the assumption of the inferiority of non–Anglo-Saxons.

What developed throughout English-speaking Canada during this period was a vicious circle of discrimination. Non–Anglo-Saxons were discriminated against because they were not assimilated, either culturally or socially, but one of the reasons they were not assimilated was because of discrimination against them. As one researcher noted in a 1917 report on "Social Conditions in Rural Communities in the Prairie Provinces," the group "clannishness" of immigrants which was so widely deplored by the public was caused as much by the prejudice of the "English" as it was by the groups' desire to remain different.[21]

There is no need to catalogue here the extensive patterns of social, economic, and political discrimination which developed against non–Anglo-Saxons.[22] Patterns of discrimination parallelled preferences of immigrant sources, with northern and western Europeans encountering relatively little discrimination, central and southern Europeans and Jews encountering more discrimination, and non-whites encountering an all-pervasive pattern of discrimination which extended to almost all aspects of their lives. Discrimination was one of the main factors which led to the transference (with only a few exceptions) of the same ethnic "pecking order" which existed in immigration policy to the place each group occupied in the "vertical mosaic," with the British (especially the Scots) on top, and so on down to the Chinese and blacks who occupied the most menial jobs.[23] Non-British and non-French groups not only had very little economic power; they also would not even significantly occupy the middle echelons of politics, education, or the civil service until after World War II.

The ethnic stereotypes which developed for eastern European and Oriental groups emphasized their peasant origins. These stereotypes played a role in determining the job opportunities for new immigrants and functioned to disparage those who would climb out of their place. Opprobrious names such as "Wops," "Bohunks," and especially "foreigner" indicated class as well as ethnic origin and these terms were used as weapons in the struggle for status. The very word "ethnic" carried, for many people, such an aura of opprobrium that even recently there have been attempts to expurgate the use of the word. Ethnic food and folklore were regarded by most Anglo-Canadians as not only "foreign," but "backward" and lower class. Folklorist Carole Henderson has aptly described the views of Anglo-Canadians toward folklore (views which continue to the present day): "Except for members of some delimited regional, and usually ethnic, subcultures such as Newfoundlanders or Nova Scotian Scots, most Anglo-Canadians simply fail to identify folklore with themselves, and tend to consider such materials to be the . . . unimportant possessions of the strange, foreign, or 'backward people in their midst.' "[24]

The 1920s and the Emergence of "Melting Pot" Ideas

The 1920s brought the second main wave of non-British and non-French immigrants to Canada and saw the emergence of the second ideology of assimilation, the "melting pot." During the early 1920s both Canada and the United States had acted to further restrict immigration from southern, central, and eastern Europe and from the Orient. Chinese were virtually excluded from Canada, and central, southern, and eastern Europeans were classified among the "non-preferred" and restricted category of immigrants. But by the mid-1920s several powerful sectors of Canadian society, including transportation companies, boards of trade, newspapers, and politicians of various political persuasions, as well as ethnic groups, applied pressure on the King government to open the immigration doors.[25] These groups believed that only a limited immigration could be expected from the "preferred" countries and that probably only central and eastern Europeans would do the rugged work of clearing marginal land. The railways continued to seek immigrants to guarantee revenue for their steamship lines, traffic for their railways, and settlers for their land. With improving economic conditions in the mid-twenties, the federal government responded to this pressure and changed its policy with respect to immigrants from central and eastern Europe.

While continuing to emphasize its efforts to secure British immigrants, in September 1925 the Liberal government of Mackenzie King entered into the "Railways Agreement" with the CPR and CNR, which brought an increased number of central and eastern Europeans. The government authorized the railways to encourage potential immigrants of the "non-preferred" countries to emigrate to Canada and to settle as "agriculturalists, agricultural workers, and domestic servants."[26]

Through this agreement, the railways brought to Canada 165 000 central and eastern Europeans and 20 000 Mennonites. They represented a variety of ethnic groups and a diversity of reasons for emigrating. Most of the Ukrainian immigrants were political refugees. Poles, Slovaks, and Hungarians were escaping poor economic conditions. German-Russians and Mennonites were fleeing civil war, economic disaster, and the spectre of cultural annihilation in Russia.[27] Often they chose Canada since they could no longer get into the United States because of its quota system and the Canadian route was the only way they could get to North America. With this new wave of immigration, the proportion of the Canadian population that was not of British, French, or native origin rose to more than 18 percent by 1931.

In responding to this new wave of immigration, many opinion leaders held to an earlier belief that Canada should be patterned exclusively on the British model, and continued to advocate anglo-conformity. In national periodicals and newspapers during the 1920s, the emphasis which was placed on the need to attract British immigrants was related to this assumption that anglo-conformity was essential to the successful development of Canadian society. "Foreign" immigrants had to be assimilated and there needed to be enough Britishers to maintain "Anglo-Saxon" traditions.[28] R.B. Bennett, later to become the Conservative prime minister during the early 1930s, attacked melting pot ideas in the House of Commons and argued "These people [continental Europeans] have made excellent settlers: . . . but it cannot be that we must draw upon them to shape our civilization. We must still maintain that measure of British civilization which will enable us to assimilate these people to British institutions, rather than assimilate our civilization to theirs."[29]

The influx of new immigrants from central and eastern Europe during the mid- and late twenties also aroused protests from a number of nativist organizations, such as the Ku Klux Klan, The Native Sons of Canada, and The Orange Order, who were convinced that Canada should "remain Anglo-Saxon."[30] Nativist sentiment in western Canada was most pronounced in Saskatchewan, where one of its leading spokesmen was George Exton Lloyd, an Anglican bishop and one of the founders of the Barr colony at Lloydminster.

In a torrent of newspaper articles and speeches, Lloyd repeated the warning that Canada was in danger of becoming a "mongrel" nation: "The essential question before Canadians today is this: Shall Canada develop as a British nation within the empire, or will she drift apart by the introduction of so much alien blood that her British instincts will be paralyzed?"[31] According to Lloyd, Canada had but two alternatives: it could either be a homogeneous nation or a heterogeneous one. The heterogeneous or "melting pot" idea had not worked in the United States (as evidenced by large numbers of unassimilated immigrants at the outbreak of World War I), and could not, he argued, work in Canada. With Lloyd, as with other individuals and organizations promoting anglo-conformity at this time, one gets the distinctive feeling that they were on the defensive. Like other English-speaking Canadians who had a strong attachment to Britain and the Empire, Lloyd saw a threat to Canada's "British" identity, not only in the increasing numbers of "continental" immigrants, but also in the declining status of things British as Canadians moved toward a North-American–based nationalism which did not include loyalty to the British Empire as its primary article of faith.[32]

During the late 1920s, a new view of assimilation, the melting pot, developed greater prominence. This view of assimilation, which arose partly as a means of defending immigrants against nativist attacks from people like Lloyd, envisioned a biological merging of Anglo-Canadians with immigrants and a blending of their cultures into a new Canadian type. Whereas Lloyd and other nativists argued that since immigrants could not conform to Anglo-Canadian ideals they should be excluded, a new generation of writers argued that assimilation was indeed occurring, but to a new Canadian type.[33] Since assimilation was occurring, nativist fears were unwarranted. Indeed, immigrants would make some valuable cultural contributions to Canada during the process of assimilation. Although these writers did not all use the "melting pot" symbol when discussing their view of assimilation, one can lump their ideas together under the rubric of the "melting pot" because they did envisage the emergence of a new society which would contain "contributions" from the various immigrant groups.

Most of these writers who defended "continental" European immigration did not seriously question the desirability of assimilation. Robert England, a writer and educator who worked for the CNR, had read widely enough in anthropological sources to be influenced by the cultural relativism of Franz Boas and other anthropologists and did in his writing question the desirability of assimilation.[34] But most of these writers were concerned primarily with attempting to promote tolerance toward ethnic minorities by encouraging their assimilation, and many became involved in programs to facilitate this assimilation.

Advocates of anglo-conformity and the melting pot both believed that uniformity was ultimately necessary for unity, but they differed on what should provide the basis of that uniformity. Advocates of the melting pot, unlike the promoters of anglo-conformity, saw assimilation as a relatively slow process, and saw some cultural advantages in the mixing that would occur.

There was not, however, always a clear distinction between anglo-conformity and the melting pot. Rhetoric indicating that immigrants might have something more to offer Canada than their physical labour was sometimes only a thinly veiled version of anglo-conformity; the melting pot often turned out to be an Anglo-Saxon melting pot. For example, John Blue, a prominent Edmonton promoter and historian, wrote in his history of Alberta in 1924 that the fears about foreign immigration destroying Canadian laws and institutions had proved groundless. "There is enough Anglo-Saxon blood in Alberta to dilute the foreign blood and complete the process of assimilation to the mutual advantage of both elements."[35]

There were a variety of reasons for the development of melting pot ideas during the 1920s.[36] The growth during the 1920s of an autonomous Canadian nationalism helped the spread of melting pot ideas. Some English-Canadian opinion leaders began to discuss the need for conformity to an exclusively Canadian norm rather than a "British" norm. One of the arguments that John W. Dafoe, the influential editor of the *Winnipeg Free Press*, and J.S. Ewart, a constitutional lawyer, used in support of their view of Canadian nationalism was that non-British immigrants could not be expected to feel loyalty to the British Empire.[37]

Melting pot advocates tended to be people who had some personal experience with immigrants, and recognized both the intense pride that immigrants had in their cultural backgrounds as well as the rich cultural sources of those traditions. But they also lived in a time when recognition of ethnicity meant mostly Anglo-Canadian use of ethnicity as a basis of discrimination or exploitation. It was also a time when some ethnic groups were still close enough to their rural peasant roots that ethnic solidarity was often not conducive to upward mobility. The view of most melting pot advocates that the disappearance of ethnicity as a basis of social organization would increase the mobility opportunities of the second generation was based on a sound grasp of the realities of the day. The lifelong campaign of John Diefenbaker for "unhyphenated Canadianism" and "one Canada" grew out of this experience with ethnicity as something that could be used to hinder opportunities, and was consistent with his emphasis on human rights, rather than group rights.[38]

124

The 1930s

Although immigration was severely cut back during the depression of the 1930s, the role of ethnic minorities in English-speaking Canada continued to be a major public concern. Paradoxically, although the depression witnessed the high point of discrimination against non–Anglo-Saxons, it was also during the 1930s that the first major advocates of cultural pluralism in English-speaking Canada began to be heard.

The depression affected non–Anglo-Saxon immigrants more than most other groups in the society. These immigrants, because of their language problems and lack of specialized skills, were concentrated in the most insecure and therefore most vulnerable segments of the economy. Since immigrants were the last hired and the first fired, a large proportion were forced onto relief. Government officials were gravely concerned about the way immigrants seemed to complicate the relief problem. Calls by some officials for deportation as the solution to the relief problem were heeded by the federal government; sections 40 and 41 of the *Immigration Act* (still essentially the same act as the one which existed in 1919) provided for deportation of non-Canadian citizens on relief, and government officials took advantage of the law to reduce their relief rolls.

While there was some continuing concern over the assimilation of non-British and non-French immigrants during the 1930s, most Anglo-Canadians were more concerned about protecting their jobs.[39]

Prior to the depression, most Anglo-Saxons were content to have the "foreigners" do all the heavy work of construction, and the dirty work of the janitors and street sweepers. But as the economy slowed down, these jobs became attractive. Whereas the pre-depression attitude was "let the foreigners do the dirty work," the depression attitude became "how come these foreigners have all of our jobs?" The 1930s also saw the high point of anti-Semitism in English-speaking Canada as the patterns of discrimination which had hindered the desires of second generation Jews for entry into the professions were extended into a vicious and virulent anti-Semitism by fascist groups.[40]

Barry Broadfoot's book *Ten Lost Years* also makes it very clear that discrimination and prejudice flourished during the depression. In the transcripts of his interviews with the "survivors" of the depression, one is struck by the all-pervasiveness of derogatory ethnic epithets in interviewees' recollections of their contact with immigrants. One does not read of Italians, Chinese, or Poles. One reads of "Dagos," "Wops," "Chinks," "Polacks," "Hunyaks."[41] One "survivor" of the depression, waxing philosophical, gives explicit expression to the prevailing attitudes of the time. He compares how the depression affected people from R.B. Bennett down to "the lowest of the low," "some bohunk smelling of garlic and not knowing a word of English."[42] Another "survivor" recalls that her boy had great difficulty finding work during the depression, and went berserk because of the blow to his self-esteem when the only job he could find was "working with a bunch of Chinks."[43]

The vicious circle of discrimination became perhaps even more vicious during the 1930s as non–Anglo-Saxons' political response to the depression further poisoned attitudes toward them. The discrimination and unemployment which non–Anglo-Saxons faced was an important factor in promoting the support of many for radical political solutions to the depression, in either communist or fascist movements. Indeed the vast majority of the support for the communists throughout Canada, and for the fascists in western Canada, came from non–Anglo-Saxons.[44] Ethnic support for these two movements, and the conflict between left and right within most central and eastern European groups and the Finns was seen as further evidence of the undesirability of non–Anglo-Saxons. The existence of fascist and communist movements in Canada was not of course due simply to the presence of immigrants bringing "old world" ideas. The leaders in both movements were predominantly of British origin,[45] and their "ethnic" support came more from immigrants reacting to depression conditions than from immigrants bringing to Canada "old world" ideas. But the depression gave further support to the notion of non–Anglo-Saxons being unstable politically; one more proof along with immigrant drinking, garlic eating, and the legendary violence at Slavic weddings, that non–Anglo-Saxons were in dire need of baptism by assimilation. Deporting immigrant radicals was seen as one alternative to assimilation and the federal government did not hesitate to use this weapon.[46]

The relationship in the public mind between ethnicity, lower social class origins, and political "unsoundness" explains why during the late 1920s so many second generation non–Anglo-Saxons who were anxious to improve their lot economically made deliberate attempts to hide their ethnic background, such as changing their names. Ethnic ties were clearly disadvantageous for those non–Anglo-Saxons seeking economic security or social acceptance. The experience of the second generation in English-speaking Canada was similar to the second-generation experience as described by a historian writing about ethnic groups in the United States. "Culturally estranged from their parents by their American education, and wanting nothing so much as to become and to be accepted as Americans, many second generation immigrants made deliberate efforts to rid themselves of their heritage. The adoption of American clothes, speech, and interests, often accompanied by the shedding of an exotic surname, were all part of a process whereby antecedents were repudiated as a means of improving status."[47]

Despite the continuing dominance of the old stereotypes concerning non–Anglo-Saxons and the continuing dominance of assimilationist assumptions, the 1930s also saw the emergence of the first full-blown pluralist ideas in somewhat ambiguous form in John Murray Gibbon's book, *The Canadian Mosaic*, and in the writings of Watson Kirkconnell, then an English professor at the University of Manitoba. These writers were much more familiar than earlier writers with the historical backgrounds of the ethnic groups coming to Canada, and they were influenced by a liberalism which rejected the assumptions of Anglo-Saxon superiority. Gibbon, a publicity agent for the Canadian Pacific Railway, wrote his book as an expansion of a series of CBC radio talks on the different ethnic groups of Canada. He traced the history of each group and related their "contributions" to Canadian society. Although he was concerned with the preservation of folk arts and music, he also went out of his way to alleviate fears of unassimilability by discussing individuals' assimilation as well as the "cement" of common institutions which bound the Canadian mosaic together. Although Gibbon was not the first writer to use the mosaic symbol, he was the first to attempt to explore its meaning in any significant way.

Kirkconnell was an essayist, poet, and prolific translator of European verse from a number of European languages. His writing on ethnic groups was based on a different approach than Gibbon's. He tried to promote tolerance toward "European Canadians" by sympathetically portraying the cultural background of the countries where the immigrants originated and by demonstrating the cultural creativity of European immigrants in Canada through translating and publishing their creative writing.[48] In his writing he attacked the assumptions of anglo-conformity, and advocated a multicultural society which would allow immigrants to maintain pride in their past:

> It would be tragic if there should be a clumsy stripping-away of all those spiritual associations with the past that help to give depth and beauty to life. . . . If . . . we accept with Wilhelm von Humboldt "the absolute and essential importance of human development in its richest diversity," then we shall welcome every opportunity to save for our country every previous element of individuality that is available.[49]

Kirkconnell was not advocating complete separation of ethnic groups so that they might be preserved. He believed that assimilation needed to occur in the realm of political and economic values and institutions but he hoped that some of the conservative values and folk culture of immigrants could be preserved.

Kirkconnell did not ignore the political differences within ethnic groups. Indeed, with the outbreak of World War II he wrote a book in which he attempted to expose and combat both fascist and communist elements in different ethnic groups.[50] But he was also active in attempts to bring various other factions of eastern European groups together in order to alleviate public criticism of divisions within ethnic groups.[51]

These advocates of pluralism believed that ethnic diversity was not incompatible with national unity. Unity need not mean uniformity. They believed that recognition of the cultural contributions of non–Anglo-Saxon groups would heighten the groups' feeling that they belonged to Canada and thus strengthen Canadian unity. But Gibbon and Kirkconnell were voices crying in the wilderness — a wilderness of discrimination and racism.

After World War II: The Emergence of Multiculturalism

The war period and early postwar period was a transitional time with respect to attitudes toward immigration and ethnicity. Although the war brought renewed hostility toward enemy aliens, a number of developments during the war eventually worked to undermine ethnic prejudice. During the arrival of the third wave of immigration in the late 1940s and 1950s, many pre-war prejudices lingered, and ethnic minorities encountered considerable pressures for conformity. But for a variety of intellectual, social, and demographic reasons, the ideology of cultural pluralism has been increasingly accepted in the post–World War II period. The postwar decline of racism and the growing influence of theories about cultural relativism opened the way for the emergence of pluralist ideas. The arrival of many intellectuals among the postwar political refugees from eastern Europe and the growth in the number of upwardly mobile second- and third-generation non–Anglo-Canadians, some of whom felt that they were not being fully accepted into Canadian society, increased the political pressures at both federal and provincial levels for greater recognition of Canada's ethnic diversity. Some suggested that this could be achieved through the appointment of senators of a particular ethnic origin, or through the introduction into the school curriculum of ethnic content and of ethnic languages as courses (and sometimes as languages of instruction).[52]

These demands for greater government recognition of "other ethnic groups" increased during the 1960s in response to the French-Canadian assertion of equal rights and the Pearson government's measures to assess and ensure the status of the French language and culture. In 1963 the Royal Commission on Bilingualism and

Biculturalism was appointed to "inquire into and report upon the existing state of bilingualism and biculturalism in Canada and to recommend what steps should be taken to develop the Canadian Confederation on the basis of an equal partnership between the two founding races, taking into account the contribution made by the other ethnic groups to the cultural enrichment of Canada." Many non-British, non-French groups, but particularly Ukrainians, opposed the view that Canada was bicultural. By 1961, 26 percent of the Canadian population was of other than British or French ethnic origin; over two hundred newspapers were being published in languages other than French and English; there were fairly well-defined Italian, Jewish, Slavic, and Chinese neighbourhoods in large Canadian cities, and there were visible rural concentrations of Ukrainians, Doukhobors, Hutterites, and Mennonites scattered across the western provinces: thus, how was it possible for a royal commission to speak of Canada as a *bi*cultural country?

This feeling that biculturalism relegated all ethnic groups who were other than British or French to the status of second-class citizens helps explain the resistance some of these groups expressed to the policies and programs that were introduced to secure the status of the French language in Canada. The place of the so-called "other" ethnic groups in a bicultural society became a vexing question for federal politicians, who had originally hoped that steps to ensure French-Canadian rights would go a long way toward improving inter-ethnic relations in Canada. The partial resolution of this dilemma was the assertion in October 1971 by Prime Minister Trudeau that, in fact, Canada is a *multi*cultural country and that steps would be taken by the federal government to give public recognition to ethnic diversity through the introduction of a policy of multiculturalism. Several provinces with large numbers of non–Anglo-Canadians have also initiated their own policies of multiculturalism.

Although most political leaders in English-speaking Canada have accepted and proclaimed the desirability of Canada's ethnic diversity, the Canadian public has not given unanimous support to pluralism. The debate over the place of ethnic groups in Canadian life continues, focusing on such questions as: Does the encouragement of pluralism only serve to perpetuate the vertical mosaic, in which class lines coincide with ethnic lines, or does it help break down class barriers by promoting acceptance of the legitimacy of cultural differences? Are the goals of current government policy — cultural pluralism and equality of opportunity — mutually compatible? Does the encouragement of ethnic group solidarity threaten the freedom of individuals in these groups, or can ethnic groups provide a liberating, rather than a restricting, context for identity? Does the encouragement of cultural diversity serve to perpetuate old-world rivalries, or will the recognition of the contributions of Canada's ethnic groups heighten their feeling that they belong in Canada and thus strengthen Canadian unity? Is government talk of multiculturalism just a way to attract the "ethnic vote," or is positive action necessary to preserve cultural pluralism when cultural diversity throughout the world is being eroded by the impact of industrial technology, mass communication, and urbanization? Does the encouragement of multiculturalism simply heighten the visibility of the growing numbers of non-whites in the country and hinder their chances of full acceptance as individuals into Canadian life, or is a public policy of multiculturalism essential to an effective campaign against racism? The nature of these arguments suggests that the prevailing assumptions about immigration and ethnicity have changed over time in English-speaking Canada. They also suggest that the discussion about the role of immigration and ethnic groups in Canadian life is still an important, and unfinished, debate.

NOTES

1. For a discussion of these three ideologies of assimilation in the United States, see Milton Gordon, *Assimilation in American Life* (New York, 1964).
2. L.G. Thomas, "The Umbrella and the Mosaic: The French–English Presence and the Settlement of the Canadian Prairie West," in J.A. Carroll, ed., *Reflections of Western Historians* (Tucson, Arizona, 1969), 135–52; Allan Smith, "Metaphor and Nationality in North America," *Canadian Historical Review* 51, 3 (September 1970).
3. The Canadian census has consistently classed the Irish as part of the "British" group.
4. Howard Palmer, *Land of the Second Chance: A History of Ethnic Groups in Southern Alberta* (Lethbridge, 1972); Norman Macdonald, *Canada Immigration and Colonization, 1841–1903* (Toronto, 1967); Harold Troper, *Only Farmers Need Apply* (Toronto, 1972).
5. Donald Avery, "Canadian Immigration Policy and the Foreign Navy," Canadian Historical Association, *Report* (1972); Edmund Bradwin, *Bunkhouse Man* (New York, 1928); H. Troper and R. Harney, *Immigrants* (Toronto, 1975).
6. Donald Avery, "Canadian Immigration Policy, 1896–1919: The Anglo-Canadian Perspective" (unpublished Ph.D. thesis, University of Western Ontario, 1973); Cornelius Jaenen, "Federal Policy Vis-à-Vis Ethnic Groups" (unpublished paper, Ottawa, 1971); Howard Palmer, "Nativism and Ethnic Tolerance in Alberta, 1880–1920" (unpublished M.A. thesis, University of Alberta, 1971); Palmer, "Nativism and Ethnic Tolerance in Alberta, 1920–1972" (unpublished Ph.D. thesis, York University, 1973).
7. H. Palmer, "Nativism and Ethnic Tolerance in Alberta, 1880–1920" (unpublished M.A. thesis, University of Alberta, 1971), ch. 1 and 2; H. Troper, *Only Farmers Need Apply* (Toronto, 1972); D.J. Hall, "Clifford Sifton: Immigration and Settlement Policy, 1896–1905," in H. Palmer, ed., *The Settlement of the West* (Calgary, 1977), 60–85.
8. H. Troper, "The Creek Negroes of Oklahoma and Canadian Immigration, 1909–11," *Canadian Historical Review* (September 1972), 272–88.
9. Rev. George Bruce, "Past and Future of Our Race," *Proceedings*, Canadian Club of Toronto, 1911, pp. 6–7; C.A. Magrath, *Canada's Growth and Problems Affecting It* (Ottawa, 1910); Goldwin Smith in *Weekly Sun*, Feb. 1, 1899, Sept. 17, 1902, Sept. 23, 1903, May 18, 1904, Aug. 16, 1905; W.A. Griesbach, *I Remember* (Toronto, 1946), 214–17, 220–21.
10. Carl Berger, *Sense of Power* (Toronto, 1970), 117–88.
11. Morton, *In a Sea of Sterile Mountains* (Vancouver, 1974); W.P. Ward, "The Oriental Immigrant and Canada's Protestant Clergy, 1858–1925," *B.C. Studies* (Summer 1974), 40–55; Ted Ferguson, *A White Man's Country* (Toronto, 1975).
12. D.J. Hall, "Clifford Sifton: Immigration and Settlement Policy: 1896–1905," in H. Palmer, ed., *The Settlement of the West* (Calgary, 1977), 79–80.
13. W.L. Morton, *Manitoba: A History* (Toronto, 1957), 161, 162.
14. J.B. Hedges, *Building the Canadian West* (New York, 1939); Frank Epp, *Mennonites in Canada, 1786–1920* (Toronto, 1974).
15. Cornelius J. Jaenen, "Ruthenian Schools in Western Canada, 1897–1919," *Paedagogica Historica: International Journal of the History of Education* 10, 3 (1970): 517–41. Donald Avery, "Canadian Immigration Policy," 374–420.
16. Avery, "Canadian Immigration Policy," 408.
17. Kate Foster, *Our Canadian Mosaic* (Toronto, 1926); J.T.M. Anderson, *The Education of the New Canadian* (Toronto, 1918); C.B. Sissons, *Bi-Lingual Schools in Canada* (Toronto, 1917); W.G. Smith, *Building the Nation* (Toronto, 1922). For a discussion of some of the concrete activities involved in these "Canadianization" programs, see R. Harney and H. Troper, *Immigrants*, ch. 4.
18. J.S. Woodsworth, *Strangers within Our Gates* (Winnipeg, 1909); Marilyn Barber, "Nationalism, Nativism and the Social Gospel: The Protestant Church Response to Foreign Immigrants in Western Canada, 1897–1914," in Richard Allen, ed., *The Social Gospel in Canada* (Ottawa, 1975), 186–226.

19. Quoted in Barbara Nicholson, "Feminism in the Prairie Provinces to 1916" (unpublished M.A. thesis, University of Calgary, 1974), 71. For the views of womens' groups on immigration and the role of immigrants in Canadian society, see pp. 83–85, 86, 114, 121, 133, 165–69, 186–87.
20. Reported in *Lethbridge Herald*, May 29, 1919.
21. J.S. Woodsworth, "Social Conditions in Rural Communities in the Prairie Provinces" (Winnipeg, 1917), 38.
22. For a fairly extensive chronicling of patterns of discrimination against a number of minority groups, see Morris Davis and J.F. Krauter, *The Other Canadians* (Toronto, 1971).
23. For an analysis of the various causes of ethnic stratification (settlement patterns, time of arrival, immigrant and ethnic occupations, ethnic values, language barriers, and discrimination and exploitation) see Book 4, *Report of the Royal Commission on Bilingualism and Biculturalism* (Ottawa, 1969), ch. 2.
24. Carole Henderson, "The Ethnicity Factor in Anglo-Canadian Folkloristics," *Canadian Ethnic Studies* 7, 2 (1975), 7–18.
25. *Canadian Annual Review* (1923), 264–65; (1924–25), 190–92.
26. *Canada Year Book* (1941), 733.
27. Olha Woycenko, *The Ukrainians in Canada* (Winnipeg, 1967); Victor Turek, *Poles in Manitoba* (Toronto, 1967), 43; J.M. Kirschbaum, *Slovaks in Canada* (Toronto, 1967), 101; Edmund Heier, "A Study of German Lutheran and Catholic Immigrants in Canada formerly residing in Czarist and Soviet Russia" (unpublished M.A. thesis, University of British Columbia, 1955), ch. 3.
28. R.B. Bennett, House of Commons *Debates*, June 7, 1929, pp. 3925–27.
29. Bennett, House of Commons *Debates*, 3925–27.
30. H. Palmer, "Nativism in Alberta, 1925–1930," Canadian Historical Association, *Report* (1974), 191–99.
31. G.E. Lloyd, "National Building," *Banff Crag and Canyon*, Aug. 17, 1928.
32. A.R.M. Lower, *Canadians in the Making* (Don Mills, Ontario, 1958), ch. 22, 27.
33. J.S. Woodsworth, "Nation Building," *University Magazine* (1917), 85–99. F.W. Baumgartner, "Central European Immigration," *Queen's Quarterly* (Winter 1930), 183–92; Walter Murray, "Continental Europeans in Western Canada," *Queen's Quarterly* (1931); P.M. Bryce, *The Value of the Continental Immigrant to Canada* (Ottawa, 1928); E.L. Chicanot, "Homesteading the Citizen: Canadian Festivals Promote Cultural Exchange," *Commonwealth* (May 1929), 94–95; E.K. Chicanot, "Moulding a Nation," *Dalhousie Review* (July 1929), 232–37. J.H. Haslam, "Canadianization of the Immigrant Settler," *Annals* (May 1923), 45–49; E.H. Oliver, "The Settlement of Saskatchewan to 1914," *Transactions of the Royal Society* (1926), 63–87; Agnes Laut, "Comparing the Canadian and American Melting Pots," *Current Opinion* 70 (April 1921), 458–62; Kate Foster, *Our Canadian Mosaic* (Toronto, 1926). Robert England, "Continental Europeans in Western Canada," *Queen's Quarterly* (1931).
34. Robert England, *The Central European Immigrant in Canada* (Toronto, 1929).
35. John Blue, *Alberta Past and Present* (Chicago, 1924), 210.
36. There were some advocates of the melting pot prior to 1920, but it did not gain widespread acceptance until the 1920s. See H. Palmer, "Nativism in Alberta, 1880–1920," ch. 1; Marilyn Barber, "Nationalism, Nativism, and the Social Gospel."
37. Douglas Cole, "John S. Ewart and Canadian Nationalism," Canadian Historical Association, *Report* (1969), 66.
38. John Diefenbaker, *One Canada* (Toronto, 1975), 140, 141, 218–19, 274.
39. H. Palmer, "Nativism in Alberta, 1920–1972," ch. 3.
40. James Gray, *The Roar of the Twenties* (Toronto, 1975), ch. 11; Lita-Rose Betcherman, *The Swastika and the Maple Leaf* (Don Mills, Ontario, 1975).
41. Barry Broadfoot, *Ten Lost Years*, 25, 70, 76, 132, 156–64, 186, 279.
42. Broadfoot, *Ten Lost Years*, 132.
43. Broadfoot, *Ten Lost Years*, 186.
44. Ivan Avakumovic, *The Communist Party in Canada: A History* (Toronto, 1975), 66–67; Lita-Rose Betcherman, *The Swastika and the Maple Leaf*, ch. 5.

129

45. See note 44 above.

46. H. Palmer, "Nativism in Alberta, 1920–1972," ch. 3.

47. M.A. Jones, *American Immigration* (Chicago, 1960), 298. For fictional treatments of the second generation's repudiation of the ethnic past in an attempt to become accepted, see John Marlyn, *Under the Ribs of Death* (Toronto, 1971) and Magdalena Eggleston, *Mountain Shadows* (New York, 1955), 122. See also *Change of Name* (Toronto: Canadian Institute of Cultural Research, 1965).

48. Watson Kirkconnell, *The European Heritage: A Synopsis of European Cultural Achievement* (London, 1930) and *Canadian Overtones* (Winnipeg, 1935). For a complete listing of Kirkconnell's work, see the list in his memoirs, *A Slice of Canada* (Toronto, 1967), 374–75. For an assessment of his work, see J.R.C. Perkin, ed., *The Undoing of Babel* (Toronto, 1975).

49. W. Kirkconnell, trans., *Canadian Overtones*, preface.

50. Watson Kirkconnell, *Canada, Europe, and Hitler* (Toronto, 1939).

51. W. Kirkconnell, *A Slice of Canada*.

52. For documentary evidence of changing ethnic attitudes in the post-war era and the emergence of multiculturalism as an idea and as a governmental policy, see H. Palmer, *Immigration and the Rise of Multiculturalism* (Toronto, 1975), ch. 3.

Article Eleven

Owen Glendower, Hotspur, and Canadian Indian Policy

J.R. Miller

Owen Glendower	I can call spirits from the vasty deep.
Hotspur	Why, so can I, or so can any man;
	But will they come when you do call for them?

—Shakespeare, *Henry IV, Part I* [1]

Scholarly writing on Canada's Indian policy of the late Victorian period has lagged behind analysis of other aspects of Native–newcomer relations. Like American academics, Canadians have made an impressive start on revising the understanding of economic, military, and social relations in the seventeenth and eighteenth centuries. However, discussions of nineteenth-century assimilative policies have persisted in an older tendency to treat the Indians as objects rather than agents, victims rather than creators of their history. The existing literature usually examines missionaries' requests for the suppression of cultural practices such as the potlatch and notes how their desires coincided with the government's anxiety to prevent Indians from squandering their capital or wasting their time. The standard interpretation then makes a logical leap from such policies as forbidding the Sun Dance or establishing residential schools to an implicit conclusion that such measures assimilated Indians.

In short, this traditional version of government policy toward Canada's Native peoples tends to treat as synonymous the aims and results of legislation banning traditional cul-

Source: "Owen Glendower, Hotspur, and Canadian Indian Policy," *Ethnohistory* 37, 4 (Fall 1990): 386–415.

tural practices or inhibiting native movement. Such treatments remind one of nothing so much as Shakespeare's dialogue between Hotspur and Owen Glendower. When the boastful Glendower claims, "I can call spirits from the vasty deep," Hotspur responds, "Why, so can I, or so can any man." Calling them is not the point. What matters is the response. "But will they come when you do call for them?"[2] Canada legislated to control and assimilate Indians late in the nineteenth century. But did the measures work? Were the Indians simply victims of these policies?[3]

This view of late-nineteenth-century policy as efficacious resembles older, outmoded views of economic, military, and social relations between Canada's indigenous peoples and European newcomers. For a long time the literature on the fur trade, for instance, treated the Indians and Inuit as victims of rapacious European traders.[4] Following Francis Parkman, military historians talked about the "use" of Indians by various European powers in the wars of the eighteenth century in North America.[5] Similarly, accounts of Christian missions in early New France emphasized the heroism of the Jesuits while paying little attention to the activities of those whom they proselytized.

Unlike the conventional treatment of late Victorian Indian policy, however, the traditional picture of the Indian as victim of European merchants, generals, and missionaries has of late been revised. Scholars like A.J. Ray and Robin Fisher have demonstrated that Indians both in the Hudson's Bay Company lands and on the Pacific were in control of the commerce in furs: Natives successfully insisted that the fur trade be carried on according to their formulas, and for purposes largely determined by them.[6] This work has been amplified and enriched by social historians who, while probing the role of Native women in fur-trade country, discovered that the social side of the commerce in peltries was controlled by Native societies, too.[7] And scholars such as Axtell, Eccles, Jaenen, and Trigger have reassessed the social and intellectual relations between Indians and Europeans in New France. They have demonstrated that missions were planted in the interior of North America primarily because the Native peoples regarded them as a manifestation of the exchange of personnel with which they had for centuries cemented commercial liaisons. Jesuits were allowed into Huronia to maintain the commercial and military alliance between the Huron and the French.[8] "Heroic" missionaries were hostages to the exchange of furs; Jesuits were "martyrs" to commercial ambitions.

The military relationship of the colonial period has also been reinterpreted to portray the Indian peoples as agents rather than objects. This development in Canadian historiography has paralleled American writing on military relations.[9] To Canadian audiences Upton explained that the Micmac did not fight as the tools of the French, but rather that they embraced Catholicism and the French alliance as their best defence against the Anglo-Americans whom they feared. And students of the American War of Independence have demonstrated conclusively that Indians operated, not as "pawns" or "tools," but according to carefully worked-out calculations of where their self-interest lay.[10] Woodlands Indians perceived that their interests lay with the more northerly, commercially inclined European power rather than with the agriculturalists to the south.[11] Pontiac sought to repel the Anglo-American farmers who were poised to sweep across the Alleghenies after the Peace of Paris in 1763. The Brant family led the Mohawk to support the British in the Revolutionary War for personal and familial reasons and because of calculations that the British posed a lesser threat to their lands than the Americans. Tecumseh and the Shawnee Prophet were operating during the War of 1812 on the same strategy that was designed to deter the advance of the agricultural frontier.[12]

What these specialists in economic, social, and military history have done is to restore indigenous peoples to their active role in Canadian history. They have demonstrated that the Native peoples, at least in the early phases of contact, controlled the fur trade, that they pursued their own interests in military matters, and that they shaped the social and intellectual relationship. Similarly, some works on education and civil policymaking in the early decades after the War of 1812 have recognized an active Indian role. Mississauga and other Indians north of the lower Great Lakes encouraged and supported efforts to educate their young until they recognized that the missionaries and government sought to assimilate Native youths as well as make them literate. And legislative initiatives in the 1850s to assert political control over Indians in the central colony of British North America encountered stiff resistance.[13] Unfortunately, studies of Indian–white relations after Confederation, the formation of the national government in 1867, have thus far proved largely resistant to reinterpretation.[14] It is now time for another look at Canada's version of the policy of the Bible and the plow.

This policy, though foreshadowed in pre-Confederation programs in central Canada, became fully developed only after 1867. Legislation of 1869 and 1876, which was reenacted in the *Indian Act of 1880*, presumed to define who was an Indian and to interfere with Indian self-government. At the same time, inducements were held out to Indians to encourage their "advancement" toward full citizenship by offering those in eastern Canada the federal franchise in 1885 and by making "allotments" of reserve land available to Indians who wished to take possession of individual plots. However, as had been the case with similar experiments earlier, Indians proved uninterested in acquiring electoral rights or freehold tenure and remarkably resistant to so-called enfranchisement, or adoption of standard citizenship status.[15] Bureaucrats responded to parallel failures in the 1870s and 1880s by resorting to what Indian commissioner Edgar Dewdney described as "sheer compulsion."[16]

Officialdom's inclination toward coercion culminated in a series of measures that were designed to control Indians politically and alter them culturally. Amendments to the *Indian Act* in 1884 prohibited the potlatch, or "the Indian dance known as the 'Tamanawas'" of the Pacific Indians, while in 1885 department regulations instituted a "pass system" designed to control movement. In western Canada, Indians who wished to travel off their reserve were expected to obtain a pass signed by the agent. The pass system was designed to inhibit the movements of Indian diplomats, to discourage parental visits to residential schools, and to provide the North-West Mounted Police (NWMP) and Indian agents with the authority to stop Plains Indians from participating in ceremonies such as the Sun Dance or the Thirst Dance on distant reserves. These coercive measures were aimed at assimilating Indians by attacking their religious rituals, removing their children from home influences, and preventing their travelling when there was work to be done in the fields. They were viewed as a necessary part of a broad campaign to inculcate agriculture in the prairie West that embraced subdivision of reserves into individual lots and enforced avoidance of mechanized horticulture.[17] These policies were stiffened in 1894–95 by regulations requiring Indian children's attendance at school and by further legislation that attacked the cultural practices of both Pacific and Plains Indians by banning "giveaway" dances or ceremonies that involved self-mutilation. Finally, in 1898 a new government withdrew the 1885 offer of the right to vote from eastern Canadian Indians.[18]

These Canadian policies were based on both British and American practices. In the British North American colonies in the middle decades of the nineteenth century, Christian missionaries and civil government had combined to promote both sedentary agriculture and education.[19] After the formation of the Dominion of Canada and the acquisition of the western plains by the new state in the 1860s, there was an increasing tendency among Canadian policymakers to look to the United States as well as to British colonial policy for suggestions as to what should be done. The destructive American Indian wars of this period were quickly rejected as a model for Canada's integration of its new lands. Recognizing that they had "to make up their mind to one of three policies—viz: to help the Indians to farm and raise stock, to feed them or to fight them," Canadian officials chose the first option for reasons of both economy and humanitarianism.[20] However, if the American military was not an appropriate model for Canadian policymakers, other aspects of American Indian policy were. Programs such as allotting lands in individual plots in an effort to break up the reserves and atomize members of bands were largely copied from the Dawes scheme.[21] And planning in the late 1870s for a new educational policy led the federal government to send a commissioner south to investigate what its neighbours were doing by way of residential schooling.[22] Finally, the thorough cooperation of state and Christian church for the prosecution of these policies was both reminiscent of contemporary American approaches and consistent with British and British North American practice.

More important than the sources of these policies of assimilation was their effect. On the whole, scholars have treated policy intent and effect as similar, if not identical, largely because they concentrated on government fiat and documents. That assimilation and coercion were the objectives of the group of policies there is no doubt. But what were the effects? Did the measures work?

Consider, for example, the notorious pass system that was set up in 1885. First, it is important to note that little about the operation, as opposed to the purpose, of the system is known. We do not know for certain how long even a pretence of enforcing it was maintained.[23] And even while it was official policy in the prairie provinces, its effects appear to have been very mixed. For one thing, it does not seem to have been implemented uniformly in the 1880s. Hayter Reed, commissioner after Dewdney's elevation to the Cabinet, referred in correspondence with his deputy minister in 1891 to "regulations already issued, but so far disregarded" when talking about Natives' mobility.[24] Agents and farm instructors, who lacked the power and the time to make Indians obey the pass regulations, attempted to hand the duty off to the NWMP.[25] But the leaders of the NWMP had serious doubts about the system and their role in enforcing it. They believed that the requirement that Indians get a pass before leaving their reserve would not stand up in court. They also feared that if Indians tested it through litigation, their victory would discredit the whole system of law enforcement. In the aftermath of the North-West Rebellion of 1885, the horsemen were most concerned not to undermine the law and themselves by attempting to enforce invalid regulations. They dragged their feet in response to agents' requests for help and, at times, refused outright to enforce the restrictions of the pass system.[26]

Indian Affairs bureaucrats themselves recognized the weakness of their position and were reluctant to provoke a confrontation over passes. The department's instruction to its agents was "to issue Passes to Indians who they know will leave in any case, and so preserve an appearance at least of control, and a knowledge of their movements."[27] It is also clear that many agents were less than thorough in their administration of the pass system. One disgruntled Mountie complained to Commissioner Reed that one of the latter's agents had given a pass to "the biggest whore master in the band," a man who "had six squaws with him."[28] In sum, what little is known about the actual operation of the pass system suggests not so much that it was effective in controlling the Indians as that it was very often a nullity.

There is similar reason to doubt the efficacy of the 1884 and 1895 measures against the potlatch and "giveaway dances." An 1884 amendment to the *Indian Act* threatened anyone "who engages or assists in celebrating the Indian festival known as the 'Potlach' or in the Indian dance known as the 'Tamanawas'" with a jail term.[29] The federal government soon found that enforcement was a problem. The provincial government of British Columbia, which quarrelled constantly with Ottawa over Indian Affairs matters, was uncooperative about enforcement of the bans on "Potlach" and "Tamanawas." And the federal government had few officials on the Northwest Coast through whom to compel compliance with the law.[30] Agents were helpless in most parts of the Coast. At the first announcement by a group of Indians that they intended to defy the ban, the local agent avoided a confrontation by acquiescing, giving as his justification the explanation that the scheduled potlatch was not really a potlatch at all.[31] The young anthropologist Franz Boas noted several years after the prohibition was legislated that "there is nobody to prevent the Indians doing whatsoever they like." He observed that an Indian who had been appointed a constable and supplied with a uniform and flag by the agent for the purpose of preventing unlawful feasts and dances responded strangely. Since his appointment, "he dances in his uniform with the flag."[32] Little wonder that the Kitwanga Indians in 1890 dismissed the anti-potlatch law, saying it "was as weak as a baby."[33]

When the occasional agent did try to enforce the ban, matters only got worse from the government's point of view. The agent at Alert Bay made the first arrest under the 1885 prohibition in 1889. Acting in his capacity as justice of the peace, he tried the accused and extracted a plea of guilty. Apparently in error, the agent or his superiors then committed the prisoner to trial in Victoria, the provincial capital. When friends of the accused Indian applied for a writ of habeas corpus, the justice immediately granted it on the grounds that the prisoner had already been tried and convicted. However, the jurist went on in a remarkable series of *obiter dicta* to lay waste the 1884 ban. He explained that the statute lacked a proper definition of "Potlach" and that the other prohibited celebration, the "Tamanawas," was "unknown." Finally, he speculated that the accused, who knew no English, probably had not understood the earlier proceedings. The judge thought, on reflection, that "there would be some difficulty in convicting at all under the Statute."[34] As the distraught agent who had begun the series of events lamented, the incident rendered the 1885 ban "a dead letter."[35]

Although a more precisely framed amendment in 1895 got around the legal difficulty, it did not lead to immediate or effective enforcement of the prohibition on potlatching. There is abundant evidence that the supposedly forbidden celebrations went on long after 1895, though no potlatcher served a prison sentence till 1920.[36] (In 1909 a Methodist missionary on Vancouver Island plaintively asked his superiors, "Can nothing be done with the Dominion Government to compel the enforcement of the Act which prohibits Potlatching?" When the principal of a residential school wanted to find out when a particular "great potlatch" was to take place, he wrote the agent to inquire — hardly evidence that potlatching was something kept hidden from the agent.)[37] A crackdown stopped the festivities for a few years, but by 1927 those Indians who still wanted to potlatch were back at it. It took the Great Depression and culture change to suppress it temporarily in the 1940s.[38] Later it would revive during a general rediscovery of traditional rites, crafts, and arts in the 1960s and later.

What is too often neglected in discussions of the anti-potlatch campaign is the role of Indian converts. The initial ban in the 1880s was a direct response to pressure from such Indians, as well as from missionaries and Indian Affairs officers.[39] Observers on the Northwest Coast noted that the minority who supported prohibition of the potlatch were Christian converts and young people who faced many decades of paying out before they could look forward to reaping their reward from the redistributive ritual.[40] Certainly there is evidence of pressure to enforce the ban from Christian converts in British Columbia. In 1888 government commissioners appointed to establish reserve limits in the Nass River area heard complaints from Indian opponents of the potlatch. They explained that they had protested to Indian Affairs officials about the practice. The officials had counselled them to "go to the heathen, and advise them to stop Potlaches, but the heathen laughed at us." They were pleased when they heard reports that the government was going to do something about the practice.[41] In 1893 the council at Kitimaat, British Columbia, ruled that "any person in the village of Kitimaat who gives a *feast* or *Potlach* will be *punished* by a fine of One hundred and forty Dollars," while the "Chiefs of Kispiox" in 1914 asked for government and church help in stopping the potlatch and "old fashioned feasts or feasts in memory of the dead."[42] Converts apparently absorbed some of the outlook of the non-Indian majority. When a spokesperson for a Kwakiutl band in 1919 wanted to "give you a few reasons" why the potlatch ban "should not only stand but . . . also be strongly enforced," she began with a patriotic argument. Here, "people as a whole will never own Allegiance to the Government or King as long as they are allowed to practice their Allegiance to the Potlatch system, for to them this excludes every other Government." "No Potlatchers," she claimed, "volunteered to serve overseas."[43] As late as 1936, a public meeting at Alert Bay was the scene of a vigorous debate between Christians and traditionalists over the potlatch and marriage customs.[44]

If not all coastal Indians opposed banning the old ways, neither did all the purveyors of new beliefs favour coercion and suppression. Some missionaries thought coercion unnecessary and undesirable. "Leave the thing alone as far as the old people are concerned; educate along definite lines with the young people and ten years at the outside should see the end of the problem," one argued.[45] Even the Department of Indian Affairs on occasion promoted supposedly forbidden traditions. Ironically and unintentionally it encouraged the officially illegal dances by conveying to the World Exposition of 1893 in Chicago a troupe of Kwakiutl who staged the illicit dances.[46]

Because a pattern similar to the anti-potlatch campaign is found in the forbidden dances of Plains Indians, we should be skeptical about the effectiveness of nineteenth-century prohibitions of these celebrations. Pressure for action against festivals such as the Sun Dance of the Blackfoot Confederacy or the Thirst Dance of the Cree and Saulteaux sometimes came from Christian converts among the Indians themselves. Church of England canon H.W. Gibbon Stocken claimed to be "writing . . . at the earnest & repeated request of several of our leading Blackfoot Christians" when he asked the deputy minister for energetic action against the "native dances, now so largely indulged in."[47] An Indian agent among the Dakota reported that "there were two cliques or factions on this reserve, a *pagan* faction and a *Christian* faction. . . . The Christians wanted to legislate the pagans into the church, first by stopping their recreations and forcing along certain lines and the pagans worked in opposition to the Christians."[48] Indian missionaries on the plains, like converts on the northwest coast, often advocated suppression. The Dakota John Thunder, a Presbyterian missionary in Manitoba, argued for action against giveaway dances, which he thought retarded his people's moral growth as well as their economic advance.[49] On the other hand, there were rare non-Native missionaries who defended Indians' right to carry out these dances. The Methodist John McDougall explained to a western audience that the Sun Dance, like the Thirst Dance, was "a religious festival." "And," he added, "I altogether fail to see why in these days of our much boasted religious liberty anyone should interfere with a few Indians in the exercise of their faith."[50] But Plains Indians did not have much need of the efforts of someone like McDougall. They proved quite adept at resisting, evading, and defying efforts to stamp out the Sun and Thirst Dances.

Local Indian leaders, some of them the products of residential schools, resorted to formal protests to the government, sometimes with the aid of Euro-Canadian lawyers whom they retained, against the agents' efforts to interfere with their dancing.[51] Residential school graduates like Dan Kennedy were also known to employ their influence against the missionary on the reserve, using the argument that removal of the cleric would put an end to interference with traditional dancing.[52] Indians also became adept at exploiting differing attitudes among white authority figures to defeat those who wanted to interfere with them. Numerous Plains bands cited the missionary McDougall in justification of their attempts to carry on with their dances.[53] In the 1890s the Blood Indians decided to ignore their agent, who threatened prosecution as they arranged a medicine pipe dance, at least partly because they knew that other agents on the Piegan and Blackfoot reserves were permitting dancing there.[54] As the years went by, it became increasingly common for Indians to use lawyers to combat Indian Affairs and for local officials to lament their charges' greater familiarity with the law and with legal weapons.[55]

Evasion was often employed by Plains Indians intent on maintaining their religious traditions in the dance. One of the easiest ways was simply to wait until the Indian agent was not expecting a dance and then hold it, as Samson's band did in the Hobbema Agency in Alberta.[56] Another method was to seek informal approval for a modified version of the forbidden dance and then to carry out the traditional ceremony. Under the 1895 amendment to the unenforceable 1884 provision on dancing, only celebrations that involved giving away property or self-mutilation were outlawed. It was a fairly simple matter for Indians to persuade the agent that they were going to hold a "modified" dance and then to indulge in the forbidden practices.[57] In theory, agents were supposed to use the pass system to prevent Indians from travelling to other reserves to participate in dances. Near the west-central Saskatchewan town of Battleford, the Cree of the Poundmaker and Little Pine bands hit on an ingenious stratagem. Since their reserves were contiguous, they built their dance hall on the boundary line so that no official could interfere.[58] And when the Poundmaker band had to replace their community hall, they made sure they built the new one well away from the prying eyes of agent and missionary. The dancing continued largely undetected.[59] Farther south, on the File Hills Farm Colony, which was designed as a Christian home for ex-pupils of the residential schools, Indian dancing also went on clandestinely.[60]

Finally, there were cases where the Indians simply defied both law and agent. An agent in northwestern Ontario who tried to dissuade a shaman from carrying on traditional feasts and dances found that the conjurer "only laughed" at him.[61] On Red Crow's Blood reserve, after several years in which the Indians had carried on modified versions of their dances, the agent in 1900 decided to prevent dancing altogether. He withheld the beef tongues that were essential to the ritual, but Indians who were employed by the Mounted Police as scouts quietly obtained tongues from police larders. Next, the agent threatened to withhold rations from any Indian who participated in the Sun Dance. When Red Crow threatened to slaughter every head in his considerable herd to feed his people, the agent capitulated, "and never again was the ceremony denied to them."[62]

Plains Indians proved so adept at resisting, evading, or defying the bans on ceremonial dancing that agents and missionaries were compelled to proceed cautiously and often to try to redirect, rather than stamp out, these activities.[63] Agents who knew that they could not suppress dancing tried to create interest in alternatives such as sports days and other summertime festivals.[64] And the Anglican missionary on the Blackfoot reserve, following in a long Christian tradition, tried to defeat "pagan" ritual by adopting and modifying it. He "made a bid for the transformation of" the tobacco dance by creating "a ceremony very much like the old one of 'Beating the bounds' which has almost gone out of the Church." He formed his converts into a procession headed by a "cross of green wood" and marched them "round the camp stopping at the East, South, west [*sic*] and North. Then we formed up in the centre of the camp and planted the cross."[65] Moreover, agents and missionaries found that efforts to discourage dancing ran up against Euro-Canadian populations that wanted the dances included in their summer fairs in order to sell tickets.[66] Efforts to stamp out dancing, like those aimed at the potlatch, proved largely ineffective because of both Euro-Canadian and Indian obstacles.

Even residential schools, which are often described as the most coercive of church–state instruments of assimilation, were no more representative of effective policy than prohibitions on Indians' traditional cultural and religious practices. These schools — a joint enterprise of the federal government and major Christian denominations, a blend of British and American practice[67] — sought to remove the children from "the demoralizing and degrading influences of the tepees" and surround them with an environment of bourgeois Christian values.[68] Here the children would be made over into acquisitive, individualistic Christians who would, ultimately, make the pass system and prohibitions on dancing or potlatching unnecessary. Residential schools were intended to lead to "not only the emancipation of the subjects thereof from the condition of ignorance and superstitious blindness in which they are, and their parents before them were sunk, but converting them into useful members of society and contributors to, instead of merely consumers of, the wealth of the country."[69]

Residential schools are usually treated as though they were effective in capturing Indian children and in crushing their will and identity. It is sometimes said that "it was the rule at that time that all treaty Indian children had to attend an Indian boarding school."[70] The authority of the Department of Indian Affairs was supposedly used to ensure that children were not only sent to these schools but also kept there. At the schools Native children were strictly forbidden to practise any Native traditional observances or to speak their own languages. Residential schooling, in short, typified the totalitarian and assimilative spirit of Canada's Indian policy in the later Victorian era and the first half of the twentieth century.[71] It amounted, as a candid missionary put it, to an effort to "educate & colonize a people against their will."[72] But is this view accurate for anything more than the intentions of those who ran the residential schools? There is no doubt that the institutions were intended to convert children to Christianity and to equip them with the skills to become self-supporting in or alongside Euro-Canadian society. But what was the result?

First, the conventional view of residential schools fails to note that the system never reached more than a minority of young Indians and Inuit. There were never more than 80 residential schools supported by the government in the entire country. Atlantic Canada did not have any until Shubenacadie was established in Nova Scotia late in the 1920s, and even thereafter most Indians in the region went to day schools or to no school at all. Much the same holds true for Quebec, where vast areas were without residential schools. In southern Ontario there were only four, and in northern Ontario many large districts lacked boarding or industrial schools. The prairie provinces, British Columbia, and the far north were the most thoroughly covered regions, not because a far-sighted federal government systematically provided full coverage, but because denominational competition among Oblates, Anglicans, Methodists, and Presbyterians fostered the rapid multiplication of missions and schools in these areas. In some cases, Indian bands petitioned unsuccessfully for the erection of a residential school for their children.[73] Many children, even in the west and the north, completely escaped the residential schools. As one Stoney put it, "I didn't even go to one hour of school because I am an Indian."[74] Thousands of young Indians similarly escaped the clutches of residential schools.[75]

Even where residential schools existed, they proved singularly difficult to keep filled with students. Missionaries in the early years were forever complaining that agents either failed to help them recruit students or even worked actively against their efforts to procure them.[76] Even after the department acquiesced in 1894 to the missionaries' cries for compulsory attendance legislation, the problem persisted. In 1908 a Methodist principal complained that "there is no law to compel an Indian to educate his child," and in 1906 the Anglican Mission Board in the Diocese of Calgary contended that Indians "send their children to school when it suits them to do so, and they keep them at home for the same reason. The only exception to this rule is, the children are allowed to please themselves whether they go or not."[77] Even allowing for clerical hyperbole, it is clear that attendance remained a problem. If this were not so, why did principals make numerous, expensive "recruiting" trips in search of students, and why did men of the cloth resort to bribing parents to get their children?[78] Once students were obtained for the schools, how could they be kept? To take only one example, Joseph Shaw was admitted to Coqualeetza Institute on 19 August 1901; he disappeared on 1 November 1903 and remained a truant till formally discharged on 3 September 1905. (He did, however, pay a visit to the school in 1906.)[79] In understaffed schools it was a lot of trouble to chase students. Agents were often uncooperative or distracted, and the police hated the chore of retrieving unhappy runaways. When the constabulary presented the bill for their services as truant officers, the evangelists became unhappy too.[80]

It is not clear that the schools, assuming they procured and held on to the students, were very successful in eradicating traditional Indian religion and cultural practices. Certainly most schools tried to force the children to conform to Euro-Canadian standards, especially in the highly visible areas of dress and grooming. It was standard procedure to scrub the students and shear the boys' hair on arrival, a practice that caused consternation in children for whom cropped hair was a sign of mourning.[81] Even after the student got over the shock of thinking that one of his loved ones had died after he left home for the school, he did not necessarily get over the rough subjection to Euro-Canadian grooming. One fellow who became a Christian worker among the Indians "never forgave the woman who cut his hair while he slept and if he followed the inclination of his own heart he would throw off all the education & go back where he would never see a white man."[82]

One area of school life that requires reconsideration is the matter of suppressing Indian languages, usually held to have universally occurred. This seems to be an exaggeration. It would have been strange for evangelists who had laboured hard to master Indian tongues —and there were many of them among the Oblates and Church Missionary Society workers in the nineteenth century in particular—not to use their linguistic skills with the children, if only outside classrooms. In many schools, at least one church service on Sunday was conducted in the Indian language, especially in those mission districts where the school chapel was also the mission's church.[83] A Methodist missionary one Sunday "held service in the schoolhouse, and had the privilege of preaching the glorious Gospel to an earnest people in the 'language wherein they were born,' which, after all, is the only way to reach the hearts and thoughts of any congregation."[84] At Lejac school "they used to pray one week in Indian and one week in . . . English."[85] In British Columbia schools the rule was, "we must not talk Indian (except when allowed)," while at some other institutions, such as the Blood Anglican school, students were able to use their own language after seven o'clock in the evening.[86] Some schoolmasters were criticized for their indifference about language.[87] But was it realistic to think all use of Indian languages could be stopped? Many schools were like Morley, Alberta, where the teachers knew that "the children were not supposed to speak Stoney, but they really couldn't stop them."[88]

There were even rare examples in which the schools turned out to be the place where students actually became acquainted with their culture. The daughter of parents who lived on the File Hills ex-pupils' colony in Saskatchewan recalled that "we didn't speak Cree in our house as our parents spoke two different languages." However, when she "went to school we learned some Cree from our schoolmates but we often found that what we learned wasn't in good taste when we repeated it to our parents." She picked up a little Cree at school, though she never mastered the language.[89] But this daughter of suppos-edly converted parents also recalled that she "learned a lot about our Indian culture and some of the language, even though we weren't allowed to speak it at school." On occasion "we went down to the lake to dance a pow-wow. We used a pail for a drum and Gracie Squatepew was always our main singer."[90]

The language question could even provoke the parents to intervene in the operation of the schools, on at least one occasion in a surprising fashion. The Anglican missionary on the Blood reserve in southern Alberta was visited by a delegation of parents whose leader told him, "I came to see you about teaching my children. They tell me that you are teach-ing them syllabics in the Blackfoot language." This man said that the parents thought that this "is wrong. We want you to teach the children the English tongue, and not syllabics. They have their own language and we have ours. Teach them English and we will be sat-isfied." The missionary acceded to the delegation's desire: "I dropped teaching them syl-labics right away. There the matter ended so far as the Bloods were concerned."[91] There were other pressures generated from among Indians in favour of the use of English. When a school population contained children from two or more language groups, English was promoted as a medium of communication that all could use.[92] Residential schools were not always the oppressive institutions they were thought to be in the area of the suppres-sion of language, and Indian parents sometimes had a significant role in the operation of these schools.

The traditional view that residential schools rigidly separated children from their parents, their homes, and their bands also should be qualified. Again, there can be no doubt that this was hoped for by government officials, who wanted the schools to socialize children away from the ways of their parents. But it frequently was not the result. Many of the boarding institutions were located close to, or even on, the reserves from which their inmates came. The Mohawk Institute in Ontario was close to the Six Nations Reserve. Crowstand in east-central Saskatchewan was on the reserve of the Cote band. In southern Alberta, in partic-ular, the boarding schools run by the Catholics and Anglicans were located on the reserves of the Sarcee, Piegan, Blackfoot, and Blood Indians. Proximity enhanced parental control of the children's movement. When "Running Rabbit made bother about his girl remaining in the Home" on the Blackfoot reserve, it was easier for the principal to "let her go" than to resist.[93] Similarly, at Alberni on Vancouver Island, the Presbyterian school was only a hop, skip, and jump from the "rancherie," or Indian encampment.[94] While the more elaborate "industrial schools" that the Department of Indian Affairs began to establish in 1883 were deliberately located far from reserves, there were always many fewer of these than of boarding schools. Most children in residential schools were not kept away from home influ-ences for long periods. Many of them visited home at least every weekend, whatever the theory of residential schooling might have held.

For other reasons also there was a great deal more interaction between the home and the child than Indian Affairs would have liked. The children at these schools were notori-ous for running away whenever they became homesick or angry at the discipline or fed up with the poor food and hard work. The diary of an Anglican missionary in southern Alberta in 1917 contains at least seventeen instances, many of them multiple escapes, of children running away during the year.[95] The high incidence of runaways was part of the reason that schools such as the Anglican Blood institution provided a weekend "monthly holiday," as well as generous Christmas, Easter, and summer breaks.[96] On Kuper Island in British Columbia, the principal pleaded with the Department of Indian Affairs for longer summer holidays, arguing that the parents would take the children salmon fishing regardless of what he or Ottawa said.[97] The flow of personnel went the other way, too. The pass system notwithstanding, Indian parents often made their way from their reserves to the school to visit their children. The principal at Lebret school in southern Saskatchewan constructed an "Indian porch" to house the unauthorized visitors, defending his action to annoyed Indian Affairs officials by saying that it was necessary to prevent the parents from removing their children from the school.[98] All such instances suggest that residential schools did not always keep parents and children apart, and that parents sometimes had some influence over the schools' operation.

Indeed, there were cases where it would be more accurate to say that the Indians were the guiding force behind the foundation of the residential school. Northwest Coast Indians demanded that the Presbyterians provide residence facilities at Alberni in which their children could stay while they were absent to work in the sealery or in the canneries.[99] Those at Kitimaat petitioned the Methodists in 1896 for a home and offered to help with the construction and maintenance of such a facility.[100] In the north, a missionary reported that "at Whitefish Lake some forty miles from Lesser Slave Lake . . . [a] Boarding School has just been erected because the Indians would not send their children to the School at the latter place."[101]

As revealing as these examples are, they pale beside the exceptional case of the Cecilia Jeffrey school in the Lake of the Woods district, near the Ontario–Manitoba boundary. In 1898 the Indians at Shoal Lake petitioned the Presbyterians in Winnipeg for a school, and two years later they were reported to be "not only willing but *anxious* for a boarding school." The local missionary warned that they "will lose confidence in us and have no further use for us" if the church did not move to meet their wishes.[102] In January 1902 an extraordinary meeting of missionaries and Ojibwa chiefs negotiated an agreement that should be quoted at length for the benefit of people who believe that residential schools were imposed on Indians and run totally by the clergy:

> 1st. That while children are young and at school they shall not be baptized without the consent of their parents but if when they reach years of understanding they wish to be baptized, relations and friends shall be invited to the baptism. . . .
>
> 4th. That a number of children shall be sent now and if they are well treated more shall be sent. . . .
>
> 6th. Little children (under 8 years) shall not be given heavy work and larger children shall attend school, at least half of each school day. . . .
>
> 8th. That parents shall be allowed to take their children to their religious festivals, but only one child at a time and the child shall not remain away over night. . . .
>
> 11th. That in case of a child running away, police aid shall not be used, but the parents shall bring back the child.[103]

As this contract made clear, the Ojibwa not only were responsible for the establishment of the school but largely dictated the terms on which it was to operate. Proselytization was forbidden, children could leave to observe traditional religious rites, and the police were not to be used to force runaways back.

Over the following few years, the Cecilia Jeffrey school continued as it had begun — under Indian control. When the Indians became annoyed because the staff made the children kneel for prayers and the matron meted out harsh discipline, they warned the local missionary that they wanted the original agreement obeyed. If "we keep our promises they will send more children but if they think we are trying to use the school as a trap to get them in and make Christians of them against their parents [*sic*] wishes, they will perhaps withdraw even the scholars we have now." The church's capitulation on the kneeling issue quieted the parents somewhat, but the protests against the matron continued.[104] The Cecilia Jeffrey case illustrated that Indians sometimes had considerable control over their children's schooling.

Parental efforts to control if and when their children entered a residential school, and how they were treated when they did, took many forms. It was quite common to keep the children out of school at the end of the summer where seasonal employment made doing so economically attractive. As the principal of the Coqualeetza Industrial Institute in the Fraser Valley noted, "It is difficult to persuade the Indians to allow their children to come to school till after the fishing season closes."[105] Once the children were in school, parents could sometimes influence the curriculum, as when they preferred instruction in English to syllabics. And they persisted in visiting the schools to check up on their children over the objections of Indian Affairs officers.

Parents also had ways of responding to school officials whom they found obnoxious. The mildest form of resistance to an unpopular staff member was to petition the Department of Indian Affairs to remove the person.[106] The fact that "the Indians from the Prince Albert District have sent in a remonstrance against the conduct of the school" was a contributing factor in the dismissal of the principal at the Battleford Industrial School.[107] Indian resistance to objectionable schooling could also be violent. At the Jesuit school on Manitoulin Island in Ontario, a boy who took exception to the unfamiliar corporal punishment grabbed his teacher by the throat and roughed him up.[108] On the Blackfoot reserve, an Indian Affairs employee was killed and the missionary-principal and his family forced to flee for their lives in 1895.[109] Another spectacular altercation between a parent and a staff member took place at the File Hills school in 1949.[110] At the Kamloops school a music instructor who had mistreated students was forced to leave, and when he returned as a teaching brother the next year, an Indian leader went to the school and successfully demanded his removal.[111] Incidents of violent resistance are not numerous in the documentary evidence (usually interviews and private correspondence between missionaries and their church's headquarters staff), but it is important to remember that missionaries were not likely to advertise their unpopularity.

More often, passive resistance was just as effective as petitions and violence were. Because of the way that the schools were financed, a certain amount of parental cooperation was essential to their survival. Since funding was based on the number of students physically present, a decline in attendance hurt the missionary organization's finances. The churches involved always found revenues from per capita grants less than their needs; therefore, a drop in enrolment-related grant revenue made a tight budgetary situation critical.[112] Denominational competition compounded the financial problem and increased the need to conciliate Indian parents. When schools of different churches occupied the same district, competition for students arose. For example, parents who were unhappy with the Methodist Coqualeetza Institute in British Columbia simply transferred their children to the Roman Catholic school on Kuper Island.[113] One consequence of competition among the schools was bribery of parents to send their children to a particular school. Another was that parents, who almost always preferred to send their children to the school closest to their home, acquired bargaining power with school officials. Institutions with reputations for mistreating or overworking children or for housing them in unhealthy conditions found recruiting more difficult. In the opinion of a bishop, the death of seven students in the Anglican school at Hay River was likely "to make recruiting impossible" in their home community the following season.[114] Parental complaints about the inadequate number of teachers and staff in their schools led the Anglicans to appeal to their members for helpers: "We are literally fighting for our continued existence as a Missionary Church in this area due to the highly organized campaign of the roman [*sic*] Church against us."[115]

The price of failing to meet such challenges by placating the parents was the demise of the schools. The Calgary Industrial School closed because it was too distant from the reserves and because the presence of other schools on the reserves gave parents alternatives.[116] As a Presbyterian missionary said of the situation in Saskatchewan, it was "almost impossible to get some of the Indians to send their children to a school on the reserve, and, of course, it is even more difficult to secure recruits for schools at a distance." Distance and a poor reputation for health conditions worked against the Presbyterians' Regina Industrial School. In western Manitoba, the "Regina School is looked upon with disfavor. It is a long way off and of the seven who were sent there only one is alive to-day, all the rest dying of tuberculosis. The parents are really afraid to let their children go."[117] In spite of herculean efforts by the Presbyterians, enrolments at Regina could not be increased sufficiently, and it closed. A similar pattern developed at an Oblate school in Alberta after the First World War. Because "Indians seem to be more and more opposed to the idea of sending their children to Dunbow," the local bishop came "to the conclusion that it is better to end the struggle and send back to their respective reserves, or to the Lebret School, the few pupils actually in the Dunbow school."[118]

Some parents fought long-term campaigns to force a school to operate as they wished. Between 1922 and 1934 the Roman Catholic Indians at Fort Frances in northwestern Ontario demanded a meeting with the provincial of the Oblates, asked for an investigation of the school's administration, withheld their children, and began to urge the Department of Indian Affairs to establish a day school. Finally, they got the principal replaced.[119] Such manifestations of organized parental resistance occurred frequently in the schools of all denominations.[120]

By means ranging from evasion to resistance, passive or violent, parents made their children's educational experiences tolerable. In unusual cases, such as the Cecilia Jeffrey school, they could set the terms on which the school was run and enforce them by withholding their children.[121] More common were the tactics of protesting, petitioning, sending the children to a competing institution, or boycotting the schools altogether. This is not to argue that the events at Cecilia Jeffrey, Lestock, Fort Frances, or Regina were typical of all residential schools. Rather, it is to suggest that the conventional picture of residential schools as totalitarian institutions run arbitrarily by all-powerful missionaries and bureaucrats is also not universally accurate.

Nor should this analysis be read as arguing that interference and coercion did not occur. Dances were interrupted and dancers prosecuted.[122] Moreover, even an ineffective pass system or an unenforceable prohibition on cultural practices could have a deterrent effect, dissuading Natives from exercising their right to move or to celebrate religious traditions.[123] This examination of Indian policy is merely an attempt to test the conventional picture of aggressive government and missionaries controlling and reshaping Indian peoples.

Students of Canadian Indian policy need to adjust the conventional picture of residential schools as well as the generally accepted view of policies aimed at political control and cultural assimilation. The pass system and the prohibitions on dancing and the potlatch were seldom or ineffectively applied. Indian peoples after the middle of the nineteenth century may have subsided into numerical inferiority to Euro-Canadian society, they may have passed into a period of economic and military irrelevance to Canadians at large, and they may have been subjected to policies intended to transform them into Christian, bourgeois citizens. However, just as their ancestors often shaped the conduct of the fur trade and served as equal partners in military alliances in the seventeenth and eighteenth centuries, Indian peoples of the late nineteenth and early twentieth centuries were actors who pursued their interests and struggled to preserve their identity. They resisted, evaded, and defied efforts to control their decision making, limit their traditional rites, and deprive them of their children. If we distinguish between the intentions of churches and government, on the one hand, and the effects of the policies, on the other, we might find that Canada's Native peoples persist throughout time as active, if lamentably ignored, actors in the country's history.

NOTES

1. William Shakespeare, *Henry IV, Part I* (Folger ed.), III, i, 57–59.
2. Ibid.
3. For examples of the conventional view of the Indian as passive victim, see Bruce Sealey and Verna J. Kirkness, eds., *Indians without Tipis: A Resource Book by Indians and Metis* (Agincourt, ON, 1973), 33; James S. Frideres, *Native People in Canada: Contemporary Conflicts*, 2d ed. (Scarborough, ON, 1983), 33; Donald Purich, *Our Land: Native Rights in Canada* (Toronto, 1986), 121–22.
4. Stanley B. Ryerson, *The Founding of Canada: Beginnings to 1815*, new ed. (Toronto, 1960), 86–88, 262.
5. Jack M. Sosin, "The Use of Indians in the War of the American Revolution: A Re-Assessment of Responsibility," *Canadian Historical Review* 46 (June 1965). See also George F.G. Stanley, "The Indians in the War of 1812," *Canadian Historical Review* 31 (June 1950).
6. Arthur J. Ray, *Indians in the Fur Trade: Their Role as Hunters, Trappers, and Middlemen in the Lands Southwest of Hudson Bay, 1660–1870* (Toronto, 1974); Robin A. Fisher, *Contact and Conflict: Indian–European Relations in British Columbia, 1774–1890* (Vancouver, 1976), chaps. 1–3. See also Kenneth Coates, "Furs along the Yukon: Hudson's Bay Company– Native Trade in the Yukon River Basin, 1830–1893," *BC Studies* 55 (Autumn 1982), 56–68.
7. Sylvia Van Kirk, *"Many Tender Ties": Women in Fur-Trade Society, 1670–1870* (Winnipeg, [1980]); Jennifer S.H. Brown, *Strangers in Blood: Fur Trade Company Families in Indian Country* (Vancouver, 1980). For examples of other fur-trade scholars who agree with Van Kirk and Brown, see Daniel Francis and Toby Morantz, *Partners in Furs: A History of the Fur Trade in Eastern James Bay, 1600–1870* (Kingston, ON, and Montreal, 1983), 53, 90; Paul C. Thistle, *Indian–European Trade Relations in the Lower Saskatchewan River Region to 1840* (Winnipeg, 1986), 9, 16; J. Colin Yerbury, *The Subarctic Indians and the Fur Trade, 1680–1860* (Vancouver, 1986), 71–72, 91.
8. Bruce G. Trigger, *Natives and Newcomers: Canada's "Heroic Age" Reconsidered* (Kingston, ON, and Montreal, 1985), chap. 5, esp. 260–71. See also James Axtell, *The Invasion Within: The Contest of Cultures in Colonial North America* (New York, 1985), esp. chap. 5; William J. Eccles, *The Canadian Frontier, 1534–1760* (New York, 1969), 44–45; Cornelius J. Jaenen, *Friend and Foe: Aspects of French–Amerindian Cultural Contact in the Sixteenth and Seventeenth Centuries* (New York, 1976), 67–68.
9. Among the most important American influences have been the following: Barbara Graymont, *The Iroquois in the American Revolution* (Syracuse, NY, 1972); Francis Jennings, *The Invasion of America: Indians, Colonialism, and the Cant of Conquest* (Chapel Hill, NC, 1975); Jennings, "The Indians' Revolution," in *The American Revolution: Explorations in the History of American Radicalism*, ed. Alfred F. Young (De Kalb, IL, 1976), 319–48, esp. 322; Jennings, *The Ambiguous Iroquois Empire: The Covenant Chain Confederation of Indian Tribes with English Colonies from Its Beginnings to*

the Lancaster Treaty of 1744 (New York, 1984); Jennings, "Iroquois Alliances in American History," in *The History and Culture of Iroquois Diplomacy: An Interdisciplinary Guide to the Treaties of the Six Nations and Their League*, ed. Francis Jennings (Syracuse, NY, 1985), 37–65; Jennings, *Empire of Fortune: Crowns, Colonies, and Tribes in the Seven Years' War* (New York, 1988).

10. Leslie F.S. Upton, *Micmacs and Colonists: Indian–White Relations in the Maritimes, 1713–1867* (Vancouver, 1979), 26; Sydney F. Wise, "The American Revolution and Indian History," in *Character and Circumstance: Essays in Honour of Donald Grant Creighton*, ed. J.S. Moir (Toronto, 1970), 200.

11. Jaenen, *Friend and Foe*, 192; Jennings, "The Indians' Revolution," 336–41.

12. E. Palmer Patterson, *The Canadian Indian: A History since 1500* (Don Mills, ON, 1970), 84. Again there are strong historiographical parallels in the U.S.: R. David Edwards, *Tecumseh and the Quest for Indian Leadership* (Boston, 1984), esp. chaps. 7–8; Edwards, *The Shawnee Prophet* (Lincoln, NE, 1983), chap. 6 and epilogue; Colin G. Calloway, *Crown and Calumet: British–Indian Relations, 1783–1815* (Norman, OK, 1987), esp. 22 and chap. 8.

13. Hope McLean, "The Hidden Agenda: Methodist Attitudes to the Ojibwa and the Development of Indian Schooling in Upper Canada, 1821–1860" (M.A. thesis, University of Toronto, 1978); John S. Milloy, "The Early Indian Acts: Developmental Strategy and Constitutional Change," in *As Long as the Sun Shines and Water Flows: A Reader in Canadian Native Studies*, ed. Ian A.L. Getty and Anthony S. Lussier (Vancouver, 1983), 56–64; Donald B. Smith, *Sacred Feathers: The Reverend Peter Jones (Kahkewaquonaby) and the Mississauga Indians* (Lincoln, NE, 1987), esp. chaps. 8–12.

14. Important exceptions to this generalization include E. Brian Titley, *A Narrow Vision: Duncan Campbell Scott and the Administration of Indian Affairs in Canada* (Vancouver, 1986); Jacqueline J. Gresko, "Qu'Appelle Industrial School: White 'Rites' for the Indians of the Old North-West" (M.A. thesis, Carleton University, 1970); Hana Samek, *The Blackfoot Confederacy, 1880–1920: A Comparative Study of Canadian and U.S. Indian Policy* (Albuquerque, NM, 1987), esp. chap. 6.

15. Milloy, "Early Indian Acts," 59–61.

16. John L. Tobias, "The Subjugation of the Plains Cree, 1879–1885," *Canadian Historical Review* 44 (December 1983), 534.

17. Sarah A. Carter, "The Genesis and Anatomy of Government Policy and Indian Reserve Agriculture on Four Agencies in Treaty Four, 1874–1897" (Ph.D. dissertation, University of Manitoba, 1987), esp. chap. 5. I am grateful to Dr. Carter for allowing me to use her dissertation.

18. Useful summaries of these policies are Titley, *A Narrow Vision*, esp. chaps. 3, 5, 6, and 8; James R. Miller, *Skyscrapers Hide the Heavens: A History of Indian–White Relations in Canada* (Toronto, 1989), chaps. 11–12.

19. See note 13.

20. David Laird (lieutenant-governor and Indian commissioner of the Northwest Territories) to Minister of the Interior, 17 April 1878, National Archives of Canada (hereafter cited as NAC), Ottawa, Records of the Department of Indian Affairs (hereafter cited as RG 10), Western Canada Files (hereafter cited as Black Series), Vol. 3664, File 9825; Miller, *Skyscrapers*, 161–62.

21. Sarah A. Carter, "Two Acres and a Cow: 'Peasant' Farming for the Indians of the Northwest, 1889–97," *Canadian Historical Review* 70 (March 1989), 38–39.

22. Nicholas F. Davin, "Report on Industrial Schools for Indians and Half-Breeds," 14 March 1879, in NAC, Sir John Macdonald Papers, Vol. 91, 35428.

23. Sarah A. Carter, "Controlling Indian Movement: The Pass System," *NeWest Review* (May 1985), 8–9; Carter, "Genesis and Anatomy," 302–12. See also Purich, *Our Land*, 129–32; F. Laurie Barron, "The Indian Pass System in the Canadian West, 1882–1935," *Prairie Forum* 13 (Spring 1988), 25–42; and B. Bennett, "Study of Passes for Indians to Leave Their Reserves" (mimeo, Treaties and Historical Research Centre, Department of Indian Affairs and Northern Development, Ottawa, 1974), esp. 7–8. I am grateful to John Leslie of the Treaties and Historical Research office for providing me with a copy of the Bennett paper.

24. RG 10, Black Series, Vol. 3675, File 11,411-4, H. Reed to L. Vankoughnet, 20 May 1891.

25. See, for example, Glenbow-Alberta Institute Archives (hereafter cited as Glenbow Archives), S.B. Lucas Papers (M 699), File 9, diary, July 1896.

26. Roderick C. Macleod, *The North-West Mounted Police and Law Enforcement, 1873–1905* (Toronto, 1976), 146; Barron, "Pass System," 35–37; Carter, "Genesis and Anatomy," 307–8. For evidence that the department knew it had no legal basis for attempting to restrict Indians to their reserves, see J.D. McLean (assistant deputy and secretary) to H.E. Calkin, J.P., 22 August 1913, RG 10, Black Series, Vol. 4076, quoted in Bennett, "Study of Passes," 6.

27. NAC, MG 29 E106, Hayter Reed Papers, Vol. 14, H. Reed to Hon. T. Mayne Daly, 25 March 1893. It is significant, too, that the printed "General Instructions to Indian Agents in Canada," issued in 1913 and reissued in 1933, nowhere mentions passes. Glenbow Archives, Blackfoot Indian Agency Papers (M 1785), Box 3, File 15.

28. Reed Papers, Vol. 17, Lawrence W. Herchmer to Hayter Reed, 7 February 1891.

29. Statutes of Canada 1884 (47 Victoria), c. 27, Sec. 3. My discussion has been greatly influenced by an unpublished manuscript on the potlatch by Douglas Cole and Ira Chaikin, which Professor Cole kindly allowed me to read.

30. Cole and Chaikin, potlatch manuscript, 51–52, 55.

31. Ibid., 46–48.

32. Franz Boas, "The Indians of British Columbia," *Popular Science Monthly* 32 (1888), 636; Boas, "The Houses of the Kwakiutl Indians, British Columbia," *Proceedings of the United States National Museum* 11 (1888), 206; quoted in Cole and Chaikin, potlatch manuscript, 50–51.

33. Quoted ibid., 59.

34. Ibid., 52–54.

35. Quoted ibid., 54.

36. Royal British Columbia Museum (hereafter cited as RBCM), Anthropological Collections Section, Nos. 250, 834, 2777 (examples only); Provincial Archives of British Columbia (hereafter cited as PABC), Sound and Moving Images Division (hereafter cited as SMID), Tape 965-1, Mrs. Edward Joyce interview; Cole and Chaikin, potlatch manuscript, 122, 168.

37. United Church of Canada Archives (hereafter cited as UCA), Toronto, Alexander Sutherland Papers, Box 5, File 97, C.M. Tate to A. Sutherland, 5 November 1909; PABC, Add. MS. 1267, Kuper Island Industrial School Papers (hereafter cited as Add. MS. 1267), Vol. 3, 266, G. Donckele to W.R. Robertson, 23 May 1903.

38. Cole and Chaikin, potlatch manuscript, chaps. 6–9.

39. NAC, Correspondence of the Secretary of State, Vol. 54, No. 4355, order in council, 7 July 1883 (gazetted 4 August 1883).

40. Cole and Chaikin, potlatch manuscript, 43.

41. Glenbow Archives, Edgar Dewdney Papers (M 320), report of meeting of reserve commissioners, Agent Todd, and Indians on board the steamer *Douglass*, 8 September 1888, p. 1394.

42. PABC, H/D/R13/R13.11, G.H. Raley Collection, notice of Kitimaat Council, 10 November 1893; ibid., H/D/R13.9 (III), Kispiox chiefs' statement of 13 February 1914.

43. Mrs. S. Cook to Deputy Superintendent General of Indian Affairs (D.C. Scott), 1 February 1919, quoted in Daisy (My-yah-nelth) Sewid Smith, *Prosecution or Persecution* (N.p., 1979), 20. Supporters of non-Christian tradition could use Christians' arguments effectively, too. One wrote to the Indian Affairs office in Ottawa to inform them that he intended to hold a potlatch. " 'I don't think there are [sic] no wrong in it, if you only look up the 10 chapter of St. Mark, ver. 17–21, in the Bible, you will see that I am just going to do the right.' " Dan Quatell to J.D. McLean, 14 July 1922; quoted ibid., 72.

44. Archives of the Anglican Diocese of British Columbia, Victoria, Text 198, File 50, report of "Special Meeting Held at Alert Bay, June 1, 1936."

45. Church of England General Synod Archives (hereafter cited as GSA), Toronto, Papers of the Missionary Society in Canada (hereafter cited as Series 75-103), Records of the Indian and Eskimo Residential School Commission (hereafter cited as IERSC 2-15), Box 23, 2433, minutes of commission, 14 May 1940, quoting Rev. F. Earl Anfield.

46. Douglas Cole, *Captured Heritage: The Scramble for Northwest Coast Artifacts* (Vancouver, 1985), 129–30.

47. RG 10, Black Series, Vol. 3825, File 60,511-1, H.W. Gibbon Stocken to Deputy Superintendent General of Indian Affairs, 6 January 1900.

48. Ibid., Vol. 3826, File 60,511-3, J. Hollies to David Laird, 15 February 1912.
49. John Thunder to David Laird, 16 July 1907, RG 10, Black Series, Vol. 3569, File 95-2, cited in Peter Douglas Elias, *The Dakota of the Canadian Northwest: Lessons for Survival* (Winnipeg, 1988), 117.
50. Clipping from *Winnipeg Free Press News Bulletin*, 27 November 1907, RG 10, Black Series, Vol. 3825, File 60,511-2. See also ibid., J. McDougall to F. Pedley, 24 May 1906. On another occasion McDougall went so far as to charge that campaigns against dancing were a violation of treaty undertakings that he, like other missionaries, had helped to convince Plains Indians to accept in the 1870s. Letter to the Editor, *Christian Guardian* (Methodist), 8 July 1914, pp. 19–20.
51. RG 10, Black Series, Vol. 3825, File 60,511-2, Levi Thomson to F. Oliver, 19 March 1906, enclosing petition dated 9 March 1906; ibid., File 60,511-1, 208133, extract from report of the Muskowpetung's agency (copy), December 1900; ibid., File 60,511-2, E.H. Yeomans to Secretary, Indian Affairs, 11 July 1907. Indians had to rely upon non-Native lawyers because no status Indian in Canada, so far as is known, was admitted to the bar until the 1950s. Information supplied by Don Purich, director, Native Law Centre, University of Saskatchewan. Concerning Indian petitions re. dancing see ibid., Chief Thunderchild and C. Fineday to Commissioner of Indian Affairs (copy), 28 June 1907; ibid., 339198, T. Cory to Secretary, Indian Affairs, 13 March 1909; ibid., File 60,511-3, notes of representations made by delegation of Indians from the west, A. Gaddie, interpreter, Ottawa, 24 January 1911.
52. UCA, Presbyterian Church of Canada, Foreign Mission Committee, Western Section, Indian Work in Manitoba and the Northwest (hereafter cited as PC, FMC, WS, IWMNW), Box 4, File 59, E. MacKenzie to R.P. McKay, 7 March 1904.
53. RG 10, Black Series, Vol. 3825, File 60,511-2, G.D. Mann to Indian commissioner David Laird, 3 July 1906, and marginal note by Laird; ibid., J.P.G. Day to Commissioner, 4 July 1908.
54. Hugh Dempsey, *Red Crow, Warrior Chief* (Saskatoon, Sask., 1980), 208, 212. Similarly, re. a Saulteaux band, see RG 10, Black Series, Vol. 3825, File 60,511-2, J.P.G. Day to Indian Commissioner, 4 July 1908.
55. RG 10, Black Series, Vol. 3825, File 60,511-2, E.H. Yeomans to Secretary, Indian Affairs (copy), 11 July 1907; ibid., File 60,511-3, R. Logan to Secretary, Indian Affairs, 8 February 1912; ibid., G.H. Gooderham to Secretary, Indian Affairs, 19 July 1912.
56. Ibid., File 60,511-2, G.G. Mann to Commissioner, 22 July 1907.
57. Ibid., File 60,511-2, W.S. Grant to Secretary, Indian Affairs, 2 July 1906; ibid., H. Nichol to Secretary, Indian Affairs, 16 February 1911; ibid., File 60,511-3, Father J. Hugonard to H. Nichol, 16 January 1913. In another instance, the Indians intended to keep their promise to conduct only a "modified" dance, but a latecomer to the festivities carried out self-mutilation rites, to the consternation of the attending Euro-Canadian officials. See "The Last Rain Dance," told by Standing Through the Earth, in *Earth Elder Stories*, by Alexander Wolfe (Saskatoon, SK, 1988), 61–64.
58. Interview with Gordon Tootoosis, Poundmaker reserve, 7 May 1987. It is extraordinary to note in the official records how infrequent are the references to the actual or even contemplated use of the pass system to prevent movement between reserves to attend festivals. See RG 10, Vols. 3825–26, File 60,511, passim.
59. Stan Cuthand, "The Native Peoples of the Prairie Provinces in the 1920s and 1930s," in *One Century Later: Western Canadian Reserve Indians since Treaty 7*, ed. Ian A.L. Getty and Donald B. Smith (Vancouver, 1978), 40.
60. Eleanor Brass, "The File Hills Colony," *Saskatchewan History* 6 (Spring 1953), 67. See also her *I Walk in Two Worlds* (Calgary, 1987), 13, 25.
61. RG 10, Black Series, Vol. 3825, File 60,511-2, R.S. McKenzie to Secretary, Indian Affairs, 24 October 1903.
62. Dempsey, *Red Crow*, 213–24. In the Blood chronicles, 1900 was recorded as the year when "Yellow Buffalo Stone Woman put up the Sun Dance by force."
63. For an example of the Department of Indian Affairs' pusillanimity concerning taking action against dancing, see Glenbow Archives, Blood Agency Papers (M 1788), Box 4, File 23, series of letters by A. de B. Owen, Joseph Howe, J.A. McGibbon, and D. Laird, 26 June to 16 July 1902.

64. RG 10, Black Series, Vols. 3285–86, passim. See also Titley, *Narrow Vision*, 170; Dempsey, *Red Crow*, 210.

65. Glenbow Archives, Tims Papers (M 1234), Box 1, File 7, J.W. House to J.W. Tims, 19 June 1939. The missionary was under no illusions about how successful this syncretic ploy was likely to be. "At the end of the ceremony I am quite sure they went back to their old customs," he noted. Blending Christian and Indian practices could backfire on the missionaries. One who tried to dissuade some Blackfoot from holding the dance they made "in preparation for tobacco sowing" on a Sunday received the reply that it was all right to hold the dance on a day of prayer because "they were going to pray." Ibid. (M 1233), Box 2, File 22, J.W. Tims Diary, 15 May 1887.

66. See, for example, University of Calgary Archives, Anglican Diocese of Calgary Papers, Box 8, General Files 64, F.W. Godsal to Canon Hogbin, 13 July 1910, and unidentified newspaper clipping entitled "The Indians and the Exhibition." In 1895 the *Calgary Herald* (10 July) had claimed that the Cree chief Piapot held his dance every year under the nose of the Indian Affairs Department in Regina, charging 25 cents' admission to the white folk who drove out from the territorial capital to see the ceremonies. *Proceedings of the Church Missionary Society, 1895–1896* (London, 1896), 395, report from the Battleford area of Christian Indians backsliding into being "present at the heathen Sun Dance, the interest in which revived in a painful degree in the summer of 1895, encouraged, Mr. Inkster says, by the morbid curiosity of white men and women." Again, there are numerous more examples in RG 10, Black Series, Vols. 3825–26, File 60,511, passim.

67. The parallels between U.S. and Canadian practice are many. See, for example, Margaret Connell Szasz and Carmelita Ryan, "American Indian Education," in *Handbook of North American Indians*, Vol. 4, *History of Indian–White Relations*, ed. Wilcomb E. Washburn (Washington, DC, 1988), 288–95; Frederick E. Hoxie, *A Final Promise: The Campaign to Assimilate the Indians, 1880–1920* (Lincoln, NE, 1984), esp. chaps. 2, 8.

68. *Calgary Herald*, 10 February 1892.

69. Report of the Department of Indian Affairs for 1891, Canada, *Sessional Papers*, No. 14 (1892), x.

70. Brass, *Two Worlds*, 4.

71. See, for example, Purich, *Our Land*, 132–34.

72. UCA, Presbyterian Church of Canada, Foreign Mission Board, Missions to the Indians of Manitoba and the North West (hereafter cited as PC, FMB, MIMNW), Box 3, File 55, H. McKay to R.P. McKay, 25 October 1903.

73. RG 10, School Files, Vol. 6038, File 157-1-1, petition of Massett, B.C., Council to Agent, 20 January 1914; A. Sutherland Papers, Box 5, File 95, C.M. Tate to A. Sutherland, 28 November 1905.

74. Nakoda Institute Archives, Oral History Program, Box 1, Norman Abraham interview. Compare the comment of a chief who said that he was glad that they had "a Reserve that the white man cannot encroach upon; but there are three things that I do not wish to see within the boundaries of our Reserve. I don't want Christianity, I don't want a school, and I don't want the law. I don't want Christianity, because we wish to follow the ways of our fathers. We are Indians, and we intend to remain Indians. I don't want schools, because I want the children to be happy and free from restraint. I don't want the law because we are good people. We never do anything wrong, and we have no use for the law." *Proceedings of the Church Missionary Society, 1898–1899* (London, 1899), 424.

75. Indeed, most Indian children for a long time escaped any kind of schooling. In 1888, when the official Indian population of Canada was 124 589, there were only 6127 enrolled in all types of schools for Indians in Canada. Report of the Department of Indian Affairs for 1888, Canada, *Sessional Papers*, No. 16 (1889), 308, 317. On the File Hills Agency in Saskatchewan in 1889, only one-third or one-quarter (depending on whether one believes the school inspector or the Indian commissioner) were in school. RG 10, Black Series, Vol. 3824, File 60,470, J.A. Macrae to Commissioner, 24 July 1889. For a close study of the inadequate coverage of British Columbia by residential schooling, see James Redford, "Attendance at Indian Residential Schools in British Columbia, 1890–1920," *BC Studies* 44 (Winter 1979–80), 41–56.

76. Tims Papers (M 1234), Box 1, File 12, J.W. Tims to Bishop of Calgary, 2 July 1895. That Tims might have had some ground for complaint is borne out by the register of Old Sun's school for 1894–1908, in which 22 of the 128 young people did not appear. Glenbow Archives, Calgary Indian Missions Papers (M 1356), Box 1, File 7, Old Sun's Boarding School history of pupils for September 1894. For a time in the early 1890s the department itself did not try "to enforce too rigidly attendance at schools. Everything that is likely to irritate the Indians is to be avoided as much as possible." Hayter Reed Papers, Vol. 17, H. Reed to Mr. Wright, 31 January 1891. Reed was concerned about Indian unrest in the United States at the time.

77. A. Sutherland Papers, Box 7, File 33, Arthur Barner to A. Sutherland, 19 September 1908; GSA, GS 75-103, IERSC 2-15, Box 18, File Nov./05–Oct./06, John Hines to "Hon. and Dear Sir," 29 November 1906.

78. Brass, *Two Worlds*, 6. See also UCA, PC, FMB, MIMNW, Box 1, File 21, H. McKay to R.P. McKay, 9 January 1901; ibid., File 32, quarterly report for Round Lake . . . 31 December 1901. "We have to pay $15 to $20 for any child that we get into the school," admitted the Presbyterian missionary, although in his official quarterly report he mentioned only that his Roman Catholic opponents on the reserve "pay $15 or $20 for a pupil & many of the Indians will give their children to those who pay most for them." A. Sutherland Papers, Box 7, File 127, John McDougall to A. Sutherland, 2 March 1906; ibid., Box 6, File 118, A. Sutherland to A.R. Aldridge, 3 March 1908.

79. United Church of Canada, Conference of British Columbia Archives, Vancouver, Coqualeetza Institute, Register of Admissions and Discharges, No. 157. See also ibid., No. 141, Simon Green: admitted September 1900, did not return from holiday July 1908, discharged officially 30 June 1909, "visited the school at Christmas 1911."

80. GSA, GS 75-103, IERSC 2-15, Box 20, IERSC Minutes, 382, minutes of 23 October 1924. At Kuper Island, when five ran off, two priests were out in a boat looking for them till four in the morning. The man who, "with a warrant," returned the children and the canoes they had stolen got a "$25 fee for returning the 5 pupils." Add. MS. 1267, Vol. 31, daily journal for 1924, entries for 2, 4, and 5 January 1924. See also Macleod, *NWMP and Law Enforcement*, 147–48.

81. Mike Mountain Horse, *My People the Bloods*, ed. H. Dempsey (Calgary, 1979), 15–16; Dan Kennedy (Ochankugahe), *Recollections of an Assiniboine Chief*, ed. James R. Stevens (Toronto, 1972), 54.

82. UCA, PC, FMB, MIMNW, Box 3, File 54, H. McKay to R.P. McKay, 25 October 1903.

83. Tims Papers (M 1234), Box 2, File 21, seven pages of prayers in syllabics on the letterhead of Calgary Industrial School. Concerning preaching in the Blackfoot language, see ibid., File 15, annual report to Church Missionary Society (draft), 31 January 1901. See also the banner in an Indian language in Christ Church Anglican Church, Alert Bay, B.C., RBCM, Anthropology Collections Section, No. 2305. Concerning Wikwemikong, see Regis College Archives, "Synopsis of the History of Wikwemikong" (typescript), entries for 1854 and 1860; ibid., Paquin, "Modern Jesuit Indian Missions," and ibid., Ontario Indian Missions Papers, file "Correspondence, Spanish, 1926–1936," C. Belanger to Father Walsh, 19 February 1936.

84. John McDougall, *Christian Guardian*, 27 January 1891, 51.

85. PABC, SMID, Tape 3533-3, Sister Patricia, S.C.J., interview. At the church on the Stoney reserve the church service was translated into Stoney. "Prayers are offered in Stoney by some of the men and in English by the Ministers." Telfer Collection, [J. Telfer], "The Stoney Indians" (typescript, n.d.).

86. PABC, H/D/R13/R13.7, Raley Collection, file of papers on Coqualeetza Industrial Institute and other schools, "Rules," A.E. Green, inspector of Indian Schools, 28 October 1906. At the Cariboo school, "we talk Shuswap when we're alone." PABC, SMID, Tape 3532-2, Celestine and David Johnson interview. A student who attended Sechelt in 1915–16 said that, while they were encouraged to speak English, "I wouldn't say [we were] punished" for speaking their own language. PABC, SMID, Tape 960-2, Clarence Joe interview. See also, re. Williams Lake, ibid., Tape 3533-1 (transcript), Sister Patricia, S.C.J., interview. Glenbow Archives, Nurse Jane Megarry Memoirs (M 4096), third (beige) book, 191.

87. Archives Deschatelets, L. 531 .M27C, Codex historicus 1907–1920 for Lestock school, 15, instructions of provincial (J.P. Magnan, O.M.I.), 27 March 1909. Ibid., L 535 .M27L 149, Brother Leach to [Provincial?], [1923], reporting that the principal at Lestock "prefered [sic] the children to speak in their own language." Concerning the willingness of school authorities to allow an Indian language to be used when outsiders were not around, see PABC, SMID, Tape 361-1, Joe C. Clemine interview.

88. Telfer Collection, notes of a conversation with Miss Jean Telfer, 16 May 1979.

89. Brass, *Two Worlds*, 13, 64.

90. Ibid., 25. This lady's interest in Cree traditions was stimulated sufficiently that she collected and published a volume of legends and stories. Eleanor Brass, *Medicine Boy and Other Cree Tales* (Calgary, 1978). The Kuper Island Conduct Book lists many instances of infractions that involved "Indian dances," "talking Indian," and "Forbidden Games." Add. MS. 1267, Vol. 38, conduct book, 1891–95.

91. Glenbow Archives, S.H. Middleton Papers (M 839), Box 2, File 7, S.H. Middleton to R. Forsberg (copy), 7 November 1960. It is also worth noting that at a day school that a Dakota band established themselves, instruction was "in both Dakota and English." Elias, *Dakota of the Canadian Northwest*, 73. And an Indian woman told a reporter that her father, himself highly educated, favoured her learning English early in life. Undated clipping from *Weekend Magazine*, UCA, E.E. Joblin Papers, Box 2, File 7.

92. PABC, SMID, Tape 3858-1, Mary England interview. The same informant (ibid.) said that parents took great pride in children who mastered English. John Jeffrey, a former student at the Chapleau, Ontario, school and an Anglican clergyman, also noted that the widely differing backgrounds of the students at Chapleau made the use of English appropriate. Audio tape, December 1989, in possession of author.

93. Tims Papers (M 1234), Box 1, File 2, diary, 8 September 1891. For a similar case in British Columbia see Add. MS. 1267, Vol. 3, 733–34, G. Donckele to W.R. Robertson, 23 July 1905.

94. UCA, PC, FMB, Missions to the Indians in British Columbia (MIBC), Box 1, File 10, B.I. Johnston to R.P. McKay, 20 February 1896.

95. Tims Papers (M 1233), Box 2, File 22, journal for 1917. In an interview, a former teacher (name withheld by request) who had served briefly at the Mohawk Institute in 1934 told me that he could not recall a day when no children ran away from the school. A request from Jesuit missionaries that the department withhold annuities from parents who failed to return schoolchildren after holidays was firmly turned down. See Regis College Archives, Wikwemikong Papers, "Various Correspondence 1909–1912," J.D. McLean to Rev. C. Belanger, S.J., 25 July 1910.

96. Middleton Papers, Box 2, File 4, school diary for 1945, entries for 2 March, 1 April, 4 May, 23 June, 1 September, and 25 December. Significantly, before adopting the policy, the principal held a "Meeting of Parents at the Reserve re. Holidays" on 9 December. At Sechelt "the children got home sometimes for weekends" to the nearby reserve. PABC, SMID, Tape 3533-3, Sister Patricia, S.C.J., interview. There were also Saturday afternoon visits home at Kitimaat (PABC, Microfilm 1360, Margaret Butcher Journal, 17 April 1917), and, at Kuper Island, once a month "four deserving students of the senior class" received a weekend leave. Archives of the Sisters of St. Ann, RG 2, Series 39, Kuper Island school papers, file "Chronicles 1944–1954," entry for 29 October 1948.

97. Add. MS. 1267, Vol. 1, 433, G. Donckele to W.H. Lomas, 3 July 1894. The same principal confessed that he was at a loss to know how to stop parents from withdrawing their children. Ibid., 583, G. Donckele to A.W. Vowell, 30 April 1895.

98. Reed Papers, Vol. 18, J. Hugonard to E. Dewdney, 5 May 1891. There was a cabin to house parents overnight at the Cariboo school. See PABC, SMID, Tape 3530-1, Lily Squinahan interview. See also Add. MS. 1267, Vol. 31, daily journal for 1924, entry of 27 May. For comments concerning the "Indian parlor" at Williams Lake, see ibid., Tape 3533-1 (transcript), Sister Patricia, S.C.J., interview. And "the parents of the pupils come from all parts of the Blood reserve to attend the Church service and to visit with their children after the service." Megarry Memoirs, third (beige) book, 238. See also Telfer Collection, "The Stoney Indians."

99. UCA, PC, FMB, MIBC, Box 1, File 1, J.A. McDonald to H. Cassells, 12 January 1892; A. Sutherland Papers, Box 6, File 108, J. Edward Rendle to A. Sutherland, 8 October 1909.

100. H/D/R13/R13.11, Raley Collection, file on Kitimaat, Chief Jessea and 41 Indians to "Dear Brothern [sic]," 23 March 1896. The "Sechelt nation" built and at least partially maintained their school. PABC, SMID, Tape 960-1, Clarence Joe interview.

101. GSA, GS 75-103, IERSC 2-15, Box 18, File Nov./05–Oct./06, W.D. Reeves to S.H. Blake, 15 October 1906.

102. UCA, PC, FMB, MIMNW, Box 1, File 14, T. Hart to W. Moore, 12 September 1898; ibid., File 20, A.G. McKitrick to R.P. McKay, 14 December 1900.

103. Ibid., Box 2, File 33, J.C. Gandier to R.P. McKay, 14 January 1902, and "agreement" of same date.

104. Ibid., Box 2, File 35, A.G. McKitrick to R.P. McKay, 7 March 1902; ibid., File 38, same to same, 2 June 1902; ibid., File 41, Indian petition dated 22 September 1902; ibid., Box 3, File 47, A.G. McKitrick to R.P. McKay, 11 March 1903; ibid., File 55, J.O. McGregor to R.P. McKay, 27 November 1903.

105. A. Sutherland Papers, Box 5, File 89, R. Cairns to A. Sutherland, 18 August 1906.

106. Ibid., Box 3, File 74, A.W. Vowell to Rev. Dr. Campbell, 13 May 1905, enclosing petition from Indians against a principal. See also Archives Deschatelets, L 281 .M274 31, list of complaints against the administration of Lebret school; GSA, GS 75-103, IERSC 2-15, Box 22, 1847, minutes of 17 July 1934, re. Lac la Ronge school.

107. Reed Papers, Vol. 14, H. Reed to Archdeacon J.A. Mackay (copy), 9 November 1894.

108. Regis College Archives, J. Paquin, S.J., "Modern Jesuit Indian Missions in Ontario."

109. *Alberta Tribune*, 12 October 1895; Toronto Globe, 4 July 1895; *Canadian Churchman*, 11 July 1895; Tims Papers (M 1234), Box 1, File 12, J.W. Tims to Bishop of Calgary (draft), 2 July 1895; Reed Papers, Vol. 14, H. Reed to T. Mayne Daly (copy), 25 June 1895. Ian A.L. Getty, "The Failure of the Native Church Policy of the CMS in the North-West," in *Religion and Society in the Prairie West*, ed. Richard Allen (Regina, SK, 1974), 30, points out that the Blackfoot had petitioned the government in 1892 to remove the missionary, whom they regarded as "too bossy." The crisis in 1895 led to his transfer to another reserve.

110. UCA, United Church of Canada, Woman's Missionary Society, Home Missions, Indian Work, File 9, L. McLean to J.P.B. Ostrander, 17 February 1949. Concerning a girl's attack on a nun at Lebret, see Archives Deschatelets, L 286 .M27L 226, J.P. Magnan (O.M.I.) to G. Leonard, 18 June 1930.

111. Celia Haig-Brown, *Resistance and Renewal: Surviving the Indian Residential School* (Vancouver, 1988), 102. At the same school a father who was angered when his daughter's head was shaved seized the priest responsible "and shook him up." Ibid., 103.

112. At the Anglican Sarcee school, for example, the government grant in 1915 was $100 per pupil, when operating costs per child were just over $160. During the remainder of the First World War, the discrepancy grew larger. Glenbow Archives, Calgary Indian Missions Papers (M 1356), Box 1, File 5, J.W. Tims's annual reports to the Church Missionary Society for the years ended March 1915 and 31 December 1919. In 1949 the Anglicans claimed that the financial shortfall in the schools' operation that was attributable to underenrolment was $51,200. GSA, GS 75-103, IERSC 2-15, Box 29, Indian School Administration circulars, Circular 14/49, 29 April 1949.

113. Add. MS. 1267, Vol. 2, 561, G. Donckele to A.W. Vowell, 7 July 1900.

114. GSA, Bishop Lucas Papers (M 75-1), Box 3, file "Correspondence A–M 1925," Bishop Lucas to T.B.R. Westgate, 20 June 1925. See also Add. MS. 1267, Vol. 1, 602, G. Donckele to A.W. Vowell, 1 June 1895; Microfilm 1360, Margaret Butcher Journal, 17 April 1917.

115. GSA, GS 75-103, IERSC 2-15, ISA, Box 25, reports of superintendents with minutes of Executive Committee 1927–1952, File 1947, circular of Alderwood to Clergy, 14 January 1947.

116. Tims Papers (M 1233), Box 1, File 6, "Impressions Regarding Missionary Effort . . . Jan. 6, 1909." For examples of opposition to sending students to far distant schools in British Columbia and Alberta, see A. Sutherland Papers, Box 6, File 108, J. Edward Rendle to A. Sutherland, 8 October 1909; ibid., Box 7, File 132, "Report of the Red Deer Industrial Institute for . . . 1907," by Thompson Ferrier.

117. UCA, PC, FMB, MIMNW, Box 4, File 66, F.F. Dodds to R.P. McKay, October 1904; ibid., File 72, F.O. Gilbart to R.P. McKay, 28 April 1905. On the difficulties at the Regina school see also Titley, *Narrow Vision*, 80–82.

118. Archives Deschatelets, HR 6676 .C73R 8, Mgr. Grandin to Mgr. J.T. McNally, Bishop of Calgary, 22 February 1922. For background see RG 10, School Files, Vol. 6039, File 160-1, part 1, D.C. Scott to W.J. Dilworth, 9 March 1915; ibid., Dilworth to Scott, 20 March 1915.

119. Archives Deschatelets, L 912 .M27C 195 and 199; ibid., L 913 .M27L 63, 102, 104, and 108. Unfortunately, the next generation of parents had to take up the struggle against another unpopular priest 30 years later. See ibid., 291, group letter of Indians to Father Provincial, May 1962.

120. See, for example, ibid., L 531 .M27C 2, Codex historicus for school at Lestock, Sask., 16 December 1934.

121. There are indications that some parents imposed limits on the duration of their children's stays at Kuper Island school when it was starting up. See Add. MS. 1267, Vol. 40, 43, quarterly return for quarter ended 30 September 1896, remarks. See also ibid., 47, quarterly return for quarter ended 31 December 1896.

122. RG 10, Black Series, Vol. 3825, File 60,511-1, extract from Sgt. Saul Martin's report from Fort Qu'Appelle, SK, 28 June 1902; Toronto *Globe*, 27 May 1903.

123. "The Last Rain Dance," 64.

Topic Six

Urbanization in Canada

In the early twentieth century, cars provided a novel, convenient method of transportation, but they also posed new challenges. A 1908 photograph by John Boyd.

154

IN 1867, Canada was an overwhelmingly rural society, with more than 80 percent of the population living in small villages and hamlets or on farms. By 1921, more than 50 percent of the Canadian population was urban. Industrialization best explains the rapid shift from a rural to an urban society. Increased industrialization accelerated urbanization. In addition to factories and workers, industrial growth required expanded financial institutions, more extensive transportation facilities, and additional public services. As a result, most cities grew rapidly in size, and many also changed in nature and function from centres of trade and commerce to industrial centres. Paul-André Linteau, René Durocher, and Jean-Claude Robert discuss the impact of industrialization in Quebec—particularly on the province's two major cities, Montreal and Quebec City—in "Urbanization in Quebec," a chapter from their book, *Quebec: A History, 1867–1929*.

Along with urbanization came modernization. In particular, the introduction of the automobile had a dramatic effect. Stephen Davies argues that "the automobile revolutionized all aspects of Canadian life." In " 'Reckless Walking Must Be Discouraged': The Automobile Revolution and the Shaping of Modern Urban Canada to 1930," Davies points out both the obvious and the subtle ways in which the automobile revolutionized the Canadian urban landscape.

On urbanization in general, see J.M.S. Careless's *The Rise of Cities: Canada before 1914*, Canadian Historical Association, Historical Booklet no. 32 (Ottawa: CHA, 1978) and his collection of essays, *Frontier and Metropolis in Canada: Regions, Cities, and Identities in Canada before 1914* (Toronto: University of Toronto Press, 1989). Students should also consult Richard Preston, "The Evolution of Urban Canada: The Post-1867 Period," in *Readings in Canadian Geography*, 3rd ed., ed. R.M. Irving (Toronto: Holt, Rinehart and Winston, 1978), pp. 19–46, and the collection of articles in *The Canadian City: Essays in Urban and Social History*, rev. ed., G.A. Stelter and A.F.J. Artibise (Ottawa: Carleton University Press, 1984 [Toronto: McClelland and Stewart, 1977]). The Canadian Museum of Civilization (formerly the National Museum of Man) has sponsored eight volumes in its series of illustrated histories of Canadian cities: J.M.S. Careless, *Toronto to 1918* (1984); James Lemon, *Toronto since 1918* (1985); Patricia Roy, *Vancouver* (1980); Max Foran, *Calgary* (1978); Alan Artibise, *Winnipeg* (1977); John Weaver, *Hamilton* (1982); John Taylor, *Ottawa* (1986); and J. William Brennan, *Regina* (1989). Bob Hesketh and Frances Swyripa have edited a collection of essays on Alberta's capital, *Edmonton: The Life of a City* (Edmonton: NeWest Press, 1995).

A detailed study of urbanization in the Maritimes is J.M.S. Careless's, "Aspects of Metropolitanism in Atlantic Canada," in *Regionalism in the Canadian Community, 1867–1967*, ed. M. Wade (Toronto: University of Toronto Press, 1969), pp. 117–29. On Nova Scotia, see also Del Muise, " 'The Great Transformation': Changing the Urban Face of Nova Scotia, 1871–1921," *Nova Scotia Historical Review* 11, 2 (1991): 1–42. On British Columbia and the Prairies, consult Paul Voisey, "The Urbanization of the Canadian Prairies, 1871–1916," *Histoire Sociale/Social History* 8 (May 1975): 77–101; A.F.J. Artibise, "The Urban West: The Evolution of Prairie Towns and Cities to 1930," *Prairie Forum* 4 (Fall 1979): 237–62; and A.F.J. Artibise, ed., *Town and City: Aspects of Western Canadian Urban Development* (Regina: Canadian Plains Research Centre, 1981).

Little has been written about the impact of urbanization on Canadian society. The most useful sources on the topic are papers published in the *Urban History Review/Revue d'histoire urbaine (UHR/RHU)*, and the major reference work in the field, A.F.J. Artibise and G. Stelter, *Canada's Urban Past: A Bibliography to 1980 and Guides to Canadian Urban Studies* (Vancouver: University of British Columbia Press, 1981).

Article Twelve

Urbanization in Quebec

Paul-André Linteau, René Durocher, and Jean-Claude Robert

Because industrialization brings workers together in factories, the growth of cities and changes in the living conditions of urban populations are among its effects. In examining these effects, however, urban historians should not confuse urbanization and industrialization. Urbanization refers to a social process in which people are grouped together in cities; in that sense it is a very old phenomenon, but one whose characteristics change over time and vary from one economic system to another. Industrialization does not create urbanization, but rather speeds up its pace and changes some of its characteristics.

General Characteristics

To describe and explain the growth of cities, geographers have developed the concept of urban function. An urban function is an economic activity that distinguishes a city, employs a significant portion of its population, and has a product that is intended for use outside the city. Until the middle of the nineteenth century, the function of Quebec's cities was essentially commercial. They were trading posts with a double role, covering both international trade, as the major staples—furs, lumber, and wheat—were brought there to be shipped out, and internal distribution, as they provided goods and services to a growing rural hinterland.

Quebec's dominant urban centres, Montreal and Quebec City, are also among its oldest. The importance of these two cities, their control of economic activity and political power, and their attraction for a significant part of the population have been evident from the seventeenth century to the present day. As the area of Quebec under cultivation expanded in the late eighteenth and early nineteenth centuries, a network of villages—points of communication between city and country—appeared, forming the skeleton of Quebec's future urban network. The dominant position of Montreal and Quebec City was not the only characteristic of the urban network that was already apparent in the commercial era; the geographer Louis Trotier has pointed out others as well. Urban centres grew up primarily along the banks of the St. Lawrence and its tributaries, and were most densely concentrated and most clearly organized into a hierarchy in the Montreal plain.

Source: From *Quebec: A History, 1867–1929* (Toronto: James Lorimer, 1983). Reprinted by permission of James Lorimer & Company Ltd., Publishers.

The 1850s and 1860s were a transition period in several respects. In those decades, the first effects of industrialization began to be felt, especially in Montreal. Montreal's growth took off, and it definitively replaced Quebec City as the nerve centre of Quebec's economic life. The population gap between the two cities widened steadily from then on. In Quebec as a whole, the organization of the urban network was changed radically by the coming of the railway. The Grand Trunk main line became a second spinal column (after the St. Lawrence) through which part of Quebec's urban system was linked together. Thanks to the railway, some villages—Saint-Hyacinthe, Sherbrooke, Lévis, Rivière-du-Loup—became intermediate centres of regional significance and experienced a period of rapid growth. As urban areas grew, it became necessary to establish political structures on the local level. Between 1840 and 1870, a series of acts set up the municipal government system as it exists today.

After 1870, the industrial function clearly became the driving force behind urban growth in Quebec. Factories began to dot Quebec's territory, draining a portion of the surplus rural population toward the cities. The commercial function did not disappear, but rather remained a significant economic base for most of Quebec's urban centres. Its effects, however, were overshadowed by those of the new industrial establishments, which were generally built in already existing towns and villages, giving them a new impetus. Very few new towns were established in this period as a direct result of industry, and there was no radical change in the existing urban network. Rather, industrial centres were superimposed on commercial ones, and urban development became even more concentrated in the Montreal plain and its neighbouring region, the Eastern Townships.

The Urban Population

As a result of industrialization, the concentration of Quebec's population in cities increased, as can be seen by looking at the percentage of the population living in urban areas in a succession of census years (Table 12.1). The census definition of an urban area is an incorporated municipality with a population of 1000 or more; in 1851, a little under 15 percent of Quebeckers lived in urban areas, while 50 years later the figure was more than a third. The growth of the urban population began to accelerate in the decade 1871–81.

The degree of urbanization in Quebec followed a similar pattern to that of Canada as a whole. Table 12.1 shows no evidence of a lag in the urbanization of Quebec in relation to that of Canada, and the percentage of Quebec's population living in urban areas was high-

Table 12.1 Percentage of the Population Living in Urban Areas, Quebec, Ontario, and Canada, 1851–1901

Year	Quebec	Ontario	Canada
1851	14.9	14.0	13.1
1861	16.6	18.5	15.8
1871	19.9	20.6	18.3
1881	23.8	27.1	23.3
1891	28.6	35.0	29.8
1901	36.1	40.3	34.9

Source: L.O. Stone, *Urban Development in Canada* (Ottawa: Dominion Bureau of Statistics, 1967), 29.

er than the Canadian percentage for every census year except 1891. There is a clearer gap between Quebec and its neighbouring province, Ontario. In the middle of the nineteenth century the two provinces showed a similar level of urbanization, but after 1871 Ontario clearly outpaced Quebec as a result of its more favourable economic circumstances.

Table 12.1 shows that Quebec underwent a significant change in the second half of the nineteenth century. But in giving us snapshots at a succession of fixed points in time, these figures can be misleading and do not always do justice to the complexity of the real world. It could be argued, for instance, that Quebec's population also underwent another process of urbanization. Throughout this period, the surplus population of the countryside flowed to the cities. Some of those who left rural Quebec remained in agriculture, in the American mid-west or western Canada, but cities were the destination for the largest part of Quebec's rural exodus. The weakness of Quebec's industrial structure relative to that of the United States made it impossible for Quebec cities to absorb all the surplus population. Those who were not absorbed within Quebec experienced urbanization outside Quebec, in the industrial towns of New England.

Migration was characteristic of North America as a whole in the second half of the nineteenth century, and it led to another phenomenon of continental significance. Much of the urban population of the time consisted of transients, either from overseas or from the rural hinterland, for whom the city was only a temporary place of residence. In a context of great geographical mobility, as people left, new arrivals came to take their place, so that the total number of people who lived in a city in a ten-year period was much larger than the population figure that showed up in a census. As major relay points in the continental communications network, Quebec City and Montreal saw part of their population periodically replaced in this way. The scope of the phenomenon has not been measured, but the geographer Raoul Blanchard examined the case of the Irish of Quebec City. For a few decades in the middle of the nineteenth century, they represented a significant proportion of the population of the city. Around 1871, with Quebec City in a period of economic stagnation, they left en masse, some for Montreal, some for other parts of North America.

Urbanization was brought about by these population movements as well as by industrialization. In the last few decades of the nineteenth century, the process was clearly under way in Quebec and could not be reversed. All regions of the province were affected by it, but its pace and scope differed from one region to another.

The Major Cities

MONTREAL

At the time of Confederation, Montreal was unquestionably the metropolis not only of Quebec but of Canada as a whole, and it maintained its dominant position throughout succeeding decades. During the period, it registered a consistently high rate of population increase, with the most rapid growth occurring between 1881 and 1891 (Table 12.2). In 1861, Montreal was a city of 90 000 people; adding the population of its still semi-rural suburbs gives a figure of almost exactly 100 000. At the end of the century Montreal proper, which now covered an expanded area, had a population of more than a quarter of a million, and adding the suburban municipalities brought the total to about 325 000, or half the urban population of Quebec.

As Raoul Blanchard pointed out, Montreal's rise was due to industry. A first period of industrial growth had occurred in the 1850s and 1860s, and was concentrated in the

Table 12.2 Population of Major Urban Centres in Quebec, 1861–1901

Municipality	1861	1871	1881	1891	1901
Montreal Region					
City of Montreal	90 323	107 225	140 247	216 650	267 730
Montreal and suburbs[1]	100 723	126 314	170 745	250 165	324 880
Saint-Jérôme	—	1 159	2 032	2 868	3 619
Joliette	—	3 047	3 268	3 347	4 220
Sorel	4 778	5 636	5 791	6 669	7 057
Saint-Hyacinthe	3 695	3 746	5 321	7 016	9 210
Saint-Jean	3 317	3 022	4 314	4 722	4 030
Valleyfield	—	1 800	3 906	5 551	11 055
Quebec City Region					
City of Quebec	42 052	59 699	62 446	63 090	68 840
Lévis	—	6 691	5 597	7 301	7 783
Lauzon	—	—	3 556	3 551	3 416
Eastern Townships					
Sherbrooke	5 899	4 432	7 227	10 110	11 765
Magog	—	—	—	2 100	3 516
Granby	—	876	1 040	1 710	3 773
Thetford Mines	—	—	—	—	3 256
Coaticook	—	1 160	2 682	3 086	2 880
Farnham	—	1 317	1 880	2 822	3 114
Others					
Hull	—	3 800	6 890	11 264	13 993
Trois-Rivières	6 058	7 570	8 670	8 334	9 981
Chicoutimi	—	1 393	1 935	2 277	3 826
Rivière-du-Loup	—	1 541	2 291	4 175	4 569

1 A suburb is defined here as a town or village on Montreal Island bordering Montreal.

Source: Censuses of Canada.

southwestern part of the city, especially along the Lachine Canal. Around 1867, Montreal's industrial structure was characterized by the presence of five major industries: sugar refining, flour milling, ironmaking, wood processing, and shoemaking. In the 1880s, a second wave of manufacturing investment rounded out this early structure. Additional enterprises were founded in the existing sectors, while new ones such as meat curing, textiles, clothing, railway rolling stock, and tobacco emerged. By the end of the nineteenth century Montreal had become an important industrial centre and accounted for half the value of Quebec's manufacturing production. Illustrations from the era show a landscape dominated by factory smoke in the southwestern and eastern parts of the city.

The advantages accruing to Montreal from its position at the centre of the transportation system were another factor in its growth. It benefited from the substantial investments in infrastructure made in the nineteenth century. The St. Lawrence River canals, the ship channel, and the city's new harbour facilities made Montreal the focal point of water transportation. It was also the base of operations for the two major railway systems, the Grand Trunk and the Canadian Pacific, which established their administrative offices and maintenance shops there, and the centre of a web of railway lines extending in many directions. Transportation was an essential factor in the marketing and distribution of the goods that were manufactured in the city. Because Montreal was so well endowed with means of transportation, the concentration of industry in the city increased and its status as a metropolis for all of Canada was enhanced.

Toward the end of the nineteenth century, Montreal's capitalist class clearly dominated the economic activity of Canada as a whole. The most visible symbol of this domination was the ascendant Bank of Montreal–Canadian Pacific tandem. These two companies seemed to be almost ubiquitous in Canada. They were controlled by a close-knit group consisting of Donald Smith, George Stephen, R.B. Angus, William C. Van Horne, and others, whose interests extended to a large number of companies in the financial, commercial, industrial, and transportation sectors.

Spatial extension was another aspect of Montreal's growth, as the area within the city limits was systematically occupied and the city began to overflow into the suburbs. Montreal's city limits had been officially designated in the late eighteenth century; within them were large areas that were not yet urbanized. These areas gradually became inhabited as the nineteenth century progressed; at the time of Confederation this progress was not yet completed. Three wards near the city limits grew substantially in the decades after Confederation—Saint-Antoine in the west end and Saint-Jacques and Sainte-Marie in the east. By the late nineteenth century, occupation of the city's original territory was almost complete, and the overflow of population into the new suburban municipalities that had been established from the late 1860s on had begun. The most important of these new suburbs were the industrial towns of Saint-Gabriel, Sainte-Cunégonde, and Saint-Henri on the banks of the Lachine Canal to the west; Saint-Jean-Baptiste and Saint-Louis to the north; and Hochelaga and Maisonneuve to the east. Between 1871 and 1901, the population of these newly urbanized areas on Montreal Island grew from 11 000 to 130 000, or from 4 percent to 20 percent of the urban population of Quebec. At the end of the century, the largest part of the population increase in the metropolitan region was occurring in these new areas.

Montreal's municipal authorities wanted to adjust the region's political structures to these new demographic and economic realities, and tried to extend the city's territory by annexing suburban towns. The process began in 1883 with the annexation of Hochelaga; in the subsequent years, three more municipalities met the same fate. The phenomenon took on new dimensions in the early twentieth century, when the annexation of nineteen suburban municipalities in twelve years brought about a spectacular increase in Montreal's territorial size.

These small municipalities were typically the creation of a handful of real estate promoters who wanted to develop land that they owned. Toward this end, they would incorporate a small town, in which they would then control the town council. Through tax exemptions or cash subsidies, they attracted companies whose employees became residents of the new town. The promoters themselves also used tax exemptions to start development projects, which the municipality financed through borrowing, the burden of which was ultimately borne by small property owners and tenants. A few years or decades later, the municipality was heavily in debt, and annexation to Montreal seemed appealing as a solution to its financial problems.

The period was thus one of rapid growth and change for Montreal. One of the most significant changes was in the city's ethnic composition. Mid-nineteenth-century Montreal was culturally and politically a British city, with an English-speaking majority between 1831 and 1865; the English-speaking proportion of the population reached a peak of 57 percent in 1844. This British preponderance was reflected in the city council, where decisions were made in the interests of the English-speaking majority. The appearance of the city also changed, and in the 1840s British-style architecture started to replace the old French architecture that had characterized the city until then, although French architecture was never completely eliminated. The situation began to be reversed around 1865, when a French-speaking majority was re-established in the city as rural French Canadians came to work in the factories and immigration from the United Kingdom slowed down. Annexation of suburban municipalities with large French-speaking majorities intensified the process. However, it was almost twenty years before the change in ethnic composition was felt on city council, and much longer before it was reflected in the city's appearance and major cultural institutions.

By 1896, Montreal had become not only a financial and commercial metropolis but also a great industrial city. However, as a result of its rapid growth, a number of problems of adjustment affected living conditions in the city: crowding, deficient sanitary conditions, a high death rate.

QUEBEC CITY

The evolution of Quebec City during this period was very different from that of Montreal. Founded in 1608, Quebec City was the oldest city in the province, and had been the principal centre of New France and later of British North America. However, it had gradually lost its political preeminence to Ottawa, and at the time of Confederation it was entering a period of relative stagnation that lasted until the end of the century.

Quebec City's population grew by 42 percent between 1861 and 1871 (Table 12.2), but its growth in the three succeeding decades was very slow. A comparison between Quebec City and Montreal brings this slowdown into sharp focus. Throughout the first half of the nineteenth century, the population of the two cities was roughly the same. A clear gap began to appear in 1851, and by 1901, the Montreal urban area had a population five times as large as the Quebec City urban area. While 22 percent of Quebec's urban population lived in the Quebec City area in 1871, that figure had fallen to 10.5 percent in 1901.

The transition from the commercial era to the industrial era was difficult for Quebec City. The difficulties the city experienced in the late 1860s were identified by Raoul Blanchard. Most significant was the decline of the timber trade. From the early nineteenth century, Quebec City was the port from which the largest part of Canadian lumber exports to England were shipped. But the replacement of squared timber by sawn lumber and the redirection of trade from Britain to the United States changed the lines of communication, so that Quebec City was no longer the pivot of wood exports. Ships built in Quebec City had carried Canadian timber to England, where the ships were resold; the slowdown in timber shipments thus adversely affected the city's shipbuilding industry. This industry was also hurt by changes in maritime technology, as the wooden vessel was replaced by the iron- or steel-hulled ship. From the 1870s on, Quebec City's shipyards declined rapidly. The port of Quebec City also experienced difficulties as a result of competition from Montreal. The dredging of the ship channel made it possible for ocean-going vessels to sail upriver as far as Montreal, and Quebec City gradually lost its importance as a terminus for transatlantic lines. Thus, as Blanchard pointed out, all of Quebec City's maritime activity was in decline, with thousands of workers losing their jobs and having to seek employment elsewhere.

Quebec City was also not well integrated into the railway system. With the Grand Trunk running along the south shore, it was the Lévis area rather than Quebec City that developed; it was not until the early twentieth century that the two banks of the river were linked by a bridge. It was only in 1879 that the North Shore Railway, connecting Quebec City with Montreal, was opened to traffic, and this long wait for railway service did not help the city get out of its slump. When the capital of Canada was established at Ottawa in 1867 there was an exodus of civil servants, which was followed by the departure of the British garrison in 1871.

While there were many unfavourable elements in Quebec City's situation, they were partly counterbalanced by the development of some compensating factors. Having lost its preeminence on a Canada-wide scale, Quebec City increasingly became a regional metropolis for eastern and central Quebec. Quebec City's immediate hinterland is fairly limited, so that new regions had to be brought under its influence and dominated, a task which occupied the Quebec City bourgeoisie during the last three decades of the century. Its main instrument was the railway. Thus, the Quebec and Lake St. John Railway allowed it to dominate the Saguenay region, the Lévis and Kennebec brought the Beauce within its orbit, and the North Shore Railway strengthened its links with the region to the west of the city. Also during this period, Quebec City attracted some industrial establishments, especially shoe factories. Some of the jobs lost through the decline of maritime activities were made up for by this industrial growth, but not enough to retain all the city's surplus population. An attempt was also made to breathe new life into the maritime sector by significantly enlarging the city's harbour facilities; this project was completed in 1890.

Thus, Quebec City's stagnation in the late nineteenth century was due to the decline of its traditional economic activities; their replacement by new activities did not occur quickly enough to stabilize its population.

This situation also had significant effects on the city's ethnic composition. In 1861, about 40 percent of its population was of British origin: by 1901 this figure had declined to 15 percent. The decline was just as dramatic in absolute numbers—from 23 000 to 10 000 in the same period. This population was mostly Irish and consisted primarily of labourers in the harbour or the shipyards; they were the first to feel the effects of the slowdown in economic activity and had no choice but to leave the city. Thus, Quebec City became increasingly French in the late nineteenth century. As Blanchard noted, this change affected the bourgeoisie as well, and there were a growing number of French Canadians among the owners of the major enterprises.

The growth of the population, limited as it was, nevertheless brought about an expansion of the city's inhabited area. This occurred in the eastern part of the city, the population of which doubled between 1861 and 1901, especially in the neighbourhoods of Saint-Roch, Saint-Sauveur, and Saint-Vallier, where new industries were established.

OTHER CITIES AND TOWNS

At the time of Confederation, Trois-Rivières was still the third-largest city in Quebec, far behind Montreal and Quebec City; in the next three decades it was passed by Hull, Sherbrooke, and Valleyfield in succession. Like Quebec City, Trois-Rivières was in a period of stagnation, and its population grew only from 6098 to 9981 in 40 years; between 1881 and 1891, it even declined slightly. The reason for this situation was the decline of the timber trade in the last quarter of the century. The economy of Trois-Rivières' hinterland was essentially agricultural or agro-forest. It was not until the early twentieth century that hydroelectricity and the pulp and paper industry gave new impetus to the region's economy and brought about the development of an urban network (Cap-de-la-Madeleine, Shawinigan, Grand-Mère, La Tuque) for which Trois-Rivières was the bridgehead.

The situation was different in the Eastern Townships, where a relatively prosperous agricultural economy led to the growth of a network of villages. In the last quarter of the nineteenth century, factories were established in a number of these centres to make use of rural manpower, turning them into small towns, each with a population of barely 3000 in 1901 — Magog, Granby, Coaticook, Farnham, Richmond, Windsor. Thetford Mines, whose growth was based on the asbestos-mining industry, was a special case. This little urban network was capped by a regional metropolis, Sherbrooke, which played a dominant role in the Eastern Townships during the period. Sherbrooke's location on the St. Francis River at its confluence with the Magog was advantageous, and it benefited further from being on the Grand Trunk Railway. It was both an industrial town and a service centre for the Eastern Townships as a whole.

There was also another regional network in Quebec, consisting of six satellite towns forming a ring around Montreal at a radius of about 60 kilometres — Saint-Jérôme, Joliette, Sorel, Saint-Hyacinthe, Saint-Jean, and Valleyfield. Their combined population was more than 18 000 by 1871, and it was 40 000 in 1901. Industrial and commercial functions and a role as service centres all contributed to their growth. The town of Joliette is a representative case. Founded in 1824, it developed slowly until the middle of the century. It was the site of a large sawmill, and the forest industry was its main economic base. When neighbouring townships were opened to settlement, it quickly became a regional service centre, a development which brought new kinds of establishments to the town and introduced a form of economic activity that was both commercial and industrial. Typical of this process was the gradual evolution of a small ironworks into a plant where farm machinery was manufactured; another ironworks offered its customers a wide variety of iron goods, from machine parts to saucepans by way of *ferrures de moulin à laver* (iron parts for wood-frame washing machines). The population of Joliette at the turn of the century was 6000; creation of a diocese of Joliette in 1904 was testimony to its importance.

At the end of the period, the process of urbanization in Quebec was well under way. Montreal's ascendancy had grown, while a network of small towns had developed primarily in the Montreal plain and the Eastern Townships.

Article Thirteen

"Reckless Walking Must Be Discouraged": The Automobile Revolution and the Shaping of Modern Urban Canada to 1930

Stephen Davies

"Civilization," wrote Dr. Frank Crane in 1918, "is a matter of transportation. The true symbol of the twentieth century, the sign of its soul, the indicator of its spirit, is the wheel." And, as Crane went on to argue, the greatest adaptation of the wheel was the automobile.[1]

Source: Adapted from "'Reckless Walking Must Be Discouraged': The Automobile Revolution and the Shaping of Modern Urban Canada to 1930," *Urban History Review* 18, 2 (October 1989): 123–38. Used by permission.

In the three decades that followed its introduction into Canada at the turn of the century, the automobile revolutionized all aspects of Canadian life. However, in a society in which the presence of the automobile has become an inseparable part of daily life, the nature and magnitude of change created by its rapid proliferation are readily overlooked. The following is an exploration of the automobile's impact on Canadian society during the first three decades of the twentieth century.[2] One can easily comprehend the physical alterations: road-building, traffic signs, and the ever-growing problem of congestion. But there is another aspect to be considered, one which must be balanced against the unbridled enthusiasm and optimism of individuals such as Crane. Change cannot always be directed or controlled, and the automobile, like other major innovations, also brought unanticipated and, in many instances, undesired consequences.

Not all change was as physically apparent as, for example, the automatic traffic signals that began to appear in Canadian cities during the 1920s. There was also a crucial, though less obvious, cultural and social reorientation. What must not be overlooked is an element of irony connected with the automobile's proliferation, in that many of the changes were the opposite of what the auto's introduction had promised. One of the unforeseen by-products of the automobile's appeal was the increasing number of restrictions and regulations imposed upon the Canadian public. The growing array of regulatory detail created one of the great paradoxes of the automobile: a vehicle ostensibly designed to increase freedom and personal mobility could become a means for the increased restriction of society. Rather than creating freedom, the automobile created the myth of carefree motoring. As Edward Sapir noted in 1924, although man may have harnessed machines to his use, he had also harnessed himself to the machine.[3] Mobility must not be confused with, nor mistaken for, freedom.

The diffusion of the automobile in Canada prior to 1930 was phenomenal. Ontario enjoyed the distinction of having the highest number of passenger vehicles of any province. Thus, it was often in Ontario that changes, generally on a scale greater than in the other provinces, were first observable. The 535 automobiles registered in Ontario in 1904 increased to 31 724 by 1914, 155 861 by 1920, 303 736 by 1925, and 490 906 by 1930.[4]

The number of autos remained considerably lower in the other provinces, but at the outbreak of World War I, Ontario ranked only fifth in automobiles per capita, with Saskatchewan a surprising first.[5] However, Ontario's rank altered rapidly, and by 1928 it ranked first (one motor vehicle per 7.3 individuals), while Saskatchewan had dropped to third (one motor vehicle per 7.8 persons).[6] The degree to which Canada readily embraced the automobile is apparent if one considers that in 1929 Canada ranked third behind the United States and the Hawaiian Islands in the world in per capita automobile registrations.[7]

The last years of World War I, and the several years immediately following it, represented the crucial period of expansion for automobile ownership in Canada. This growth can be attributed to a combination of both intellectual and economic factors. At one level, the automobile's rapid spread reflected an alteration of perceptions regarding its role in Canadian society. By the 1920s it was no longer simply a rich man's toy but had been transformed, as the *Canadian Motorist* argued in 1915, into a necessity rather than a luxury.[8]

An important economic consideration was the effect the war had on the automobile's rise in numbers. Wartime inflation and demand had increased automobile prices in Canada, but that rise was more than offset by higher wages. By 1920, automobile prices had begun to drop. This decline, and the introduction of new financing plans such as those first extended by GMAC in 1919, stimulated automobile purchases. In the four years following 1920, the selling price of the average automobile dropped by approximately 38 percent.[9] In fact automobile prices dropped continuously throughout the 1920s. The average selling price for an automobile in 1921 was $906, a figure which declined to $695 by 1926.[10]

The attendant expansion in ownership meant a physical alteration of the urban landscape in one manner or another. The most obvious change was the increased number of vehicles visible on the streets of Canada's cities. As registrations rose, so too did traffic congestion. While the growth of the former was generally lauded as concrete proof of the country's progress, the latter was accepted as an unfortunate by-product of that progress. A comparison of traffic on Dundas Street ten miles west of Toronto in 1908 and 1912 graphically illustrates the changes in traffic patterns wrought by the automobile. In a ten-hour period in mid-August 1908, one site on Dundas witnessed the passing of six automobiles. By 1912, 382 automobiles passed that same spot within the ten-hour period, leading the president of the Ontario Good Roads Association to remark how the automobile had "revolutionized traffic conditions everywhere."[11]

Yet the true revolution was yet to come, as comprehensive traffic surveys conducted in 1914 and 1922 demonstrate. In these studies more than 200 stations were monitored on various roads throughout southern Ontario during the summer months. Two examples suffice to convey a sense of how dramatically traffic had increased in only eight years. On the Toronto–Hamilton Highway at Long Branch Park, an average of 268.8 automobiles a day passed in 1914, with the maximum for one day reaching 382. That same spot in 1922 witnessed an average of 8236.4 automobiles a day, with a maximum of 12 296 on Labour Day. A survey conducted at Fruitland, on the Hamilton–Niagara Road, arrived at similar figures. In 1914 that road bore an average of 189 vehicles a day, with a one-day high of 253. By 1922 the traffic passing the same spot had risen to a daily average of 2 849.8 with a one-day maximum of 5030.[12] Taken together, traffic surveys and registration figures create some understanding of the physical implications of the automobile. Undoubtedly it heralded an age of personal mobility, but it also introduced a new range of problems, of which increased traffic flow and congestion were only a part.

One overlooked alteration to the urban environment, and indeed to the country as a whole, was the decline of the automobile's nearest competitor, the horse. The traffic censuses of Ontario conducted in 1914, 1922, and 1925 give some notion of the shift under way. At Port Credit on the Toronto–Hamilton Highway, the daily average of horse-drawn vehicles in 1914 was 158.7, which by 1922 had declined to 25.3.[13] In Toronto the change was even more startling. A survey of traffic on Dundas Street at Bloor in 1914 showed 349 automobiles and 248 horse-drawn vehicles passing in a day. By 1925 the daily total of automobiles had risen to 7 943, while horse-drawn vehicles had declined to a mere 15. "One noticeable feature of this tabulation," noted the Toronto and York Road Commission, which had undertaken the Dundas and Bloor survey, "is the constant dwindling, almost to the vanishing point, of horse-drawn traffic on the main roads, pointing to the conclusion that the main roads of the future must be designed primarily for motor traffic."[14]

Even roads removed from the larger urban centres witnessed a decline of horse-drawn vehicles. For instance, a survey on the Guelph–Owen Sound Road saw the number of horse-drawn vehicles decline to 30.2 per day in 1922 from a level of 39.0 in 1914.[15] The declines varied from area to area and were sometimes only slight, particularly in predominantly agricultural areas. At best the number of horse-drawn vehicles in use remained static in the face of a rising population.[16]

The decline of horse-drawn vehicles was indicative of fundamental changes taking place in cities, towns, and villages. The movement from horse to horseless carriage meant that urban life acquired a quicker pace in the first decades of the twentieth century. Along with this faster pace of life, the dominance of the automobile meant a distinct change in urban sights, sounds, and smells. Taken together, such changes had created by 1930 a greatly altered urban environment.

Traffic congestion by the automobile was not a significant problem in Canada prior to 1910. The chief constable of Toronto reported in 1907 no problems with congestion, though he was perturbed about automobile speeding. A 1910 report on transit in Toronto could still conclude that, as for ordinary vehicular traffic, there existed no "extraordinary congestion."[17]

By the end of the first decade of the century, however, indications were already present that increasing automobile traffic was to have a serious impact on Canadian cities. As the Civic Improvement Committee for Toronto reported in 1911, problems engendered by the automobile's proliferation were becoming increasingly clear. The report noted that a "courageous endeavor" was required if the transportation problem was not to prove detrimental to the interests of the city.[18] Apparently this growing apprehension had some effect for, in 1913, members of the Toronto police force were sent to New York City and London, England, to learn how to handle traffic more effectively.[19] Though concern was not limited to Toronto, it had the greatest concentration of automobiles in Canada and generally experienced problems of congestion first and to a greater degree. Even Ottawa, which had fewer than 1900 automobiles at the end of World War I, was reporting serious traffic problems by 1920.[20]

Growing automobile congestion meant that two new concerns had to be addressed in urban planning. One was where to park vehicles, and the other was how to keep them moving quickly and efficiently. By 1916, the *Canadian Motorist*, a publication representing motorists across Canada, was noting how parking was a problem for all urban centres. "The automobile," the *Canadian Motorist* editorial pointed out, "is a latecomer in the general scheme of things and the best must be made of inadequate parking facilities. Cities of the future no doubt will be planned in such a way as to provide for the parking of cars in convenient and accessible parts of the business district."[21]

Yet even as the *Canadian Motorist* was putting forward its case, the Toronto City Council, equally aware of the problem, had already designated streets where parking was permissible. On all other streets, in an effort to reduce traffic slowdown, drivers could be given a summons by the police for leaving their automobiles unattended for more than a few minutes.[22] This approach, however, offered little more than a temporary solution. Toronto's chief constable lamented in 1926 that the city's streets were "just an open air garage."[23] By the following year the problem had intensified, prompting the chief constable to call for a strict enforcement of parking bylaws:

> Vehicles should be prohibited from standing unattended in that district [downtown] or for a period longer than necessary to take on or discharge passengers, or load or unload merchandise.[24]

Automobile parking was only part of the larger crisis imposed on urban planning by the automobile's presence. Civic bureaucracies became increasingly preoccupied, from World War I onwards, with the problems created by automobile traffic.[25] As Blaine Brownell has argued in the case of the United States, and it is a point equally applicable to the Canadian situation, one by-product of the automobile's rapid spread was a significant evolution in urban planning.[26] Planning for the automobile was, according to Brownell, an evolutionary process, whereby "most planners perceived at least the broad outlines of the motor vehicle's impact, and even the necessity of redesigning the city to accommodate the innovation."[27] In this context the automobile exerted yet another unexpected influence. The growing necessity for traffic planning helped advance the status—not to mention the business—of urban planning and consulting.[28]

In 1926 Toronto's chief constable, still concerned with regulating traffic in the city, introduced recommendations that would quickly and permanently alter the urban landscape. Noting that traffic problems were common in most cities, he suggested using "Mechanical Automatic Controls" for all street intersections in the downtown Toronto area.[29] Acting on that recommendation, in 1928 Toronto installed automatic traffic signals at 71 intersections.[30] In addition, given the realization that, as the chief constable expressed it, "our present streets were not laid out with any idea of the amount of traffic they would be called upon to carry," recommendations were put forward to improve traffic flow by revising existing street patterns. This trend had been under way in many cities since the early 1920s. Ottawa's planning commission, for example, had been busy throughout the decade "rounding corners" to facilitate a faster movement of traffic.[31] Toronto's planning commission responded in a similar fashion to the new problems of the automobile, noting that the primary need of the city was the development of a series of through and paved streets for modern vehicular traffic.[32] Such alterations provided the city of 1930 with a look that unmistakably distinguished it in appearance from the city that had existed only two decades previously.

One of the rarely considered legacies of the automobile has been its impact on the form of urban residential structures. "As an architectural unit," the *Canadian Motorist* argued in 1915, "the garage is rapidly coming into its own."[33] The automobile garage was not merely a useful accessory but, by 1915, was touted as an essential component of housing design. Thus, garages were no longer an afterthought, but were being integrated into new housing structures whenever possible. According to the *Canadian Motorist*, this integration had gained favourable acceptance. As the journal noted:

> The merits of such an arrangement have gained wide popularity for this style of a garage. In the new residential districts of our Canadian cities thousands of such are to be seen. Sometimes they are located under verandas and porches, frequently under conservatories, sun rooms, dens, breakfast rooms, etc. When so located, they are, of course, part of the architectural scheme of the house—indeed part of the house itself.[34]

Thus, along with the more obvious changes in street appearance and structure, the automobile ushered in a new era of housing design whereby residential structures were altered or entirely redesigned to accommodate the new technology.

However, the automobile's introduction had far more serious implications than just the transformation of housing styles. Automobiles also introduced a new element of risk and destruction to Canadian streets, for as their number grew, so too did the number of related deaths and injuries. By the late 1920s, Ontario, with the largest automobile population in the country, was experiencing the highest number of such fatalities. In 1927, for example, Ontario had 387 motor fatalities, a figure that represented more than 40 percent of Canada's automobile-related deaths. With a significantly smaller population than Ontario, British Columbia had only 77 such fatalities.[35] In terms of fatal motor accidents per 100 000 persons, Ontario, with 12.1, ranked second behind British Columbia (with 13.4).

The cities had the most lethal concentration of motor vehicles. Although Toronto experienced only one motor fatality in 1907, the number had reached 17 by 1912, 48 by 1922, and 87 by 1927.[36] Thus, in 1927, Toronto accounted for more than 10 percent of the country's total number of deaths related to motor vehicles. And yet Toronto did not have the highest number of urban automobile fatalities. Montreal held that dubious distinction with 126 deaths. Nearly one-quarter of all Canadian automobile fatalities occurred in the two cities.[37] Such was the paradoxical nature of the automobile that a vehicle which promised increased freedom and mobility also meant death and injury for thousands.

167

The new element of danger did not pass unnoticed. When, in 1913, advertisements for the Hupmobile pointed out that the countryside was "better, cleaner and safer than city streets," it was not merely rhetoric.[38] City streets had become dangerous places, particularly for children. Inspired partly by the presence of the automobile, and partly as an attempt to instill a degree of moral and social guidance in the young, local playground movements developed in the early twentieth century. In an editorial that commented on the opening of a new playground in 1918, a Hamilton newspaper underscored the role which the automobile had played:

> Playgrounds are becoming more a necessity than ever. The automobile and the motor truck have driven the children off the streets.[39]

Hamilton had established its first playground in 1909, but as advertisers pointed out, the streets remained a dangerous place for children. Even with the establishment of playgrounds throughout the city, Hamilton children, and the children of all urban centres, continued to fall victim to the automobile. From January to September 1922, 789 street accidents occurred in Hamilton. Of those, 162 involved children under the age of 14, of whom 41 were injured while playing on the streets. Influenced by the growing number of fatalities, an editorial queried:

> Should we encourage properly supervised playgrounds, or, by neglect, make the streets unhealthy "plague" grounds, a menace to the safety and sanity of child life?[40]

Playgrounds, like the addition of automatic traffic signals, or the newly designed traffic routes, contributed to a new look for the urban environment of the post-1920 period. Many of the physical changes caused by the automobile were minor or of a subtle nature, but their cumulative effect was to substantially alter the face of the Canadian city by 1930.

The overt physical alteration of the urban environment was only part of a much wider social transformation created by the automobile's presence. The automobile, or more specifically the new mobility provided by the automobile, caused a reassessment and reorientation of established spatial norms. This alteration of established spatial relationships, particularly the relationship between rural and urban society, perhaps held the greatest consequences. Within a relatively short period of time the automobile became synonymous with a new freedom of space, distance, and speed.

However, because of the inherently restrictive nature of the urban environment, the countryside became the logical location to experience the new boundaries of mobility as defined by the automobile. The rural environment, with its open spaces and unchecked speeds, became the ideal location to experience the full potential of the automobile's ability for spatial reorientation.

The attraction of the rural environment for the urban dweller was not based solely on the possibilities of speed. While the countryside represented the appeal of the outdoors with all the associated virtues (independence, open space, and a slower pace of life), the automobile remained the key to enjoying those virtues. A 1908 article in the Toronto *Globe* asked its readers,

Who is the owner of an automobile who has not many a time used it to hurry far away from the madding crowd to the quiet spots of nature, where he can breathe freely and receive the endless inspirations of fine scenery?[41]

Moreover, the opportunities opened by the automobile were themes reinforced by advertising. Automobile advertising placed an emphasis on the virtues of rural space. Automobiles were portrayed as the means of escape from the urban maelstrom—they held out the hope of tranquility in a hurried world.

Copywriters often waxed eloquent about the joys to be found in the nonurban environment. One Chevrolet advertisement in 1929 reminded the reader:

> There's a shady woodland nook awaiting you. Beside the blue waters of a placid lake are rest and relaxation. A laughing, leaping brook is calling you to come! Break down the barriers of everyday. There's happiness ahead.[42]

A Ford advertisement nine years earlier had enticed the reader "out beyond the pavement" to "the unexplored woodlands and remote farmlands." The automobile became a necessity to explore such areas, for as Ford pointed out:

> Nature's loveliest beauty spots, her choicest hunting grounds are far removed from the railroads, away from the much travelled highways.[43]

Advertisements with an outdoor theme did more than comment on the superiority of the outdoors: by implication, if the rural environment was healthy, the urban environment must be unhealthy. A Chevrolet advertisement in 1924 urged readers to escape "from the dust of the city" to where one could "drive through the fresh air to some inviting spot amid the beauties of nature."[44] Some advertisements were more forceful in denouncing the city, juxtaposing the benefits of the country with the liabilities of the city, and making the choice between the two appear obvious. That year Ford asked potential customers, "which shall it be this summer?" and then went on to lay out two choices:

> City streets for a playground, or the open country where the air is perfumed with the scent of growing things and the butterflies dance in the sunshine? The Ford car is the friend of childhood—the modern Magic Carpet that will transport them and you from the baking asphalt to the shady country lanes whenever you wish to go.[45]

Thus, the assessment that the countryside represented an environment that was, according to Hupmobile, "better, cleaner and safer than city streets" was not simple advertising rhetoric, particularly in the light of the death toll previously discussed.[46]

Advertisers did not so much create the contrast between urban and rural environments as they exploited themes already prevalent in society and adopted them as marketing techniques. And, as the ease of travel from one locale to another by the automobile created a greater interaction between the two environments, comparisons were made increasingly easy. By contrasting the two environments, advertisers reinforced the differences, real and imagined, between the two. The irony was that just as urban families came to experience the countryside, they changed it.

Until the 1920s in Ontario, when the provincial government assumed responsibility for highway traffic and locational signs, private organizations such as the Ontario Motor League undertook the task of erecting signs throughout the province. Road signing to aid touring motorists often unintentionally altered the character of rural society. Sign campaigns threatened a sense of identity which, for many small rural communities, had remained unchanged for years before the coming of the automobile. One possible consequence of the motor league's sign efforts was illustrated in the case of Green River, Ontario:

> The unwary traveller might pass through and go for miles beyond still looking for it, did he not know that the church set among the trees on one side of the stream and the small general store on the opposite side of the stream, each hidden from the other, were two positive evidences that it was a village.[47]

Since the post office at Green River displayed no sign, the members of the motor league arbitrarily decided where to place a name sign announcing the village, a necessary step "so that the travelling tourist might know when he came to certain villages."[48]

The local population, however, displayed little enthusiasm for the process. When a nearby farmer was asked whether it was an appropriate place for a Green River sign, he replied, "Well, boys, I guess it is as good as any, as the store and post office are across the crick."[49] The apparent indifference of local inhabitants was understandable, given that in their minds there already existed a clearly defined local identity of place and circumstance, even if it went unsigned. If signs did not create an identity for such communities, they did so for outside interests such as touring motorists. Signs, and the motorists they served, meant that communities such as Green River were slowly integrated into the wider fabric of provincial life with their "new" identity. In turn such communities were forced to sacrifice some of the local identity that relative isolation and anonymity had provided.

In any consideration of the mobility and freedom provided by the automobile, the question of speed is crucial. Speed, and the fascination with it, were integral parts of the early-twentieth-century consciousness. And the automobile was, as *Maclean's* noted in 1914, "the sign of a quicker-moving age."[50] Speed naturally became an important selling feature (for some manufacturers the prime selling point) in automobile advertising. The Auburn billed itself as "America's Fastest Stock Car," while the Willys-Knight pointed out that its six-cylinder model "Accelerates like a Flash—5 to 40 miles in 14 1/2 seconds."[51]

Judging from police reports and newspaper accounts, owners certainly were partaking of the sensations a speeding auto provided. It soon became apparent that regulation was necessary to check the appetite for speed. By 1911 Hamilton employed plainclothes policemen on the city's thoroughfares to time the speed of, and to apprehend, offending "buzz wagons." Shortly thereafter the Hamilton police resorted to using officers disguised as tramps in order to time suspected speeders, an early instance of unmarked speed traps.[52] Despite official checks and traps, the public's thirst for speed appeared unquenched. The difficulty lay in controlling the belief that, as it was expressed in *Maclean's*, "the automobile has been invented in vain if it is to be forbidden to travel quickly."[53]

Ontario's actions to deal with motorists in general, and not just speeding drivers, were typical of the regulatory revolution that the country as a whole underwent. In 1903 the province introduced its first motor vehicles act (3 Edw. VII c. 27), which formed the nucleus of all subsequent motor vehicle legislation. The 1903 act consisted of 12 sections; 7 were concerned with administrative details and the remaining 5 dealt with such items as speed limits. By 1912 the *Motor Vehicles Act* of Ontario had expanded to 55 sections, and by 1923 to 227 sections, subsections, and clauses; this expansion highlighted the province's growing concern for all aspects of automobile use. Driving was no longer a matter of paying a registration fee and taking the vehicle directly onto the road.

The substance of these regulations, and, as importantly, their form, would alter early-twentieth-century Canadian society. The *Canadian Motorist* pointed out in 1914:

> Regulations governing the use of motor vehicles in Canada at the present time vary in each Province of the Dominion, and motorists who have occasion to drive from one province to another are frequently perplexed and sometimes greatly inconvenienced by the divergent laws as to speed, display of numbers and lights, and other less important features of motoring.[54]

In February 1915, the same journal noted with approval the plan undertaken by the Association of Police Chiefs of America to develop a standard set of rules and regulations with respect to the automobile.[55] The following year it endorsed the compilation of a standard code of traffic regulations by the street traffic committee of the Safety First Federation of America, which would "be welcomed by everyone conversant with the present chaotic conditions caused primarily by the varying traffic ordinances in force in our municipalities."[56] The committee was hopeful that such regulation would be enforced in every city in North America with 5000 or more residents.[57] Thus, the automobile had, by the time of World War I, set in motion a process that would revolutionize the character of the urban environment. Local characteristics would never be entirely eliminated, but more and more cities came to resemble one another under the influence of a commonly shared technology. Ironically, it was the very technology which purported to be an expression of individualism that contributed significantly toward a more homogeneous urban environment.

Automobile legislation was unique in an important respect, in that it often meant the regulation of Canadian society as a whole, nonmotorists as well as motorists. A case in point was the reduced status of the urban pedestrian. Animosity quickly developed between the motorist and the pedestrian after the turn of the century, each claiming priority over the other. In the struggle to assert their claims, pedestrians gained an early sympathy in some quarters. The pedestrian, as the premier of Ontario made clear in 1910,

> has the first right of the road. The chauffeur who thinks that, because he gives warning of his approach, he is entitled to the road, is utterly and entirely wrong. He comes after the pedestrian and even after the man on the bicycle. It is not the pedestrian who must get out of the way of the automobile, but the automobile that must get out of the road of the pedestrian, even if he is standing still.[58]

Yet within a decade, as the number of motor vehicles grew at an unprecedented rate, a reversal of positions was under way. Initially, calls were made for the "re-education" of the pedestrian. One contributor to the *Canadian Motorist* in 1916 argued that the automobile's presence required a change of attitude among pedestrians, but unfortunately a large number of pedestrians had

> not yet graduated from the parochial, or colonial, or wayback attitude, whatever one may call it, in spite of the enormous increase in all kinds of vehicular traffic.[59]

Education alone did not appear to have a significant effect on reducing the conflict between the two, particularly in view of the rising number of pedestrian-related automobile accidents. Many arguments in support of automobiles were built upon accident statistics to demonstrate that, if automobiles were indeed dangerous, pedestrians brought that danger upon themselves. By 1925, the *Canadian Motorist* argued that "reckless walking" must be discouraged and "pedestrian traffic, like all other traffic, regulated."[60] It was not surprising, therefore, that the journal should smile upon legislation passed in Connecticut that made "reckless walking" an indictable offence.[61] The logical extension of this attitude regarding pedestrian education, and one increasingly favoured by many, was the regulation of the pedestrian.

By 1920 changes were under way to redefine the relationship between pedestrian and motor vehicle in Canada's cities. F.C. Biggs, the Minister of Public Works for Ontario, stated in 1921:

> The sooner this House or the cities wake up and ask pedestrians to cross the street at street intersections and not anywhere they have a mind to hop off the sidewalk, the sooner we are going to get away from 90 per cent of the accidents in the Province.[62]

Biggs, a boisterous good-roads advocate and auto enthusiast, was a biased witness to events. Nevertheless, his statement signalled an official recognition of a change of attitude due to the automobile. Moreover, Biggs was not alone in demanding the regulation of the nonmotorist. What provided freedom and mobility for one segment of the urban population brought regulation and loss of freedom for another. Claims of prior rights by pedestrians were dismissed by an editorial in the *Canadian Motorist* in 1923 as "so much idle prattle."[63] By that time it had become evident that pedestrians had lost the primacy of consideration to motorists on the nation's streets.

By the onset of the Great Depression, Canada had experienced major alterations brought about by the automobile's presence. It was a transition filled with conflicts and decisions, the long-term consequences of which had been unforeseen. Given the pattern of concentration, it was to be expected that the urban environment would exhibit striking examples of that change. In everything from sound and smell, to housing design, to street patterns and congestion, the automobile profoundly affected urban life. Although the potential for increased mobility was immediately recognized, the degree to which it ultimately would alter established patterns of temporal and spatial reality (patterns based on nineteenth-century transportation technology) went unappreciated.

The automobile also irreversibly altered stable established forms of interaction between the rural and urban environments. Similarly, the presence of the automobile required a greater level of societal control than had previously existed. The effects of regulation spread beyond the motoring public, and all city dwellers were subject to restriction forced by the automobile. The automobile was fraught with irony, particularly evident in the paradox of freedom versus regulation—a technology that traded heavily on the possibilities of personal liberation simultaneously introduced an escalating level of restriction on personal conduct. The introduction of the automobile into Canadian society not only demonstrated how unpredictable a technology's ultimate effects might be, but also underscored how technological innovations affect the public in ever-widening and increasingly complex circles.

NOTES

1. *Canadian Motorist* (hereafter *CM*) (June 1918): 387.
2. The termination date of 1930 has been chosen because most of the changes precipitated by the automobile were either already in place or at least under way by that date. As well, the exceptional social and economic conditions of the Great Depression and their impact on the spread of the automobile in Canada would in themselves require a separate study.

3. Edward Sapir, "Culture, Genuine and Spurious," *American Journal of Sociology* 29 (Jan. 1924): 408.

4. Ontario, *Sessional Papers*, 1942. Annual Report of the Department of Highways, Report of Motor Vehicle Registrations, 1941.

5. *CM* (April 1914): 168.

6. *Preliminary Report: Registration of Motor Vehicles, 1922–24, 1926–56* (Ottawa, 1956).

7. Ibid.

8. Don Kerr and Stan Hanson, *Saskatoon: The First Half-Century* (Edmonton, 1982), 258; *CM* (Feb. 1915): 35.

9. *The Automobile Industry in Canada, 1924* (Ottawa, 1925).

10. *The Automobile Industry in Canada, 1921* (Ottawa, 1922); *Automobile Statistics for Canada, 1926* (Ottawa, 1927).

11. Ontario, *Sessional Papers*, 1923. President's Address, Eleventh Annual Convention, Ontario Good Roads Association.

12. Ontario, *Sessional Papers*, 1915. Annual Report on Highway Improvement, 1915, appendix D; 1923. Annual Report on Highway Improvement, 1922, appendix G. The 1914 census was conducted for a twelve-hour period, from 7 A.M. to 7 P.M. However, because of the prevalence of night traffic, the 1922 census was conducted from 6 A.M. to 10 P.M.

13. Ontario, *Sessional Papers*, 1915. Annual Report on Highway Improvement, 1915, appendix D; 1923. Annual Report on Highway Improvement, 1922, appendix G. In this comparison I have considered only one-horse carriages, which most closely correspond to the passenger automobile. However, even two-horse vehicles, which would be used in hauling or for light industry, also declined at approximately the same rate, according to census figures.

14. *Report of the Toronto and York Roads Commission* (Toronto, 1926), 33.

15. Ontario, *Sessional Papers*, 1915. Annual Report on Highway Improvements, 1915, appendix D; 1923. Annual Report on Highway Improvement, 1922, appendix G.

16. The rise of the automobile at the expense of the horse is readily apparent in the decline of the carriage and wagon industry. In Ontario in 1920 there were 217 manufactuers of carriages and wagons, which by 1930 had declined to only 80 such producers. Other forms of transportation also experienced a decline with the growing popularity of the automobile. The automobile meant the eventual decline of the steamboats that served the resort areas of Lake Simcoe and Georgian Bay. Even Ontario's inter-urban railways, built expressly for the efficient movement of passengers, suffered a decline in passsenger levels during the 1920s because of the automobile. *Preliminary Report of the Carriage and Wagon Industry in Canada, 1920* (Ottawa, 1922); *Preliminary Report on the Carriage and Wagon Industry in Canada, 1929 and 1930* (Ottawa, 1932); John Craig, *Simcoe County: The Recent Past* (The Corporation of the County of Simcoe, 1977); *Report of the Commission Appointed to Inquire into Hydro-Electric Railways* (Ontario, Sessional Papers, 1922), 53; John F. Due, *The Intercity Electric Railway Industry in Canada* (Toronto, 1966), 25, 33–36, 53, 61–95.

17. *Annual Report of the Chief Constable of the City of Toronto, 1907, 1910.*

18. Ibid., 1911.

19. Ibid., 1913.

20. *CM* (Feb. 1918): 71; J.H. Taylor, *Ottawa: An Illustrated History* (Toronto, 1986), 146.

21. *CM* (July 1918): 445.

22. *CM* (Dec. 1916): 496.

23. *Annual Report of the Chief Constable of the City of Toronto, 1926.*

24. Ibid., 1927.

25. James Lemon, "Tracey Deavin Lemay: Toronto's First Planning Commissioner, 1930–1954," *City Planning* (Winter 1984): 4–5.

26. Blaine Brownell, "Urban Planning, the Planning Profession, and the Motor Vehicle in Early Twentieth Century America," in *Shaping an Urban World*, ed. G.E. Cherry (London, 1980), 60.

27. Ibid., 69.

28. Ibid., 67.

29. *Annual Report of the Chief Constable of the City of Toronto, 1926.*

30. Ibid., 1928.
31. Taylor, *Ottawa*, 48.
32. *Report of the Advisory City Planning Commission* (Toronto, 1929), 11.
33. *CM* (Oct. 1915): 345.
34. *CM* (Sept. 1915): 306. The *Canadian Motorist* also added a note of warning to owners of houses with garages joined by conservatories. Noting the danger to plants when the doors are thrown open in winter, the journal advised that there would be no problem "so long as the chauffeur sees to it that the communicating door between the conservatory and the garage is kept shut."
35. *Deaths Due to Motor Vehicle Accidents* (Ottawa, 1934).
36. Ibid.; *Annual Report of the Chief Constable of the City of Toronto*, 1907; *CM* (Feb. 1923): 76.
37. *Deaths Due to Motor Vehicle Accidents* (Ottawa, 1934).
38. *Maclean's* (July 1913).
39. *Hamilton Times*, 6 July 1918.
40. *Hamilton Spectator*, 6 May 1924.
41. *Globe*, 21 March 1908.
42. *Maclean's* (1 May 1929).
43. *Maclean's* (15 Oct. 1920).
44. *Canadian Magazine* (May 1924).
45. *Maclean's* (July 1924).
46. *Maclean's* (July 1913).
47. P.E. Doolittle, "The Pleasure of Erecting Road Signs," *CM* (April 1914): 146–47.
48. Ibid., 182.
49. Ibid.
50. James Grantham, "The Law and the Motor," *Maclean's* (May 1914): 29.
51. *Maclean's* (1 May 1927); *Canadian Magazine* (April 1927).
52. *Hamilton Herald*, 14 June 1911; *Hamilton Herald*, 19 Aug. 1912.
53. Grantham, "The Law and the Motor," 30.
54. *CM* (Aug. 1914): 319.
55. *CM* (Feb. 1915): 40.
56. *CM* (Feb. 1916): 38.
57. *CM* (May 1916): 163.
58. *Toronto Daily Star*, 10 March 1910.
59. *CM* (Aug. 1916): 292.
60. *CM* (Jan. 1925): 19.
61. *CM* (Jan. 1923): 31.
62. Ontario, Legislative Assembly, *Debates*, 8 March 1921.
63. *CM* (Feb. 1923): 89.

The Impact of Industrialization

Women workers sorting ore in the Huntington Copper Mining

Company near Bolton, Quebec, 1867.

176 | **CANADA'S** rapid transition from an agricultural and rural to an industrial and urban society caused great change and upheaval. Many Canadian families had to adjust to living in urban centres and to having one or, in many cases, both parents, as well as the older children in the household, working outside the home. Such changes affected the family on every level, from its composition and its social dynamics to its decision-making processes. In "Gender at Work at Home: Family Decisions, the Labour Market, and Girls' Contributions to the Family Economy," Bettina Bradbury examines how preconceived notions of gender and class influenced the decisions of working-class families in Montreal as to which of their members should seek wage-earning work.

Individual working-class men also experienced upheaval and the need to make significant adjustments. Many had to work long hours in monotonous jobs that afforded them no sense of self-worth or pride of accomplishment. Rather, they became "cogs in the wheel of industrialization." Working conditions in poorly ventilated, highly congested factories were often appalling: living conditions in working-class ghettos were no better. In late-nineteenth-century Montreal, Joe Beef's Canteen became a place of refuge and escape for many working-class people. In "Joe Beef of Montreal: Working-Class Culture and the Tavern, 1869–1889," Peter DeLottinville re-creates the cultural life of Montreal's working class as experienced at Joe Beef's Canteen.

On the subject of women who work outside the home, see the relevant sections in Alison Prentice et al., *Canadian Women: A History*, 2nd ed. (Toronto: Harcourt Brace, 1996); Marjorie Griffin Cohen, *Women's Work, Markets, and Economic Development in Nineteenth-Century Ontario* (Toronto: University of Toronto Press, 1988); and Graham S. Lowe, *Women in the Administrative Revolution: The Feminization of Clerical Work* (Toronto: University of Toronto Press, 1987). Mary Kinnear, ed., *First Days, Fighting Days: Women in Manitoba History* (Regina: Canadian Plains Research Centre, 1987) contains several essays on women workers. See also Janice Acton et al., eds., *Women at Work: Ontario, 1850–1930* (Toronto: Women's Educational Press, 1974), and Wayne Roberts, *Honest Womanhood: Feminism, Femininity and Class Consciousness among Toronto Working Women, 1893 to 1914* (Toronto: New Hogtown Press, 1976). A comparative study of men and women workers in the Ontario towns of Paris and Hanover is provided by Joy Parr in *The Gender of Breadwinners: Women, Men, and Change in Two Industrial Towns, 1880–1950* (Toronto: University of Toronto Press, 1990). On the impact of industrialization on women and/or the family, see Bettina Bradbury's *Working Families: Age, Gender and Daily Survival in Industrializing Montreal* (Toronto: McClelland and Stewart, 1993) and the essays in Section 4 of her *Canadian Family History: Selected Readings* (Toronto: Copp Clark Pitman, 1992), as well as Peter Gossage, *Families in Transition: Industry and Population in Nineteenth-Century Saint-Hyacinthe* (Montreal/Kingston: McGill-Queen's University Press, 1999), and R. Marvin McInnis's "Women, Work and Childbearing: Ontario in the Second Half of the Nineteenth Century," *Histoire sociale/Social History* 24, 48 (November 1991): 237–62.

Three excellent primary sources exist for a study of the impact of industrial growth in Canada at the turn of the century. The first is *The Royal Commission on the Relations of Labour and Capital, 1889*. An abridged version has been published under the title *Canada Investigates Industrialism*, edited and with an introduction by Greg Kealey (Toronto: University of Toronto Press, 1973). The other two sources are collections of documents: *The Workingman in the Nineteenth Century*, ed. M.S. Cross (Toronto: Oxford University Press, 1974), and *The Canadian Worker in the Twentieth Century*, ed. I. Abella and D. Millar (Toronto: Oxford University Press, 1978). Three worthwhile collections are *Canadian Working Class History: Selected Readings*, ed. Laurel Sefton MacDowell and Ian Radforth (Toronto: McClelland and Stewart, 1992); *Essays on Canadian Working Class History*, ed. G. Kealey and P. Warrian (Toronto: McClelland and Stewart, 1976); and *Canadian Labour History: Selected Readings*, ed. D.J. Bercuson and David Bright (Toronto: Copp Clark, 1994). Terry Copp provides an in-depth study of working-class life in Montreal in his *The Anatomy of Poverty: The Conditions of the Working Class in Montreal, 1897–1929* (Toronto: McClelland and Stewart, 1974). A counterpart to Copp's work is Greg Kealey's *Toronto Workers Respond to Industrial Capitalism, 1867–1892* (Toronto: University of Toronto Press, 1980). A second valuable study on Toronto is Michael Piva's *The Conditions of the Working Class in Toronto, 1900–1921* (Ottawa: University of Ottawa Press, 1979). For Ontario in general, see Paul Craven, ed., *Labouring Lives: Work and Workers in Nineteenth-Century Ontario* (Toronto: University of Toronto Press, 1995). On Atlantic Canada, see Daniel Samson, ed., *Contested Countryside: Rural Workers and Modern Society in Atlantic Canada, 1800–1950* (Fredericton: Acadiensis Press, 1994). David Bright looks at the history of the labour movement in Calgary in his *The Limits of Labour: Class Formation and the Labour Movement in Calgary, 1883–1929* (Vancouver: University of British Columbia Press, 1998).

For a discussion of working-class culture, see Bryan Palmer's *A Culture in Conflict: Skilled Workers and Industrial Capitalism in Hamilton, Ontario, 1860–1914* (Montreal/Kingston: McGill-Queen's University Press, 1979), and his *Working-Class Experience: The Rise and Reconstitution of Canadian Labour, 1800–1991*, 2nd ed. (Toronto: McClelland and Stewart, 1993).

Article Fourteen

Gender at Work at Home: Family Decisions, the Labour Market, and Girls' Contributions to the Family Economy

Bettina Bradbury

Introduction

"Gender at work" can be read in two ways. In the first, work is a noun, and the central question is "How do definitions of skill, of appropriate work for men and women, get negotiated within the workplace by men and women, workers and capital?" Recent discussions of the sexual division of labour in diverse industries, of "gender at work," of the social construction of skill, and of the role of unions in perpetuating women's unequal

Source: *Canadian and Australian Labour History*, ed. Gregory S. Kealey and Greg Patmore (Sydney: Australian Society for the Study of Labour History and the Committee on Canadian Labour History, 1990), pp. 119–40. Reprinted by permission.

position in the workforce have made major contributions to our understanding of the complexities of the relationships between gender and class, between patriarchy and capitalism. Historical research in this field is rich and fascinating, and is reshaping both women's history and working-class history in Canada as elsewhere.[1]

178

"Gender at work" can also be read, if my grammar is correct, as a verb. Here the question posed would be "How does gender work as a process in society which means that men and women end up with different work and life experiences?" To answer this question involves consideration of factors other than those found in the workplace. In this paper I would like to argue that while workplace-centred approaches go a long way toward explaining sex segregation within specific trades, they ignore different levels of decision making and other institutions that have already gendered the workforce before it arrives at the factory gate.[2] Equally, while approaches stressing the strength of patriarchal ideology or the importance of domestic labour help explain why married women remained out of the workplace, they fail to grasp the complex interactions between patriarchy and capitalism. Furthermore they are more difficult to apply when dealing with the work of daughters rather than their mothers.

Within families, decisions were made about who should stay home to look after children and do housework and who should earn wages which had wide-reaching impact on the composition of the workforce. Such decisions were never made in an ideological or economic vacuum; they represented a complex and often unconscious balance between basic need, existing ideology and practice regarding gender roles, the structure of the economy, and the particular economic conjuncture. Schools taught specific skills and implanted tenacious ideas about future roles. At its broadest level this paper represents a simple plea to those looking at divisions of labour in the workplace to also consider the work done by historians of the family and education. In Canada such work offers some clues about this broader process, although little research systematically examines the question.[3] To the extent that historians interested in how gender is worked out within the workplace and in the unions ignore what happens prior to men's and women's arrival at work, their explanations will fail to consider the wider and deeper sexual division of labour, which not only relegated women to jobs defined as less skilled in workplaces shared with men and to feminine ghettos, but also determined that large numbers would simply not enter the workforce or would do so only sporadically.

More specifically, the paper focuses on one aspect of the question, namely, how family decisions in interaction with the nature of local labour markets influenced sons' and, in particular, daughters' contributions to the family economy.[4] The paper concentrates on the micro-level, examining what I have been able to deduce about family decision-making processes regarding which family members should seek wage labour in two Montreal working-class wards between the 1860s and 1890s. A brief description of the major sectors employing males in Montreal is followed by an assessment of the importance of additional wage earners to working-class families. The respective work of sons and daughters within the family economy is evaluated.

I argue that the sexual division of labour within the family, and the need for additional domestic workers as well as extra wage labourers, meant that the context, timing, and contours of boys' and girls' participation in wage labour were different. By looking at the role of girls in the family economy and not just in the labour market,[5] we can better see how the major changes accompanying the emergence of industrial capitalism in Montreal did not modify the dominant sexual division of labour.

Montreal Families and Wage Labour, 1860–1890

The years 1860 to 1890 were characterized by the growing dominance of industrial capital in the economic structure of Montreal and the increasing dependence on wage labour of a major proportion of its population. Canada's first and largest industrial city, "the workshop" of Canada, had a wide and complex array of industries. Most important were those relating to rail and water transportation, shoemaking, clothing, and food and beverages. The metallurgy sector, dominated by production for the railroads, provided jobs for skilled immigrants from Great Britain, and some French Canadians with a long tradition of working in metal. In shoemaking and dressmaking, as in numerous other smaller trades, artisanal production was rapidly, if unevenly, giving way to production in large factories. Minute divisions of labour accompanied the utilization of new types of machinery throughout the period, drawing immigrants and French Canadians new to the city into the myriad of largely unskilled jobs that were being created. Broadly speaking, the male workforce was divided into four groups. Best paid and most secure were the relatively skilled workers involved in the new trades that emerged with the industrial revolution—the engineers, machinists, moulders, and others who worked in the foundries and new factories. More subject to seasonal and conjunctural unemployment were skilled workers in the construction trades. A third group comprised those workers in trades undergoing rapid deskilling and reorganization; most important among these were the shoemakers. General unskilled labourers made up the other major subgroup within the working class. About 25 cents a day separated the average wage of each of these groups, setting the stage for potential differences in their standard of living and their family economy.[6] Women and girls worked largely in separate sectors of the economy, particularly as domestic servants and dressmakers and in specific kinds of factory work. In virtually every sector, their wages were half those of males or less.[7]

The Importance of Additional Earners in the Family Wage Economy

These disparities of approximately 25 cents a day had the potential to separate the working class into identifiable fractions, each capable of achieving a different standard of living in good times, and each vulnerable in diverse ways to the impact of winter, cyclical depressions, and job restructuring. Throughout most of the period, the most skilled had more flexibility in their budget and a greater chance of affording to eat and live at a level that may also have helped to ward off the diseases that spread only too quickly through the poorly constructed sewers and houses of the city. This greater margin of manoeuvre which higher daily wages, greater job security, and the possession of skills that were scarce and usually in demand gave to the skilled was not constant. It was particularly likely to be eroded in times of economic depression or of rapid transformations in the organization of work.

While some skilled workers organized successfully during this period, the major element of flexibility in the family income, for skilled and unskilled alike, lay not so much in the gains that organization could offer, but in the ability to call on additional family members to earn wages, to gain or save money in other ways, or to limit the necessity of spending cash. Decisions about who additional family workers would be were therefore crucial in determining the contours of the family economy and of the labour force. An examination of the importance of secondary wage earners and of who they were in terms of their age and sex allows a better grasp of the interaction between family labour deployment decisions, the "gendering" of the workforce, and the structure of the economy. This section therefore assesses the importance of additional wage earners in families headed by men in different types of occupations.[8] The following section then attempts to determine who such workers were.

The average number of workers reported by the families of the two working-class areas studied here, Ste. Anne and St. Jacques wards, fluctuated over the family life cycle. Among young couples who had not yet borne children, the wife would occasionally report an occupation, and sometimes another relative lived with the couple, contributing to the number of workers in the household, so that until 1881 families averaged just over one worker at this first stage of a couple's married life. Most families then passed through a long period of relative deprivation as children were born, grew, and required more food, clothing, and larger living premises. Between the time when the first baby was born and some children reached twelve or thirteen, the families of Ste. Anne and St. Jacques continued to have only slightly more than one worker. Then children's contribution began to make up for the difficult years. In 1861, families where half the children were still under fifteen averaged 1.34 workers; once half were fifteen or more they averaged 1.97. In subsequent decades the expansion of wage labour made children's contribution even more important. Whereas in 1861 the average family with children over the age of eleven had only 0.48 of them at work, in 1881 it had 1.16. By 1871 the average family with offspring aged fifteen or more had nearly as many children living at home and working as there had been total number of workers a decade earlier. From 0.85 children at work, the number reported increased to 1.85. The total number of family workers increased from an average of under two at this stage in 1861 to nearly three a decade later. Children's wages became more and more important as children came to constitute a wage-earning family's major source of security.

The prosperity that this number of workers could have secured was temporary. It depended largely on the ability of parents to keep their wage-earning children in the household. As older sons or daughters began to leave home to work or marry, the average dropped down again. If both members of a couple survived they would find themselves struggling again in their old age on a single wage, or no wage at all. For aged working-class widows and widowers, the situation was particularly bleak if there were no children able to help.[9]

Over these years the patterns of the working-class and non-working-class families diverged. In 1861 the non-working class, particularly in St. Jacques, included a high proportion of artisans and shopkeepers, men whose family economy required not the wages, but the work of wives and children. As a result, the average number of workers and of children at work in their families was higher than in all other groups except the unskilled. Over the next two decades, artisans became less and less common. Family labour was increasingly limited to enterprises like small corner groceries. Professionals and some white-collar workers became more important among the non-working-class populations. After 1871, the reporting of jobs by children was least likely among this group.

It was within the working-class family economy that the most dramatic changes occurred over this period, although there were significant and changing differences between the skilled, the unskilled, and those in the indentured trades. The inadequacy of the $1.00 a day or less that a labourer could earn remained a constant throughout this period. As a result, unskilled families consistently relied on additional workers when they were able to. In 1861 they averaged 1.45 workers, compared to 1.27 among the skilled. Over the next two decades the growing number of jobs available allowed them to increase the average number of family workers to 1.62, then 1.66. Among those with working-age offspring, the average number at work increased by 123 percent, from 0.60 in 1861 to 1.34 two decades later.

For these unskilled workers, the period before children were old enough to work was the most difficult. It is worth examining how some such families managed at the critical stage of the family life cycle and later, as children matured. Olive Godaire, wife of labourer Pierre, worked, probably at home as a dressmaker, in 1861, to help support their three children, aged two to eight. Ten years later, it was her eighteen-year-old daughter who was taking in sewing, while a ten-year-old boy was apprenticed to be a tinsmith.[10] In the case of labourer John Harrington's family, the period when the father was the only earner within the nuclear family lasted for at least eighteen years. When John and Sarah's children were under ten, they took in boarders and had John's 50-year-old father, also a labourer, living in the household. Whatever money these extra family and household members contributed would have helped compensate for John's low wages or irregular work, and they continued to take in boarders over the next ten years. Their oldest son, Timothy, was still going to school in 1871, and the family was cramped in a rear dwelling where rent was minimal. Somewhere between 1871 and 1881, the boys joined their father in seeking general labouring jobs. For the first time, the family lived alone, without additional household members. With three wage earn-ers—indeed, three labourers—they must have enjoyed a standard of living that was relatively high compared to the previous year.

The degradation of work conditions and lower wages that typified trades like shoe-making appear to have been counteracted by families' sending growing numbers of their members to seek steady work. In 1861, families in such trades had only 1.08 workers—fewer than any other group. By 1881, they averaged 1.62 workers. Most dramatic was the increased importance of the contribution of children resident at home. Among families with children of working age, the average number of children reporting a job nearly tripled over the two decades, from 0.55 to 1.51. At that date, a few families, like that of Angeline and Alexis Larivière, had four workers. Their two daughters, 22-year-old Josephine and sixteen-year-old Marie-Louise, worked as general labourers. The twenty-year-old son, Charles, was a stone-cutter.[11]

The relative superiority of the wages of skilled workers seems clear in 1861, when they appear to have been able to manage with fewer workers than other groups—averaging only 1.27. A decade later, with 1.5 workers, they still needed fewer than the rest of the working class. The depression that hit in 1874, however, appears to have eroded much of the superiority of the skilled workers. In 1881, after seven years of major depression, which was only just lifting and which must have left many a family heavily indebted, the pattern of family labour deployment was similar to that of the unskilled and those in the indentured trades.

This convergence of experiences within the working class over this period is not sur-prising, given the impact of the depression, combined with the degeneration of work con-ditions in some skilled trades. In the metal-working trades, for example, trade was said to be dead in the winter of 1878. Half the local unionized workers were said to be "working at any kind of labouring work." Two years earlier, a moulder drew attention to the des-perate condition of Montreal mechanics, "working on a canal at 60 cents per day, men who have served years in securing a trade, the wages they receive being only a mockery of their misery."[12]

Families clearly attempted to shape their own economies by adjusting the numbers of wage earners to fit their expenses when they were able to do so. Additional wage earners were not only needed, but were used by all fractions of the working class, with differences stemming from the economic conjuncture, the nature of the labour market, and their own life cycle and earning power. In this way, working-class families influenced the city's labour pool and enhanced their own survival. The increasing availability of wage labour in the factories, workshops, and construction sites of Montreal meant that even in times of depression more and more sons and daughters could and did find work. The reliance of employers in certain sectors on women and youths resident at home depressed male wages generally, while offering families the opportunity to counter a father's low earnings.

Economic transformation thus interacted dialectically with family needs, reshaping the labour market, the family economy, and the life course of children. This interaction is clearest in the case of workers in those sectors undergoing the most dramatic transformation. The continued reorganization of production in trades like shoemaking was reflected not only in the greater increase in the number of their children seeking waged work over the period, but also in a tendency to delay marriage and reduce family size. In the labour market in general, children living at home became a much more significant proportion of workers.[13] In the sewing trades, for example, one-quarter of the workers had been co-resident children in 1861; by 1881, 55 percent were.

Age, Gender, and Additional Family Earners

To try to grasp the decision-making processes behind these patterns of change in the average numbers of family members reporting work over this period, it is necessary to determine who the family workers were in terms of age and gender, and to examine the families from which they came.

Older sons still living at home were the most usual second earners in a family. The number of really young children or married women reporting a job was insignificant beside the importance of children in their late teens or twenties, despite the attention focused on such young workers by contemporaries.[14] Once sons, in particular, reached fifteen or sixteen, they were expected to work. "In our culture," reported Alice Lacasse, the daughter of a French-Canadian immigrant to New Hampshire, "the oldest children always went to work."[15] Wage labour for boys over fifteen became the norm in this period, as more and more were drawn into the labour force. Growing numbers of girls did report a job, but the proportion of boys at work remained consistently higher than that for girls in all age groups. And the pattern of involvement over a girl's life course continued to be completely different from a boy's.

By the age of fifteen or sixteen, 30 percent of the boys who lived at home in these two wards were reporting a job in 1861. Others no doubt sought casual labour on the streets, working from time to time, at other times roaming together in the gangs of youths that dismayed middle-class contemporaries, and filled up the local police courts. In 1871, when times were good, and industrial capitalism more entrenched, nearly 46 percent of boys this age could find a job, while in the depression of the 1870s and early 1880s, the percentage dropped back to 37 percent. After the age of sixteen, and increasingly over the period, boys' involvement with wage labour or other work would grow steadily as they aged. At ages seventeen to eighteen, 50 percent reported a job in 1861, nearly 68 percent two decades later. By age 21 nearly 90 percent of boys listed a job at the end of the period.

Among the girls of Ste. Anne and St. Jacques wards, the work found and the pattern of job reporting over their lives was very different from that of the boys. Once boys passed their early teens, they found work in a wide variety of jobs in all sectors and workplaces of Montreal. Girls, in contrast, remained concentrated within specific jobs and sectors. For girls as for boys, the chances of finding work clearly expanded with the growth of Montreal industry. At ages fifteen to sixteen, for instance, only 13 percent reported a job in 1861, compared to 30 percent in 1881. At the peak age at which girls reported working, nineteen to twenty, 25 percent worked in 1861, nearly 38 percent in 1871, and 35 percent in 1881. Even then, however, the visible participation rate of girls was only half that of boys.[16] After age twenty, the experiences of boys and girls diverged quickly and dramatically, as most, but never all, women withdrew from the formal labour market while most men found themselves obliged to seek work for the rest of their lives.

183

For those girls who did earn wages, then, paid labour was apparently undertaken for a brief period of their lives prior to marriage. At any one time, most girls aged fifteen or more who remained at home with their parents in these wards reported no job at all. Joan Scott and Louise Tilly have suggested that within the "industrial mode of production" "single women are best able to work, since they have few other claims on their time."[17] The discrepancy in the formal wage labour participation rates for boys and girls in these two Montreal wards suggests to me that single women did, in fact, have other claims on their time. In particular, the heavy and time-consuming nature of nineteenth-century housework, the prevalence of disease, the wide age spread among children in most families, and the myriad of other largely invisible pursuits and strategies necessary to survival for the working-class family meant that many of these girls were needed by their mothers to help with work at home. Their role in the division of labour within the family is highlighted on one census return where members' roles were explicitly described. Louis Coutur, a carter who was 50 in 1861, reported that his 21-year-old son was a shoemaker and that his wife's job was "housework."[18] It seems fair to assume, making allowance for the under-enumeration of steady labour and casual work among daughters, that most of the girls who listed no job or school attendance worked periodically, if not continually, at domestic labour as mother's helpers in and around the home. It is thus in the light of family decisions about the allocation of labour power at home, as well as in the structure of jobs available in the marketplace, that the patterns of children's wage labour as well as of their schooling must be interpreted.

At home, girls served an apprenticeship in the reproduction of labour power—in babysitting, cleaning, mending, sewing, cooking, and shopping and, by the end of the century, in nursing and hygiene.[19] Religious leaders were explicit about the need for mothers to educate their daughters in their future roles. "Apply yourselves especially to the task of training your daughters in the functions they will have to perform for a husband and family, without neglecting your other children," wrote Père Mailloux in a manual for Christian parents that was republished several times between the middle and end of the nineteenth century.[20] When girls attended school, the subjects learned were not very different. Education for females, except in a few expensive academies out of reach of the working class, taught only the most basic and general of subjects and housekeeping-type skills. Whereas boys' schools offered bookkeeping and geography, girls' schools offered music, needlework, and sewing.[21] Curriculums aimed to prepare girls for their future role as housekeeper, wife, and mother.[22] The minister of education was explicit. He feared that too many young women were being educated above their station in life, and suggested that bookkeeping and domestic economy constituted the best basis of female education.[23]

Girls, then, were increasingly likely to become secondary wage earners within the working-class family economy during this period, but remained less likely to report a job than were boys. The importance of their contribution to domestic labour, the lower wages they could make in the formal labour market, or an ideological repulsion to girls' labour either within the working class or among capitalists constitute partial explanations for their lower rate of participation. In the absence of interviews or written memoirs, it is important to examine the work patterns of specific families more closely to see what reasons can be deduced from the evidence.[24]

Even among the families apparently in greatest need, sons seem to have been sent out to work in preference to daughters. If any families needed to draw on as many workers as possible, it should have been those headed by the labourers or shoemakers of these wards. In such families, food costs alone for a family with several growing children rapidly outstripped a man's incoming wages. Yet even these families appear to have avoided sending girls out to work, if possible. Among labourers' families in Ste. Anne in 1881, for example, 66 percent of those who had boys over ten reported having a son at work, while only 28 percent of those with girls the same age did so. If older brothers were working, girls generally did not. Girls of age twenty or more would stay at home while a teenage son worked. Their respective roles seem clearly defined. Twenty-six-year-old Ellen Mullin, for example, reported no occupation. Two brothers, aged nineteen and 23, worked as carters. Ellen's role was to help her mother with the domestic labour for the three wage earners and her fourteen-year-old younger brother.[25]

In Ste. Anne, even families without sons, or with young sons only, seem to have been either unwilling to send girls to work or unable to find work that was seen as suitable in the neighbourhood. Forty-two-year-old Octave Ethier must surely have had trouble supporting his four daughters, aged one to seventeen, and his wife on his labourer's wages. Yet neither seventeen-year-old Philomène nor fifteen-year-old Emma reported having a job.[26]

The girls in labourers' families who did report an occupation fell into two categories. Half were the oldest child, either with no brothers or only brothers who were much younger than they were. Nineteen-year-old Sarah Anne Labor, for instance, was the oldest in a family of six children. The closest brother was only seven. She worked as a soap maker. Her wages, and the fact that the family shared the household with several other families, must have helped make ends meet.[27]

The second group of girl workers in Ste. Anne and St. Jacques came from labourers' families that sent almost all their children to work regardless of gender. Catherine Harrigan, for instance, was fourteen. She worked as a servant. Her two brothers, aged fifteen and twenty, were labourers like their father. In the family of St. Jacques labourer Damase Racette, four girls, aged seventeen to 25, were all dressmakers, as was his wife, Rachel. A 27-year-old son was a cigar maker.[28] This latter group of families appears the most desperate, perhaps because of recurrent illness or the habitual drunkenness of a parent. When Commissioners Lukas and Blackeby were examining the work of children in Canadian mills and factories in 1882, they reported finding too many cases in the cities and factory districts where parents with "idle habits" lived "on the earnings of the children, this being confirmed" in their eyes by one instance where three children were at work, having a father as above described.[29] Yet, such a family could simply have been taking advantage of the fact of having more children of working age to make up for years of deprivation on the inadequate wages most family heads could make. Two years later, reports made to the Ontario Bureau of Industries stressed the inadequate wages of family heads as the major cause of children's working, while mentioning that dissipation of the husband or father was less often a cause.[30] When a father was chronically ill or a habitual drunkard, the wages of several children would indeed have been necessary to support a family. The use of daughters and of children aged ten to twelve to earn wages in this minority of labourers' families contrasts with the absence of such workers in other labourers' families, highlighting the relative infrequency of a daughter's work, even among those in greatest need.

Was it in part working-class ideology that kept girls at home if at all possible, seeing the workplace as unfit for them, or was it rather a pragmatic response to the fact that boys' wages rapidly outstripped those of girls? Pragmatism, made necessary by the exigencies of daily life, must certainly have played an important part. It made good sense to have boys earn wages rather than girls, for while young children of each sex might earn a similar wage, once they reached fifteen or sixteen, girls' wages were generally half those of young men. On the other hand, when there was work available that girls could do, more were likely to report a job. Thus, the labourers of St. Jacques were more likely to have daughters at work than those of Ste. Anne. St. Jacques labourers' families with children aged eleven or over had an equal percentage of girls and boys at work. The fact that nearly 80 percent of these girls worked in some branch of the sewing industry shows how families took advantage of the availability of this kind of work in the neighbourhood.

Family labour deployment decisions, then, were forged in the context of their own needs, invariably arising partly from the size, age, and gender configurations of the family, as well as from the kind of work the family head could find. They were realized in relationship with the structure of the local labour market, of job possibilities, and of local wage rates for men and women, boys and girls. And they were influenced by perceptions, ideologies, and gut reactions about what was appropriate for sons and daughters. Thus, it was not just the fact that sewing was available in St. Jacques ward that made this such a popular choice for daughters living in that ward, for putting out could theoretically operate anywhere in the city or the surrounding countryside. It was, I suspect, the very fact that it could be done at home that was crucial. For, while domestic service no doubt took some young women from families in these wards away from their own families and into the homes of others, sewing usually kept daughters working at home.[31]

Home-work offered parents, and mothers in particular, several advantages. First, they could oversee their daughters' work and behaviour, avoiding the individualism that working in a factory might encourage and skirting the dangers and moral pitfalls that at least some contemporaries associated with factory work for young, unmarried women.[32] More important, girls sewing at home, like their mothers, could combine stitching and housework, take care of younger children, run odd errands, or carry water as needed, because they were right there and were always paid by the piece.

The clustering of two to five family members, all seamstresses, commonly found in the census returns for St. Jacques ward suggests very strongly that here was a centre of the home-work that was crucial to Montreal's sewing and shoemaking industries during this period. It was not uncommon to find three to four sisters, ranging in age from eleven to 28, all working, presumably together, as sewing girls. In the Mosian family of St. Jacques ward, for instance, four daughters worked as seamstresses in 1871. The father was a labourer, and although the wife reported no occupation, she probably also did some sewing at home at times.[33] In 1881, the family of Marie and Michel Guigère had reached a relatively secure stage in their family life cycle. With nine children at home, aged two to 23, this joiner's family reported seven workers. Four of the girls, aged thirteen to 23, were seamstresses; one son worked as a labourer; and the thirteen-year-old son was an apprentice. The girls could combine sewing with helping their mother keep house for other workers, care for the younger children, shop, cook, clean, and also look after her husband's 70-year-old father, who lived with them. Marie too probably helped sporadically with sewing.[34]

Some parents with the liberty to choose must have been reluctant to expose their daughters to the long hours, continual supervision, exhausting work, and brutal forms of discipline that existed in some of Montreal's workshops and factories. Work at home could counteract such factors of "repulsion"[35] in some of the sectors employing girls. Cigar-making factories provided jobs for girls and boys in Ste. Anne and St. Jacques alike. While some manufacturers appear to have been decent men, neither fining nor beating their employees, others, in an apparently desperate attempt to control their youthful workforce, resorted to physical violence, heavy fines, even locking up children, as they strove to mould this young generation of workers to industrial work. Children, like adults, in these factories worked from six or seven in the morning until six at night, and sometimes later.[36] Unlike adult males, they were subject to a vast array of disciplinary measures aimed at making them more productive and more responsible as workers. One child reported:

> If a child did anything, that is, if he looked on one side or other, or spoke, he would say: I'm going to make you pay 10 cents fine, and if the same were repeated three or four times, he would seize a stick or a plank, and beat him with it.[37]

Mr. Fortier's cigar-making factory was described as a "theatre of lewdness." There was said to be "no such infamous factory as M. Fortier's . . . nowhere else as bad in Montreal." There, one cigar maker described apprentices as being "treated more or less as slaves."[38] It was the evidence of the treatment of one eighteen-year-old girl that really shocked both the public and the commissioners examining the relations between labour and capital in 1888. Georgina Loiselle described how Mr. Fortier beat her with a mould cover because she would not make the 100 cigars as he demanded.

> I was sitting, and he took hold of me by the arm, and tried to throw me on the ground. He did throw me on the ground and beat me with the mould cover.
> Q. Did he beat you when you were down?
> A. Yes, I tried to rise and he kept me down on the floor.[39]

The case of Mr. Fortier's cigar factory was not typical. It created a sensation when the evidence was heard. At least some of the mothers of girls working there got together, perhaps encouraged by Mr. Fortier, to give evidence to counteract the impact of such bad publicity. "I am the mother of a family and if I had seen anything improper I would not have stayed there," explained a Mrs. Levoise. "I have my girl working there."[40]

While conditions in other Montreal factories were not as extreme, there was sufficient evidence of beatings, other draconian forms of discipline, and heavy fines to explain why many girls and their parents may have wished to avoid factory labour. In cotton factories there was some evidence of boys and girls being beaten. Furthermore, fines in at least one Montreal cotton factory could reduce pay packages by between $1.00 and $12.00 in two weeks. Work there began at 6:25 A.M. and finished at 6:15 P.M. When extra work was required, employees had to stay until 9 P.M., often without time off for supper.[41] There were some perks to working in the textile industry. Nineteen-year-old Adèle Lavoie explained that the girls were accustomed to "take cotton to make our aprons." Apparently this was usually allowed, but on at least one occasion she was accused by the foreman of having taken 40 to 50 yards. When a search of her house produced no results, she reported that the foreman returned to the factory to insult and harass her sister. When she did not produce the cotton, "he stooped at this time and raising the skirt of my sister's dress, he said she had it under her skirt."[42]

Airless, hot, dusty factories, such sexual abuse by foremen, work conditions, and the long hours were all factors that may have discouraged parents from sending girls into factory work. More significant were the wages they earned. For children under fourteen or so, wages varied little by sex. After that, male and female differentials hardened. Girl apprentices in dressmaking, mantlemaking, and millinery sometimes earned nothing for several years until they learned the trade; then they received around $4.00 a week only. "Girls" in shoe manufactories received $3.00 to $4.00, compared to the $7.00 or $8.00 earned by men. A girl bookbinder made between $1.50 and $6.00 weekly, compared to an average of $11.00 for male journeymen. Even on piece-work, girls and women generally received less than men. In general, wage rates for women were approximately half those of men.[43]

Over this period, more and more working-class boys would have reached manhood accustomed to wage labour. Because of duties at home and low wages, however, their sisters, whether they worked in or outside the home, were much more likely to move backwards and forwards between paid work and housework in response to the family's economic needs and their position in the household. Once boys, and particularly those who had been fortunate enough to acquire a skill in demand in the marketplace, reached their late teens, their earning power might rival that of their father. Wage labour offered such children potential freedom from their family in a way that had not been possible in family economies based on shared work and the inheritance of property. Such freedom was seldom possible for girls, unless they were willing to complement wage labour with prostitution.

Age, Gender, and Changing Patterns of Residence, Schooling, and Domestic Labour

Yet, boys in general do not appear to have taken dramatic advantage of such potential freedom. Nor did girls.[44] In 1861, living with others was still an important stage in the lives of some young people of both sexes. Among the seventeen-year-old girls residing in Ste. Anne and St. Jacques, 35 percent were boarding with other families, living with relatives, or working and living in as a servant. Twenty years later, only 12 percent of girls that age were not living with their parents, and half of these were already married. Among boys aged eighteen, 34 percent were not living with their parents in 1861, compared to only 17 percent two decades later. Living longer at home with their parents was a fundamental change in the life cycle of boys and girls alike during this period of industrial expansion.[45]

Behind the percentages of children living with their parents or elsewhere lies a complex history of tension between family needs and individual desires, of children balancing off the advantages of the services offered at home against the relative independence that living with strangers, or even relatives, might offer.[46] For all families who had passed through at least fifteen years of budget stretching, house sharing, and debt building while their children were young, the relative prosperity that several workers could offer was to be jealously guarded. It was precisely "because young adults could find jobs" that it "was in the interest of parents to keep their children at home as long as possible."[47] The patterns of residence of children suggest that, whatever conflicts there were overall, in these two wards of Montreal between 1861 and 1881, it was increasingly the parents who were the winners.

The motives behind individual decisions, the weight of traditions of family work, are difficult to grasp in the absence of written records. The factors constraining or encouraging one choice or another are clearer. Most children would have left home once they had a job only if their wages were adequate to pay for lodgings and they felt no commitment to contributing to the family income.[48] Clearly, more older boys earned enough to pay for room and board than did girls. Thus, in 1871, when work was readily available, 29 percent of the 23-year-old males living in these wards were boarding or with relatives, 39 percent were living with their parents, and 32 percent had married. Among girls the same age, the low wages they could make severely limited their options. Only 15 percent were boarding, 41 percent were still with their parents, and 44 percent were already married. The contraction of work and the lower wages that accompanied the depression that hit in 1874 limited the possibility of leaving home to lodge with others or to marry. In 1881, the percentage of 23-year-old boys married had dropped to 25 percent; only 10 percent were boarding or living with relatives. Sixty-five percent remained at home with their parents, presumably pooling resources to survive the difficult times. The depression appears to have hastened the decline of this stage of semi-autonomy. What occurred in subsequent years remains to be determined.

The different roles of boys and girls in the family economy are confirmed in the different patterns of school attendance by age and sex. In general, school and work appear to have been complementary rather than in competition. Some children began school at four years old. By age seven, approximately 60 percent of boys and girls were receiving some education. In 1881, this percentage rose to a peak of 78 percent for eight- and nine-year-old boys, and around 80 percent for girls aged nine to twelve, then fell off rapidly once both sexes reached thirteen. The proportion of children receiving some schooling increased, but not dramatically, between 1861 and 1881. Age, gender, and the economic conjuncture created variations within this overall trend. Most important was the more erratic pattern in the attendance of boys that hints at relationships between age, gender, schooling, and wage labour that require further investigation. Overall, the percentage of ten- to fourteen-year-old girls at school increased slowly but steadily, from 57 percent in 1861 to 68 percent in 1881.[49] The increase was greater in St. Jacques than Ste. Anne, but the pattern was similar. Among boys in each ward, in contrast, the proportion at school was lower in 1871 than any other year, and the proportion of ten- to nineteen-year-olds at work increased. In Ste. Anne, in particular, the factories, workshops, and general labouring jobs attracted growing numbers of these youths. The percentage of fifteen- to nineteen-year-old boys reporting working in that ward increased from 38 in 1861 to 64 a decade later. While a certain number of families appear to have taken advantage of boom periods to draw their sons, in particular, out of school, the majority of families appear to have got the best of both worlds. Most working-class boys went to school for varying lengths of time before they reached thirteen or so, and then sought wage labour.

These figures confirm the greater importance of a son's wage contribution to the family economy. Girls' role is clear in the high proportion that continued to report neither a job nor school attendance. Transformations of the economy and the passage of time were slow to modify this gender difference in the relationship between girls' and boys' schooling and their roles in the family economy. A study conducted in Quebec in 1942, just before school was finally made compulsory in that province, found that among children quitting school before the age of sixteen, 61 percent of girls gave as their reason, "Maman avait besoin de moi," while 50 percent of boys stated, "Ma famille avait besoin d'argent." Only 10 percent of girls gave that reason.[50] The centrality of girls' domestic labour in a different Canadian city, Toronto, is corroborated by evidence showing that potential foster parents in that city at the turn of the century were four times more likely to seek girls than boys, specifically for their usefulness as domestics and nursemaids.[51]

Conclusion

Gender was clearly at work in both senses of the word in nineteenth-century Montreal. On the one hand, the labour market was characterized by a sexual division of labour which, despite the rapid and dramatic changes occurring in the period, limited the numbers of jobs where capitalists considered employing women. This was not immutable, as the cases where "girls" were used as strikebreakers made clear. Montreal's labour market included major sectors, particularly sewing and shoemaking, that employed large numbers of girls and women. Yet, the figures of labour-force participation rates for the two wards studied here suggest strongly that girls and women seldom entered the workforce in proportions equivalent to their brothers or boys the same age, and that over their life courses their participation was totally different.

The reasons why lie at least partially within the workings of the family-wage economy. Working-class families in Montreal clearly both needed and used additional family workers to counteract low wages, and to improve their standard of living. The number of extra workers varied with the skill of the family head and the worth of that skill in the labour market. Thus, while skilled workers managed, in good times, with fewer family workers than the unskilled or those in indentured trades, economic depression eroded such superiority. Yet in whatever complex and probably tension-loaded decisions were made about who would seek what kind of work, boys were much more likely to be the auxiliary wage earners than girls.

To explain why brings us, in a sense, to the heart of the debate about the relative importance of patriarchy and capitalism in explaining women's oppression.[52] That the domestic labour of wives has been crucial both to family survival and to women's inequality has long been recognized both empirically and theoretically. But where do daughters fit in? Fathers, one could argue, by keeping girls at home along with their mothers to serve their daily need for replenishment, ensured that the work of all women was viewed as intermittent and secondary to that of the major wage earners.[53] Alternatively, the accent can be put on the nature of specific industries, or more generally on the capitalist labour market, which, by setting women's wage rates at half those of men, made it logical to send boys to work rather than girls.[54] Unequal access to work on the same terms as men thus not only perpetuated women's position in the home, but tragically disadvantaged those single women and widows who alone, or supporting children or elderly parents, had to live on such wages.

Clearly a dialectic is at work here. Neither empirically nor theoretically can the workings of patriarchy or capitalism be neatly separated from each other.[55] The nature of the interaction between the two and the weight of one over the other will vary historically and geographically. Among Montreal families, decisions were made in part in relation to existing jobs and wage rates, and such decisions perpetuated and reified the idea that women's work was temporary, performed before marriage or in moments of family crisis.[56] Admitting the dialectic adds complexity to the explanation but remains, I suspect, insufficient, because the emphasis remains on the formal, wage-earning labour market. Domestic labour in the nineteenth century was fundamental to family survival, to the transformation of wages into a reasonable standard of living, and to the reproduction of the working class. Historians have recognized the importance of this job for the working-class wife and mother; the role of daughters has been examined less explicitly.[57] Yet, for nineteenth-century mothers whose children were widely spaced in age and in whose homes technology had made virtually no inroads to lighten their labour, the help of daughters was invaluable. Housewives had no control over the amount of wages the husband earned, and little over how much was turned over to them. Housework was labour intensive and time consuming. One of the only ways in which wives could control the content and intensity of their work was to get children to help. Wherever possible, once girls reached an age where they could be of use to the mother, they were used to babysit, to run errands, to clean, sew, and cook. If this could be combined with wage-earning activities, as in the case of home-work in the sewing industry, then such girls did work more formally. If there were no brothers of an age to earn, daughters might work in factories, offices, or shops, or as domestics. But the need of mothers for at least one helper at home would mean that the rate of formal labour-force participation for girls would generally be lower than that for boys.[58] Patriarchal ideas within the working class, elements of male pride and self-interest, economic pragmatism, and the daily needs of mothers and housewives thus inter-acted, creating a situation in which most girls served an apprenticeship in domestic labour prior to, or in conjunction with, entering the workforce.[59] In cities and towns where the labour market was completely different, where whole families or women were explicitly sought by employers, this division of labour, indeed, the very institutions of marriage and the family, could be modified. The question of how to ensure that the necessary domestic labour was performed, however, would remain fundamental.[60] The working out of roles by gender at home would continue to influence the configurations of gender at work.

NOTES

1. Heidi Hartmann, "Capitalism, Patriarchy, and Job Segregation by Sex," *Signs* 1 (Spring 1976): 137–69; Judy Lown, "Not So Much a Factory, More a Form of Patriarchy: Gender and Class during Industrialisation," in E. Garmarnikow et al., *Gender, Class, and Work* (London, 1983); Sonya O. Rose, "Gender at Work: Sex, Class, and Industrial Capitalism," *History Workshop Journal* 21 (Spring 1986): 113–31; Nancy Grey Osterud, "Gender Divisions and the Organization of Work in the Leicester Hosiery Industry," in Angela V. John, *Unequal Opportunities: Women's Employment in England, 1800–1918* (Oxford: Basil Blackwell, 1986), 45–70; Sylvia Walby, *Patriarchy at Work: Patriarchal and Capitalist Relations in Employment* (Minneapolis: University of Minnesota Press, 1986); Ruth Milkman, *Gender at Work: The Dynamics of Job Segregation by Sex during World War II* (Urbana: University of Illinois Press, 1987). For Canadian articles touching on the question, see Gail Cuthbert Brandt, "The Transformation of Women's Work in the Quebec Cotton Industry, 1920–1950," in *The Character of Class Struggle: Essays in Canadian Working Class History, 1840–1985*, ed. Bryan D. Palmer (Toronto: McClelland and Stewart, 1986); Mercedes Steedman, "Skill and Gender in the Canadian Clothing Industry, 1890–1940," in *On the Job: Confronting the Labour Process in Canada*, ed. Craig Heron and Robert Storey (Montreal: McGill-Queen's University Press, 1986), 152–76; Marta Danylewycz and Alison Prentice, "The Evolution of the Sexual Division of Labour in Teaching: A Nineteenth-Century Ontario and Quebec Case Study," *Histoire sociale/Social History* 6 (1983): 81–109; Marta Danylewycz and Alison Prentice, "Teachers, Gender, and Bureaucrating School Systems in Nineteenth-Century Montreal and Toronto," *History of Education Quarterly* 24 (1984): 75–100; Jacques Ferland, "Syndicalisme parcellaire et syndicalisme collectif: Une interpretation socio-technique des con-flits ouvriers dans deux industries québécoises, 1880–1914," *Labour/Le Travail* 19 (Spring 1987): 49–88.

2. This argument is obviously not mine alone. It is fundamental to much of the discussion of the workings of patriarchy and to the domestic labour debate, where too often it remains at an abstract theoretical level or based on cursory historical data. It is worth making here because much theoretical work places too much emphasis on either capitalist relations or reproduction and patriarchy, simplifying the complexity of relations between the two, while historical litera-ture on the workplace or the family tends to treat the relation between the two simplistically.

190

3. Joy Parr's recent articles offer the first major sustained analysis in which decisions and conditions in the home and in the workplace and the relationship between the two are constantly and systematically examined. See especially "Rethinking Work and Kinship in a Canadian Hosiery Town, 1910–1950," *Feminist Studies* 13, 1 (Spring 1987): 137–62; and also "The Skilled Emigrant and Her Kin: Gender, Culture, and Labour Recruitment," *Canadian Historical Review* 68, 4 (Dec. 1987): 520–57, reprinted in *Rethinking Canada: The Promise of Women's History*, 2nd ed., ed. Veronica Strong-Boag and Anita Clair Fellman (Toronto: Copp Clark Pitman, 1991), 33–55. Gail Cuthbert-Brandt does so in a different sense in "Weaving It Together: Life Cycle and the Industrial Experience of Female Cotton Workers in Quebec, 1910–1950," *Labour/Le Travailleur* 7 (Spring 1981). Mark Rosenfeld's recent article " 'It Was a Hard Life': Class and Gender in the Work and Family Rhythms of a Railway Town, 1920–1950," *Historical Papers* (1988), and reprinted in this volume [i.e., *Canadian and Australian Labour History*], carefully unravels how the rhythms of work in the running trades structured the family economy and gender roles in Barrie, Ontario, a railway town.

4. No Canadian work directly confronts this question either in the econometric sense in which Claudia Goldin poses it in "Family Strategies and the Family Economy in the Late Nineteenth Century: The Role of Secondary Workers," in *Philadelphia: Work, Space, Family and Group Experience in the Nineteenth Century*, ed. Theodore Hershberg (New York: Oxford University Press, 1981), 277–310, or in the more feminist and qualitative way that Lynn Jamieson poses it in "Limited Resources and Limiting Conventions: Working-Class Mothers and Daughters in Urban Scotland c. 1890–1925," in *Labour and Love: Women's Experience of Home and Family, 1850–1940*, ed. Jane Lewis (Oxford: Basil Blackwell, 1986), 49–69.

5. Marjorie Cohen makes a similar argument without elaborating on its implications for daughters in stating that "the supply of female labour was limited by the labour requirements of the home." *Women's Work, Markets, and Economic Development in Nineteenth-Century Ontario* (Toronto: University of Toronto Press, 1988), 139. Her insistence on the importance of domestic production and women's work in the home for rural and urban families alike and for an understanding of the wider economy represents an important contribution to economic history as well as to the history of women and the family in Canada.

6. On the average, in the early 1880s, for example, a labourer earned around $1.00 a day, a shoemaker $1.25, a carpenter $1.50, and various more highly skilled workers anything from $1.75 (blacksmith) up. See Bettina Bradbury, "The Working-Class Family Economy, Montreal, 1861–1881" (Ph.D. diss., Concordia University, 1984), 18; Canada, Parliament, *Sessional Papers*, 1882, Paper No. 4, Appendix 3, Annual Report of the Immigration Agent, 110–11, lists wages in a variety of trades.

7. In this, Montreal and Canada were little different from other cities and countries, nor has much of the discrepancy been eliminated today.

8. The figures used in this paper are derived from research done for my Ph.D. thesis, currently under revision for publication. A 10 percent random sample was taken of households enumerated by the census takers in Ste. Anne and St. Jacques in 1861, 1871, and 1881. This resulted in a total sample of 10 967 people over the three decades. They resided in 1851 households and 2278 families as defined by the census takers.

9. For a brief and preliminary examination of how widows of all ages survived, see my "Surviving as a Widow in Nineteenth-Century Montreal," *Urban History Review* 17, 3 (1989): 148–60, reprinted in *Rethinking Canada*, 2nd ed., ed. Strong-Boag and Fellman.

10. These life histories were re-created by tracing families between the censuses of 1861, 1871, and 1881.

11. Mss. Census, St. Jacques, 1881, 17, p. 110.

12. *Iron Moulders Journal*, Jan. and June, 1878, Report of Local 21; *Iron Moulders Journal*, Jan. 1876, Report of Local 21 and open letter from Local 21 to the editor, cited in Peter Bischoff, "La formation des traditions de solidarité ouvrière chez les mouleurs Montréalais: la longue marche vers le syndicalisme, 1859–1881," *Labour/Le Travail* 21 (Spring 1988): 22. Bischoff suggests, sensibly, that among moulders the homogenizing experience of these years of depression left them more open to the idea of including less skilled workers in their union in the 1880s. The widespread appeal of the Knights of Labour could be seen in the same light.

13. In 1861, for example, only 16 percent of those reporting jobs in these two wards were children residing at home; twenty years later nearly one-third of all reported workers were offspring living with their parents. Peter Bischoff found a similar trend among moulders. The percentage of moulders for the entire city of Montreal that were sons living with their parents rose from 25 percent in 1861 to nearly 40 percent in 1881. Peter Bischoff, "Les ouvriers mouleurs à Montréal, 1859–1881" (M.A. thesis, Université de Québec à Montréal, 1986), 108.

14. There is no doubt that the wage labour both of young children and married women was under-enumerated. However, as no labour laws existed in Quebec until 1885, and education was not compulsory until 1943, it is unlikely that fear of repercussions would have inhibited parents from responding as it might have elsewhere. It seems fair to assume that the under-reporting of children's jobs, and probably married women's, would have been no greater in Montreal than in other cities of Canada, England, or America, and probably less.

15. Tamara K. Hareven and Randolph Langenbach, *Amoskeag: Life and Work in an American Factory City* (New York: Pantheon Books, 1978), 262.

16. Caution has to be exercised when using reported jobs for women and children. There is a tendency now in some of the literature on the subject to suggest that gender differentials in work-force participation are largely a result of women's work not being adequately enumerated. While I am sure that some under-enumeration of women's work occurred in Montreal, as elsewhere, I don't think that under-enumeration can explain away the differential. Nor is the phenomenon easy to measure. More important, I think, was the nature of women's work, which, because of its lack of regularity, its more informal nature, was less likely to be reported. On the problem of under-reporting, see, in particular, Sally Alexander, "Women's Work in Nineteenth-Century London: A Study of the Years 1820–1850," in *The Rights and Wrongs of Women*, ed. Juliett Mitchell and Ann Oakley (London: Penguin Books, 1976), 63–66; Karen Oppenheim Mason, Maris Vinovskis, and Tamara K. Hareven, "Women's Work and the Life Course in Essex County, Massachusetts, 1880," in Tamara K. Hareven, *Transitions: The Family and the Life Course in Historical Perspective* (New York: Academic Press, 1979), 191; Margo A. Conk, "Accuracy, Efficiency and Bias: The Interpretation of Women's Work in the U.S. Census of Occupations, 1890–1940," *Historical Methods* 14, 2 (Spring 1981): 65–72; Edward Higgs, "Women, Occupations, and Work in the Nineteenth-Century Censuses," *History Workshop* 23 (Spring 1987).

17. Joan Scott and Louise Tilly, *Women, Work, and Family* (New York: Holt, Rinehart and Winston, 1979), 231.

18. Mss. Census, 1861, St. Jacques, 11, p. 7750.

19. By the end of the century the need for this kind of education of daughters was being explicitly preached by Montreal doctors and by church representatives, and was formalized in Quebec with the creation of *écoles ménagères* after the 1880s. Carole Dion, "La femme et la santé de la famille au Québec, 1890–1940" (M.A. thesis, Université de Montréal, 1984).

20. A. (Père) Mailloux, *Le manuel des parents Chrétiens* (Quebec, 1851, 1910), cited in Carole Dion, "La femme et la santé de la famille," 60–65.

21. L.A. Huguet-Latour, *L'Annuaire de Ville Marie: Origine, utilité, et progrès des institutions catholiques de Montréal* (Montreal, 1877), 165–70.

22. Marie-Paule Malouin, "Les rapports entre l'école privée et l'école publique: L'Académie Marie-Rose au 19e siècle," in *Maîtresses de maison, maîtresses d'école*, ed. Nadia Fahmy-Eid and Micheline Dumont (Montreal: Boreal Express, 1983), 90.

23. Québec, *Documents de la Session*, 1874, "Rapport du Ministre de l'instruction publique," vii.

24. In Lynn Jamieson's study of working-class mothers and daughters in Scotland, which is based on interviews, she makes it clear that mothers made different demands upon boys and girls in terms of the contributions they should make to the family economy. Mothers "pre-occupied with their housekeeping responsibilities" were much more likely to keep girls home from school to help with housework than to encourage boys to go out and earn. If a father died, for example, daughters or sons might enter full-time paid employment, but if a mother died "only daughters left school early to become full-time housekeepers." "Working-Class Mothers and Daughters in Scotland," in *Labour and Love*, 54, 65.

25. Mss. Census, Ste. Anne, 1881, 5, p. 1.
26. Mss. Census, Ste. Anne, 1881, 5, p. 1.
27. Mss. Census, Ste. Anne, 1881, 9, p. 208.
28. Mss. Census, St. Jacques, 1881, 17, p. 340.
29. "Report of the Commissioners Appointed to Enquire into the Working of the Mills and Factories of the Dominion and the Labour Employed Therein," Canada, Parliament, *Sessional Papers*, 1882, Paper No. 42, p. 2.
30. Annual Report of the Ontario Bureau of Industries, 1884, cited in Cohen, *Women's Work*, 128.
31. The fact that domestic service was Montreal's leading employment for girls, and that it usually involved living in, complicates this analysis of the work of children. Girls could work away from home as domestics and contribute their pay to their parents; they would not, however, figure among the average number of workers found in census families, nor would their experience be captured in the proportion of girls having a job. On the other hand, neither is that of any boys who left to find work in construction shanties, lumbering camps, railroad work, etc. The figures given in the text are always the percentages of those living in the ward, and with their parents, who reported a job. Those who lived and worked elsewhere are thus always removed from both the numerator and the denominator.
32. On the commissioners' concerns about this, see Susan Mann Trofimenkoff, "One Hundred and One Muffled Voices," in *The Neglected Majority: Essays in Canadian Women's History*, ed. Susan Mann Trofimenkoff and Alison Prentice (Toronto: McClelland and Stewart, 1977). How the working class viewed these morality issues requires examination.
33. Mss. Census, St. Jacques, 1871, 6, p. 137.
34. Mss. Census, St. Jacques, 1881, 12, p. 101.
35. Sydney Pollard, *The Genesis of Modern Management: A Study of the Industrial Revolution* (London: Edward Arnold, 1965), 162.
36. Royal Commission on the Relations of Capital and Labour (RCRCL), *Quebec Evidence*, evidence of Wm. C. McDonald, tobacco manufacturer, p. 529.
37. RCRCL, *Quebec Evidence*, anonymous evidence, p. 42.
38. RCRCL, *Quebec Evidence*, pp. 44–47.
39. RCRCL, *Quebec Evidence*, p. 91.
40. RCRCL, *Quebec Evidence*, evidence of Mrs. Levoise.
41. RCRCL, *Quebec Evidence*, evidence of a machinist, Hudon factory, Hochelaga, pp. 273–74.
42. RCRCL, *Quebec Evidence*, evidence of Adèle Lavoie, pp. 280–82.
43. RCRCL, *Quebec Evidence*, evidence of Patrick Ryan, cigar maker, p. 37; machinist, Hudon Mills, p. 271; Samuel Carsley, dry goods merchant, p. 15; Oliver Benoit, boot and shoemaker, p. 365; Henry Morton, printer, p. 297; F. Stanley, foreman at the Star, p. 331.
44. Here I am referring to the percentage of children at home as opposed to boarding, living with relatives, or living in someone else's house as a servant. The samples taken in each census do not allow me to follow children over time and identify those who actually left home.
45. The same process occurred in Hamilton, and in other cities that have been studied. See Michael Katz, *The People of Hamilton*, 257, 261; Mary P. Ryan, *The Cradle of the Middle Class: The Family in Oneida County*, New York, 1790–1865 (New York: Cambridge University Press, 1981), 168–69; Richard Wall, "The Age at Leaving Home," *Journal of Family History* 8 (Fall 1983): 238.
46. For a careful analysis of the relationship between women's wages, costs of board, and decisions about where to live, see Gary Cross and Peter Shergold, "The Family Economy and the Market: Wages and Residence of Pennsylvania Women in the 1890s," *Journal of Family History* 11, 3 (1986): 245–66.
47. Paul Spagnoli, "Industrialization, Proletarianization and Marriage," *Journal of Family History* 8 (Fall 1983): 238.
48. Michael Anderson's careful analysis of which children left home shows that boys in Preston, Lancashire, were more likely to do so than girls. He believes children made "a conscious calculation of the advantages and disadvantages, in terms of the standard of living which they could

enjoy," based on the wages they could make, their father's wage, and the amount they were required to hand over to their parents. *Family Structure*, 67, 127–29.

49. A similar, but greater, increase in girls' school attendance is described for Hamilton by Michael B. Katz and Ian E. Davey in "Youth and Early Industrialization," in *Turning Points: Historical and Sociological Essays on the Family*, ed. John Demos and Sarane Spence Boocock.

50. "Le problème des jeunes qui ne fréquent plus l'école," *École Sociale Populaire* 351 (April 1941), 26, cited by Dominique Jean, "Les familles québécois et trois politiques sociales touchant les enfants, de 1940 à 1960: Obligation scolaire, allocations familiales et loi controlant le travail juvenile" (Ph.D. diss., Université de Montréal, 1988).

51. "First Report of Work Under the Children's Protection Act," p. 26; "Third Report of Work Under the Children's Protection Act," p. 10, cited in John Bullen, "J.J. Kelso and the 'New' Child-Savers: The Genesis of the Children's Aid Movement in Ontario" (Paper presented to the CHA Annual Meeting, Windsor, Ont., June 1988), 35–38.

52. The usefulness of taking a category of women other than wives and mothers to test the soundness of contemporary feminist theory on this question is clear in the article of Danielle Juteau and Nicole Frenette, who start with an examination of the role of nuns in late-nineteenth- and early-twentieth-century Quebec, and use their insights to critique much contemporary feminist theory. "L'évolution des formes de l'appropriation des femmes: Des religieuses aux 'mères por-teuses,'" *Canadian Review of Sociology and Anthropology* 25, 2 (1988).

53. One of the great advantages of the domestic labour debate was its recognition of the importance of housework and reproduction of labour power to capitalism. Less clear in much of the writing was the failure of most writers to acknowledge the interest of men in the perpetuation of domestic labour. For an elaboration of this critique, see Walby, *Patriarchy at Work*, 18–19.

54. Ruth Milkman criticizes labour-segmentation theory, early Marxist-feminist writing, and Hartmann's description of patriarchy for paying insufficient attention to the effect of industrial structure on the sexual division of labour and struggles over "woman's place" in the labour market. Looking much more concretely than theorists have done at specific industries, she argues that "an industry's pattern of employment by sex reflects the economic, political, and social constraints that are operative when that industry's labour market initially forms." *Gender at Work*, 7.

55. Herein lies the problem of the "dual systems" approach of Hartmann and others. Heidi Hartmann, "Capitalism, Patriarchy and Job Segregation by Sex," *Signs* (1977); Varda Burstyn, "Masculine Dominance and the State," in Varda Burstyn and Dorothy Smith, *Women, Class, Family, and the State* (Toronto: Garamond Press, 1985); Sylvia Walby succeeds better than others in drawing out the links between the two, but insists on their relative autonomy in *Patriarchy at Work*.

56. Canadian historians, whether in women's history or working-class history, are only just beginning to unravel this complex, dialectical relationship between the structure of the economy and the needs of the family, in interaction with both capital's and labour's definitions of gender roles. It is an unravelling that must continue if we are to understand how gender was at work and continues to work outside the workplace as well as within it.

57. Some of the problems faced by feminist theoreticians grappling with the relationship between women's oppression by males within marriage, their subordination in the labour market, and the wider forces of patriarchy stem from the assumption that only wives perform domestic labour. This seems to me a profoundly ahistorical view, and one that downplays the importance of the family as a place of socialization and training.

58. Here would be an example of mothers making choices that made their lives easier, but that in the long run perpetuated, even exaggerated, men's more privileged position in the marketplace. On this, see Gerder Lerner, *The Creation of Patriarchy* (Oxford: Oxford University Press, 1986), cited in Bonnie Fox, "Conceptualizing Patriarchy," *Canadian Review of Sociology and Anthropology* 25, 2 (1988): 165.

59. Psychological, Freudian theories about gender identity seem less important here than the practical day-to-day experience in the home and the role model of the mother. Nancy Chodorow, *The Reproduction of Mothering* (Berkeley: University of California Press, 1978).

60. For a superb description of the complex ways in which women in Paris, Ontario—a knitting town where job opportunities for women were much greater than for men—dealt with domestic labour, see Joy Parr, "Rethinking Work and Kinship in a Canadian Hosiery Town, 1910–1950," *Feminist Studies* 13, 1 (Spring 1987): 137–62.

Article Fifteen

Joe Beef of Montreal: Working-Class Culture and the Tavern, 1869–1889

Peter DeLottinville

Montreal was a city of contrasts. The casual tourist, following the advice of his *Strangers' Guide to Montreal*,[1] would spend days viewing florid Gothic and ornate Italian church architecture, the engineering marvel of Robert Stevenson's Victoria Bridge, and the various monuments to commercial power. This faithful *cicerone*, however, would not give the tourist the total picture of a nineteenth-century urban landscape. The official face of Canada's first city consisted of monuments to individual industry, public morality, and social harmony. Absent from the official guide were the inhabitants of the narrower streets —the factory workers, the frequenters of taverns, the waterfront street gangs, or the crowds of longshoremen outside the Allen Line office waiting for work. What the tourist needed to see was a monument to Montreal's working class. Had he accidentally wandered into Joe Beef's Canteen, the tourist might have found it, where the rules and procedures of official Montreal had little value.

During the late nineteenth century, Joe Beef's Canteen was a notorious part of that underworld which existed in the Victorian city.[2] Located in the centre of the waterfront district, the Canteen was the haunt of sailors and longshoremen, unemployed men and petty thieves. Middle-class Montreal saw this tavern as a moral hazard to all who entered and a threat to social peace. Yet if critics called the Canteen's owner, Charles McKiernan, the "wickedest man" of the city, working-class residents along the waterfront claimed McKiernan as their champion. His tavern was a popular drinking spot, but also a source of aid in times of unemployment, sickness, and hunger. For its patrons, Joe Beef's Canteen was a stronghold for working-class values and a culture which protected them from harsh economic times.

Primarily, this essay describes the working-class culture which grew around Joe Beef's Canteen and analyzes that culture in terms of the community which supported it. The efforts of middle-class organizations to improve the conditions of the waterfront labourers are examined in the light of this culture. Finally, by placing this culture within the major developments influencing Montreal during the 1880s, the decline of Joe Beef's Canteen can be understood. Through this process a clearer understanding of the relationship between cultural change and historic development can be reached.

Source: "Joe Beef of Montreal: Working-Class Culture and the Tavern, 1869–1889," *Labour/Le Travailleur* 8/9 (1981/1982): 9–40. © Canadian Committee on Labour History.

196

As the recent lively debate bears witness,[3] the concept of working-class culture in historical analysis is both fruitful and problematic, and before entering into a detailed discussion of the working-class tavern, it is necessary to define this concept and establish the limitations of its application. Working-class culture covers a wide range of recreational, social, and job-related activities from labour day parades and trade union picnics to charivaris and the secret ceremonies of the Knights of Labor. While each form of culture can only be understood within its specific time and place, there was a common thread which made particular cultures working-class cultures. As Raymond Williams has stated, working-class culture embodies "a basic collective idea and the institutions, manners, habits of thought and intentions which proceed from this."[4] By assuming an "active mutual responsibility"[5] between workingmen, working-class culture offered an alternative to the individualist, competitive philosophy of the nineteenth-century middle class. Nothing was as common as a tavern in nineteenth-century Montreal, and because of this, working-class taverns probably represented one of the most basic forums of public discussion. Drawing their customers from the neighbouring streets, such meeting places were the first to sense a change in mood, or experience the return of economic prosperity. Joe Beef's Canteen, while attracting a wider clientele than most taverns, was essentially the same type of focal point for the dockyard workers. The uncommon aspect of the Canteen was the remarkable ability of Charles McKiernan, the tavern's owner, to transform this rather commonplace forum into a dynamic force for the working class of Montreal.

The depression which accompanied the 1870s had a great impact on those who, like the patrons of Joe Beef's Canteen, were at the bottom end of the economic scale. Gareth Stedman Jones, in his study of casual labour and unemployment, *Outcast London*, demonstrated that middle-class London saw the casual labourers of East London as unregenerated workers who had yet to accept the industrious habits of their fellow workingmen of the factories.[6] These "dangerous classes," much like the patrons of the Canteen, were perceived as a threat to social order. While Montreal's waterfront could not compare to the horrors of East London, Montreal's middle classes were concerned about a "dangerous class" united by a forceful, if eccentric, spokesman who articulated labourers' frustrations and demands. Joe Beef would have been taken much less seriously had his success not coincided with the increasing number of factory workers, both skilled and unskilled, who appeared on the streets of Montreal. Municipal authorities, encouraged by middle-class reformers, paid more attention to questions of public order and morality in the face of such a mass of new residents. Drunkenness, blood sports, and street brawls associated with the waterfront taverns could not be permitted to flourish if all workers were to adopt the disciplined virtues of the new industrial society.

Charles McKiernan was born on 4 December 1835, into a Catholic family in Cavan County, Ireland. At a young age, he entered the British Army and, after training at the Woolwich gunnery school, was assigned to the 10th Brigade of the Royal Artillery. In the Crimean War, McKiernan's talent for providing food and shelter earned him the nickname of "Joe Beef," which would stay with him for the rest of his life. In 1864, McKiernan's Brigade was sent to Canada to reinforce the British forces at Quebec. By then a sergeant, McKiernan was put in charge of the military canteens at the Quebec barracks and later on St. Helen's Island. If army life had seemed an alternative to his Irish future, then McKiernan saw better opportunities in North America. In 1868, McKiernan bought his discharge from the Army and with his wife and children settled in Montreal, opening the Crown and Sceptre Tavern on St. Claude Street.[7]

By settling in Montreal, McKiernan joined an established Irish community which accounted for 20 percent of the total population. Centred in Griffintown, the largely working-class Irish had their own churches, national and charitable societies, political leaders, and businessmen.[8] And as a tavern owner, McKiernan entered a popular profession in a city with a liquor licence for every 150 inhabitants.[9] The increasing number of taverns caused one temperance advocate to lament that if trends continued Montreal was destined to become "the most drunken city on the continent."[10] The Crown and Sceptre, commonly known as "Joe Beef's Canteen," had a central location, with Griffintown and the Lachine Canal to the east and the extensive dockyards stretching out on either side. Business was good for Charles McKiernan.

In spite of the large numbers of taverns, Joe Beef's Canteen had an atmosphere, and a reputation, which was unique. Located in the waterfront warehouse district and at night identified only by a dim light outside the door, the Canteen housed a fantastic assortment of the exotic and the commonplace. One visitor described it as "a museum, a saw mill and a gin mill jumbled together by an earthquake; all was in confusion."[11] The barroom was crudely furnished with wooden tables and chairs, sawdust covering the floor to make cleaning easier. At one end of the bar, great piles of bread, cheese, and beef supplied the customers with a simple meal. Behind the bar a large mirror reflected a general assortment of bottles, cigar boxes, and curios. One bottle preserved for public display a bit of beef which lodged—fatally—in the windpipe of an unfortunate diner. The quick-witted McKiernan served his patrons with an easy manner. An imposing figure with a military bearing and fierce temper, the owner had few problems with rowdyism.[12]

Joe Beef's Canteen had a special type of patron, and McKiernan aptly referred to his establishment as the "Great House of Vulgar People." His clientele was mostly working class. Canal labourers, longshoremen, sailors, and ex-army men like McKiernan himself were the mainstays of the business. Along with these waterfront workers, Joe Beef's Canteen attracted the floating population along the Atlantic coast. W.H. Davies, in his *Autobiography of a Super-Tramp*, remarked that, "not a tramp throughout the length and breadth of the North American continent . . . had not heard of [Joe Beef's Canteen] and a goodly number had at one time or another patronized his establishment."[13] McKiernan's tavern was also a well-known rendezvous for the "sun-fish" or "wharf-rats" of the harbour who lived a life of casual employment and poverty. Newspaper reporters often dropped into the tavern to check on petty criminals who mingled with the crowd. Unemployed labourers visited the Canteen in the early morning to look for a day's labour and often remained there throughout the day in the hope of something turning up. In all it was not a respectable crowd[14] and, no doubt, was shunned by the more self-respecting artisans of the neighbourhood.

For working-class Montreal, the tavern held attractions beyond the simple comforts of food and drink. With no public parks in the immediate area, and only occasional celebrations by national societies and church groups, their daily recreational activities were centred around places like Joe Beef's Canteen. McKiernan's tavern was exceptionally rich in popular recreations. A menagerie of monkeys, parrots, and wild cats of various kinds were from time to time exhibited in the Canteen, but it was McKiernan's bears which brought in the crowds. Joe Beef's first bear, named Jenny and billed as the "sole captive" of the "courageous" 1869 expedition to the North West, never retired sober during the last three years of her life. One of her cubs inherited the family weakness. Tom, who had a daily consumption of twenty pints of beer, was often "drunk as a coal heaver" by closing. Indeed, Tom was one of the regulars, usually sitting on his hind quarters and taking his pint between his paws, downing it without spilling a drop. Local temperance men had always pointed out that drink turned men into animals, but in observing Tom's habits Joe Beef could point out this curious reversal of behaviour which the Canteen produced.[15] Other bears were kept in the tavern's cellar and viewed by customers through a trap door in the barroom floor. Occasionally, McKiernan brought up the bears to fight with some of his dogs or play a game of billiards with the proprietor.

The tavern was not an ideal place for animals and one observer remarked on the mangy, dirty, and listless character of the bears.[16] Beatings were often used to rouse the animals into their "naturally" ferocious state. Sometimes McKiernan was mauled during these demonstrations and once a buffalo on exhibit sent him to hospital for a number of days.[17] A Deputy Clerk of the Peace, inspecting the tavern to renew its licence, was bitten by one of Joe Beef's dogs.[18] There was little public outcry over these conditions. Montreal's Royal Society for the Prevention of Cruelty to Animals was still a fledgling organization in the 1870s which spent its time regulating butchers' practices and prosecuting carters for mistreatment of their horses. As long as they presented no public danger, McKiernan's menagerie was left undisturbed.

Although lacking formal education, Charles McKiernan considered himself a man of learning and regularly read the *New York Journal*, the *Irish American*, the *Irish World*, and local newspapers. He employed a musician (which was illegal under the terms of his licence) to entertain his customers. Regular patrons played the piano in the tavern. McKiernan, however, led much of the entertainment. Drawing on personal experience and varied readings, McKiernan eagerly debated topics of the day, or amused patrons with humorous poems of his own composition. He had a remarkable ability to ramble on for hours in rhyming couplets. Sometimes to achieve this end, he distorted the accepted English pronunciation beyond recognition. This disgusted some middle-class visitors to the Canteen, but regular customers clearly enjoyed these feats of rhetoric.[19] Behind the bar, two skeletons were hung from the wall and served as props for McKiernan's tales. From time to time, the skeletons represented the mortal remains of McKiernan's first wife, his relatives in Ireland, or the last of an unfortunate temperance lecturer who mistakenly strayed into Joe Beef's Canteen one night.

From the occasional poetry which McKiernan printed in the newspapers, the style and subjects of these evenings can be seen. Concentrating on the figures of authority in the workingman's life, the employer, the Recorder, the landlord, or the local minister, McKiernan's humour allowed his patrons a temporary mastery over the forces which dominated their lives outside the Canteen doors. Inside the Canteen, the rights of the common man always triumphed. On local issues, McKiernan complained about the lack of municipal services for the waterfront community. He demanded,

> Fair play for Sammy, Johnny and Pat as
> well as the Beaver Hall Bogus Aristocrat![20]

Legal authority, most familiar to his patrons through the Recorder's Court, was also denounced, but feared. An engraving of the Recorder looked down on the patrons from above the bar, and wedged into the frame were a number of dollar bills and notes which served as a reserve fund. McKiernan used this fund to pay fines imposed upon his regular customers.[21] Since most depended upon day labour, even a short jail term could spell disaster for the labourers' families. Imprisonment in lieu of fines was a very contentious issue, as the vehemence of the following poem illustrates.

> They have taken me from my father,
> They have taken me from my mother,
> They have taken me from my sister,

They have taken me from my brothers,
In this wintry season of woe
And for the sake of *one* paltry, lousy *Dollar*,
Down to jail, for to die, like a Dog, amongst *Bugs* and *Vermin*, I had to go.
I died amongst howling and laughter,
I died howling for a drink of water
But you living *Tyrants*, and *Two Legged Monsters* take warning and remember that cold, cold
Saturday Morning!!!
For man's vengeance is swift, though God's vengeance is with some, rather slow.[22]

McKiernan himself was no stranger to the Recorder's Court. In July 1867, the tavern keeper faced charges from a disgruntled patron who had been roughly thrown into the street for rowdyism. On different occasions, McKiernan's musician and a former servant complained of beatings they had received for drunkenness on the job.[23] Along with the violations of his liquor licence, such incidents illustrated that Joe Beef's legal opinions were grounded in experience.

Another prominent subject in Joe Beef's Canteen was the economic depression which hovered over Montreal for much of the 1870s. As casual labourers, the Canteen's patrons were severely affected by commercial slumps. In "Joe Beef's Advice to Biddy, the Washerwoman," McKiernan wrote,

I must tell you that Kingston is dead, Quebec is
Dying and out of Montreal, Ottawa and Toronto hundreds are flying
In the country parts unless you can
Parlez-vous, There is nothing for you to do
And in John's office it is all the cry
No Union printers for work need apply
And if the landlord his rent you cannot
Pay your sewing machine he will take
Away. So in the fall God help the
Poor of Montreal.[24]

The unwillingness of the private and public authorities to provide adequate relief systems also attracted Joe Beef's notice. In a parody of the economic theories of industrialists, McKiernan professed,

Joe Beef of Montreal, the Son of the People,
He cares not for the Pope, Priest, Parson or King
William of the Boyne; all Joe wants is the Coin.
He trusts in God in the summer time to keep him
from all harm; when he sees the first frost and
snow poor old Joe trusts to the Almighty Dollar
and good maple wood to keep his belly warm.[25]

These were problems which his patrons had little difficulty in understanding.

Central to all of McKiernan's pronouncements was the belief that the common problems of casual labourers and the poor of Montreal should overcome the religious and national differences which separated them. Joe Beef did "not give a damn Whether he is an Indian a Nigger a Cripple a Billy or a Mich"[26] when attempting to help the unemployed. What the unemployed and casual labourer lacked, in McKiernan's opinion, was a common voice. Since no one else was likely to assume that role, Joe Beef became the self-appointed champion of the waterfront workers. His success was remarkable as he gained the confidence of his neighbours and attracted the attention of many residents who were unaware of the poor conditions on their doorstep. He made friends with both English and French journalists, and Joe Beef's Canteen and the waterfront community appeared regularly in the press. While such publicity was good for the Canteen, few accused McKiernan of self-interest. "Joe Beef" became so well known that few knew precisely who Charles McKiernan was. And despite his Irish background, Joe Beef had considerable appeal to French-Canadian workers as well, if one can judge popularity from the coverage Joe Beef received in the French-language press.

The recreational aspects of Joe Beef's Canteen covered only a narrow spectrum of the interaction between the tavern owner and his patrons. As the focal point of social activities, Joe Beef's Canteen also provided the initiative for a number of social services which were a logical outgrowth of the close relationship between McKiernan and his neighbourhood. His role in alleviating problems of housing, job hunting, health care, and labour unrest indicated the possibility of a collective response to the common problems among casual labourers of Montreal's waterfront.

The most visible service which Joe Beef's Canteen offered was a cheap place to stay for transient and single workers. In the Crown and Sceptre, the barroom was situated next to a dining room and sleeping quarters. The sleeping area contained about 40 wooden sofas which served as beds. At eleven o'clock, boarders deposited ten cents at the bar and were handed a blanket. The men then spread a mattress over the wooden sofa, stripped off all their clothes, and went to sleep. McKiernan insisted that all his boarders sleep naked as a matter of cleanliness. Those found dirty were ordered upstairs to use one of the wash tubs. Each boarder also had to have his hair cut short, and those failing to meet the standards were sent to Joe Beef's "inspector of health," or barber, to comply. No conversation was permitted after eleven o'clock and everyone was roused out of bed at seven sharp. These rules were enforced personally by McKiernan in his best British Army sergeant's manner. Three-quarters of the tavern's boarders were boys between the ages of twelve and fourteen who earned their living selling newspapers. For twenty cents a day, they received their food and lodging and, although the conditions set down by Joe Beef might be draconian, they were clearly preferred to similar facilities offered by church organizations. Indeed, the Crown and Sceptre proved such a popular place that one of the prime reasons for moving to Common Street in 1876 was the lack of space. His waterfront location had room for 200 men.[27]

Fees for room and board were often waived for those without the means to pay such modest sums. McKiernan's tavern was also close to the sources of casual employment, which was an important consideration when a day's work might depend on arriving early on the job site. McKiernan often loaned shovels to men engaged in snow shovelling and other jobs. And as the natural resting place for all types of labourers on the docks, Joe Beef's Canteen was an ideal location to learn who might be hiring in the future. In this way, the tavern allowed transient workers to familiarize themselves with the local labour market and to make a decision whether to stay in Montreal or move on.[28]

Other social services grew informally as local residents turned to McKiernan for assistance in times of trouble. When a Lachine Canal labourer was injured during a blasting operation, fellow workers brought him to Joe Beef's to recuperate. After two men got into a drunken brawl and the loser stripped naked in the street, the crowd brought the man to Joe Beef's for care. A young immigrant who collapsed on the docks also ended up in the tavern for convalescence. While Joe Beef's served as a neighbourhood clinic, McKiernan's folk cures left much to be desired. The young immigrant was treated with a vinegar-soaked towel bound tightly around his head. McKiernan also professed faith in cayenne pepper and whiskey to cure cramps and Canadian cholera. All this in twenty minutes.[29] Still, many people in the nineteenth century attributed medicinal powers to alcohol, and McKiernan did state an intention to take courses at the Montreal General Hospital to improve his knowledge of basic medicine.

These experiences led the tavern owner to lobby established medical institutions to improve health care services for waterfront residents. In December 1879, he set up a collection box in his tavern for the Montreal General Hospital and invited his customers to contribute. Donating one-tenth of his receipts from all his dinners and a similar share of his boarding house income, McKiernan hoped to raise $500 a year. In the following years, McKiernan offered $100 to the Montreal General if they would provide a doctor to attend the poor in their homes. The hospital declined the offer. Unsuccessful in a more formal improvement of health care services, McKiernan continued to provide emergency relief. When the body of a suicide was buried in August 1883, the tavern keeper provided a tombstone.[30]

The question of class allegiance was most clearly defined by the incidents of labour unrest which periodically disrupted the city. In December 1877, over 1000 labourers working on the enlargement of the Lachine Canal abandoned their picks and shovels after a reduction in wages. The Irish and French workers paraded behind a tricolour flag along the canal banks and drove off those who refused to participate in the strike. Following a riot at the offices of canal contractor William Davis, during which the strike leader was shot, the Prince of Wales Rifles were called out to protect the canal and those workers who continued to work at reduced wages.[31] The strikers demanded a wage increase to a dollar a day, a nine-hour day, regular fortnightly payments, and an end to the "truck system" of payment.[32] Among the Montreal citizens, there appeared to be some sympathy with the poor working conditions of the labourers, notably from the *Montreal Witness* and local MP Bernard Devlin,[33] but the militant behaviour of the strikers was generally condemned.

Strongest support for the strikers came from the waterfront community. Practical in all things, McKiernan realized that strikers, like the army, travel on their stomachs. On the morning of 20 December, he sent 300 loaves of bread, 36 gallons of tea, and a similar quantity of soup. These supplies required two wagons to be delivered. In addition to feeding the strikers, McKiernan took in as many as the Canteen could hold. One night 300 people found shelter under his roof. Throughout the strike McKiernan was observed "carting loaves and making good, rich soup in mammoth boilers, as if he were a commissary-general with the resources of an army at his back."[34] No doubt his military training was put to the test in maintaining order in his kitchen. That background also made the tavern keeper aware of the awkward position of the Prince of Wales Rifles who had been hastily summoned to guard the canal. To ensure that the soldier ate as well as a striker, McKiernan despatched a wagon of bread to the men on duty. The soldiers saw the humour in Joe Beef's assistance and gave most of the bread away to the crowd.[35] Some of the tension between striker and soldier was successfully released.

McKiernan, of course, was not popular with the canal contractors for his whole-hearted support of the labourers. William Davis, pointing suspiciously to the fourteen taverns in the immediate area, wrote that the strike was caused by outside trouble makers. Another contractor was more direct in his accusations. "All of the trouble which we have had on the canal this winter has been caused mostly by men that never worked a day on the canal and have been started in a low Brothel kept by one *Joe Beef* who seems to be at the head of it all."[36] Despite this claim, McKiernan had only a supporting role in the labourers' actions, but such comments indicated the success of McKiernan's efforts to aid the strike.

Besides using his Canteen to take care of the strikers' physical needs, McKiernan also used his skills as an orator to attract public attention to the strikers' demands. By 1877, Joe Beef was a figure of some notoriety in Montreal and the local press found that his exploits made good copy. His support of the strike was reported extensively in Montreal and even in one Ottawa newspaper. The strikers' first meeting took place outside Joe Beef's Canteen and the tavern owner was asked to say a few words. Those nightly discussions in the tavern had given McKiernan a remarkable ease with language, and his talent for speaking in rhyming couplets was not wasted. Most of his speech to the crowd was in rhyming form, which so impressed the *Montreal Witness* reporter that he apologized for only reporting the substance of the speech and not its form as well. McKiernan explained his actions in the following terms.

> I have been brought up among you as one of yourselves since I was a boy running about bare-footed. When I heard of the strike on the Lachine Canal, I thought I would try to help you, for I knew that men employed there had much to put up with. So I sent you bread to help you hold out. I could not send you whiskey, because you might get drunk, and commit yourselves. In this way you might have injured your cause, and perhaps made the volunteers fire on you. (Laughter) . . . The greatest philanthropists in the world are in Montreal, and the public here will sympathize with you. They will not see you tyrannized over. But if you are riotous, depend upon it, as sure as you are men before me, the law will take it in hand and crush you. I have nothing against the contractors and you will succeed by speaking rightly to them. You will get your $1 a day for nine hours, or perhaps for eight hours (cheers) or perhaps more (loud cheers). But keep orderly; mind your committee.[37]

The speech was received with "deafening" cheers.

These mass meetings organized by the strike committee were an important part of their efforts to secure better working conditions. Since the canal enlargement was a federal project, Alexander Mackenzie's government was anxious to have it completed before the next election. Failure to live up to this previous election promise would cost the Liberals votes in Montreal.[38] By rallying public support for their cause, the strikers hoped that Ottawa would intervene on their behalf and compel the contractors to make concessions. As the strike continued, the size of the mass meetings grew. In Chaboillez Square 2000 people assembled to hear McKiernan and other speakers. Joe Beef lectured on the theme of the "Almighty Dollar."

> My friends, I have come here tonight to address you on "the Almighty Dollar." The very door bells of Montreal ring with the "Almighty Dollar." The wooden-headed bobbies nail you, and you have to sleep on the hard floor provided by the City Fathers, and the next morning the fat Recorder tells you: "Give me the 'Almighty Dollar,' or down you go for eight days." The big-bugs all have their eyes on the "Almighty Dollar," from the Bishop down, and if you die in the hospital, they want the almighty dollar to shave you and keep you from the students. No one can blame you for demanding the "Almighty Dollar" a day. The man who promises 90¢ a day and pays only 80¢ is no man at all. The labourer has his rights.[39]

Public support for the strikers did not alter the fact that the labourers were without income, and after eight days on strike, they returned to the canal at the old wages.[40]

The canal labourers, however, refused to admit defeat. In mid-January, a strike committee went to Ottawa with funds raised by McKiernan and others in order to plead their cause before Alexander Mackenzie. They reduced their demands to the single request that the contractors pay them every fortnight in cash.[41] Mackenzie was sympathetic but noncommittal. When the committee returned to Montreal, the mass meetings became overtly political and the problems of the canal labourers were attributed to the inaction of the Liberal government.[42] Meanwhile, Mackenzie had ordered an investigation into the Lachine situation which revealed the widespread use of store payment which considerably reduced the real wages of the labourers. Sensing a political disaster in the making, the government ordered the contractors to end store payments.[43] All contractors complied immediately and the labourers won a modest victory. McKiernan's efforts, while not the only factor in this outcome, did help the strikers publicize their demands and eased their physical hardships. In doing so, he demonstrated the potential strength of a waterfront community united in a common cause.

The canal labourers' strike was McKiernan's most extensive effort in aiding strikers, but not his only involvement. During a strike against the Allen line, ship labourers used the Canteen as a rallying point and the flag they used in their parades came from the tavern. In April 1880, when the Hochelaga cotton mill workers struck, Joe Beef again assumed his role as people's commissary-general by supplying the strikers with bread.[44] Such incidents illustrated how the working-class culture which centred around the tavern could be mobilized to produce benefits for the Canteen's patrons. But in doing so, McKiernan also attracted the criticism of middle-class reformers who felt that such a culture encouraged workers in a dangerous behaviour which threatened the social stability of Montreal.

During the 1870s, middle-class reformers began to enter into the waterfront community to assist the workingman in overcoming his social and economic poverty. The YMCA, the Salvation Army, as well as local employers and clergy, all found themselves confronted by an existing culture and community services centred around Joe Beef's Canteen. Their response to McKiernan's activities illustrated the immense social differences between the middle and working class of Montreal. One visitor to the city described Joe Beef's Canteen as a "den of robbers and wild beasts" over which McKiernan presided, "serving his infernal majesty in loyal style." The patrons were "unkempt, unshaven, fierce-looking specimens of humanity," and "roughs of various appearances, ready apparently, either to fight, drink, or steal, if the opportunity offered." In conclusion, this visitor wrote, "As we came away from his canteen where we felt that dirt, bestiality, and devilment held high carnival, my friend said, 'I believe Joe is worse than his bears and lower down in the scale of being than his monkeys. No monkey could ever be Joe's ancestor, though he is the father of wild beasts that prey on society.' "[45] While Montreal's middle class did not engage in the "slumming parties" which were popular in London, portrait painter Robert Harris and his companion William Brymmer visited the Canteen to satisfy their curiosity.[46] The actions of middle-class men on the waterfront revealed a fundamental misunderstanding of the nature of the working-class behaviour which they observed.

The common middle-class picture of the waterfront community was one of drunkenness, immorality, and lawlessness. Waterfront taverns like the Canteen, or French Marie's, were described by the Montreal Police Chief as "hot beds of all that is vicious" whose patrons were "always on the look out for mischief, and whose chief and most relished pastime seems to consist in attacking the police, rescuing prisoners, and spreading terror."[47] Sub-Chief Lancy reported that the only reason why police did not close down Joe Beef's Canteen was that "it is better to have all these characters kept in one place so that they might be dropped upon by the detectives."[48] Indeed, there was much truth to police complaints about public order on the waterfront, but they were less than candid in public statements about the role which men like Charles McKiernan played in the maintenance of order. The Black Horse Gang, composed of working-class youths, roamed the waterfront for years, extorting drinking money from lone pedestrians and robbing drunken sailors. Implicated in at least one death, the Black Horse Gang rarely faced prosecution because their violent reputation intimidated many witnesses from pressing charges. And the Black Horse Gang did frequent Joe Beef's Canteen, or at least until October 1876, when McKiernan threw four of its members out into the street for rowdiness. Ironically, one of the gang members attempted to lay charges against the tavern owner for injuries resulting from the incident.[49] The waterfront also harboured "Joe Beef's Gang," which in November 1878 was involved in a market square battle with local butchers.[50]

Violations of public order, however, must be distinguished from acts of criminality. Indeed, McKiernan was known to assist the police in their efforts to capture criminals. Police arrested ten men on charges of highway robbery in September 1880 following a tip from McKiernan. In minor cases, the tavern owner was called upon to give character references for waterfront residents. McKiernan's censure was enough to send a local street gang leader to two months' hard labour. When the prisoner tried to retaliate by charging Joe Beef's Canteen with violations of its liquor licence, the judge, grateful for the favour to the court, refused to admit the evidence.[51] McKiernan, like many working-class people, did not consider occasional drunkenness or acts of rowdyism sufficient cause to send men to jail, especially if imprisonment meant certain ruin for a labourer's family. The informal, if sometimes rough, justice which McKiernan enforced upon his patrons was obviously preferable to the legal penalties of the court. While not publicly admitting such an accommodation, the Montreal police found that such informal cooperation worked in their favour.

The difference between the middle-class attitude toward the police and that of the waterfront residents was illustrated by the experience of the YMCA's first venture into the area. As an alternative to the saloon, the YMCA established a reading room on Craig Street. In January 1877, eight men were arrested there for creating a disturbance, and the *Montreal Witness* accused McKiernan of offering a reward to the men who closed down the operation. The tavern owner refuted these charges by pointing out that the incident had occurred only because of the YMCA's mishandling of the situation. As McKiernan explained, "Joe Beef never called on one policeman to arrest any of those men who frequent *his* place. If those eight had only been sent to him he would have given them work and food and sent them back better behaved."[52] By using the police to settle their problems, the YMCA violated one of the unwritten rules of behaviour on the waterfront.

The influence of waterfront taverns upon sailors visiting Montreal was a constant concern among ship owners. Searches for deserting sailors often started with a visit to Joe Beef's Canteen and a quick check of its customers. As an alterative to the tavern, the Montreal Sailors Institute was established in 1869 "a stone's throw" from nine taverns. Open from May to November, the Institute had a reading room, writing desks, stationery, and sabbath services. Food, for a price, could be bought but not alcohol. In 1879, the Institute sold 4885 cups of coffee and confidently concluded that "Every cup lessen[ed] much the demand for whiskey." Encouraging sailors to sign abstinence pledges, the Institute recognized that sober sailors were dependable sailors.[53] But like the YMCA, the Institute had little understanding or sympathy for the working-class culture of the neighbourhood. The Institute manager, Robert R. Bell, described tavern patrons as "the lowest and most depraved human beings."[54] Dock workers, in particular, he found "a class much given to alcoholic liquors."[55] Bell lamented the inability to enforce the Sunday liquor laws and suggested the local policemen were in league with the tavern keepers. In his attempts to save the waterfront workers from their own culture as well as from economic hardship, Bell was typical of the middle-class professionals who came into the area. With 60 percent of the Institute's budget earmarked for the salary of Bell and his two assistants, and liberal contributions from local ship owners,[56] the motives behind such projects were viewed suspiciously by the waterfront workers.

The most ardent attempts to reform the moral and social habits of the waterfront workers came from Montreal's clergy. The importance of the church in nineteenth-century social welfare services need not be recounted here,[57] but the resources of Montreal's various churches dwarfed anything which the waterfront community could organize on its own. McKiernan's public attitude toward all denominations of clergy was openly hostile. He wrote that "Churches, Chapels, Ranters, Preachers, Beechers and such stuff Montreal has already got enough."[58] The cartoon from *Le Canard* illustrated quite clearly that Joe Beef would look almost anywhere for salvation before turning to the church. Respectable Montreal was shocked in 1871 when McKiernan buried his first wife. On leaving the cemetery, he ordered the band to play the military tune, "The Girl I Left Behind Me." This so outraged the *Montreal Witness* that its editor only described the funeral as a "ludicrous circumstance" without going into details.[59] And, probably to his great delight, McKiernan actually convinced the census taker in 1881 that he was a practising *Baptist!*[60]

Clergy who ventured onto the waterfront, however, were sometimes pleasantly surprised at McKiernan's behaviour. John Currie, a Presbyterian minister, ventured into Joe Beef's Canteen to preach to its patrons as an "act of Faith." After some initial heckling from the tavern owner, Currie was allowed to finish his sermon. On its conclusion, McKiernan offered any man who went to Currie's services a dinner and night's lodging for free.[61] The YMCA and a "Hot Gospeller" at different times held religious services in the dining room attached to Joe Beef's Canteen. The apparent contradiction in McKiernan's public and private behaviour originated with his general distrust of a clergy which was essentially middle class. Once he viewed individual ministers at close range and found them willing to treat his patrons as their equals—at least before the eyes of God—then the tavern keeper had no objection to their work. As Joe Beef reported to the press,

> A Preacher may make as many proselytes as he chooses in my canteen, at the rate of ten cents a head. That's my price . . . for if I choose to give myself the trouble I could make them embrace any faith or none at all or become free thinkers.[62]

Not all preachers received a welcome into Joe Beef's Canteen. Mr. Hammond, a travelling revivalist whose views on tobacco and drink were at odds with McKiernan's, was invited to the Canteen for a debate. Before the evening was out, Mr. Hammond had been chased around the Canteen by a pack of Joe Beef's bears and dogs to the general amusement of the tavern's patrons.[63] When the Salvation Army first appeared in Montreal, McKiernan supported them. With their military bearing and brass-band approach to salvation, they were a natural to play outside the Canteen, and McKiernan paid them to do so. This harmonious relationship abruptly ended when an Army officer called the Canteen "a notorious *rendez-vous* of the vicious and depraved."[64] Shortly afterwards the band was arrested for disturbing the peace and McKiernan was suspected of being behind the complaint.

These clashes between the local clergy, reform groups, the police, and Joe Beef were carefully chronicled by the editor of the *Montreal Witness*, John Dougall. Dougall founded the *Witness* to instruct the general public in the Christian way of life and frequently drew upon Joe Beef for examples of modern depravity. Dougall was not unsympathetic to the economic hardships of Montreal's working class. He gave extensive coverage to the 1877 canal labourers' strike and attacked industrialists for their lack of concern over the moral implications of modern industry upon employees. But Dougall was convinced that the working-class culture which centred around taverns was a dangerous influence for all workingmen. As one contemporary described Dougall, he was "a fighter in the cause of temperance, of political purity, of public morals, of municipal righteousness, of Free Trade and of aggressive Christianity."[65] The unyielding earnestness of Dougall's public statements made him a frequent target for Joe Beef's satires. A typical verse stated,

> Bitter beer I will always drink,
> and Bitter Beer I will always draw
> and for John and his song singing
> Ranters never care a straw.[66]

When the *Witness* dismissed six of its printers for belonging to the International Typographers Union, McKiernan naturally sided with the union's efforts to have the men reinstated.[67]

Dougall characterized Joe Beef as the "hunter for the souls of men"[68] and, instead of seeing the social services which surrounded the Canteen as a positive contribution to the community, believed that these were merely clever ways of entrapping unsuspecting workers into a world of drink and sin. The death of John Kerr in April 1879 confirmed Dougall's conviction. Kerr was a regular at the Canteen who made his living doing odd jobs around the docks. One day in April, Kerr did not go out to work and by nightfall had drank himself to death. During the Coroner's inquest, McKiernan explained his policy of never calling in the police. When men got rowdy, he simply put them in a room under the bar to sleep it off. Customers, McKiernan went on, were never treated roughly and they were "all in good health. We never club them; you know you can squeeze a man to make him do what you want, without beating him."[69] Kerr, a well-behaved man and often sick, was never treated in this manner. Yet the existence of the "Black Hole" (as the jury foreman described it) caught Dougall's attention. In a scathing editorial, the *Witness* charged that McKiernan preyed on the unemployed in a merciless way.

> What an empire within an empire is this, where law is administered and Her Majesty's peace kept without expense to Her Majesty. How joyfully should Government renew the licence of this carer of the poor, who can squeeze a man even to the last cent he wants, even to go uncomplainingly to prison, or to working for him all day with the snow shovel he provides, and bringing home his earning daily and nightly to hand over the counter for the poison which is his real pay.[70]

Dougall demanded the Canteen's licence be revoked. The coroner's jury, however, did not see anything illegal in the unconventional practices of Joe Beef.

"Into Africa" was the phrase that one visitor to the waterfront used to describe his experience, and the social isolation of the middle and working classes of Montreal in the 1870s was quite remarkable. Yet these initial failures for the reformers did not stop their efforts, and throughout the coming decades they continued to establish links between the waterfront and the rest of the city. McKiernan, though suspicious, was not entirely hostile to these men addressing themselves to the obvious problems of the casual labourers. Their working-class culture was still strong enough to ensure that social assistance did not mean social control. Forces beyond the control of the waterfront community, however, were already weakening that culture.

The world of Joe Beef, which developed during the 1870s, continued to function throughout the 1880s, but its dynamic qualities appeared to be on the wane. Joe Beef's public profile certainly declined in the 1880s. The eventual disintegration of this culture cannot be attributed to any single factor either within the working-class community or from some of the larger developments of the decade. A combination of factors, including a decasualization of dockwork, the rise of the Knights of Labor, plus new attitudes toward leisure and urban conditions, made the survival of Joe Beef's Canteen beyond the death of its owner unlikely.

As a waterfront tavern, Joe Beef's Canteen depended upon the patronage of the long-shoremen who unloaded and loaded the ships in the Montreal harbour. Longshoremen worked irregular hours, sometimes as long as 36 hours at a stretch. Crews were hired by stevedores who contracted with a ship's captain to unload the vessel for a fixed price and provided the necessary equipment. Longshoremen, therefore, spent long periods of time on the docks either working, or contacting stevedores about the prospects for employment. With between 1700 and 2500 men competing for work, individuals had to spend much of their time ensuring that they earned the average wage of $200 per season.[71] Given these job conditions, the attraction of a waterfront tavern where one could eat, sleep, drink, and scout around for employment cannot be underestimated.

The nature of employment on the docks began to change in the mid-1880s. H. & A. Allen Company, one of the larger shipping firms in the port, introduced a system of contract labour. Over 100 longshoremen signed contracts directly with the shipping company, which guaranteed steady employment for the season. The contract specified that each contract employee would have to pay 1 percent of his wages toward an accident insurance plan, as well as agree to have 10 percent of his total wages held back until the end of the season. Any man who left before the term of his contract forfeited claim to these wages. With a rate of 25 cents per hour, the pay of the Allen contract employees was slightly better than that of regular longshoremen, but these relinquished their traditional rights to refuse work which did not suit them.[72] Longshoremen testifying before the 1889 Royal Commission on the Relations of Capital and Labour were certainly critical of the contract system, which most felt gave the company a guaranteed labour supply without contributing greatly to the welfare of the longshoremen.[73] While the contract system accounted for only a fraction of the total labour force on the docks, the Allen Company's desire to "decasualize" their labour force was an indication of the future. Such a system made a convenient tavern unnecessary.

It was no coincidence that the Allen Company attempted to introduce the contract system among longshoremen at the same time that labour organizations appeared on the waterfront. Edmund Tart told the Royal Commission that he belonged to a "secret trades organization" which existed on the docks.[74] Possibly a local of the Knights of Labor, the union had its own benefit plan to offset the Allen Company insurance scheme. Patrick Dalton, a longshoreman for the Allen Company, testified against the contract system. Pointing to the organization of the Quebec City longshoremen, Dalton stressed that only the organization of all longshoremen could guarantee higher wages. Dalton concluded by saying that labour unions were not fundamentally concerned with wages, but with bettering "the condition of the men, socially and morally."[75]

The rise of the Knights of Labor in the mid-1880s produced profound changes in the dynamics of working-class development, and the culture surrounding Joe Beef's Canteen was shaken up by their emergence. Along with lawyers, bankers, and capitalists, the Knights of Labor banned tavern owners from their ranks. Testifying before the Royal Commission on the Liquor Traffic, Louis Z. Boudreau, president of the Montreal Trades and Labour Council, reflected this attitude toward drink when he stated that "people we meet in the Trades and Labor Council are not drinking men as a whole. They are a good class of men."[76] As skilled workers accepted the need for temperance, the unskilled water-front labourers might also reexamine the benefits of tavern life. This did not signal an alliance between organized labour and the temperance advocates who attacked Joe Beef in the 1870s. Spokesmen for organized labour criticized most of these temperance work-ers for failing to realize that much of the drunkenness among workingmen resulted from economic hardship. Clearly, William Darlington, a prominent Montreal Knight of Labor, shared McKiernan's distrust of the clergy's attempt to reform the workingman. Darlington told the Liquor Commission that "the workingmen feel that the church is a religious insti-tution without Christianity, and that the clergy is simply a profession, got up for the pur-pose of making money in some instances, and in others, for preaching in the interest of capital against labour. . . . They find out in reality that the Knights of Labor preach more Christianity than the churches."[77] Despite such similarities, there was no room for Joe Beef in the Knights of Labor.

Outside of the working-class neighbourhoods, other forces were emerging which shaped public attitudes toward Joe Beef's Canteen. Throughout the 1880s, Montreal's middle-class residents grew more critical of the police force's inability to enforce the liquor laws. This new mood was captured by the Law and Order League (also known as the Citizens League of Montreal) which was formed in 1886. The League's purpose was to pressure police to enforce the liquor and public morality laws by publicizing open viola-tions. Operating in cooperation with the Royal Society for the Prevention of Cruelty to Animals, the League was able to effect a dramatic increase in the number of prosecutions against tavern owners.[78] Under such pressure, the police were less likely to work infor-mally with Joe Beef on matters of public order.

New attitudes toward leisure activities were also coming to the fore during the 1880s. With the growth of the YMCA and the Amateur Athletic Associations, urban youths were encouraged to spend their time in organized sport and develop the socially useful traits of "teamwork, perseverance, honesty and discipline — true muscular Christianity."[79] As one YMCA lecturer told his audience, recreation had to "invigorate the mind and body, and have nothing to do with questionable company, being regulated by Christian standards."[80] While such campaigns were not designed to recruit former members of street gangs, but rather the middle-class youth and clerks from the new industrial factories, these new approaches to recreation did have an impact on general tolerance of the waterfront cul-ture. Prize fighting, probably a favoured sport of Joe Beef's patrons, was publicly denounced as a barbaric and dangerous sport.[81] With the growing alliance between the RSPCA and the Law and Order League, the Canteen's menagerie could not have survived a public outcry. New recreational opportunities for working-class Montreal, such as the opening of Sohmer Park in the early 1890s,[82] indicated that the necessity to centre all recreational life around the tavern was diminishing.

There was also a perceptible shift in public attitudes toward poverty and the city slums. With the reformers' concentration on the physical aspects of their city — clean water, paved streets, public parks, and adequate fire protection — urban slums were no longer seen only as places for poor people to live, but as potential threats to public health. Herbert Ames, a pioneer in efforts to clean up Montreal, stated that in matters of public health a simple rule existed — "the nearer people live to each other, the shorter they live."[83] Such programs as the Fresh Air Fund, which sent mothers and children of the slums to a coun-try retreat for temporary escape from the noise and smoke of the city, testified to the con-cern among middle-class reformers about the dangerous effects of an industrial city.[84] The

Montreal Star carried a series of reports on the terrible living conditions in Montreal's slums.[85] In 1885 during a smallpox epidemic, riots broke out when health authorities tried to vaccinate working-class people against the disease.[86] The great physical dangers which the slums created for the city, let alone the social danger, forced local authorities to take a closer look at the waterfront neighbourhoods.

Many of these fears and developments seem to have been familiar to the reporter who visited the Canteen in 1887. While the bears received the familiar treatment, the reporter was quite disturbed at the new attitude among the patrons. He wrote, "Nothing is more striking than the demeanor of the poor folk who fill the room. No oaths are uttered, no coarse jests, no loud talking, and never a laugh is heard. A very quiet, not to say sombre, lot of men. One would like to see a little more animation and liveliness, to hear now and then a good hearty laugh."[87] Nor was this brooding silence unique to Joe Beef's Canteen, as the reporter found several other taverns similarly devoid of their regular good cheer. These dull vacant looks, the reporter went on, "are the kind of faces one meets in the east end of London and other similar districts; but we should hardly expect to find them here. They are here, though, you see."[88] The reporter's reference to East London was repeated a few years later by the author of *Montreal by Gaslight*, a muckraking study of the city's "underworld." For the local observer, the most frightening prospect for his city was to duplicate the urban miseries of the East End of London. In *Montreal by Gaslight*, the author warned against the social consequences of drink and crushing poverty. "Last and greatest of all, think you that the modern plague of London is not known to us? Are we not infected?"[89] Along the waterfront, the silence of the labourers was feared to be the incubation period of this great urban disease. Of its eventual outbreak, one author wrote, "It may be that some day labor will raise and demand that for which it now pleads. That demand will mean riot, strike, and even civil war."[90] *Montreal by Gaslight* was written as a warning that a solution must be found before it was too late. The general outcome of such fears was that middle-class Montreal began to pay more attention to its waterfront area just as the social and economic circumstances which gave rise to Joe Beef's Canteen were changing.

The rough life along the waterfront had its own hazards and on 15 January 1889 Charles McKiernan died of heart failure in his Canteen while only 54 years of age. His death was received with great sadness in many quarters of the city and the funeral attracted large crowds. As the *Gazette* reporter commented, "Every grade in the social scale was represented in those assembled in front of the 'Canteen.' There were well known merchants, wide awake brokers, hard working mechanics and a big contingent of the genus bum, all jostling one another for a glimpse of the coffin containing what remained of one, whatever may have been his faults, who was always the poor man's friend."[91] After a short Anglican service, McKiernan's body was carried out of the tavern and the procession started for Mount Royal Cemetery. Among those in the procession were representatives from 50 labour societies who acknowledged for the last time Joe Beef's support of the trade union movement. The exception to this general sympathy was the *Montreal Witness*, which published its own death notice.

> Joe Beef is dead. For twenty five years he has enjoyed in his own way the reputation of being for Montreal what was in former days known under the pet sobriquet of the wickedest man. His saloon, where men consorted with unclean beasts was probably the most disgustingly dirty in the country. It has been the bottom of the sink of which the Windsor bar and others like it are the receivers. The only step further was to be found murdered on the wharf or dragged out of the gutter or the river, as might happen. It was the resort of the most degraded of men. It was the bottom of the pit, a sort of *cul de sac*, in which thieves could be corralled.

The police declared it valuable to them as a place where these latter could be run down. It has been actively at work over all that time for the brutalizing of youth—a work which was carried on with the utmost diligence by its, in that sense, talented proprietor.[92]

Perhaps more than any of Joe Beef's lampoons, this editorial showed the limits of the *Witness*'s Christian charity.

With McKiernan's death, Joe Beef's Canteen declined. The transient customers were the first to suffer. Thomas Irwin, a "protege" of the Canteen, was arrested a few days after McKiernan's death for stealing a piece of flannel. In explaining his crime, Irwin stated "There is no use for me trying to make my living now that poor old Joe is dead and gone. I must get a home somewhere in winter; won't you admit that? Well, I stole to get a lodging."[93] For the wharf-rats and sun-fish, Joe Beef's was closed. His bears met an ignoble end as well. In April police officers shot Joe Beef's bears on the request of McKiernan's widow. She planned to have them stuffed.[94] By 1893 the Canteen was gone. The Salvation Army bought the tavern and under the banner of "Joe Beef's Converted" continued many of the services to transient workers which McKiernan had pioneered. Masters at adapting popular culture to their religious beliefs, the Salvation Army transformed one of their most troublesome enemies into a prophet for bread and salvation.[95]

In assessing the significance of Charles McKiernan to the Montreal working class in the 1870s and 1880s, one must remember that when McKiernan arrived in 1868 he did not create the working-class culture associated with Joe Beef's Canteen. That culture, which had grown out of the daily routines of the casual labourers on the docks, already existed. What Joe Beef accomplished was to give that culture a public face and voice, a figure upon which the local press and reformers could focus. In doing so, Joe Beef saved that culture from the obscurity which generally surrounds work cultures. The material necessary for that culture was amply demonstrated by the numerous community services which grew up around the tavern. This waterfront culture possessed its own values of mutual assistance, hard work, good cheer, and a sense of manly dignity. The necessity to "act like men," which McKiernan urged upon striking canal labourers, was an important code of ethics which the tavern owner used as a measure of all things. Clergy who treated his patrons "as men" were allowed into the Canteen, but organizations which resorted to the police to settle problems deserved condemnation for such unmanly behaviour. Even McKiernan's denunciations of Montreal industrialists, the "Big Bugs," or John Dougall were denunciations of individuals and not social classes. Indeed, the tendency to personalize every problem facing the waterfront community pointed out the necessity for longshoremen to find some larger institutional framework through which they could preserve the values that their work culture generated. The Knights of Labor provided this opportunity, but the Knights built upon the traditional values preserved and strengthened by Joe Beef.

While Joe Beef's controversies with the middle-class reformers who entered into his neighbourhood were genuine, the lasting influence of such incidents appeared small. For all his bluster, Joe Beef was a limited threat to the social order of Montreal. As a spokesman for rough culture, Joe Beef satirized only the pretensions and hypocrisy which he saw in the smooth behaviour of middle-class men. He did not advocate class antagonism, but a fair deal. For a short time, Joe Beef's influence was able to reach a fair deal with municipal authorities. What frightened some observers was the possibility that the growing numbers of unskilled factory workers, that unknown quantity of industrial transformation, would adopt the working-class culture of Joe Beef, with its violence and disregard for legal and moral authority. No doubt these observers were pleased that the new factory hands followed the lead of respectable skilled workers within the Knights of Labor.

The culture represented by Joe Beef was certainly different than that of the skilled tradesmen of Montreal. Only with difficulty can one imagine an experienced typographer making regular trips to the Canteen to see the bears. Though rough and respectable cultures interacted, they were clearly separate.[96] The culture surrounding the casual labourers grew out of a physically demanding life of marginal economic benefit, obtained through the common exertion of labour. In these respects, Joe Beef's world was closer to the world of Peter Aylen and the Shiners of the Ottawa Valley than to that of the typographers in the offices of the *Montreal Witness* or of the cotton mill workers of Hochelaga.[97] The waterfront world had its own internal hierarchy as Joe Beef vigorously defended his patrons against middle-class charges of drunken violence, but then threw them into the street when they got rowdy. While McKiernan's background, as his Irish verses confirm,[98] was rural, he lived in an industrial city and had to contend with the economic and social restrictions which this implied. Realizing the growing power of the police and social reformers to define the limits of acceptable behaviour, Joe Beef attempted to convince these men of the validity of working-class culture. He was not very successful. To the very end, McKiernan was rooted in the culture of his tavern and neighbourhood. For him, the liquor business was not a means of upward mobility and the tavern owner's sons remained working class.

Joe Beef's Canteen illustrated the complex nature of working-class culture. In the narrow, traditional sense of culture as artistic creation, the satiric verses, engravings, or cartoons by McKiernan and others about Joe Beef contributed in a minor way to the nineteenth-century radical literature in Canada. Local historians of Montreal were well aware of this tradition left behind by Joe Beef.[99] In the broader sense of culture as popular culture, the tavern life of bears, debates, and songs acknowledged a recreational culture created by the working class and not for them. The coming of rational recreation would weaken this tradition, but McKiernan's death had little long-term effect on this level. Finally, Joe Beef's Canteen represented a material culture of community services relating to the employment, housing, and health of the working-class neighbourhood. This culture was the most important manifestation of the Canteen in terms of class conflict.[100] All aspects of culture surrounding Joe Beef's Canteen demonstrated the integral nature of the life of the labouring men along the waterfront who would probably not have recognized distinctions between recreation and work, between a popular and material culture.

To label Joe Beef's Canteen a "pre-industrial" fragment in an industrial world obscures the fact that working-class culture was a fluid culture borrowing from its own past and from contemporary middle-class culture. Middle-class disgust at Joe Beef's antics grew largely out of his ability to parody their most pious thoughts. While Joe Beef rejected these new industrial virtues, this hardly distinguished him from thousands of other Montreal labourers and skilled workers. In many ways, the culture of Joe Beef had reached its own limits. Successful in bargaining social questions of public conduct and order, McKiernan played only a supporting role in the economic struggles in the factories and on the docks. The attempt to form new alliances between skilled and unskilled, men and women, tradesman with tradesman, would be made not by the Joe Beefs of the nineteenth century but by the Knights of Labor.

NOTES

1. *Montreal Illustrated*; or *The Strangers' Guide to Montreal* (Montreal, 1875). For a more thematic guide to the city in the 1880s, see S.E. Dawson, *Hand-Book for the City of Montreal and Its Environs* (Montreal, 1883). *Lovell's Historic Report of the Census of Montreal* (Montreal, 1891) is a

good example of how the material progress of Montreal was equated with social and moral improvements. As Lovell stated, "Peace, happiness and prosperity abound, and brotherly love forms a link that might be prized in any city. The policeman is seldom needed. Intemperance is becoming a thing of the past." (45) Lovell's private census should not be confused with the Dominion census conducted that same year. The *Montreal Star*, in its 16 September 1886 issue, carried special stories on the city's capitalists and their contribution to social development.

2. This underground Montreal is given a muckraker's treatment in *Montreal by Gaslight* (Montreal, 1889), which contains a chapter on Joe Beef's Canteen. Charles McKiernan's landlord, F.X. Beaudry, was closely connected with the local prostitution trade, as his obituary (*Montreal Witness*, 25 March 1885) details. On gambling dens, see *Montreal Witness*, 14 September 1876, and *Montreal Star*, 30 October 1889. The *Star*, 23 January 1872, carries an article on a local cockfight.

3. The most recent contributions to this debate are Kenneth McNaught, "E.P. Thompson vs. Harold Logan," *Canadian Historical Review* 62 (1981): 141–68; Gregory S. Kealey's "Labour and Working-Class History in Canada: Prospects in the 1980s," and David J. Bercuson's "Through the Looking Glass of Culture," both from *Labour/Le Travailleur* 7 (1981): 67–94, 95–112. The history of Joe Beef hopefully shows some of the merits of a cultural approach to working-class history.

4. Raymond Williams, *Culture and Society* (London, 1960), 327.

5. Williams, *Culture and Society*, 330.

6. Gareth Stedman Jones, *Outcast London* (Oxford, 1971). Comparisons between Montreal and London, at least on general terms, are not as tenuous as might first appear. Contemporary observers of the waterfront often compared these slums to those of East London. Herbert Ames's attempt to introduce model housing for the workingman was modelled on the efforts of Octavia Hill's plan to help the London poor (*The City Below the Hill* [Toronto, 1972], 114). McKiernan received his training at Woolwich, which William Booth studied before founding his Salvation Army. The Salvation Army was one of the more successful groups in the waterfront neighbourhood.

7. *Montreal Star*, 16 January 1889. See also Edgar A. Collard's *Montreal Yesterdays* (Toronto, 1962) for a good general assessment of Charles McKiernan, and the Montreal City Archives clipping file R. 3654.2 "*Rues*, Commune, Rue de la," for general press coverage of McKiernan by Collard and other Montreal historians.

8. Dorothy Suzanne Cross, "The Irish in Montreal, 1867–1896," (M.A. thesis, McGill University, 1969) gives a general account of the Montreal Irish community. For contemporary descriptions, see John Francis Maguire's *The Irish in America* (Montreal, 1868), and Nicholas Flood Davin, *The Irishman in Canada* (Toronto, 1877).

9. *Montreal by Gaslight*, 10. Other well-known taverns were Tommy Boyle's The Horseshoe, which catered to those who followed prize fighting, and the Suburban, which had a reputation for giving the poor man a helping hand (94–105).

10. *Montreal Star*, 14 February 1888. Liquor licences, which included hotels, restaurants, saloons, and groceries, increased from 723 in 1879 to 1273 in 1887. Joe Beef's Canteen had a hotel licence.

11. *Montreal Witness*, 4 April 1881.

12. *Toronto Globe*, 14 April 1876; *Halifax Herald*, 28 June 1880; *Montreal Star*, 3 October 1887.

13. W.H. Davies, *The Autobiography of a Super-Tramp* (London, 1964), 131, cited in Clayton Gray, *Le Vieux Montreal* (Montreal, 1964), 16.

14. *Montreal Witness*, 4 April 1881. In an account of Joe Beef's encounter with the census taker, the problems of tracing the transient population were made clear. Of all the one-night guests which the Canteen provided for, only ten men were found by the census taker. Two of these, an Irish musician and a Spanish cook, were probably employees of the tavern. Also listed were an English coachmaker, an Irish blacksmith, an American barber, a Scottish commercial agent, an English (Quaker) leather merchant, an Irish accountant, an English labourer, and an Irish tanner. McKiernan's fifteen-year-old son was listed as a rivet maker and was likely serving an apprenticeship. See Public Archives of Canada (hereafter PAC), RG 31, Census of Canada, 1881, Manuscript, Montreal, West Ward, Division 3, p. 1.

15. *Toronto Globe*, 14 April 1876.

16. *Montreal by Gaslight*, 115.

17. *Montreal Star*, 10 September 1883; 11 September 1883; 3 October 1883.

18. *Montreal Witness*, 17 March 1881; 22 March 1881.

19. *Montreal Herald*, 21 April 1880; *Montreal Witness*, 6 August 1875. Jon M. Kingsdale, "The Poor Man's Club: Social Functions of the Urban Working Class Saloon," *American Quarterly* 25 (1973): 472–89, provides an excellent background to the discussion which follows and demonstrates that many of the Canteen's services were common to nineteenth-century taverns.

20. *La Minerve*, 2 August 1873.

21. *Toronto Globe*, 14 April 1876; *Halifax Herald*, 28 June 1880; *Montreal Star*, 3 October 1887.

22. *La Minerve*, 20 January 1874.

23. *Montreal Star*, 14 July 1876; *Montreal Witness*, 22 October 1873; 12 November 1877.

24. *La Minerve*, 7 November 1873. John was John Dougall of the *Montreal Witness* who had recently dismissed some union employees. Although the Canteen was a male bastion, McKiernan was not unaware of the growing number of women workers in the Montreal labour force. For the employment of women, see Dorothy Suzanne Cross's "The Neglected Majority: The Changing Role of Women in Nineteenth Century Montreal," *Social History* 12 (1973): 202–203.

25. *Montreal Yesterdays*, 273–74.

26. *La Minerve*, 28 December 1878.

27. *Toronto Globe*, 14 April 1876.

28. The integration of transient labour into urban centres was very important and a failure to do so is described in Sydney L. Harring's "Class Conflict and the Suppression of Tramps in Buffalo, 1892–1894," *Law and Society Review* 11 (1977): 873–911. See also James M. Pitsula's "The Treatment of Tramps in Late Nineteenth-Century Toronto," *Historical Papers* (1980), 116–32.

29. *Montreal Star*, 5 February 1877; *Witness*, 2 August 1876; *Star*, 3 October 1879.

30. *Star*, 15 January 1878; 29 December 1879; 27 February 1880; 25 March 1880; 1 April 1880. H.E. MacDermot in his *History of the Montreal General Hospital* (Montreal, 1950) wrote that Joe Beef's Canteen was "a particularly staunch supporter, and entries of donations from 'Proceeds of iron box, barroom, of Joe Beef' are frequent, or from 'his own skating Rink,' as well as contributions for the care of special patients" (55). MacDermot's work was cited in Edgar Collard's "All Our Yesterdays," *Montreal Gazette*, 9 January 1960. William Fox Beakbane, who drowned at Allan's wharf on 29 July 1883, was buried in the McKiernan family plot in Mount Royal Cemetery (*Star*, 10 August 1883).

31. *Witness*, 17 December 1877; 19 December 1877. Strike leader Lucien Pacquette spent several days in hospital recovering from his wound. For contractor William Davis, this was not the first time his workers reacted violently to his labour practices. A year earlier someone tried to blow up the contractor's house and severely damaged the building (*Witness*, 20 December 1877).

32. *Witness*, 17 December 1877.

33. *Witness*, 19 December 1877, 20 December 1877. Bernard Devlin (1824–80) came to Quebec in 1844 and published the *Freeman's Journal and Commercial Advertiser*. He ran unsuccessfully for the 1867 Parliament against Thomas D'Arcy McGee, who accused Devlin of being secretly in support of the Fenians. Devlin served as a Liberal MP for Montreal West from 1875 to 1878 (DCB 10: 250).

34. *Star*, 20 December 1877; *Witness*, 24 December 1877.

35. *Star*, 19 December 1877.

36. PAC, Dept. of Public Works, RG11, B1(a), vol. 474, p. 2534, Whitney & Daly to F. Braun, 22 January 1878.

37. *Witness*, 21 December 1877.

38. *Witness*, 22 December 1877.

39. *Witness*, 21 December 1877.

40. *Witness*, 26 December 1877.

41. *Ottawa Citizen*, 18 January 1878. The *Citizen* carried a copy of a strikers' petition to Mackenzie which was signed by 122 people including McKiernan. Most of the signers were untraceable in local business directories, but some local grocers and dry goods merchants did support the

214

strikers' demands and this suggests some degree of neighbourhood support. Original petition in PAC, RG11, B1(a), vol. 473, pp. 2514–20.

42. *Ottawa Citizen*, 24 January 1878. An admitted weakness of this study is the failure to document the political connections which McKiernan had with municipal politicians. Federally, McKiernan was a Conservative and this no doubt played some part in his attack on Mackenzie. During the 1872 election, McKiernan led a group of sailors into a Liberal polling station and began serenading them with a concertina. When surrounded by an angry crowd, McKiernan pulled out a pistol and fired into the air. In the tumult which followed McKiernan and his companions were beaten and had to be rescued by the police. *Montreal Witness*, 28 August 1872.

43. PAC, RG11, B1(a), vol. 473, pp. 2514–69. Not all contractors paid their workers in truck, and those who did argued that the workers benefited from the arrangement. Davis argued that monthly pay periods increased productivity. "On Public Works as a Rule, a large number of men lose time after pay day, and, thereby disarrange and retard the progress of the Works." (Davis to Braun, 21 January 1878, p. 2532). John Dougall of the *Montreal Witness*, however, published an account of the supplies given to a labourer instead of cash. For $1.75 owing in wages, the worker received whiskey, sugar, tobacco, cheese, and bread valued at $1.05. The goods were on display throughout the strike at Joe Beef's Canteen (*Witness*, 22 January 1878).

44. *Star*, 17 April 1880; *Witness*, 21 April 1880.

45. *Halifax Herald*, 28 June 1880.

46. PAC, MG28, I 126, vol. 15, Royal Canadian Academy of Art scrapbook; *Montreal Gazette*, 7 February 1916, cited in *Montreal Yesterdays*, 271.

47. "Third Report of the Select Committee of the House of Commons respecting a Prohibitory Liquor Law," *House of Commons Journals*, 1874, Testimony of F.W. Penton, 9.

48. *Montreal Gazette*, 22 April 1880. The importance of battles between the police and working-class people is illustrated by Robert D. Storch in "The Policeman as Domestic Missionary: Urban Discipline and Popular Culture in Northern England," *Journal of Social History* 9 (1976): 481–509.

49. *Star*, 30 October 1876. The Black Horse Gang's activities are reported in the *Witness*, 26 May 1875; 27 May 1875; *Star*, 1 February 1876; *Witness*, 24 July 1880; 10 May 1882. Street gangs in general are discussed in the *Witness*, 31 May 1875.

50. *Witness*, 19 November 1878; 18 November 1878. The *Witness* story on the incident was protested by "Joe Beef's Gang" who turned up in the editor's office and claimed that they were "respectable mechanics and that the butchers are on the contrary not noted for their respectable behaviour."

51. *Witness*, 28 September 1880; 24 July 1879.

52. *Witness*, 8 February 1877.

53. *Annual Report of the Montreal Sailors Institute for the Year Ending January, 1870* (Montreal, 1870), 5; *Annual Report of the Montreal Sailors Institute of 1870* (Montreal, 1871), 8.

54. Royal Commission on the Liquor Traffic, *House of Commons Sessional Paper*, no. 21, 1894, 584.

55. *House of Commons Sessional Paper*, no. 21, 1894, 589.

56. *House of Commons Sessional Paper*, no. 21, 1894, 586.

57. The difference of religious sentiment was reflected in the organization of benevolent associations. Roman Catholic Montreal had its own hospitals and dispensaries, thirteen benevolent institutions caring for the aged, orphaned, and widowed. Nine Catholic charitable societies also contributed to the welfare of the impoverished citizens. Protestant Montreal, besides having its hospitals, had sixteen benevolent institutions for the same clientele as the Catholic institutions as well as homes for female immigrants and sick servant girls. Religious differences were further complicated by the national origins of Montreal residents. To aid fellow countrymen there were several national societies including the St. George, St. Andrew, St. Patrick, St. Jean Baptiste, Irish Protestant, Italian, Welsh, Scandinavian, and Swiss benevolent organizations. See *Lovell's Historic Report of the Census of Montreal* (Montreal, 1891), 62–63, 72–73. See also Janice A. Harvey's "Upper Class Reaction to Poverty in Mid-Nineteenth Century Montreal: A Protestant Example," (M.A. thesis, McGill University, 1978) for descriptions of Protestant charities.

58. *Montreal Yesterdays*, 273–74.

59. *Montreal Star*, 29 September 1871; *Montreal Yesterdays*, 272–73. McKiernan's 25-year-old wife Mary McRae and her baby died on 26 September 1871, and it is uncertain whether the contemporary accounts correctly interpreted McKiernan's actions. Interestingly enough, McKiernan's republican sentiments exhibited themselves on his wife's gravestone. Her inscription read in part,
> I leave a husband and four orphan babes
> To mouth their mother's loss
> Who will never return.
> But let that tree, which you see
> Be the tree of Liberty
> And in its stead never let the tree of [Bigotry]
> Be planted between them and me.

60. *Montreal Witness*, 4 April 1881; PAC, RG31, Census of Canada, 1881 Manuscript, Montreal, West Ward, Division no. 3, p. 1.
61. *Montreal Yesterdays*, 279–80.
62. *Toronto Globe*, 14 April 1876; *Montreal Star*, 31 July 1876.
63. *Halifax Herald*, 28 June 1880. For Mr. Hammond's preaching style see *Montreal Star*, 18 March 1880.
64. Edgar Collard, "Of Many Things," *Montreal Gazette*, 28 February 1976. For the legal problems of the Salvation Army, see the *Montreal Star*, 19 August 1886; 3 September 1886; 14 September 1886.
65. *Montreal Star*, 9 January 1911. See J.I. Cooper's "The Early Editorial Policy of the Montreal Witness," Canadian Historical Association, *Report* (1947), 53–62, and Dougall's obituary in the *Montreal Star*, 19 August 1886.
66. *La Minerve*, 13 March 1873.
67. *Montreal Star*, 26 November 1872; 27 November 1872; 28 November 1872.
68. *Montreal Witness*, 8 February 1877.
69. *Montreal Witness*, 4 April 1878.
70. *Montreal Witness*, 5 April 1879.
71. Royal Commission on the Relations of Capital and Labour, 1889, Quebec Evidence, vol. 1, pp. 150–86.
72. Royal Commission on the Relations of Capital and Labour, Testimony of R.A. Smith, 156-60; James Urquhart, 173–75.
73. Royal Commission on the Relations of Capital and Labour, Testimony of Patrick Dalton, 183–85.
74. Royal Commission on the Relations of Capital and Labour, Testimony of Edmund Tart, 175–81.
75. Royal Commission on the Relations of Capital and Labour, Testimony of Patrick Dalton, 186.
76. Royal Commission on the Liquor Traffic, 512.
77. Royal Commission on the Liquor Traffic, 583.
78. *Montreal Star*, 28 January 1886. On the Law and Order League, see *Star*, 16 August 1887; 24 January 1889; 16 February 1889, 10 March 1887.
79. Alan Metcalfe, "The Evolution of Organized Physical Recreation in Montreal, 1840–1895," *Social History* 21 (1978): 153. For the role of the YMCA in the new attitude toward leisure activities, see David Macleod, "A Live Vaccine: The YMCA and Male Adolescence in the United States and Canada, 1870–1920," *Social History* 21 (1978): 5–25. An excellent study of recreation in England is Peter Bailey, *Leisure and Class in Victorian England* (Toronto, 1978).
80. *Montreal Star*, 15 November 1873.
81. For denunciations of prize fighting see *Star*, 4 January 1887; 9 May 1887; 20 May 1887; 23 May 1887; 15 September 1887.
82. *Montreal Star*, 6 June 1893; 13 July 1893. Richard Bell of the Montreal Sailors Institute preferred that sailors drink at Sohmer Park rather than in the waterfront taverns. Royal Commission on the Liquor Traffic, 584–89.
83. Herbert B. Ames, "Why We Should Study the Municipal System of Our City," *Abstract of a Course of Ten Lectures on Municipal Administration* (Montreal, 1896), 7.

84. *Montreal Star* contains several articles promoting the Fresh Air Fund: see 11 June 1887; 18 June 1887; 25 June 1887; 6 July 1887. On the Fresh Air Home, see *Star*, 23 June 1888.
85. *Star*, 24 December 1883; 29 December 1883.
86. *Star*, 29 September 1885.
87. *Star*, 3 October 1887.
88. *Star*, 3 October 1887.
89. *Montreal by Gaslight*, 10.
90. *Montreal by Gaslight*, 35.
91. *Montreal Gazette*, 19 January 1889.
92. *Montreal by Gaslight*, 119.
93. *Star*, 24 January 1889.
94. *Star*, 29 April 1889.
95. *Star*, 26 May 1893; 27 May 1893. R.G. Moyles, in *The Blood and Fire in Canada* (Toronto, 1977), remarked that this was a new venture for the Salvation Army. "Whereas other men's hostels had been designed as rescue centres for ex-prisoners and for total derelicts, Joe Beef's was a hostel for transients, providing a cheap bed for the unemployed man with little money and a cheap meal for the poor city labourer" (69).
96. Peter Bailey's "Will the Real Bill Banks Please Stand Up? Towards a Role Analysis of Mid-Victorian Working-Class Respectability," *Journal of Social History* 12 (1979), offers some interesting insights into the differences between rough and respectable workingmen.
97. Michael S. Cross, "The Shiners' War: Social Violence in the Ottawa Valley in the 1830's," *Canadian Historical Review* 54 (1973): 1–26. For a description of an early Ottawa tavern see W.P. Lett, "Corkstown," *Recollections of Old Bytown* (Ottawa, 1979), 81–86.
98. See the attitudes reflected in "Spurn Not the Poor Man," *La Minerve*, 7 January 1874; "I am Long Past Wailing and Whining," *La Minerve*, 27 January 1874; and "The Big Beggarman," *La Minerve*, 13 January 1874. Poetic style makes it unlikely that these verses are from McKiernan's pen, but by printing them with his advertisements he demonstrated a sympathy with their author.
99. Frank W. Watt, "Radicalism in English Canadian Literature since Confederation" (Ph.D. thesis, University of Toronto, 1957). Watt does not mention McKiernan but Watt's description of a literature disillusioned with nation building and inclined to associate patriotic feelings with the motives and methods of capitalist exploitation could accommodate much of McKiernan's verse.
100. Bryan D. Palmer's *A Culture in Conflict* (Montreal, 1979) contains the fullest discussion of the importance of culture in Canadian class conflict. See also Gareth Stedman Jones, "Working-Class Culture and Working-Class Politics in London, 1870–1900," *Journal of Social History* 7 (1974): 460–508.

Topic Eight

Late-Nineteenth-Century Cultural
Values in English-Speaking Canada

Toronto Lacrosse Club team. By the late nineteenth century, lacrosse
had become immensely popular among white middle-class men.

THE CULTURAL history of the Victorian and Edwardian ages has received a great deal of study in Britain but much less in English-speaking Canada, despite the formative influence of the culture of that period. What work has been done has tended to focus on what we call high culture — music, art, and literature. Only recently have historians turned to popular culture — attitudes reflected in the issues, events, and icons that affect "ordinary people."

The following two articles reflect this new trend in cultural studies with a particular emphasis on gender studies. In "Historical Attitudes toward Women and Childbirth," Wendy Mitchinson looks at the attitudes and values medical doctors brought to their study of women's physical nature, their sexuality, and childbirth. As she notes, these "scientific experts" and "objective observers" of the human body read into such medical terms as "hysteria," "ovaries," and "uterus" the social mores and gender bias of the dominant male society to which they belonged. In "Idealized Middle-Class Sport for a Young Nation: Lacrosse in Nineteenth-Century Ontario Towns, 1871–1891," Nancy B. Bouchier reconstructs the values of the emerging dominant middle-class male population. She does so through a study of the emergence of amateur lacrosse as a legitimate and respectable sport for inculcating socially acceptable qualities and characteristics in male youth in the southwestern Ontario towns of Ingersoll and Woodstock in the late nineteenth century. In their efforts to inculcate male qualities of strength, endurance, and manliness with middle-class values of respectability, team work, self-sacrifice, and moral purity, sport leaders enlisted the church leaders' support to establish a middle-class male cultural hegemony. In the end, however, they met with resistance with conflicting values that underlay competitive and professional sports.

In what ways does a study of popular culture offer a different perspective on Victorian society than one of "high culture"? Although Mitchinson and Bouchier study quite different subjects within the same period, do they make similar observations and conclusions of the society's cultural values? What do both studies tell us about cultural attitudes in the Victorian era, and in what ways do their studies advance our understanding of the age?

A useful collection of essays dealing with cultural attitudes in the context of gender is *Gender and History in Canada*, ed. Joy Parr and Mark Rosenfeld (Toronto: Copp Clark, 1996). Wendy Mitchinson studies the attitude of Victorian doctors to women and childbirth in greater depth in *The Nature of Their Bodies: Women and Their Doctors in Victorian Canada* (Toronto: University of Toronto Press, 1991). Also useful are the essays in *Caring and Curing: Historical Perspectives on Women and Healing in Canada*, ed. Diana Dodd and Deborah Gorham (Ottawa: Carleton University Press, 1994), and Angus McLaren, *Our Own Master Race: Eugenics in Canada, 1885–1945* (Toronto: McClelland and Stewart, 1990).

On the larger issue of gender relations from a female perspective, see the essays in Franca Iacovetta and Mariana Valverde, eds., *Gender Conflicts: New Essays in Women's History* (Toronto: University of Toronto Press, 1992), and in Veronica Strong-Boag and

Anita Clair Fellman, eds., *Rethinking Canada: The Promise of Women's History*, 2nd ed. (Toronto: Copp Clark, 1991). For the Maritimes, see Janet Guilford and Suzanne Morton, eds., *Separate Spheres: Women's Worlds in the 19th Century Maritimes* (Fredericton: Acadiensis Press, 1994), and Colin Howell and Richard J. Twoney, eds., *Jack Tar in History: Essays in the History of Maritime Life and Labour* (Fredericton: Acadiensis Press, 1991). For British Columbia, see the special issue on gender history of *BC Studies* (November 1995). The Dionne quintuplets as cultural icons are examined in a special issue of the *Journal of Canadian Studies* (Winter 1994–95); see, as well, Pierre Berton's *The Dionne Years* (Toronto: McClelland and Stewart, 1977).

Although male gender studies are less numerous, students should consult Michael Kaufman, *Cracking the Armour: Power, Pain and the Lives of Men* (Toronto: Viking, 1993), and the essays in his edited collection, *Beyond Patriarchy: Essays by Men on Pleasure, Power and Change* (Toronto: Oxford University Press, 1987).

A number of good regional studies have been written in gender-related history. For the Maritimes, see Judith Fingard, *The Dark Side of Life in Victorian Halifax* (Halifax: Potters Field, 1989); Colin Howell, *Northern Sandlots: A Social History of Maritime Baseball* (Toronto: University of Toronto Press, 1995); Suzanne Morton, *Ideal Surroundings: Domestic Life in a Working-Class Suburb in the 1920s* (Toronto: University of Toronto Press, 1995); Eric Saeger, *Ships and Memories* (Vancouver: University of British Columbia Press, 1993), especially the chapters on masculinity and family, pp. 106–17 and 97–105, respectively. For Ontario, see Karen Dubinsky, *Improper Advances: Rape and Heterosexual Conflict in Ontario, 1880–1929* (Chicago: University of Chicago Press, 1993); Thomas Dunk, *It's a Working Man's Town: Male Working-Class Culture in Northwestern Ontario* (Montreal/Kingston: McGill-Queen's University Press, 1991); Ruth Frager, *Sweatshop Strife: Class, Ethnicity and Gender in the Jewish Labour Movement of Toronto, 1900–1939* (Toronto: University of Toronto Press, 1992); Franca Iacovetta, *Such Hard-Working People: Women, Men and the Italian Immigrant Experience in Postwar Toronto* (Montreal/Kingston: McGill-Queen's University Press, 1992); Joy Parr, *The Gender of Breadwinners: Women, Men and Change in Two Industrial Towns, 1880–1950* (Toronto: University of Toronto Press, 1990), a study of Hanover and Paris, Ontario; Joan Sangster, *Earning Respect: The Lives of Working Women in Small-Town Ontario, 1920–1960* (Toronto: University of Toronto Press, 1995), a study of Peterborough, Ontario; and Carolyn Strange, *Toronto's Girl Problem: The Perils and Pleasures of the City, 1880–1930* (Toronto: University of Toronto Press, 1995). For British Columbia, see Jean Barman, *Growing Up British in British Columbia: Boys in Private School* (Vancouver: University of British Columbia Press, 1984).

On sports and masculinity, see Alan Metcalfe, *Canada Learns to Play: The Emergence of Organized Sport, 1897–1914* (Toronto: McClelland & Stewart, 1987); and the relevant essays in Morris Mott, ed., *Sports in Canada: Historical Readings* (Mississauga, ON : Copp Clark Pitman, 1989). For a discussion of an emerging middle-class culture in English-speaking Canada, see Andrew C. Holman, *A Sense of Their Duty: Middle-Class Formation in Victorian Ontario Towns* (Montreal/Kingston: McGill-Queen's University Press, 1999); and Lynne Marks, *Revivals and Roller Rinks: Religion, Leisure, and Identity in Late Nineteenth Century Small-Town Ontario* (Toronto: University of Toronto Press, 1996); and on cultural hegemony, Keith Walden, "Speaking Modern: Language, Culture, and Hegemony in Grocery Window Displays, 1887–1920," *Canadian Historical Review*, 70, 3 (1989): 285–310.

Article Sixteen

Historical Attitudes toward Women and Childbirth

Wendy Mitchinson

The study of past attitudes toward women's physical nature and sexuality has been very limited in Canada.[1] This is surprising considering the rapid development of women's history within the last five years and the importance attributed to the physical differences between men and women in both the nineteenth and twentieth centuries. In the nineteenth century feminists and anti-feminists may have debated where the division between sex roles was but for the most part both agreed that there should be one.[2] Inevitably that division was based on the biological differences between men and women, as these were the most obvious and most basic.

By the latter part of the nineteenth century physicians were recognized as the "experts" on those differences, which most Canadians believed dictated separate spheres for each sex. They were not, however, disinterested observers. Medical knowledge is not absolute; it changes with time and often the study of medicine says more about a culture than about science.[3] Certain words in the medical lexicon were as value filled as those outside it. If "family," "home," and "mother" were key words in understanding the private lives of Canadians in the nineteenth century, words such as "hysteria," "ovaries," and "uterus" were equally significant in reflecting medical attitudes toward women. Although physicians based their beliefs on medical "facts," they also extrapolated from those facts and the direction they took was more often than not influenced by the mores of their society.

The direction was also influenced by their attempt to increase their own importance to society. Throughout the nineteenth century they had been striving to form themselves into a profession with control over standards and access to practice. By the end of the century they had succeeded. Nevertheless they were constantly aware of pressure from irregular practitioners and others to return to an earlier and more open system of medical practice which had encompassed so many forms of medical treatment and education. In response, the regular practitioners attempted to maintain and even expand their influence by speaking out on matters not only of medical health but also of social health.[4] This could and did have serious repercussions for women, since, in the latter half of the nineteenth century, science was developing into a significant polarity to religion. However, science and religion were not necessarily opposed. In fact, as will be seen, physicians often rationalized the withholding of medical knowledge on moral or religious as well as on medical grounds.[5] Doctors were, after all, part of society and as a result of their successful attempt to professionalize were becoming prominent spokesmen for the beliefs, medical and non-medical, of that society.

One example was the way in which medical science invested the concept of true womanhood with scientific legitimacy. Physiologists had discerned that woman's brain weighed less than man's.[6] While this suggested inferior capabilities to many, physicians were not content to leave it at that but explained in detail that women were in truth different from men:

Source: "Historical Attitudes toward Women and Childbirth," *Atlantis: A Woman's Studies Journal* 4.2, Pt. II (Spring 1979): 13–34. Reprinted by permission of the author and the Institute for the Study of Women, Mount Saint Vincent University.

for there can be no doubt that—putting aside the exceptional cases which now and then occur—the intellectual powers of Woman are inferior to those of Man. Her intuitive powers are certainly greater than his; her perceptions are more acute, her apprehensions quicker; and she has a remarkable power of interpreting the feelings of others, which gives to her, not only a much more ready sympathy with them, but that facility in guiding her actions so as to be in accordance with them, which we call tact.[7]

Woman's character balanced man's.[8] This was a basic tenet of late-nineteenth-century Canadian society. Medical opinion did not form it; it only reflected it and bolstered it. However, considering that physicians were in a position to impose their beliefs on their patients, the influence this gave them was significant.

Studying medical attitudes toward women is fraught with problems. The first is that historians are often untrained in medical terminology. The second is that little critical writing on the medical profession in Canada has been done and so the medical context for such a study is limited.[9] A third difficulty is distinguishing Canadian medical practice from that of the United States, England, or Europe. What I have done is to examine Canadian medical journals, and textbooks used in Canadian medical schools.[10] Although much of the material is non-Canadian in origin, the fact that the Canadian medical profession circulated it and thus implicitly promoted it is an indication of the direction in which it was heading. In any event many Canadian doctors were trained outside Canada.[11] A fourth difficulty linked with the use of such data is that it is almost impossible to know how influential this literature was. Even the circulation of the various medical journals is unknown.[12] As well, how many women actually consulted physicians? Given the limited number of doctors (in 1871, only 2792) and the large number of women (1 721 450) scattered across Canada, the number is probably minimal,[13] especially when for most of the century, the tendency was not to consult physicians. However, in the later decades of the nineteenth century the medical profession was gradually becoming the arbiter of all medical knowledge. If women did not consult physicians personally, the knowledge the latter had and disseminated was nevertheless influential.

This paper will study only two aspects of medical attitudes toward women. The first is the medical view of woman's physiological nature. This section will argue that physicians, by providing a "scientific" support for the domestic image of women, discouraged higher education for women. Also, because they accepted the domestic image of woman, they refused her access to birth control information, which ultimately cost many women their lives in childbirth. The second aspect examined is the way in which physicians viewed childbirth and treated their patients. This section stresses the way in which medical attitudes supported the importance of and need for an attending physician, and also the way in which new medical technology often brought disadvantages as well as advantages to the patient. Both sections reveal that doctors were strongly influenced by the mores of their society and their own self-interests as members of that society. Beyond certain biological basics there is no single way of giving birth. Each society has its own traditions and procedures. By studying Canadian medical practice we can gain insight into Canadian attitudes toward women.

Childbirth is a good place to begin. Nancy Cott's description of late-eighteenth-century New England is applicable to much of Canada in the last half of the nineteenth century. In both countries the separation of place of work and place of residence had brought about the emphasis on women's domestic role:

More than ever before . . . the care of children appeared to be mothers' sole work and the work of mothers alone. The expansion of non agricultural occupations drew men and grown children away from the household, abbreviating their presence in the family and their roles in child rearing. Mothers and young children were left in the household together just when educational and religious dicta both newly emphasized the malleability of young minds.[14]

222

Motherhood was woman's outstanding source of prestige. However, as this role gained in prestige so did the specialty of obstetrics. "The high cultivation of Obstetrics," as the *Canada Lancet* declared in 1874, "will be held to worthily distinguish the present epoch in medical history."[15] While women were being seen more and more in their maternal role, men were taking over the management of the birth process. The role division between the sexes so prevalent in other areas of society had even touched what was closest to woman, childbirth.

I

The most obvious place to begin the study of the treatment of childbirth in the late nineteenth century is the state of medical knowledge about the female reproductive system. What did it mean to be a woman? The clearest demonstration to physicians was the menstrual cycle, the central fact of puberty. In keeping with a century which esteemed the scientific, medical texts abounded with carefully gathered statistics to determine at what age menstruation was most likely to begin. After much study, the consensus was that it began between the ages of 13 and 16.[16] By studying women all over the world and keeping detailed records, textbooks also concluded that certain conditions would bring about earlier menstruation in women: warm climate, luxurious living, early stimulation of mental faculties and premature sexual stimulus. It also apparently occurred earlier in women living in towns and in brunettes as opposed to blondes.[17] Physicians generally had no explanation to account for the above phenomena but continued to present their findings.

Such findings were harmless enough and appealed to the desire to quantify, which was becoming an important part of scientific inquiry in the late nineteenth century. However, physicians were not content to simply measure. They pursued their investigations into a realm that was open to value judgements, namely, the emotional effects of menstruation on women. In their descriptions, cultural expectations for women were revealed:

> The most noticeable feature of this transition may be the development of self-consciousness; as the young girl becomes conscious of sex differences she is apt to develop a shyness toward members of the opposite sex not noted in very early life. However, the most important psychological change is the shifting of the emphasis from a self-centered one to a consideration of others. It's the successful accomplishment of this transition which assures a normal, well adjusted adult [female] both sexually and socially.[18]

The physiological function of menstruation brought about not only the physical differences between men and women but the emotional and psychological differences as well. Society did not impose the service role on woman. According to medical opinion, woman's own body did so. A woman's struggle to expand her activities in society would, according to such beliefs, fly in the face of her very physical being and thus be doomed to failure. The comfort such beliefs gave to the status quo need not be stressed.

Why was menstruation seen as such a disturbing phenomenon? Did it really disrupt a woman's life? In theory it did not have to. The *Canadian Practitioner*, in 1884, suggested that "menstruation should be performed without pain."[19] Yet despite the recognition that it was a normal physiological function, physicians tended to be cautious and stressed the need for prudence, encouraging women, particularly the middle-class women who were their patients, to think of themselves as fragile during this time.[20] They seemed to feel that many women did experience extreme discomfort. In 1877 the *Canada Medical and Surgical Journal* reported a study done in the United States where 1000 circulars were sent out to women asking about their experience during menstruation. Of the 268 women who replied, only 35 percent claimed they were free of discomfort.[21] Of course we cannot accept this as proof since we do not know the sample that was used, but it is at least tenuous corroboration of the medical viewpoint. If true, one of the contributing causes could have been the tendency of many upper-class women to wear tight corsets, which placed undue pressure on the reproductive system, perhaps resulting in painful menstruation.[22] Whatever the reason and whether fact or fantasy, physicians believed many women were uncomfortable during menstruation, especially in the early years, and advised mothers to "secure rest and quiet" for their daughters. One textbook even advised bed rest for several days each month.[23]

One reason why physicians in the past tended to make conclusions which today's society would find unwarranted is, of course, the value system of their society. In suggesting that women needed rest every month, physicians were not suggesting anything which the rhetoric of domesticity would find surprising. They were, in fact, supporting the dominant view of woman as being more fragile than man, overlooking the fact that this same fragile creature could undergo and survive the trauma and pain of childbirth. Another reason to explain their belief in the fragility of women was the limitation of knowledge. Physicians did not really understand the physiology of menstruation.[24] Not until 1832 was the human ovum discovered and even after that the precise cause of menstruation was not clear. One physician even suggested that menstruation had not existed in earlier times but that it was a pathological condition which "has become a fixed habit of the female sex in consequence of the vitiating influence of civilization."[25] The result was that speculation occurred, and comparisons were often made with the animal kingdom which were not always complimentary to women. "The Function of Menstruation," as the *Montreal Medical Journal* explained it, "is surely one of the most remarkable in the animal economy . . . It is confined to the human female and certain monkeys."[26] Menstruation was also compared to the rut in animals.[27] The implication certainly was that women were lower on the evolutionary scale than men.

By making such statements physicians were enhancing their own prestige. In this specific instance their opinion bolstered conventional wisdom and thus they were listened to. They had become society's spokesman. This could not help but carry over when they gave their opinion on other issues perhaps even less connected to medical health than this one. Doctors certainly did not limit their statements to what they felt they knew about the physiological functioning of the female body. Indeed, they spoke out about the implications of that functioning for woman's role in life. Physicians' beliefs about the physical nature of women, especially the reproductive process, led them to discourage higher education for women and refuse women birth control information. The former would limit the sphere of woman; the latter would, by encouraging women to have children, keep them in the sphere considered appropriate to their nature.

II

Physicians had control over information concerning the body and were not about to share it. One textbook explained that while girls should be taught hygiene they should not be taught anatomy and physiology: "A little learning in anatomy and physiology is truly a dangerous thing."[28] The author feared that knowledge about the female body would only focus women's attention on it and lead to hypochondria and eventual ill health.[29] Knowledge would also allow women to judge the quality of the treatment they received.

Because many doctors believed they were the ultimate source of information on the female body, they tended to pontificate on subjects which were only tangential to medicine. One was the desire of women to further their education:

> Once bring men and women into keen competition for bread, for place, for honors, for power, and you break down the barriers Nature has set up, and tend to destroy those differences which she has taken eons to form.[30]

What is interesting about the above quotation is not its sentiment — many nineteenth-century Canadians disapproved of higher education for women — but the biological evolutionary rationale behind it and the overview of human development which it reflected. Physicians believed that men and women were basically equal until puberty:

> After puberty woman does not keep pace with the companion of her youth in this regard; her mental growth becomes slower and more limited. After the menopause there is an apparent tendency to become in her mental qualities more like the male.[31]

After puberty the reproductive function dominated woman. Physicians felt men and women should be educated differently and were aghast that North Americans emphasized education for both sexes to the degree they did.[32] Doing so weakened the nervous system and led to precocity in children. This tendency was particularly dangerous for young women during the early years of puberty. Women must allow their bodies to develop and prepare for the maternal function; this they could not do if they were kept studying all day.[33]

> Education has great influence in the development of gynecological diseases. Too great assiduity in study in early youth concentrates the nerve-energy on the brain, and deprives the uterus and ovaries of their share at a time when these organs are undergoing an enormous development, and preparing for the important functions of womanhood and motherhood.[34]

If women did not get the rest they needed, dire results would follow: disease, feebleness of the muscular system, dysmenorrhoea (painful menstruation), and even sterility.[35] Such arguments were taken up by the opponents of higher education for women.

Many physicians believed that young women could not do mental work and develop their bodies at the same time. This did not mean, however, that physicians were against education for women. On the contrary, many supported training for women, but the training they envisioned was of a domestic nature. "Too much brain work, too little housework, is another crying evil of our land," exclaimed William Goodell in *Lessons in Gynecology*.[36] The dominating social role of woman and medical theory conveniently went hand in hand. People generally believed what they wanted to. In the case of physicians it can be argued that they saw and approved of woman's social role and thus argued backwards from that to her physical nature instead of looking at the pure physical being and arguing to the social role. However, considering that social role obviously has some bearing on physical health, in the specific case of women in the clothes they wore and the environment they lived in, the deductions physicians were making may not have been unreasonable. Social context and physical health are not separate. Each affects the other. We cannot assume that the women of the nineteenth century enjoyed our standard of health. Neither can we assume that the "scientific" arguments put forward by physicians to limit woman's sphere were not strong rationalizations for the status quo.

In many respects doctors' attitudes toward higher education for women were influenced by their own vested interests. The opposition to higher education for women would be of benefit to those physicians already practising. Women physicians, after all, would be competition for them. In the 1880s, when several medical schools had opened their doors to women, the *Canada Medical Record* stressed the desirability of controlling the number of medical graduates so that all practitioners could be assured a decent living.[37] When it became clear that it was going to be impossible to prevent women from studying, many physicians believed these new doctors should be restricted in their practice. Again it was the *Canada Medical Record* which argued that women should limit themselves to the easier aspects of medical practice.[38] In fact, it suggested that they take over midwifery and care of the poor, since male doctors were not particularly interested in those areas as there was not enough money in them.[39] One of the reasons given for letting women take over midwifery among the poor was that it would eliminate the untrained midwives that so many women in childbirth used. Eliminating these women had long been an ambition of the regular doctors. They provided competition and also undermined the prestige of the profession by offering a medical service without training. Replacing them with qualified female physicians would further extend the profession's control over an area it had yet to dominate.[40]

III

A second area of particular concern to women which the profession felt it should control was contraception. Many Canadians wanted to limit the size of their families. This was reflected most vividly in the declining birth rate in Canada, especially in the cities. While some medical journals felt the decline was due to the disinclination of men to marry as a result of the pressures of modern society,[41] most believed it was a result of birth control. If true, Canadians received little help from the medical profession, since most doctors refused to provide information on any effective means of contraception.

William Goodell, in *Lessons in Gynecology*, mentioned that husbands and wives were constantly beseeching physicians for means to prevent pregnancy but that physicians must morally refuse.[42] Others agreed, arguing that contraception made marriage a form of prostitution, cheapened sex, and dulled sexual enjoyment and so led to unfaithfulness. Still others kept to the supposed medical repercussions: nervous disease, insomnia, insanity, and impotence.[43] The practical consequences of these beliefs and attitudes could be cruel. In the Goodell text, physicians were told that the author refused to treat a woman with uterine troubles until her husband gave up the practice of coitus interruptus to prevent childbirth.[44] The physician's actions were depicted as worthy of emulation.

The refusal of physicians to countenance contraception was not simply a medical decision but also a social one. Of major concern to many doctors was the fact that contraception was being practised by the "better classes."[45] These were, of course, the women whom the physicians were treating and the ones on whom they depended for their livelihood. Doctors accused women of limiting their families for selfish reasons; that is, to maintain their figures and so they could go out in society.[46] Another indication that the disapproval of contraception was social and not totally medical was the fact that the medical profession believed it knew of a harmless means of contraception for patients for whom pregnancy would be dangerous.[47] If it could recommend it for these patients with no ill effects, why would it not recommend it to others?

The answer lies in the wider context of society. In late-nineteenth-century Canada, woman's role was seen as that of mother. Industrialization had brought with it the separation of place of work and place of residence. As a result, woman's place was the private sphere, the home; man's the public sphere, the workplace. It was felt that each balanced the other in a healthy society. Contraception was a denial of woman's highest function and a denial of that balance.[48] If women rejected their maternal role and as a consequence their focus on the home, society was deemed the sufferer. Physicians, as caretakers of physical health, easily extended their concern to social health, and thus the refusal to provide contraceptive devices may have been seen by them as a protection of society itself.

The only contraception physicians were willing to suggest for the healthy was the rhythm method.[49] There was only one problem with this method. Medical scientists in the nineteenth century understood so little about the reproductive cycle that they believed a woman's most fertile period was the exact opposite to when it was. Textbook after textbook declared "there is a greater aptitude for Conception immediately before and after that epoch [menstruation] than there is at any intermediate period."[50] The rhythm method thus defined would not only have been useless as a means of contraception but would have been an actual inducement of pregnancy. As a result of the medical stance, women were left to what knowledge they could gain through word of mouth or were forced to resort to the more dangerous practice of abortion.

Many women seemed willing to do so. In 1870, the *Canada Health Journal* referred to abortion as "The Great Crime of the Age."[51] Certainly the medical profession feared that the number of abortions was increasing. There was the occasional mention of abortion trials but since prosecution seldom occurred unless the woman died, the number of such trials was limited. However, the profession had other indicators. According to the *Canada Lancet*, physicians were constantly being asked to perform abortions. One doctor in Windsor and Essex County, for example, estimated that he had had 50 requests in one year.[52] Medical journals also mentioned the frequency of newspaper advertisements of abortifacients such as Clarke's Female Pills and Hooper's Female Pills, which blatantly warned about the danger of their use by pregnant women.[53]

Physicians were bitterly opposed to such means. "Better never read a paper, if it were necessary, than to risk the introduction of a serpent into the bosom of their family."[54] The medical profession argued that the fetus was alive as soon as it was conceived, and so abortion was a crime against life and therefore against God.[55] This moral judgement affected medical treatment, for the hatred of abortion was such that it sometimes placed a patient's life in danger. One article in the *Canada Lancet* discussed the advantages and disadvantages of the particular treatment of a pregnant woman who had a history of fetal craniotomies due to a pelvic deformity. Rather than abort the child, the decision was taken to perform a Caesarian section, which, in 1875, was almost tantamount to a death sentence for the woman.[56]

Physicians felt threatened by abortions. Certainly they were an attempt on the part of women to control their own bodies and thus a challenge to the medical profession. As previously mentioned, many physicians did not want women to understand their own bodies, let alone control them. As well, physicians felt vulnerable. If they refused to perform an abortion they feared they would be accused by the patient of doing so anyway in a spirit of revenge.[57] This fear could only be rational if the doctors recognized the determination of their women patients to have abortions and admitted that from the patient's point of view the medical profession was working for the status quo and against women in refusing abortions.

To overcome the problem of not being seen to respond to the needs of the patient, medical journals described in detail the possible consequences of abortion: ill health, sterility, or inability to carry a child full term.[58] Certainly many of these consequences were possible. As well, prior to the 1880s, surgical abortion, in the best of hands, carried a far higher risk of mortality than childbirth.[59] These medical rationales provided recognition that the physician knew better than the patient what was good for her. As a result the physician could see himself in a paternal role. This was part of the whole "mystique" which was beginning to surround the medical profession in these years. It must be remembered that from the early decades of the nineteenth century "regular" physicians had been attempting to have themselves recognized as a profession with complete control over standards, access to medical information and practice. Originally this was to eliminate the numerous irregular practitioners[60] but this desire for exclusivity also influenced the relationship between physician and patient.

By the end of the century, physicians were in a position of power with respect to their patients. Understandably this power came from their access to medical knowledge. However, many physicians desired to exert their influence in non-medical areas. For example, one physician in the *Canada Lancet*, in 1875, stated that abortion was practised more among Protestants than Catholics, and cited the influence of the priests in the confessional as the main deterrent for Catholics. This physician felt the medical profession should fill the moral void in society and impress upon women, like the priest in the confessional, that abortion was murder.[61] As in the case of contraception, the transition on the part of the doctor was being made from medical judge to moral judge.

The attitudes of physicians to contraception and abortion were motivated by three forces. Practitioners were protecting their vested interests as men and as professionals, but, as well, they were trying to protect their patients. Doctors did not question society's attitudes toward women because they were not really forced to, and for most Canadians woman's maternal role was a fact of life that was immutable. As professionals, physicians wanted to protect themselves in their exclusivity. This they had managed to do by controlling access to the increasing wealth of medical technology and theory. Because they alone had access to this information they could only logically believe that they knew best for their patient. One result was increasing medical interference in childbirth.

IV

Physicians clearly believed respectably married women should have children. Children were a "needful condition to health and happy marriages."[62] So convinced were some physicians that the maternal role was natural to women that they advocated marriage and motherhood as cures for uterine disease.[63]

If physicians believed women should have children, they also rather conveniently believed women in the civilized society of the late nineteenth century needed medical assistance in giving birth to those children. Physicians rationalized the emergence of the man midwife in the same way men rationalized their control over other areas of economic endeavour. They had the expertise and, according to physicians, this medical expertise was increasingly needed in the management of childbirth. The term "management" itself suggests an attempt to control or widen their power. They announced loudly and clearly — women were no longer fit to have babies without aid. Ironically the civilization which

228

had raised women to new moral heights as mothers had weakened them physically. Medical practitioners were generous enough to admit that this weakness in woman was not inherent but learned. Nevertheless, the customs of civilized life had undermined her: the lack of outdoor exercise, overwork of the brain, her manner of dress, imprudence during menstruation and after parturition, prevention of conception and inducement of abortion, insufficient food, and habitual constipation.[64]

In the *Canada Medical Record* of 1889, one article went into a lengthy explanation of the way in which men and women were evolving and how this was affecting the birth process.[65] First the sexual feeling in women was dying out through the pressure of social constraints on women to repress their feelings. This in itself was not a bad occurrence, for sexual feeling in a woman was not necessary for propagation and "the women who have no such feelings are perhaps the best off." However, as the feeling declined in women, it correspondingly increased in men. Reproduction for a man was an active process and only men with strong sexual feelings had children. Social Darwinism was put forward:

> For, owing to the keenness of the struggle for existence, in greater part due to extravagance, no man will enter into the expense and responsibilities of matrimony unless compelled to do so by the force of his sexual feelings.

At this point the logic of the argument tends to dissipate. Since only men with strong sexual feelings have children, the author concluded that their sons would inherit this same sexual drive. Men with weak sexual desires would not have children. The result would be a society in which men had increasingly strong sexual drives. Survival of the fittest (or in this case the sexiest) would hold sway. Interestingly enough, daughters did not inherit their father's sexual inclinations but rather their mother's. Thus the future envisioned was of virile men and sexually passive women.

Yet this still does not account for the need for interference in childbirth. However, at the same time this development was occurring, the pelves of women were getting smaller and the heads of male children were becoming larger (due to the importance of brain power in modern nineteenth-century life). "While nature if left to herself would exterminate at their birth these big-headed men who are able to amass so much wealth, civilization comes to their rescue and saves them." The rescue, of course, came in the guise of the specialist, the obstetrician. While the author does not condone such interference, in fact he suggested removing the uterus of such women to stop the breeding of such men. The majority of physicians clearly were the beneficiaries of the theory since it meant that the demand for their services would increase.[66] It provided them with the rationale to interfere in what had long been women's "business." That they wanted to was obvious. Their general attitude toward midwives was that they belonged to some by-gone era. However, medical men with training, and most significantly technology, were now taking over. It was their control of technology which gave them an edge over midwives, for only medical practitioners were trained in the use of forceps, specula, sounds, curettes, and the myriad of other instruments which made up the arsenal of the nineteenth-century obstetrician.[67] This gave them the wherewithal to interfere in childbirth more than any midwife would dare. The instrumental interference separated them from midwives.

Yet at times physicians seemed ambivalent. Although they benefited from their belief that civilization was rendering women less capable of giving birth without assistance, they also seemed to yearn back to a time when women were more capable of having children naturally. It was their mission, they believed, to rectify the situation, to make women healthy so they could have children.[68] It was their goal to restore women to their proper function. This they tried to do by making childbirth easier and safer.

They would first meet their patients to diagnose pregnancy. In the very early part of the century one lecturer suggested that since examining a woman internally for pregnancy was disagreeable to modest ladies, it should be done in their own homes with their "servants" about them.[69] This is perhaps indicative of the class of women who actually consulted a doctor about pregnancy. By the latter decades of the century the preferred practice, according to medical texts, was attendance in a doctor's office, a possible reflection of the increasing stature of the medical profession.

The signs of pregnancy were seen to be more or less what they are today, although myths did abound. Of these one author of a textbook gave "greater importance to the more voluptuous sensation, the more erethism experienced by some females during a prolific coition, by which a few of them can recognize with a degree of certainty that they have become pregnant."[70] This belief survived well into the century.[71]

Once the diagnosis of pregnancy was confirmed, there seemed to be little if any followup during pregnancy unless there were complications. Most physicians did not see their patients again until they actually went into labour. When this occurred, the physician was sent for. Few babies were born in hospitals; most were born at home. In the mid part of the century this meant that during labour the patient was often surrounded by her friends and neighbours, a practice not always approved of by the medical fraternity. Indeed one physician questioned whether these onlookers were really interested in the welfare of the patient or were simply curious about "whether the patient was to die or live."[72] After mid-century very seldom were such gatherings mentioned in the medical journals of the day. The birth process had become something between patient and physician, something private. This too reflects the increasing stature of the medical practitioner and his/her gradual control over the birth process.

Some practices in the early years suggest a more relaxed attitude toward birth than later became the case. One text advised that a doctor should be sensitive to whom a pregnant woman wanted in the room with her; i.e., some women wanted their husbands while others did not.[73] Several texts mentioned allowing the woman to take whatever position felt comfortable during birth.[74] For most physicians, however, the position was dictated by where they had been trained: if in England, the woman would be lying on her left side; if in France, Germany, or America, she would be placed on her back.

Other practices in the early period make the modern reader wonder what purpose the presence of a physician served. The most prevalent of these was the idea that the physician should not see the body of the patient but rather have the patient covered at all times. If birth was to be assisted it was to be done by touch. In fact the concept of demonstrative midwifery in mid-century was a highly contentious issue.[75] This was a time when men were just coming into use as midwives in Canada and the morality of having men in the birth chamber was widely debated. Most women probably gave birth on their own, with the help of friends or a female midwife. However, when something went wrong in labour the tendency was to call in a physician.[76]

The main problem in childbirth which would necessitate medical intervention was an abnormal presentation, that is, a non-head presentation. In such cases the physician had three choices: podalic version, the turning of the child for correct presentation, that is, a foot presentation; use of forceps; or a cutting operation on either the mother or child. All three had been developed by the mid-eighteenth century and were used well into the nineteenth.[77] Not until the era of antiseptics and anaesthetics was there a major change in treatment eliminating one of the above methods, namely the cutting operation on the child, and accentuating another, the use of forceps.

The most extreme intervention was the cutting operation. When the child was too large or the mother unable to give birth safely, physicians frequently were forced to choose between the life of the child and that of the mother. Almost all Protestant doctors agreed that the life of the mother had priority.[78] The result was to "divide (the child) in pieces" so that delivery could be accomplished safely for the mother.[79] One of the reasons such operations were resorted to was that the cutting operations on the mother in an attempt to save both mother and child were extremely risky. Nevertheless they were performed.

Symphysiotomy consisted of enlarging the pelvis (usually deformed) so that a natural delivery could occur. To do so the union between the two pubic bones was divided and the bones pushed forcibly outwards so as to increase the capacity of the contracted pelvis.[80] However, it was seldom performed because it could leave the patient a permanent cripple. In 1893 only three cases in Canada had ever been performed.[81]

The laparotomy consisted of delivering a baby which had escaped the uterus through a rent by cutting the abdominal wall.[82] Given the lack of antiseptics until the 1870s, this operation (like all operations) had a high maternal mortality rate. For a similar reason Caesarian section was also dangerous. In the United States, between 1876 and 1886, in 37 operations performed, 29 women died.[83] One text suggested that the Caesarian section be used only as a last resort and only to save the life of the child.[84] With antiseptics, however, such operations were much safer and soon replaced the cutting operations on the child.

Women faced other dangers in childbirth as well. Until the introduction of antiseptics in the 1870s, puerperal fever was a major killer, with many a doctor carrying death from one patient to another. Especially bad were hospitals, some of which, like the Toronto General in mid-century, were noted for their uncleanliness.[85]

At the very least, childbirth in the late nineteenth century could be extremely uncomfortable. Bleeding the patient was still fairly prevalent at mid-century. The *Upper Canada Journal of Medical, Surgical and Physical Sciences* reported one woman being bled of 30 ounces of blood to bring her out of puerperal convulsions.[86] Some physicians inserted vinegar into the uterus to stop post-partum hemorrhage,[87] while another favoured treatment was the use of electricity. One pole of the galvanic current was placed in the uterus while the other was placed over the abdomen. The result was a powerful contraction of the uterus which would (it was hoped) stop hemorrhage.[88]

It would be easy to criticize the medical profession for some of its treatment of women in childbirth.[89] But such criticisms would come from hindsight and do not really provide insight into the dynamics of change within the profession. What does give insight is a closer examination of some of the advances made, the attitude of physicians to them, and the way in which they affected treatment, sometimes for the worse. The three examined are antiseptics, anesthesia, and forceps.

Not everyone was willing to accept antiseptics when they were first introduced in the 1870s. As late as 1885 one physician in Montreal was still ridiculing their use:

I think we might recognize a momentum in antiseptic theories—a momentum that seems to be carrying us into irrational and absurd practices, that after a time we shall be compelled to give up, but not without the loss of prestige and influence with the public. According to the present rate of progression we shall soon, when called upon to attend a case of midwifery, be compelled to retire to our bath-rooms, wash and scrub in disinfectant solutions, don a fresh suit of disinfected clothes, and, like the Romish priests, when called to administer the communion at a person's residence, we shall go forth, preceded by couriers to clear the way and open doors, etc., etc., not daring to touch even a door bell knob, last, possibly, an unclean mendicant has first handled and defiled it.[90]

A better description of modern surgery could not be found. Fortunately for patients, if the evidence of the medical journals is to be believed, most Canadian doctors accepted anti-septics gratefully.

Anesthesia in labour was also generally adopted, its first use being as early as 1848.[91] However, some physicians were uneasy about the effect it would have on women's moral well-being. The American specialist Meigs opposed it, considering the pain of childbirth to be "a desirable, salutary, and conservative manifestation of life force."[92] Tyler Smith in his major text, *Parturition and the Principles and Practice of Obstetrics*, argued that pain was a nat-ural part of childbirth and referred to the morality of that pain. Without it he feared women would descend to the level of the lower animals and substitute sexual orgasm for it:

> Provident Nature has, moreover, specially exempted women from the dominion of all pas-sion save that of maternity at the time of childbirth. I believe this exemption and moral supe-riority arises, in a very great degree, from the physical suffering of parturition. The natural throes deliver womankind from those emotions natural to the inferior animals. Here it is that we see more clearly than under any other circumstances, the *morality of pain* . . . The pains of natural labour are hard to bear, . . . but they ennoble the sufferer morally.[93]

Most physicians, however, did not seem to share this fear, and, given the cutting opera-tions which did occur during this period, patients must have been thankful for it. However, the opinions expressed by Meigs and Smith do underline the concern of physicians for more than medical well-being and show how willing some were to make judgements in areas outside their expertise. Such judgements were clearly influenced by society's attitude toward women at that time and the desire of physicians to become spokesmen for their society and extend their influence to non-medical areas.

While most of us probably see antiseptics and anesthesia as beneficial, they did make it easier for physicians to resort to surgery. If in many cases this was justified, in others it was deemed to be, by at least one physician, a desire on the part of his colleagues to gain a rep-utation.[94] Antiseptics and anesthesia allowed physicians to interfere more in natural processes because they could do so more safely than before.

Whether they should do so in childbirth was a major controversy in the last half of the nineteenth century. At the centre of the storm was the use or overuse of forceps. The con-troversy went in cycles. In the 1850s there was great concern over "meddlesome mid-wifery,"[95] with the result that many women were left in labour for hours without interference of any kind.[96] Reacting to this situation, many physicians increased their use of forceps so that by the 1880s and 1890s, the concern was once again too much interfer-ence. Opponents of "meddlesome midwifery" argued that childbirth was a natural physi-ological function which needed no outside assistance unless there were complications. Physicians were not to try to improve upon nature.[97] Those who did could come in for some scathing attacks. One physician denounced "meddlesome midwifery," declaring that "The forceps are sometimes used to save time, sometimes to gain a little notoriety, some-times for the double fee, and sometimes from ignorance."[98]

Ironically the medical profession itself may have been partially responsible for the inter-ference. Reading the medical journals of the time, one would conclude that childbirth was a difficult process which required the mechanical aid of an expert. This, of course, reflected the tendency of physicians to write papers on their more difficult cases. Unfortunately this could not help but influence the inexperienced practitioner who read these journals. Little guidance was given. No one seemed to know how often forceps were used in practice or should be used. In 1877, one physician reported using forceps in one out of every 27 cases while another reported using them as often as in one out of thirteen.[99] Unfortunately, in the hands of the "amateur," the use of forceps could be tragic. In the *Canada Medical Record* of 1898, one article suggested that many of the cases needing gynecological care and even surgery were the result of poor childbed treatment, specifically the overuse of forceps.[100]

The "meddlesome midwifery" opponents did not condemn forceps out of hand. Forceps were an important tool which would and did save the lives of women. What they objected to was the use of forceps becoming a standard medical procedure in cases which did not warrant it. They objected to it becoming fashionable and to physicians treating it as a child does a new toy, playing only with it until he tires of it or something else takes its place. But medical science seemed to work that way. Each advance in treatment seemed to bring with it disadvantages and it took time for the medical profession to work out an acceptable compromise. In the case of forceps it was the advent of the lifesaving anesthesia and antiseptics which lessened the pain and danger of medical interference in childbirth and to a certain extent were responsible for "meddlesome midwifery."

V

Childbirth was a fact of life for most married women in late-nineteenth-century Canada. While many if not most of these women were not treated by physicians, the knowledge held by the profession did dictate the way in which they were cared for. Childbirth was something experienced only by women, yet in the nineteenth century it was increasingly managed by men. Most of these physicians were hardworking, caring individuals. However, they were a product of their time. They believed women were controlled by their reproductive function and, while this made woman special, it also made her, from the physicians' viewpoint, inferior to man. This could not help but be reflected in their treatment of women. The medical profession withheld contraceptive knowledge from women and provided opponents of higher education for women with arguments. The rationale for both was the need to protect woman's reproductive system. The consequence of both was to limit woman's control over her own life and to extend the influence of the medical profession into areas where the barriers between medical issues and non-medical issues were, to say the least, hazy. Even when advances in medicine such as antiseptics and anesthesia were made that could help women in childbirth, they were often accompanied by disadvantages, for example, when the introduction of forceps led to their overuse, and to "meddlesome midwifery." This could be dangerous, since, as the century advanced, women increasingly consulted physicians with respect to childbirth. Childbearing was considered the preeminent function of women by the medical profession. Without it, they were less than women. Because of it, they were less than men.

NOTES

1. Michael Bliss, in "Pure Books on Avoided Subjects," C.H.A. *Historical Papers* 1970, made an appeal for such a study.
2. Rosalind Rosenberg, "In Search of Woman's Nature," *Feminist Studies* 3 (4) (Fall 1975), p. 142.
3. Ann Wood, "The Fashionable Diseases," *Journal of Interdisciplinary History* 4 (1) (Summer 1973), p. 25; P. Bart, "Social Structure and Vocabularies of Discomfort," in C. Edgley, ed., *Life as Theatre: A Dramaturgical Source Book* (Chicago: Aldine, 1975), p. 192; William Tyler Smith, *Parturition and the Principles and Practice of Obstetrics* (Philadelphia, 1849), p. 19.

4. I would like to thank Professor Jean-Claude Guedon for suggesting the above point.

5. Some doctors did not even need moral reasons. In one manuscript entitled "Lectures on the Theory and Practice of Midwifery" by J. Lowdar, the author felt that in the birth of twins, the doctor shouldn't even inform the patient until the second was already born. Special Collections, Tupper Medical Library, Dalhousie University.

6. Alexander Skene, *Medical Gynecology; A Treatise on the Diseases of Women from the Standpoint of the Physician* (N.Y. 1895), p. 72.

7. William Carpenter, *Principles of Human Physiology* (London, 1869), pp. 911–912; Skene, op. cit., p. 80.

8. Skene, op. cit., pp. 76–77. For an intensive look at how important this balance between the sexes was in nineteenth-century society, see Nancy Cott, *The Bonds of Womanhood* (New Haven: Yale University Press, 1977).

9. Elizabeth Gobbs, "Professionalization of Canadian Medicine, 1850–1970," C.H.A. *Historical Papers* 1978, unpublished paper; William Canniff, *The Medical Profession in Upper Canada, 1783–1850* (Toronto, 1894); W.B. Howell, *Medicine in Canada* (N.Y., 1933); John J. Heagerty, *Four Centuries of Medical History in Canada and a Sketch of the Medical History of Newfoundland* (Toronto, 1928); Hugh MacDermot, *One Hundred Years of Medicine in Canada, 1867–1967* (Toronto, 1967). Most of the above are very narrative, with little attempt made to provide a social context.

10. I looked only at the English-language journals and texts because France and England had two different medical traditions and it would have complicated this preliminary work to have attempted to cope with both.

11. This was especially true in the Maritimes. Kenneth Mackenzie, "A Century of Medicine in Nova Scotia," *Nova Scotia Medical Bulletin* 32 (1953), p. 290.

12. C. Roland, "Ontario Medical Periodicals," C.H.A. *Historical Papers* 1978, unpublished, p. 2.

13. *Census of Canada*, 1871, Vol. 1, 341, p. 31.

14. Nancy Cott, *The Bonds of Womanhood* (New Haven: Yale University Press, 1977), p. 46; Ann Douglas, *The Feminization of American Culture* (New York: Knopf, 1977), p. 75.

15. *Canada Lancet* 7 (Oct. 1874), p. 57.

16. Henry Garriques, *A Text-book of the Diseases of Women* (Philadelphia, 1894), p. 114; Carpenter, op. cit., pp. 832–833; William Tyler Smith, *The Modern Practice of Midwifery: A Course of Lectures on Obstetrics* (New York, 1858).

17. Alfred Galabin, *A Manual of Midwifery* (Philadelphia, 1886), p. 53; Arthur Edis, *Diseases of Women: A Manual for Students and Practitioners* (Philadelphia, 1882), p. 133.

18. Edmund R. Novak and Emil Novak, *Novak's Textbook of Gynecology* (Baltimore: Williams and Wilkins, 1965), p. 82; Tyler Smith, *Parturition . . .*, op. cit., p. 89; Galabin, op. cit., p. 53; Tyler Smith, *A Course of Lectures*, op. cit, p. 89; Theophilus Parvin, *The Science and Art of Obstetrics* (Philadelphia, 1885), p. 90; P. Cazeaux, *Theoretical and Practical Treatise on Midwifery* (Philadelphia, 1837), p. 103.

19. *Canadian Practitioner* (Dec. 1884), p. 361.

20. Paul Mundé, *A Practical Treatise on the Diseases of Women* (Philadelphia, 1891), p. 40; John Thorburn, *A Practical Treatise on the Diseases of Women* (London, 1885), pp. 96–97.

21. *Canada Medical and Surgical Journal* (July 1877), p. 22.

22. The clothing women wore was of concern to the medical profession. See Charles Penrose, *A Text-book of Diseases of Women* (Philadelphia, 1905, 5th edition), p. 19; Alexander Skene, *Medical Gynecology* (New York, 1895), pp. 12–14; William Goodell, *Lessons in Gynecology* (Philadelphia, 1890), p. 548; *Canada Medical Record* (Dec. 1888), pp. 69–70; Theodore Thomas, *A Practical Treatise on the Diseases of Women* (Philadelphia, 1868), pp. 56–57.

23. John Baldy, *An American Text-book of Gynecology* (New York, 1844), p. 97.

24. Richard Leonardo, *History of Gynecology* (New York: Proben, 1944), p. 255.

25. Paul Mundé, "Quarterly Report of Obstetrics and Diseases of Women and Children," *American Journal of Obstetrics and Diseases of Women and Children* (1875), p. 353.

26. *The Montreal Medical Journal* XXV/9 (March 1897), p. 681.

233

27. Garriques, op. cit., p. 115.

28. Skene, op. cit., pp. 33–34.

29. Ibid.

30. *Canada Medical and Surgical Journal* (Oct. 1887), p. 185.

31. Skene, op. cit., p. 80.

32. *Dominion Medical Monthly and Ontario Medical Journal* (Sept. 1893), p. 68; *The Sanitary Journal* VI (1874), p. 56.

33. *Canadian Practitioner* (June 1891), p. 261; *Canada Lancet* VI/7 (March, 1874), p. 233.

34. Garriques, op. cit., p. 125; *Canada Medical Record* VII (Sept. 1879), p. 311.

35. *Canada Lancet* VI/7 (March 1874), p. 233; *Montreal Medical Journal* XXV (March 1897), p. 682, Mundé, op. cit., p. 37; *The Sanitary Journal* 1 (1874), p. 56.

36. William Goodell, *Lessons in Gynecology* (Philadelphia, 1890), p. 549; Skene, op. cit., p. 33.

37. *Canada Medical Record* (July 1888), p. 239.

38. Ibid., p. 238.

29. Ibid., VIII (June 1890), p. 215.

40. The medical profession dominated childbirth only among the middle class; i.e., the class who could afford their services.

41. *Canada Lancet* (Nov. 1894), p. 98. Unless Canadians were unlike other people, the birth control alternative is the most obvious. See Linda Gordon, *Woman's Body, Woman's Right: A Social History of Birth Control in America* (New York: Viking Press, 1976); Patricia Knight, "Women and Abortion in Victorian and Edwardian England," *History Workshop* 4 (August 1977), pp. 57–69; Angus McLaren, "Women's Work and Regulation of Family Size," *History Workshop* 4 (August, 1977), pp. 70–81.

42. Goodell, op. cit., p. 562.

43. *Kingston Medical Quarterly* III/1 (October 1898), p. 165; Goodell, op. cit., p. 573; p. 570; *Canada Medical Journal and Monthly Record* 3 (1867), p. 226; p. 228; *Canadian Practitioner* 18 (April 1883), p. 296.

44. Goodell, op. cit., p. 566.

45. Paul Mundé, ed., *A Practical Treatise on the Diseases of Women* (Philadelphia, 1891), p. 43; *Canada Health Journal* I/5 (May 1840), p. 66.

46. *Canada Lancet* IV/4 (Dec. 1871), pp. 185–86; *Canada Health Journal* I/5 (May 1870), p. 67.

47. *Canada Lancet* 25 (July 1893).

48. *Kingston Medical Quarterly* II (Oct. 1898), p. 165.

49. *Canada Medical Record*, June 1889, p. 194.

50. William Carpenter, *Principles of Human Physiology* (Philadelphia, 1847), p. 834; P. Cazeaux, *Theoretical and Practical Treatise on Midwifery* (Philadelphia, 1837), p. 123; *Canadian Practitioner* (April 1884), p. 115; Garriques, op. cit., p. 117.

51. *Canada Health Journal* I/5 (May 1870), p. 65.

52. *Canada Medical and Surgical Journal* 12 (1884), p. 252; *Provincial Medical Journal* (May 1868), pp. 13–16; *Canada Lancet* 7 (June 1875), p. 291.

53. *Canada Lancet* IV/4 (Dec. 1871), pp. 185–86; *Canada Health Journal* I/5 (May 1870), p. 66.

54. *Medical Chronicle* (1856), p. 35.

55. *Canada Health Journal* I/5 (May 1870), pp. 67–68; *Kingston Medical Quarterly* 3 (1) (Oct. 1898), p. 165.

56. *Canada Lancet* VII (June 1875), p. 289.

57. *Canada Lancet* (March 1889), p. 218.

58. *Canada Health Journal* I/5 (May 1870), p. 70.

59. Dr. Charles Roland kindly pointed this out to me.

60. See E. Gibbs, "Professionalization of Canadian Medicine," op. cit., for a detailed description of this process.

61. *Canada Lancet* (June 1875), p. 291.

62. Goodell, op. cit., p. 570; Skene, *Medical Gynecology*, p. 85.

63. Mundé, op. cit., p. 511.
64. Mundé, op. cit., pp. 35, 46, 52; Charles Penrose, *A Text-book of Diseases of Women* (Philadelphia, 1905), p. 18; *Canada Medical Record* (Nov. 1889), p. 27.
65. For a detailed study of sexual theories, see Jill Conway, "Stereotypes of Femininity in a Theory of Sexual Evolution," *Victorian Studies* XIV/1 (Sept. 1970), pp. 47–63.
66. *Canada Medical Record* (Nov. 1889), p. 29.
67. *Canada Lancet* VII (Oct. 1874), p. 57.
68. Goodell, op. cit., p. 550; *The Sanitary Journal* (1876), p. 335.
69. Lowder Manuscript, p. 99, see footnote 5.
70. Cazeaux, op. cit., p. 238.
71. See M. Bliss, op. cit.
72. *Upper Canada Journal of Medical, Surgical and Physical Science* I (July 1851), p. 152.
73. Cazeaux, op. cit., p. 392
74. *Canada Medical Record* 6 (Jan. 1878), p. 82; Tyler Smith, *A Course of Lectures on Obstetrics*, op. cit., pp. 358–59. Playfair suggested that it was up to the woman whether she wanted her husband with her or not. William Playfair, *A Treatise on the Science and Practice of Midwifery* (London, 1880), p. 276.
75. *British American Journal of Science* (Nov. 1850), p. 333.
76. *Medical Chronicle* (Dec. 1854), pp. 261–62.
77. Harvey Graham, *Eternal Eve, the History of Gynecology and Obstetrics* (New York: Doubleday, 1951), p. 213.
78. Alfred King, *A Manual of Obstetrics* (Philadelphia, 1884), p. 210.
79. Ibid., p. 204.
80. Graham, op. cit., p. 160.
81. *Dominion Medical Monthly* I/1 (July 1893), p. 26.
82. King, op. cit., p. 201.
83. A. Charpentier, *Cyclopaedia of Obstetrics and Gynecology*, IV (New York, 1887), p. 207.
84. King, op. cit., pp. 198–99.
85. *Medical Chronicle* (1855), pp. 494–97.
86. *Upper Canada Journal of Medical, Surgical and Physical Science* (August 1851), p. 195; Walter Radcliffe, *Milestones in Midwifery* (Bristol, 1967), pp. 82–83.
87. *Canadian Journal of Medical Science* (Jan. 1880), p. 45.
88. *Canada Lancet* VI/7 (March 1874), p. 219; *Upper Canada Journal of Medical, Surgical and Physical Science* 2 (July 1852), pp. 66–67.
89. As a matter of record, the medical treatment of men for nervous and sexual disorders was equally horrendous. See Gail Pat Parsons, "Equal Treatment for All: American Medical Remedies for Male Sexual Problems: 1850–1900," *Journal of the History of Medicine* 32 (Jan. 1977), pp. 55–71.
90. *Canada Medical Record* (May 1885), p. 171; *Canada Lancet* (Sept. 1885), p. 26.
91. *British American Journal of Medical and Physical Science* (Feb. 1948), p. 324.
92. Radcliffe, op. cit., p. 81.
93. Tyler Smith, op. cit., p. 128.
94. *Dominion Medical Monthly and Ontario Medical Journal* (June 1899), pp. 277–80.
95. *Canada Medical Record* (Feb. 1876), p. 129.
96. Tyler Smith, *A Course . . .*, op. cit., p. 30.
97. *Canada Lancet* 18 (Sept. 1885), p. 25; *Maritime Medical News* (Oct. 1898), p. 337; *Canada Medical Record* (Feb. 1889), p. 99; *Maritime Medical News* (July 1892), p. 125.
98. *Canada Lancet* 18 (Sept. 1885), p. 73.
99. *Canadian Journal of Medical Science* (Oct. 1877), p. 339; *Maritime Medical News* (May 1897), p. 153; G. Bedford, *The Principles and Practice of Obstetrics* (New York, 1861), p. 574.
100. *Canada Medical Record* (1898), p. 4.

Article Seventeen

Idealized Middle-Class Sport for a Young Nation: Lacrosse in Nineteenth-Century Ontario Towns, 1871–1891

Nancy B. Bouchier

During the late nineteenth century, social groups attempting to establish a cultural hegemony used sport as a site for their struggles over culture.[1] Although the coalition of interests best denoted as the respectable Victorian middle class won this battle, the victory was neither complete nor truly coherent. Thus, a study of the local adoption of amateur lacrosse in Ingersoll, and its nearby arch-rival Woodstock, Ontario,[2] provides a way of exploring how social groups in small localities used sport to experience, and contribute to, the formulation of a hegemonic culture.[3]

One outcome of this late-nineteenth-century process is a most enduring legacy. It is the notion that games somehow build character, and, by extension, that sport is a potent vehicle for achieving and reinforcing certain social goals, and rectifying the physical and moral ills of society. Perhaps best known through the phrase "muscular Christianity,"[4] this notion deeply pervaded the amateur sport movement that created the institutional framework necessary for sport competition to thrive during the last century, and for the acceptance of sport as an integral aspect of our education system today.[5]

In their quest to project their world view of respectability through team sport, sport reformers approached it from a rational, utilitarian perspective.[6] Their claims about sport's character-building qualities and the sporting performances choreographed to buttress these claims constitute the stories that Canadian sport reformers were telling about themselves and their world.[7] By doing so, they rendered sport an arena for the acting out of the hegemonic process. Since in the process the voices of those who they deemed to be their opponents have been muted, not recorded, or suppressed through time, detractors remain a hazy group. Thus, we are left mainly with the legacy of those who held the dominant agenda for sport. However, we do have some clues to the identity, actions, and perhaps belief of those who resisted their efforts.

Amateur lacrosse is a particularly ripe sport in which to study the phenomenon of sport as a site for an emerging hegemony. It advanced the popular, late-nineteenth-century notion that games build character, and it bore a particular "Canadian" stamp. It provides a fascinating example of the larger sport-reform phenomenon during the era of Canada's birth as a nation and a particular vision of how sport could cultivate "Canadian character." Although lacrosse had origins in Indian religion, tradition, and society, white urban men with a specific social agenda devised its organized form.[8] These men took the Indian game and "reinvented" it in the effort to create a version of a Canadian sporting culture that projected their particular vision of reality and belief system (that was class-bound, racist, and gender-specific).[9] Lacrosse was conceived by them as a vehicle for cultivating Canadian nationalism, manliness, and respectability in male youth, and to keep the leisure activities of males in check. Projecting lacrosse as a quintessentially Canadian sport, lacrosse propa-

Source: *Journal of Canadian Studies*, 29, 2 (Summer 1994): 89–110. Reprinted with permission.

gandists, like propagandists for other popular sports of the day, received support from social reformers, religious leaders, and educators.[10] They maintained that such sports cultivated and contributed to the emerging urban-industrial Canadian nation.

This research addresses several interrelated issues in the use of sport in hegemonic struggles over culture through an examination of the development of lacrosse in the two towns during the sport's heyday, between 1871 and 1891. It first identifies certain social themes embraced both locally and nationally by the organized lacrosse movement, particularly nationalism, manliness, and youth reform through rational recreation. These themes mark lacrosse as a sport with a social agenda based upon a particular vision. Then, using demographic data on the Ingersoll and Woodstock clubs, it identifies the organizers and players who masterminded and carried out this process of reforming local sport. The research also shows that middle-class reformers were keenly aware of harmful diversions (such as swearing, drinking, gambling, immorality) that surrounded sport, and were concerned about the acceptability of certain sports themselves (such as horseracing, dog and cockfighting, bull and bear baits, and pugilism).[11] The reformers sought to monopolize the forms and meanings that local sport was to take. By the late 1880s, town councils allowed these men, who were connected to an evolving cult of respectability, to organize annual community civic holidays through their local Amateur Athletic Associations (AAAs), which regulated community sport. Finally, the research shows the ways in which sport reformers infused urban boosterism into their social agenda for lacrosse.

AAA efforts to define legitimate activities for others, like similar efforts to sublimate and marginalize unacceptable traditions, remained ongoing in the hegemonic process. While they did manage to systematize and rationalize some familiar sports and to remove others from the athletic grounds while promoting utilitarian, respectable, and representative team sports such as lacrosse, the social agenda of sport reformers met with resistance.[12] Ironically, boosterism fuelled playing field violence during intense competition as well as rowdiness in the stands. Such responses caused problems for idealistic visions of sport, prompting middle-class sport reformers to make concessions in order to maintain their hegemony.

Like other social thinkers concerned with physical health, youth, and Canadian society, the headmaster of Woodstock College, J.E. Wells, believed that physical development played an essential role in the shaping of a national character in Canadian youth. Some seven years after Confederation, he wrote in the *Canadian Monthly and National Review* that physically well-developed youth were needed for young Canada to assume "the attitudes and tones, and to some extent the responsibilities of, nationality." Wells believed that Canadians possessed certain inheritable qualities, which, tempered by climatic conditions, would "prove most favourable to mental as well as physical development." The latter was viewed as the key to national development: "bone and muscle and nerve fibre must be necessary antecedents of brain power."[13] This, in turn, undergirded nation building. Like other educational institutions, Wells's Woodstock College, which later became McMaster University, sought to stimulate the mental and physical development of youth through "a rational program of gymnasium work and outdoor sports featuring lacrosse."[14]

Wells was not alone in his concerns and efforts. Proselytizers for lacrosse throughout Canada shared this nationalist orientation and, through it, hoped to create a culture of purposeful sport.[15] For example, Dr. William George Beers, the Montreal dentist credited with facilitating the early development of the Canadian Dental Association, spearheaded the creation of the National Lacrosse Association in 1867, advocating that lacrosse could shape boys into manly Canadian nationalists.[16] With an almost evangelical fervour his

Lacrosse: The National Game of Canada (1869) proposes a nationalist agenda for his vision of sport.[17] Beers pushed his point as far as he could:

> It may seem frivolous, at first consideration, to associate this feeling of nationality with a field game, but history proves it to be a strong and important influence. If the Republic of Greece was indebted to Olympian games; if England has cause to bless the name of cricket, so may Canada be proud of Lacrosse. It has raised a young manhood throughout the Dominion to active, healthy exercise; it has originated a popular feeling in favour of physical exercise and has, perhaps, done more than anything else to invoke the sentiment of patriotism among young men in Canada; and if this sentiment is desirable abroad, surely it is at home.[18]

Despite such claims, lacrosse is not our national sport: we simply do not have one. Still, the myth persists. It was initiated in the nineteenth century by men such as Beers, and W.K. McNaught, author of *Lacrosse and How to Play It* (1873), who commended lacrosse as having "a nationalizing influence upon all who come in contact with it, and, for this reason alone, if for no other, it ought to be encouraged." More recently, Canadian sport historian Don Morrow has argued that the notion that lacrosse is our national sport continues to be supported through "a kind of consensual validity: if something is claimed to be true enough times, it is often accepted as truth — then and now."[19]

Part of the lacrosse myth's success can be attributed to late-nineteenth-century efforts to point to the Aboriginal origins of the game in order to vindicate and justify the sport as a national symbol. In his writings Beers made all of the necessary connections. For example, he romanticized Indians a noble savages, themselves a feature of the rugged Canadian northern landscape, which white men were successfully conquering through their nation-building pursuits.[20] By extension, he believed that the Indian game could be used toward nationalist ends. Beers was certainly not alone in this effort. In "The Northern Character: Theme and Sport in Nineteenth Century Canada," Canadian sport historian David Brown traces the blending of the northern theme with Victorian beliefs in muscular Christianity.[21] He points out that Beers developed and fused the themes of northern character and national sport in *Lacrosse: The National Game*, at the same time that R.G. Haliburton published *The Men of the North and Their Place in History*. Beers's approach, Brown argues, "provided Canadian nationalists with another medium through which they could promote their country and its benefits vigorously on both a national and international scale."[22]

Lacrosse promoters credited the physical robustness that they believed Indians had (but which white urban males, who were doomed to sedentary occupations, lacked) to the vigorous demands that lacrosse made on their physiques. They linked this attribute to their ability to conquer the Canadian wilderness by reshaping it to suit middle-class, white-male, urban culture. It would produce "the greatest combination of physical and mental activity white man can sustain." They believed that they significantly elevated the moral tone of lacrosse. Beers bluntly claimed his version of lacrosse was "much superior to the original as civilization is to barbarism."[23]

Repeated themes — "nation building," "boyish sport," and "young manhood" — were central to the promotion of lacrosse as a rational recreation aimed primarily at Canadian male youth. The concern of social and sport reformers with the "problem" of urban youth helped to fuel lacrosse's reform agenda. As high school enrolments increased (nearly doubling in Ontario between 1875 and 1895), and as the apprenticeship system declined, middle-class males were dependent on their families for longer periods of time than had previously been the case.[24] With children and adolescents increasingly under female scrutiny — in schools and in the home — some social observers feared that boys were becoming increasingly feminized and were lacking in male role models.[25] Many argued that, unchecked, this situation would result in males becoming physically weak and, therefore, powerless. Keenly concerned about this, parents and social reformers sought appropriate spare-time activities to occupy young males. Through these activities they hoped to expose them to masculine role models and to teach them the importance of manly physical activity in an increasingly sedentary world.

In both Ingersoll and Woodstock clergymen repeatedly stressed the relationship between manliness and the leisure habits of male youth. Sermon titles reveal their preoccupations: "How Does Physical Welfare Affect Moral Conduct?"; "Young Man's Leisure"; "Where Do You Spend Your Time?"; "True Manhood"; and "A Manly Man."[26] As Ingersoll's Rev. P. Wright asserted in 1872, the lack of a conception of true manhood was a "fruitful source of failures in young men." He determined that, with a grasp of this concept, "evil has no chances for young men." Simply cultivating brute strength and courage in youth was not sufficient for the pursuit of manliness: each element had to be "suitably controlled."[27]

To Canadian social and sport reformers lacrosse was one solution to the problem of urban male youth. Lacrosse was a means to the end of cultivating manliness in youth and developing character so that young men would remain on the path of righteousness. Its newness appealed to the reform-minded since it was socially insulated from taverns and other unsavoury institutions where illegal and publicly castigated sports, such as pugilism and cockfighting, thrived in an environment of alcohol and gambling. As George Beers put it, lacrosse did not have "debasing accompaniments such as the bar room association" that plagued other sports.[28] When responding to the Commission Appointed to Enquire into the Prison and Reformatory System about potential cures for youth idleness, Woodstock's gaoler offered: "I would keep children employed at something or other," for example, "good honest play, a game of lacrosse or similar amusement."[29] Presumably, similar efforts to keep boys on the right path led to the granting of the title "Tzar" of the Beavers Lacrosse Club to Woodstock's Chief Constable T.W. McKee.[30]

Lacrosse superbly embodied the notion that games build character, a key ingredient in nineteenth-century conceptions of muscular Christianity.[31] Historians J.A. Mangan, David Brown, and other scholars have shown how this powerful ideology of sport was a class-bound phenomenon rooted in British mid-nineteenth-century public school reform.[32] Public school sports played under the watchful eye of men such as Dr. Thomas Arnold at the Rugby school aimed to instill valued character traits such as team work, self-sacrifice, courage, manliness, and achievement. School masters believed that these traits were transferable to other real-life situations. Popular novels by English authors Charles Kingsley and Thomas Hughes, and writings by American Thomas Wentworth Higginson, among others, brought these beliefs to life.[33] They projected sport as a means of character building and not an end in itself.

Such arguments undercut prevailing ascetic-pietist objections to sports as useless, immoral, and socially improper.[34] Protestant clergymen, educators, and social observers had, until this time, encouraged moderate forms of physical activity simply to keep people's bodies and minds refreshed and fit for work, but they still held deep suspicions of the fun and frivolity surrounding sporting activities.[35] Higher motives for sport were thus needed to transform rowdy, idle diversion to a morally uplifting, socially sanctioned activity appropriate to the social and physical changes of an increasingly industrialized society. According to Canadian sport historian Gerald Redmond, muscular Christianity's social construction attempted "to reconcile the centuries-old Christian faith with the new realities of the modern world to the apparent satisfaction of Victorian and Edwardian consciences."[36] It met with a considerable degree of success: its rise marked the evolution from a tradition of ascetic Protestantism to one of a moral athleticism. Church leaders and religious institutions emerged as patrons, rather than critics, of sport.[37] After the turn of the century, such support lent credibility to incorporating sport into the public school curriculum as a means of providing for the social and moral education of students, while at the same time physically educating their bodies.

Amateur lacrosse upheld muscular Christian principles. In fact, the National Lacrosse Association received its most prestigious award, the Claxton Flags, from a charter member and sometime president of North America's first Young Men's Christian Association.[38] The deed of gift records Montreal millionaire, philanthropist, and social reformer James T. Claxton's desire to "promote by every means in his power the fostering of clean, amateur athletics amongst the youth of Canada."[39] This occurred long before the YMCA embraced sport as a means of cultivating the spiritual, social, and physical dimensions of man.[40]

The muscular Christian influence on lacrosse resulted in demands that players develop a rational, educated strength: speed and agility were to be carefully circumscribed by an idea of right action.[41] To this end, the rules of lacrosse restricted what players were to do, both physically and socially.[42] Bruises, cuts, scrapes, and broken bones were likely to occur if 24 players on the field, sticks in hand, were simply to charge after a single ball. A "scientific" approach aimed to eliminate violence and injury by de-emphasizing physical contact for the presumed higher social skills believed to be obtained through the activity.[43] This system of beliefs relegated brute force to the status of being inherently unmanly. Organized clubs aimed to reinforce learning experiences through the creation of a sporting "freemasonry" of those similarly indoctrinated.[44]

Expressions of manly camaraderie were commonplace: lacrosse club members shared grief in their losses and celebrated their accomplishments.[45] For example, local merchant Edward W. Nesbitt, secretary of Woodstock's Beavers, received an exquisite silver tea service from the club at a testimonial to him honouring his forthcoming marriage in 1879. A beautiful parchment scroll, elaborately detailed in gold, accompanied the gift. Its inscription with its echoes of the Sermon on the Mount speaks volumes about the club's social and moral goals:

> We feel it is no empty boast when we say that it is an honour to belong to the Beaver Lacrosse Club of Woodstock. The Young men who organized this Club nine years ago have retired and now occupy positions of trust and honour in our community leaving their places in the Club to be filled by other and younger men who bid fair to follow in the footsteps of their predecessors. At home and abroad the name of the Beaver Lacrosse Club has been and is now a synonym of honesty, uprightness, and fair dealing. Taking defeat in the same good natured and gentlemanly manner that they have scored victories, and on all occasion, recognizing the golden rule *To do to others as they wished to be done by.*[46]

In 1871, some four years after the creation of the National Lacrosse Association, Ingersoll and Woodstock sportsmen turned their attentions to cultivating this stylized approach to sport. Their involvement in lacrosse coincided with local baseball clubs losing their single-handed dominance of the towns' interurban, amateur team competition.[47] Not surprisingly they had turned first to baseball, a likely candidate for their reform efforts, since it was a highly familiar and popular activity among children and youth.

In 1864 Woodstock's first known sports club for young men, the Young Canadian baseball club, created the Silver Ball award (which came to be popularly known as the emblem of the Canadian Baseball Championship), to stimulate interurban, challenge-match competition.[48] Over the next five years Woodstock's home team defended its Canadian championship title, with a home field advantage, against rivals from Ingersoll, Guelph, and other Ontario towns. The *New York Clipper*, the premier sporting journal of the day, kept North American readers abreast of Woodstock and Ingersoll team activities.[49]

By the late 1860s and early 1870s, however, a growing emphasis on winning had begun to undercut organized baseball's early social orientation and to tarnish its clean image. With rowdyism, gambling, and professionalism on the rise in amateur baseball, local reformers began to promote lacrosse as *the* organized sport of the day. It was precisely at the point when intense competition and pressure to win resulted in the Woodstock Young Canadians losing their Canadian championship to their arch-rival, the Guelph Maple Leafs, that matters worsened. Associations between baseball and rowdyism surfaced among players and fans, illustrating the difficulties reformers faced in eradicating alternate traditions. At an 1868 Silver Ball match between the Young Canadians and the Maple Leafs, fights broke out as toughs roamed the stands, "no one" daring "to interfere with them in their nefarious work."[50]

According to sport reformers, baseball's respectability wavered because teams paid players under the table and heated competition sparked lively betting.[51] Baseball reformers repeatedly sought new solutions to these dilemmas — creating new leagues to reaffirm their intention, requiring amateur documentation from players to limit the involvement of itinerant professional athletes, having amateur sponsoring agencies fund team expenses through gate receipts to lessen the impact of money on the game. Yet the behaviours of players, fans, and others ensured that the plague persisted. In 1884, the Woodstock amateur club presented their strongly worded view of the matter: "we have no sympathy whatever with 'professional sport,' as it is now carried on in the interests of speculators and gamblers . . . the result of a professional baseball match has no more interest for us than the result of a fight between two ownerless street curs."[52]

In the midst of such controversy, local sport reformers turned their focus on lacrosse, packaging it as a purer, and a particularly Canadian, team sport. They were confident in the ability of the existing national-level regulatory agency (the NLA) to oversee the sport locally. Demographic data on Ingersoll and Woodstock club organizers and players reveal the identities of the people who masterminded and carried out this reforming of local sport. The organizers of Ingersoll and Woodstock lacrosse clubs are readily found in local historical records. The names of the men who ran local lacrosse clubs between 1871 and 1890 read like a local social register; indeed, their names are still present on local buildings, street signs, and memorials.[53]

Seventy-two Ingersoll and Woodstock men who organized local lacrosse between 1871 and 1890 show striking demographic similarities, and while the data includes a considerable range of affluence and power (especially regarding occupation), some important conclusions can be drawn. For example, they operated within an exclusively male network. Presumably they never officially prohibited females from involvement because existing social and cultural constraints had already done this work.[54] And, with only three exceptions, for almost twenty years group members were exclusively Protestants.[55] Beyond this, their shared social background united the reformers and differentiated them from other local males. If one applies a taxonomy to census data and uses it as a proxy for class, those data reveal that, as a group, these men had a very different occupational pattern than the overall local workforce.[56] (See Table 17.1.)

Only a very small group of manual workers, drawn from labour's small aristocracy of skilled artisans, were lacrosse organizers. Middle-class men (holding non-manual occupations in banks, law offices, mercantile establishments, and publishing offices) dominated lacrosse organizations. As such, they vastly overrepresented their segment of the local workforce hierarchy.

Table 17.1 Occupational Characteristics of Ingersoll and Woodstock Lacrosse Executives Compared to Local Male Workforces, 1871–1890*

Occupational Categories	Lacrosse Organizers	Male Workforce+
Non-manual	94%	26%
Manual skilled	6%	48%
Manual unskilled	0%	26%
Total number	72	2883

*In rounded figures.
+Combined, Ingersoll and Woodstock male workforces over 16 years derived from 1881 manuscript censuses.

Their local voluntary association and political involvement also afford highly suggestive glimpses into the social similarities and shared values of these sport reformers. To summarize the data in Table 17.2, lacrosse organizers engaged in remarkably similar voluntary activities. At least two-thirds of them were officers in more than one sports club, and slightly less than one-half of them held offices in reform-based societies and other fraternities. Beyond this, one in three sat on the local town council, while roughly one in six sat on the board of trade.

Though exclusively male sport clubs, reform societies (for example, Royal Templars of Temperance), and fraternal lodges (for example, the Independent Order of Odd Fellows), these men created environments in which notions of respectability could be formulated and then promoted. The ritual, literature, and social practices of their various organizations emphasized certain key ingredients that they deemed to be essential to their cause: responsibility, sobriety, honesty, thrift, support for the dominant religion, and personal and sexual morality. Christopher Anstead has shown how, with their policing of individual members' behaviour, these groups spread the ideology of respectability to a wider audience.[57] Other voluntary activities, such as membership in the board of trade and election

Table 17.2 Voluntary Organization Profiles of Ingersoll and Woodstock Lacrosse Club Executives, 1871–1890*

Type of Organization	% Involved	
	One Organization	More than Two
Sports clubs	100%	66%
Social/fraternal orders	44%	24%
Town council	32%+	–
Board of trade	15%	–
Total number	72	

*In rounded figures.
+Six held the office of mayor or reeve.

to the town council, provided avenues for other commitments, such as boosting their town's economic development through supporting aspects of industrial growth.

Because lacrosse clubs drew members from different social backgrounds than club organizers, there was a need for cooperation, presumably based in consent, from certain members of the subordinated classes. Between 1880 and 1889, three-quarters of club members were between 15 and 21 years of age — a small cohort drawn from what was only 14 percent of the local male population. Their membership was touted by the press as a matter of social prestige and envy for other boys.[58] As seen in Table 17.3, the youth in these clubs came from more socially diverse backgrounds than club organizers. Proportionately more lacrosse players came from a home where the household head worked with his hands than did lacrosse organizers. Still, no players came from homes of unskilled workers.

In short, amateur lacrosse in Ingersoll and Woodstock was a class-based phenomenon like the amateur movement itself. Lacrosse reformers, like reformers for other sports, wished to restructure local sport along carefully circumscribed social lines, and they appear to have elicited support through working-class youth involvement. Just as sport organizers in both towns adopted lacrosse as a vehicle for their reform agenda, they also envisioned creating a local institution to carry out their agenda for sport on a grander scale. One way to achieve this agenda was through the creation of a multi-sport amateur agency which aimed to regulate all local sport.

In April 1884, Woodstock's Beaver lacrosse club, together with the local amateur baseball and bicycle clubs, organized a local multi-sport regulatory agency, the Woodstock Amateur Athletic Association (WAAA). Two years later Ingersoll sports reformers, including leaders of the Dufferin lacrosse club, followed suit and created the Ingersoll Amateur Athletic Association (IAAA), which was incorporated in 1889.[59] In both cases these umbrella organizations for sports clubs (notably for lacrosse, baseball, cycling, and tennis) were designed to encourage and regulate amateur sports. The respective town councils also authorized their AAAs to be responsible for creating community sporting and social entertainments for the Queen's Birthday and Dominion Day civic holidays.[60] This "stamp" of approval from local government ensured sport reformers important opportunities to display and disseminate their version of sport.

Under AAA governance local sport was structured in ways that middle-class sport reformers preferred; these preferences were institutionalized and their underlying

Table 17.3 Occupational Characteristics of Ingersoll and Woodstock Lacrosse Players Compared to Male Workforces, 1880–1889*

Occupational Categories	Lacrosse Players	Male Workforce+
Non-manual	46%	26%
Manual skilled	54%	50%
Manual unskilled	0%	24%
Total number	147	2883

*In rounded figures for occupation of household head.
+Combined, Ingersoll and Woodstock male workforces over 16 years estimated for 1885, derived from 1881 and 1891 manuscript censuses.

rationales were articulated through exclusive gentleman's clubs.[61] AAA constitutions asserted their reform orientation through the mandate, "the encouragement of athletic sports, the promotion of physical and mental culture among, and the providing of rational amusements for members."[62] Like other middle-class voluntary associations, the AAAs had strict rules carefully circumscribing the conduct of members. Club rooms prohibited all drink, gambling, betting, lotteries, and profane language. Those defying the rules of "gentlemanly conduct," were expelled.[63]

Modelling their own associations on the exclusive and powerful Montreal Amateur Athletic Association (1881), IAAA and WAAA organizers sought to suppress all but carefully restricted amateur sports which bore the mark of muscular Christianity.[64] Stressing what they called morality and justice in sport, they emphasized efficiency and organization, and denigrated any alternative in order to elevate their own vision for sport. Determined to establish amateur sport as *the* natural and only legitimate version of sport, they strove to marginalize other practices. To this end, local AAA officials attempted to suppress certain sports by eliminating them from the landscape of community sport, especially holiday competitions, and by limiting which sports were granted AAA club affiliation. Amateur regulations demanding that athletes be "carded" in order to compete, while limiting club membership, also worked toward this goal.

Local AAA sport reformers and town councillors alike believed that socially exclusive amateur sports would enhance their town's physical and moral greatness. Yet the AAAs were joint-stock ventures capitalized through membership fees—and one had to first pass a blackballing to enter AAA ranks. Socially exclusive, they were nevertheless designated by town councils to represent the town. Thus the AAAs upheld the façade, though not the substance, of democracy.[65]

The social fabric of a group of 103 Ingersoll and Woodstock AAA executives similarly belies any notion of democracy. The AAA officials, while individually possessing a considerable range of affluence and power, exhibited certain social traits as a group that sharply set them apart from the local populace. Like the lacrosse executives, they almost all held non-manual occupations of a professional, commercial, or administrative nature. (See Table 17.4.)

Like sport reformers generally, IAAA and WAAA organizers tended to be engaged in other voluntary and fraternal activities by which they shaped and reflected their worldview of respectability and capitalism. (See Table 17.5.)

Table 17.4 Occupational Characteristics of IAAA and WAAA Executives and Local Male Workforces, 1884–1896*

Occupational Category	AAA Executives	Male Workforces[+] 1891
Non-Manual	95%	26%
Manual skilled	5%	51%
Manual unskilled	0%	23%
Total number	103	4400

*In rounded figures.
[+]For occupation of household head in the workforce of males over 16. Combined and averaged between 1891 Ingersoll and Woodstock manuscript censuses.

Table 17.5 Voluntary Profiles of IAAA and WAAA Executives, 1884–1896*

Type of Organization	Organization Executives % Involved
Amateur sport clubs Executives	100%
Fraternal order Executives[+]	63%
Town Council	23%[+]
Board of Trade	16%
Total number	103

*In rounded figures.
[+]Data on social and fraternal order membership kindly supplied by Christopher Anstead.

The intricate ties between the amateur clubs and the agendas of social reform and boost-erism promoted by their organizers can also be seen in interurban lacrosse competition and in the ways in which it was supported locally.[66] By infusing sporting events with their vision, they aimed to reinforce their appearance as natural social and political leaders.

From the early 1870s club organizers and town councillors had featured lacrosse matches on Dominion Day holidays.[67] Thousands flocked into town to view these events. After noon-time parades, speeches form local dignitaries, and picnics, the afternoon sport performance began. The profits derived from ten cent admission fees to holiday matches alone could support a club's expenses for the entire season. To ensure successful holiday-sport events, Woodstock clubs, like clubs from Montreal and Toronto, arranged exhibition matches against Indian teams from nearby reserves.[68] The war-painted Indians also per-formed war dances and concerts after the matches. Appropriately costumed, they played their tightly choreographed role, though whatever they themselves thought of that role remains unknown. There is no doubt, however, that the lacrosse propagandists created the extravaganzas to symbolize and celebrate what Canada as a young nation had become. The productions aimed to fortify and celebrate one version of pride in locality and Canadian nation, while evoking images of the sport's distant origins in Aboriginal culture.[69]

One sketch published in the 1893 Dominion Day edition of the *Sentinel* gave the desired effect of reinforcing what lacrosse propagandists saw as the intimate connection between lacrosse and the Canadian nation. The sketch consisted of a crest with symbols for each province surrounded by scenes of Canadian wilderness. A well-placed lacrosse stick in the diagram gave the illusion that lacrosse, geography, and climate worked together to unite the Canadian nation.[70]

To sport reformers lacrosse offered all sorts of possibilities for creating and maintain-ing a cultural hegemony. Lacrosse teams, seen by local government to be legitimate agents of local boosterism, were projected to represent the town's merit, and were them-selves considered capable of cultivating high civic standards. Throughout the year citizens followed Ingersoll and Woodstock teams through NLA divisional competition. Club vic-tories often prompted community-wide celebrations; for example, in 1888 Ingersoll citi-zens petitioned the mayor to declare a half-holiday so they could celebrate the advancement of the Dufferins to the southern district championship. In 1901, on the occasion of Woodstock's birth as a city, the *Sentinel* proclaimed that the Beavers had given Woodstock "an enviable reputation in the realm of sport."[71] This reputation, it implied, was both a symptom and an emblem of the type of drive and determination that had nurtured the town's rise to city status. Team uniforms, themselves symbols of order and respectability, and team names reinforced ties to the home town, providing myth-makers with opportunities to tell stories about themselves and their reality; in such narratives sports fields became symbolic battlegrounds.[72]

Community organizations, mayors, local professional men, and merchants strongly supported club efforts. As early as 1871 even Woodstock's Ladies Benevolent Society publicly offered their support. They graced the Beavers with a $15 donation and embroidered goal flags, "worked in gold [and] surmounted by a Beaver." Like the Claxton Flags, which were the emblem of the Canadian championship, they were a treasure to behold. Individuals also handed out rewards to club players for their social and sporting skills.[73] In keeping with the thrust of amateurism, the awards were symbolic rather than monetary. In 1874 Dr. Turquand, sometime executive of the Royal Arcanum, ten-year town council veteran, and sometime mayor, donated a silver cup for Woodstock's best all-round player. In 1880 Samuel Woodroofe, local jeweller, sometime WAAA executive, and executive of the local bicycle and football clubs, donated a silver medal for a club running competition. He shrewdly placed it in his store window for a week, thus calling attention to the team and drawing in curious customers. In 1888, sometime president of the WAAA and newly elected president of the Canadian Lacrosse Association, local grocer E.W. Nesbitt donated a diamond pin for the best all-round player who showed punctual attendance.[74]

Yet the residual element of a displaced rowdiness could be found within the connection between team and town that was fostered by capitalist boosterism, and shaped by the hand of middle-class businessmen. With its growing popularity in the late 1870s and 1880s and with the increasing associations between lacrosse teams and the corporate community, the gap between what sport reformers hoped to achieve through lacrosse, and what actually happened, widened significantly.[75] Pressures for victory, coupled with intense fan and player identifications with the home team, undermined reformers' efforts.[76] So, too, did greater player commitment to winning for the glory of the team and the honour of the town. Of course, rewards for proper conduct and punctual attendance would have been needless if individual players had been behaving in desired ways.

Despite prohibitions, frequent newspaper reports of money won and lost showed that fans still bet on sport competition, especially when their home team was involved. In 1879 Simcoe's team and their backers arrived for a match in Woodstock "supplied with heaps of wealth," which Beaver supporters "readily took up."[77] It was only a short step from betting to game fixing and under-the-table payments to amateur players. In July 1887 the Brantford Brants had courted Beaver players Kennedy, Kelly, and Laird with offers of jobs that guaranteed a sizable $20 per week salary during season play. One week later certain Brantford fans reportedly offered Beaver player (and Patterson Factory worker) Ed. Kennedy $20 to throw a game. The local press decried the action and praised Kennedy's refusal to take part in the schemes. The *Sentinel* claimed: "this is the sort of thing that is ruining lacrosse, it is the betting spirit that leads to such attempts at fraud. Unless betting and the influence of betting men is stamped out, amateur lacrosse is dead — in fact it don't deserve to live."[78]

Efforts to eradicate betting and other prohibited behaviours at local playing grounds were to no avail. Obviously, many resisted. Some flatly refused to behave in prescribed ways while at games. Others simply refused to participate in the community event. They found nearby spots — the cemetery hill overlooking the WAAA grounds, for example — where they could sit on tombstones and watch the performances *gratis*. Resisting the WAAA social agenda, such hill-sitters garnered the best of both worlds. They had the pleasure of watching an afternoon's sport on their own terms: segregated from those who would presume to tell them how to behave, they could enjoy a good drink, a cuss, and a bet among like-minded people while watching a game of lacrosse. Better yet, they were physically distanced from, but quite visible to, frustrated WAAA executives. Abhorred by the recalcitrants "flaunting" their disdain for the WAAA agenda and its visions of what was appropriate personal behaviour, the frustrated WAAA officials appeared flabbergasted that their appeals to honour and decency fell on deaf ears: the hill-sitters were unmoved by WAAA threats to publish the names of "sneaks" and to photograph them in the act.[79]

Lacrosse organizers also had difficulty constraining other forms of resistance, like violent behaviour on the field. Tremendous player commitment to winning stretched the limits of rules on the playing field. The emphasis of lacrosse increasingly shifted from the process of character building to the goal of mere victory. Lacrosse play also shifted from cultivating and displaying an educated strength toward exhibiting unrestrained brutality. Like hockey today, the sport bred player violence during emotion-packed competition. This, of course, ironically enhanced the sport's appeal to those inclined toward unsavoury, or brutal sport.

During one visit to Ingersoll in 1888, for example, Woodstock players found themselves under attack in the heavily charged environment of lacrosse competition.[80] During the match (refereed by what the Woodstock press referred to as "daisy" umpires), one Woodstonian player checked his opponent. Hundreds of Ingersoll fans responded by mobbing him and his teammates. The melee lasted fifteen minutes. After the field cleared and play recommenced, one obscenity-screaming spectator (who just happened to be the local police chief), chased down a rough Woodstock player and, catching him by the throat, thrashed him.

Lovers of the sport throughout southwestern Ontario knew well the antipathy between the two towns that was prompted by playing-field battles. Commenting on this state of affairs, an Embro *Courier* editorial pointed a harsh finger at overzealous fans: "if the spectators of these two towns would keep quiet and not interfere so, much of the bad feeling between the boys would die out." The Tillsonburg *Liberal* similarly blamed the spectators who, it maintained, should "keep their mouths shut and not interfere with the players disputes which occur on the field." The *Chronicle* responded to the indictment, acknowledging the displaced rowdiness inherent in intense interurban competition: "if you expect the spectators in rival towns to keep quiet you make a great big mistake." Fan behaviour at lacrosse competition, encouraged by boosterism, thus undercut images of respectability, especially with fans howling "like maniacs."[81] And while this rowdiness was mostly in the stands, rather than at the centre of public display, it was still problematic for sport reformers since it was far from invisible.

Often the local press, an instrument of persuasion in the hegemonic process, stepped into the battle, admonishing locals to be "gentlemanly." But even the papers exhibited elements of displaced rowdyism when, for example, after the Woodstock match in question, the *Chronicle* suggested that "had the spectators stepped in and hammered some of them and maimed them for life the punishment would be no less than they deserve.[82]

This situation, although testifying to lacrosse's immense popularity as a form of action-packed competition and entertainment, undercut attempts to reform the sport. With its rising popularity, by the 1890s lacrosse increasingly became an antithesis to the vision of Canadian youth and sport first expounded by middle-class sport reformers. As the gap between ideation and behaviour widened, lacrosse clearly did not live up to expectations of it as a truly national game that united social groupings under the leadership of a small, select group of men.

The social reform agenda for sport, and the search for sport forms that appeared to solve the social, physical, and moral ills of society, are resilient legacies from the sports-conscious decades of the last century. So, too, is the manipulation of sport to buttress a certain vision of reality. In the case of lacrosse, middle-class reformers aimed to make their (racist, class- and gender-bound) reality credible, and, in so doing, to legitimize their role as the natural leaders of society. With working-class youth filling lacrosse clubs, they appear to have enlisted some cooperation and support from subordinated groups. Even so, their hegemony was never complete, nor truly coherent. The notions of building character through wholesomely Canadian amateur team sport and of playing for the honour of the town, institution, or country one represented just did not comfortably fit, and residual elements —violence, and rowdyism in particular—remained. Yet, at the same time the notions upon which the amateur lacrosse movement was built laid a general foundation for organized sport to assume its prominent role in Canadian culture today. The contradictions in the belief that games build character while, at the same time, that sport competition says something about the competitors and, more importantly, the places or institutions that they represent, thrives today in Canadian sporting culture.

NOTES

1. For a discussion of a hegemonic struggle, see Keith Walden, "Speaking Modern: Language, Culture, and Hegemony in Grocery Window Displays, 1887–1920," *Canadian Historical Review* 70, 3 (1989): 285–310. A now dated discussion of the trend of Gramscian-influence historical research is found in T.J. Jackson Lears, "The Concept of Cultural Hegemony: Problems and Possibilities," *American Historical Review* 90, 3 (June 1985): 567–93.

2. Both communities are located in Oxford County in southwestern Ontario. Between 1871 and 1891 Ingersoll, the smaller of the two, had a population that hovered between 4000 and 4200 people. Woodstock, the County Seat, though initially smaller than Ingersoll, experienced a doubling of its population size, from nearly 4000 to over 8600 people. By 1901 Woodstock achieved city status. For the history of both towns see Brian Dawe, *Old Oxford is Wide Awake! Pioneer Settlers and Politics in Oxford County 1793–1855* (Woodstock: John Deyell Co., 1980); and Colin Read, *The Rising in Western Upper Canada 1837–1838* (Toronto: University of Toronto Press, 1982). On Ingersoll see James Sinclair, *A History of the Town of Ingersoll* (Ingersoll, c.1924); George N. Emery, "Adam Oliver, Ingersoll and Thunder Bay District," *Ontario History* 68, 1 (1976): 25–44; Ronald Adair Shier, "Some Aspects of the Historical Geography of the Town of Ingersoll" (B.A. thesis, University of Western Ontario, 1967). On Woodstock see Marjorie Cropp, "Beachville the Birthplace of Oxford" (reprint Beachville Centennial Committee, 1967); and John Ireland (pseud.), "Andrew Drew and the Founding of Woodstock," *Ontario History* 60 (1968): 231–33.

3. See Mark Dyreson, "America's Athletic Missionaries: Political Performance, Olympic Spectacle, and the Quest for an American National Culture, 1896–1912," *Olympika* 1 (1992): 70–90 for a good analysis of America's professionalizing middle class's attempts to engineer a cultural hegemony through sport and the making of an American national culture in the context of progressive-era modernity.

4. On muscular Christianity see Peter McIntosh, *Sport and Society* (London: C.A. Watts, 1963), 69–79; Gerald Redmond, "The First Tom Brown's Schooldays and Others: Origins of Muscular Christianity in Children's Literature," *Quest* 30 (Summer 1978): 4–18; Guy Lewis, "The Muscular Christianity Movement," *Journal of Health, Physical Education and Recreation* (May 1966): 27–30; J.A. Mangan, *Athleticism in the Victorian and Edwardian Public School: The Emergence and Consolidation of an Educational Ideology* (Cambridge: Cambridge University Press, 1981); Idem. *The Games Ethic and Imperialism. Aspects of the Diffusion of an Ideal* (Markham: Viking Press, 1986);

David Brown, "Athleticism in Selected Canadian Private Schools for Boys to 1918" (Ph.D. dissertation, University of Alberta, 1984).

5. For a survey of the rise of organized sport in Canada, see Don Morrow, et al., *A Concise History of Sport in Canada* (Toronto: Oxford University Press, 1989) and Idem., "Canadian Sport History: A Critical Essay," *Journal of Sport History* 10,1 (September 1983) 67–79. Other related works include: Alan Metcalfe, *Canada Learns to Play. The Emergence of Organized Sport 1807–1914* (Toronto: McClelland & Stewart, 1987); Richard Gruneau, *Class, Sports and Social Development* (Amherst: University of Massachusetts Press, 1983); Morris Mott, *Sports in Canada. Historical Readings* (Toronto: Copp-Clark, 1989); Sid Wise, "Sport and Class Values in Old Ontario and Quebec," *His Own Man. Essays in Honour of A.R.M. Lower*, eds. W.H. Heick and Roger Graham (Montreal/Kingston: McGill-Queen's University Press, 1974) 93–117.

6. Peter Bailey, *Leisure and Class in Victorian England. Rational Recreation and the Quest for Control, 1830–1885* (Toronto: University of Toronto Press, 1966); and Chris Waters, "'All Sorts and Any Quantity of Outlandish Recreations': History, Sociology, and the Study of Leisure in England, 1820–1870," *Canadian Historical Association Historical Papers* (1981): 8–33.

7. Clifford Geertz, "Notes on the Balinese Cockfight," *The Interpretation of Cultures* (New York: Basic Books, 1973) 417.

8. I use the term Indian because the lacrosse writers of the era used this term. Their ethnocentrism limited their ability to see Aboriginal peoples as having any "culture." For a view of the game from the Indian oral tradition, see *Tewaarathon (Lacrosse): Akwesasne's Story of Our National Game* (North American Indian Travelling College, 1978). On European interpretations of lacrosse in Indian cultures see Stewart Culin, "Games of the North American Indians," *Twenty-fourth Annual Report of the Bureau of American Ethnology* (Washington: Government Printing Office, 1907); George Catlin, *Letters and Notes on the Manners, Customs and Condition of the North American Indians*, vol. 2 (London: The Egyptian Hall, 1871); and Michael A. Salter, "The Effect of Acculturation on the Game of Lacrosse and on Its Role as an Agent of Indian Survival," *Canadian Journal of the History of Sport and Physical Education* 3, 1 (May 1972): 28–43.

9. On organized lacrosse, see Don Morrow, "The Institutionalization of Sport: A Case Study of Canadian Lacrosse," *International Journal of History of Sport* 9, 2 (August 1992): 361–51. See also, Robert W. Henderson, *Ball, Bat and Bishop* (New York: Rockport Press, 1947); Alexander M. Weyand and M.R. Roberts, *The Story of Lacrosse* (Baltimore: H & A Herman, 1965); T.G. Vellathottam and Kevin G. Jones, "Highlights in the Development of Canadian Lacrosse to 1931," *Canadian Journal of the History of Sport and Physical Education* 5, 2 (December 1974): 37; Christina A. Burr, "The Process of Evolution of a Competitive Sport: A Study of Lacrosse in Canada, 1844 to 1914" (M.A. Thesis, University of Western Ontario, 1986); and Metcalfe 181–218.

10. The motto of the National Lacrosse Association, "Our Country, Our Game," and the title of William George Beer's great treatise, *Lacrosse the National Game of Canada*, give the impression that lacrosse is Canada's national sport. See Kevin G. Jones and T. George Vellathottam, "The Myth of Canada's National Sport," *CAPHER Journal* (September–October 1974): 33–36; *Globe and Mail*, 20 December 1868; Morrow 53–54.

11. For example, the activities found in Edwin C. Guillet, *Pioneer Days in Upper Canada* (Toronto: University of Toronto Press, 1979), especially chapters IX and X. For a good social analysis of a particularly castigated sport, see Elliott J. Gorn, "'Gouge and Bite, Pull Hair and Scratch': The Social Significance of Fighting in the Southern Backcountry," *American Historical Review* 90, 1 (February 1985): 18–43.

12. For an extended discussion, see Christopher J. Anstead and Nancy B. Bouchier, "From Greased Pigs to Sheepskin Aprons: Rowdiness and Respectability in Victorian Ingersoll's Civic Holidays," unpublished manuscript, 1993.

13. J.E. Wells, "Canadian Culture," *Canadian Monthly and National Review* (1875): 459–67. This item was brought to my attention in David Brown, "Prevailing Attitudes Towards Sports, Physical Exercise and Society in the 1870's: Impressions from Canadian Periodicals," *Canadian Journal of History of Sport* 17, 2 (December 1986): 58–70.

249

14. See *Sentinel-Review Express Industrial Edition* February 1906; *Woodstock College Memorial Book* (Woodstock: Woodstock College Alumni Association, 1951). On physical education and sports programs in Canadian schools: Frank Cosentino and Maxwell L. Howell, *A History of Physical Education in Canada* (Toronto: General Publishing Co., 1971); M.L. Van Vliet, *Physical Education in Canada* (Scarborough: Prentice-Hall, 1965); Brown, "Athleticism in Selected Canadian Private Schools"; Jean Barman, *Growing Up in British Columbia: Boys in Private School* (Vancouver: University of British Columbia Press, 1984), chap. 4; G.G. Watson, "Sports and Games in Ontario Private Schools: 1830–1930" (M.A. thesis, University of Alberta, 1970).

15. Nationalism through sport thrived elsewhere, too. See Donald Mrozek, *Sport and American Mentality, 1880–1910* (Knoxville: University of Tennessee Press, 1983); Peter Levine, *A.G. Spalding and the Rise of Baseball* (New York: Oxford University Press, 1985). On cultural motifs and nationalism see Eric Hobsbawm, *Nations and Nationalism since 1780: Programme, Myth, Reality* (New York: Cambridge University Press, 1990).

16. Peter Lindsay, "George Beers and the National Game Concept. A Behavioral Approach," *Proceedings of the 2nd Canadian Symposium on the History of Sport and Physical Education* (Windsor: University of Windsor, 1972), 27–44. On the Canadian nationalist theme in sport see: Morrow, "Lacrosse as the National Game," in *A Concise History of Sport*, 45–68; Alan Metcalfe, "Towards an Understanding of Nationalism in Mid-Nineteenth Century Canada—A Marxian Interpretation," *Proceedings of the 2nd Canadian Symposium on the History of Sport and Physical Education*, 7–14; R. Gerald Glassford, "Sport and Emerging Nationalism in Mid-Nineteenth Century Canada," in ibid. 15–26.

17. George Beers, *Lacrosse: The National Game of Canada*. His other lacrosse-related publications include: "Canadian Sports," *Century Magazine* 14 (May–October 1879): 506–27; Goal Keeper (pseud.) *The Game of Lacrosse* (Montreal: The Montreal Gazette Steam Press, 1860); "The Ocean Travels of Lacrosse," *Athletic Leaves* (September 1888): 42, "A Rival to Cricket," *Chambers Journal* 18 (December 1862): 366–68.

18. Beers, *Lacrosse: The National Game* 59.

19. W.K. McNaught, *Lacrosse and How to Play It* (Toronto: Robert Marshall, 1873) 21. Morrow, *A Concise History of Sport*, 54.

20. Beers, "Canadian Sports," 506–27; "Canada in Winter," *British American Magazine* 2 (1864): 166–71; "Cheek," *Canadian Monthly* 11 (1872): 256–62; "Canada as a Winter Resort," *Century* (1854–55): 514–29.

21. David Brown, "The Northern Character Theme and Sport in Nineteenth Century Canada," *Canadian Journal of History of Sport* 20, 1 (May 1989): 52. See also Carl Berger, "True North Strong and Free," *Nationalism in Canada*, ed. Peter Russell (Toronto: McGraw-Hill, 1966), 3–26; Idem., *The Sense of Power. Studies in the Ideas of Canadian Imperialism 1867–1914* (Toronto: University of Toronto Press, 1970), 128–53.

22. Brown, 47–48, 52.

23. Beers, *Lacrosse: The National Game*, 32, 33. The comparison continues: "or [as] a pretty Canadian girl to any uncultivated squaw."

24. M.C. Urquhart and K.A.H. Buckley, *Historical Statistics of Canada* (Toronto: Macmillan, 1965), 591. On schools and reform: Susan E. Houston, "Politics, Schools, and Social Change in Upper Canada," *Canadian Historical Review* 53 (September 1972): 249–71; Idem, "Victorian Origins of Juvenile Delinquency: A Canadian Experience," *History of Education Quarterly* 20 (Fall 1972): 254–80; Houston and Alison L. Prentice, *Schools and Scholars in Nineteenth Century Ontario* (Toronto: University of Toronto Press, 1988); and Alison L. Prentice, *The School Promoters. Education and Social Class in Mid-Nineteenth Century Upper Canada* (Toronto: McClelland and Stewart, 1977).

25. This point has recently been a focus of sport history scholarship. See Steven A. Riess, "Sport and the Redefinition of Middle Class Masculinity," *International Journal of the History of Sport* 8, 1 (May 1991): 5–27; J.A. Mangan and James Walvin, eds., *Manliness and Morality. Middle Class Masculinity in Britain and Americas, 1800–1940* (Manchester: Manchester University Press, 1987). See also: E. Anthony Rotundo, "Body and Soul: Changing Ideals of Middle Class Manhood,"

Journal of Social History 14 (1983): 23–38; Joseph Maguire, "Images of Manliness and Competing Ways of Living in Late Victorian and Edwardian Britain," *British Journal of Sports History* 3, 3 (December 1986): 265–87; David Howell and Peter Lindsay, "Social Gospel and the Young Boy Problem, 1895–1925," *Canadian Journal of History of Sport* 17, 1 (May 1986): 79–87; David I. MacLeod, "A Live Vaccine. The Y.M.C.A. and Male Adolescence in the United States and Canada," *Social History/Histoire Sociale* 11, 21 (1978): 55–64.

26. Reprints of Sermons, in whole or part, found in *Woodstock Sentinel*, 20 November 1887; *Woodstock Herald*, 14 March 1845; *Ingersoll Chronicle*, 25 October 1888, 30 January 1868.

27. *Chronicle*, 7 November 1872. In 1867 Ingersoll male youths were exhorted not to "make a great bluster and be rough and hard, thinking to be manly. Be a little quiet in the house, gentle with your little sisters, and not tiring mother with a great deal of noise. . . . When your work is over and its the right time for sport kick up your heels and have lots of fun outdoors" (*Chronicle*, 20 June 1867). One Mr. Harstone from nearby St. Mary's evoked similar arguments. In his appeal to the town council for the establishment of a public park, he clearly connected the issues of youth, social reform, and sport: "boys who grow up fond of sports make the best citizens. Cultivate the spirit of good manly sport and they will avoid many vices. Where towns do not give support to athletic sports, the greatest numbers are found going into the wrong paths" (*St. Marys Journal-Argus*, 8 September 1871). On 29 January 1889 the *Sentinel* reported on a lecture given in nearby Brantford by the Rev. Dr. Nichol who spoke at the YMCA rooms on vices peculiar to young men. He "warned his hearers very strongly against practices that were destroying the manhood of thousands and supplying our insane asylums with occupants." Presumably playing fields "suitably controlled," in cathartic fashion, sexual urges and the dreaded "secret vice" of masturbation.

28. Beers, *Lacrosse: The National Game*, 35.

29. Ontario, *Report of the Commissioners Appointed to enquire into the Prison and Reformatory System Sessional Papers* XXIII Part III (No. 7), 1891, 529. Thanks to Susan Houston for bringing this item to my attention.

30. *Sentinel*, 19 April 1880.

31. McIntosh, *Sport and Society*, 69–79; Lewis, "The Muscular Christianity Movement"; Redmond, "The First Tom Brown's Schooldays and Others."

32. Mangan, *Athleticism in the Victorian and Edwardian Public School*; Idem, *The Games Ethic and Imperialism*; Brown, "Athleticism in Selected Canadian Private Schools"; Watson, "Sports and Games in Ontario Private Schools"; Gruneau, *Class, Sports and Social Development* 101–3; Eric Dunning, "Industrialization and the Incipient Modernization of Football," *Stadion* 1, 1 (1975): 103–39.

33. This is best exemplified in Thomas Hughes's widely read classic *Tom Brown's Schooldays* (1857), in the fiction of Charles Kingsley, and in Thomas Wentworth Higginson's "Saints and their Bodies." The writings of Canadian novelist Ralph Connor are also reminiscent of this approach. See Bruce Haley, "Sport and the Victorian World," *Western Humanities Review* 22 (Spring 1968): 115–25; Idem, *The Healthy Body and Victorian Culture* (Cambridge: Cambridge University Press, 1978).

34. On the ascetic-pietist legacy and sport, see Barbara Schrodt, "Sabbatarianism and Sport in Canadian Society," *Journal of Sport History* 4, 1 (Spring 1977): 22–23; Dennis Brailsford, "Puritanism and Sport in Seventeenth Century England," *Stadion* 1, 2 (1975): 316–30; Peter Wagner, "Puritan Attitudes Towards Physical Recreation in 17th Century New England," *Journal of Sport History* 3 (Summer 1976): 139–51; Nancy Struna, "Puritans and Sports: The Irretrievable Tide of Change," *Journal of Sport History* 4 (Spring 1977) 1–21.

35. Gerald Redmond, "Some Aspects of Organized Sport and Leisure in Nineteenth Century Canada," *Sports in Canada. Historical Readings*, ed. Morris Mott (Toronto: Copp Clark Pitman, 1989), 97–98.

36. Ibid., 98.

37. Howell and Lindsay, "The Social Gospel and the Young Boy Problem, 1895–1925"; C.H. Hopkins, *History of the YMCA in North America* (New York: Associated Press, 1951). Also see Diane Pederson, "Keeping Our Good Girls Good," *Canadian Women Studies* 7, 4 (1986): 20–24.

38. On early formation of the National Lacrosse Association see Peter Lindsay, "A History of Sport in Canada, 1807–1867" (Ph.D. dissertation, University of Alberta, 1969), 114–32.

39. Claxton's obituary from *Sunday World*, 1908, as cited in Harold Clark Cross, *One Hundred Years of Service with Youth: The Story of the Montreal YMCA* (Montreal: Southam Press, 1951), 144. The flags, donated by the Montreal millionaire wholesaler in November 1867, were valued at $250.

40. These dimensions were to become symbolized through the association's hallmark, the triangle. See Cross, *One Hundred Years of Service with Youth*. Local connections between lacrosse and the YMCA in Woodstock also predated the association's full-scale involvement in sport. At its outset in 1871 the Woodstock YMCA's aim, "the improvement of the religious, mental, and social conditions of young men in Woodstock," overlooked sport. Yet within two years the Beavers and the YMCA contemplated combining their energies to form a gymnasium. By 1874 the Beavers were using YMCA club rooms for lacrosse meetings. (*Sentinel*, 24 October 1873, 29 May 1874). On Woodstock's YMCA: W. Stewart Lavell, *All This Was Yesterday The Story of the YMCA in Woodstock, Ontario, 1868–1972* (Woodstock: Talbot Communications, 1972).

41. This point is taken from John Weiler, "The Idea of Sport in Late Victorian Canada," *The Workingman in the Nineteenth Century*, ed. Michael Cross (Toronto: University of Toronto Press, 1974), 228–31.

42. On rational recreation see Bailey, *Leisure and Class in Victorian England;* Idem., "'A Mingled Mass of Perfectly Legitimate Pleasures': The Victorian Middle Class and the Problem of Leisure," *Victorian Studies* 21, 2 (Winter 1978): 7–28.

43. Beers, *Lacrosse: The National Game of Canada*, 51–56. Burr analyzes the evolution of the *science* of the game in "The Process of Evolution of a Competitive Sport."

44. Beers, *Lacrosse: The National Game*, 50. Beers's use of the term "freemasonry" is apt and intended to appeal to his middle-class male audience. Lacrosse and nineteenth-century freemasonry shared a number of key elements: secret bonding; a sub-community within a corporate community which also exists within a national and provincial network; an esoteric body of knowledge; and a particular style of dress. On fraternal societies see Christopher J. Anstead, "Fraternalism in Victorian Ontario: Secret Societies and Cultural Hegemony" (Ph.D. dissertation, University of Western Ontario, 1992); J.S. Gilkeson, *Middle Class Providence, 1820–1940* (Princeton: Princeton University Press, 1986).

45. The Beavers, for example, paid for the funeral of their mascot, little Jimmy Kinsella, who died in an accident at Karn's Organ Factory, *Sentinel*, 22 January 1887. On club celebrations for individuals, *Chronicle*, 7 July 1887, *Sentinel*, 30 June 1887.

46. "Testimonial to Edward W. Nesbitt. Woodstock 26 November 1879." Woodstock Museum (my italics).

47. On June 16 1871 the *Sentinel* reports, "with the loss of the late lamented Silver Ball lacrosse seems to be the favoured game this season." Journalist Henry Roxborough argues that because of baseball's immense popularity in the area, the adoption of lacrosse generally lagged in southwestern Ontario. Henry Roxborough, *One Hundred Not Out. The Story of Nineteenth Century Canadian Sport* (Toronto: Ryerson Press, 1966), 40. On the Guelph–Woodstock rivalry that led to the Woodstonians' dethroning see *Guelph Evening Mercury*, 5 August 1868; *Guelph Evening Telegram*, 27 September 1923; and William Humber, *Cheering for the Home Team: The Story of Baseball in Canada* (Erin: The Boston Mills Press, 1983).

48. *Hamilton Spectator*, 11 August 1864; *Chronicle*, 13 and 20 July; 21 and 26 August 1869. The Silver Ball, long lost, is pictured in *Star Weekly*, 19 July 1924. This earliest attempt to create a Canadian "national" baseball association in 1864, led by Woodstock's Young Canadian Club, relied almost completely on the American model of the national Association of Baseball Players (NABBP). The Canadian association, like most baseball ventures throughout the period between 1860 and 1885, structured competition on a challenge match, or exhibition basis. See Hamilton *Times*, 24 August 1864 and *Spectator*, 11 and 24 August 1864; Ingersoll *Chronicle*, 26 August, 7 October 1864; *The New York Clipper*, 14 September 1864.

49. *The New York Clipper*, 14 September 1864; 1 October 1864; 27 June 1868; 19 and 26 June, 17 July 1869; 28 May 1871.

50. *Guelph Evening Mercury*, 5 August 1868. Apparently "stragglers" from Guelph, who did not make the costly $1 trip to Woodstock, but who reportedly "had staked small piles on the game," congregated at Guelph's telegraph office to keep abreast of match developments. In the ensuing weeks after the near-riot, Woodstock and Guelph newspapers continued the rivalry: Guelph's *Evening Mercury* likened Woodstock to "a huge snake after getting a nock [sic] on the head, [which] writhes about in a fearful mental agony" (see 6, 8, 15 August 1868). Also see *Guelph Evening Telegram*, 27 September 1923; Humber, *Cheering for the Home Team*, 29, refers to this incident as well.

253

51. See Humber, *Cheering for the Home Team* 27–37; Metcalfe, *Canada Learns to Play*, 85–98 and 164–66. Metcalfe rightly notes that baseball was alienated from the mainstream of the amateur sport movement and that it was "significantly different form the other [amateur] sports in that its movement toward league competition came at a slower rate" (88). Baseball lacked well-rooted protectionist agencies (a sporting press; a "national" baseball association; or an institutional tradition) in the face of the American professional model, especially after 1871.

52. On the 1876 Canadian League see *The New York Clipper*, 22 April, 6 May 1876; *Bryce's 1876 Canadian Baseball Guide* (London, Ontario, 1876); *Canadian Gentleman's Journal of Sporting Times*, 28 April 1876; George Sleeman Collection, Regional Collections; File 4065, D.B. Weldon Library, University of Western Ontario; *Star Weekly* 19 July 1924. Other short-lived ventures, in 1880, 1884, and 1890 were centred in southwestern Ontario. *Sentinel*, 24 May, 30 July 1880; *Empire*, 24 May 1880; *Globe*, 22 May 1880; *Globe*, 17 May 1884; *Sentinel*, 14 May 1889; *Chronicle*, 11 and 17 April 1890; *Sentinel*, 18 April 1884.

53. The names of sport players and executives were extracted from reports in local newspapers and Canadian and American sport periodicals, team photographs, various local history sources, and sport-related collections. They were hand-linked to corresponding manuscript census rolls for the urban populations of Ingersoll and Woodstock. Demographic data (age, place of birth, religion, marital status, occupation, and the name and occupation of household head) were derived from the record linkage. Occupation information was corroborated, supplemented, and verified through town directories, tax assessment rolls, local histories, and local genealogies. Data on social and fraternal orders kindly supplied by Christopher Anstead.

54. On the sporting activities of females and social constraints impinging on them see Patricia Vertinsky, *The Eternally Wounded Woman: Women, Exercise and Doctors in the Late Nineteenth Century* (Manchester, England: Manchester University Press, 1990); Helen Lenskyj, *Out of Bounds. Women, Sport, and Sexuality* (Toronto: The Women's Press, 1986); and Michael Smith, "Graceful Athleticism or Robust Womanhood: The Sporting Culture of Women in Victorian Nova Scotia, 1870–1914," *Journal of Canadian Studies* 23, 1/2 (Spring/Summer 1988): 120–37.

55. Religion itself played a significant role in community social-class formation. A systematic relationship exists between the religious and social-class background distributions in the populations. For a statistical analysis of this phenomenon, see Nancy B. Bouchier, "'For the Love of the Game and the Honour of the Town': Organized Sport, Local Culture and Middle Class Hegemony in Two Ontario Towns, 1838–1895" (Ph.D. dissertation, University of Western Ontario, 1990), 90–92.

56. The occupational classification is based on Gerard Bouchard and Christian Pouyez, "Les Catégories Socio-Professionelles: Une Nouveau Grille de Classement," *Labour/Le Travail* 15 (Spring 1985): 145–63.

57. This understanding of fraternal orders is the central argument of Anstead, "Fraternalism in Victorian Ontario." See also Mary Ann Clawson, *Constructing Brotherhood: Class, Gender and Fraternalism* (Princeton, 1989); Brian Greenberg, "Workers and Community: Fraternal Orders in Albany, New York, 1845–1885," *The Maryland Historian* (1977).

58. *Sentinel*, 20 June 1887.

59. *Sentinel*, 4, 11, 18 April 1884; *Chronicle*, 3 and 10 June 1886; *Woodstock Amateur Athletic Association Constitution and Bylaws* (Woodstock: Sentinel-Review Co. Printers, 1908). This followed resolution of difficulties over obtaining acceptable playing field space. *Sentinel*, 4, 11, 18 April 1884; *Chronicle*, 3 and 10 June 1886, 29 March 1889, 1 April, 30 May 1890; *Ingersoll Amateur Athletic Association Constitution and Bylaws* (Ingersoll, 1889).

60. Nancy B. Bouchier, "'The 24th of May is the Queen's Birthday': Civic Holidays and the Rise of Amateurism in Nineteenth Century Canadian Towns," *International Journal of the History of Sport* 10, 2 (August 1993): 159–92. Sport clubs often hosted some form of sports events during the Queen's Birthday and Dominion Day holidays. For example, the Montreal Lacrosse Club organized matches against teams from the St. Regis and Caugnawaga Reserves (*Gazette*, 23 May 1884, 22 May 1885).

61. On gentlemen's clubs see Gilkeson, *Middle Class Providence* especially chap. 4, "The Club Idea." On clubs, sport, and Toronto's interlocking social elite, see R. Wayne Simpson, "The Elite and Sport Club Membership, Toronto, 1827–1881" (Ph.D. dissertation University of Alberta, 1987). On the social-class background of other sports clubs see Bouchier, "'For the Love of the Game and the Honour of the Town,'" especially chap. 4.

62. WAAA, *Constitution and Consolidated Bylaws* (Woodstock: Sentinel-Review Co. Printers, 1908), Article II; *IAAA Constitution and Bylaws* (Ingersoll, 1889), Article II.

63. In *Canada Learns to Play* Metcalfe argues that amateurism, with its requisites for gentlemanly behaviour, was a form of social reproduction squarely rooted in the English social-class system, and that the philosophical basis of amateurism originated in the patterns of eighteenth-century English aristocratic social reproduction. Many scholars concur with this line of thought. Mangan and Brown show that the emphasis placed on muscular Christian sports in the reformed British public school system replaced the anti-utilitarian approach to sport heretofore taken by England's elite. Dunning and Gruneau suggest further that the muscular Christian precepts of the "games-build-character" approach to sport popularized by the public schools indicated a mutual accommodation between declining aristocratic interests and a rising industrial bourgeoisie. See Metcalfe, 120–21; Mangan, *Athleticism in the Victorian and Edwardian Public School*; Brown, "Athleticism in Selected Canadian Private Schools"; Gruneau, 101–3; Dunning, "Industrialization and the Incipient Modernization of Football." WAAA, *Constitution and Consolidated Bylaws*, Article IX; *IAAA Constitution and Bylaws*, Article IX.

64. See Don Morrow, "The Powerhouse of Canadian Sport: The Montreal Amateur Athletic Association, Inception to 1909," *Journal of Sport History* 8, 3 (Winter 1981): 20–39; Idem, *A Sporting Evolution*; Alan Metcalfe, *Canada Learns to Play*; Charles Ballem, *Abegweit Dynasty, 1899–1954. The Story of the Abegweit Amateur Athletic Association* (Charlottetown, 1986); Gerald Redmond, "Some Aspects of Organized Sport and Leisure in Nineteenth Century Canada," *Sport in Canada. Historical Readings*, ed. Morris Mott (Toronto: Copp Clark Ltd., 1979), 81–106; Wise, "Sport and Class Values."

65. WAAA, *Constitution and Consolidated Bylaws*, Article VI; *IAAA Constitution and Bylaws*, Article VI. On the socially exclusive nature of amateurism see Alan Metcalfe, "The Growth of Organized Sport and the Development of Amateurism in Canada, 1807–1914," *Not Just a Game. Essays in Canadian Sport Sociology*, ed. Jean Harvey and Hart Cantelon (Ottawa, 1988), 33–50.

66. Anstead and Bouchier, "From Greased Pigs to Sheepskin Aprons."

67. Between 1871 and 1890, Ingersoll featured lacrosse on eight Dominion Day holidays, while Woodstock did so on eleven holidays.

68. In 1871 the Beavers paid the Grand River Indians $60 to compete against them in the 24 May match. Ten cent admissions covered this outlay and brought a $159 profit to the club (*Sentinel*, 7 July 1871). Other Indian teams were the Tuscaroras, Onondagas, Muncitown, Sioux, and Six Nations. *Sentinel*, 7 July 1871, 31 May, 23 August 1872, 26 June 1874, 23 May, 4 July 1879, 30 April 1880, 23 June 1882, 25 May 1887. *Chronicle*, 9 May 1877. George Gray, a Woodstonian, recorded his observations about two such matches in his diary 3 July 1871 and 24 May 1872. Woodstock Museum, George A. Gray Diaries, 1857–1878.

69. This is very much in keeping with the dominant theme of the 1876 and 1883 Canadian lacrosse tours to Britain. Don Morrow, "The Canadian Image Abroad: The Great Lacrosse Tours of 1876 and 1883," *Proceedings of the 5th Canadian Symposium on the History of Sport and Physical Education* (Toronto: University of Toronto Press, 1982), 17. On sporting tours and empire see David W. Brown, "Canadian Imperialism and Sporting Exchanges: The Nineteenth Century Cultural Experience of Cricket and Lacrosse," *Canadian Journal of History of Sport* 18, 1 (May 1987): 55–66.

70. *Sentinel-Review*, 1 July 1893.
71. *Chronicle*, 14 September 1888. *Sentinel*, "Birth of the Industrial City," 9 July 1901.
72. On the relationship between team and town, see Morris Mott, "One Town's Team: Souris and its Lacrosse Club, 1887–1906," *Manitoba History* 1, 1 (1980): 10–16; Carl Betke, "Sports Promotion in the Western Canadian City: The Example of Early Edmonton," *Urban History Review* 12, 2 (1983): 47–56.
73. *Sentinel*, 7 July 1871. *Chronicle*, 13 July 1871, 30 June 1885, 19 May 1887, 10 May 1888.
74. *Sentinel*, 1 April 1874. *Sentinel*, 21 May 1880. Also 21 November 1884. *Sentinel* 16 May 1888.
75. On escalating violence and rowdyism in lacrosse see Metcalfe, 181–218; Idem, "Sport and Athletics: A Case Study of Lacrosse in Canada, 1840–1889," *Journal of Sport History* 3, 1 (Spring 1976): 1–19; Burr, "The Process of the Evolution of Lacrosse."
76. Barbara S. Pinto, "'Ain't Misbehavin': The Montreal Shamrock Lacrosse Club Fans 1868 to 1884." Paper presented to the North American Society for Sport History (Banff, Alberta, 1990).
77. *Sentinel*, 22 and 29 August 1879, 25 August 1882, 15 September 1886, 28 and 30 June 1887; *Chronicle*, 23 June 1887; *Sentinel*, 22 August 1879.
78. *Sentinel*, 20 July 1887. *Chronicle*, 23 June 1887. *Sentinel*, 30 July 1887.
79. *Sentinel*, 3 July 1885.
80. *Sentinel*, 6 September 1888.
81. Reported in *Sentinel*, 7 August 1885. Related to the incident *Sentinel*, 7 and 14 August 1885; *Chronicle*, 6 August 1885. *Sentinel*, 30 July 1887. *Tillsonburg Liberal* editorial reprinted with comments *Chronicle*, 28 June 1888. *Chronicle*, 28 June 1888.
82. *Sentinel*, 30 July 1887.

Topic Nine

World War I

On sentry duty in a front-line trench in France, September 1916.

258   **IN 1914,** Canada participated in its first large-scale war. Over the next four years, the nation of fewer than ten million people provided more than half a million men as soldiers, sailors, and airmen, as well as several thousand women as nursing sisters, to the Allied war effort. More than 60 000 Canadians died fighting in the struggle, while many more returned to Canada mentally and physically impaired.

Not all eligible Canadians volunteered for war service, however. One group in particular was targeted for criticism: French Canadians. From the outset, French Canadians in Quebec had lagged behind English Canadians in proportion to their enlistment numbers. French Canadians had no strong attachment to either Britain or France, having lived in North America for three centuries. They also distrusted Britain and suspected imperial ambitions behind Anglo-Canadian enthusiasm for the war. In addition, the Canadian government mismanaged the enlistment effort in Quebec by failing to give the French language a meaningful place in Canada's armed services. French Canadians had to serve under English-speaking officers in English-speaking units (with the exception of the Royal 22nd Regiment, the famous "Vandoos"). Furthermore, the educational policies of two English-speaking provinces did not help. At a time when the federal government was pressuring French Canadians to fight for democracy in Europe, the provincial governments of Ontario and Manitoba eliminated publicly supported bilingual schools. While the main attack against Quebeckers who failed to enlist in the war effort came from English-speaking Canadians, the following debate between Henri Bourassa, who opposed French-Canadian enlistment, and his cousin Talbot Papineau, who had enlisted and was fighting on the war front, reminds us that the debate occurred among French-speaking Canadians themselves.

In "Fortunes of War," historian Sandra Gwyn uses the letters of Talbot Papineau, Charlie Stewart, and Agar Adamson to reconstruct the horrors of trench warfare in the battle of St. Eloi in April of 1916. She gives the reader a sense of what it was like for a soldier to be in trench warfare, and the "blood and guts" of war. She adds the human feelings and the personal tragedies of war that are too often omitted in "official" military accounts.

For a compelling account of the war years from the perspective of social history, see Desmond Morton and Jack Granatstein, *Marching to Armageddon: Canadians and the Great War, 1914–1919* (Toronto: Lester and Orpen Dennys, 1989); Daniel Dancocks, *Spearhead to Victory: Canada and the Great War* (Edmonton: Hurtig, 1987); and Desmond Morton, *When Your Number's Up* (Toronto: Random House, 1994). For an overview of the war years, see the relevant chapters in R.C. Brown and R. Cook's *Canada, 1896–1921: A Nation Transformed* (Toronto: McClelland and Stewart, 1974). A quick overview is found in Roger Sarty and Brereton Greenhous, "The Great War," *Horizon Canada* 85 (1986): 2017–23. A number of biographies of key politicians during World War I contain useful discussions of the war years. The most important are R.C. Brown's *Robert Laird Borden: A Biography*, vol. 3, *1914–1937* (Toronto: Macmillan, 1980); J. Schull's *Laurier: The First Canadian* (Toronto: Macmillan, 1965); Robert Rumilly's *Henri Bourassa* (Montreal:

Chantecler, 1953); and R. Graham's *Arthur Meighen*, vol. 1, *The Door of Opportunity* (Toronto: Clarke, Irwin, 1960). On Canada's most important military commander in World War I, see A.M.J. Hyatt, *General Sir Arthur Currie: A Military Biography* (Toronto: University of Toronto Press, 1987).

John Swettenham's *To Seize the Victory* (Toronto: Ryerson, 1965) and Robert James Steel's *The Men Who Marched Away: Canada's Infantry in the First World War, 1914–1918* (St. Catharines: Vanwell, 1989) describe Canadian participation at the front, as does Sandra Gwyn's *Tapestry of War: A Private View of Canadians in the Great War* (Toronto: HarperCollins, 1992), from which "Fortunes of War" is excerpted. On Canada's involvement in the Ypres Salient, see Daniel Dancocks, *Welcome to Flanders Fields: The First Canadian Battle of the Great War, Ypres, 1915* (Toronto: McClelland and Stewart, 1988). Pierre Berton tells the story of Canada's greatest battle in *Vimy* (Toronto: McClelland and Stewart, 1986). On the nature of trench warfare, see Bill Rawling, *Surviving Trench Warfare: Technology and the Canadian Corps, 1914–1918* (Toronto: University of Toronto Press, 1992); and Tim Cook, *No Place to Run: The Canadian Corps and Gas Warfare in the First World War* (Vancouver: University of British Columbia Press, 1999).

On the issue of conscription, see Elizabeth Armstrong's *The Crisis of Quebec, 1914–1918* (New York: Columbia University Press, 1937); J.L. Granatstein and J.M. Hitsman's *Broken Promises: A History of Conscription in Canada* (Toronto: Oxford University Press, 1977; new edition, 1984); Desmond Morton's "French Canada and War, 1868–1917: The Military Background to the Conscription Crisis of 1917," in *War and Society in North America*, ed. J.L. Granatstein and R. Cuff (Toronto: Nelson, 1970), pp. 84–103; Brian Cameron's "The Bonne Entente Movement, 1916–17: From Cooperation to Conscription," *Journal of Canadian Studies* 13 (Summer 1978): 1942–55; the relevant chapters in John English, *The Decline of Politics: The Conservatives and the Party System, 1901–1920* (Toronto: University of Toronto Press, 1977); and Jean Pariseau, "La participation des Canadiens français à l'effort des deux guerres mondiales: Démarche de ré-interprétation," *Canadian Defence Quarterly/Revue canadienne de défense* 13, 2 (Autumn 1983): 43–48. Henri Bourassa's views are presented in Joseph Levitt, ed., *Henri Bourassa on Imperialism and Bi-culturalism, 1900–1918* (Toronto: Copp Clark, 1970). The Papineau–Bourassa debate over conscription is reviewed in Sandra Gwyn, *Tapestry of War: A Private View of Canadians in the Great War* (Toronto: HarperCollins, 1992). Thomas Socknat's *Witness against War: Pacifism in Canada, 1900–1945* (Toronto: University of Toronto Press, 1987) reviews the pacifists' response to the war.

Two novels help to re-create the atmosphere of Canada during World War I: Philip Child's *God's Sparrows*, published in 1937 and reprinted in 1978 with an introduction by Dennis Duffy (Toronto: McClelland and Stewart), and Timothy Findley's award-winning *The Wars* (Toronto: Clarke, Irwin, 1977). Grace Morris Craig's *But This Is Our War* (Toronto: University of Toronto Press, 1981) is both her own recollection of the war years at home in Ontario and a collection of letters from her two brothers at the front.

Modris Ekstein's *Rites of Spring: The Great War and the Birth of the Modern Age* (Boston: Houghton Mifflin, 1989) looks at the Great War from a broader perspective. Jonathon F. Vance's *Death So Noble: Memory, Meaning and the First World War* (Vancouver: UBC Press, 1997) is an excellent study of the image of the Great War in the popular culture of the interwar years.

Article Eighteen

An Open Letter from Capt. Talbot Papineau to Mr. Henri Bourassa

(A copy of this letter was sent to Mr. Bourassa by Mr. Andrew-R. McMaster, K.C., on July 18, 1916. It was published, on July 28, in most Montreal, Quebec, Ottawa, and Toronto papers, both English and French.)

In the Field,
France, March 21, 1916.

To Monsieur Henri Bourassa,
Editor of Le Devoir,
Montreal.

My dear Cousin Henri, —

I was sorry before leaving Quebec in 1914 not to have had an opportunity of discussing with you the momentous issues which were raised in Canada by the outbreak of this war.

You and I have had some discussions in the past, and although we have not agreed upon all points, yet I am happy to think that our pleasant friendship, which indeed dates from the time of my birth, has hitherto continued uninjured by our differences of opinion. Nor would I be the first to make it otherwise, for however I may deplore the character of your views, I have always considered that you held them honestly and sincerely and that you were singularly free from purely selfish or personal ambitions.

Very possibly nothing that I could have said in August 1914 would have caused you to change your opinions, but I did hope that as events developed and as the great national opportunity of Canada became clearer to all her citizens, you would have been influenced to modify your views and to adopt a different attitude. In that hope I have been disappointed. Deeply involved as the honour and the very national existence of Canada has become, beautiful but terrible as her sacrifices have been, you and you alone of the leaders of Canadian thought appear to have remained unmoved, and your unhappy views unchanged.

Too occupied by immediate events in this country to formulate a protest or to frame a reasoned argument, I have nevertheless followed with intense feeling and deep regret the course of action which you have pursued. Consolation of course I have had in the fact that far from sharing in your views, the vast majority of Canadians, and even many of those who had formerly agreed with you, were now strongly and bitterly opposed to you. With this fact in mind, I would not take the time from my duties here to write you this letter did I not fear that the influence to which your talent, energy, and sincerity of purpose formerly entitled you, might still be exercised upon a small minority of your fellow countrymen, and that your attitude might still be considered by some as representative of the race to which we belong.

Source: *Canadian Nationalism and the War*. Published in Montreal, 1916.

Nor can I altogether abandon the hope—presumptuous no doubt but friendly and well-intentioned—that I may so express myself here as to give you a new outlook and a different purpose, and perhaps even win you to the support of a principle which has been proved to be dearer to many Canadians than life itself.

I shall not consider the grounds upon which you base your opposition to Canadian participation in this more than European—in this World War. Rather I wish to begin by pointing out some reasons why on the contrary your whole-hearted support might have been expected.

And the first reason is this. By the declaration of war by Great Britain upon Germany, Canada became "ipso facto" a belligerent, subject to invasion and conquest, her property at sea subject to capture, her coasts subject to bombardment or attack, her citizens in enemy territory subject to imprisonment or detention. This is not a matter of opinion—it is a matter of fact—a question of international law. No arguments of yours at least could have persuaded the Kaiser to the contrary. Whatever your views or theories may be as to future constitutional development of Canada, and in those views I believe I coincide to a large extent, the fact remains that at the time of the outbreak of war Canada was a possession of the British Empire, and as such as much involved in the war as any country in England, and from the German point of view and the point of view of International Law equally subject to all its pains and penalties. Indeed proof may no doubt be made that one of the very purposes of Germany's aggression and German military preparedness was the ambition to secure a part if not the whole of the English possessions in North America.

That being so, surely it was idle and pernicious to continue an academic discussion as to whether the situation was a just one or not, as to whether Canada should or should not have had a voice in ante bellum English diplomacy or in the actual declaration of war. Such a discussion may very properly arise upon a successful conclusion of the war, but so long as national issues are being decided in Prussian fashion, that is, by an appeal to the Power of Might, the liberties of discussion which you enjoyed by virtue of British citizenship were necessarily curtailed and any resulting decisions utterly valueless. If ever there was a time for action and not for theories it was to be found in Canada upon the outbreak of war.

Let us presume for the sake of argument that your attitude had also been adopted by the Government and people of Canada and that we had declared our intention to abstain from active participation in the war until Canada herself was actually attacked. What would have resulted? One of two things. Either the Allies would have been defeated or they would not have been defeated. In the former case Canada would have been called upon either to surrender unconditionally to German domination or to have attempted a resistance against German arms.

You, I feel sure, would have preferred resistance, but as a proper corrective to such a preference I would prescribe a moderate dose of trench bombardment. I have known my own dogmas to be seriously disturbed in the midst of a German artillery concentration. I can assure you that the further you travel from Canada and the nearer you approach the great military power of Germany, the less do you value the unaided strength of Canada. By the time you are within fifteen yards of a German army and know yourself to be holding about one yard out of a line of five hundred miles or more, you are liable to be enquiring very anxiously about the presence and power of British and French forces. Your ideas about charging to Berlin or of ending the war would also have undergone some slight moderation.

No, my dear Cousin, I think you would shortly after the defeat of the Allies have been more worried over the mastery of the German consonants than you are even now over a conflict with the Ontario Anti-bilinguists. Or I can imagine you an unhappy exile in Terra del Fuego eloquently comparing the wrongs of Quebec and Alsace.

But you will doubtless say we would have had the assistance of the Great American Republic! It is quite possible. I will admit that by the time the American fleet had been sunk and the principal buildings in New York destroyed the United States would have declared war upon Europe, but in the meantime Canada might very well have been paying tribute and learning to decline German verbs, probably the only thing German she *could* have declined.

I am, as you know, by descent even more American than I am French, and I am a sincere believer in the future of that magnificent Republic. I cannot forget that more than any other nation in the world's history—England not excepted—she has suffered war solely for the sake of some fine principle of nationality. In 1776 for the principle of national existence. In 1812 for the principle of the inviolability of American citizenship. In 1860 for the preservation of National unity and the suppression of slavery. In 1896 for the protection of her National pride and in sympathy for the wrongs of a neighbouring people.

Nor disappointed as I am at the present inactivity of the States will I ever waiver in my loyal belief that in time to come, perhaps less distant than we realize, her actions will correspond with the lofty expression of her national and international ideals.

I shall continue to anticipate the day when with a clear understanding and a mutual trust we shall by virtue of our united strength and our common purposes be prepared to defend the rights of humanity not only upon the American Continent but throughout the civilized world.

Nevertheless we are not dealing with what may occur in the future but with the actual facts of yesterday and today, and I would feign know if you still think that a power which without protest witnesses the ruthless spoliation of Belgium and Serbia, and without effective action the murder of her own citizens, would have interfered to protect the property or the liberties of Canadians. Surely you must at least admit an element of doubt, and even if such interference had been attempted, have we not the admission of the Americans themselves that it could not have been successful against the great naval and military organizations of the Central Powers?

May I be permitted to conclude that had the Allies been defeated Canada must afterwards necessarily have suffered a similar fate.

But there was the other alternative, namely, that the Allies even without the assistance of Canada would *not* have been defeated. What then? Presumably French and English would still have been the official languages of Canada. You might still have edited untrammeled your version of Duty, and Colonel Lavergne might still, publicly and without the restraining fear of death or imprisonment, have spoken seditiously (I mean from the Prussian point of view of course). In fact Canada might still have retained her liberties and might with the same freedom from external influences have continued her progress to material and political strength.

But would you have been satisfied—you who have arrogated to yourself the high term of Nationalist? What of the Soul of Canada? Can a nation's pride or patriotism be built upon the blood and suffering of others or upon the wealth garnered from the coffers of those who in anguish and with blood-sweat are fighting the battles of freedom? If we accept our liberties, our national life, from the hands of the English soldiers, if without sacrifices of our own we profit by the sacrifices of the English citizen, can we hope to ever become a nation ourselves? How could we ever acquire that Soul or create that Pride without which a nation is a dead thing and doomed to speedy decay and disappearance?

Article Eighteen • An Open Letter from Capt. Talbot Papineau to Mr. Henri Bourassa

263

If you were truly a Nationalist — if you loved our great country and without smallness longed to see her become the home of a good and united people — surely you would have recognized this as her moment of travail and tribulation. You would have felt that in the agony of her losses in Belgium and France, Canada was suffering the birth pains of her national life. There even more than in Canada herself, her citizens are being knit together into a new existence because when men stand side by side and endure a soldier's life and face together a soldier's death, they are united in bonds almost as strong as the closest of blood-ties.

There was the great opportunity for the true Nationalist! There was the great issue, the great sacrifice, which should have appealed equally to all true citizens of Canada, and should have served to cement them with indissoluble strength — Canada was at war! Canada was attacked! What mattered then internal dissentions and questions of home importance? What mattered the why and wherefore of the war, whether we owed anything to England or not, whether we were Imperialists or not, or whether we were French or English? The one simple commending fact to govern our conduct was that Canada was at war, and Canada and Canadian liberties had to be protected.

To you as a "Nationalist" this fact should have appealed more than to any others. Englishmen, as was natural, returned to fight for England, just as Germans and Austrians and Belgians and Italians returned to fight for their native lands.

But we, Canadians, had we no call just as insistent, just as compelling to fight for Canada? Did not the *Leipzig* and the *Gneisnau* possibly menace Victoria and Vancouver, and did you not feel the patriotism to make sacrifices for the protection of British Columbia? How could you otherwise call yourself Canadian? It is true that Canada did not hear the roar of German guns nor were we visited at night by the murderous Zeppelins, but every shot that was fired in Belgium or France was aimed as much at the heart of Canada as at the bodies of our brave Allies. Could we then wait within the temporary safety of our distant shores until either the Central Powers flushed with victory should come to settle their account or until by the glorious death of millions of our fellowmen in Europe, Canada should remain in inglorious security and a shameful liberty?

I give thanks that that question has been answered not as you would have had it answered but as those Canadians who have already died or are about to die here in this gallant motherland of France have answered it.

It may have been difficult for you at first to have realized the full significance of the situation. You were steeped in your belief that Canada owed no debt to England, was merely a vassal state and entitled to protection without payment. You were deeply imbued with the principle that we should not partake in a war in the declaration of which we had had no say. You believed very sincerely that Canadian soldiers should not be called upon to fight beyond the frontier of Canada itself, and your vision was further obscured by your indignation at the apparent injustice to a French minority in Ontario.

It is conceivable that at first on account of this long-held attitude of mind and because it seemed that Canadian aid was hardly necessary, for even we feared that the war would be over before the first Canadian regiment should land in France, you should have failed to adapt your mind to the new situation and should for a while have continued in your former views; — but now — now that Canada has pledged herself body and soul to the successful prosecution of this war — now that we know that only by the exercise of our full and united strength can we achieve a speedy and lasting victory — now that thousands of your fellow citizens have died, and alas! many more must yet be killed — how in the name of all that you hold most sacred can you still maintain your opposition? How can you refrain from using all your influence and your personal magnetism and eloquence to swell the great army of Canada and make it as representative of all classes of our citizens as possible?

Could you have been here yourself to witness in its horrible detail the cruelty of war — to have seen your comrades suddenly struck down in death and lie mangled at your side, even you could not have failed to wish to visit punishment upon those responsible. You too would now wish to see every ounce of our united strength instantly and relentlessly directed to that end. Afterwards, when that end has been accomplished, then and then only can there be honour or profit in the discussion of our domestic or imperial disputes.

And so my first reason for your support would be that you should assist in the defence of Canadian territory and Canadian liberties.

And my second would be this: —

Whatever criticism may today be properly directed against the Constitutional structure of the British Empire, we are compelled to admit that the *spiritual* union of the self-governing portions of the Empire is a most necessary and desirable thing. Surely you will concede that the degree of civilization which they represent and the standards of individual and national liberty for which they stand are the highest and noblest to which the human race has yet attained and jealously to be protected against destruction by less developed powers. All may not be perfection — grave and serious faults no doubt exist — vast progress must still be made — nevertheless that which has been achieved is good and must not be allowed to disappear. The bonds which unite us for certain great purposes and which have proved so powerful in this common struggle must not be loosened. They may indeed be readjusted, but the great communities which the British Empire has joined together must not be broken asunder. If I thought that the development of a national spirit in Canada meant antagonism to the "spirit" which unites the Empire today, I would utterly repudiate the idea of a Canadian nation and would gladly accept the most exacting of imperial organic unions.

Hitherto I have welcomed your nationalism because I thought it would only mean that you wished Canada to assume national responsibilities as well as to enjoy its privileges.

But your attitude in the present crisis will alienate and antagonize the support which you might otherwise have received. Can you not realize that if any worthy nationality is possible for Canada it must be sympathetic to and must cooperate with the fine spirit of imperial unity? That spirit was endangered by the outbreak of European war. It could only be preserved by loyal assistance from all those in whom that spirit dwelt.

And so I would also have had you support Canadian participation in the war, *not* in order to maintain a certain political organism of Empire, but to preserve and perpetuate that invaluable *spirit* which alone makes our union possible.

The third reason is this: You and I are so called French Canadians. We belong to a race that began the conquest of this country long before the days of Wolfe. That race was in its turn conquered, but their personal liberties were not restricted. They were in fact increased. Ultimately as a minority in a great English-speaking community we have preserved our racial identity, and we have had freedom to speak or to worship as we wished. I may not be, like yourself, "un pur sang," for I am by birth even more English than French, but I am proud of my French ancestors, I love the French language, and I am as determined as you are that we shall have full liberty to remain French as long as we like. But if we are to preserve this liberty we must recognize that we do not belong entirely to ourselves, but to a mixed population, we must rather seek to find points of contact and of common interest than points of friction and separation. We must make concessions and certain sacrifices of our distinct individuality if we mean to live on amicable terms with our fellow citizens or if we are to expect them to make similar concessions to us. There, in this

Article Eighteen • An Open Letter from Capt. Talbot Papineau to Mr. Henri Bourassa

265

moment of crisis, was the greatest opportunity which could ever have presented itself for us to show unity of purpose and to prove to our English fellow citizens that, whatever our respective histories may have been, we were actuated by a common love for our country and a mutual wish that in the future we should unite our distinctive talents and energies to create a proud and happy nation.

That was an opportunity which you, my cousin, have failed to grasp, and unfortunately, despite the heroic and able manner in which French-Canadian battalions have distinguished themselves here, and despite the whole-hearted support which so many leaders of French-Canadian thought have given to the cause, yet the fact remains that the French in Canada have not responded in the same proportion as have other Canadian citizens, and the unhappy impression has been created that French Canadians are not bearing their full share in this great Canadian enterprise. For this fact and this impression you will be held largely responsible. Do you fully realize what such a responsibility will mean, not so much to you personally—for that I believe you would care little—but to the principles which you have advocated, and for many of which I have but the deepest regard? You will have brought them into a disrepute from which they may never recover. Already you have made the fine term of "Nationalist" to stink in the nostrils of our English fellow citizens. Have you caused them to respect your national views? Have you won their admiration or led them to consider with esteem, and toleration your ambitions for the French language? Have you shown yourself worthy of concessions or consideration?

After this war what influence will you enjoy—what good to your country will you be able to accomplish? Wherever you go you will stir up strife and enmity—you will bring disfavour and dishonour upon our race, so that whoever bears a French name in Canada will be an object of suspicion and possibly of hatred.

And so, in the third place, for the honour of French Canada and for the unity of our country, I would have had you favourable to our cause.

I have only two more reasons, and they but need to be mentioned, I think, to be appreciated.

Here in this little French town I hear all about me the language I love so well and which recalls so vividly my happy childhood days in Montebello. I see types and faces that are like old friends. I see farm houses like those at home. I notice that our French-Canadian soldiers have easy friendships wherever they go.

Can you make me believe that there must not always be a bond of blood relationship between the Old France and the New?

And France—more glorious than in all her history—is now in agony straining fearlessly and proudly in a struggle for life or death.

For Old France and French civilization I would have had your support.

And in the last place, all other considerations aside and even supposing Canada had been a neutral country, I would have had you decide that she should enter the struggle for no other reason than that it is a fight for the freedom of the world—a fight in the result of which like every other country she is herself vitally interested. I will not further speak of the causes of this war, but I should like to think that even if Canada had been an independent and neutral nation she of her own accord would have chosen to follow the same path of glory that she is following today.

Perhaps, my cousin, I have been overlong and tedious with my reasons, but I shall be shorter with my warning—and in closing I wish to say this to you.

Those of us in this great army, who may be so fortunate as to return to our Canada, will have faced the grimmest and sincerest issues of life and death—we will have experienced the unhappy strength of brute force—we will have seen our loved comrades die in blood and suffering. Beware lest we return with revengeful feelings, for I say to you that for those who, while we fought and suffered here, remained in safety and comfort in Canada and failed to give us encouragement and support, as well as for those who grew fat with the wealth dishonourably gained by political graft and by dishonest business methods at our expense — we shall demand a heavy day of reckoning. We shall inflict upon them the punishment they deserve — not by physical violence — for we shall have had enough of that — nor by unconstitutional or illegal means — for we are fighting to protect not to destroy justice and freedom — but by the invincible power of our moral influence.

Can you ask us then for sympathy or concession? Will any listen when you speak of pride and patriotism? I think not.

Remember too that if Canada has become a nation respected and self-respecting she owes it to her citizens who have fought and died in this distant land and not to those self-styled Nationalists who have remained at home.

Can I hope that anything I have said here may influence you to consider the situation in a different light and that it is not yet too late for me to be made proud of our relationship?

At this moment, as I write, French and English Canadians are fighting and dying side by side. Is their sacrifice to go for nothing or will it not cement a foundation for a true Canadian nation, a Canadian nation independent in thought, independent in action, independent even in its political organization — but in spirit united for high international and humane purposes to the two Motherlands of England and France?

I think that is an ideal in which we shall all equally share. Can we not all play an equal part in its realization?

I am, as long as may be possible,

Your affectionate Cousin,

TALBOT M. PAPINEAU.

Mr. Bourassa's Reply to Capt. Talbot Papineau's Letter

Montreal, August 2nd, 1916.

Andrew-R. McMaster, Esq., K.C.,
189 St. James St.,
City.

Dear Sir,

On my return from an absence of several weeks, I found your letter of the 18th ult., and the copy of a letter apparently written to me by your partner, Capt. Talbot Papineau, on the 21st of March.

Capt. Papineau's letter, I am informed, appeared simultaneously, Friday last, in a number of papers, in Montreal, Quebec, Ottawa, and elsewhere. You have thus turned it into a kind of political manifesto and constituted yourself its publisher. Allow me therefore to send you my reply, requesting you to have it transmitted to Capt. Papineau, granting that he is the real author of that document. I can hardly believe it. A brave and active officer as he is has seldom the time to prepare and write such long pieces of political eloquence. Then, why should Capt. Papineau, who writes and speaks French elegantly, who claims so highly his French origin and professes with such ardour his love of France, have written in English to his *"dear cousin Henri"*? How is it that a letter written on the 21st of March has reached me but four months later, through your medium? For what purpose did you keep it so long in portfolio? and why do you send me a copy, instead of the letter itself?

It is, you say, an "open letter." It was, nevertheless, meant to reach me. It opens and ends with forms of language bearing the touch of intimate relationship—more so even than could be expected from the rare intercourse which, in spite of our blood connection, had so far existed between your partner and myself. The whole thing has the appearance of a political manoeuvre executed under the name of a young and gallant officer, who has the advantage or inconvenience of being my cousin. That Capt. Papineau has put his signature at the foot of that document, it is possible; but he would certainly not have written it in cool thought, after due reflection. It not only expresses opinions radically opposed to those I heard from him before the war; it also contains inaccuracies of fact of which I believe him honourably incapable.

He mentions "some discussions in the past," "differences of opinion," which have left "uninjured" a "pleasant friendship," dating, he says, "from the time of [his] birth." From his childhood to his return from Oxford, I do not think we had ever met, and certainly never to exchange the slightest glimpse of thought or opinion. Of matters of national concern we talked but once in all my life. From that one conversation I gathered the impression that he was still more opposed than myself to any kind of imperial solidarity. He even seemed much disposed to hasten the day of the Independence of Canada. Since, I met him on two or three occasions. We talked of matters indifferent, totally foreign to the numerous questions treated with such eloquent profuseness and so little reasoning in his letter of the 21st of March.

How can he charge me with having expressed "unhappy views" "at the outstart of the war," in August 1914, and held them stubbornly "unchanged" till this day? In August 1914, I was abroad. My first pronouncement on the intervention of Canada in the war is dated September 8th, 1914. In that editorial, while repelling the principles of Imperial solidarity and their consequences, and maintaining the nationalist doctrine in which Capt. Papineau—and you as well—pretends to be still a believer, I pronounced myself in favour of the intervention of Canada, *as a nation*, for the defence of the superior interests uniting Canada with France and Britain. My "unhappy views" were thus analogous to those of your partner. It is but later, long after Capt. Papineau was gone, that my attitude was changed and brought me to condemn the participation of Canada in the war,—or rather the political inspiration of that participation and the many abuses which have resulted therefrom. The reasons of that change are well known to those who have read or heard with attention and good faith all my statements on the matter. To sum them up is now sufficient.

The free and independent participation of Canada—free for the nation and free for the individuals—I had accepted, provided it remained within reasonable bounds, in conformity with the conditions of the country. But the Government, the whole of Parliament, the press, and politicians of both parties all applied themselves systematically to obliterate the free character of Canada's intervention. "Free" enlistment is now carried on by means of blackmailing, intimidation, and threats of all sorts. Advantage has been taken of the emotion caused by the war to assert, with the utmost intensity and intolerance, the doctrine of Imperial solidarity, triumphantly opposed in the past by our statesmen and the whole Canadian people, up to the days of the infamous South African War, concocted by Chamberlain, Rhodes, and the British imperialists with the clear object of drawing the self-governing colonies into "the vortex of European militarism." That phrase of your political leader, Sir Wilfrid Laurier, is undoubtedly fresh in your mind. After having given way to the imperialistic current of 1899, Sir Wilfrid Laurier and the liberal party had come back to the nationalist doctrine. The naval scare of 1909 threw them again under the yoke of imperialism; the war has achieved their enslavement: they united with the tory-jingo-imperialists of all shades to make of the participation of Canada in the war an immense political manoeuvre and thus assure the triumph of British imperialism. You and your partner, like many others, have followed your party through its various evolutions. I have remained firmly attached to the principles I laid down at the time of the South African war and maintained unswervingly ever since.

As early as the month of March 1900, I pointed out the possibility of a conflict between Great Britain and Germany and the danger of laying down in South Africa a precedent, the fatal consequence of which would be to draw Canada into all the wars undertaken by the United Kingdom. Sir Wilfrid Laurier and the liberal leaders laughed at my apprehensions; against my warnings they quoted the childish safeguard of the "no precedent clause" inserted in the Order in Council of the 14th of October 1899. For many years after, till 1912, and 1913, they kept singing the praises of the Kaiser and extolling the peaceful virtues of Germany. They now try to regain time by denouncing vociferously the "barbarity" of the "Huns." Today, as in 1900, in 1911, and always, I believe that all the nations of Europe are the victims of their own mistakes, of the complacent servility with which they submitted to the dominance of all Imperialists and traders in human flesh, who, in England as in Germany, in France as in Russia, have brought the peoples to slaughter in order to increase their reapings of cursed gold. German Imperialism and British Imperialism, French Militarism and Russian Tsarism, I hate with equal detestation; and I believe as firmly today as in 1899 that Canada, a nation of America, has a nobler mission to fulfill than to bind herself to the fate of the nations of Europe or to any spoliating Empire — whether it be the spoliators of Belgium, Alsace, or Poland, or those of Ireland or the Transvaal, of Greece or the Balkans.

Politicians of both parties, your liberal friends as well as their conservative opponents, feign to be much scandalized at my "treasonable disloyalty." I could well afford to look upon them as a pack of knaves and hypocrites. In 1896, your liberal leaders and friends stumped the whole province of Quebec with the cry "WHY SHOULD WE FIGHT FOR ENGLAND?" From 1902 to 1911, Sir Wilfrid Laurier was acclaimed by them as the indomitable champion of Canada's autonomy against British Imperialism. His resisting attitude at the Imperial Conferences of 1902 and 1907 was praised to the skies. His famous phrase on the "vortex of European militarism," and his determination to keep Canada far from it, became the party's by-word — always in the Province of Quebec, of course. His Canadian Navy scheme was presented as a step toward the independence of Canada.

Then came the turn of the Conservatives to tread in the footsteps of the Nationalists; they soon outstripped us. A future member of the conservative Cabinet, Mr. Blondin, brought back to life an old saying of Sir Adolphe Chapleau, and suggested to pierce the Union jack with bullets in order to let pass the breeze of liberty. The tory leaders, Sir Robert Borden, Sir George Foster, the virtuous Bob Rogers, and even our national superKitchener, Sir Sam Hughes, while trumpeting the purity of their Imperialism, greeted with undisguised joy the anti-imperialist victory of Drummond-Arthabaska, and used it for all it was worth to win the general elections in 1911.

By what right should those people hold me as a "traitor," because I remain consequent with the principles that I have never ceased to uphold and which both parties have exploited alternately, as long as it suited their purpose and kept them in power or brought them to office?

Let it not be pretended that those principles are out of place, pending the war. To prevent Canada from participating in the war, then foreseen and predicted, was their very object and *raison d'être*. To throw them aside and deny them when the time of test came, would have required a lack of courage and sincerity, of which I feel totally incapable. If this is what they mean by "British loyalty" and "superior civilization," they had better hang me at once. I will never obey such dictates and will ever hold in deepest contempt the acrobats who lend themselves to all currents of blind popular passion in order to serve their personal or political ends.

This, let it be well understood, does not apply to your partner. His deeds have shown the sincerity of his political turn. Without agreeing with his new opinions, I admired his silent courage in running to the front at the first call. His verbose political manifesto — supposing he is really responsible for it — adds nothing to his merits. Still less does it enhance the dignity and moral worth of the politicians and pressmen of all kinds, who, after having denounced war and imperialism, and while taking great care not to risk their precious body, have become the apostles of war and the upholders of imperialism.

I will not undertake to answer every point of the dithyrambic plea of my gallant cousin. When he says that I am too far away from the trenches to judge of the real meaning of this war, he may be right. On the other hand, his long and diffuse piece of eloquence proves that the excitement of warfare and the distance from home have obliterated in his mind the fundamental realities of his native country. I content myself with touching upon one point, on which he unhappily lends credit to the most mischievous of the many anti-national opinions circulated by the jingo press. He takes the French Canadians to task and challenges their patriotism, because they enlist in lesser number than the other elements of the population of Canada. Much could be said upon that. It is sufficient to signalize one patent fact: the number of recruits for the European war, in the various Provinces of Canada and from each component element of the population, is in inverse ratio of the enrootment in the soil and the traditional patriotism arising therefrom. The newcomers from the British Isles have enlisted in much larger proportion than English-speaking Canadians born in this country, while these have enlisted more than the French Canadians. The Western Provinces have given more recruits than Ontario, and Ontario more than Quebec. In each Province, the floating population of the cities, the students, the labourers and clerks, either unemployed or threatened with dismissal, have supplied more soldiers than the farmers. Does it mean that the city dwellers are more patriotic than the country people? or that the newcomers from England are better Canadians than their fellow citizens of British origin, born in Canada? No; it simply means that in Canada, as in every other country, at all times, the citizens of the oldest origin are the least disposed to be stampeded into distant ventures of no direct concern to their native land. It proves also that military service is more repugnant to the rural than the urban populations.

There is among the French Canadians a larger proportion of farmers, fathers of large families, than among any other ethnical element in Canada. Above all, the French Canadians are the only group exclusively Canadian, in its whole and by each of the individuals of which it is composed. They look upon the perturbations of Europe, even those of England or France, as foreign events. Their sympathies naturally go to France against Germany; but they do not think they have an obligation to fight for France, no more than the French of Europe would hold themselves bound to fight for Canada against the United States or Japan, or even against Germany, in case Germany should attack Canada without threatening France.

English Canada, not counting the *blokes*, contains a considerable proportion of people still in the first period of national incubation. Under the sway of imperialism, a fair number have not yet decided whether their allegiance is to Canada or to the Empire, whether the United Kingdom or the Canadian Confederacy is their country.

As to the newcomers from the United Kingdom, they are not Canadian in any sense. England or Scotland is their sole fatherland. They have enlisted for the European war as naturally as Canadians, either French or English, would take arms to defend Canada against an aggression on the American continent.

Thus it is rigorously correct to say that recruiting has gone in inverse ratio of the development of Canadian patriotism. If English-speaking Canadians have a right to blame the French Canadians for the small number of their recruits, the newcomers from the United Kingdom, who have supplied a much larger proportion of recruits than any other element of the population, would be equally justified in branding the Anglo-Canadians with disloyalty and treason. Enlistment for the European war is supposed to be absolutely free and voluntary. This has been stated right and left from beginning to end. If that statement is honest and sincere, all provocations from one part of the population against the other, and exclusive attacks against the French Canadians, should cease. Instead of reviling unjustly one-third of the Canadian people — a population so remarkably characterized by its constant loyalty to national institutions and its respect for public order, — those men who claim a right to enlighten and lead public opinion should have enough good faith and intelligence to see facts as they are and to respect the motives of those who persist in their determination to remain more Canadian than English or French.

In short, English-speaking Canadians enlist in much smaller number than the newcomers from England, because they are more Canadian; French Canadians enlist less than English Canadians because they are totally and exclusively Canadian. To claim that their abstention is due to the "baneful" influence of the Nationalists is a pure nonsense. Should I give way to the suggestion of my gallant cousin, I would be just as powerless as Sir Wilfrid Laurier to induce the French Canadians to enlist. This is implicitly acknowledged in Capt. Papineau's letter: on the one hand, he asserts that my views on the participation of Canada in the war are denied by my own friends; on the other he charges the mass of the French-Canadian population with a refusal to answer the call of duty. The simple truth is, that the abstention of the French Canadians is no more the result of the present attitude of the Nationalists than the consequence of the liberal campaign of 1896, or of the conservative appeals of 1911. It relates to deeper causes: hereditary instincts, social and economic conditions, a national tradition of three centuries. It is equally true, however, that those deep and far distant causes have been strengthened by the constant teaching of all our political and social leaders, from Lafontaine, Cartier, Macdonald, Mackenzie, to Laurier inclusively. The only virtue, or crime, of the Nationalists is to persist in believing and practising what they were taught by the men of the past, and even those of today. This is precisely what infuriates the politicians, either *blue* or *red*. To please the Imperialists, they have renounced all their traditions and undertaken to bring the French Canadians under imperial command. Unable to succeed, they try to conceal their fruitless apostasy by denouncing to the hatred of the jingos the obtrusive witnesses of their past professions of faith.

The jingo press and politicians have also undertaken to persuade their gullible followers that the Nationalists hinder the work of recruiters *because* of the persecution meted out to the French minorities in Ontario and Manitoba. This is but another nonsense. My excellent cousin, I am sorry to say, — or his inspirer — has picked it up.

The two questions are essentially distinct; this we have never ceased to assert. One is purely internal; the other affects the international status of Canada and her relations with Great Britain. To the problem of the teaching of languages we ask for a solution in conformity with the spirit of the Federal agreement, the best interests of Confederation, and the principles of pedagogy as applied in civilized countries. Our attitude on the participation of Canada in the war is inspired exclusively by the constant tradition of the country and the agreements concluded half a century ago between Canada and Great Britain. Even if the irritating bilingual question was non-existent, our views on the war would be what they are. The most that can be said is, that the backward and essentially Prussian policy of the rulers of Ontario and Manitoba gives us an additional argument against the intervention of Canada in the European conflict. To speak of fighting for the preservation of French civilization in Europe while endeavouring to destroy it in America, appears to us as an absurd piece of inconsistency. To preach Holy War for the liberties of the peoples overseas, and to oppress the national minorities in Canada, is, in our opinion, nothing but odious hypocrisy.

Is it necessary to add that, in spite of his name, Capt. Papineau is utterly unqualified to judge of the feelings of the French Canadians? For most part American, he has inherited, with a few drops of French blood, the most *denationalized* instincts of his French origin. From those he calls his compatriots he is separated by his religious belief and his maternal language. Of their traditions, he knows but what he has read in a few books. He was brought up far away from close contact with French Canadians. His higher studies he pursued in England. His elements of French culture he acquired in France. The complexity of his origin and the diversity of his training would be sufficient to explain his mental hesitations and the contradictions which appear in his letter. Under the sway of his American origin, he glories in the Revolution of 1776; he calls it a war "for the principle of national existence." In good logic, he should approve highly of the tentative rebellion of the Sinn Feiners, and suggest that Canada should rise in arms to break the yoke of Great Britain. His American forefathers, whom he admires so much, fought against England and called upon France and Spain to help them against their mother-country, for lighter motives than those of the Dublin rebels. The Imperial burden they refused to bear was infinitely less ponderous than that which weighs today upon the people of Canada.

With the threat contained in the conclusion of his letter, I need not be concerned. Supposing always that he is truly responsible for that document, I make broad allowance for the excitement and perturbation resulting from his strenuous life. He and many of his comrades will have enough to do in order to help Canada to counteract the disastrous consequences of the war venture in which she has thrown herself headlong. To propagate systematically national discord by quarrelling with all Canadians, either French or English, who hold different views as to the theory and practice of their national duty, would be a misuse of time. Moreover, it would be a singular denial of their professions of faith in favour of liberty and civilization.

As to the scoundrels and bloodsuckers "who have grown fat with the wealth dishonourably gained" in war contracts, I give them up quite willingly to their just indignation. But those worthies are not to be found in nationalist ranks: they are all recruited among the noisiest preachers of the Holy War waged for "civilization" against "barbarity," for the "protection of small nations," for the "honour" of England and the "salvation" of France.

Yours truly,

Henri BOURASSA

P.S. — I hope this will reach you before you leave for the front: no doubt, you have been the first to respond to the pressing call of your partner.   H.B.

Article Nineteen

Fortunes of War

Sandra Gwyn

Instead of ending by Christmas, the war had ended in a "race to the sea" that itself had ended in a draw. The famed Schlieffen Plan, a strategy derived from Hannibal's victory at the Battle of Cannae, by which the Germans planned to crush the allied armies by a pincer-like assault, had failed — just — because there weren't quite enough Germans to bring it off and because the French had rushed reinforcements out of Paris in taxi-cabs. Barbed wire and the machine gun now ruled the battlefield. Nothing could get through them, nor, later, at Gallipoli, around them. Both sides, their generals weaned on Alexander, Caesar, Marlborough, Frederick the Great, Napoleon, still believed in the "the breakthrough." Both maintained their regiments of cavalry, ready to be unleashed in one glorious charge across open fields. To prepare for that day, both dug protectively into the earth, unfurled strands of barbed wire, and set up strongpoints for their machine guns. These were merely temporary bastions from which the breakthrough would be launched.

Trapped in a technological timewarp, the two armies settled into a war like none before or since. From just south of the mouth of the Yser, on the coast of Belgium, down to Beurnevisin on the Swiss frontier, stretched 400 miles of twisting, looping, but roughly parallel lines of trenches. Into this immensely long but narrow space were compressed more men and more armaments than had ever been assembled before in even the widest of spaces. Three and a half years, and millions of dead young men, later, the lines followed almost exactly the same looping course between the mouth of the Yser and the hamlet of Beurnevisin. At times, as at Verdun or at Passchendaele, the line did shift a few miles eastwards or westwards. Later, it shifted back the same number of miles. "This isn't war," said Lord Kitchener early in 1915. He was right. It was mutual suicide.

"The idea of the trenches," writes Paul Fussell in his 1975 masterpiece, *The Great War and Modern Memory*, "has been assimilated so successfully in metaphor and myth that it is not easy now to recover a feeling for the actualities." A front-line trench could be as close as a few dozen yards from its enemy counterpart, although, quite randomly, the gap between them was sometimes as wide as a mile. In theory (as we shall discover shortly, practice was often quite different) a trench was about eight feet deep and four or five feet wide, thickly surrounded by barbed-wire entanglements, and the floors covered with wooden duckboards (in the damp soil of Flanders, these were often covered with a foot or more of sludgy water). To the front and rear were parapets of sandbags. Along the top of the parapet there were snipers' plates made of thick steel, with holes just large enough to accommodate a rifle barrel and the human eye. At the back of the trenches there was usually a row of dugouts, reached by dirt stairs and used for officers' quarters. (Officers' meals were usually provided by a cook; other ranks did their own cooking, such as it was, sometimes using coal braziers and toward the end of the war, Primus stoves. Mostly, they simply opened tins of bully beef or the infamous meat-and-vegetable Maconochie stew.) A well-built trench did not run straight but zigzagged every few yards so that a shell or bomb that landed in it could kill only those in each "zig." With all these zigs, the allied front alone encompassed some 12 000 miles of trenches. Communication trenches, running roughly at right angles to the front line, served to bring up supplies such as food and ammunition, and to bring back the dead and wounded. Behind these were more trenches parallel with the front line, to serve as a defence in depth for up to half a mile to the rear. Forward of the front line, shallow ditches known as "saps" thrust out into no man's land and served as posts for observation and grenade-throwing. In some instances, as at Vimy, as visitors can still see today, opposed "saps" might be less than twenty yards apart. A standard tour of duty in the front line was about four days. It was spent entirely head-down. To look up and out, other than through a periscope, was to die to a sniper or to a burst of machine-gun fire.

Within this "Troglodyte World," in Fussell's phrase, normal biorhythms were turned upside-down. His description of trench routine speaks for the Canadians as well as for the British. "During the day, men cleaned weapons and repaired those parts of the trench damaged during the night. Or they wrote letters, deloused themselves, or slept. The officers inspected, encouraged, and strolled around looking nonchalant to inspire the men. They censored the men's letters and dealt with the quantities of official inquiries brought to them by runner. . . . Daily 'returns' of the amount of ammunition and the quantities of trench stores had to be made. Reports of the nightly casualties had to be sent back. And letters of condolence, which as the war went on became form-letters of condolence, had to be written to the relatives of the killed and wounded." After evening stand-to, the real work began. No man's land came alive as small parties of men inched through the wire, scurrying from shell-hole to shell-hole, hugging the ground when a flare arched up, trying to pick up intelligence by listening to the enemy's whispered conversations, trying to snatch a prisoner, trying to demoralize the enemy with a sudden storm of hand grenades upon his trenches, or, as the textbooks demanded, just trying to keep up their own aggressive spirits. To relieve the tension and the monotony, almost everyone became a chain-smoker. Cigarettes were smoked behind cupped hands; no one, except newcomers, lit more than one from a single match. Only with the dawn could everyone begin to relax: its coming meant there would be no attack — except when it did come.

The first 40 miles of the allied line of trenches, a mainly quiescent sector north of Ypres, was held by the Belgians. The next 90 miles, down to the river Ancre in northwest France, was held by the British and Colonial forces. The French manned the rest, to the south, their stronghold the fortress of Verdun on the River Meuse. The British and Colonial part of the line normally comprised some 800 battalions of about a thousand men each. They were concentrated in two main sectors: the Somme area in Picardy, which would take centre stage in 1916, and the Ypres Salient in Flanders. This latter was an untidy bulge, about nine miles long at its widest point and protruding about four miles eastward into the German lines. Vulnerable to attack on three sides, and under constant artillery fire on its exposed flanks, the Salient was a military insanity but a political necessity: it encompassed almost all of the little bit of Belgium that had been held onto at such an appalling cost, and therefore had to go on being held no matter how appalling the future cost. It was here that the Patricias first entered the line, on January 7, 1915, as part of the British 27th Division.

One of the best ways to recapture the *idea* of the trenches is to make a pilgrimage through the Ypres Salient. At first, the placid and prosperous Flemish farm country evokes little that's resonant. Only the occasional shell craters, now serving as waterholes for cattle and geese, or an unnatural wave in a field of cabbage or corn, serve as reminders of battles long ago. Even the daily sunset ceremony at the Menin Gate in Ypres, although moving, lacks a quality of immediacy. Then, when the suburbs of Ypres are still in the rearview mirror, the road-signs marked "Passchendaele" flash into view. Suddenly, the tragic dimension of the war becomes recognizable as the pilgrim realizes how small was the battlefield over which so much blood was spilled. The description that best sets it in context for Canadians is that of Ralph Allen in *Ordeal By Fire*:

> During the three years between early 1915 and early 1918, the whole of the Canadian ground forces fought and died, and if fortunate, lived, in an area hardly bigger than three or four Saskatchewan townships. Their every value and perspective had to be adjusted accordingly. From one small piece of quagmire, another piece of quagmire fifty yards away could look as enticing as the towers of Cathay. The slightest bulge on the flat, sodden, dangerous plains became a hill or a mountain. On a reverse slope, a company or a battalion could buy respite from the incessant artillery barrages. On a forward slope, it could be wiped out. In the desperate lore of the front, hummocks not large enough to make a toboggan slide became as high and as famous as Everest or the Matterhorn.

The other quality of the Ypres Salient that soon intrudes upon a visitor is the ambience. Brooding and melancholy, it is that of a vast graveyard. Meticulously maintained cemeteries and memorials encroach everywhere upon the farmland: the huge British cemetery at Tyne Cot, close to Passchendaele; the giant statue of the "Brooding Soldier" at Vancouver Corner commemorating the 18 000 Canadians who faced the enemy nearby after the first German gas attacks in April 1915. As memorials go, the regimental cemetery of the Princess Patricia's at Voormezele, a village about four miles south of Ypres, is one of the smaller, mentioned in few of the official guidebooks. For us, though, because a number of our characters are now at rest there, it is a place filled with resonance.

Talbot Papineau and Charlie Stewart, recovered from the burns and accompanied by a detachment of 40 men, caught up with the Patricias on February 1; Agar Adamson and his draft of 200 arrived by way of Rouen three weeks later. They found the regiment near the village of St. Eloi, at the extreme southeast elbow of the Salient, engaged in a stubborn defence of a strongpoint that had been christened "The Mound" and that was just that, a hump of brickmakers' clay some twenty feet high and 70 feet long, standing beside the road at the southern approach to Ypres. Elsewhere in the area, the Germans held the high ground. "You never saw such a scene of utter desolation and destruction," was Papineau's first impression on arriving at regimental headquarters in the cellar of a ruined farmhouse that Colonel Farquhar had christened Shelley Farm, not in honour of the poet. "Every barn and house has been smashed to pieces. We passed a whole village smashed to ruins, church and all, not a stray dog or cat living. The Germans would throw up their famous lightning rockets and our whole party would throw themselves down flat in the mud til the darkness came again." Yet his first tour of front-line duty was an easy one, without casualties, and being young and full of mettle, he found it exhilarating. "It's like a game," he wrote his mother on February 5, "dodging and running and creeping and lying down. As it grows dusk we meet our guides and in the dark, in a single file, we are led silently across the fields. All about is the sharp crack of rifle fire. We follow hedgerows and avoid the open. Then we creep up to the opening of the trench, and one by one jump in. I wait until my men are all in and jump after. I have not been badly frightened yet. That will come, I suppose. This is so much like a *fête-de-nuit*, a thunderstorm and duck shooting, that I positively like it."

We can suspect that Papineau was being economical with the truth to spare Caroline's feelings. Soon — "I have faith in your courage" — he began telling her more. Yet he did not describe in detail the horrors that soon became routine, still less the black mood of hopelessness that after six weeks of fruitless fighting was starting to creep up on the regiment.

Adamson spared Mabel nothing. "At the present moment, the Germans have the best of it," he wrote within days of arriving. "Their bomb and mortar throwing is perfect, also their flares, and we are infants at it. Their trenches are beautifully made, they have their men do nothing else, and they are drained and all communicate with each other. Their sniping is organized, the snipers having fixed rifles with telescopic sights firing from about 300 yards. Their particular game is to enfilade the trenches. They fire all day, picking certain points where they know the men will be working, and at night keep up a steady fire about every 30 seconds, generally from both sides of the advance trenches."

The trenches inherited by the Patricias beggared description. Recently taken over from French troops, who had relied much more heavily upon their artillery than their infantry, they weren't trenches at all, only shallow ditches knee-deep in water, protected by a few sandbags and isolated from one another. Number 21, the most notorious death-trap of all, in which Adamson found himself in his first day in the line, "consisted of sandbags about 5 feet high and no trench whatever." Getting in and out involved crawling zigzag through half a mile or more of the mud, and was the most dangerous part. "We lose a lot of men in this way," he continued. "The routes have to be changed constantly as the Germans always find out, and the only way of knowing is by our number of casualties."

We can imagine Mabel shuddering as she read such reports by the dining room fire at Basil Street. Each letter she opened was grimmer. The putrefying stench of wet and decaying human and animal flesh, Agar told her, was incomparably worse than he'd anticipated, and far beyond the power of the smelling salts she'd sent him. "I counted seven dead horses just outside my trench yesterday," he wrote on March 3. "There is also a dead Frenchman there and has been for a long time. We got orders reading, 'Keep the Shelley Farm on your right, and pass between the broken tree and the dead Frenchman on your right,' so the poor fellow was being of some use in death.... One of the most disgusting sights was a couple of pigs deliberately feeding on the decomposed body of a soldier. You will be glad to hear it was their last meal, and they remain to add to the stench." A few days later, making improvements to a trench, his men dug into a mass grave. "We had to get the correct depth to give the living men shelter. The only thing to be done was to dig right on regardless of what we went through. The grave was some months old and it was a most horrible operation, especially when the flares were turned on and you saw the awful sights you were digging and picking to pieces. It was too much for some men, who had to be relieved."

Almost as bad as the stench and the sights was the continual pounding of the artillery. "It affects the strongest of us," Agar went on. "The noise and the shaking of the earth gives us the most dreadful headaches and turns us deaf." Even on an uneventful day, the tension of being in the front lines was ever-present. "It gets on one's nerves, always having to be on the alert, as one never knows where or what they will do, and I think when you find they have not done anything, and you have really got out with the whole company safe, the relief is almost as bad as the strain."

Thus far, physical casualties to the Patricias had been relatively slight: 70 killed and wounded since early January. But the dreadful conditions produced much sickness—pneumonia, typhoid, rheumatism, a condition called "trench foot," a low-grade form of frostbite produced by standing for hours in cold water—so that by the time Adamson arrived, the regiment was nearly 400 men under strength. "The suffering of the men is very great after they come out of the trenches," he reported. "Their hands and feet are all swelled up and a stiffening of the joints sets in." As damaging to morale in these early days was the large number of deaths that were caused by carelessness and inexperience. The first officer to be killed, Captain D.O.C. Newton, a former aide to the Governor General and great beau around Ottawa, lost his way at night in no man's land and was shot by one of his own sentries. A fortnight later, a Captain Fitzgerald jumped out of his trench in broad daylight to inspect a dead body and was instantly shot dead by a sniper. "He practically committed suicide, so foolish was he," Papineau wrote home. On the same day, he continued, "Lieutenant Price was killed. His guide led him incorrectly into the trenches, and he was shot in the chest." The moment when Talbot himself stopped thinking of the war as a *fête-de-nuit* came shortly before noon on March 3, when Captain J.S. Ward, the Okanangan fruit farmer who had become his close friend, jumped up too hastily to inspect the neighbouring trench. "He sank back in my arms," wrote Talbot. "He had been shot in the back of the head. He bled frightfully. The brain matter was easing out. I loved old Ward. He was one of the best fellows I know. It was terrible for me to see him like that so suddenly. He was conscious and could recognize me, although his mind wandered. He was in great pain, and I gave him a good deal of morphine. He would hold my hand sometimes. He said, 'Talbot, you're an angel.' He called for 'Alice, where's Alice?' A terrific snowstorm blew up. I never saw such darkness and such wind. Flocks of birds flew before it. Later there was thunder and lightning. How long those hours were. It was not until 8:30 P.M. that the stretcher party came." Ward died a few days later.

Two other casualties not recorded in official regimental records dealt the Patricias another blow. On January 7, the first day the regiment was in the front line, two officers had broken under the strain. One was a Captain Smith, "accused of lying and cold feet," as Papineau reported. The other was Major J.W.H. McKinery, a big blustery man, Adamson's former company commander. "It appears that he 'blew up,'" Agar wrote Mabel. "He hid himself in the only safe place in the trench for 48 hours, cursing and swearing at his subalterns and NCOs all the time, and as soon as he got out bolted for the dressing station to have imaginary wounds attended to. The NCOs told the CO that if they were ordered to go into the trenches with him again, they would refuse and stand a court-martial." As a cover story, it was put out that both men had been sent back to England on sick leave. Few people believed this — "It is surprising how men come back from the front just ill or tired out," Mabel noted skeptically in a letter to her mother — and the resulting gossip damaged the regiment's reputation. (Both men subsequently were struck "off strength" and reassigned to low-echelon staff duties.)

On February 27, Farquhar conceived of a way to hit at the enemy before being hit by him. He requested permission to make a sudden local attack on a new trench that the Germans were sapping directly in front of The Mound, and so less than twenty yards away from the Patricias' line. Described as a "reconnaissance in force," this was the first engagement fought by a Canadian regiment in Europe. It was also the first of the "trench raids" for which the Canadians were to become famous. Talbot Papineau was one of the 90 or so men chosen to take part. Nearly eight decades later, his private account, a sixteen-page letter to his mother scribbled hastily in pencil, remains the most riveting account of this singular Canadian military initiative.

"We have made an attack at last and I have led it," begins Papineau's letter. At midnight, he and the other raiders had assembled at Shelley Farm. Already, Hamilton Gault and another officer, Lieutenant Colquhoun, who unfortunately had been spotted by the enemy and taken prisoner, had reconnoitred the territory. They were divided into three groups. The first, led by Lieutenant C.E. Crabbe, consisted of about 30 snipers and riflemen, plus three grenade-throwers headed by Papineau. Their objective was to rush the German sap and clear it. The other two parties were to act as cover, and to break down the enemy parapet. "The moon was well down and dawn was coming," continued Papineau.

"The colonel said, 'There are six snipers that will go ahead of you then you will go with your bomber-throwers. Crabbe will be behind you with his men. All right! Lead on!'"

I was pretty scared! My stomach seemed hollow. I called my men and we fell into line and began creeping forward flat on our bellies. I had a bomb ready in my hand. We lay for a moment exposed and then suddenly we were all up and rushing forward. My legs caught in barbed wire, but I stumbled through somehow. I set my fuse and hurled my bomb ahead of me. From that moment, all hell broke loose. I never thought there could be such noise. I had my revolver out. A German was silhouetted and I saw the flash of his rifle. I dropped on my knees and fired point blank. He disappeared. I said to myself, "I have shot him." I fired into the trench at whatever I thought was there. Then my revolver stopped. I lay flat and began to reload. I was against the German parapet. I looked behind me and could see only one man apparently wounded or dead near me. I thought, "The attack has failed. I am alone. I will never get out." A machine gun was going and the noise was awful.

Then I saw Crabbe coming. He knelt near me and fired over me with a rifle. I had got a cartridge home by this time and Crabbe and I went over the edge into the trench. It was deep and narrow, beautifully built, dried by a big pump, sides supported by planks, looked like a mine shaft. A German was lying in front of me. I pushed his head down to see if he was dead. He wasn't. I told a man to watch him. Then I began to pull down some of the parapet and sandbags. Three or four men were there too with shovels. The German machine guns were going like mad. It was beginning to grow light.

Presently we were told to evacuate the trench. I passed the order, then climbed out and made a run for our own line. Another man and I went over head first. The man that came after me was shot through the lungs. The next man got it in the stomach. They fell on me in the mud. I could not budge. Then over on top of us all came a German! He held up his hands and a couple of our men took him away. Gault was there and he worked pulling the wounded men off each other. One or two men came piling over with fixed bayonets and almost put our eyes out. I was finally pulled out of the mud. It was not quite light. I had to get back to my own trench. I beat it across the open expecting to get it any minute. I was so exhausted I wobbled from side to side in the mud. However, I reached home and dived for cover. I was tired but mostly glad to be back.

The stretcher bearers were carrying the wounded out past the back of my trench. The last party got halfway, then dropped their stretcher and ran. Gault crawled out to the man with a couple of volunteers and they dragged the stretcher into a ditch and then to a hedge. Gault was shot through the wrist. He will probably get the VC.

In practical terms, the raid achieved little, at a cost of twenty casualties. No ground was gained; the damage inflicted upon the German trench was slight; indeed, within minutes, as Papineau noted, the enemy was back in it throwing bombs. For the next three days, infuriated at having been outwitted even briefly, the Germans battered the regiment with mortar, rifle fire, and grenades and gave Adamson, now McKinery's replacement as commander of No. 2 Company, what he described as "the most awful day I ever put in."

"I could do nothing," he told Mabel. "There was only one rifle working owing to the mud and the debris knocked up by the bombs. We just lay there all day huddled together with constant fire pulling our breastwork down inch by inch. I lost 6 killed and 21 wounded." Nor was there any long-term gain; a fortnight later, after more severe fighting and many more casualties—including Charlie Stewart, badly hit in the stomach—the Germans captured The Mound and the first battle of St. Eloi was lost.

Yet within the context of early 1915, the raid was an important achievement. It demonstrated enterprise and daring. The Divisional Commander telegraphed "Well done PPCLI." Field Marshal Sir John French himself telegraphed "his great appreciation." Within the regiment itself, morale had been recouped and honour restored. Papineau and Crabbe both received the new decoration for junior officers, the Military Cross, and were the first Canadians to do so. Hamilton Gault won the first Canadian DSO for his gallant rescue of the wounded soldier. As mattered most of all, the newspapers having reported the affair, the future of the Patricias was secure at least for the time being.

This was to be "Fanny" Farquhar's last legacy to the Patricias. On March 19, shortly after receiving instructions to leave St. Eloi for the centre of the Salient, Farquhar was hit by a chance bullet while showing the commanding officer of the relieving battalion around. Adamson, leading his own company back to billets after a hard 48 hours in the trenches, learned what had happened when he stopped briefly at the dressing station. "I found the Colonel on the floor," he wrote Mabel. "The surgeon was dressing his wound. He was groaning and suffering a great deal. From the very first there was no hope." That same day, Adamson was also mourning the death of Sergeant Cork, his trusted emissary during the battle with Colonel James. "I had just spoken to him," he told Mabel. "He said he had received your remedy for chilblains and was going to write to thank you for it. He was shot through the spine a few minutes afterwards."

Two nights later the Patricias buried their colonel in the new regimental cemetery at Voormezele, a few yards away from Sergeant Cork's grave. "We all seem to think he would like to be with his men," Adamson wrote. "It was his own idea to rope off a separate piece of ground for them." Only 40 officers and men were allowed to attend since the ground was continually raked by enemy fire. Nowadays, for the contemporary visitor, thanks to an eloquent letter that Papineau wrote Lady Evelyn, it requires no stretch of the imagination for the tidy rows of poplars around the cemetery and the well-tended rosebushes surrounding the graves, to dissolve into that long-ago muddy field just back of the front lines. "We paid our last respects to the Colonel. It was the first beautiful evening we had had. The lovely sunset still tinged the sky, a new moon and little stars were quiet and clear overhead. A warm stillness and peacefulness seemed with us as we stood by the grave, but just beyond there was the constant crackle of rifles, now and then the whine of a bullet or the loud explosion of a bomb. Peace upon one side, war upon the other . . ."

Papineau's letter went on to say all the right things. "As a Canadian, I feel a national debt of gratitude to him. An Imperial officer, who could have commanded the highest position in the British army, he accepted the task of creating as well as commanding a new and untried Canadian regiment. He knew how to combine the discipline and dignity of the regular British army with the easy independence and democracy of a volunteer Canadian regiment. . . . He himself is with us no longer but his influence and his memory will endure."

Yet, nearly 80 years on, Agar's stumbling description of his own feeling is the more telling. "We are all very much depressed but have to keep up an appearance of cheerfulness, and speak of it as if it were only the fortunes of war. . . . What really makes a real man is something very hard to fathom. I suppose it is a case of training, but I really think it is more than that. It must be a matter as difficult as the definition and reason for the production of a real genius."

On March 25, the Patricias marched to Poperinghe, a peaceful market town turned into a bustling transport centre and forward base. There they spent the next week luxuriating in hot baths and the first change of clothes in a month. (Adamson and the other officers had their baths in a hotel: the men splashed around in huge converted beer vats in the main square.) There was even a divisional race meeting with a steeplechase in which both Adamson and Papineau took part. Everyone roared with laughter at the regimental four-in-hand, a carriage painted yellow and black, with two men inside dressed up as a bride and bridegroom. A few moments later, recounted Adamson, "a very fat French nurse and a fatter priest turned up. General Plumer said it was the most perfect makeup job he had ever seen. He was quite upset when he found out it was a real woman and priest and that she was the matron of the hospital at Poperinghe."

Soon the Second Battle of Ypres would begin. Compared to it, the desperate weeks at St. Eloi would seem like a militia manoeuvre.

Topic Ten

The Interwar Years

Road construction at Kimberly-Wasa, BC, May 1934. During the

Great Depression, the federal government established relief

projects for unemployed single men.

THE INTERWAR years were decades of upheaval and discontent as Canadians adjusted to new postwar conditions in the 1920s and then to the Great Depression in the 1930s. All regions, social classes, and ethnic groups were affected in some way by these unsettling conditions.

In the West, the 1920s saw the rise of a new political protest movement: the Progressives. They were followed in the thirties by the rise of Social Credit in Alberta and the Co-operative Commonwealth Federation in Saskatchewan. All of these political movements have been seen as common expressions of protest on the Prairies. In "The Pattern of Prairie Politics," Nelson Wiseman challenges this view of Prairie homogeneity to argue that political movements varied from province to province in terms of political ideology and social, economic, and cultural values, and that these provincial differences reflected the dominant ethnic composition of each province at the time of its formation.

The Maritimes also had a history of protest since Confederation. The postwar years proved to be a particularly disquieting period, as Maritimers reexamined their position in Confederation and compared their region's slow rate of growth with the more rapid growth of central Canada and the West. Many Maritimers saw themselves as victims of a central government that was more interested in satisfying the demands of the influential regions of central and western Canada, demands that were in conflict with those of the Maritime region. In "The Origins of the Maritime Rights Movement," E.R. Forbes analyzes the motivations of the different groups that participated in this effective protest movement.

The Great Depression brought about great social upheaval in Canada. The prices of primary commodities fell drastically, unemployment soared, Canadian consumers' purchasing power was greatly diminished, and secondary manufacturing declined. Thousands of people had to go on relief—in other words, to accept government assistance. The Conservative government of Prime Minister R.B. Bennett, in power from 1930 to 1935, experimented with make-work projects, as well as with relief camps that were designed to provide single men with basic food and accommodation along with menial jobs, but neither program succeeded in reducing the number of unemployed. When the Liberals came to power under William Lyon Mackenzie King in 1935, they pressured the prime minister to appoint a National Employment Commission to investigate the unemployment and relief situation, and a Royal Commission on Dominion–Provincial Relations. Both commissions strongly recommended that the federal government take responsibility for unemployment relief by setting up a national employment service and a nationwide unemployment insurance system. In "Canadian Unemployment Policy in the 1930s," James Struthers outlines the rationale behind the attitudes of the Bennett and Mackenzie King governments toward unemployment and relief projects.

For an overview of the 1920s, consult John Herd Thompson, with Allen Saeger, *Canada, 1922–1939: Decades of Discord* (Toronto: McClelland and Stewart, 1985). On the Progressive movement, the standard work remains W.L. Morton's *The Progressive Party in Canada* (Toronto: University of Toronto Press, 1950). See, as well, Walter Young, *Democracy and Discontent*, 2nd ed. (Toronto: McGraw-Hill Ryerson, 1978). On the ideology of progressivism, see David Laycock's *Populism and Democratic Thought in the Canadian Prairies, 1910–1945* (Toronto: University of Toronto Press, 1990), and Jeffrey Taylor's "The Language of Agrarianism in Manitoba, 1890–1925," *Labour/Le Travail* 23 (Spring 1989): 91–118. The link between the Progressive movement and the social gospel movement is shown in R. Allen's "The Social Gospel as the Religion of the Agrarian Revolt," in *The West and the Nation: Essays in Honour of W.L. Morton*, ed. C. Berger and R. Cook (Toronto: McClelland and Stewart, 1976), pp. 174–86. On the role of the United Farmers of Alberta and its Farm Women of Alberta section, see Bradford James Rennie, *The Rise of Agrarian Democracy: The United Farmers and Farm Women of Alberta, 1909–1921* (Toronto: University of Toronto Press, 2001).

A more comprehensive treatment of the postwar protest in the Maritimes can be found in E.R. Forbes's *The Maritime Rights Movement, 1919–27* (Montreal/Kingston: McGill-Queen's University Press, 1979). Students will find the essays on the Maritimes in *Canada and the Burden of Unity*, ed. D. Bercuson (Toronto: Macmillan, 1977) of value in placing the Maritime Rights movement in a broader perspective.

Much has been written on the decade of the Great Depression. For overviews, see Thompson with Saeger, *Canada, 1922–1939: Decades of Discord* (cited above); H.B. Neatby's *The Politics of Chaos: Canada in the Thirties* (Toronto: Macmillan, 1972); and Pierre Berton's popular account, *The Great Depression, 1929–1939* (Toronto: McClelland and Stewart, 1990). On western politics, see Walter Young, *Democracy and Discontent*, 2nd ed. (cited above). Two collections edited by Michiel Horn are helpful: *The Dirty Thirties: Canadians in the Great Depression* (Toronto: Copp Clark, 1972), a collection of primary and secondary sources, and *The Depression in Canada: Responses to Economic Crisis* (Toronto: Copp Clark, 1988).

James Struthers's work on unemployment relief in the thirties is presented in greater detail in *No Fault of Their Own: Unemployment and the Canadian Welfare State, 1914–1941* (Toronto: University of Toronto Press, 1983). For developments in Ontario, see his *Limits of Affluence: Welfare in Ontario, 1920–1970* (Toronto: University of Toronto Press, 1994). Also useful is Dennis Guest's *The Emergence of Social Security in Canada* (Vancouver: University of British Columbia Press, 1980). In "A Profession in Crisis: Charlotte Whitton and Canadian Social Work in the 1930s," *Canadian Historical Review* 62 (1981): 169–85, Struthers looks at Canada's best-known social worker of the period; see also P.T. Rooke and R.L. Schnell, *No Bleeding Heart: Charlotte Whitton, A Feminist on the Right* (Vancouver: University of British Columbia Press, 1987). On the impact of the Great Depression on women and families in Montreal, see Denyse Baillargeon, *Making Do: Women, Family and Home in Montreal during the Great Depression* (Waterloo: Wilfrid Laurier University Press, 1999).

Article Twenty

The Pattern of Prairie Politics

Nelson Wiseman

Canadian historians and social scientists have usually depicted prairie politics as a response, a reaction, to external impositions: the tariff, the withholding of authority over natural resources by the federal government, discriminatory transportation policies, and bilingualism, among others. This approach tells us substantially about east–west Canadian

Source: "The Pattern of Prairie Politics," originally published in *Queen's Quarterly* 88, 2 (Summer 1981): 298–315. This revised and updated version appears in *Party Politics in Canada*, 7th ed., ed. Hugh G. Thorburn (Toronto: Prentice-Hall Canada, 1996), pp. 428–45. Reprinted by permission of the author.

284

relations. By itself, however, it tells us little about the diversity of political traditions *on* the prairies. What is needed is an interpretive analysis which comes to terms with intra-regional differences. Why is Manitoba the only prairie province where the Conservatives and Liberals have consistently won seats in provincial elections? Why has Saskatchewan been governed by the CCF-NDP for most of the past half-century? Why did Alberta spawn such a durable and unorthodox farmers' government (the UFA) then, overnight, become the bastion of an equally unorthodox Social Credit regime? A contemporary manifestation of contrasting provincial patterns was the 1993 federal election: the Reform party won 22 of Alberta's 26 seats, fewer ridings in Saskatchewan than either the Liberals or the NDP, and only a single constituency in Manitoba. Why the uneven performance?

Answers to these questions do not lie in an exploration of the east–west relationship. Nor do the answers lie in analyses which focus strictly on party systems or economic conditions. An economic analysis cannot explain why, in both the "free trade" elections of 1911 and 1988, Alberta overwhelmingly endorsed proponents and Manitoba embraced opponents. An analysis of party systems may be used to explain why, at the provincial level, Saskatchewan and Alberta rejected the two older parties in favour of third parties: the CCF and Social Credit. It will not explain, however, why these two third parties were at opposite poles of the Canadian political spectrum. Identifying and accounting for the differences among the three prairie provinces, therefore, is essential. But this too is insufficient because striking diversities are to be located not only among but also *within* the provinces. By the 1890s, for example, Manitoba had been remade in the image of western Ontario. Yet in 1919, Winnipeg exhibited a level of class consciousness and class conflict that was decidedly more reminiscent of the European than the North American scheme of things. In Saskatchewan, until 1945, the Liberal party was consistently stronger than in any other English-Canadian province. But it was this same province that returned North America's first social democratic government, a CCF government whose ideology was rooted in the British Labour party. Inconsistent political patterns seem no less profound in Alberta, where governing parties that are defeated at the polls have faded almost immediately.

The analysis employed here utilizes the concepts of ideology and ethnicity. Elements of Canadian toryism, liberalism, and socialism[1] have been present in varying proportions in each province. Representatives of these ideological tendencies on the prairies in their formative years include people as diverse as Rodmond Roblin, John Diefenbaker, Charles Dunning, John Dafoe, J.S. Woodsworth, Tommy Douglas, Henry Wise Wood, and William Aberhart, none of whom was born on the prairies. Because the prairie provinces and their societies were moulded in the late nineteenth and early twentieth centuries, this is not surprising. Ideas and ideologies first appeared on the prairies as importations.

It is very unlikely that a Rodmond Roblin or a Tommy Douglas, preaching what they did, could have become premiers of Alberta. William Aberhart would not likely have succeeded in Manitoba or Saskatchewan. Politicians are reflectors of their society, their environment, their times. They may be examined in terms which transcend quirks of personality. Their ideas and actions may be seen as reflections of the popular and ideological-cultural basis of their support.

The historical key to prairie politics is in the unravelling of the dynamic relationship between ideological-cultural heritage and party. In Manitoba, the imported nineteenth-century Ontario liberal party tradition (with "a tory touch") maintained political hegemony until the NDP's election in 1969. In Saskatchewan, the dominant tone of politics reflected a struggle between Ontario liberal and British socialist influences. In Alberta, American populist-liberal ideas gained widespread currency beginning in the very first decade of that province's existence. In all three provinces, minorities of non-Anglo-American origins, in their voting, helped make and break governments. These minorities, however, did not determine the ideological colouration of any major party.

Prairie political culture may be seen as the product of the interaction of four distinct waves of pioneering settlers. The first wave was a Canadian one. More precisely, it was largely rural Ontarian. This wave was a westward extension of English Canada's dominant charter group. Ontarians were a charter group in each prairie province but their impact was greatest in Manitoba. It seemed both fitting and telling that one of Manitoba's premiers (Hugh John Macdonald) was the son of Canada's first prime minister. Tory-touched Canadian liberalism was the ideological core of nineteenth-century Ontario and its prairie offshoot.

A second distinct wave in prairie settlement was a new, modern, British group. Coming near the turn of this century, it was largely urban and working class. Transformed and battered by nineteenth-century industrialism, Britain's working class had begun to turn to socialism. Despite the cultural and ideological differences between the Ontario and new-British waves, their social status in the west was roughly equal, both groups being British subjects and Anglo-Saxon pioneers in British North America. The new-British wave had its greatest impact in the cities, most powerfully in the then largest prairie city, Winnipeg. In Saskatchewan relatively large numbers of new British and European-born immigrants settled in rural areas; they produced Canada's most successful provincial social democratic party. It seemed both fitting and telling that Saskatchewan's premier in this labour-socialist tradition (Tommy Douglas) was British-born and grew up and was politically socialized in Winnipeg's new-British labour-socialist environment.

The third wave in prairie settlement was American. More specifically it was midwest, great plains American. Like the Ontario wave, but unlike the new-British wave, it came out of an agrarian setting with deeply rooted agrarian values and settled, in overwhelming numbers, in rural areas. American Anglo-Saxons became the only non-Canadian, non-British charter group on the prairies. The dominant ideological strain carried by the American wave was similar but not identical to that carried by the Ontarians. It was, to be sure, liberal, but its liberalism was devoid of toryism. It was a radical "populist" liberalism. It stressed the individual rather than the community or the state as a tory or socialist would. This wave's greatest impact was in rural Alberta, the continent's last agricultural frontier. Populist liberalism expressed itself in an unconventional farmers' movement/government known as the United Farmers of Alberta (UFA) and in the long tenure of Social Credit. It seemed both fitting and telling that this wave's leading representative figure (Henry Wise Wood) was a veteran Missouri populist known as "the uncrowned king of Alberta."

The fourth and last wave of prairie settlement consisted of continental Europeans. Because of their numerous national origins, they were the most diverse of the four waves. However, neither were they a charter group nor did they have a significant ideological impact (the eastern European influence in the Communist party being a minor exception). The non-Anglo-Saxons were "alien" and suspect in the eyes of the other three groups. At times their very presence was attacked and challenged; at best they were tolerated. The ideological and political role of the continental wave became largely one of deference. The continental wave had its greatest urban impact in Winnipeg and its greatest rural impact in Saskatchewan. These areas were also those in which the new-British wave had its greatest impact. The combined voting strength of these two waves was to lead to CCF-NDP victories in Saskatchewan and Manitoba in later years. The Old World ideological attributes of the continentals were dismissed as illegitimate. Thus, continentals deferred to the parties based on the other three groups, but the continentals represented the largest swing factor in voting of the four waves. They helped elect and defeat parties anchored by the other waves; they neither anchored nor led a major party.

The foregoing description of the four distinct waves of prairie settlers is not intended to imply that all Ontarians were tory-touched liberals, that all new Britons were labour-socialists, that all Americans were populist-liberals, or that all continentals deferred ideologically and politically. Furthermore, it should be understood that not all Ontarians voted for the Liberals and Conservatives, not all new Britons voted CCF, and not all Americans voted UFA-Social Credit. The contention here is simply that without the new-British impact the CCF would not have been created; similarly, without the American impact the UFA-Social Credit phenomenon in Alberta would not have been anything like what it was; and without the Ontarians, prairie Liberal and Conservative parties would not have gained early hegemony. The conceptual framework underlying this analysis is that Manitoba, Saskatchewan, and Alberta were most influenced in their formative years by the political cultures of early-twentieth-century Ontario, Britain, and the American midwest, respectively. What we have here is a bare and simple macrocosmic sketch of the ethnocultural and ideological bases of prairie politics in the first half of this century.

The evidence for the interpretation presented here is to be found in prairie historiography, but it is generally disregarded. The notion that Ontario, British, American, and continental European people and influences have helped shape prairie politics is not a new idea. But it might as well be, because it is an idea that has never been developed. There are ten excellent books in a series titled "Social Credit in Alberta: Its Background and Development." Not one of these books, however, devotes one paragraph to the American impact on Alberta, an impact unparalleled in Canada.

The impact of transplanted ideas was greater in Canada's west than in the United States because the physical impact of immigrants was greater. In 1914, for example, the year of greatest immigration to the U.S. in the decade, one immigrant arrived for every 80 in the population. In Canada, by contrast, one immigrant arrived for every eighteen in the population in 1913. The bulk of them, whether from Britain, continental Europe, or the United States, went west. Moreover, Canada's frontier experience was different from that of the U.S. South of the border, a soft frontier meant immigrants acculturating as settlement spread slowly westward. North of the border, a hard frontier meant getting off a boat and immediately boarding a transcontinental train. Immigrants and their ideas appeared more suddenly and in greater relative proportions on the Canadian prairies than in the American west.

Initially, Ontarians prevailed on the prairies. They occupied the best agricultural lands and secured homesteads along the new Canadian Pacific Railway. Their power was most profound in Manitoba, which, having entered Confederation in 1870, offered the most accessible frontier. The Ontarians were soon followed by waves of Britons, Americans, and continentals. The British came from the most urbanized industrial society in the world, but one that offered no rise in real wages between 1895 and 1913. More than a century of slowly developing working-class consciousness was represented by this new-British group. The American settlers, in contrast, came largely from the rural midwest. The Jeffersonian physiocratic notion that the soil was the sole source of wealth guided their thinking. Their interest in the Canadian frontier was fuelled by Canadian government propaganda which employed the agrarian ideal, the Horatio Alger tradition, and the log cabin stereotype, all prominent features of American liberal mythology. The continental immigrants were largely from eastern and central Europe, where land tenancy systems were in some cases only a half-century removed from feudalism. Of these three groups the Americans were the most likely and the British the least likely to homestead. Many Britons and continentals were to find their way into the new and growing prairie cities: Winnipeg, Regina, Calgary, and Edmonton.

In addition to differences in immigrant distribution among the provinces, there were differences within each province. Although there were equal numbers of Americans and Britons in Alberta, in the 1920s, for example, Americans outnumbered Britons in all fifteen of Alberta's rural census divisions, by a ratio of two to one. In a province where the rural MLAs prevailed this meant an extraordinary American political influence. In twelve of the fifteen rural census divisions in Alberta, Americans also outnumbered continental-born settlers. All three exceptions were in the northeast — the part of the province that provided the strongest rural opposition that both the American-influenced United Farmers of Alberta and Social Credit encountered.

In Saskatchewan, in the 1920s, Britons only slightly outnumbered Americans. The relative rural homogeneity of Saskatchewan, however, produced a dramatically different equation than in Alberta: the overwhelming majority of Britons settled in rural areas. Paradoxically, Saskatchewan had fewer Britons than either Alberta or Manitoba, but the Britons it did have penetrated rural Saskatchewan in a way that the Britons in neighbouring provinces did not. Furthermore, in Alberta the majority of American settlers were Anglo-Saxons; in Saskatchewan Anglo-Saxons were in a minority among Americans. This was important because a condition for political success was an Anglo-Saxon background. Because the largest number of Britons who entered Manitoba and Alberta headed for the cities, the ideology of labour-socialism in those provinces was systematically underrepresented by rurally weighted electoral maps.

The four distinct waves of immigrants differed in religion as well as political ideology. Methodists and other social gospellers had their greatest impact in places like Winnipeg, where the British-born labourist wave was particularly strong. Catholicism, brought over by many continental Europeans, was strongest in Saskatchewan and contributed to the Liberals' long hold on power there. Anglicans, with roots in both Ontario and Britain, reinforced Conservative tendencies in all three provinces. Many fundamentalists, representing an exceptionally high 20 percent of Alberta Protestants, came to that province as American Bible Belt populists.

Ethnic voting studies have not been able to provide a coherent interpretation of prairie politics because studying "ethnic" voting by listing "Anglo-Saxons" as against Germans, Ukrainians, and French, for instance, fails to appreciate that some "Anglo-Saxons" were from the "Red" Clyde of Glasgow, others from Perth County, Ontario, and still others from the populist state of Kansas. Different types of divisions existed of course within other ethnic groups. Between the 1920s and 1950s the key distinguishing features in Anglo-Saxon voting in Winnipeg were class status and birthplace. For example, in one part of Winnipeg represented almost continuously between the 1920s and 1980s by MPs J.S. Woodsworth and Stanley Knowles, large numbers of British-born, low-income residents voted overwhelmingly for the CCF. The city's highest-income Anglo-Saxon area with relatively fewer British-born, in contrast, voted overwhelmingly Liberal and Conservative. In both areas Canadian-born Anglo-Saxons far outnumbered other Anglo-Saxons. This revealed that second and third generations reflected inherited ideological-cultural traditions which continued to be expressed in party voting.

Although their demographic impact was great, continental immigrants did not play a leading role in early political developments. Rather, they yielded to the politics of the charter groups. Large numbers of them were isolated in rural ethnic colonies; many were in marginal farming areas where federal agents had directed them. In response to their new opportunity, and in their related effort to prove their loyalty to their new country, these minorities voted Liberal in Alberta from 1905 to 1921, and Liberal in Saskatchewan from 1905 to 1944. In Manitoba too the Liberals were the main beneficiaries of this vote, although occasionally, as in 1914, proof of loyalty expressed itself in a Conservative vote. Winnipeg was an exception to the rest of the prairies only in that its working-class continentals were sufficiently numerous, concentrated, and class-conscious to form a vibrant Communist party after 1920. The politics of deference, however, did little to raise the status of the European minorities. Racial prejudice against the continentals was widespread.

Ontarian influence seemed dominant in all three provinces until at least 1921. During World War I, for example, all three provincial premiers, their ministers of agriculture, and a majority of MLAs were Ontarians. In Manitoba the grit agrarianism of Ontario expressed itself in the selection of every premier from the 1880s until Ed Schreyer in 1969. Its distinct mark was reflected in the transplantation of the Ontario municipal system and in the School Question. In Saskatchewan this same, essentially Protestant and English grit, outlook dominated the Saskatchewan Grain Growers Association (SGGA), the province's federal and provincial Progressives, and the Liberal party. But in Saskatchewan, unlike Ontario and Manitoba, the dominance of this liberal grit tradition was dependent upon support from other elements in the population, specifically non-Anglo-Saxons, of which Saskatchewan had English Canada's highest percentage. Moreover, Saskatchewan's version of grit agrarianism was to encounter a powerful ideological competitor in the form of British-style socialism. The votes of the continentals helped elect a prairie version of the British Labour party in 1944.

American populist influences were greater in Saskatchewan than in Manitoba but they were secondary and not nearly as significant as in Alberta. In Alberta, the American-style populist farmers association (the UFA) determined the complexion of successive provincial governments for years. Alberta populism, like American populism, attracted some socialists, but it rejected socialist ideology. CCF socialism, embraced in Saskatchewan, was rejected by Alberta farmers on the peculiarly American grounds that it represented a repudiation of their "rugged individualism."

Manitoba: The Ontario of the Prairies

Manitoba was the province most true to the values of rural Ontario. In the language rights debates it was more Orange than Ontario. Manitoba imported its early American-inspired farm organizations—the Grange and the Patrons of Industry—only after they had become established in Ontario. Manitoba's Tory farmers rejected any suggestion of possible secession from Confederation and American annexation in the 1880s.

A good representative of Manitoba's tory-touched liberalism was Rodmond Roblin, premier from 1900 to 1915. His toryism was reflected in the debate over direct legislation, an idea brought to the prairies from the United States. Every political party on the prairies supported the proposal except Roblin's Conservatives in Manitoba. Roblin attacked direct legislation as "A Socialistic and Un-British Plan." This permitted him to appeal to a fundamentally liberal but tory-touched rural Manitoba. According to Sir Rodmond, direct legislation represented a form of "degenerate republicanism," much too strong a phrase to use successfully in Alberta, but not in Manitoba.

T.A. Crerar was a typical Ontarian in rural Manitoba. As a member of the dominant charter group on the prairies, Crerar became a spokesperson for the west but remained a product of the east. Between 1919 and 1922 he was offered the premierships of both

Ontario and Manitoba. Crerar's liberalism was expressed in his leadership of the Progressive party and as the architect of federal Liberal-Progressive rapprochement. He insisted that his party was not appealing to any specific class in society. Alberta's Henry Wise Wood, in contrast, insisted that it must make a class appeal to farmers by demanding occupational representation or what became known as "group government." Wood's approach was typical of the American left, wholly within the confines of monolithic American liberalism, defining class in liberal (equality of opportunity) rather than socialist (equality of condition) terms. Crerar's liberalism, closer to British liberalism, denied any connection with class politics. Crerar represented the tory-touched rural liberalism of Manitoba; Wood reflected the radical populist liberalism of Alberta.

Although Manitoba Liberal and Conservative governments relied on rural support from continental-born immigrants, few Europeans, of either British or continental origins, were to be found in the higher echelons of either of these parties. Nor were many to be found in the United Farmers of Manitoba (UFM). "Canadian Ukrainians do not have any influence," declared one Ukrainian paper in 1932, the year of the CCF's birth: "We are poor and need political help. Ukrainian farmers and workers depend for their livelihood on the more powerful. This forces us to support a politically influential party. Affiliation with small radical parties brings Ukrainians only discredit and ruin."[2] Such deference, however, did little for continental immigrants in the city. In the 1930s none of Winnipeg's banks, trust companies, or insurance firms would knowingly hire a Jew or anyone with a Ukrainian or Polish name. Nor would Anglo-Saxon premiers pick them for their cabinets.

Labour-socialist politics in Manitoba were as much determined by newly arrived Britons and Europeans as agrarian politics were determined by Ontarians. Winnipeg became the home of Canada's first Independent Labour party (ILP) and, by 1899, 27 separate unions appeared at the May Day parade. A year later, the editor of Winnipeg's labour newspaper, *The Voice*, was elected to the House of Commons. Within a decade the labour-socialist sectarianism of Europe was reproduced in Winnipeg. Two groups working outside of the dominant ILP influence were the Social Democratic party and the Socialist Party of Canada. By 1921 the two permanent parties that emerged were the British-led ILP and the continental-based Communist party. Every imprisoned 1919 strike leader, except one, came from Britain to Winnipeg between 1896 and 1912. So too did most of the ILP leadership. The Communists, on the other hand, drew their inspiration from the Russian Revolution and scientific socialism. A small and insignificant British minority, including One Big Unionist and strike leader R.B. Russell, stayed out of both camps. In Manitoba, as in Britain, labourism won over Marxism and syndicalism. By 1923, when the Ontario ILP was falling apart, the Manitoba ILP could boast that it held more than two dozen municipal and school board seats, the mayoralty of Winnipeg, and representation in both federal and provincial parliaments. This modern, turn-of-the-century British labourist tradition had its greatest Canadian urban impact in Winnipeg and Vancouver, an impact that accounts for the historical strength of the CCF-NDP in these cities.

Until at least 1945 much of the politics of the large Ukrainian community in Winnipeg was still tied to the Russian Revolution and its aftermath. Those against the Revolution supported the Liberals. The CCF, for many virulent anti-Communists, was a socialist step in a hated communist direction. Those supporting the Revolution embraced the Communist party. The CCF, for many Communist sympathizers, was a naive, liberal, social democratic, reformist gang. After World War II, however, ethnic assimilation contributed to strengthening the CCF-NDP position within both the former Liberal and Communist Ukrainian groups. An example of the shift from the CP to the NDP is the contrast between Jacob and Roland Penner, father and son. The former was for decades

Winnipeg's leading Communist, the latter became the NDP's Attorney General in 1981. The CP withered because the older continental-born generation died and the party lost its base. In contrast, the ideology of British labourism, in the form of the ILP-CCF, survived and took root. Other socialist traditions among British and continental immigrants either accommodated themselves to this dominant influence on the left or they generally faded as did the SPC and CP.

Liberal, Conservative, and Farmer governments dominated provincial politics. Winnipeg counted for little in the government's considerations, and centre and north Winnipeg, where the British and European-born had settled, counted for less. It was unpenalized neglect because the rurally biased electoral map ensured agrarian dominance. Between 1920 and 1949, for example, Winnipeg had only 10 seats in a 55 seat legislature. In the 1922 election, labour votes equalled those for 27 non-labour MLAs, but Labour won only 6 seats. In 1945 the CCF received as many votes as the Liberal-Progressives and almost double the Conservative total, but the CCF won only 10 seats to the Liberals' 24 and the Conservatives' 13.

Successive Manitoba governments reflected an alliance of Anglo-Saxons in the southwest wheat belt and in south Winnipeg. This alliance went under various labels at different times: Liberal, Conservative, United Farmers of Manitoba, Progressive, Liberal-Progressive, Brackenite, Coalition, and even Non-Partisan. What distinguished it from its main ideological opponent was class and heritage, not ethnicity. In 1919 the warring Strike Committee and Citizens Committee had one feature in common: Anglo-Saxon backgrounds. In working-class Winnipeg, the European minorities lined up behind the British-born Strike Committee because the Citizens Committee gave them little choice, condemning them as alien radicals. In rural Manitoba these minorities deferred to the established Canadian-born anti-strike forces.

These divisions were reflected in voting patterns. There seemed little basis for farmer–labour cooperation in Manitoba. They shared little in common. Labour issues, such as the eight-hour day, were ridiculed in the countryside. Every rural newspaper in Manitoba condemned the 1919 strike. Labour's attitude to Manitoba's farmers was equally suspicious; until 1927 UFM members were ineligible to join the ILP.

Manitoba's farm leaders went the way of Ontario's. Alberta's UFA, Saskatchewan's UFC (SS), and even Ontario's UFO affiliated with the federal CCF in 1932 (although the latter disaffiliated in 1934). The UFM, like its forerunners a half-century before, was true to the values of rural Ontario and remained aloof. In the late 1940s agrarian politics in Manitoba began to shift somewhat with the rise of the Manitoba Farmers Union (MFU). The MFU's membership came largely from more northerly, less prosperous, continental-born, and second-generation Canadian farmers. By the 1950s, ethnic interaction over the course of 40 years made possible the viability of such an organization. To the MFU leadership the Manitoba Federation of Agriculture, like its UFM predecessor, represented the wealthier, established, Anglo-Saxon, Liberal farmers. After John Diefenbaker and Conservative premier Duff Roblin left their respective leadership posts in 1967, the provincial NDP capitalized on gaining informal MFU support in certain rural areas. It was a breakthrough that helped the NDP win enough rural seats to form a government in 1969. For a combination of reasons, including the fact that he was the son-in-law of the first president of the MFU, Ed Schreyer was the only figure in the Manitoba NDP who could attract such support.

Manitoba was ripe for an NDP victory in 1969 in a way that Ontario was not. In Ontario the impact of Anglo-Saxon voters, most of them long established in Canada, was more powerful than in Manitoba. This is another way of pointing out that Ontario is ideologically older than Manitoba in its conservatism, particularly in the rural areas, but in the cities too. There was a significant new-British labourist impact in Ontario (for example, Toronto mayor Jimmie Simpson in the 1930s) but, because of Ontario's relative age, it was not as profound as it was further west.

Manitoba had enough of Ontario in it to have sustained the only provincial Conservative party west of Ontario that has never collapsed. But it also had enough of modern Britain and continental Europe to provide CCF member J.S. Woodsworth and provincial Communist leader Bill Kardash with parliamentary seats between the 1920s and 1950s. Manitoba also had enough of the prairies in it to produce national and provincial Progressive parties in the 1920s. Their Ontario-born liberal leadership, however, led both of them back to the Liberal party.

Saskatchewan: British Labourism on the Prairies

As in Manitoba, provincial politics in Saskatchewan initially meant transplanting Ontarian politics. The provincial Liberal government operated at the pleasure of the Saskatchewan Grain Growers Association, the dominant political and economic organization in the province. Both the Liberals and the SGGA were led by the same figures and most of them had Ontario roots. The Progressive debacle in Ottawa, however, and the inability of the SGGA to break with the Liberals fuelled the formation of a rival agrarian organization: the Farmers Union of Canada. It was founded and first led by L.B. McNamee, a former British railway worker and trade unionist. This difference between the SGGA's Ontarian leadership and the Farmers Union British leadership broadly represented the difference between Ontario liberal and British socialist influences. The division became a central feature of Saskatchewan politics.

The success of the Farmers Union led to the formation of the United Farmers of Canada (Saskatchewan Section or SS) and that, in turn, led directly to the Farmer-Labour party, led by British socialists and Canadians sympathetic to socialism. It then took three elections and ten years, from 1934 to 1944, to catapult this party to power under a CCF label. This became possible because enough continental-origin voters transferred their preferences from the Liberals to the CCF.

Liberalism at first seemed unbeatable in Saskatchewan. Although it came later than in Manitoba, the Ontario impact was the first in Saskatchewan and it was, as in Manitoba, generally Liberal. While the national, Manitoba, and Alberta Liberal parties were rejected in the early 1920s, the Saskatchewan Liberals carried on. All six of Saskatchewan's daily newspapers supported them. A key factor for the Liberals in Saskatchewan was the province's large numbers of Catholics and eastern and central Europeans. In the European rural districts the provincial Liberals reaped the rewards of the federal government's immigration program.

In Saskatchewan, however, unlike Manitoba and Alberta, there was a significant new-British *rural* presence. Although Saskatchewan attracted fewer Britons than either Manitoba or Alberta, it had almost as many British-born farm operators as the other two provinces combined. This British influence, coming later than the Ontario influx, took a longer time to assert itself. The farmer–labour connection in the Farmers Union was unique among prairie farm organizations of any significant size. Much of its support came from farmers in continental-based areas, areas that switched from the Liberals to the CCF between 1934 and 1944. The SGGA, like the neighbouring UFM and UFA, had largely ignored the non-Anglo-Saxon farmers and had little following in areas settled by Europeans. All three organizations were rooted in the oldest and most established areas.

The United Farmers of Canada (Saskatchewan Section or SS), a product of a merger of the growing Farmers Union and the declining SGGA in the mid-1920s, was socialist in a way that no other Canadian farm organization had ever been. That socialism, like Saskatchewan's early made-in-Ontario liberalism, was imported. The two most important permanent officials of the new UFS (SS) were former members of the British Labour party and the Socialist Party of the United States. The UFC (SS)'s socialist, British, labourist, and agrarian heritages could be summed up by isolating two planks in its 1930 platform: "Abolition of the competitive system and substitution of a cooperative system of manufacturing, transportation, and distribution," and "Free trade with the mother country." The UFC (SS) endorsed a land nationalization scheme patterned on the British Labour Party's rural program. It also forged a political alliance with the Saskatchewan Independent Labour party. Formed in the late 1920s, the ILP was largely composed of teachers, some unionists, and British socialists. It was modelled on the successful Manitoba ILP. When the UFC (SS) and the ILP came together in 1932 they formed the Farmer-Labour party and elected a British-born Fabian, M.J. Coldwell, as their leader.

A contributing factor to the rise of socialism in Saskatchewan was that the cooperative movement was stronger there than in any other province. Moreover, Saskatchewan's cooperators were more socialist than their provincial neighbours. The cooperative movement became an integral part of the CCF's constituency in Saskatchewan and the movement's growth was aided by a provincial government branch headed by a British immigrant and veteran of the British cooperative movement. This "British" link reappears often in Saskatchewan history.

The story of the CCF's success in Saskatchewan need not involve, as most sources do, a discussion of the Depression. When the Farmer-Labour (CCF) party ran in 1934 it was largely an unknown entity in politically cautious and deferential continental-origin areas. It had to contend, moreover, with the Catholic Church. Catholic opposition to the CCF was important in Saskatchewan because it was the most Catholic of the prairie provinces. A papal encyclical and a 1934 statement by the Archbishop of Regina attacking socialism as contrary to the Catholic faith aided the Liberals. The Liberals swept both the Ontario-anchored regions and the continental, particularly Catholic, areas. Voting among Anglo-Saxons was divided, however, between areas that were largely Ontarian in origin and areas that contained large numbers of British-born. In both the 1934 and 1938 elections, cultural rather than economic factors provided the clues to unravelling the voting patterns.

The CCF succeeded because it was British-led and ideologically British-based. The CCF's Britishness, its cultural acceptability, made it difficult to attack as alien. Its cultural legitimacy made it politically acceptable. It could therefore become an alternative to the Liberals for Saskatchewan's continental-origin citizens. Even more than in Manitoba, continental-origin citizens represented a large potential swing factor in voting. This helps explain why the CCF-NDP's success in Saskatchewan came a quarter century before it did in Manitoba and why it was more profound in terms of votes and seats. The large rural British presence, combined with a large rural continental presence relative to Manitoba and Alberta, made it easier for continental-origin citizens in Saskatchewan to attach themselves to the CCF. This was further facilitated in 1943 when the Catholic barrier to CCF aspirations was lowered: the Church declared its support for the cooperative movement, expressed concern respecting social welfare, and told its members they were free to vote for any party that was not communist. The CCF victory in 1944, therefore, was no surprise.

The surge in CCF support in 1944 was most dramatic in the previously Liberal, continental-origin areas. Many CCF rural leaders were of non-Anglo-Saxon origins, a dramatic contrast to the overwhelming Anglo-Saxon character of the Liberal and Conservative leaders. The swing among continentals from the Liberals to the CCF was no less pronounced in urban areas. Between 1934 and 1944, for example, support for the CCF rose 218 percent in the most European part of Regina.

American influences in Saskatchewan were secondary to the Ontario and British influences. In contrast to Alberta, however, the Americans in Saskatchewan tended to help the fortunes of British-led anti-Liberal organizations such as the Farmers Union and the CCF. In Saskatchewan, unlike Alberta, the majority of Americans were non-Anglo-Saxons. Moreover, few of them in Saskatchewan had English as a mother tongue. Among these European-Americans in Saskatchewan were large numbers — larger than in Alberta — of Scandinavians. European and American Scandinavians in Saskatchewan were much more receptive to socialism than Anglo-Saxon Americans — the majority American group in Alberta. Therefore, European-Americans, such as Scandinavians, encountered a powerful, legitimate, and culturally acceptable ideological ally in Saskatchewan in the form of the British-influenced CCF. In Alberta, in contrast to Saskatchewan, there were both fewer British farmers and fewer European-Americans. British labour-socialism was not a leading ideological force in rural Alberta as it was in Saskatchewan. In Alberta, European-Americans represented a minority among Americans in rural areas. They had no corresponding powerful rural British labour-socialist strain to attach themselves to. Thus, in Alberta, there never arose a socialist agrarian rival to the UFA as there did to the SGGA in the form of the Farmers Union.

The connection between British birth and labour-socialist politics has been demonstrated in Manitoba. It was also reflected, as late as 1942, in Alberta, where four of five CCF provincial executive members were British-born, and in British Columbia, where nine of the fourteen CCF MLAs were British-born. In Saskatchewan, in slight contrast, there were four Americans yet only three Britons among the eleven-member British-led CCF caucus at this date. Some of the Americans elected as CCF MLAs in 1944 had voted for Socialist Eugene Debs in the United States. In the United States, as the Socialist party withered, socialist supporters of European origins on the American great plains returned to the established American parties. In Saskatchewan, by contrast, as the socialist-farmer-labour movement grew, American socialist sympathizers of European ancestry, not overwhelmed by American liberalism as they were in the U.S., had alternatives not restricted to the established parties.

In the late 1950s Saskatchewan produced another political phenomenon, John Diefenbaker, who made it possible for the Conservatives to become a national party for the first time since 1935. In the 1940s, Manitoba preferred the Liberals, Saskatchewan the CCF, and Alberta Social Credit. Diefenbaker, unlike other national leaders, was neither Anglo-Saxon nor was he identified with central Canadian financiers. This made it possible for European-origin farmers to flock, for the first time, to the Conservative banner. Ethnic interaction and the passing of earlier prejudices no longer crippled the Conservatives in Saskatchewan's European-origin areas. At the same time, Diefenbaker's toryism and commitment to agricultural interests made him equally acceptable to rural, Anglo-Saxon, prairie farmers. They recognized him as an established, Ontario-born Canadian and not as a European, naturalized one. Diefenbaker's populist image, another side of this phenomenon, helped him in Alberta, where agrarian populism, as in the United States, eased its way into agribusiness. The prairies could therefore embrace the federal Conservative party after the 1950s because it was a qualitatively different party under Diefenbaker than it had been under Arthur Meighen, R.B. Bennett, John Bracken, and George Drew.

Seymour Lipset's *Agrarian Socialism* is something of a misnomer in reference to Saskatchewan. The Saskatchewan CCF-NDP consistently fared better in cities than in the countryside. More precisely, it had been a case of British-style socialism succeeding in an unexpected agricultural setting. M.J. Coldwell, Tommy Douglas, Woodrow Lloyd, and Allan Blakeney were never farmers. Nor was British-born and longtime Toronto MP Andrew Brewin, who drafted Saskatchewan's "showpiece" labour legislation in the 1940s. Saskatchewan did produce one British-born non-socialist premier: Charles Dunning. But he represented an older part of Canada's British heritage. Dunning succeeded as easily in Prince Edward Island, which he went on to represent as finance minister in Mackenzie King's cabinet. The only part of the Maritimes that would have sent a Tommy Douglas to Ottawa was Cape Breton, because it had been subject to the same type of new-British influx as Saskatchewan. This connection between British-birth and socialist inclinations was revealed in the 1970s, when Douglas represented Nanaimo (British Columbia) as an MP. In the 1920s, Nanaimo was the most British city in Canada, almost half its residents having been born in the British Isles. The British labourist-socialist connection became, paradoxically, most successful in Canada's most agrarian province.

By the late 1970s, the Liberals disappeared from the Saskatchewan legislature for the first time. Liberals defected in droves to the Conservatives, who went from 2 percent of the vote in 1971 to 54 percent in 1982. This represented no ideological realignment; the Conservatives, who became free-enterprising liberals indistinguishable from the Liberals, merely replaced the latter as the preferred anti-socialist standard-bearer in Saskatchewan's bipolar political system. The provincial Conservatives, moreover, had been remade and recast, calling themselves populists and opening their membership so that they were no longer an anathema to the ethnic minorities. Saskatchewan's Liberals, like their Manitoba and Alberta cousins, suffered from their identification with the federal Trudeau Liberals with the result that there was only one elected provincial Liberal in all of Western Canada in the late 1970s. More than ever, the Saskatchewan NDP appeared as an unmistakable urban party. As such it lost power in the 1980s, its rural weakness being a major but only temporary impediment to its success. The return to office of the NDP in 1991 and the election of more NDP MPs from the province than from the rest of Canada in 1993 reconfirmed Saskatchewan as the party's strongest outpost.

Alberta: The American Midwest on the Prairies

The politics of rural Alberta were as much influenced by the values of the American great plains as the politics of rural Manitoba were influenced by the standards of rural Ontario. In Alberta the various cultural waves, from Ontario, Britain, continental Europe, and the United States, came closest to arriving simultaneously. Early Ontario settlers in rural Alberta, as in Saskatchewan, encountered another ideological strain. It was not, however, a socialist challenge as it had been in Saskatchewan. It was, rather, a more militant, more radical, less tory form of petit-bourgeois liberalism than was the Canadian norm. It was not so much a challenge as a reinforcement, a radicalization, of the natural liberalism of transplanted Ontarians. There seemed little need, as there had been in Saskatchewan, for two rival agrarian organizations or for an ideologically distinct opposition party. The older parties simply reoriented themselves. The Liberals and Conservatives became competitors vying for support from the American-influenced UFA. An MP remarked in the House of Commons that Alberta, "from the border northward to Edmonton, might be regarded as a typical American state."

American populism pervaded Alberta politics. Many Canadian- and British-born settlers, to be sure, were found in the vanguard of the agrarian movement. But Americans and American ideas played an influential role in Alberta that was unparalleled in Canada. An early example in the UFA was that both sides in the debate over whether or not to enter electoral politics argued their cases with references to experiences south of the border, one side referring to the sad end of the People's party and the other side pointing to the Non-Partisan League's success in North Dakota.

When Social Credit came to power in 1935 there was no significant shift of ideological allegiance in rural Alberta. UFA members had been nurtured on inflationary monetary theories in the United States and at UFA conventions throughout the 1920s. The overwhelming majority of UFA members found socialism alien and voted for a technocratic, "pragmatic" remedy in Social Credit. It was a response with American (Free Silver, Greenbackism), not Canadian, antecedents. Social Credit had much in common with American monetary reform schemes like the Townsend Plan, which, in 1936, claimed over three million adherents. Although the Social Credit label originated in Britain, Alberta's version of Social Credit had stronger material links to the United States. In Britain, Social Credit's appeal was strongest among the Catholic, the urban, and the cosmopolitan. In Alberta, in contrast, Social Credit was viewed most suspiciously in Catholic areas and was most popular in the rural and Protestant, particularly American fundamentalist, areas.

The American influence in rural Alberta expressed itself in many ways. More than one in five Alberta residents at one point was American-born, while the national ratio was less than one in 25. Canadian branches of the American Society of Equity, containing large numbers of transplanted Nebraskans and Dakotans, were the core of the UFA when it was formed in 1909, and about one-half of the directors on the UFA's board were American-born, outnumbering both British- and Canadian-born.

In sharp contrast to T.A. Crerar and Manitoba's farmers, Henry Wise Wood and the UFA's break with the Liberals was final and complete. The division between the UFA brand of third-party populism and the Manitoba brand of third-party parliamentarism, one longing for a reconciliation with the Liberals, came at the founding convention of the national Progressives in 1920. Wood intended that the UFA govern Alberta with no reference to the older parties. This never happened in Ontario-anchored Manitoba. This difference meant that the Liberal party was doomed in Alberta. In Ontario, Manitoba, and Saskatchewan — in contrast to Alberta — most of the federal Progressives who had been elected to replace Liberals became Liberals.

American-style populism prevailed in Alberta because a heavily rurally oriented electoral map, like Manitoba's, meant agrarian dominance. The new-British labour-socialist impact in Calgary and Edmonton was insufficient to offset American populist-liberal dominance in the rural areas. Although one-third of Calgary was British-born and although Calgary served as the site of the founding conventions of both the OBU and the CCF, as well as being the constituency of Labour MP William Irvine, Calgary was in the largely rural province of Alberta and was thus also subject to an American impact: it became the headquarters of the Society of Equity, the Non-Partisan League, the UFA, prairie evangelism, and Social Credit, all of which had American roots. In 1993 it elected Preston Manning, William Aberhart's godson.

Alberta's preoccupation with monetary theories was a result of the American influence. Low agricultural prices in the United States led American farmers to fight for the free coinage of silver and an inflation in the money supply. When J.W. Leedy, the former populist governor of Kansas, and U.S. credit expert George Bevington and many other Americans emigrated to Alberta, they brought along their monetary theories. Throughout the 1920s and 1930s, UFA conventions became debating forums for the monetary theorists. The monetary issue was second to none. In Manitoba and Saskatchewan, in contrast, it was rarely debated. When C.H. Douglas's Social Credit theories appeared, they had much in common with notions already present in the UFA. The UFA contributed to this link by distributing Douglas's books throughout the 1920s. Social Credit, therefore, could be regarded as a supplement rather than as an alternative to UFA thinking.

Wood's retirement from the UFA presidency led to a crystallization of the majority and minority positions in the UFA. The American-influenced majority was occupied with monetary reform; a British-influenced minority was more interested in socialist efforts at the national level. Both positions gained recognition at the 1931 UFA convention: Bevington's annual inflationary money resolutions were endorsed, and British-born, socialist-leaning Robert Gardiner became the new UFA president. Gardiner led his federal Ginger Group caucus into an even closer working arrangement with J.S. Woodsworth's Labour group. When the UFA's federal leadership in 1932 took the UFA into the CCF, Gardiner's caucus in Ottawa became isolated from the majority sentiment in rural Alberta. Neither Wood, nor UFA Premier Brownlee, nor his cabinet ever endorsed the "farmer-labour-socialist" alliance as the CCF described itself.

Social Credit was the political heir of the American-influenced monetary reform wing of the UFA. Aberhart succeeded only because the monetary reformers in the UFA had tilled the soil so well for him. It was the UFA, he continually reminded his audiences, that had introduced Social Credit thinking into Alberta. By 1935 UFA locals throughout the province were clamouring for some form of Social Credit. During the election campaign Social Credit was really not a partisan issue: few dared attack it. It became, rather, an assumption. Even the Liberals promised to implement Social Credit theory, and the Alberta Federation of Labour indicated enthusiasm for its ideas as well. Aberhart's Social Credit message was consistent with Alberta's populist history. The American monetary reformers had done their work well. Social Credit's sweeping victory in 1935 was therefore no surprise. Had Social Credit not appeared, another party would have arisen preaching much the same gospel.

American analogies are logical in Alberta. There is something to the argument that Aberhart comes closest among Canada's premiers to looking and sounding like a radical, populist, American governor. Many of his supporters referred to him as Alberta's Abraham Lincoln. Preston Manning was repeatedly compared in the 1990s to Ross Perot. But no one could compare prairie CCF leaders such as Douglas, Coldwell, or Woodsworth to American populists. One could identify them with a Norman Thomas but, to be more accurate, one would have to look to a Briton like Ramsay MacDonald, Labour's first prime minister.

Alberta's voting patterns may be related directly to the patterns of settlement and to the ideological-cultural heritages of the settlers. Initial Ontario settlers in the south, particularly those who came before 1896 and settled along the CPR line, voted for the party of the railroad, the federal Conservatives. The early-twentieth-century American influx altered this. The American impact was most pronounced in southern and eastern Alberta, an area representing the key to political power in the province just as the southwest represented that key in Manitoba. The southern, American-settled parts of Alberta which were most favourable to prohibition in 1915 became the most favourable to the UFA from 1921 to 1935, to Social Credit from 1935 to the early 1970s, and to the Reform party in the 1980s and 1990s.

Continental-origin and French-Canadian voters in northern Alberta represented a Liberal electoral base for the same reasons as in Saskatchewan and Manitoba: the Liberals were the party of immigrants and Catholics. The UFA, in contrast, was overwhelmingly Anglo-Saxon, composed of Canadian-, American-, and a sprinkling of British-born farmers. UFA and Social Credit majorities were produced by an electoral map which ensured that the party that swept the south was the party that won elections. UFA and Social Credit voter support was never as strong in the continental and French-Canadian north as in the Ontario and American south. These patterns reflected how much the UFA and Social Credit had in common with each other and how little either had in common with the CCF.

The new-British labour-socialist element in Alberta was largely isolated in the urban centres. Consequently, the CCF floundered. The British-anchored provincial CCF never managed to win more than two seats in Alberta. Significantly, both CCF MLAs in the 1950s were from the north and were second-generation Ukrainians, as were large numbers of their constituents. These northeastern areas were among the very few where, in the 1920s, continental-born farmers outnumbered American-born ones. The CCF success here confirmed the shift, although in a much less dramatic fashion than in Saskatchewan, from the Liberals to the CCF among non-Anglo-Saxons of continental, particularly eastern European, origin. In Saskatchewan, large numbers of rural continentals had swung their votes to support the party of large numbers of rural Britons, the CCF. In Alberta, however, there were both fewer continentals and fewer rural Britons. Thus, the CCF was a relatively minor force in Alberta's rural areas.

Manifestations of American and fundamentalist Christian influences in Alberta abound. One example of a republican liberal tendency was the Alberta government's refusal in 1938 to appear before the Royal Commission on Dominion–Provincial Relations, addressing its comments instead to "the Sovereign People of Canada." Parliamentary government was described as a form of state dictatorship. Another example was the complaint of a Nebraska-born MLA who called the caucus form of government undemocratic and criticized the Speech from the Throne for making more of the 1937 coronation festivities than of Social Credit. Could such a sentiment respecting the coronation have been expressed at Queen's Park or in any other English-Canadian provincial legislature? Preston Manning's constitutional and political reform proposals — on the Senate, on deleting group rights and adding property rights to the Charter, on free votes for MPs, and on referendums — are all modelled on American arrangements. Solon Low, Alberta's treasurer and then the national Social Credit leader in the 1950s, was the son of Mormon immigrants from Utah. In the 1980s, the Western Canada Concept elected Gordon Kessler, an MLA in the constituency of the departing Social Credit leader and a graduate of Utah's Brigham Young University. That Kessler, Low, Aberhart, Ernest and Preston Manning have all been fundamentalist Christians sets Alberta apart from the Canadian norm and is a stark contrast to Manitoba's NDP cabinet in the 1970s, which contained four Unitarians.

Conclusion

Although prairie politics continue to be tied to prairie history, the passage of time has brought changes. In 1994, the only Conservative governments in the land were both on the prairies. Once the anti-immigrant party, the Conservatives refashioned themselves and succeeded among many of the grandchildren of the ethnic pioneers. The politics of deference on the part of the ethnic minorities are no longer practised or anticipated. The European-origin minorities became established economically, culturally, and politically. By the 1970s, for example, Jews served as leaders of Manitoba's Conservative and Liberal parties and as the provincial chief justice. When the latter retired, he was replaced by a Franco-Manitoban. This would have been inconceivable in the 1950s, and unlikely in the 1960s. Slavs made up one-third of Howard Pawley's first NDP government and were present, in increasing numbers in influential positions, in the administrations of all three provinces. One served as the Governor General and, for the first time ever, the 1990s featured three prairie premiers none of whom are of Anglo-Saxon origins.

European ethnic minorities are in the mainstream, rather than at the periphery, of prairie politics. Their increasingly active role was fostered by their integration, acculturation, and assimilation. Urbanization and mobility, as well as changes in laws, education, and values, have also played a role. "Multiculturalism" became part of the national constitutional fabric with all the parties courting minorities rather than excluding them from active participation. The British or Anglo-Saxon charter group, moreover, decreased in relative numbers, making up just over a third of the populations of Manitoba and Saskatchewan in the 1980s. Today they are underrepresented in the provincial legislatures.

Today's new ethnic minorities include diverse groups of Asians and Natives who are not as numerous or established as the European-origin minorities. Nevertheless, today they too have relatively easy access to the political system, contesting and winning ridings for all the major parties. Today, unlike the 1920s, it is Ontario and not the prairies that is home to most new immigrants. A prairie population that was once more than 40 percent foreign-born is now overwhelmingly Canadian-born and socialized. In Alberta today more are fluent in Chinese than in Ukrainian, more born in Asia than in Britain, and for every two American immigrants, there is one from Africa. In Manitoba more people speak Punjabi than either Yiddish or Icelandic. In Saskatchewan there are now many more clerical and service employees than farmers.

Ideological differences among the parties continue to be reflected symbolically and in pubic policy agendas. Although parties of different stripes may behave similarly once in office, provincial differences in nuance, style, and substance persist. Manitoba Conservative Sterling Lyon, for example, exhibited a trace of toryism in objecting in 1980 to a revised constitution that entrenched individual rights at the expense of parliamentary sovereignty. Conservative Peter Lougheed, in contrast, offered historically more populist and liberal Alberta a referendum bill in 1980 that could be used to settle constitutional as well as non-constitutional matters. Allan Blakeney's career as a civil servant and then as a socialist politician in Saskatchewan reflected the NDP's ideological concern with building a professional civil service, one sensitive to social democratic values. Thus, under NDP tutelage, an experienced band of central planners and bureaucrats has moved easily from province to province within and outside the prairies as NDP governments have come and gone.

Projecting the past into the future is perilous because society, and thus political culture, is ever-changing, however slowly. Nevertheless, continuities, however frayed, may be discerned. Manitoba, Saskatchewan, and Alberta continue to exhibit distinctive patterns in provincial party politics and federal voting behaviour. Manitoba's Conservative regime, currently opposed by a fading NDP and resurgent Liberals, is cautious and conservative. It projects constancy and stability in a province where the Conservatives were also in office when this century began. Federally, Manitoba voted for the Liberals in 1993, consistent with its Ontarian traditions. Saskatchewan may prove to be the home of English North America's first and last social democratic government in this century. The British Labourist model for its early years is increasingly less relevant in terms of both personnel and policies as time creeps on. In Alberta, brash assaults by Ralph Klein, the new Conservative premier, on the welfare state are consistent with that province's populist and right-wing liberal (what is now commonly called "neoconservative") predilections.

The social democratic impulse on the prairies is now in retreat. This is evidenced by the NDP's obliteration in Alberta's 1993 election after its modest but steady gains in the 1980s. That it came less than two years after the Saskatchewan NDP's return to office reminds us of how different the political traditions of these geographically adjacent provinces remain.

In Manitoba the two historically social democratic ridings in north central Winnipeg have, for the first time since the 1910s, left the fold in two successive federal elections. This represents a fundamental structural decline for the NDP. Whether Reform can expand beyond its solid regional base, as Social Credit failed to do, remains to be seen. That its support, however strong or weak, will continue to be more robust in Alberta than in Manitoba will yet again confirm the differing cultural legacies of these two provinces.

NOTES

1. See Gad Horowitz, "Conservatism, Liberalism, and Socialism in Canada: An Interpretation," *Canadian Journal of Economics and Political Science* 32, 2 (May 1966).
2. Canadian Farmer, Winnipeg, June 8, 1952. Quoted in Thomas Peterson, "Manitoba: Ethnic and Class Politics," in *Canadian Provincial Politics*, ed. Martin Robin (Scarborough: Prentice-Hall, 1978), 84.

Article Twenty-One

The Origins of the Maritime Rights Movement

E.R. Forbes

Canadian historians have devoted considerable attention to postwar agitation on the Prairies: they have virtually ignored similar agitation in the Maritimes, the regional protest movement which became known by the slogan "Maritime Rights." The few comments it has received, in biographical literature or in sweeping analyses of long periods of history, have been largely concerned with its political manifestations.[1] Such a preoccupation is not surprising. Both Liberals and Conservatives were vociferous in their efforts to portray themselves as the champions of the movement. Shortly before the Antigonish-Guysborough by-election of 1927 a Protestant clergyman set out to review the issues of the campaign from the pulpit. Both candidates, he noted, were clamouring for attention as the defenders of "Maritime Rights." This aspect of their campaign, he said, reminded him of the behaviour of his own young children one evening when he and his wife were getting ready to go visiting. The little girl set up an awful howl from the moment the babysitter arrived. She bawled and bawled. Finally, just as her parents were going out the door, her brother turned, slapped her sharply, and declared, "Shut up, I wanna cry."

There was much more to "Maritime Rights" than the conspicuous wail of the politicians. One cannot begin to tell here the story of the movement—the intensive organizational campaign with its delegations to Ottawa, economic conferences, and country-wide speaking tours; the erratic swings in the popular vote from one party to another as Maritimers searched desperately for solutions to their problems; and the inevitable royal commissions sent in to defuse the agitation[2]—but one can at least attempt a more basic introduction through the analysis of the motives of the different social groups which

Source: E.R. Forbes, "The Origins of the Maritime Rights Movement," *Acadiensis*, v. 1 (Autumn 1975): 55–66. Reprinted by permission.

participated in it. Their behaviour suggests that the issues involved went much deeper than mere political manoeuvring or even, as Professor G.A. Rawlyk has suggested, the attempt by the local "Establishment" to undercut other forms of social protest.[3] All classes in the region, although often in conflict on other issues, were united in their support of Maritime Rights. Each was aware that its own particular aspirations were incapable of realization until the region's declining influence was checked or reversed.

The social categories employed here will be those used by the people themselves. Maritimers spoke frequently in this period of their "classes." They were not referring to any clear Marxian structure nor did they imply the status-based stratification of the modern sociologist. Essentially they were talking about broad occupational interest groups. Such divisions were partly theoretical: the members of each group or "class" were assumed to have interests in common of which not all might be conscious. But they also had an empirical basis through such exclusively occupational organizations as the Maritime Division of the Canadian Manufacturers Association, retail merchants' associations, the United Farmers, federations of labour, and, by the end of the decade, the Maritime Fishermen's Union. These were the kinds of groupings to which New Brunswick Premier P.J. Veniot referred early in 1923 when he reported to Mackenzie King that, after looking "carefully into the [Maritime Rights] movement," he had found it was "purely non-political and embraces [the] efforts of all classes to obtain what is sincerely considered fair play for [the] Maritime Provinces."[4]

The development of Maritime regionalism, of which the Maritime Rights movement formed the climax, took place largely in the first two decades of the century. Previously, popular loyalties had been focused on larger imperial or national entities or on smaller political, cultural, or geographical units. The shift was dictated by a growing realization of the need for cooperation. Cooperation was essential if the three Atlantic provinces were to counteract the eclipse of their influence which resulted from the rise of the West and the growing metropolitan dominance of Central Canada. Another factor contributing to the growth of regionalism was the progressive ideology of the period, which increased the pressure upon the small governments for expensive reforms while at the same time suggesting the possibility of limitless achievement through a strategy of unity, organization, and agitation. Consequently, regional awareness increased sharply in the three provinces. Their leaders joined forces to fight losses in representation, which followed every census after 1891; to increase their subsidies, which had fallen far behind those of the Prairies; and to defend the Intercolonial Railway, whose pro-Maritime policies came under attack from both the Prairies and Central Canada.[5]

The manufacturers' stake in the regionalization of the Maritimes was most obvious, particularly for the defence of the Intercolonial Railway. By the end of the nineteenth century that railway had become an important agent of industrialization in the region. Its management had accepted the principle that half a loaf was better than none and had reduced rates to develop traffic. It created a basic freight rate structure which was between 20 and 50 percent lower than that in force in Ontario and offered in addition special rate concessions based upon "what the traffic would bear."[6] Built into the structure was a system of "arbitraries" or especially low rates between the Maritimes and Montreal on goods destined for points further west. These rates enabled the secondary manufacturers in the Maritimes to penetrate markets in Western and Central Canada to obtain the sales volume necessary for competitive production.[7] With such encouragement, capital investment in manufacturing in the Maritimes quadrupled between 1900 and 1920.[8] The old dream of some Nova Scotian entrepreneurs that their province would play the role of a great industrial metropolis to a Canadian hinterland was far from realization. But the Maritimers' optimism for their manufacturing potential persisted. The Halifax *Morning Chronicle* in 1906 explicitly touted Nova Scotia's pioneer program in technical education as encouraging the industrialization which would reverse the region's declining status in Confederation. The Saint John *Standard* in 1916 enthused about a hydroelectric project to harness the Bay of Fundy tides, which, by providing cheaper energy for manufacturing, would raise the Maritimes "to a position of commercial supremacy as compared with any other part of the Dominion."[9]

Such aspirations received a severe check with the integration of the Intercolonial into a national system. The happy partnership between the Intercolonial management and the local producers had come under attack both from competing Central Canadian manufacturers and Prairie farmers preoccupied with their demand for the equalization of freight rates.[10] The Borden government apparently decided to get rid of the anomaly of a Maritime-oriented railway once and for all. In November 1918, it shifted the Intercolonial's headquarters to Toronto, transferred its senior officials to other lines, and replaced them with appointees from the Canadian Northern. The following year, the Intercolonial was placed under the de facto jurisdiction of the Board of Railway Commissioners, which raised the rates to the Ontario level.[11] The process was completed in time to provide an inflated base for the 40 percent general rate increase of 1920. In Ontario and Quebec freight rates increased 111 percent between 1916 and September 1920; in the Maritimes basic rates rose between 140 and 216 percent and the simultaneous cancellation of special rates, such as the special commodity rate on sugar, led to still greater increases.[12]

The rate changes not only threatened the local entrepreneurs' dreams of industrial grandeur, but left them seriously exposed to the pressure for metropolitan consolidation. For many, the campaign for Maritime Rights became a struggle for survival. In 1919 a group of manufacturers mounted a delegation to Ottawa, demanded the restoration of the Intercolonial to independent management, and revived the Maritime Board of Trade as a channel for their agitation.[13] They continued to play a prominent role in the leadership of the movement through such representatives as W.S. Fisher of Saint John, a former Canadian Manufacturers Association president, who served as a spokesman for another delegation to Ottawa in 1921, and D.R. Turnbull, managing-director of the Acadia Sugar Corporation, who, in 1925, became Nova Scotia's representative on the newly formed Maritime Rights Transportation Committee.[14]

Maritime merchants were also seriously affected by the integration of the Intercolonial into a national system. The wholesalers were injured by the shift in supply purchasing for the railway from the Maritimes to Toronto.[15] They were weakened further, in relation to their metropolitan competitors, by the sharp increase in "town distributing rates" — especially low rates which had enabled them to import quantities of goods from Central Canada, break them up, and send them out to individual towns and villages at little more than the cost of direct shipment. Similarly higher rates on the Intercolonial accelerated the shift away from Maritime ports as distributing points for products entering from abroad. H.R. Silver, a commission merchant, reported a decline in molasses shipments out of Halifax from 130 carloads in 1916 to 17 in 1921.[16] Retailers were also adversely affected. They had to pay more for their goods and had difficulty in passing the full charge on to their customers. The Halifax *Maritime Merchant* commented tersely in 1920 upon the general effect of the increase: "Added to the handicap already suffered by firms seeking western business, the new rate will be hard on the merchants and add materially to the cost the local consumer must pay."[17]

The issue which generated the greatest heat from the merchant and commercial interests of Halifax and Saint John was the development of their ports as entrepôts for Canada's winter trade. The two cities were engaged in a Darwinian struggle with the American seaports and with each other. The key to victory was volume and variety of traffic. The more traffic, the lower the port charges and ocean rates; the lower the rates, the greater the traffic. The Maritime ports were most conscious of their rivalry with Portland, Maine, which had traditionally enjoyed the advantage of a very active canvass for trade from the Grand Trunk Railway.[18] The Maritime ports' aspirations for Canadian trade, aroused initially by Confederation, had blossomed under the "national policy" of the Laurier government. Laurier had promised that the National Transcontinental Railway would channel exports, particularly grain, through national ports. In 1903, he appointed a royal commission to investigate other means of routing trade through "all-Canadian channels," and in 1911, he pledged that his government would restrict the Imperial preference to goods entering through Canadian ports.[19]

Such expectations were rudely shaken by the federal takeover of the Grand Trunk. With it, the Canadian government inherited a strong vested interest in the commercial success of Portland. At Halifax, prominent Liberals urged the return of a Conservative cabinet minister in the by-election of 1920 to give the Maritimes at least a voice in defending their port's interest.[20] Early in 1922 the Halifax and Saint John boards of trade appointed a joint committee, consisting largely of merchants and manufacturers, to coordinate their agitation on such issues as the restoration of the Intercolonial and the routing of trade through Maritime ports.[21] The merchants' position in the Maritime Rights movement continued to be a prominent one through the organized activities of boards of trade and the role of individuals such as W.A. Black, of the leading merchant-shipping firm of Pickford and Black. At 76 years of age, against "his physicians' advice, his wife's fears and his family's opposition," Black came out of retirement to fight the Halifax by-election of 1923 on a platform of Maritime Rights.[22]

Another business group, the lumbermen, also joined the agitation. For them, the impact of the increased freight charges was compounded in 1921 by increased American duty on timber products under the Fordney tariff. Angus MacLean of The Bathurst Company, later president of the New Brunswick Lumberman's Association, appealed to Mackenzie King for relief on both issues.[23] When none was forthcoming he and other so-called "Lumber lords" of New Brunswick, such as Archie and Donald Fraser, owners of the second-largest lumber company in the Maritimes, threw their very considerable support behind the Conservative "Maritime Rights" candidates in the federal election of 1925.[24] In that year, MacLean became the titular leader of the protest movement as president of the Maritime Board of Trade.

Although labour in the Maritimes was at the peak of its "class" consciousness in 1919, it joined with the business groups in the agitation. Between 1916 and 1920, reported union membership in the Maritimes had quadrupled to about 40 000.[25] Spurred by the anticipation of a "new era" to follow the war[26] and beset by the grim reality of galloping inflation,[27] the workers attempted new techniques in organization and challenged their employers in a series of strikes in 1919 and 1920. At the same time they were conscious that their aspirations for a greater share of the fruits of their labour could not be achieved if their industries were destroyed from other causes. Early in 1919 the *Eastern Federationist*, published by the Trades and Labour Council of Pictou County, argued that the freight rate increases violated the "rights of the Maritime Provinces' people under the terms of Confederation."[28] After the Amherst "General Strike" in May and June of 1919, the *Federationist* was particularly incensed by reports that the Canada Car Company was planning to transfer its Amherst operation to Montreal. The thrust of the editor's bitterness was directed at both the capitalists involved and the trend toward metropolitan consolidation, which posed a continual threat to Maritime industry and jobs.[29] Similarly the Halifax *Citizen*, the organ of the local Trades and Labour Council, severely criticized the removal of the railway headquarters from Moncton and commended the activities of the Maritime Board of Trade president, Hance J. Logan, in seeking Maritime union as a counterweight to the declining political influence of the region. Bemoaning the unfair treatment accorded the Maritimes by the rest of the country, the *Citizen* concluded that there was "very little hope of any justice for us under present conditions."[30] The journal periodically returned to this theme and remained a consistent supporter of Maritime Rights.

The Railway Brotherhoods, which, after the United Mineworkers, constituted the largest bloc of organized labour in the region, were directly involved in the Maritime Rights campaign. During the first decade of the century the brotherhoods had won the acceptance of the principle of seniority in promotions and layoffs on the Intercolonial.[31] In theory at least, the humblest employee could aspire to the highest office on the road. Under the new regime after 1918, that principle went by the board. According to one estimate, 400 employees were transferred out of the Moncton headquarters and any replacements came from other government roads. In addition, the repair shops declined and staff was reduced all along the line. To some workers it seemed the principle of seniority had been replaced by the principle that no Maritimer need apply.[32]

Labour did not need to be coaxed into the Maritime Rights movement by the Halifax *Herald* or other politically oriented journals in the 1920s; large segments were already there, drawn by a consideration of their own immediate interest. The railway centres provided the most consistent voting support for Maritime Rights candidates throughout the 1920s. F.B. McCurdy attributed his victory in the important Colchester by-election of 1920 to the railway workers' belief that in the cabinet he would "be strong enough to afford some relief in the railway grievance." He blamed his defeat in the general election of 1921 on his inability to do so.[33] Labour also threw its support behind W.A. Black in the Halifax by-election of 1923.[34] Neil Herman, labour organizer, Social Gospel clergyman, and some-time editor of the Halifax *Citizen*, was a founder and executive member of the Halifax Maritime Club.[35] He later accompanied its president, H.S. Congdon, in a tour of Central Canada to drum up newspaper support for the movement. When the so-called "Great" Maritime Rights delegation went to Ottawa in February 1925, J.E. Tighe, president of the Saint John local of the International Longshoreman's Association, was one of four speakers who addressed the members of Parliament on Maritime problems.[36]

The farmers were only slightly behind labour in their support for Maritime Rights. They too had expected to play a greater role in the new society which was supposed to follow the war; instead they were confronted by the realities of rural depopulation and community disintegration.[37] They challenged the business groups with new or intensified political, occupational, and economic organization. But their problems were in part those of the region. The new freight rates hit them, both as producers and consumers. Some were also angered by federal policies which seemed not only to encourage new immigrants to bypass their region but also to promote westward migration at their expense. As much as they might resent the growth of industrial towns and their own relative loss in status, the farmers were conscious of their dependence on these towns for their markets. Even those who sold their apples or potatoes in Great Britain or the West Indies usually earned a significant proportion of their income in local markets—an important hedge against the sometimes widely fluctuating international prices.[38]

For a brief period the farmers' regional concern was obscured by their participation in what they believed was a national "class" movement. But their organizations, such as the Canadian Council of Agriculture, were dominated by the Prairies. Manitobans

T.A. Crerar and George Chipman also sought to direct the movement in the Maritimes through the *United Farmers' Guide*. The *Guide*, theoretically the organ of the New Brunswick and Nova Scotia United Farmers Associations, was in fact a subsidiary of the *Grain Growers' Guide*.[39] The two regionalisms were soon in conflict. Western organizers tried in vain to get unequivocal statements against the tariff from the United Farmers of Nova Scotia and were cool to suggestions that "necessary" protection for local industries should be retained.[40] At the same time, they offered no support for the Maritime positions on such issues as the Intercolonial, freight rates, and subsidies. Most Maritime farmers realized they could not achieve their regional goals through a movement which was, in federal politics at least, "an agrarian and sectional bloc from the continental West, the representation of the monolithic wheat economy."[41] In 1921 support for the western-affiliated United Farmers Associations rapidly dwindled. By mid-summer "a majority" in the Maritime Co-operative Companies was reported anxious to dispose of the *United Farmers Guide* in which they had initially invested but were unable to control.[42]

The agricultural interests of Prince Edward Island had been involved in the Maritime Rights movement from the outset. At the Maritime Board of Trade meeting in 1919 they were happy to associate with the broader issues of the movement their own special problems. These were two: the need for a second car ferry and the completion of the widening of their narrow-gauge railways to permit a more rapid, reliable, and cheaper delivery of their products to mainland markets.[43] In 1921 the mainland farmers met in conference with representatives of manufacturing, merchant, and shipping groups to launch a delegation to Ottawa to demand the return of the Intercolonial to independent management.[44] Thereafter, farm leaders assumed an increasingly important role in the Maritime Rights agitation. In 1923, for example, A.E. McMahon, president of the United Fruit Companies and a former vice-president of the United Farmers of Nova Scotia, became president of the Maritime Board of Trade, and, a year later, of the Maritime Development Association. One of the primary purposes of the latter organization was the rehabilitation of the rural areas through immigration and colonization.[45]

The fishermen's contribution to the Maritime Rights movement was largely restricted to the intensification of the discontent which underlay it. Their aspirations had been relatively moderate. The victims of a declining salt fish trade with the West Indies, they hoped to restore their industry through the expansion of their sales of fresh fish in Central Canada and New England. The former had been encouraged by a federal subsidy of one-third of the express rate to Montreal on less than carload lots, the latter by a *modus vivendi* with the United States which had permitted them to land and sell their catches directly at American ports.[46] In 1919, the federal subsidies on fresh fish were terminated just as the trade was hit by the higher freight rates.[47] Needless to say, the fish merchants passed on their losses to the largely unorganized fishermen. Meanwhile, the door to the New England market was slammed shut by the American cancellation of the *modus vivendi* and the introduction of the Fordney tariff.

In the election of 1921, some fishermen seem to have accepted the Liberal promises of reciprocity to restore the American markets.[48] When this failed to materialize, their desperate plight led many (for example, the Yarmouth halibut fleet) to pack up and move to the United States.[49] Those who remained formed one group in Maritime society which seemed genuinely prepared to contemplate secession in their frantic search for markets. It was surely no coincidence that both Howard Corning, who proposed the famous secession resolution of 1923, and the lawyer Robert Blauveldt, self-proclaimed secessionist and Maritime Rights publicist,[50] were residents of Yarmouth county.

The role of professional classes in the Maritime Rights movement was prominent, but their motivation ambiguous. It is often difficult to discern whether lawyers, doctors, clergymen, academics, and journalists were speaking for themselves or for the other groups in society by whom they were directly or indirectly employed. Certainly they played an important function in articulating and rationalizing the aspirations of the other groups. This role was explicit in some cases. The Nova Scotia government retained H.F. Munro of Dalhousie University to aid in the preparation of its submission to the Duncan Commission. The boards of trade hired freight rate experts, professional organizers, and lawyers to prepare, publicize, and help present their cases before the federal government and its various commissions. Significant also was the relationship between Maritime Rights journalists and the interests who paid their salaries, or patronized their newspapers through advertising and subscriptions. The lumberman-industrialist Angus MacLean, for example, was reportedly "the principal owner" of the Saint John *Telegraph Journal*.[51] That paper in 1925 promoted the cross-country speaking-tours of president J.D. McKenna and editor A.B. Belding as part of its campaign for Maritime Rights. Similarly C.W. Lunn, who was credited with the initial popularization of the defence of the Intercolonial as guaranteed under the "compact of confederation," aspired to a labour readership and was even hired for a brief period to write for the *Eastern Federationist*.[52] More tenuous but still significant was the relationship between clergymen and the congregations which they represented. It is clear, for example, that the priests who protested the Duncan Commission's failure to help the fishermen were acting as agents for the fishermen in their parishes. Their intervention resulted in the Royal Commission investigation of the fisheries in 1928.[53]

In articulating the progressive reform ideology, which provided an important element in the developing Maritime regionalism, the professionals' motivation was also ambiguous. As various American scholars have pointed out, "progressivism," with its optimism, social criticism, and focus on government as an agent of reform, might be inspired by many and mixed motives.[54] To farmers, labour, and their representatives, "progressivism" could be the desire to improve the lot of the weak and exploited, namely themselves. On the part of the business-oriented it might be concern for efficiency, the replacement of old-fashioned party structures, and the development of a more dynamic role by government which might more effectively serve the interests of the entrepreneur. To the professionals, besides any humanitarian concern, "progressivism" might mean an improved status or an expansion of their role in society in social work, health services, or the government bureaucracy.

In the Maritimes, the clergy and academics were most prominent in articulating the various strains of an amorphous progressive ideology. The clergy, imbued with the social gospel, promoted a variety of reforms ranging from prohibition to widows' pensions and occasionally engaged in wholesale attacks on the capitalist system.[55] Academics used a more secular terminology but they too championed a wide range of reforms for the welfare of the community. Dr. F.H. Sexton hailed Nova Scotia's program of technical education — he happened to be its superintendent — as a valuable means of "social service" in improving the lot of the miners and industrial workers.[56] That it was also a service for local industry went without saying. Dr. Melville Cummings of the Truro Agricultural College and Rev. Hugh MacPherson of Saint Francis Xavier University displayed a similar zeal for agricultural education and farmers' cooperatives as the means of rural regeneration. President George B. Cutten of Acadia University, having failed to persuade governments to undertake the hydroelectric development of the Bay of Fundy, organized the Cape Split Development Company in an attempt to interest private capital in the scheme.[57]

All these progressive proposals placed strong pressure on provincial governments to inaugurate or expand programs for which revenue was not readily available. This fact led progressive elements into an ephemeral campaign for Maritime union, which was expected to provide a more efficient use of available resources,[58] and into a more substantive campaign for Maritime unity, one object of which was to wrest from the federal government a "fair" share of Dominion revenues.

Increased federal subsidies were sought, for example, by professionals concerned about the declining quality of instruction in the schools as higher salaries drew experienced teachers westward. But, since fiscal need had never been accepted as a justification for higher subsidies, Maritime governments developed the claim that they were entitled to monetary compensation for grants of land from the public domain — grants such as had been given to Ontario, Manitoba, and Quebec in the boundary settlements of 1912. They also demanded subsidies in lieu of the increasingly lucrative "school lands" funds held in trust by the federal government for the Prairie provinces. The Maritime Educational Convention at Moncton in 1918 and a Catholic educational conference at Antigonish a year later both discussed the subsidy claims as a matter vital to educational reform.[59] In the latter year the Conservative Halifax *Herald* enthusiastically endorsed a Liberal resolution which outlined the Maritime claims in the Nova Scotian legislature. The "serious material injustice" inflicted upon the Maritimes through "the unfair distribution which has been made of federal assets by successive governments" had, according to the *Herald*, starved local government services or supplied them "in such a niggardly manner that progress is almost impossible." The *Herald* advocated the launching of "a concerted movement and [sic] properly directed activity. *We suggest that a maritime popular league should be forthwith organized, with provincial and county and town and village branches in all parts of the Maritime provinces, until the whole country has been enlightened, aroused and arrayed in a support of the resolution unanimously adopted by the Nova Scotia legislature.*"[60] Although as their problems increased, Maritimers sought more fundamental solutions, the subsidy claims remained one of the basic components of the campaign for Maritime rights.

The Maritime Rights agitation which had emerged by 1919 was a regional protest movement which saw all classes united in their demands on the rest of the country. This did not mean that different classes did not have distinct aspirations of their own; on the contrary, they were probably more conscious of them in 1919 than in any other period before or since. Each held a dream of progressive development in which its own collective interests were directly involved: for the manufacturers, their growth as the major industrial suppliers of the country; for the urban merchants, the final attainment of their communities' status as the entrepôts of Canada's trade; for labour and farmers, the emergence of a new, more democratic society in which they would break the economic and political dominance of the business classes; for the fishermen, the chance to rehabilitate their industry through the new fresh fish trade; and for the professionals, the elevation of Maritime society through education. But none of these aspirations was capable of realization with the continued decline of the economic and political status of the Maritimes in the Dominion. Just as electricity might channel the usually conflicting molecular energies of an iron bar to produce a magnetic force, so the federal government's adverse policies served to realign the various "classes" in the Maritimes to produce a powerful social force — regionalism. This force, dressed up in a variety of complex rationalizations, became the Maritime Rights movement of the 1920s.

NOTES

1. See J.M. Beck, *The Government of Nova Scotia* (Toronto, 1957), 338–40; W.R. Graham, *Arthur Meighen*, vol. 2, *And Fortune Fled* (Toronto, 1963), ch. 11; H.B. Neatby, *William Lyon Mackenzie King: 1924–1932; The Lonely Heights* (Toronto, 1963), 67 and 220–24; K.A. MacKirdy, "Regionalism: Canada and Australia" (Ph.D. thesis, University of Toronto, 1959), 245–50; and G.A. Rawlyk, "The Maritimes and the Canadian Community," in *Regionalism in the Canadian Community, 1867–1967*, ed. M. Wade (Toronto, 1969), 113–15. The only previous study which focused directly on Maritime Rights was Michael Hatfield, "J.B. Baxter and the Maritime Rights Movement" (B.A. honours essay, Mount Allison University, 1969).
2. E.R. Forbes, "The Maritime Rights Movement, 1919–1927: A Study in Canadian Regionalism" (Ph.D. thesis, Queen's University, 1975).
3. G.A. Rawlyk, "The Farmer–Labour Movement and the Failure of Socialism in Nova Scotia," in *Essays on the Left*, ed. Laurier LaPierre et al. (Toronto, 1971), 37–38.
4. P.J. Veniot to W.L.M. King, 27 February 1923, W.L.M. King Papers, Public Archives of Canada (hereafter PAC).
5. See Canada, *Sessional Papers* (1910), no. 100; Halifax *Wesleyan*, 12 May 1909; Saint John *Standard*, 30 October 1913; W. Eggleston and C.T. Kraft, *Dominion Provincial Subsidies and Grants* (Ottawa, 1939), 188–89; and the "Presentation to His Royal Highness in Council of the claims of the Provinces of New Brunswick, Nova Scotia and Prince Edward Island, for Compensation in Respect of the Public Lands of Canada, transferred to Certain Provinces of Canada or held in trust for their Benefit, January 29, 1913," R.L. Borden Papers, p. 5249, PAC.
6. R.A.C. Henry and Associates, *Railway Freight Rates in Canada* (Ottawa, 1939), 266 and 268, and Transcripts of the hearings of the Royal Commission on Maritime Claims, 462–65, Atlantic Provinces Transportation Commission (hereafter APTC).
7. See S.A. Saunders, *The Economic History of the Maritime Provinces* (Ottawa, 1939), 27.
8. *Canada Year Book* (1922–23), 220, 415–16.
9. Halifax *Morning Chronicle*, 17 August 1906, and Saint John *Standard*, 25 March 1916.
10. Judgement of the Board of Railway Commissioners, 15 March 1919, R.L. Borden Papers, pp. 131067–9, PAC; Canada, *Debates* (1917), 787, 4339–77.
11. Transcript of hearings of the Board of Railway Commissioners [BRC], 1920, p. 11703, PAC.
12. Calculated from percentages in BRC transcripts 1926, p. 6602, and from "standard mileage rates" in R.A.C. Henry, *Railway Freight Rates*.
13. *The Busy East of Canada* (Sackville), September 1919.
14. "Report of Meeting with the Prime Minister and the members of the Government, Delegation from the Maritime Province," 1 June 1921, R.B. Bennett Papers, p. 10142, PAC, and F.C. Cornell to H.D. Cartwright, 12 October 1925, Maritime Provinces Freight Rate Commission Papers, APTC.
15. E.M. Macdonald to Mackenzie King, 8 December 1922, W.L.M. King Papers, PAC.
16. F.C. Cornell, "Memorandum re the Transportation Problems and Freight Rate Structure of the Province of Nova Scotia," 1926, p. 10, and Transcripts, BRC, 1926, pp. 6765–67, PAC.
17. *Maritime Merchant*, 16 September 1920, p. 104.
18. Transcripts, Royal Commission on Maritime Claims, p. 2173, APTC.
19. "Report of the Royal Commission on Transportation . . . 1903," Canada, *Sessional Papers* (1906), no. 19a; Canada, *Debates* (1922), 708–10.
20. Halifax *Herald*, 18 September 1920.
21. Minutes of the Council of the Saint John Board of Trade, 13 July 1922, New Brunswick Museum.
22. Hector McInnes to Arthur Meighen, November 1923, Arthur Meighen Papers, p. 051956, PAC.
23. A. MacLean to W.L.M. King, 25 April 1922 and 8 October 1924, W.L.M. King Papers, PAC.
24. J.C. Webster to Arthur Meighen, 26 September 1925, and R. O'Leary to Meighen, 3 September 1925, Arthur Meighen Papers, PAC.

25. *The Fifth Annual Report on Labour Organization in Canada, 1916* (Ottawa, 1917), 206–207, and the *Tenth Annual Report on Labour Organization in Canada, 1920* (Ottawa, 1921), 279.
26. For examples of their optimistic rhetoric, see the Sydney *Canadian Labour Leader*, 8 February 1918; the New Glasgow *Eastern Federationist*, 19, 26 April 1919; and the Moncton *Union Worker*, February 1920.
27. *Labour Gazette*, January 1921, p. 117.
28. *Eastern Federationist*, 8 March 1919.
29. *Eastern Federationist*, 7 June 1919.
30. Halifax *Citizen*, 21 May and 10 September 1920.
31. "Being an address by Mr. Geo. W. Yates, Assistant Deputy Minister of Railways, Before the History and Political Science Club of Western Ontario, Feb. 16, 1923," Arthur Meighen Papers, pp. 157485-9, PAC.
32. *The Busy East*, June and July 1923.
33. F.B. McCurdy to Robert Borden, 21 December 1921, Robert Meighen Papers, PAC.
34. H.L. Stewart to W.L.M. King, 9 December 1923, W.L.M. King Papers, PAC.
35. "Minutes of the Maritime Club of Halifax," 11 February 1924, H.S. Congdon Papers (courtesy of Mr. H.H. Congdon, Huntsville, Ontario).
36. Saint John *Telegraph Journal*, 27 February 1925.
37. See A.A. Mackenzie, "The Rise and Fall of the Farmer–Labour Party in Nova Scotia" (M.A. thesis, Dalhousie University, 1969), and L.A. Wood, *A History of Farmer Movements in Canada* (Toronto, 1924).
38. *Proceedings of the Select Special Committee of the House of Commons to inquire into Agricultural Conditions* (Ottawa, 1924), 475.
39. Three of the five members of the directorate were Manitobans. C.F. Chipman to "The Editor," *Maritime Farmer*, 13 March 1920, T.A. Crerar Papers, The Douglas Library, Queen's University.
40. J.M. Pratt to T.A. Crerar, 9 November 1920, and G.G. Archibald to T.A. Crerar, 4 October 1920, T.A. Crerar Papers, The Douglas Library, Queen's University.
41. W.L. Morton, *The Progressive Party in Canada* (Toronto, 1950), 129.
42. S.H. Hagerman to G.F. Chipman, 18 June 1921, T.A. Crerar Papers, Douglas Library, Queen's University.
43. *The Busy East*, September 1919. See also M.K. Cullen, "The Transportation Issue, 1873–1973," in *Canada's Smallest Province: A History of Prince Edward Island*, ed. F.W.P. Bolger (Charlottetown, 1973), 255–57.
44. *The Busy East*, May 1921.
45. Charlottetown *Evening Patriot*, 23 January 1925.
46. *Report of the Royal Commission Investigating the Fisheries of the Maritime Provinces and the Magdalen Islands* (Ottawa, 1928), 32, 61–65.
47. "Fifty-third Annual Report of the Fisheries Branch . . . 1919," *Sessional Papers* (1919), no. 44, p. 11.
48. G.B. Kenny reported to Hector MacInnes after a trip along the Eastern Shore that the Liberal candidates had "actually got many people to believe that real free trade with the U.S. is in sight." 21 November 1921, Hector MacInnes Papers (courtesy of Donald MacInnes, Halifax, N.S.).
49. Transcripts of the hearings of the Royal Commission Investigating the Fisheries . . . 1928, p. 3476, APTC.
50. R. Blauveldt to H.S. Congdon, 30 September 1924, H.S. Congdon Papers.
51. J.H. McGaffigan to Arthur Meighen, 28 February 1924, Arthur Meighen Papers, PAC.
52. See Halifax *Morning Chronicle*, 16 November 1921; C.W. Lunn to H.S. Congdon, 13 April 1929, H.S. Congdon Papers.
53. Transcripts, Royal Commission to investigate the Fisheries . . . 1927, p. 6.
54. See, for example, R.H. Wiebe, *The Search for Order, 1877–1920* (New York, 1967); Gabriel Kolko, *The Triumph of Conservatism* (New York, 1963); and D.W. Noble, *The Progressive Mind, 1890–1917* (Chicago, 1970).

55. See E.R. Forbes, "Prohibition and the Social Gospel in Nova Scotia," *Acadiensis* 1, 1 (Autumn 1971): 15–19, and his review of Richard Allen, *The Social Passion*, in *Acadiensis* 2, 1 (Autumn 1972): 98.
56. Halifax *Daily Echo*, 24 May 1913.
57. *Industrial Canada*, August 1918.
58. See J.M. Beck, *The History of Maritime Union: A Study in Frustration*, 31–44.
59. O.T. Daniels, *The Claims of the Maritime Provinces for Federal Subsidies in Lieu of Western Lands* (Halifax, 1918) and *Proceedings of the Second Annual Educational Conference, Antigonish* (1919).
60. Halifax *Herald*, 10 May 1919.

Article Twenty-Two

Canadian Unemployment Policy in the 1930s

James Struthers

I

One of the problems of discussing unemployment during the Great Depression is the danger of becoming overcome by a sense of déjà vu. Today unemployment officially stands at over 12 percent of the workforce; perhaps as many as 2 000 000 Canadians are without work and according to the Economic Council of Canada the jobless total is unlikely to drop below 10 percent until 1987. Yet despite these appalling figures, our government, as in the 1930s, tells us it cannot act to create jobs because its first priority must be to reduce the deficit in order to restore business confidence.

Although the arguments behind today's economic policies are certainly different from those of the 1930s, many of the essential moral homilies remain unchanged. Canadians in the 1980s, like their parents and grandparents of the 1930s, are being told they can't expect to hope for recovery without practising severe restraint, self-discipline, hard work, and much tightening of belts. Despite these frightening parallels, however, we haven't yet been surrounded by soup kitchens, relief camps, food vouchers, bankrupt provincial governments, and trainloads of hungry single men "riding the rods" in search of work or relief. Yet all these sights and problems were characteristic of the failure of governments to respond to unemployment during the 1930s. Why this was so I will attempt to explain in this paper.

To a large extent the unemployment policies pursued by R.B. Bennett and Mackenzie King in the 1930s were continuations of approaches and attitudes toward joblessness that had been widespread in Canada before 1930. Canadians had become well acquainted with cyclical unemployment — or trade depressions as they were then called — well before the "dirty thirties." The 1870s, the early 1890s, and the years 1907–08, 1913–15, and 1920–25, were all periods of heavy unemployment in this country. From this perspective it is best to

Source: *Windy Pine Occasional Paper no. 1*, Canadian Studies Program, Trent University, 1984. Reprinted by permission.

think of the Great Depression as simply the most intense and long-lasting of a series of "waves" of unemployment which battered all western industrial economies during the last half of the nineteenth and first third of the twentieth centuries.

Because of our climate we were also quite familiar with seasonal unemployment. Canada is infamous for being an "eight months country." Each winter tens of thousands of Canadians working in the country's great outdoors industries—construction, agriculture, forestry, fishing, and transportation—routinely lost their jobs, often for up to six months of the year, due to bad weather. Even in the boom years of the so-called "roaring twenties" (1926–29), winter unemployment rates averaged well over 10 percent of the workforce. So the sight of hungry, jobless men walking the streets in search of work or relief was quite familiar to most urban-dwellers in Canada.

Why, then, did the Great Depression take us so much by surprise? Why, for example, didn't Canada follow Great Britain's lead in 1911 by devising new institutions and policies, such as a national system of unemployment insurance and a state employment service, to cope with the problem of joblessness? There were a number of reasons for our unpreparedness but three were particularly important. In the first place, seasonal unemployment was predictable. Winter was a fact of Canadian life; therefore, newspapers, politicians, businessmen, and others argued that workingmen should save up enough money during the summer to tide themselves and their families over the winter. Moreover, it was simply assumed (without any evidence) that wages for seasonal labour were high enough to allow them to do so. To provide the seasonally unemployed with relief, it was argued, would discourage habits of thrift, frugality, and self-reliance.

As for cyclical unemployment, attitudes toward this problem were shaped by two factors. First, recovery in the past had always occurred eventually. The market did correct itself. Therefore, all a country could do was to "tough it out" by practising restraint and doing nothing to discourage business confidence, especially on the part of foreign investors. Second, Canada was a New World society with a developing farm frontier. It was also a country which, in the three decades before 1930, had become increasingly preoccupied with rural depopulation. And it was a country in which farmers were still politically powerful and were continually complaining about the shortage of farm help at affordable wages. For these reasons, legislation such as unemployment insurance, which might be appropriate in more crowded, congested, and highly urbanized societies such as Great Britain, was deemed by business and farm leaders to be inappropriate for Canada. There was always work for the unemployed, even if only for room and board and little more, they argued, on the nation's farms during the winter. If life in the city was made too easy through doles and unemployment insurance for the idle, might not even more men and women be encouraged to leave the land altogether?

Finally, working-class political pressure, in the form of strong trade unions and labour parties, was extremely weak in Canada before World War II. Farmers and businessmen, on the other hand, were politically powerful. Hence governments responded to their views on the unemployment question and not to the views of those who were most likely to become unemployed.

As a result of these attitudes, Canadian governments, although well acquainted with unemployment before 1930, were hopelessly ill-equipped for dealing with it. No one kept unemployment statistics; there was no efficient state employment service; no public welfare departments existed at the federal or provincial level and there were only four at the municipal level. In all of Canada before 1930 there were less than 400 trained social workers. Relief, where available, was granted by private religious charities or by nineteenth-century poor law "Houses of Industry," both of which operated at the local level. In

Toronto as late as 1932, jobless men still had to line up at the local House of Industry, first built in the 1830s, to get a bag of groceries or a basket of coal and were expected to saw wood or break rocks in exchange for this miserly relief. Moreover, with the brief exception of the years 1920–21, when the threat of unemployed World War I veterans loomed large throughout Canada, provincial governments along with Ottawa denied any responsibility for coming to the aid of the jobless. Public relief where given was an exclusively local matter financed solely out of local taxes, chiefly on property. One of the sad ironies of the "dirty thirties" was that although no other country, except perhaps the United States, was more economically devastated by the Great Depression than Canada, no other country was as ill-prepared for dealing with its consequences. On the eve of 1930 we lacked even the bare bones of a permanent welfare structure for relieving those in need.

II

The origins of Canadian unemployment policy in the depression lie within the 1930 federal election. On the one hand, Mackenzie King went into the election—at a time when unemployment was about 12 percent—denying that there was a jobless problem and bragging that he would not give a "five cent piece" to any Tory provincial government for unemployment relief. King also claimed that the whole idea of an unemployment crisis was simply a Conservative pre-election plot.

Bennett, on the other hand, made what from our perspective today seem like recklessly extravagant promises. He claimed he would "end unemployment," "abolish the dole," and provide "work and wages for all who wanted it." Not surprisingly, Bennett won the election, largely on the strength of his promises to do something about the unemployment crisis.

Despite the boldness of his rhetoric, however (which reflected his egotism, arrogance, and over-confidence in his own abilities), Bennett really had very traditional ideas about how to deal with unemployment. Like King, he believed the problem in 1930 was largely a seasonal and temporary phenomenon which would quickly right itself. Unlike King, Bennett, as a good Tory, also believed that sharply boosting the protective tariff would stimulate investor confidence, create jobs by reducing reliance on imports, and ultimately force other nations to lower their trading barriers against Canadian exports. It was through these tariff hikes that Bennett hoped to "end unemployment."

But these hikes would take time to produce results. Since Bennett had promised to provide jobs immediately, he also introduced a $20 000 000 emergency relief act in the summer of 1930 to tide people over what was expected to be a difficult winter. Sixteen million dollars was to be spent on public works, and, most significantly, the projects were to be administered by local and provincial governments who together were expected to contribute 75 percent of their cost. Unemployment relief, Bennett insisted like King before him, was primarily a local responsibility. Ottawa's help was on a temporary, emergency basis only, and would last only until the effects of his tariff hike were felt.

Through providing money for relief projects such as provincial road-building, Bennett also hoped to deal with another pressing problem. Transient, unemployed single men, largely immigrants, were trapped in Canadian cities because the lumber, construction, and agricultural industries which normally drew them out of cities were closed down. Such men, cut off from family ties, coming from different cultural backgrounds, and with nothing to lose, were considered to be a serious menace to law and order. Bennett's relief projects would draw them out of the cities and put money into their pockets for the winter months ahead.

Between the fall of 1930, when he first took office, and the spring of 1932, Bennett adhered to this policy of using public works or relief works, as they were called, to fight unemployment. Indeed, throughout the fiscal year 1931–32 his government spent almost $50 000 000, or more than twice as much as it had the previous year, on this approach. Nevertheless, by the spring of 1932 unemployment stood above 20 percent of the workforce and the federal deficit was over $151 000 000, almost half of total government revenue for that year. As a result, Bennett quickly became disillusioned with public works as a means of relieving unemployment.

In the first place, he had used this approach only as a temporary stopgap expedient. Neither he nor anyone in his government were believers in Keynesian deficit-spending as a way out of depression; therefore there was no expectation that public employment could be used in itself as a recovery strategy. Moreover, by 1932 it had become obvious that the depression was more than a "temporary" problem. Second, by 1932, local and provincial governments, especially in the west, could no longer afford to pay their 75 percent share of the cost of these increasingly expensive relief works and Bennett had no intention of assuming a larger share of the cost. Finally, Bennett and Canadian businessmen were increasingly alarmed at the size of the federal deficit and the level of taxation which in themselves appeared to be a threat to investor confidence, and hence a barrier to recovery.

For all these reasons, then, Bennett reversed his unemployment policy in the spring of 1932, virtually abandoning reliance on public works, and instead depended almost solely on direct relief or the provision of a "dole" to tide the unemployed over the worst of the depression until recovery began. His chief unemployment policy, now that tariffs and public works had failed, was to attempt to eliminate the deficit and to balance the federal budget. This meant keeping expenditure on the jobless down to the lowest level consistent with their physical survival. At the same time, Bennett also refused to modify his policy that unemployment relief was primarily a provincial and local responsibility. His government would pay only one-third the cost of direct relief in any town or city and would contribute nothing to the costs of its administration.

III

Once Bennett opted for a policy of direct relief as his sole remaining means of dealing with unemployment, he entered into a nightmare of contradictions, ironies, and paradoxes which he had never anticipated and which would ultimately destroy his administration. Five such anomalies were of particular importance. The first was the paradox of residency requirements for relief. Since local governments, under Bennett's policy, had to assume anywhere from one-third to one-half the cost of relief on a rapidly diminishing and highly regressive property tax base, they attempted to limit their own relief costs in the only way possible, namely, by restricting eligibility for relief to their own municipal residents. Only those who could prove anywhere from six months' to, in some cases, three years' continuous residence in a city before applying for the dole were deemed eligible to receive it. In a country like Canada, with a geographically diverse and highly mobile labour market, many of the unemployed who had been on the road looking for work could not qualify for relief when they needed it. To get the dole they had to return to their home town, which they had left in the first place because there was no work. Bennett's policy, then, discouraged the unemployed from looking for work outside their town or city for fear of becoming ineligible for relief.

Transients also posed a contradiction. Tens of thousands of Canada's unemployed were immigrant, seasonal workers — bunkhouse men — who by the very nature of their work on the frontier could not qualify for relief in any city. Bennett's earlier public works policy had, in part, been intended once again to get them out of urban areas. Now, without public works, they had no choice but to drift back into Canadian cities where they could find neither relief nor work. As a result, transient single men "riding the rods" from town to town were quickly recognized as a serious menace to law and order. Since the cities refused to assume responsibility for them, and since Bennett refused to assume responsibility for relief, he decided on another alternative suggested to him by General Andrew McNaughton of the Canadian army—relief camps, run by the Defence Department. Here the men could be kept out of the cities, provided with room, board, and clothing and put to work on useful projects to preserve their morale. There was only one hitch. Since Bennett had already abandoned public works as a relief policy, the men couldn't be paid a wage, not without arousing serious unrest from married unemployed men on direct relief. Instead they were paid a 20¢ daily "allowance" in return for their labour in the camps.

Why would single men go into such camps for 20¢ a day? Cut off from direct relief in the cities, they had no choice except starvation, which is why the 20 000 men in the camps after 1933 quickly referred to them as "slave camps" and ultimately organized the relief camp strike and "On to Ottawa Trek" of 1935, which ended in a bloody two-hour riot with the RCMP in Regina. As one camp inhabitant cynically put it in 1933, "You come in broke, work all winter and still you are broke. It looks like they want to keep us bums all our lives."

Relief standards posed a third source of contention. By insisting on primary local and provincial responsibility for the financing of relief, and by assuming no share in the cost of administering relief, Bennett's government ensured that relief scales—that is, how much money or its equivalent in food vouchers a family would receive—varied dramatically from city to city, depending on the health of local economies and the political complexion of local city councils. A survey by the Canadian Welfare Council of relief standards in 50 Canadian cities during September 1936 showed just how far such scales of aid could differ. In London, Ontario, a family of five could receive no more than $40.39 a month for food, fuel, and shelter costs. That same family in Toronto could get $58.87; in Hamilton $34.40; in Ottawa $45.32; in Quebec City $26.66; in Calgary $60.00; and in Halifax a mere $18.86. Such gross variations in support within cities of comparable living costs was, of course, morally indefensible. Within Ontario, the Canadian Association of Social Workers discovered, in a survey of 107 municipalities, that not one provided the food allowance recommended by the Ontario Medical Association as the minimum necessary to maintain nutritional health. Food allowances in Toronto alone were 40 percent below the minimum standard which the League of Nations defined as necessary to maintain health. Since Bennett had promised, when elected in 1930, to "abolish the dole," such gross variations and substandard levels of support in a policy of direct relief which his administration had initiated was political catastrophe.

The bankruptcy of first local and then provincial governments was the fourth disastrous consequence of Bennett's relief policy. By insisting that local and provincial governments were to be held primarily responsible for the cost of relief, Bennett's unemployment policy concentrated the fiscal cost of the depression where its impact was greatest—that is, in western Canada. By 1932, all four western provinces were technically bankrupt because of the cost of paying their two-thirds share of direct relief and were only kept solvent by continual federal loans and grants. By 1937 Ottawa would be paying 85 percent of all relief costs in Saskatchewan; 71 percent in Alberta; 69 percent in British Columbia; and 68 percent in Manitoba; while still insisting that relief was a local responsibility. In Ontario and Quebec, in contrast, Ottawa paid only 29 percent and 32 percent, respectively, of relief costs.

To give an equally paradoxical example of the contradictions of this policy, in Forest Hill, a very wealthy area of Toronto with few unemployed, per capita relief costs to taxpayers averaged only $4.00 a month in 1934. In East York, a working-class borough only a few miles away, with almost 50 percent of its population on relief, the cost of the dole averaged $2.50 a month per taxpayer. Yet the people of Forest Hill, in many cases, were the employers of those living in East York. By drawing municipal boundary lines around themselves, they could enjoy the lowest relief taxes in Canada and shove the burden of the depression onto their unfortunate employees.

The final irony of direct relief was the fact that you had to be totally destitute to receive it. Insurance policies, bank savings, home equity, automobiles, everything of value had to be liquidated, in many municipalities, before a family could become eligible for the dole. Hence, what was the point of saving for a rainy day if you knew beforehand that all your assets would be confiscated before you could become eligible for aid? Far better to spend your money while you had it, since if you lost your job you would soon be just as badly off as the man down the road who had saved nothing.

IV

Because of contradictions such as these, by 1933–34 Bennett was desperately looking for alternatives to his relief policy. There were two directions he could go. The first, urged increasingly by the provinces, the municipalities, organized labour, some social workers, and the unemployed, was to take over total responsibility for unemployment relief instead of continuing to contribute on a one-third basis. Had Bennett followed this option, residency requirements for relief could have been abolished; the provinces, particularly in the west, and the municipalities would once again have been fiscally solvent; and most importantly the levels of assistance for families on the dole across Canada could have been raised to a national minimum standard sufficient to ensure that everyone received at least enough food, shelter, and clothing to remain healthy and to enjoy reasonably decent living standards.

Bennett had absolutely no interest in taking this route, however. In the first place, it would have cost far more to the federal government, already concerned primarily in reducing, not increasing, its deficit. Second, it would have necessitated the creation of a permanent federal welfare bureaucracy at a time when Bennett was still convinced that the unemployment crisis was temporary. Finally, and most important, Bennett and his advisers believed that a national minimum standard of relief would increase the numbers of those unemployed. Why? Because wage rates for those already working in Canada, particularly unskilled labourers, had been so lowered by the depression (clothing workers in Montreal and Toronto, for example, often made only $10.00 for a 60-hour work week) that for a large segment of Canada's working class a dole which provided healthy and decent living standards would be preferable to work.

This was certainly the conclusion of Charlotte Whitton, Canada's best-known social worker, an arch social conservative, and Bennett's key adviser on relief policy in the 1930s. In a 1932 report to the government on relief in western Canada, Whitton told Bennett that 40 percent of those living off the dole on the prairies didn't really need it; that the very existence of direct relief in the west was drawing tens of thousands of farm families into the western cities during the winter, thus artificially boosting the unemployment rate; and that by contributing to local and provincial relief efforts, Bennett's government had only succeeded in making thousands of immigrant and poor rural families "permanently dependent at a scale of living which they never had and never will be able to provide for themselves."

With this kind of advice coming from the chief executive of the Canadian Welfare Council, it was small wonder that Bennett himself concluded in 1934 that the people had become "more or less relief-conscious and were determined to get out of the Government, whether it be municipal, provincial, or federal, all they could." Instead of opting to take over total responsibility for unemployment relief, Bennett decided over the winter of 1934 to move in exactly the opposite direction: to sever all of Ottawa's ties with the dole and turn the whole ugly, embarrassing business completely back to the provinces and municipalities.

From this perspective, unemployment insurance, which the British had pioneered in 1911, began to appear more and more attractive as a policy alternative for the Bennett government. In the first place, at a time when unemployment still hovered at 20 percent of the workforce, Bennett simply could not withdraw from direct relief and abdicate all responsibility for the jobless. He had to have some political alternative to put in its place. Unemployment insurance fit the bill nicely for a number of reasons. Businessmen, particularly bankers and insurance company and real estate executives, favoured such a measure by 1934. These financial organizations now held many worthless municipal and provincial bonds and had become convinced that direct municipal relief was a highly inefficient way to finance the costs of unemployment. Far better, such businessmen argued, to build up an unemployment fund in good times through insurance premiums which could be used to aid the jobless during depressions. Better yet, unemployment insurance seemed to reinforce thrift. Since the premiums were compulsory, it forced workers to defer part of their incomes for a rainy day. Thus, unlike the dole, it didn't reduce everyone to complete and utter destitution before they could become eligible for aid. Moreover, because 80 percent of the cost of unemployment insurance could be financed by compulsory premiums paid by workers and employers, it would cost the federal government only a fraction of what was presently being spent on relief. As a result, unlike the dole, unemployment insurance would not interfere as directly with the widely shared desire among businessmen to see a balanced federal budget.

Finally, precisely because it was called unemployment "insurance," actuarial science, not nutritional standards of human need, could provide an arbitrary ceiling on benefits which in any case would always be kept to a fixed percentage of existing wage rates. In this way unemployment insurance seemed to pose no threat to the market-determined distribution of income. Under the legislation Bennett eventually introduced in the early months of 1935, Canadians had to work a minimum of 40 weeks over two years to be eligible for any benefits whatsoever, which in any case were set at a maximum of $11.40 a week for a family of five, almost 40 percent below the $17.30 a week which the Montreal Council of Social Agencies recommended as the minimum amount necessary to maintain health.

Under Bennett's unemployment insurance act, then, only those workers who were most regularly employed could qualify for benefits and the levels were set low enough to ensure that in no case would life on unemployment insurance be preferable to any form of work offered by Canadian employers anywhere in the country. In other words, unemployment insurance, as drafted by Bennett's advisers, was designed to reinforce the work ethic and to provide a perfect political cover for a federal withdrawal from relief. It was not designed to reduce poverty or to provide unemployed Canadians with a level of support adequate to maintain health and decency.

Most important, unemployment insurance offered nothing to the 1.2 million Canadians who were already on relief in 1935. Since their family breadwinners were obviously not working, they could not pay any premiums or qualify for benefits. It was a good idea for future depressions, but unemployment insurance really provided no solution to the problems of the 1930s.

Nevertheless, Bennett proceeded with his strategy. In June 1934, he told the premiers that all federal support for relief would be cut off on August 1. After tremendous political pressure, he subsequently modified this policy to a 22 percent federal cutback in relief spending. Then, in September, Bennett asked the provinces whether they would be willing to surrender their exclusive jurisdiction over unemployment insurance to Ottawa. Outraged by his high-handed pressure tactics and unilateral cutbacks, the premiers understandably refused. As a result, faced with an election and almost certain defeat in 1935, Bennett simply introduced his unemployment insurance bill in Parliament as part of his package of New Deal reforms, knowing full well that without provincial agreement the bill was probably unconstitutional and hence useless, as indeed it turned out to be.

After five years in office, Bennett went down to spectacular defeat in the 1935 election, his party losing all but 39 seats. He also left a very meagre legacy for his successor, the Liberal leader Mackenzie King. The attempt to provide work for the jobless had been abandoned after 1932; relief standards across Canada were grossly inadequate everywhere; four provincial governments were technically bankrupt; single unemployed men in the relief camps had walked out and rioted in their attempt to reach Ottawa; and unemployment insurance, the only creative piece of legislation on the jobless crisis to emerge from Bennett's administration, was clearly unconstitutional.

V

In what ways, if any, did Mackenzie King pursue different policies for the remainder of the depression? Unlike Bennett in 1930, King made no promises in the 1935 election beyond pledging to provide sober, orderly government. As a result, he had no political I.O.U.'s to redeem. In fact, the most striking aspect of King's unemployment policy is that from December 1935 until the spring of 1938 it was virtually a carbon copy of Bennett's. In the first place, he continued to insist that the jobless were primarily a local and provincial responsibility. Second, after a quick hike in federal relief contributions immediately after the election, King began systematically to cut back on Ottawa's support of the dole to such an extent that by 1937, in cities such as Winnipeg, Ottawa was paying only 20 percent of relief costs and on a national basis, only 30 percent, compared to the one-third share Bennett had paid throughout most years of his administration. Like the Tory prime minister, King's first priority was to balance the budget.

King's administration also refused to define any national minimum standard of relief, based on medical or nutritional standards. Instead, his government defined a national maximum. In October 1937 King's minister of Labour, Norman Rogers, announced that Ottawa would in no province pay more than 30 percent of the dole's cost, and in every city the standard of living on relief had to be kept below the average going rate for unskilled labour in the surrounding area, in order that "work incentives" could be enforced. This policy was adopted at a time when most provinces had no minimum wage for men.

Although King did abolish Bennett's hated relief camps for single men in 1936, the alternative he put in place was, in many ways, much worse. This was a farm placement scheme which paid about 45 000 of Canada's single unemployed $5.00 a month to work on farms across the country. This was less than the infamous 20¢ daily "allowance" the men had received in the camps, and there was no guarantee that food, clothing, shelter, and medical care provided by individual impoverished farmers across Canada would be comparable to what the army had offered in the relief camps. As one army commander pointed out when the camps were shut down in 1936 and many men refused to leave, "the men prefer to stay where they have 'regular hours' and good food, rather than leave for farms, where they have to work harder, longer hours, and for lower wages, with a possibility that they may not collect their wages in the fall." Although cynical in its conception, King's farm placement scheme nonetheless did solve the problem of chronic unrest among transients. Spread out individually across Canada rather than concentrated in the camps, single men proved almost impossible to organize politically after 1936.

King's overall unemployment strategy duplicated Bennett's in two other ways. As Bennett had done after 1932, until the severe recession of 1938, King rejected public works as an antidote to unemployment, in marked contrast to the massive works schemes pioneered by Franklin Roosevelt's New Deal south of the border. Instead, King relied totally on direct relief as a means of caring for the jobless. King also refused to enact an unemployment insurance plan, claiming that the political opposition to the measure by New Brunswick, Quebec, and Alberta made impossible the unanimous consent which he claimed was necessary for a constitutional amendment.

In only two areas did King take actions significantly different from Bennett's. In April 1936 he appointed a National Employment Commission, chaired by Montreal industrialist Arthur Purvis, to investigate the unemployment and relief situation and to come up with recommendations for reform. Second, in August 1937, he appointed a Royal Commission on Dominion–Provincial Relations, chaired by Supreme Court justice Newton Rowell, to investigate and attempt to straighten out the tangled web of federal–provincial financial relations, particularly the continuing inability of the western provinces to stay fiscally solvent without federal loans and grants.

The most significant result of both these commissions is that they ended up saying the same thing. The NEC, which reported in January 1938, and the Rowell-Sirois Commission, as it came to be called, which reported in May 1940, both argued that the first step in combatting unemployment and restoring fiscal solvency to the provinces and local governments was for Ottawa to put in place immediately a national employment service and system of unemployment insurance, and to assume total financial and administrative responsibility for unemployment relief. In short, both commissions argued that Ottawa should take the route both Bennett and King had rejected throughout the entire depression, namely to accept primary responsibility for unemployment. The jobless crisis, both commissions argued, was a national problem, reflecting Canada's national economy; consequently, relief to those without work should be first and foremost a national responsibility. Only Ottawa through its unlimited taxing power, they argued further, possessed the fiscal strength to pay for these relief costs. Finally, reflecting the new Keynesian sophistication being developed within the department of finance, both commissions concluded that only Ottawa could inject enough purchasing power into the economy through insurance and relief payments and public works to push levels of demand up high enough to stimulate economic growth and thus ultimately to eliminate unemployment.

It would be pleasant to report that after receiving this sensible advice, King realized the error of his ways and reversed his economic policies. In fact, he did no such thing. When he discovered that the NEC was about to recommend federal control of relief, King pulled out every stop he could to kill the commission's final report. When that proved impossible, thanks to Arthur Purvis's integrity, King simply ignored it. Why? The reason was best expressed by Mary Sutherland, King's closest confidant on the NEC and the author of a dissenting minority report. In it, Sutherland articulated the basis for Ottawa's continued resistance throughout the 1930s to accepting primary responsibility for the jobless. "No matter which government is responsible for and administers relief," Sutherland wrote, "there will be constant pressure to increase the benefits and to enlarge the base of admittance to benefits. If responsibility is centralized in the Dominion government, the counter-pressure from local taxpayers will be eased. The irksome, unwelcome, and hard check provided by necessity, by municipal officials, harrassed by mounting demands on diminishing revenues, will be removed."

In short, Sutherland, like King and R.B. Bennett, believed that national responsibility for relief would cost too much and would erode the work ethic. If Ottawa controlled relief, it would have to define a national minimum standard of support, or in effect a national poverty line, across the country. In a country like Canada with widely diverse regional wage rates and living standards, such a national minimum would inevitably be higher than existing wage rates for many of the working poor. The result would be to attract this class out of work and onto relief, thus increasing unemployment. Sutherland's argument was, in this sense, almost identical to the one first put forward by Charlotte Whitton in her 1932 report on relief in western Canada. Only by keeping relief a local responsibility and local governments on the edge of bankruptcy could relief costs and benefit levels be kept to the barest minimum.

Ironically, putting more purchasing power directly into the hands of the jobless and their families in the form of higher relief benefits was exactly what was needed in order to push up consumption and effective demand to levels that would in turn encourage investment and employment. But as long as the Bennett and King administrations continued to approach the relief question from the angle of its effects upon the work ethic of individuals rather than upon the purchasing power of all the unemployed, they simply could not see this. As a result, in their relief policy, as in their wider economic policies of balanced budgets, a sound dollar, and regressive taxation, Bennett and King inhibited the chances of recovery.

VI

In 1940, after World War II had begun, Canadians finally did see enacted a constitutionally valid scheme of unemployment insurance. The pressures of war and the need for national unity had dissolved the political objections of the three dissenting provinces. More important, King's own fear of postwar unemployment, and of how jobless veterans would respond to relief of the 1930s variety, now galvanized him into making unemployment insurance a first priority of the government, particularly with an election looming on the horizon in 1940. Wartime mobilization and the potential labour shortage also gave the federal government a vital need for creating a national employment service, a motive which had not been present during the heavy labour surplus of the 1930s. Finally, the necessity for massive war expenditures gave Ottawa an overpowering political argument for trying out new Keynesian ideas such as deliberately incurring large deficits, a policy which would have left most Canadian businessmen aghast in the depression.

The tragedy of unemployment policy in the 1930s is that strategies for dealing with joblessness which were politically possible, indeed essential in the context of the war, were not deemed possible, given Canada's political landscape in the depression. The essential continuity and the essential failure of the policies pursued by both R.B. Bennett and Mackenzie King lay in their refusal to accept that the unemployed were a national responsibility. This refusal, in turn, was rooted in what might be termed the dilemma of "less eligibility" in a market economy. In a private enterprise system, business and the market set wage levels and living standards. During the 1930s, for many working Canadians, these standards and wages were below what was necessary to ensure a decent and healthy standard of living. As a result, both the Bennett and King governments believed they could not provide higher relief benefits for the jobless without attracting many of the working population onto the dole. Without direct state intervention or trade union pressure to improve working conditions and living standards for low-income Canadians, or in other words, without massive intervention into the marketplace, the government felt limited in the benefits it could provide for the unemployed. And in the political context of the 1930s, given the absence of a serious political threat from the left or a strong labour movement, the pressure simply was not there for either Bennett or King to move in a direction that would have been regarded by Canadian businessmen as serious meddling in their affairs.

Only war, with the full employment it would bring and the strong labour union organization it would permit, could create a political climate in which it would be possible to effect these kinds of permanent structural reforms to underpin working-class incomes. By 1945, then, Canadians were finally ready to fight the Great Depression of the 1930s.

World War II

Veronica Foster, known as "The Bren Gun Girl," takes a break on
the Bren Gun production line at John Inglis Co. Ltd. in Toronto,
May 1941. The Bren Gun became one of the most widely used
machine guns of its kind and was a staple for line troops during
World War II.

TWENTY YEARS after the Great War, Canada entered World War II (1939–1945). The causes of the two world wars differed, as did Canada's reasons for entering and the nature of its participation. In both cases, Canada contributed large numbers of men and women, and enormous financial, agricultural, and industrial resources to the war effort. In "The War Changed Everything," historians J.L. Granatstein and Desmond Morton explain why it was necessary for Canada to join that war. They also recount the myriad ways in which World War II dramatically changed Canada by making comparisons to the experiences of World War I.

Xenophobia, the rise of animosity and hatred against ethnic Canadians, became one of the negative repercussions of World War II on the home front for those ethnic Canadians whose places of origin were countries at war with Canada. Japanese Canadians living on the west coast particularly felt the brunt of racial attitudes and a backlash against their presence in the country. Xenophobia was the result of long-standing racial intolerance and the immediate fear of a possible Japanese attack. The Canadian government responded to these fears by evicting Japanese Canadians to the interior of British Columbia or points farther east, disregarding the fact that the majority of Japanese Canadians were born in Canada or had become Canadian citizens. Historian Peter Ward recounts the expulsion and the motives behind it in "British Columbia and the Japanese Evacuation."

On the impact of the war, see Desmond Morton, *Canada and War*: *A Military and Political History* (Toronto: Butterworths, 1981); Norman Hillmer et al., eds., *A Country of Limitations*: *Canada and the War in 1939* (Ottawa: Canadian Committee for the History of the Second World War, 1996); and J.L. Granatstein and Desmond Morton, *A Nation Forged in Fire*: *Canadians and the Second World War, 1939–1945* (Toronto: Lester & Orpen Dennys, 1989). On Canada's participation in the war, see W.A.B. Douglas and Brereton Greenhous, *Out of the Shadows*: *Canada in the Second World War*, rev. ed. (Toronto: Dundurn Press, 1995); David J. Bercuson, *Maple Leaf against the Axis*: *Canada's Second World War* (Toronto: Stoddart, 1995); Ted Barris and Alex Barris, *Days of Victory*: *Canadians Remember, 1939–1945* (Toronto: Macmillan, 1995); Desmond Morton and J.L. Granatstein, *Victory 1945*: *Canadians from War to Peace* (Toronto: HarperCollins, 1995); and Mark Zuehlke, *Ortona* (North York, ON: Stoddart Publishing, 1999). Useful collections of essays include Peter Neary and J.L. Granatstein, eds., *The Good Fight: Canada and the Second World War* (Toronto: Copp Clark Longman, 1994); and Marc Miller, ed., *Canadian Military History: Selected Readings* (Toronto: Copp Clark Pitman, 1993).

Peter Ward's *White Canada Forever: Popular Attitudes and Public Policies towards Orientals in British Columbia* (Montreal/Kingston: McGill-Queen's University Press, 1978) is a comprehensive study of the British Columbia response to Asian immigration. For an alternative view, see Patricia Roy's "British Columbia's Fear of Asians, 1900–1950," *Histoire sociale/Social History* 13 (May 1980): 161–72, and her book, *A White Man's Province: British Columbia Politicians and Chinese and Japanese Immigrants, 1858–1914* (Vancouver: University of British Columbia Press, 1989). See also Patricia Roy et al., *Mutual Hostages: Canadians and Japanese during the Second World War* (Toronto: University of Toronto Press, 1990), and J.L. Granatstein and Gregory Johnson, "The Evacuation of the Japanese Canadians, 1942: A Realist Critique of the Received Version," in *On Guard for Thee: War, Ethnicity, and the Canadian State, 1939–1945*, ed. N. Hillmer et al. (Ottawa: Canadian Committee for the

History of the Second World War, 1988). Ann Gomer Sunahara's *The Politics of Racism: The Uprooting of Japanese Canadians during the Second World War* (Toronto: Lorimer, 1981) is a carefully documented study of this same issue; it should be read in conjunction with Ward's study. A popular summary is Thomas Berger's "The Banished Canadians: Mackenzie King and the Japanese Canadians," in his *Fragile Freedoms: Human Rights and Dissent in Canada* (Toronto: Clarke, Irwin, 1981), pp. 93–126.

On the question of redress, see Roy Miki and Cassandra Kobayashi, *Justice in Our Time: The Japanese Canadian Redress Settlement* (Vancouver: Talon Books, 1991), and Maryba Omatsu, *Bittersweet Passage: Redress and the Japanese Canadian Experience* (Toronto: Between the Lines, 1992).

Article Twenty-Three

The War Changed Everything

J.L. Granatstein and Desmond Morton

Was it all worth it? Had Canada lost 47 000 lives and squandered thirteen billion dollars in vain? Had we fought one evil empire only to saddle much of Europe with another? Or had we fought only to restore corrupt capitalism?

Such questions, not uncommon in university classrooms half a century after 1945, prove that some people never learn and others all too easily forget. Revisionist "scholars" who argue that Adolf Hitler was a statesman, that the Holocaust never happened, that Winston Churchill's greatest error was his refusal to strike a deal with a triumphant Germany in the summer of 1940, exploit a freedom young Canadians died to protect. And they are wrong.

The Second World War was the one good war. The struggle between democracy and fascism was, quite literally, a struggle between light and darkness. Hitler's Third Reich invaded Austria, Czechoslovakia, Poland, Denmark and Norway, the Netherlands, Belgium, France, Yugoslavia, Greece, and the Soviet Union. Had Britain not kept its fleet intact and its air force battling in the skies, Hitler's armies would have invaded England. North America would eventually have been next. Italy's Benito Mussolini supported Hitler's conquests and tried his own, though with less success. Japan's corporate and military elite gave Hitler his greatest ally in world conquest. Its powerful army, navy, and air force ravaged China and seized every British, Dutch, and American colony it could reach.

For centuries, nations invaded their neighbours with cruelty and without provocation, but behind Hitler's steel-helmeted legions rode an army of bureaucrats with plans and orders to exploit the conquered people for Germany's Nazi elite. Close behind the soldiers came the Gestapo and the SS extermination squads with orders to rid Europe of those whom the Nazis decreed to be *Untermenschen* — Jews, Gypsies, Slavs, homosexuals, the disabled, the mentally disturbed. Initially, the squads merely shot their victims. When that proved inefficient, Nazi officials ordered more concentration camps and gas chambers. Men, women, and children were crammed in until the weak vanished under foot, only to

Source: *Canada Remembers* (Ottawa: Department of Supply and Services, Government of Canada, 1994), pp. 75–81.

be asphyxiated. Giant gas ovens destroyed the corpses. Nazi engineers devised ways to collect gold fillings from calcified corpses and to keep molten grease from corpses from dousing the burners.

Was this a regime with which Britain and Canada could have made peace? Or was peace possible with an Imperial Japan? After its troops had destroyed their enemies and imprisoned the survivors (including 1500 Canadians) in bestial conditions, the killing went on. For its "Great East Asia Co-Prosperity Sphere," Japan slaughtered millions of Chinese, Filipinos, and other Asians. This was no war of liberation but an imperial conquest as cruel and arrogant as any in recorded history.

For all their faults, Canada and the other democracies had no real alternative to fighting Germany, Italy, and Japan. Unfortunately it took them so long to draw a line and defend it. Perhaps it was the wrong line in the wrong place but the alternatives remain almost unthinkable. No one, winner or loser, fights a war with clean hands, perfect foresight, and a balanced sense of justice. Even a good war has terrible moments, such as the firestorms of Hamburg, Dresden, Tokyo, and Nagoya, the nuclear devastation of Hiroshima and Nagasaki, with the unexpected collateral horror of radiation sickness.

If ever a war had to be won, it was the Second World War. Had the Allies lost the war, the world could not look the way it does today. The revisionists would not have had to wait 50 years to revive the nightmare of Hitlerism.

What the War Changed for Canada

When war came on September 10, 1939, Canada was still trapped in the Great Depression. For a decade, Canadians had been caught in a downward cycle of business failure, unemployment, and debt. Close to a quarter of Canadian families had suffered the humiliation of accepting welfare payments. Their sons, denied help because there must be a job somewhere, rode boxcars across the country in search of a meal and a warm place to sleep. Couples postponed marriage until times got better and found themselves with years to wait. Even meagre relief payments had bankrupted municipalities and provinces. Between 1928 and 1939, the national debt had almost doubled, though governments cut any spending that could be cut. Like other nations, Canada tried to protect jobs by raising tariff walls—and watched whole industries collapse for the lack of export markets. Prairie farmers watched as drought killed their crops, scorching winds blew away their topsoil, and grasshoppers devoured what remained. In a region that called itself "the world's breadbasket," people starved.

Economists would argue that there was recovery from the depths of 1933, that profits and dividends gradually climbed back to 1929 levels, and those prairie farmers who had the means and courage to plant a crop that year harvested a bumper crop. That was little comfort to most Canadians. One person in six was still out of work and a good crop gave bankers an incentive to foreclose.

By 1945, Canada was transformed. With almost a million Canadians in uniform, industries competed for workers and a few even enticed mothers with a promise of day nurseries. The gross national product, the measure of all the goods and services Canadians produced, reached $11 billion, double the prewar level.

In the 1914–1919 war, Canadian factories turned out millions of artillery shells and opened a primitive aircraft industry. The Second World War saw a quantum leap in the extent and complexity of munitions production. Canadian workers, male and female, produced everything from light machine guns to binoculars. Canadian factories rolled out tanks, naval guns, radar sets, and huge four-engined Lancaster bombers. Shipyard workers on both coasts and the Great Lakes built merchant ships, corvettes, minesweepers, and fast, sophisticated Tribal-class destroyers.

There was work — and unlimited overtime too — for all who wanted it. Farmers and fishermen could sell anything they brought to market, and governments, conscious of a starving world, pleaded with them to do more. Huge new plants devoured electricity and bauxite to produce aluminum. Gold, copper, nickel, and coal all commanded wartime prices. A mysterious mineral called uranium was suddenly in demand. Indeed, the allied war effort seemed to have a need for everything Canada could produce and some things, like synthetic rubber, that only wartime ingenuity could create.

Wartime wealth became a catalyst for equally dramatic changes in Canada's social structure. The gospel of laissez faire had survived the 1930s intact. Indeed, an emerging class of business leaders, like George McCullagh of the newly merged *Globe and Mail*, urged a new ruthlessness. If they had prospered, all the more reason to blame society's losers for their own fate. Such notions did not die, but they paled in the ultimate struggle of war. To survive, Canada needed its citizens to make sacrifices, even of life itself. To mobilize its strength, the country demanded a finer vision than a return to 1939.

In 1940, the long struggle to persuade Canada to follow Britain and the United States in adopting unemployment insurance was won. Wartime, with its prospect of full employment and rising incomes, became a wonderful opportunity to build up a fund to cushion the ultimate transition to peace and to drain off spending power that otherwise could fuel wartime inflation. The war rescued a stagnant labour movement. Defence workers joined unions, learned their value, and fought wartime regulations that held their wages to 1929 levels. Union leaders favoured long-term legal protection over short-term wage gains. In February 1944, they got their reward: P.C. 1003. The government guaranteed employees the right to form unions, bargain collectively, present grievances, and strike — provided a formal contract had expired. Canadian labour had a bill of rights that would last far beyond the war.

Canadians had debated family poverty for decades, conscious that there would never be a time when Canada could afford a solution. That time also came in 1944. Parliament approved a baby bonus scheme that put a monthly payment for each child in the mother's purse. The scheme would cost a quarter of a billion dollars a year — almost half of all federal government spending in 1939.

Appalled by its deficit, Ottawa in 1919 had told the average returning soldier to land on his own two feet. Disabled veterans did receive pensions, training, and financial help; however, the refusal to recognize the degree to which able-bodied veterans required assistance in returning to civilian life left a lasting grievance. Veterans were in charge of veterans' programs in the Second World War: They would not let it happen again. The result of wartime wealth, fears for the postwar, and relentless pressure gave Canada the richest reestablishment package in the world. The Veterans' Charter promised free university and technical training, a generous gratuity, and credits to buy anything from a refrigerator to a small business. The money did more than compensate those who had served Canada; it helped to rescue the economy from a postwar slump.

In 1945, no one knew if these and other measures would be enough to save Canada from a new depression when the munitions plants closed and hundreds of thousands of service members landed in Civvy Street. What mattered was that buoyed by the success of wartime economic management, Ottawa now believed that it could take responsibility for Canadians and their well-being. When it campaigned for reelection on June 11, 1945, the Liberal government of W.L. Mackenzie King campaigned not on wartime achievements but on the promise of a "New Social Order." The Liberals won, the wartime boom continued with scarcely a check, and Canada continued its longest sustained period of prosperity.

Canada and the World

Canada's reward for the 60 000 dead of the earlier Great War had been membership in the League of Nations and its agencies, but Canada's delegate in 1923, Raoul Dandurand, had preached that Canada was "a fire-proof house, far from inflammable materials." From 1919, Canadian politicians and officials had resisted any commitment to collective security under the League's Covenant. Whatever feeble pressure Canada could exert in the late 1930s had favoured appeasement of the European dictators.

Here, too, the war changed everything. Canada's astonishing war effort laid the groundwork. A country of 11 500 000 people became a major military power, with the world's third-largest navy, fourth-largest air force, and an overseas field army of five divisions and two armoured brigades, with the reserve manpower to keep them in action. Added to the country's immense industrial and agricultural contribution to the Allied war effort, the great powers had to listen when Canada spoke. And Canada, at last, had something to say.

Represented by some of the ablest diplomats ever assembled to serve their country, the government decided what mattered to Canada and what did not. Grand strategy was left to the great powers; issues of long-term economic significance were not. When Britain and the United States created a Combined Food Board to allocate supplies, as a major producer, Canada demanded a place. When the British balked, Ottawa threatened retaliation and finally got its seat. The prime minister, Mackenzie King, even found a principle to define Canada's policy: Wherever Canada filled the functions of a major power, it would insist on a share of decision making. When it came to the production of food and raw materials, the provision of relief supplies to liberated nations, even the regulation of civil aviation, Canada insisted on its "functional principle" and won much of what it wanted.

When the great powers met at Dumbarton Oaks in 1944 to plan a United Nations that would keep lesser countries in their place, Canadian officials were indignant, but they kept their fury under control. At the UN's founding conference at San Francisco in the spring of 1945, Canadian diplomat Lester Pearson organized behind the scenes, giving smaller countries a stronger voice in the General Assembly and other UN bodies while manoeuvring to make sure that no major power got so angry that it walked out. The little, isolationist Canada of 1920–1939 had grown up. Canada's representatives now argued for their conception of the world and, as "helpful fixers," did much to bring it into being.

The world was no paradise when the guns fell silent in 1945. Canadians had the strength to become the first of the world's middle powers, but their sovereignty in North America was more constrained. At Ogdensburg in upstate New York in August 1940, wartime necessity had persuaded the government to strike its first defence alliance with the United States. As Britain faced its finest and perhaps its final hour, Mackenzie King and President Franklin Delano Roosevelt had agreed to establish the Permanent Joint Board on Defence, a combined military–civilian body that was to make recommendations to the two governments on the defence of the continent. The next year, King and Roosevelt signed the Hyde Park Agreement, an arrangement that allowed Canada to continue paying for its enormous wartime purchases from the United States by obliging the Americans to buy more goods in Canada.

The necessity for cooperation seemed obvious in the spring of 1941 and it was even more apparent after December 7, 1941, when Japan's attack on Pearl Harbor forced the

United States into the war. With a victorious Japan running wild in the Pacific and even seizing the tip of the Aleutians off Alaska, Ottawa welcomed an American decision to establish airfields in the northwest, an oil pipeline from Norman Wells to Whitehorse, and an Alaska Highway that would link Edmonton and Fairbanks. It was natural that a Canadian brigade, partly composed of conscripts, would join an American expedition that recaptured Kiska in the Aleutians.

The Americans, as a postwar politician once stated, "are our best friends, whether we like it or not." At war's end, Canada paid its friends in full for their wartime installations in the North. It was the best way to ensure that the Stars and Stripes continued to fly in as few places as possible. Wartime experience with Washington, so different from that in Whitehall, taught Canadians that the new relationship had to be handled with care. The task was made no easier by reviving concerns about the secret intentions of the Soviet Union. A few of those secrets escaped when Igor Gouzenko, a cipher clerk at the Soviet Embassy in Ottawa, defected on September 5, 1945, with documents identifying Soviet spy networks in Canada. These were secrets Mackenzie King would almost have preferred not to know. As Soviet armies tightened Moscow's grip on eastern Europe and Moscow tried to forge a security ring around the Soviet frontiers, planners in Ottawa felt the first real military threat to North America in a century. In any Soviet–American war, Canadian territory would be no man's land. Canada could not opt out. There could be no return to the prewar days when $23 million paid for untrained reserves and a few thousand regulars.

Could Canada's sovereignty survive as an outwork of Fortress America? By 1948, the country that had feared commitments and condemned collective security was pressing the nations of the North Atlantic for a treaty to link them in a common system of defence. When the North Atlantic Treaty Organization was formed, one of its Canadian architects, Escott Reid, called it "our providential solution." When North Korea hurled its forces against South Korea in 1950, Canada was among the first to respond to a UN call for help and warships, aircraft, and a brigade of troops served under the United Nations command. In 1951, another brigade and the first of twelve fighter squadrons went to Europe. Such bold commitments would have been inconceivable to Canadians fifteen years before. Seemingly, the war had taught Canadians a lesson: Unpreparedness and weak resolve benefit none but aggressor states and unprincipled dictators.

Canada and Canadians

Postwar prosperity made Canada very different from the country that Canadians who engaged in that war had known. After 1945, Canada was a land of both opportunity and security. Steady growth in output, productivity, and purchasing power seemed to promise that there would always be more. Canadians also had unprecedented protection from the economic catastrophes of life — poverty, sickness, unemployment. The combinations made Canadians both more optimistic and compassionate than they had ever been. It was harder to believe that there were too many spoons for the soup.

Canada had always been a poor country, with much of the meanness poverty usually induced. Prewar Canadians often knew little beyond districts and neighbourhoods that were small, largely homogeneous and exclusive. There was usually no room in them for Japanese or Chinese Canadians and scant tolerance for Jews or blacks or those with "different" attitudes or beliefs. Minorities did not have to be visible to suffer the lash of discrimination: French Canadians, Catholics, Ukrainians felt it whenever they ventured beyond the regions and social classes where circumstances or history had made them a majority. Immigrants often ran into barriers of contempt and hatred. Even the wealthy in the midst of poverty were more timid, afraid of change, and socially conservative than their affluent descendants.

The war helped soften such attitudes. Human rights legislation, a response to the Holocaust, originally targeted anti-Semitism but inevitably broadened to fight all forms of racial discrimination. The wartime sacrifices by Canadians of every ethnic origin inspired a young Liberal, Paul Martin, to establish an inclusive Canadian citizenship. The undermining of grosser forms of prejudice benefited the flood of postwar immigrants who reached Canada's shores from Europe. Eventually even the old barriers to immigration from Asia, the West Indies, and Africa collapsed.

Affluence offered Canadians and immigrants alike a new social and physical mobility. An automotive industry that had helped put most of the British army on wheels could supply almost every Canadian family and, be it a new model or an old clunker, it carried families from inner-city slums to the new suburbs of Scarborough, the South Shore, or Burnaby, where home ownership and a new middle class and consumer-driven conformity awaited. Canada loosened up, lightened up, and became a kinder, gentler place.

For some Canadians, of course, the war changed everything: 47 000 Canadians died in their prime, and another 55 000 suffered wounds in action. Many lost limbs, suffered hideous disfigurement, or came home hopelessly damaged in mind or body. Who can ever assess the loss? Someone who failed to return might have found a cure for cancer, written the great Canadian novel, or led us all to a better life. Children grew up without fathers; tens of thousands more would never be born. Is there any measure of the psychological agony of those who served and those who waited? Men and women, not frozen statistics, paid a terrible price for a better Canada. Canadians must never forget those who paid in full for all we gained. It makes those gains even more worth defending.

Article Twenty-Four

British Columbia and the Japanese Evacuation

W. Peter Ward

On 27 February 1942 the Canadian government announced plans to remove all persons of Japanese ancestry from the coastal region of British Columbia. During the seven months which followed, more than 22 000 Japanese, aliens, and Canadian citizens alike, were forced to abandon their homes and move eastward under government supervision. The majority were sent to settlements in the interior of the province, while others went to more distant points beyond the Rockies. Yet when war with Japan was first declared, on 7 December 1941, the federal government saw no need for such drastic action. Left to their own devices, Prime Minister King and his Cabinet would not have compelled most of the Japanese to leave the coast. After war's outbreak, however, the Liberal government could not resist the swelling tide of anti-Japanese feeling on

Source: "British Columbia and the Japanese Evacuation," *Canadian Historical Review* 57, 3 (September 1976): 289–309. Reprinted by permission of University of Toronto Press Incorporated.

the Pacific. Ultimately, King and his government concluded that only evacuation would quiet the popular outcry and avert public disorder.

But if the expulsion was a direct result of wartime stress, it was also the consequence of strained race relations in British Columbia. Since the late 1850s west-coast society had been divided by a deep racial cleavage and, over the years, only limited integration had occurred in patterns of work, residential accommodation, and social contact. The white community had vented its persistent anti-Asian sentiments through petty discrimination, verbal abuse, and even mob violence. Driven by economic threats (both real and apparent) as well as cultural conflicts and psychological tensions, politicians, editors, farm and business organizations, patriotic clubs, and nativistic societies had all assailed the Asian immigrant at one time or another. Periodically, federal, provincial, and municipal governments had also approved legislation and enforced covenants which discriminated against Orientals. These official measures served to legitimate popular prejudice. In sum, long before Canada went to war with Japan, British Columbians had passively tolerated and actively promoted hostility toward their Asian minorities.[1]

Many whites who peered across this racial cleft viewed Orientals through a haze of prejudice, for their images of Asians were drawn from a few widely accepted negative stereotypes.[2] In the case of the Japanese these stereotyped attitudes, which hardened perceptibly during the interwar years, emphasized four characteristics: their unassimilability, their economic competitiveness, their high birth rate, and their lingering loyalty to Japan. None of these stereotypes was particularly accurate, although some did contain at least a kernel of truth. But it was their substance, not their accuracy, that mattered most to British Columbians.

During the early and middle 1930s anti-Japanese feeling was not particularly intense in British Columbia. But in the closing months of 1937 a new source of strain bore down upon the west coast's racial cleavage. Japan attacked China once again and, in Canada, reports of this aggression provoked the first strong outburst of anti-Japanese feeling in a decade. Much of it was directed at Japan herself. Across the nation indignant Canadians boycotted Japan's products and protested her war atrocities.[3] At the same time British Columbians aimed new barbs at the local Japanese. Animus was most intense in coastal centres — especially Vancouver, Victoria, and their surrounding districts — where provincial xenophobia traditionally had been strong. In part, at least, Canada's Japanese merely became the scapegoats of Japan's militarism. But some whites saw them as a separate cause for concern. Japan's military adventures had roused anxiety on the coast by stirring up the region's traditional fears of isolation and vulnerability, and this new, tense atmosphere breathed fresh life into the community's dormant animus. Moreover, it confirmed the threatening impression left by the popular Japanese image. Older Japanese stereotypes, like those which emphasized low standards of living and unfair competition, were burnished anew by abrasive racial tension. They shone even more brightly in the menacing light of Japanese militarism, for Japan was presumed to have designs upon British Columbia. It was rumoured that hundreds of illegal Japanese immigrants were present on the coast, that Japanese spies and military officers lived surreptitiously in the community, and that a Japanese fifth column potential was growing in the province. Thus in 1937, when old antipathies fused with new anxieties, another wave of anti-Asian sentiment surged over the province.

Archdeacon F.G. Scott, a former popular Anglican wartime padre, precipitated the new outbreak in mid-November 1937, one week after the Japanese had taken Shanghai. In a widely reported interview with the *Toronto Daily Star* he suggested that Japanese officers were living, disguised, in Japanese fishing villages along the west coast.[4] A few coastal residents ridiculed Scott's claims. Others, however, vouched for their truth, and his supporters won the day, for a public outcry followed his remarks. Captain MacGregor Macintosh, a Conservative member of the legislature of British Columbia, first endorsed Scott's report and then, early in 1938, raised charges of widespread illegal Japanese immigration.[5] Led by A.W. Neill, an Independent and perennial foe of the Oriental immigrant, provincial members of Parliament from all major parties demanded a halt to Japanese immigration.[6] Simultaneously, in Vancouver, Alderman Halford Wilson urged city council to limit the number of licences for Japanese merchants and to impose zoning restrictions upon them.[7] Meanwhile, Vancouver's major daily newspapers launched their own anti-Japanese campaigns.[8] In Ottawa the prime minister received a flurry of protest notes while the outspoken Alderman Wilson's mail brought him letters of support.[9]

Judged in the light of past anti-Oriental incidents, this was not a major outburst. Its central figures, Wilson and Macintosh, made no attempt to organize a protest movement. They merely spent their energies in making public demands for more restrictive legislation. Nor was popular hostility as intense as it had been during the mid-1880s or the summer of 1907, when anti-Asian riots had occurred in Vancouver. Because the level of social strain was relatively low and dynamic organizational leadership was absent, this precluded the development of a major racial crisis. Nevertheless, signs still pointed to increasing public tension, and the weight of this concern was soon felt in Ottawa.

But Prime Minister Mackenzie King was loath to grasp the nettle. King probably wished to placate British Columbia's xenophobes, or at least quiet them, if he could. At the same time, however, he was subject to countervailing pressures. He was anxious not to embarrass British interests in Asia by taking any initiative which might provoke Japanese ire. Japan's renewed militarism had heightened his own inherent sense of caution. But pressure from the west coast grew so intense that, ultimately, he could not ignore it. Urged first by Premier T.D. Pattullo of British Columbia and then by Ian Mackenzie, the only west-coast representative in the Cabinet, King early in March 1938 promised a public inquiry into rumours of illegal Japanese immigration.[10]

But the mere promise of an investigation did not still the insistent demands for an end to Japanese immigration. Macintosh even called for the repatriation of all Japanese residents in Canada, regardless of their citizenship.[11] Then on 24 March the Board of Review charged with the investigation held its first public hearing in Vancouver. Over the next seven weeks it conducted a series of further meetings in major centres throughout the province and, once the hearings commenced, popular unease appeared to dissipate. The hearings themselves put an end to scattered public protest by offering a forum to the vociferous. Furthermore, the meetings forced critics to prove their allegations or remain silent, and many chose the latter refuge. In fact, public concern subsided to such an extent that, when the board's findings were published early in 1939, the report scarcely attracted notice.[12]

But while hostility ebbed appreciably, it was not completely dispelled, and over the next two years the west-coast Japanese remained the targets of rumours, suspicion, and criticism. Then in the spring of 1940, a wave of animosity began to well up once again. The anxious wartime atmosphere shaped by Canada's recent belligerency once more heightened traditional prejudices and aggravated racial tensions in west-coast society. At the same time, and for the same reason, Japan's Asian military campaign again began to rouse concern. The growth of general unease once more strengthened feelings of vulnerability and insecurity in the community. Prompted by mounting anxiety, the cry again went up that illegal Japanese immigrants were infiltrating the country; renewed demands were made for an end to all Japanese immigration as well as for stronger Pacific coast defences.

It was Alderman Halford Wilson who headed this new campaign of protest. Throughout the summer of 1940 he warned of Japanese subversion and called for closer restrictions on all Japanese residents.[13] Wilson still made no attempt to organize a popular movement but he did remain the most insistent of the Japanese community's critics. Himself aside, it is difficult to know for whom Wilson actually spoke. Few British Columbians in 1940 were willing to follow his lead in public. Yet undoubtedly there were many who endorsed the general thrust of his remarks, if not their specific aim. Certainly his crusade was a measure of the times, for anti-Japanese nativism was once more on the rise.[14] And in Ottawa as well as Victoria this resurgence soon became a source of some concern.[15] The worry was that Wilson's comments might put the torch to public opinion and touch off racial disorder.

While provincial and federal authorities grew increasingly alarmed at the prospect of racial turmoil, senior military officers in British Columbia were also concerned by the presence of Japanese on the coast. Intelligence officers had kept watch on the Japanese community since 1937 and, from the outset, they had accepted the prevailing assumption that Japanese residents, regardless of their citizenship, would endanger national security in time of war. As early as June 1938 the Department of National Defence had explored the prospect of widespread Japanese wartime internment.[16] In 1940, during the summer's crest of popular anti-Japanese feeling, the Pacific Command's Joint Service Committee approved contingency plans to meet both an external Japanese attack and an internal Japanese insurrection. The committee also endorsed an intelligence report which warned of possible sabotage from the west-coast Japanese fishing fleet. Japanese residents, it reported, "could very easily make themselves a potent force and threaten the vital industries of British Columbia." If war broke out, the committee believed, every Japanese resident in British Columbia should be considered a potential enemy.[17]

In contrast, the RCMP tended to minimize the Japanese threat. Since 1938 officers in "E" Division, stationed in Vancouver, had also kept the Japanese under surveillance. In 1940 they assigned three constables to observe the community and also employed Japanese informants. Through continual investigation the force concluded that Japanese residents posed no real threat to Canada. On the contrary, it observed what it believed to be convincing evidence of Japanese loyalty to Canada. Signs of this were especially clear in the community's strong support for Victory bond drives and Red Cross work, the Nisei desire to volunteer for military service, and the widespread wish among Japanese not to arouse white antagonism. "This office," the officer commanding at Vancouver reported late in October 1940, "does not consider that the Japanese of British Columbia constitute a menace to the State."[18]

Was there substance to this apparent threat of Japanese subversion? The Board of Review in 1938 had found no proof of wholesale illegal immigration. Nor had the RCMP discovered any indication of serious danger and, surely, this was the organization best able to judge.[19] It had scrutinized the Japanese community more carefully than had any other agency. Neither military intelligence nor popular rumour was founded on such close observation, and the claims of each should be judged accordingly. All available signs pointed in one direction only: no significant evidence of Japanese treachery could be seen at this time. Nor would any be discovered at a later date. The threat of Japanese subversion was in essence a fiction based on xenophobic traditions and perceptions clouded by fears and anxieties. Yet despite its insubstantial basis, the threat was real enough to many British Columbians and it was the goad which stirred popular animus to life once more.

This resurgence of anti-Japanese sentiment again placed the King government in an uncomfortable position. Whatever it felt about the demands of west-coast nativists, more than ever, in the summer of 1940, it wished to avoid irritating Japan as this might jeopardize British interests in the Pacific, if not induce war itself. As well, by this time Canada was preoccupied by European conflict and presumably the federal government wished to avoid distractions. Therefore it hesitated as long as seemed possible before taking action. But by September 1940, when rumours first were heard that Oriental Canadians would be included in the first call for military service, the question could no longer be ignored. Just as Japan announced her alliance with the Axis powers, these reports provoked a sharp cry of protest. Bowing before the rising winds of criticism, the Cabinet War Committee omitted Asian Canadians from the first draft and then formed a special committee to investigate the question of Orientals and British Columbia's security.[20]

The committee soon confirmed that anti-Japanese feeling was running high in the province and that this, rather than Japanese subversion, was the greatest potential source of danger to the community. Its major recommendations were therefore aimed at reducing public tension. In order to scotch persistent rumours of illegal Japanese immigration, it urged a new registration of all Japanese residents, both citizens and aliens alike. It also proposed the creation of a standing committee to advise the government on problems relating to Orientals in British Columbia.[21] King and his Cabinet, because of the delicate state of Anglo-Japanese relations, were anxious to avoid even the threat of civil disorder in British Columbia. Thus they implemented these suggestions in the hope that they would promote public calm. Intent on disarming British Columbia's xenophobes, the government included MacGregor Macintosh on the Standing Committee. And in order to reassure the Japanese, it nominated Professor H.F. Angus, a long-time champion of civil rights for Japanese Canadians.[22]

If the King government hoped its new initiative would calm popular fears, it must soon have been disabused of its optimism. During the first half of 1941 the public temper remained aroused. A few signs indicated, in fact, that some British Columbians were growing even more suspicious of the Japanese. Agitation thus continued, even though still no credible leadership had emerged to give protest a focus. Halford Wilson kept up his one-man campaign, repeatedly urging that, in the interest of national security, all Japanese fishing boats should be sequestered.[23] Furthermore, ongoing tension remained a source of concern to federal officials who still feared a racial incident. Wilson was singled out as the chief cause for alarm and unsuccessful efforts were made to persuade him to keep silent.[24] Meanwhile, in military circles, fear of public disturbance was matched by continued suspicion of the Japanese themselves. As an intelligence report noted in July 1941, widespread Japanese sabotage was unlikely in the event of war but it remained a possibility unless proper security precautions were taken and the Japanese themselves were protected from white provocation.[25]

In the final months before Pearl Harbor was bombed, racial tensions began to abate. But even then conditions favoured a new anti-Japanese outburst. Influenced by the community's xenophobia, its traditional racial cleavage, and its anxieties born of war and isolation, British Columbians continued to suspect their Japanese neighbours. The west-coast Japanese could not be trusted. Their allegiance was in doubt. Given the opportunity, it was assumed, some among them would betray the province to the enemy. The federal government, while alarmed by British Columbia's Japanese problem, was ill prepared to meet the issue head on. It feared that Japan might use a racial disturbance as a *casus belli*, but aside from forming the Standing Committee, it had done very little to prevent an outbreak.

Canada declared war on Japan on 7 December 1941, within hours of Pearl Harbor. The King government immediately recognized the likelihood of violent anti-Japanese demonstrations in British Columbia. At the same time it had to deal with a new enemy alien problem, for war's outbreak altered the status of many Canadian residents of Japanese origin.[26] Faced with the prospect of racial incidents as well as an alien menace, the dominion government quickly took preemptive action. Thirty-eight Japanese nationals were interned on the grounds that they might endanger the community, and the west-coast Japanese fishing fleet was immobilized. On the advice of the RCMP, all Japanese-language newspapers and schools voluntarily closed their doors. Meanwhile, Prime Minister King, senior police and military officers, and Vancouver's major newspapers all reassured the public and called for calm. As King declared in a radio address to the nation on 8 December: "the competent authorities are satisfied that the security situation is well in hand. They are confident of the correct and loyal behaviour of Canadian residents of Japanese origin."[27]

But many west-coast whites were not so easily mollified. Neither prompt federal action nor loyal protestations from leading Japanese did much to assuage their fears. War's outbreak had once more opened the floodgates of fear and hostility. Roused by war on the Pacific, the west coast resumed its attack on the province's Japanese. Again, enmity was strongest in and around Vancouver and Victoria, long the province's two focal points of anti-Asian sentiment. In the week following Pearl Harbor some Japanese in Vancouver were victimized by scattered acts of vandalism. Several firms began discharging their Japanese employees. Fear of Japanese subversion again spread in the province.[28] In private, British Columbians began protesting to their members of Parliament. The weight of public concern also bore down on provincial newspapers. Columnist Bruce Hutchison informed the Prime Minister's office that, at the *Vancouver Sun*, "we are under extraordinary pressure from our readers to advocate a pogrom of Japs. We told the people to be calm. Their reply was a bombardment of letters that the Japs all be interned."[29]

To encourage calm, police, government, and military officials issued further assurances that the Japanese problem was well in hand.[30] But their statements seemed to have little effect. Popular protest continued to grow and, in response, alarm in government and military circles increased too. On 20 December, F.J. Hume, chairman of the Standing Committee, told King: "In British Columbia particularly, the successes of the Japanese to date in the Pacific have to a great extent inflamed public opinion against the local Japanese. People here are in a very excited condition and it would require a very small local incident to bring about most unfortunate conditions between the whites and Japanese."[31] Major General R.O. Alexander, commander in chief of the Pacific Command, was also concerned: "The situation with regard to the Japanese resident in British Columbia is assuming a serious aspect. Public feeling is becoming very insistent, especially in Vancouver, that local Japanese should be either interned or removed from the coast. Letters are being written continually to the press and I am being bombarded by individuals, both calm and hysterical, demanding that something should be done."[32] Alexander feared that public demonstrations, to be held in the near future according to rumour, might lead to racial violence.

After a brief lull over Christmas the public outcry grew more strident than ever. Increasing numbers of west-coast whites, regardless of all reassurance, were certain that the local Japanese community endangered west-coast security. By early January 1942 patriotic societies, service clubs, town and city councils, and air-raid precaution units, most of them on Vancouver Island or in the Vancouver area, had begun to voice protest.[33] Repeatedly they urged that all Japanese, regardless of citizenship, be interned, as quickly as possible. Other spokesmen suggested somewhat less drastic action, but whatever the precise demands of the public they all assumed the need for some form of Japanese evacuation. And with each passing day opinion seemed to grow more volatile. Even moderates like J.G. Turgeon, the Liberal MP from the Cariboo, were alarmed at the seeming danger. On 6 January he warned the prime minister:

> the condition of this province is dangerous, so far as the Japanese are concerned. If the Government do not take drastic action, the situation will get out-of-hand. The Government will suffer, and so will the Japanese, personally and through destruction of property.
>
> I am therefore forced to recommend that very strong measures to [*sic*] taken, and quickly. Either delay, or lack of thorough action, may cause violence.[34]

Beneath this new hostile outburst, which war with Japan had precipitated, lay two primary social strains.[35] The first was British Columbia's traditional racial cleavage, one marked in recent years by strong anti-Japanese prejudice. This permanent gulf between whites and Asians had created enduring social tensions which perpetually tended toward outbreaks of racial animosity. The structure of west-coast race relations was conducive to such an end. The second strain was the growing sense of anxiety which accompanied war's outbreak, a condition created by the atmosphere of ambiguity which surrounded the Pacific war. In the weeks following Pearl Harbor, the level of generalized public anxiety created by war increased appreciably. In itself the opening of a new theatre of war was a new source of unease because it raised new uncertainties in an already war-troubled world. More specifically, the ambiguity which enveloped Japan's military activities in the weeks after 7 December also conditioned the growth of anxiety. The startling number of her targets, the suddenness of her assaults, the speed of her military expansion, and the seeming ease of her victories surprised and frightened many west-coast whites. The enemy seemed everywhere in the Pacific. No one knew where he might next attack and some feared it would be British Columbia. In such conditions civil defence preparations themselves became a source of unease for they reflected the assumption that a Japanese attack was indeed imminent. During the first week of war, air raid precaution units were called for duty, defence regulations were posted, and nightly blackouts were enforced. Far from offering reassurance, these activities further unsettled an already apprehensive public.

In the years since the expulsion it has occasionally been suggested that two economic motives caused the anti-Japanese outburst: one the desire of some British Columbians to acquire Japanese property at bargain prices, the other a wish to rid the province, once and for all, of Japanese economic competition. These conclusions, however, are informed by little more than hindsight. There is no body of evidence to indicate that either factor significantly shaped public opinion or government policy. In the Fraser and Okanagan valleys some residents did request stringent restrictions on Japanese landholding, a proposal which reflected interracial tensions of economic origin. But the great majority of those who protested had no obvious economic interest to defend against Japanese encroachment and, evidently, no strong desire to profit at the expense of evacuees.[36]

It was because of wartime social strains that a sense of crisis mounted in British Columbia. And as these tensions grew they sharpened the coast's hostility toward the Japanese minority. Japanese militarism and the province's legacy of racial tension combined to cast the old image of the Yellow Peril in a new and lurid light. As many British Columbians peered through the fog of their anxieties, they saw little but the menacing outline of Japanese subversion. Furthermore, while the growing sense of crisis narrowed whites' perceptions, these perceptions, in turn, intensified public unease. Thus, social tensions and racial imagery were mutually reinforcing. Had British Columbians seen their Japanese neighbours clearly, they would have observed an isolated, defenceless minority, gravely alarmed by its plight and anxious to demonstrate its loyalty to Canada. But fear and prejudice prevented them from taking a closer look. Consequently, the Japanese appeared nothing but a threat and therefore the call went up for their expulsion.

In addition, aroused public opinion pressed down upon a group of politicians particularly susceptible to prejudice against Asians. On a personal level, most political leaders in British Columbia probably shared the stereotyped attitudes of their constituents. Furthermore, ever since Confederation anti-Orientalism had pervaded the provincial political culture. Over the years conservatives, liberals, and socialists alike had freely employed the rhetoric of racialism. The Conservative and Liberal parties had regularly nailed anti-Oriental planks to their election platforms, both federal and provincial, and after 1933 the CCF, despite its professed concern for civil liberties, had been divided on the question. Seldom, if ever, had the anti-Asian cry been a decisive issue in electoral contests: the broad consensus among west-coast politicians had prevented that. Yet, by World War II racial prejudice had long been common currency in political discourse. Some politicians merely dealt in the small change of petty racialism; others, like Wilson and Macintosh, traded in larger denominations — nativism and xenophobia. Ian Mackenzie, upon whom the weight of west-coast opinion fell in 1942, stood between the two extremes. He was undoubtedly confirmed in his anti-Asian sentiments, yet not outspokenly so. Certainly, on the eve of war in the Pacific, most British Columbian politicians shared some of Mackenzie's convictions. Consequently, when anti-Japanese feeling welled up after Pearl Harbor, they also shared the public's growing concern and responded sympathetically to popular pressure.

In Ottawa Mackenzie King was also a target of rising protest. His experience with west-coast hostility toward Asians had been longer and more intimate than that of any other federal politician. In 1907 and 1908 he had held three royal commissions to investigate Oriental immigration and racial disturbances in Vancouver. Throughout the 1920s and 1930s, as prime minister, the issue confronted him repeatedly. As was usual with King, his comments on the Oriental problem were always extremely circumspect. Prior to his premiership he concluded that the roots of west-coast tensions were economic, not racial, and he saw their satisfactory resolution in negotiation with Asian nations to seek mutually acceptable immigration levels.[37] In office his government used both diplomacy and legislation to enforce restrictions on immigration from China and Japan. During the later 1930s, however, when anti-Japanese feeling increased on the west coast, King felt constrained from any further restrictive action by international tensions. His view of the issue after the outbreak of war with Japan remains unclear. He did not share the anxieties of west-coast residents yet he ultimately accepted the possibility of a Japanese invasion of British Columbia.[38] Probably his primary concern was for the instability of west-coast opinion and the threat to public order which it posed. If subsequent government policy was any measure of King's thought, he was willing to accept any expedient solution to reduce public tension.

Under heavy popular pressure, the federal government ordered yet another review of the Japanese problem in British Columbia. On 8 and 9 January 1942 a committee of federal and provincial government, police, and military officials met in Ottawa to discuss means of allaying west-coast alarm. The central question explored was whether or not the Japanese should be removed from coastal areas; but the meeting could not agree on an answer. Several representatives who had just arrived from British Columbia, together with Ian Mackenzie, the meeting's chairman, argued that all able-bodied male Japanese nationals should immediately be removed. The majority of the delegates, however, few of whom had recently been in British Columbia, opposed such drastic action. Consequently the meeting submitted a moderate report which suggested both an extension of existing minor restrictions on the liberties of all Japanese and the creation of a quasi-military work corps for Canadian Japanese who wished to support the war effort.[39]

But the conference's report was only one opinion. From British Columbia there came ever more insistent demands for an evacuation program, and within the Cabinet Ian Mackenzie, King's closest political friend from the province, pressed for such a solution.[40] Consequently, when the government announced its revised plans on 14 January, the new policy bore the unmistakable imprint of west-coast opinion. The King government accepted most of the Ottawa conference's proposals, but in addition it proposed to remove all enemy aliens, regardless of age, sex, or nationality, from protected areas soon to be defined in British Columbia. The program was aimed primarily at Japanese nationals although it embraced Germans and Italians as well. The statement also promised that a Japanese Civilian Corps would soon be formed for work on projects deemed in the national interest.[41] The covert hope was that Japanese-Canadian men would volunteer for it in large numbers, thus permitting the government to remove them from the protected areas without an unpleasant resort to compulsion.[42]

It was felt that, by yielding to some of the west coast's demands, the partial evacuation policy would calm British Columbian fears. Concerned for the safety of Canadian prisoners in Japan's hands, anxious to avoid needless expense and disruption in time of war, and touched with a lingering sense of justice and humanity, the King government refused to make further concessions. But the plan was also rather equivocal in that it neither defined the protected areas nor promised when evacuation would begin. In effect it still gave the federal government considerable freedom of action. For a few brief moments the gesture seemed satisfactory. Premier John Hart of British Columbia, whose government had already demanded similar measures, applauded the decision, and the *Vancouver Sun* praised the King government's common sense. The storm of protest abated temporarily.[43]

Within ten days, however, agitation began to increase once again. The public outcry mounted throughout February until, during the last week of the month, it reached unprecedented volume. Pressed by the fear of enemy subversion, thousands of west-coast whites petitioned Ottawa for the immediate evacuation of all Japanese. Individuals, farm organizations, municipal councils, civil defence units, constituency associations, service clubs, patriotic societies, trades unions, citizens committees, chambers of commerce — even the Vancouver and District Lawn Bowling Association — all demanded the total evacuation of Japanese from coastal areas.[44] One group of prominent Vancouver residents telegraphed Ian Mackenzie that, "owing to widespread public alarm over enemy aliens on the Pacific coast and especially respecting those astride vital defence points and with a view to stabilizing public opinion and in the interest of public safety," they urged the immediate evacuation of all Japanese.[45] Never before had west-coast race relations been so seriously strained.

By and large British Columbians appear to have reached their conclusions about the Japanese menace with little prompting. More or less simultaneously thousands recognized an obvious threat and identified the equally obvious solution. In the generation of this consensus neither popular leaders nor popular journalism played a predominant role. Halford Wilson and MacGregor Macintosh, once the two chief critics of the west-coast Japanese, were submerged beneath the rising tide of hostility. In fact the protest movement had no preeminent leaders whatsoever. Nor did provincial papers become leaders of opinion, even though some took up the popular cry. During the crisis west-coast journalism helped sustain the prevailing mood, but most papers merely reflected the popular mind. Agitation was the product of a widespread outburst of hostility, one which was rooted in long-standing antipathies as well as immediate wartime pressures.

The very structure of the protest movement supports this contention for it clearly revealed how extensive was the anti-Japanese consensus. Although public anxiety had flared up immediately after Pearl Harbor, no effective anti-Japanese movement had begun to emerge until late January. In its earliest stage protest was random; it had no central leadership and no institutional focus. But when the movement began to take form, protest was mobilized by a broad range of the traditional social, economic, administrative, and political organizations already entrenched in British Columbia. The Provincial Council of Women, the Vancouver Real Estate Exchange, the Canadian Legion in Gibson's Landing, the Kinsmen's Club of Victoria, the North Burnaby Liberal Association, the B.C. Poultry Industries Committee, the Corporation of the District of Saanich, the National Union of Machinists, Fitters, and Helpers (Victoria Local Number 2), and scores of other similar groups all pressed their demands for evacuation. These organizations not only represented major interest groups in the province but their influence cut across most social, economic, and political bounds in west-coast society. They represented the interests and opinions, the fears and hostilities of tens of thousands of British Columbians. If there were some who did not share prevailing attitudes, they remained largely silent when confronted by the tyranny of the consensus.

One further sign of mounting social pressure was the growing incidence of rumours of Japanese subversion. Some told of Japanese who owned high-powered vehicles and short-wave equipment, who lived near sites of great strategic value, who swelled with insolent pride at Japan's successive victories. Others hinted at active Japanese disloyalty — and, in the hothouse atmosphere of growing public tension, stories grew to outlandish proportions. Military intelligence officers were informed in mid-January that Japanese in Vancouver had fixed infrared and ultraviolet beacons on their roofs, devices which, when viewed through special binoculars, would guide enemy flights over the city.[46] Rumour itself is usually the product of serious social strain.[47] These persistent rumours were one more indication of the growing racial crisis on Canada's west coast. The outbreak of war with Japan had spread a grave sense of looming threat among west-coast whites. Yet for all its immediacy this threat remained somewhat vague and nebulous. The enemy was identified, his whereabouts were not. Rumours helped resolve this ambiguity. They suggested that some of the enemy were very close at hand. While this in itself was cause for concern, it also helped to clarify the confusions of war with a distant, elusive power. Because rumours singled out the nearest available enemy, they helped reduce the ambiguity which had spawned them in the first place. And, once in circulation, they, too, stirred the ever-widening eddies of hostility and alarm.

It seemed clear, as well, that one immediate reason for the renewed upsurge of protest in February was that many British Columbians, anxious for total evacuation, had misinterpreted the government's policy announcement of 14 January. The *Vancouver Sun* had taken it to mean that "all Japanese and other enemy aliens" were to be removed from protected areas, an assumption shared by several provincial members of Parliament. "My understanding," wrote Ian MacKenzie, "was that all able-bodied, adult enemy aliens would have to be removed from protected areas. My further understanding was also that all able-bodied *Canadian nationals* would have to be moved, but that *first* they should be given an opportunity to volunteer in the Civilian Corps."[48] This confusion aside, the federal government also failed to implement its program immediately. Neither the evacuation plans nor the designated protected areas were announced until 23 January, and the delay itself provoked some concern. Furthermore, when finally announced, the plans indicated that evacuation was not to be completed before 1 April, a date which seemed far too remote to those who believed the Japanese threat was imminent. Once the plans were made public there was a further delay while the relocation machinery was set up. The task of arranging to move, house, and care for several thousand Japanese proved a time-consuming one and it was complicated further by the strong opposition of residents in the British Columbian interior, especially the Okanagan Valley, to proposals that the Japanese all be settled inland.[49] Several times the immediate departure of Japanese from Vancouver was announced and then postponed. Consequently, few, if any, Japanese left their homes before mid-February. In the eyes of concerned west-coast whites the government's partial evacuation policy increasingly seemed a mixture of confusion, delay, and prevarication. It appeared that Ottawa did not understand, let alone sympathize with, British Columbia's predicament.

Japan's startling military success continued to play on west-coast fears as well. By mid-January Japanese troops had overrun much of Malaya, the Philippines, Burma, and British North Borneo. They had occupied Thailand, captured Hong Kong (taking more than 1600 Canadian troops prisoner), sunk Britain's most modern battleship, and crippled her Pacific fleet. Late in January they had laid siege to the island of Singapore. News of this swift succession of decisive victories dominated the front pages of the provincial press. Furthermore, these accounts repeatedly emphasized that Japanese subversion and fifth-column activity had played a central role in Japan's program of conquest. Already convinced of their own vulnerability, British Columbians grew more alarmed when worse news succeeded bad. As the military crisis deepened across the Pacific, so public tension grew on Canada's west coast.

Parliament reconvened on 22 January as the racial crisis mounted. Members of Parliament from British Columbia, no doubt as concerned as their protesting constituents, themselves began to press for total evacuation. Howard Green, the Conservative member from Vancouver South, opened the attack in the Commons on 29 January.[50] The threat of Japanese treachery confronted the Pacific coast, he said, and therefore all Japanese should be removed from the province. Other British Columbian members made similar claims before the House over the next three weeks. In private they were even more insistent. On 28 January British Columbians in the Liberal caucus demanded that Japanese Canadians who failed to volunteer for the Civilian Corps be evacuated as quickly as possible. In succeeding weeks, as popular protest reached its greatest heights, King faced successive demands for relocation from provincial politicians — Conservative, Liberal, and Independent alike.[51]

Meanwhile, government officials in British Columbia sustained their pressure as well. At the height of the popular outcry the attorney-general of British Columbia told Ian Mackenzie:

> Events have transpired recently which add to the danger we have already been subjected to by the presence of Japanese on this Coast.
>
> I cannot urge too strongly the seriousness of this situation and the danger the people of British Columbia feel upon this matter.
>
> Nothing short of immediate removal of the Japanese will meet the dangers which we feel in this Province.[52]

At the same time the minister of labour campaigned for total evacuation. The lieutenant-governor informed Mackenzie King that he had "rarely felt so keenly about any impending danger as I do about the Japanese on this coast being allowed to live in our midst." He suggested that, at very least, Japanese males be quickly interned. Since mid-January senior officers of the Pacific Command had grown more concerned as well. By the time public protest reached its peak, they, too, subscribed to demands for total evacuation.[53]

It was Ian Mackenzie who ultimately bore the brunt of this storm of protest. First he received warnings and notes of alarm, then petitions urging evacuation, and finally demands that he resign. But Mackenzie shared the concerns of his west-coast constituents. In the first weeks after the outbreak of war he grew convinced that all able-bodied Japanese men should be removed from strategic areas. In consequence, he considered the partial evacuation policy inadequate. He also believed that the 1 April deadline was too remote. Furthermore, as pressure upon him grew, Mackenzie's alarm at the instability of public opinion increased in like proportion. On 22 February, when news reached him of a series of mass protest meetings planned for 1 March, his anxiety heightened further.[54] Two days later he informed Cabinet colleagues of the heated state of west-coast opinion and of a call for his own resignation. As he told the minister of justice:

> The feeling in British Columbia in regard to the Japanese is so aflame that I consider we should take the necessary powers (if we have not got them now) to remove Canadian Nationals, as well as Japanese Nationals, from the protected areas.
>
> I have no report on how the Vancouver Corps has succeeded, but I greatly fear *disorder* from reports actually received, unless all able-bodied males of Japanese origin are immediately evacuated.[55]

Publicly Mackenzie appeared unperturbed, urging calm on his west-coast correspondents, but privately he was extremely exercised.[56]

Within the Cabinet others shared something of Mackenzie's alarm, particularly his concern for possible public disturbances. The prime minister agreed that there was "every possibility of riots" on the west coast, and feared that in such an event there would be "repercussions in the Far East against our own prisoners." The situation was awkward, he recognized, because "public prejudice is so strong in B.C. that it is going to be difficult to control."[57] Thus, under heavy external pressure and alarmed by the evident danger of racial violence, the federal government finally took decisive action. On 24 February, only hours after Mackenzie had written his warning to Cabinet colleagues, the government approved an enabling measure which permitted total evacuation. Three days later the announcement was made that all persons of Japanese ancestry would have to leave the protected zones.[58] In the hope of reducing social tensions, the King government had finally capitulated to public pressure.

The province did not all at once breathe a sigh of collective relief. Tension remained high for several days thereafter. From Ottawa Ian Mackenzie believed that public disorder was still possible. Hostility surged onward in the Okanagan Valley, where many local residents feared that the new federal policy would bring a large Japanese influx. Slowly, however, the strain of racial crisis began to ease. The two mass meetings held on 1 March were quiet and orderly. Mackenzie received a note of praise from supporters in Vancouver. The flood of protests to Ottawa began to recede.[59]

When the Cabinet approved the order which permitted evacuation, the editors of the *Sun* looked forward to the day the move would be complete. They hoped that the coast was "Saying Goodbye, Not Au Revoir" to the Japanese.[60] But while some had undoubtedly seen the crisis as a chance to solve the province's Japanese problem for all time, this scarcely explains the previous weeks' outburst of hostility. War with Japan had sharpened the animus, narrowed the vision, and roused the fears of a community already deeply divided along racial lines. In the minds of west-coast whites, intimations of vulnerability and isolation had long nursed a sense of insecurity, and after Pearl Harbor many British Columbians had felt themselves exposed as never before to attack from Japan. In addition, they had grown convinced that the resident Japanese were a threat to the community's security. These beliefs had virtually no foundation in fact. In essence they were facets of the traditional Japanese image held by white British Columbians, stereotypes further distorted in the heat of war. Its fears fed by these perceptions, the west coast loosed a torrent of hostility. Sensitive to the public temper, and alarmed by the prospect of racial disturbance, the federal government attempted preventative action. But neither minor restrictions on civil liberties nor the promise of partial relocation could satisfy the west-coast public for long. It demanded total Japanese evacuation. In the end its wishes were met.[61]

NOTES

1. The major works on Orientals in Canada are Tien-fang Cheng, *Oriental Immigration in Canada* (Shanghai, 1931); Charles H. Young and Helen R.Y. Reid, *The Japanese Canadians* (Toronto, 1938); Charles James Woodsworth, *Canada and the Orient: A Study in International Relations* (Toronto, 1941); Forrest E. LaViolette, *The Canadian Japanese and World War II: A Sociological and Psychological Account* (Toronto, 1948); William Peter Ward, "White Canada Forever: British Columbia's Response to Orientals, 1858–1914" (Ph.D. thesis, Queen's University, 1972).

2. On the nature and significance of Oriental stereotypes, see Ward, "White Canada Forever," 37–67 and 132–48, and LaViolette, *The Canadian Japanese*, 3–28.

3. A.R.M. Lower, *Canada and the Far East — 1940*, Institution of Pacific Research Inquiry Series (New York, 1940), 23–28.

4. *Vancouver Sun*, 17 Nov. 1937.

5. *Vancouver Sun*, 24 Nov. 1937; *The Colonist* (Victoria), 19 Jan. 1938.

6. Canada, House of Commons, *Debates* (17 Feb. 1938), 550–75.

7. *The Province* (Vancouver), 22 Feb. 1938.

8. *The Province*, 2, 17, 18, and 24 Feb. 1938; *Vancouver Sun*, 10, 12, 14, and 28 Feb. 1938.

9. Two representative letters to King are: R.S. Hanna to King, 14 Feb. 1938, William Lyon Mackenzie King Papers, MG 26, J2, vol. 147, file 1-209, Public Archives of Canada [PAC]; Forgotten Native of Japanada to King, n.d., King Papers. Letters to Wilson in 1938 can be found in the Halford Wilson Papers, vol. 1, file 1, Public Archives of British Columbia [PABC].

10. T.D. Pattullo to King, 26 Jan. 1938, King Papers, MG 26, JI, vol. 256, 218388-9; Ian Mackenzie to King, 26 Feb. 1938, King Papers, vol. 253, 216060; King to Mackenzie, 1 March 1938, King Papers, vol. 253, 216062–3A. At this time Mackenzie was the minister of national defence. After the outbreak of war he was transferred to Pensions and National Health.

11. *Vancouver Sun*, 23 March 1938.

12. The Board of Review concluded that rumours of illegal Japanese immigration had been greatly exaggerated. It estimated that about 120 Japanese were living illegally in the province. Board of Review [Immigration], *Final Report*, 29 Sept. 1938, 38.

13. H.L. K[eenleyside], Memorandum, 11 June 1940, Department of External Affairs Records, RG, G-1, vol. 2007, file 212, part 1, PAC; *The Province*, 7 and 15 Aug. 1940.

14. See also Wilson Papers, vol. 1, file 4; *Vancouver Sun*, 29 June and 10 Aug. 1940; *The Province*, 21 and 24 Aug. 1940.

15. K[eenleyside], Memorandum, 11 June 1940, External Affairs Records, vol. 2007, file 212, part 1, PAC; Gray Turgeon to King, 7 Aug. 1940, King Papers, MG 26, JI, vol. 297, 252824–5; King to Lapointe, 8 Aug. 1940, King Papers, vol. 297, 252828.

16. Extract from Report on Japanese Activities on the West Coast of Canada, 10 March 1937, External Affairs Records, vol. 1803, file 729, PAC; Major General E.C. Ashton, Chief of the General Staff, Memorandum, Acquisition by Japanese Interests of Timberland and Mineral Concessions on the Pacific Coast, 13 Nov. 1937, Ian Mackenzie Papers, MG 27, 3-B-5, vol. 30, file X-23, PAC; L.R. LaFlèche, deputy minister, Department of National Defence, to F.C. Blair, director of immigration, 2 June 1938, Department of National Defence Records, file HQ 6-0-7, Department of National Defence Archives.

17. Brigadier C.V. Stockwell, district officer commanding Military District 11, to the secretary, Department of National Defence, 4 Sept. 1940, Defence Records, file HQS, vs 38-1-1, vol. 5.

18. Superintendent C.E. Hill, "E" Division, RCMP, to the Commissioner, 25 Aug. 1938, Government of Canada, Immigration Branch Records, RG 76, vol. 86, file 9309, vol. 16, PAC; R.R. Tait, assistant commissioner, RCMP, to Keenleyside, 28 Oct. 1940, External Affairs Records, vol. 2007, file 212, part 1, PAC. The entire contents of this file substantiate the observations made in this paragraph.

19. The RCMP did, however, identify a small number of Japanese who might endanger the state in time of war, and these individuals were arrested and detained immediately after war on Japan was declared.
20. Pattullo to King, 23 Sept. 1940, King Papers, MG 26, JI, vol. 293, 248363; King to Pattullo, 27 Sept. 1940, T.D. Pattullo Papers, Vol. 70, file 4, 21, PABC; Wilson to the Finance Committee, City of Vancouver, 24 Sept. 1940, Wilson Papers, vol. 1, file 4; A.D.P. Heeney, Memorandum for the Prime Minister, 27 Sept. 1940, King Papers, MG 26, J4, vol. 361, file 3849.
21. Report and Recommendations of the Special Committee on Orientals in British Columbia, Dec. 1940, typescript, King Papers. The committee also recommended that, because testimony before it almost unanimously favoured a complete end to Japanese immigration, the government should forbid it when the international situation permitted. This recommendation was not published because King feared it might strain existing relations with Japan and inflame anti-Oriental opinion in British Columbia. Government of Canada, Privy Council, Minutes and Documents of the Cabinet War Committee, RG 2, 7C, vol. 4, Minutes, 2 Jan. 1941, 8–9, PAC; Keenleyside to Sansom, [3 Jan. 1941], External Affairs Records, vol. 1868, file 263, part 4, PAC; Additional Statement by the Members of the Special Committee on Orientals in British Columbia for consideration by the Prime Minister and members of the Cabinet War Committee, n.d., King Papers, MG 26, JI, vol. 307, 259432–3.
22. Keenleyside to King, 2 Dec. 1940, King Papers, MG 26, JI, vol. 289, 244808–10.
23. *The Province*, 9 Jan. and 11 Feb. 1941; *Victoria Times*, 26 Feb. 1941; *Vancouver Sun*, 8 April and 26 July 1941. One sign of growing suspicion was the increasing sensitivity of west-coast whites to Japanese using cameras. For example, see *Nanaimo Free Press*, 8 Feb. 1941.
24. Keenleyside to S.T. Wood, commissioner, RCMP, 20 Feb. 1941, External Affairs Records, vol. 2007, file 212, part 2, PAC; F.J. Mead, assistant commissioner, RCMP, to the commissioner, 28 Feb. 1941, External Affairs Records, vol. 2007; H.F. Angus to Mayor F.J. Hume, chairman, Standing Committee on Orientals, 25 July 1941, External Affairs Records, vol. 2007.
25. Flying Officer W.A. Nield, Report on the State of Intelligence on the Pacific Coast with Particular Reference to the Problem of the Japanese Minority, 27 July 1941, Defence Records, file HQ S67-3, vol. 1.
26. All Japanese nationals immediately became enemy aliens and, in addition, restrictions imposed on them were also imposed on all Japanese Canadians naturalized after 1922.
27. LaViolette, *The Canadian Japanese*, 44; Declaration of the Existence of a State of War Between Canada and Japan, 8 Dec. 1941, King Papers, MG 26, J5, D58190-4; Vancouver Sun, 8 Dec. 1941; *Nanaimo Free Press*, 8 Dec. 1941; *The Province*, 8 Dec. 1941.
28. After Pearl Harbor the major daily newspapers in Vancouver and Victoria published steady streams of letters on the Japanese problem, most of which voiced suspicion of the west-coast Japanese and demanded federal action to remove the threat which they posed. For reports of vandalism, see *The Province*, 8, 9, and 11 Dec. 1941. For rumours of Japanese subversion, see Weekly Internal Security Intelligence Report, 13 Dec. 1941, Western Air Command, Defence Records, file HQ S67-3, vol. 1. With the exception of fishermen, those Japanese who lost their jobs were soon reabsorbed by the labour market. C.H. Hill, assistant commissioner, RCMP, Intelligence Report, 16 Dec. 1941 and 13 Jan. 1942, External Affairs Records, file 3464-G-40, Department of External Affairs, Archives Branch [EAA].
29. Hutchison to Pickersgill, [16 Dec. 1941], King Papers, MG 26, J4, vol. 347, 239219–20.
30. *The Province*, 19 Dec. 1941; Hill to the commissioner, RCMP, 20 Dec. 1941, External Affairs Records, file 3464-H-40C, EAA.
31. Hume to King, 20 Dec. 1941, External Affairs Records, vol. 1868, file 263, part 4, PAC.
32. Alexander to chief of the General Staff, 30 Dec. 1941, Defence Records, file HQ 6-0-7. Alexander's concern was shared by those officers commanding Canada's Pacific coast naval and

air forces. Commodore W.J.R. Beech to the general officer commanding-in-chief, Pacific Command, 27 Dec. 1941, Defence Records; L.S. Stevenson to the secretary, Department of National Defence for Air, 2 Jan. 1941, Defence Records, file HQ S67-3, vol. 1. In Ottawa the chief of the General Staff did not subscribe to these fears. Lt.-Gen. K. Stuart to Keenleyside, 26 Dec. 1941, External Affairs Papers, file 3464-H-40C, EAA.

33. Petitions to the federal government can be found in King Papers, MG 26, J2, vol. 294, file p-309, vol. 14; Mackenzie Papers, vol. 24, file 70-25, vol. 1, vol. 25, file 70-25, vols. 2 and 3, vol. 25, file 70-25E; External Affairs Records, file 773-B 1-40, parts 1 and 2, EAA.

34. Turgeon to King, 6 Jan. 1942, External Affairs Records, file 773-b-1-40, part 1.

35. For a useful theoretical discussion of the hostile outburst as a social phenomenon, see Neil J. Smelser, *Theory of Collective Behavior* (New York, 1962), especially ch. 8.

36. *Langley Advance*, 15 and 22 Jan. 1942; see also note 49.

37. W.L. Mackenzie King, *Industry and Humanity: A Study in the Principles Underlying Industrial Reconstruction* (Toronto, 1918), 75–76.

38. King Diary, 20, 23, and 24 Feb. 1942, King Papers, MG 26, J13.

39. Conference on the Japanese Problem in British Columbia, Minutes, 8 and 9 Jan. 1942, External Affairs Records, vol. 1868, file 263, part 4, PAC; Mackenzie to King, 10 Jan. 1942, Mackenzie Papers, vol. 32, file x-81; Keenleyside to Mackenzie, 10 Jan. 1942, Mackenzie Papers. The minority recommendation for partial evacuation was appended to the report.

40. Pacific Command to National Defence Headquarters, 12 Jan. 1942, telegram, Defence Papers, file HQ 6-0-7; Mackenzie to King, 10 Jan. 1942, Mackenzie Papers, vol. 32, file x-81.

41. Statement of the prime minister, 14 Jan. 1942, Mackenzie Papers, vol. 24, file 70-25, vol. 1.

42. Mackenzie to Bryce M. Stewart, deputy minister of labour, 23 Jan. 1942, Mackenzie Papers, vol. 32, file x-81, vol. 2; Keenleyside to Mackenzie, 26 Jan. 1942, Mackenzie Papers; Keenleyside, The Japanese Problem in British Columbia, Memorandum to Mr. Robertson, 27 Jan. 1942, Mackenzie Papers.

43. *Vancouver Sun*, 14 Jan. 1942; the lull was obvious to military intelligence officers in British Columbia. Major C.H. Bray, Intelligence, Pacific Command, to the director, Military Operations and Intelligence, National Defence Headquarters, 29 Jan. 1942, Department of Labour Papers, RG 27, Lacelle Files, vol. 174, file 614.02:11-1, vol. 1, PAC.

44. See above note 33.

45. M.C. Robinson and others to Mackenzie, 23 Feb. 1942, Mackenzie Papers, vol. 25, file 70-25, vol. 2.

46. Weekly Internal Security Intelligence Report, 17 Jan. 1942, Western Air Command, Defence Records, file HQ S67-3, vol. 1. For another example of rumour, see Gwen Cash, *A Million Miles from Ottawa* (Toronto, 1942), 25–26.

47. On the nature and significance of rumour, see Gordon W. Allport and Leo Postman, *The Psychology of Rumor* (New York, 1965), especially ch. 2.

48. *Vancouver Sun*, 14 Jan. 1942; Mackenzie to Stewart, 23 Jan. 1942, Mackenzie Papers, vol. 32, file x-81, vol. 2. The emphasis was Mackenzie's.

49. Although some fruit and vegetable growers in the Okanagan Valley requested Japanese workers for the duration of the war in order to ease the wartime labour shortage, the proposal roused a strong outburst of bitter opposition in the valley. Protest was channelled through municipal councils, newspapers, boards of trade, and dissenting farm organizations. In addition, proposals that the Japanese be moved east of the Rockies met opposition from several provincial governments. *Penticton Herald*, 15, 22, and 29 Jan. 1942; *Kelowna Courier*, 22 Jan. and 12 Feb. 1942; Keenleyside, Memorandum for Mr. Robertson, 4 Feb. 1942, External Affairs Records, file 3464-G-40, [EAA].

50. House of Commons, *Debates* (29 Jan. 1942), 156–58.

51. Mackenzie to Robertson, 28 Jan. 1942, Mackenzie Papers, vol. 32, file x-81, vol. 2; R.W Mayhew to King, 12 Feb. 1942, King Papers, MG 26, J1 vol. 330; G. McGeer to King, 13 Feb. 1942, Gerald Grattan McGeer Papers, box 2, file 9, PABC; Olaf Hanson and others to King, 21 Feb. 1942, King Papers, MG 26, J1, vol. 336.

52. R.L. Maitland to Mackenzie, 17 Feb. 1942, Mackenzie Papers, vol. 32, file x-81, vol. 2.

53. *Vancouver Sun*, 16 Feb. 1942; Pearson to A. MacNamara, associate deputy minister of Labour, 17 Feb. 1942, Labour Records, RG 27, Lacelle Files, vol. 174, file 614.02: 11–1, vol. 1; W.C. Woodward, lieutenant-governor, to King, 11 Feb. 1942, King Papers, MG 26, J1, vol. 336; Alexander to the secretary, Chiefs of Staff Committee, Department of National Defence, 13 Feb. 1942, Defence Records, Chiefs of Staff Committee, Miscellaneous Memoranda, vol. 3, Feb. 1942; Joint Services Committee, Pacific Coast, Minutes, 19 and 20 Feb. 1942, Defence Records.

54. Mackenzie to L. St. Laurent, 14 Feb. 1942, Mackenzie Papers, vol. 24, file 70-25, vol. 1; Mackenzie to King, 22 Feb. 1942, King Papers, MG 26, J1, vol. 328.

55. Mackenzie to St. Laurent, 24 Feb. 1942, Mackenzie Papers, vol. 25, file 70-25, vol. 2. At the same time, Mackenzie sent similar letters to colleagues King, Power, Ralston, Macdonald, and Mitchell.

56. Mackenzie to J.R. Bowler, dominion secretary, Canadian Legion, 26 Feb. 1942, Mackenzie Papers, vol. 25.

57. King Diary, 19 Feb. 1942.

58. Order-in-Council PC 1486, 24 Feb. 1942; House of Commons, *Debates* (27 Feb. 1942), 917–20.

59. Cash, *A Million Miles from Ottawa*, 33; *The Province*, 2 March 1942; *The Colonist*, 3 March 1942; Ann Thompson, Vancouver Liberal Council to C.N. Senior [private secretary to Mackenzie], 27 Feb. 1942, Mackenzie Papers, vol. 25, file 70-25, vol. 2.

60. *Vancouver Sun*, 26 Feb. 1942.

61. While racial tensions swelled in British Columbia after Pearl Harbor, a similar crisis occurred on the American Pacific Coast. There, as in Canada, residents in coastal areas who were of Japanese origin were forced to move inland to camps constructed for their reception. The American decision for evacuation, however, was based solely on military considerations and was taken by military officers who had been given a free hand by President Roosevelt. There was no collaboration between the Canadian and American governments in the decision-making process and, while the events of the two evacuations ran in close parallel, neither country's policy appears to have influenced the other. For accounts of the American evacuation, see Morton Grodzins, *Americans Betrayed: Politics and the Japanese Evacuation* (Chicago, 1949); Stetson Conn, "The Decision to Evacuate the Japanese from the Pacific Coast (1942)," *Command Decisions*, ed. Kent Roberts Greenfield, Prepared by the office of the Chief of Military History, Department of the Army (New York, 1959); Roger Daniels, *Concentration Camps USA: Japanese Americans and World War II* (New York, 1972).

Topic Twelve

Foreign and Military Policy, 1930–1949

Lester B. Pearson addresses one of the committees at the

United Nations Conference on International Organization in

San Francisco, 1945.

346   **THE PERIOD** from 1919 to 1945 saw the development of important definitions in Canadian foreign and military policy. Canada had emerged from World War I as an autonomous nation in practice, if not yet in theory. Canadians had contributed greatly to the Allied cause in terms of troops (650 000 soldiers), equipment, and provisions. In return, Prime Minister Robert Borden had won for Canada the right to representation as an autonomous nation and as a member of the British delegation at the Paris Peace Conference. Canada had also gained membership in the General Assembly of the newly elected League of Nations. Further gains in autonomy came in the 1920s, when Prime Minister William Lyon Mackenzie King refused to join in the common British Imperial foreign policy urged by British leaders in response to the Chanak crisis of 1922. The cause of Canadian independence was advanced with the signing of the Halibut Treaty of 1923 between Canada and the United States. Three years later, with the signing of the Balfour Report at the Imperial Conference of 1926, Britain recognized the autonomy of all its dominion states, in free association as members of the British Commonwealth of Nations. The British Parliament's passage of the Statute of Westminster in 1931 confirmed Canada's complete independence.

Preoccupied throughout the 1930s with protecting its newly won independence, Canada overlooked the seriousness of the international situation that was developing during that decade. Independence became its rationale for refusing to support the League of Nations, the only international organization capable of controlling European aggression. In "'A Low Dishonest Decade': Aspects of Canadian External Policy, 1931–1939," James Eayrs critically reviews Canada's foreign policy in the 1930s.

Analysts of Canadian foreign and military policy in the post–World War II era have argued that Canada underwent a dramatic shift in perspective from isolationism in the 1930s to internationalism in the 1940s. They cite Canada's more active involvement in the United Nations than in the League of Nations, its willingness to take a more active role in the British Commonwealth of Nations than in the British Empire, and its greater involvement along with the United States in trying to resolve conflicts in eastern Europe, southeast Asia, and the Middle East through the North Atlantic Treaty Organization (NATO). In "The Cold War and the Limits of 'Internationalism' in Canada's Foreign Relations, 1945–1949," historian Hector Mackenzie challenges this conventional perspective of the so-called "golden age in Canadian diplomacy." He argues that the shift in policy was not as consistent as believed, nor as dramatic or different from what came before. Even in this period, Canada pursued "internationalism" from a Canadian national perspective, one based first and foremost on the traditional relationship with Britain and the United States known as the North Atlantic Triangle.

Canadian Foreign Policy: Historical Readings, ed. J.L. Granatstein (Toronto: Copp Clark, 1986) is a useful collection of articles. James Eayrs, in *In Defence of Canada*, vol. 2, *Appeasement and Rearmament* (Toronto: University of Toronto Press, 1965), provides an exhaustive analysis of Canadian foreign policy in the late 1930s. Two alternatives to Eayrs's critical views of Canada's position of isolationism are H. Blair Neatby's "Mackenzie King and National Unity," in *Empire and Nations: Essays in Honour of Frederic H. Soward*, ed. H.L. Dyck and H.P. Krosby (Toronto: University of Toronto Press, 1969), pp. 54–70, and J.L. Granatstein and R. Bothwell's "'A Self-Evident National Duty': Canadian Foreign Policy, 1935–1939," *Journal of Imperial and Commonwealth History* 3 (1975): 212–33. A good documentary collection on the 1930s is R. Bothwell and G.N. Hillmer, *"The In-Between Time": Canadian External Policy in the 1930's* (Toronto: Copp Clark, 1975). For an overview of the interwar years, see C.P. Stacey, *Canada and the Age of Conflict*, vol. 2, *1921–1948: The Mackenzie King Era* (Toronto: University of Toronto Press, 1981); Richard Veatch, *Canada and the League of Nations* (Toronto: University of Toronto Press, 1975); and Norman Hillmer and J.L. Granatstein, *Empire to Umpire: Canada and the World to the 1990s* (Toronto: Copp Clark Longman, 1994).

On Canadian foreign policy in the late 1940s and 1950s, see James Eayrs, *In Defence of Canada: Growing Up Allied* (Toronto: University of Toronto Press, 1980); Denis Smith, *Diplomacy of Fear: Canada and the Cold War, 1941–1948* (Toronto: University of Toronto Press, 1988); John Hilliker and Donald Barry, *Canada's Department of External Affairs*, vol. 2, *Coming of Age, 1946–1968* (Montreal/Kingston: McGill-Queen's University Press, 1995); Robert Spencer, *Canada in World Affairs: From UN to NATO, 1946–1949* (Toronto: University of Toronto Press, 1959); and David J. Bercuson, *Blood on the Hills: The Canadian Army in the Korean War* (Toronto: University of Toronto Press, 1999). A valuable collection of essays is *Canada and the Early Cold War 1943–1957*, compiled by the Department of Foreign Affairs and International Trade (Ottawa: Canadian Government Publishing, 1998).

Contemporary accounts by members of the Canadian foreign service include Escott Reid, *Radical Mandarin: The Memoirs of Escott Reid* (Toronto: University of Toronto Press, 1989); and his *On Duty: A Canadian at the Making of the United Nations, 1945–1949* (Toronto: McClelland and Stewart, 1983); and John W. Holmes, *The Shaping of Peace: Canada and the Search for World Order, 1943–1957*, 2 vols. (Toronto: University of Toronto Press, 1979, 1982).

Postwar Canada–U.S. relations are discussed in Robert Bothwell, *Canada and the United States: The Politics of Partnership* (Toronto: University of Toronto Press, 1992); J.L. Granatstein and Norman Hillmer, *For Better or for Worse: Canada and the United States to the 1990s* (Toronto: Copp Clark, 1991); and R.D. Cuff and J.L. Granatstein, *Ties That Bind: Canadian–American Relations in Wartime from the Great War to the Cold War* (Toronto: Samuel Stevens Hakkert, 1977). For relations in the defence sector, see Joseph T. Jockel's *No Boundaries Upstairs: Canada, the United States and the Origins of North American Air Defence, 1945–1958* (Vancouver: University of British Columbia Press, 1987).

Article Twenty-Five

"A Low Dishonest Decade": Aspects of Canadian External Policy, 1931–1939

James Eayrs

There has not yet taken place in Canada that debate on the wisdom of appeasement in which British statesmen and scholars have been engaged since the appearance of Professor Feiling's *Life of Neville Chamberlain*. If this seems a remarkable fact, it is not hard to explain. Had the Canadian government of that day urged a more sturdy resistance to the Nazi tyranny, it is doubtful that events would have taken a significantly different course. German policy was unresponsive to the action or inaction of the Dominions; and it seems unlikely that Chamberlain would have been deflected from the path of the appeaser any more by the prime minister of Canada than he was by the prime minister of New Zealand, which is to say not at all. Canada's external policy during the years 1931–1939, so far from requiring extended apology, appears to most of its historians to possess the self-evident vindication of having brought a united and determined nation to Britain's side on September 10, 1939. The evidence which might sustain a contrary interpretation is still scanty. Documents from the files of the Department of External Affairs have yet to be published; the private papers of the prime ministers of the period are withheld from the scholar's domain;[1] both R.B. Bennett and Mackenzie King retained a jealous hold upon the External Affairs portfolio and conducted foreign policy possessively, even stealthily, so that few of their colleagues and subordinates have been able to throw strong light upon shadowy though crucial episodes; and a tradition unlike that prevailing at Westminster (where politics and literature — or politics and journalism — honourably combine) assists in their concealment. These are some (but by no means all) of the circumstances accounting for the remarkable early appearance of an Authorized Version of events not yet three decades removed.

The time is now approaching when a revisionist interpretation will be possible; one or two significant steps in this direction have already been taken.[2] The present paper has a more modest purpose. It attempts to discuss some aspects of Canadian external policy during the 1930s to which insufficient attention has perhaps been paid, and to bring to more familiar themes evidence previously overlooked. Although the title[3] may suggest an excess of moral indignation, its point of view is rather that of Lord Vansittart, who, writing of Dominion policies during the period in which he laboured with such prescience and to such little avail, remarked, perhaps too generously: "One could not blame them, one could not admire them, one could not admire anybody."[4]

The New World and the Old

In 1919 Canadians turned away from Europe, leaving behind their dead. However misguided it might appear to those of a later generation drawn as their fathers had been into "the vortex of militarism," isolationism in Canada was a natural response to the four-year ordeal on the Western front. The Great War remade the map, but left unchanged the scale and the projection. How could a conflict in which major gains were measured by hundreds of yards, and a million lives exchanged for a few desolated acres of mud, affect in any way the traditional concepts of geography? It brought half a million Canadians to Europe but Europe no closer to Canada. The world was still wide. To the Oceans and the Fleet might now be added as purveyor of security the great and friendly guardian to the South. Canada was a "fire-proof house, far from inflammable materials";[5] and its fortunate inhabitants peered indistinctly at the distant continent from which invasion seemed so improbable. "At present danger of attack upon Canada is minor in degree and second-hand in origin," Mackenzie King had insisted as late as 1938;[6] and although his military advisers were less certain of Canada's immunity,[7] their misgivings were not allowed to disturb unduly the complacency of the public or the size of the defence estimates.

Isolationism was the product of geography; it was shaped by distrust, a distrust born of the Great War and confirmed at the council tables of Paris. "It was European policy, European statesmanship, European ambition, that drenched this world with blood," N.W.

Rowell told the First Assembly of the League of Nations. "Fifty thousand Canadians under the soil of France and Flanders is what Canada has paid for European statesmanship trying to settle European problems. I place responsibility on a few; I would not distribute it over many; but nevertheless it is European."[8] These bluntly accusing words, an official of the Canadian delegation wrote privately at the time, "hurt and stung many people," and in his view "marred the performance."[9] But they conveyed, however tactlessly, the sense of Canadian feeling; and the prime minister wrote to their author to express his "appreciation of the stand you took in stating to the Conference, as frankly as you did, the price the world has paid for the European diplomacy of the last hundred years."[10] Nor, as it seemed, had the trauma of the trenches changed Europe for the better. Ancient enmities and grievances arose once more, or were replaced or supplemented by new disorders; the scope for intrigue and for disaster was if anything enhanced. "Everywhere there are signs of trouble," wrote one of Canada's representatives at the Paris Peace Conference in 1919. "Egypt is now disturbed with the fever for self govt. — the vicious results of Wilson's doctrine of ill or nondefined self determination. Asia Minor and Turkey are disorganized — Roumanians threatened on three sides by Bolshevists and Hungarians — Russia poisoned and poisoning — Hungary communist and Germany in near chaos. 'Tis surely a sad mess out of which to evolve a new Europe."[11]

Distrust and disapproval of Europe's statecraft and statesmen passed easily into an assertion of North American moral superiority. In Canada as in the United States there was nourished the conviction that the New World in its national life and international behaviour exhibited standards above and beyond those of the Old. Like Mr. Herbert Hoover, Canadians

> returned in 1919 from several years abroad . . . steeped with two ideas: first, that through three hundred years [North] America had developed something new in a way of life of a people, which transcended all others of history; and second, that out of the boiling social and economic cauldron of Europe, with its hates and fears, rose miasmic infections which might greatly harm or even destroy . . . the hope of the world.[12]

Rare was the Canadian who, addressing himself at Geneva or at home to the theme of his country's place in world affairs, did not elaborate this contrast. "[W]e think in terms of peace," remarked Senator Dandurand in 1924, "while Europe, an armed camp, thinks in terms of war."[13] "After listening to and participating in the proceedings of the League," Mackenzie King declared in 1928, "I have come back to Canada with a more profound conviction than ever that there is no land on the face of the globe in which the lot of men, women and children is cast in a pleasanter place than in this Dominion."[14] In 1936 he referred to Canada's "tremendous, absorbing and paramount tasks of achieving economic development and national unity, which with us take the place of the preoccupation with the fear of attack and the dreams of glory which beset older and more crowded countries";[15] a few weeks later, at Geneva, he contrasted his country's friendly relations with the United States and Europe's "violent . . . propaganda and recriminations hurled incessantly across the frontiers, the endeavours [in Europe] to draw all countries into one or other extremist camp, the feverish race for rearmament, the hurrying to and fro of diplomats, the ceaseless weaving and unravelling of understandings and alliances, and the consequent fear and uncertainty of the peoples";[16] and in March 1939, soon after Hitler's seizure of Czechoslovakia, he referred despairingly to the "continent that cannot run itself," in implied contrast to that North American continent which could.[17]

Such comparisons were frequently joined to moral exhortation. The rostrum of the Palais des Nations became for successive Canadian spokesmen a pulpit from which Europe was urged to forswear her foolish ways, to abandon intrigue, violence, hostility, to adopt those institutions which (they claimed) had brought a century of peace to North America. Canada and the United States, Mackenzie King informed the Ninth Assembly of the League of Nations, had ceased "to rely upon force, we have looked to reason as the method of solving our differences, and reason has supplied us from time to time with conference, conciliation or arbitration in a form . . . sufficient to settle our various differences as they have arisen."[18] Let there be a European Rush-Bagot Treaty, a European International Joint Commission — tranquillity would follow for a hundred years. As a prescription for Old World ills, these New World remedies were altogether inadequate, arising as they did from a wholly different situation.

> The toad beneath the harrow knows
> Exactly where each tooth-point goes;
> The butterfly upon the road
> Preaches contentment to that toad.

Moreover, they were compounded of a series of fictions unrelated to things as they were. "Not a single soldier, not a single cannon," the Canadian delegate had told the Fifth Assembly of the League, faced the famous frontier. This was simple falsehood. The International Joint Commission had been able to function without major difficulty only because each government had refrained from submitting disputes other than those over waterways. As for the Rush-Bagot Agreement, "the truth is," Mackenzie King had written privately in 1922, "our American friends have been steadily evading [it], until it has become more or less of a mockery to speak of its terms in the manner in which we do."[19]

However ill-justified, Canada's moralizing at Europe led logically not to isolation but engagement. Ought not the practitioners of the New World's higher mortality try by more active participation in the affairs of the Old to lead it into the paths of righteousness? That is not what happened. More potent than the zeal of the missionary was the desire to escape contamination. The less the New World came in contact with the Old, the better; the more, the greater the chance of succumbing to those "miasmic infections" which threatened to invade and to destroy the healthy bodies politic of North America. "Bolshevism," wrote the editor of the *Canadian Annual Review* in 1918, "had a basis wherever Russians and Jews and other foreigners gathered together" in Canada's cities; if foreigners brought Bolshevism, Canadians should keep clear of foreigners. "We are told there are enormous numbers of people on the continent of Europe who want to come [here]," remarked a former Minister of Immigration in 1922. "I want to say I regard it of the dimensions of a national menace that there is any danger whatever of the bars being let down."[20] Questioned in 1920 on Canada's readiness to accept a mandate for Armenia, the leader of the opposition wrote that the proposal "would provoke general protest from one end of the Dominion to the other," for "a sort of reaction has set in . . . with respect to interference by the Governments of this Continent with European Affairs."[21] As the twenty years' crisis developed and deepened, isolationism became if anything more firmly rooted in the Canadian people and their governors. Early in 1922 the Canadian government refused to contribute funds in the form of an interest-free loan for the relief of famine in Russia, and turned down a Soviet request for credit to buy Canadian seed wheat. In 1924 it ignored an appeal to contribute to the relief of famine in Albania. In 1925 it refused the invitation to sign the Geneva Protocol, and it was largely at Canada's insistence that an article was inserted in the text of the Locarno Agreements specifically exempting the Dominions from their provisions. "I do not see," Ernest Lapointe observed some years later, "that Canada should assume obligations in connection with the boundaries between France and Germany . . . [or] guarantee any boundaries in central Europe or elsewhere."[22] And an influential member of the Canadian government wrote before sailing for the Imperial Conference in the spring of 1937:

> The conference will be interesting, and probably in some ways revealing; but the more I see of the whole thing, the more I am certain that our destiny is on the North American continent and that if Europe is going to insist on destroying itself, it is no part of our mission to destroy ourselves in attempting to prevent it.[23]

The League and the Nation

If other countries entered the League of Nations in something of the spirit expressed by Smuts' phrase — "the tents have been struck and the great caravan of humanity is once more on the march" — Canada may be said to have been mainly concerned lest she be called upon to do more than her share of the work in breaking camp or be compelled to march without the consent of her Parliament. It is usual to attribute the reserve with which Canadians watched the Geneva experiment to the coercive characteristics of the Covenant, and to suppose that so long as the League confined itself to conciliatory methods it could count upon Canadian approval. This view has the weighty support of Professor Mansergh, who writes that "from the first the League was welcomed as a means of furthering international co-operation, as a forum for debate and discussion," and that it was only "as a means for enforcing, as distinct from maintaining, peace" that it aroused the suspicion and censure of successive Canadian governments.[24] Certainly it is difficult to overestimate the agitated concern lest through Articles X and XVI of the Covenant the newly independent Dominion be placed at "the beck and call of a Council not responsible to the nation for its actions," or, even worse, become involved "in conflicts in some faraway section of Europe, or in some distant portion of South America."[25] Fears such as these lead to that policy; "remarkable," as Professor Mansergh observes, "for its consistency," by which Canada tried at first to have Article X removed entirely from the Covenant; that proving unsuccessful, introduced an interpretative resolution which, though it failed by one vote to receive the unanimous support required for adoption, had the desired effect of weakening the obligations of League membership; and finally, when the League was confronted with the two decisive tests of its procedures for collective security, did what could be done to weaken the effectiveness of sanctions.

But this interpretation may be misleading. It implies a degree of attachment to the League as a non-coercive agency for peaceful conciliation which, whatever might be said in public, no Canadian minister really felt. For Canadian suspicion of Geneva derived basically from Canadian distrust of Europe; and it was as a European institution that the League appeared from Canada. "The League was born ostensibly as a world League," commented a former official of the Department of External Affairs in 1926, "but really is a European League with the non-Europeans tacked on. The most distinctive and powerful New World people went out of it." A Canadian had no more legitimate concern "with the administration of Danzig or of the Saar Valley" than had "a Nova Scotian . . . [with] the municipal government of Vancouver."[26] "Let us . . . conciliate Quebec and Ontario," remarked a member of Parliament in 1923, "before we start conciliating Roumania and

Ukrainia."[27] "The League of Nations is a preposterous and expensive farce," wrote Sir Clifford Sifton, "and amounts to nothing more than a part of a machine designed to involve us in European and Imperialistic complications. Canada ought to call a halt on this business."[28] The views of those in office were much the same. Sir Joseph Pope, the Undersecretary of State for External Affairs until 1925, dismissed the Covenant as "not worth the paper it is written on," and wrote in his diary: "Our reps are making a great stir at the League of Nations, advertizing Canada and incidentally themselves. I think it all absurd, and am convinced that Canada's true policy right now is to develop her resources and to leave European questions such as the Bessarabian frontier &c to our Imperial states-men and the trained experts of Downing Street."[29] His successor, O.D. Skelton, while holding "the trained experts of Downing Street" in somewhat lesser regard, was no more sympathetic to the Geneva experiment. Mackenzie King, as his official biographer remarks, "was the type of uplifter who might have been expected to give the League his full and enthusiastic support," but his attitude toward the League in its formative years "was one of studied neglect."[30] In the 1930s this was to develop into an attitude of pro-found hostility, especially after the "Riddell incident" of November 1935. W.A. Riddell, the Canadian Permanent Delegate at Geneva, left in some perplexity as a consequence of the General Election a few days earlier, proposed on his own initiative the imposition of cer-tain sanctions against Italy, and in the brief period until his action was repudiated by the Canadian government, set Canada's policy upon a course it had never before taken. In his published recollection of this celebrated episode, Dr. Riddell attributes his repudiation part-ly to the fact that the prime minister and the undersecretary of state for External Affairs were at the time out of the country, leaving the Department of External Affairs in charge of "two French Canadians," Ernest Lapointe and Laurent Beaudry. On reporting to Mackenzie King in Ottawa, Dr. Riddell writes, he found him, "as always, most gracious," while Lapointe seemed "cold, critical and overbearing."[31] But beneath a mask of practiced cordiality King was no less angered than Lapointe, probably more so, by Riddell's initia-tive. A Canadian newspaperman has recorded an interview with the prime minister soon after the event:

> Had a few words with Mr. King re the Italo-Ethiopian settlement and he spoke with surpris-ing frankness. I never knew before Mr. King's general attitude towards the League and for-eign affairs. King complained angrily about Dr. Riddell's gasoline [*sic*], steel and coal proposal. "I am certainly going to give him a good spanking," was the way he put it. . . . He said that excessive idealism in politics should be avoided. Canada's policy, he believed, should be dic-tated by considerations of geographical location and population. After all we are but 10 mil-lions on the north end of a continent and we should not strive to over-play our part. . . . He is very dubious about foreign commitments, and, also, about getting into the League too deeply. He said that the only real difference of opinion he had ever had with Lapointe was with regard to Canada's acceptance of the presidency of the League Assembly [in 1925]. He had opposed it on the ground that it would stimulate League thought in Canada, tend to lead us more deeply into League affairs and, possibly, foreign commitments.[32]

"We should not strive to over-play our part." This theme was henceforth to be heard in nearly all of the prime minister's infrequent public statements on the European crisis until the outbreak of war, a refrain in praise of diffidence. "After all, . . . there is such a thing as a sense of proportion in international affairs," he said in the House of Commons in February 1936. "Do hon. members think that it is Canada's role at Geneva to attempt to regulate a European war?" If he had not disavowed Riddell's proposal, "the whole of

Europe might have been aflame today."[33] A few days later he added: "Our country is being drawn into international situations to a degree that I myself think is alarming."[34] Within a fortnight Hitler was to invade the Rhineland.

The Law and the Jungle

If distrust of European politics contributed to isolationist sentiment in Canada in the years between the wars, it also helped to thwart understanding of what was happening to Europe during the deepening crisis of the later 1930s. With a very few exceptions, notably J.W. Dafoe,[35] Canadians did not recognize Fascist Italy and Nazi Germany for what they were. Totalitarianism was thought to be merely an aggravation of that malaise from which Europe traditionally suffered; there was little if any suspicion that it might be a distinctively twentieth-century phenomenon arising from the tensions and insecurities of twentieth-century man. The fascist apparition was no new menace for which the old responses would no longer suffice, but a rebirth of the intrigues, the rivalries, the nationalisms of prewar European diplomacy. Thus it required no special explanation; created no new problems; needed no exceptional precautions.

A significant section of the Canadian public was indeed disposed to view fascism in its Mediterranean setting not merely without alarm but with undisguised approval. The lofty sentiments of Fascist doctrine elaborated by Mussolini's publicists, with their apotheosis of order, discipline, family, nation, their pseudo-syndicalist remedies for industrial unrest, gained powerful support among the elite of French Canada. "The work of Mussolini and of the Fascist Party finds among a certain number of my compatriots admirers," remarked Mr. Paul Gouin in 1938. "They have the same attitude towards the corporative movement of Salazar. . . . We may ask ourselves if it would not be to the advantage of our Province and of Canada to borrow what is best in these different formulae, while naturally avoiding their excesses."[36] Few French-speaking Canadians saw anything for adverse comment in the description of General Franco's forces offered by the newly appointed Papal Delegate to Canada and Newfoundland as that "army of heroes, justly called Christ's militia,"[37] any more than they resented the valedictory pronounced by Maxime Raymond in the House of Commons on the occasion of the departure of the Mackenzie–Papineau Brigade: "This, I admit, does not give me any sorrow; it will rid us of these undesirable people, provided they do not return home here."[38] If there was no emulation in French Canada of General O'Duffy's Blueshirts, who went from Eire to fight in Spain for Franco, it was due not to want of sympathy for the Nationalist cause but to the even stronger hold of isolationism.

National Socialism was something else again. No religious or ideological link could bind Quebec to a regime which had so soon and so obviously singled out the Catholic Church for brutal destruction. But diagnosis of the Nazi movement was hindered in Canada by the magnitude of domestic crisis and by the isolationist tradition. Events in Germany were consistently misconstrued as a nationalist revival of the conventional type, distinguished, perhaps, by the odd fanaticism of its leaders, by the strut and swagger of its rank and file, but for all that a movement which might be comprehended in traditional terms, appeased and contained by traditional methods. When Hitler entered the Rhineland there was aroused among English-speaking Canadians little of the emotion produced by Mussolini's attack on Ethiopia. On the contrary, there was a widely held conviction that in reoccupying the demilitarized zone Hitler was only avenging the wrongs of Versailles, taking possession of what rightfully belonged to Germany. Why shouldn't a man walk into his own backyard? With the significant exception of Dafoe's *Free Press*, nearly all Canadian newspapers urged, on March 9, 1936, a sympathetic understanding of Hitler's position. "Canadians who do not allow themselves to be swayed by a personal dislike for Hitler and his unpleasant colleagues," wrote the editor of the Vancouver *Sun*, "will feel a measure of sympathy for this new attitude of the German people. . . . Canada is only a spectator. There are not enough moral principles at stake to induce her to become otherwise. . . . Whatever morality lies in the scales seems to be, this time, on Germany's side of the balance." "After eighteen years," the Edmonton *Bulletin* observed, "Europe can afford to restore Germany to full standing in the concert of nations." "Nothing can ever be gained," argued the editor of the Montreal *Gazette*, "by persistently treating Germany as though she were national enemy No. 1 in perpetuity. It would likewise be dangerous and futile to regard Adolf Hitler in no other light than as one whose designs are wilfully antagonistic to forces that hate war."

It is possible that had Canada been represented in Germany by a diplomat of insight and influence, a less reassuring image of National Socialism would have reached its government and people. As it was, the Canadian government, having no diplomatic mission at Berlin, necessarily relied on whatever Whitehall might select for its instruction from the dispatches of Sir Nevile Henderson — dispatches which conveyed a sadly erroneous interpretation of Nazi policy.[39] This unhelpful source was supplemented by the assessment of the Canadian High Commissioner at London, so closely associated with the group which moved with such great and disastrous effect between Cliveden, Printing House Square, and Downing Street that nothing he learned from its members seems likely to have provided a useful corrective to the misleading dispatches passed on by the Dominions Office. "Walked about the grounds in the forenoon with Vincent Massey, talking politics," wrote Thomas Jones in his diary on June 7, 1936. "I begged him to stress the urgency of dealing with Germany and not to wait upon France."[40]

But the most misleading impression was derived more directly. In 1937 Mackenzie King decided to go from the Imperial Conference to Germany. There he met and talked with Hitler and other leading personalities of the Third Reich. It was not a wholly useful confrontation. It is true that King did not allow so unique an opportunity to pass without stressing in Berlin what he felt unable to disclose in London, namely, that in the event of "a war of aggression, nothing in the world would keep the Canadian people from being at the side of Britain."[41] Heeded or not heeded, this message was at least delivered, and more valuable service could hardly have been rendered. But its value was diminished by the way in which the Canadian prime minister fell victim to the Führer's remarkable capacity for mesmerizing his visitors. "There is no doubt that Hitler had a power of fascinating men," Mr. Churchill wrote in his memoirs; and added the sage advice: "Unless the terms are equal, it is better to keep away."[42] And between the prime minister of Canada and the perpetrator of the Nazi *Schrecklichkeit* the terms were far from equal. The extent of Hitler's advantage may be measured by the opinions with which King returned to Canada. According to Mr. Bruce Hutchison, to whom he related them soon afterward, King found Hitler

> a simple sort of peasant, not very intelligent and no serious danger to anyone . . . obsessed with the recovery of neighboring territory inhabited by Germans, a natural feeling. When he had brought these territories into the Reich . . . he would be satisfied . . . he would not risk a large war. His ambitions were centered entirely in Germany and the narrow irredentist regions beside it. For this reason [there would be] . . . no early trouble in Europe.[43]

And to the Canadian people Mackenzie King declared, three weeks after his talks with the German leaders:

Despite every appearance to the contrary, I believe the nations of Europe have a better under-standing of each other's problems to-day than they have had for some years past. Moreover, despite all appearances, they are prepared, I believe, in an effort to work out a solution, to co-operate to a greater degree than has been the case for a long while. . . . Of this I am cer-tain . . . that neither the governments nor the peoples of any of the countries I have visited desire war, or view the possibility of war between each other, as other than likely to end in self-destruction, and the destruction of Europe civilization itself.[44]

That the destruction of European civilization was precisely the object of the man he had so recently talked with in the Reichskanzlei was a thought unlikely to have crossed the mind of the Canadian prime minister; for, as was remarked of him in a different connec-tion, "Mr. King never quite got it into his head during his economic studies at Toronto and Harvard that our civilization is dominated by carnivorous animals."[45]

Empire and Reich

In 1923 the prime minister of Canada had protested vigorously and decisively against the Imperial Conference "assuming the rights of a cabinet in the determination of foreign pol-icy . . . expressing approval of the present [British] Government's foreign policy . . ., try-ing to shape the affairs of Europe."[46] By 1937 Mackenzie King's suspicions of "Downing Street domination" had been sufficiently allayed to allow him to do what he had never done before—to endorse at an Imperial Conference a united Commonwealth policy on international affairs. As it happened, the policy for which the Dominions offered their col-lective approval and support was the ill-fated policy of appeasement. "[T]he settlement of differences that may arise between nations," asserted the section of the *Proceedings* of the Conference dealing with foreign affairs, "should be sought by methods of co-operation, joint enquiry and conciliation . . . differences of political creed should be no obstacle to friendly relations between Governments and countries . . . nothing would be more dam-aging to the hopes of international appeasement than the division, real or apparent, of the world into opposing groups."[47] These sentiments, which, as Professor Mansergh rightly remarks, are "hardly consistent with the dignity of a great Commonwealth confronted with the shameless aggression of European tyrants unmatched for their cruelty and faith-lessness since the Dark Ages,"[48] continued to be uttered by Mackenzie King during the interval between the end of the Conference and the beginning of war. For the first time since becoming prime minister in 1921, he found himself able to pay public tribute to "the unremitting care and anxiety which those responsible for the foreign policy of Britain have devoted to their task"; he spoke of "their strong and determined effort to establish peace."[49] This was followed by a series of press statements in praise of British policy. When the news of the proposed mission to Berchtesgaden reached him, Mackenzie King announced that he had "conveyed to Mr. Neville Chamberlain the deep satisfaction with which my colleagues and I have learned that his proposal for a personal conference with Herr Hitler . . . has been agreed to" and described "this far-seeing and truly noble action on the part of Mr. Chamberlain" as "emphatically the right step." A further statement issued after the British Cabinet's decision to support the principle of self-determination for Sudeten Germans referred to the "courage and vision" displayed by the government of the United Kingdom in seeking "to avert recourse to force by finding a peaceful and agreed solution of the present clash of interests in Central Europe." Following Chamberlain's radio address of September 27, 1938 ("How horrible, fantastic, incredible it is that we should be digging trenches and fitting gas-masks because of a quarrel in a far away country"), Mackenzie King proclaimed the Canadian government's "complete accord with the statement Mr. Chamberlain has made to the world today." Word of the impending visit to Munich called forth the most ecstatic endorsement of all:

> The heart of Canada is rejoicing tonight at the success which has crowned your unremitting efforts for peace. . . . My colleagues in the Government join with me in unbounded admiration at the service you have rendered mankind. . . . On the very brink of chaos, with passions flaming, and armies marching, the voice of Reason has found a way out of the conflict.

It may be safely assumed that these utterances were carefully noted and transmitted to Berlin by the German consul general at Ottawa, Herr Windels; and to the extent that the disordered diplomatic apparatus at the Wilhelmstrasse was capable of bringing them to the attention of the Führer they can only have reinforced his belief that the British Empire was too weak and too craven to oppose his plans for the subjugation of Eastern Europe as a prelude to the destruction of the West. Appeasement, the only foreign policy on which the Commonwealth has ever been in substantial agreement, thus came close to accomplishing its ruin. Offered in the hope of peace, it led it straight to war.

Yet while Mackenzie King had by 1937 become able to support Britain's appeasement of Germany, his earlier fear of centralized control persisted in the realm of defence. All attempts on the part of the United Kingdom to cooperate militarily and industrially with Canada in advance of the outbreak of war were rebuffed. "From 1936 onwards," the official history of the Royal Air Force recalls reproachfully, "Canada, which enjoyed an ideal strategic position and a convenient proximity to the vast industrial resources of the United States, was repeatedly approached [with the request to make facilities available for training of pilots and aircrew]; but the Canadians, largely for domestic reasons, felt unable to accept our proposals."[50] At the Imperial Conference of 1937 "the principal Supply Officers' Committee tried to pilot through . . . an agreement with Canada about wartime supplies of bauxite and aluminium," but failed largely because of Canadian opposition.[51] In the summer of 1938 the Board of Trade entered into negotiations with the Canadian government to make provision in advance of war for adequate supplies of certain strategic materials; but Ottawa being unwilling to assume such commitments, by September 1939 "virtually no preparations had been made for the war-time purchase of raw materials in North America."[52] Munitions fared little better; with the exception of a contract for Bren machine guns, nothing was done by the Canadian government to assist United Kingdom defence officials in their effort to stimulate the manufacture of arms in the overseas Dominions.[53]

It is thus a major irony of Commonwealth history that Canadian influence on British policy was at this stage brought to bear in the worst of all possible ways. In external policy, as Professor Mansergh observes, "what was most of all required was not a greater consensus of Commonwealth opinion but the more vigourous expression of independent and conflicting opinion";[54] in defence policy what was most of all required was a united effort to create a deterrent of imperial power. The Canadian response was to voice with unaccustomed fervor approval of British statecraft while resisting Britain's efforts to improve the Empire's defences. While "no evidence so far published suggests that doubts about the unity of the Commonwealth were a major factor in encouraging German aggression,"[55] a firmer signification of the Commonwealth's will to resist might have given Hitler pause; in any event the opportunity was both too good and too rare to be squandered. Certain it is that a fuller measure of defence preparation would have made his defeat less costly and precarious. The margin of superiority with which Britain faced the Axis in the summer of 1940 remained excruciatingly narrow. Had the RAF failed, for want of aircraft or of pilots, to deflect and defeat the Luftwaffe, would not those responsible for Canadian policy during the prewar years have to share the blame?

Statecraft and Unity

On January 20, 1937, the Canadian prime minister spoke in confidence to a meeting of his parliamentary supporters. He urged them to reject the views of Mr. Arthur Meighen, the Conservative leader in the Senate, "that the amount in the [defence] estimates was not enough, that we were concerned with the defence of the Empire as a whole; that the first line of our defence was the Empire's boundaries." Equally he urged them to reject the alternative offered by J.S. Woodsworth, the leader of the socialist group in the House of Commons, who, he said, "would do nothing at all" for defence. "The safe policy is the middle course between these two views. . . . Let us explain that policy to our people and let us above all strive at all times to keep Canada *united*."[56] This insistence upon the overriding importance of national unity appears again and again in Mackenzie King's statements on external policy during the years immediately preceding World War II. It served to explain his reluctance to participate in projects or pronouncements likely to deter potential aggressors. To do so, as he remarked in the House of Commons on May 24, 1938, "would bring out deep and in some cases fundamental differences of opinion, [and] would lead to further strain upon the unity of a country already strained by economic depression and other consequences of the last war and its aftermath."[57] Of the wisdom of this policy its architect betrayed neither doubt nor misgiving, and believed it fully vindicated by events. On September 8, 1939, he spoke as follows in the House of Commons:

> I have made it, therefore, the supreme endeavour of my leadership of my party, and my leadership of the government of this country, to let no hasty or premature threat or pronouncement create mistrust and divisions between the different elements that compose the population of our vast dominion, so that when the moment of decision came all should so see the issue itself that our national effort might be marked by unity of purpose, of heart and of endeavour.[58]

It is a matter for debate whether this "supreme endeavour" was not altogether too restricted. Politics is the art of the possible. But how much was possible during the years before the war? More, perhaps, than the prime minister of Canada allowed the nation, or himself, to believe. Never was Mackenzie King more satisfied than when enunciating the dictum that his country was difficult to govern. It was, and is, difficult to govern, in the sense that government is at all times and in all places an exacting and complicated craft. Compared to the ordeals which nearly every twentieth-century nation has undergone — destruction and occupation in war, civil conflict, malevolent and scouring tyrannies — Canadians might consider their situation extraordinarily favourable. Nor were those wearying comparisons between the continent of the undefended frontier and "the continent which cannot run itself" too easily reconciled with plaintive references to exceptional domestic difficulties invoked to justify inaction. So much harping upon the need for unity and the obstacles in its path exaggerated the degree of internal discord, just as repetition of the difficulties encountered in governing the country obscured the fact that it was a good deal less difficult to govern than most. Was it not misleading "to emphasize the precariousness of Canada's export markets, but not the value of her exports; to speak of regional and cultural tensions within but not of the growing sense of unity; of the conflicting pulls of geography and history to which indeed every 'settled' country is subject, but not of the immense strength of Canada's position in the heart of the English-speaking world"?[59] When the history of these years is set out in detail, many of the portents of disunity in the Dominion will be seen to have been greatly overdrawn. For example, it is commonly believed that had the United Kingdom gone to war over Czechoslovakia in September 1938, the CCF (Socialist) party in Canada would have demanded a policy of neutrality. But Professor McNaught has discovered that "correspondence in the Saskatchewan C.C.F. files . . . leaves no doubt that the C.C.F. leaders who defeated the Woodsworth–Farmer neutrality motion in the emergency National Council meeting in [September] 1939 had concluded at least as early as September, 1938, that 'it is already decided that if Britain declares war, Canada must accept the situation.' "[60]

A direct result of reducing Canadian policy to the lowest common denominator of public agreement was the condition of the nation's defences, "utterly inadequate," as the official historian of the Canadian Army observes, "by comparison with the scale of the coming emergency."[61] Another harmful consequence was the effect upon United Kingdom policy. Just as the Canadian government seized with alacrity upon stress and strain in the Dominion's domestic affairs as an excuse for passivity in all external policies save that of appeasement, so the British government fastened upon the difficulties of members of the overseas Commonwealth to justify its own cautious conduct. Disunity in the Dominions plays a major part in the arguments of apologists for Britain's prewar policy. "The fact remains that the Commonwealth Governments were unwilling to go to war on the issue of Czechoslovakia," a former British foreign secretary has written of that period. "Dominion opinion was at the time overwhelmingly against a world war. This opposition was continually in our minds. Time after time we were reminded of it, either by the High Commissioners in London, or by Malcolm MacDonald, the Secretary of State for the Dominions. As early as March 18, 1938, we had been told that South Africa and Canada would not join us in a war to prevent certain Germans from rejoining their fatherland."[62] While "the actual policy Mr. Chamberlain followed in September 1938 owed little or nothing to dominion inspiration,"[63] there can be no doubt that dispiriting responses from the Dominions were used by him to discourage those within the British Cabinet who urged a less cowardly posture in the face of German threats.[64] In Canada's case their effect was the more damaging for their misrepresentation of the real intention of its government. For had war broken out at the time of Munich, the prime minister "was prepared to call Parliament within two weeks and submit to it a policy of Canadian participation. . . . The Cabinet was unanimous."[65]

Over half a century ago the French historian André Siegfried had noted the timidity of Canada's political leaders. "They seem," he wrote, "to stand in fear of great movements of public opinion, and to seek to lull them rather than to encourage them and bring them to political fruition."[66] It will be observed that Canadian political leadership at the time of M. Siegfried's examination was provided by Sir Wilfrid Laurier; and that it was upon Sir Wilfrid Laurier's leadership that Mackenzie King had faithfully modelled his own. "You do Sir Wilfrid Laurier an injustice in regarding him as an opportunist," King had written a friend during the controversy over naval policy in 1909. "He is other than that. . . . We have had no man in Canada who had done as much to reconcile differences of race and creed and to make of the people one nation. If he hesitates to go to the length that some desire, it is because he does not wish disruption and believes that a united progressive Canada is a more valuable asset to the Empire, and will be so through time, than a Canada divided in opinion, or professing an obligation it is not in a position to meet."[67] But hesitation for the sake of unity was not the inevitable response of all Canadian leaders to the tensions of their plural society; there were those to whom its tensions the more insistently demanded bold and imaginative statecraft. "In our Dominion where sections abound," Mr. Arthur Meighen once declared, "a Dominion of races, of classes and of creeds, of many languages and many origins, there are times when no Prime Minister can be true to his trust to the nation he has sworn to serve, save at the temporary sacrifice of the party he is appointed to lead."[68] Faithfully practising this doctrine, Mr. Meighen was compelled to retire from public life. Mackenzie King's very different concept of political leadership, no less faithfully practised and resulting in political longevity only once surpassed in the history of the Commonwealth, must face a very different kind of criticism. It "would have been improved," his official biographer has conceded,

> had he been more venturesome and more willing to offer forthright advice to the nation. King's tactics enabled him to secure and retain office—the indispensable first step. But King, too frequently, stopped right there; and because he was reluctant to press on and try to realize some independent conception of the national interest, his policies slipped into the mire of pure expediency. King was always reluctant to venture into the unknown. He avoided taking risks, and he would postpone action, if by so doing he could ensure a greater degree of safety. He dreaded unnecessary discussion which might lead to disagreement and even threaten the existing party solidarity on which the whole security of his position rested. He was not prepared to use his own power extensively in an effort to modify the character and scope of those common elements on which he sought to base his policy. He was too willing at times to yield his own judgment when confronted with opposing opinion. He was slow to admit that he had a duty as leader to exert a moderate pressure in the direction in which he believed the country should move.[69]

This verdict is the more severe coming as it does from "one who is in general sympathy with Mr. King and his work and career."[70] There is no part of Mackenzie King's long responsibility for Canadian affairs to which it may with more justice be applied than to his conduct of external policy during that "low dishonest decade" when the world lay "defenceless under the night" and so few free men in power dared to "show an affirming flame."

NOTES

1. The Bennett Papers have been deposited by Lord Beaverbrook, their owner, at the Library of the University of New Brunswick. The King Papers are in the Public Archives of Canada and became the property of the Crown in 1975. The present writer, having assisted in the preparation of the official biography of W.L. Mackenzie King, has had access to this immense collection; he has permission from Mr. King's Literary Executors to quote from the King correspondence to the end of 1923, the period covered by the published first volume of the official biography. [*Editors' note:* Eayrs was writing this in 1960.]
2. See K.W. McNaught, "Canadian Foreign Policy and the Whig Interpretation: 1936–1939," Canadian Historical Association, *Report of the Annual Meeting* (1957), 43–54.
3. It is taken from the poem by W.H. Auden, "September 1, 1939": "As the clever hopes expire/Of a low dishonest decade."
4. *The Mist Procession: The Autobiography of Lord Vansittart* (London, 1958), 529.
5. League of Nations, Official Journal, Special Supplement no. 23, *Records of the Fifth Assembly* (1924), 222. It is interesting that this most celebrated of Canadian utterances on foreign affairs goes unremarked in the unpublished autobiography of Senator Raoul Dandurand, its author.

6. Canada, *House of Commons Debates* (1938), 3: 3179.

7. See Colonel C.P. Stacey, *Six Years of War: The Army in Canada, Britain and the Pacific* (Ottawa, 1955), 10.

8. League of Nations, *Records of the First Assembly* (1920), 379.

9. Loring C. Christie to Sir Robert Borden, Dec. 12, 1920, Borden Papers (Public Archives of Canada).

10. Arthur Meighen to N.W. Rowell, Jan. 10, 1921, Rowell Papers (PAC).

11. Diary of Sir George Foster, entry for April 7, 1919 (PAC).

12. *The Memoirs of Herbert Hoover: The Cabinet and the Presidency, 1920–1933* (New York, 1951), v.

13. League of Nations, Official Journal, Special Supplement no. 23, *Records of the Fifth Assembly* (1924), 221.

14. "Address Delivered by the Right Hon. W.L. Mackenzie King on November 9th, 1928, at a Banquet of the League of Nations Society in Canada" (Ottawa, 1928), 22.

15. Canada, *H. of C. Debates* (1936), 4: 3862.

16. League of Nations, *Verbatim Record of the Seventeenth Ordinary Session of the Assembly*, Sept. 29, 1936, p. 1.

17. Canada, *H. of C. Debates* (1939), 3: 2419.

18. League of Nations, Official Journal, Special Supplement no. 64, *Records of the Ninth Assembly* (1928), 60.

19. Mackenzie King to Wallace Nesbitt, Oct. 2, 1922, King Papers.

20. Sir Clifford Sifton, "Immigration," in *Addresses Delivered before the Canadian Club of Toronto, 1921–2* (Toronto, 1923), 185–86.

21. Mackenzie King to Aneuran Williams, Feb. 18, 1920, King Papers. A portion of this letter is quoted in R. MacGregor Dawson, *William Lyon Mackenzie King: A Political Biography*, vol. 1, *1874–1923* (Toronto, 1958), 404.

22. Canada, *H. of C. Debates* (1928), 2: 1960.

23. T.A. Crerar to J.W. Dafoe, April 17, 1937, Dafoe Papers (PAC).

24. Nicholas Mansergh, *Survey of British Commonwealth Affairs: Problems of External Policy, 1931–1939* (London, 1952), 112.

25. Canada, *H. of C. Debates* (1919, Special Session), 102, 103.

26. Loring C. Christie, "Notes on the League of Nations Meeting of March, 1926," April 14, 1926, Borden Papers.

27. Canada, *H. of C. Debates* (1923), 4: 4001.

28. Sir Clifford Sifton to J.W. Dafoe, Nov. 19, 1920, Dafoe Papers.

29. Entry for Dec. 11, 1920, Pope Papers (PAC).

30. Dawson, *William Lyon Mackenzie King*, 1: 403.

31. W.A. Riddell, *World Security by Conference* (Toronto, 1947), 140.

32. Grant Dexter to J.W. Dafoe, Dec. 17, 1935, Dafoe Papers.

33. Canada, *H. of C. Debates* (1936), 1: 97, 98.

34. Quoted in F.H. Soward et al., *Canada in World Affairs: The Pre-War Years* (Toronto, 1941), 23.

35. Of whose newspaper it was well remarked that "what the Free Press thinks today, Western Canada will think tomorrow and the intelligent part of Eastern Canada will think a few years hence." Frank H. Underhill, "J.W. Dafoe," *Canadian Forum* 13 (Oct. 1932): 22.

36. Quoted in Henri Saint-Denis, "Fascism in Quebec: A False Alarm," *Revue de l'université d'Ottawa* (Jan. 1939), 4. See also "S," "Embryo Fascism in Quebec," *Foreign Affairs* 16 (April 1938): 454–66.

37. *Le Devoir* (Montreal), July 14, 1938.

38. Canada, *H. of C. Debates* (1937), 1: 910.

39. During the Munich crisis in the fall of 1938, Henderson wrote of "Hitler's own love for peace, dislike of dead Germans and hesitation of risking his regime on a gambler's throw." Quoted in

Felix Gilbert, "Two British Ambassadors: Perth and Henderson," in Gordon A. Craig and Felix Gilbert, *The Diplomats, 1919–1939* (Princeton, 1953), 543.

40. Thomas Jones, *A Diary with Letters, 1931–1950* (London, 1954), 218. See also Thomas Jones to Lady Grigg, March 8, 1936, Jones, *A Diary*, 179–81; *The History of "The Times": The 150th Anniversary and Beyond, 1912–1948*, part 2, *1921–1948* (London, 1952), 938; John Evelyn Wrench, *Geoffrey Dawson and Our Times* (London, 1955), 369.

41. Canada, *H. of C. Debates* (1944), 6: 6275.

42. Winston S. Churchill, *The Second World War*, vol. 1, *The Gathering Storm* (London, 1949), 250.

43. Bruce Hutchison, *The Incredible Canadian* (Toronto, 1953), 226.

44. Speech given over the National Network of the Canadian Broadcasting Corporation, July 19, 1937.

45. Frank H. Underhill, "The Close of an Era: Twenty-Five Years of Mr. Mackenzie King," *Canadian Forum* 24 (Sept. 1944): 125.

46. Quoted in Dawson, *William Lyon Mackenzie King*, 1: 474.

47. Imperial Conference, 1937, *Summary of Proceedings*, pp. 14, 16.

48. Mansergh, *Survey . . .: Problems of External Policy*, 89.

49. Canada, *H. of C. Debates* (1938), 3: 3182.

50. Denis Richards, *Royal Air Force, 1939–1945*, vol. 1, *The Fight at Odds* (London, 1953), 72–73.

51. *History of the Second World War*, United Kingdom Civil Series, M.M. Postan, *British War Production* (London, 1952), 89.

52. *History of the Second World War*, United Kingdom Civil Series, J. Hurstfield, *The Control of Raw Materials* (London, 1955), 254.

53. See *History of the Second World War*, United Kingdom Civil Series, H. Duncan Hall, *North American Supply* (London, 1954).

54. Nicholas Mansergh, *Survey of British Commonwealth Affairs: Problems of Wartime Co-operation and Post-War Change, 1939–1952* (London, 1958), 17.

55. Mansergh, *Survey . . .: Problems of External Policy*, 446.

56. Quoted in Stacey, *Six Years of War*, 14.

57. Canada, *H. of C. Debates* (1938), 3: 3184.

58. Canada, *H. of C. Debates* (1939, Special War Session), 1: 25.

59. Mansergh, *Survey . . .: Problems of External Policy*, 111.

60. McNaught, "Canadian Foreign Policy," 54 n. 40.

61. Stacey, *Six Years of War*, 35.

62. Viscount Templewood, *Nine Troubled Years* (London, 1954), 323.

63. Mansergh, *Survey . . .: Problems of External Policy*, 439.

64. See *Old Men Forget: The Autobiography of Duff Cooper* (London, 1954), 239–40.

65. "Back Stage in Ottawa," *Maclean's Magazine* 2 (Nov. 1, 1938).

66. André Siegfried, *The Race Question in Canada* (London, 1907), 142.

67. Mackenzie King to Lord Stanhope, July 23, 1909. Quoted in Dawson, *William Lyon Mackenzie King*, 1: 215.

68. Arthur Meighen, *Unrevised and Unrepented: Debating Speeches and Others* (Toronto, 1949), 319.

69. Dawson, *William Lyon Mackenzie King*, 1: 417–18.

70. Dawson, *William Lyon Mackenzie King*, 1: viii.

Article Twenty-Six

The Cold War and the Limits of "Internationalism" in Canada's Foreign Relations, 1945–1949

Hector Mackenzie

Canada's postwar international relations have usually been described as a reversal of earlier attitudes and a break with past policies. Canadian stances and actions in the "low dishonest decade" of the 1930s have been most often, and with good reason, portrayed as negative and irresponsible. Whether the focus of examination has been imperial affairs, continental dealings with the United States, or participation in the League of Nations, there has been ample evidence for a harsh indictment of Canada's foreign relations before 1939.[1] With that dark tableau as a backdrop, the subsequent decade has seemed especially luminous. Most accounts have endeavoured to explain an apparent transformation of Canada's international relations during and immediately after the Second World War. Words and deeds have been cited to demonstrate that Canada was much more involved in world affairs after that conflict than before.[2]

The overall impression conveyed has been that the shift in perspective and conduct was so complete that attitudes and assumptions that had prevailed less than ten years before were virtually excluded when Canada weighed its options in "the shaping of peace." Thus, in the elaboration of foreign policy and in the evaluation of national defence and collective security, finance and trade, Canada embarked on the avowedly "internationalist" course which has tended to characterize its external relations ever since.[3] The quintessential "middle power"[4] pursued its enlightened self-interest, steering a course toward "multilateralism," only occasionally straying, regretfully but pragmatically, in the direction of "bilateralism."[5] Recent experience provided a warning rather than a guide.

With respect to the United Nations, however, Canada's performance demonstrated a different approach to international relations than after the First World War and during the interwar years. Before, during, and after the San Francisco Conference of 1945, Canadian representatives blended idealism with practical concern for the viability of the organization.[6] Throughout, they were determined to secure for Canada both rights and duties. Canada was engaged in most aspects of the restoration of peace and the reconstruction of the international community. Perhaps most remarkably, when the United Nations seemed unable to assure the security of Western Europe, Canada joined with its closest allies, Britain and the United States, to start the negotiations which led to the North Atlantic Treaty. The tensions of the cold war apparently supplied the necessary impetus for action by Canada.[7] For a country whose government had so recently and unequivocally proclaimed its resolve to avoid commitments in advance of war to participate in a military alliance in peacetime seemed to observers then and since to be a thorough and deliberate repudiation of the pronouncements and actions of the past.

But a closer scrutiny of the evidence suggests that this seeming reversal or dramatic departure in Canada's foreign relations may not have been as sudden or as complete as most commentaries have suggested. Some scholars have cast doubt on the negative generaliza-

Source: An earlier version of this article appeared as an occasional paper published by the Centre for International and Security Studies of York University, Toronto. Reprinted by permission of the author.

tions about Canada's detachment and indifference in the late 1930s.[8] As for the greater involvement of Canada in international affairs after the Second World War, that was influenced by various factors, including the onset of the cold war, but the specific policies pursued by the Canadian government were neither so consistent nor so different from what came before as most analyses imply. On the contrary, what is remarkable about Canada's view of the rest of the world, and its response to international events from 1945 to 1949, is the continuity which lurks beneath the surface of this supposed sea change. This was undeniably a time of transition for Canada in world affairs. But the shift was more gradual and cautious than one might suspect from a perusal of Canada's commitments.

To some extent, the apparent turnabout may be ascribed simply to heightened awareness of both power and vulnerability in the aftermath of Canada's contribution to victory. Complacency and irresponsibility were impossible after 1945. . . . Circumpolar views of the world were not as comforting as Mercator's projection once had been. Geography no longer seemed to protect Canada, situated as it was between two antagonistic superpowers.[9] Moreover, with so much of Europe and Asia still recovering from the devastation of a global conflict, Canada could not pretend that its decisions had no impact overseas or that others would fill whatever void it left.

Manifestations of a similar engagement in other sectors of policy have lent credence to the impression that there was a more comprehensive reappraisal of Canada's position underway. As a panoply of multilateral institutions was created to deal with the vast array of social, economic, and political problems that confronted the postwar world, Canadians were among those who helped to redefine the world order. The irresponsible bystander of former years had somehow metamorphosed into an assertive and compulsive joiner. More than simply a participant, Canada sometimes played the part of advocate, negotiator, or partner. Numerous agencies with diverse functions bore the imprint of the individual and collective influence of Canadians: the International Civil Aviation Organization (ICAO), the World Bank or International Bank for Reconstruction and Development (IBRD), the International Monetary Fund (IMF), the General Agreement on Tariffs and Trade (GATT), the World Health Organization (WHO), and many other instruments for cooperative action among nations.[10]

Often these multilateral organizations had no prewar counterparts, so that the opportunity for engagement itself was novel. Usually their creation was inspired by one or more of the major powers, with Canada and other nations obliged to react. Even so, Canada's response to the specialized agencies seemed more positive than it might have been before. There were also apparently signs of a reassessment of Canada's interaction with the rest of the world in its performance within familiar institutions, such as the Commonwealth, as well as in the conduct of its bilateral relations, especially, though not exclusively, those with Britain and the United States.

This depiction of Canada's international relations suggests a "revolution" in Canadian diplomacy in the immediate aftermath of the Second World War, with the cold war as the setting, if not the cause.[11] As Robert Bothwell has argued, that interpretation has been reinforced by a bias toward "periodization" in scholarly analyses of Canadian history.[12] On closer examination, however some of the factors which purportedly contributed to a reversal had more ambiguous or contradictory consequences. To raise questions about the impression conveyed of fundamental change in Canada's international relations, it is necessary to take a closer look at some of the influences on decision making in the critical years, from 1945 to 1949.

Understandably, there has been a tendency to stress the influence of character as well as circumstance on Ottawa's approach to international relations after the war. A prominent place in most accounts is given to the change in leadership of the Department of

External Affairs. In September 1946, William Lyon Mackenzie King handed over the position of Secretary of State for External Affairs to Louis St. Laurent. Generally, this move has been depicted favourably as belated acknowledgement that Mackenzie King no longer dominated this subject and that the portfolio imposed burdens too great for a prime minister, especially one whose age, health, and demeanour supposedly displayed symptoms of impending retirement. Even those who extol Mackenzie King's achievements during the Second World War make no similar effort to defend his postwar record.[13] Thus, the decline and subsequent departure of Mackenzie King is seen as loosening reins which had held more adventurous spirits in check. That liberation is regarded as more than offsetting the loss of a supposed advantage for the Department of External Affairs in Cabinet of having the powerful voice of the prime minister as its advocate. That influence at the head of the table had often been a dubious asset with unpredictable consequences.

Even after he relinquished his ministerial responsibility for foreign affairs, Mackenzie King asserted his knowledge and authority in that sphere. Soon after his appointment, however, St. Laurent projected a distinct image and attitude. That change in style was evident in a major address which he delivered early in his tenure. What was most remarkable about the Gray Lecture which St. Laurent gave at the University of Toronto in January 1947 was that such a self-conscious statement of Canadian policy, with an open invitation to public discussion of the subject, was made at all.[14] St. Laurent, unlike his predecessor, had become a politician reluctantly and late in life. Less than five years after Mackenzie King had persuaded him to join his wartime government, St. Laurent was responsible for Canada's foreign policy. He approached questions much as an experienced lawyer reviewing a brief, anxious to be convinced first before he attempted to persuade others of the wisdom of a recommended course. Episodes from the past, which played such an important and idiosyncratic part in shaping Mackenzie King's reaction to current events, usually had little or no resonance for St. Laurent. Though St. Laurent was not much younger than Mackenzie King, his reliance on even younger advisers and his sense of detachment from past battles — won and lost — conveyed the impression that a generational shift in leadership had taken place. That was especially welcome to those who had chafed under the wary direction of Mackenzie King.

St. Laurent was Secretary of State for External Affairs for barely more than two years, but that was long enough to establish a partnership closely identified with the "golden decade" — often lengthened to an "age" or "era" — of Canadian diplomacy.[15] First as deputy minister and principal adviser to St. Laurent, then as his successor and Cabinet colleague, Lester B. Pearson enjoyed a relationship of mutual trust and confidence with his superior that fostered a positive and creative approach to Canada's international relations.[16] "Mike" Pearson had been one of the initial recruits for the foreign service by the second Undersecretary of State for External Affairs, O.D. Skelton.[17] He was familiar with and to the Department of External Affairs. So well did Pearson know his staff that he was able to make effective use of their differences in making up his own mind.[18] What that meant for his officials was a unique opportunity to assess the implications for Canada of its involvement in world affairs and to take advantage of their country's exceptional power and influence in the wake of the Second World War.[19] . . .

Those who had joined the Department of External Affairs during the bleak interwar years and who represented Canada abroad after 1945 — such as Norman Robertson, High Commissioner in London until early 1949, when he returned to Ottawa as Clerk of the Privy Council and Secretary of the Cabinet; Hume Wrong, ambassador in Washington from 1946 to 1953; Escott Reid; and Charles Ritchie — were an impressive group, with greater depth and experience than before, as well as more favourable circumstances. . . . But there were still occasions when Canadian views were strongly influenced by essential foreign information and advice, particularly that passed on by the more elaborate diplomatic networks of the British Foreign Office and the American Department of State. That feature of Canadian decision making reminds us that there were practical problems of adjustment in the transition from wartime plans to postwar commitments. Ottawa may have been better able to meet those challenges after the war, but it still relied on help from its principal allies.

Moreover, it is facile to attribute differences in performance to a change in the cast. So far as senior decision makers are concerned, the metamorphosis was not so comprehensive as implied by references to a "golden age." The decisions most closely identified with that tribute, to participate in the United Nations and to negotiate a North Atlantic defence pact, were both taken with that paragon of caution, Mackenzie King, at the helm. His attitudes and experiences still cast a long shadow in his final years as prime minister, as when he blocked a proposal for a customs union with the United States or when the Cabinet decided that Canadian aircraft and personnel would not assist in the Berlin Airlift.[20] Colleagues and subordinates usually deferred, however grudgingly, to Mackenzie King's political judgement. . . .

Whether or not the roster and responses of policymakers in Ottawa were changing, the world which they confronted was different, and that had a considerable bearing on their decisions. For that reason, a brief examination of the international context is critical. . . . After the war, Britain was obviously eclipsed by the emerging superpowers, the United States and the Soviet Union. With hindsight, we may conclude that the pace and extent of the decline of the United Kingdom in the immediate postwar world have been exaggerated. Especially in the early years of reconstruction, there was a difficult and incomplete adjustment by the British public and statesmen to the revised hierarchy of international power and its implications. That problem was most acute in the realm of international finance and trade, but it also affected commitments in defence and foreign policy. What that meant for Canada was that a major power on which it relied for information and occasional advocacy was relatively less important and that, therefore, Canada's indirect influence was also diminished. As well, Britain's defensive response to its own decline sometimes alienated its intimate ally.[21]

While rhetoric about the "North Atlantic Triangle" soared, practical developments suggested that those cold waters separated rather than united Britain and Canada on some critical bilateral and multilateral issues.[22] Yet one could also cite numerous examples of collaboration and cooperation which contradicted this impression. For reasons of history, personal and family associations, cultural and political traditions, investment and financial links, as well as that elusive but forceful influence, sentiment, the British Isles and the rest of the Commonwealth did not suddenly sink below the horizon for English-speaking Canada. On the contrary, both public and policymakers paid close and sympathetic attention to British affairs.[23] Nor did most Canadians assume that the United Kingdom's postwar decline was a permanent or irreversible feature of global politics. Significant commitments, such as Canada's reconstruction loan to Britain in March 1946, were premised on opposite assumptions.[24]

Whether or not it was well understood, Britain's decline did have one positive impact on the making of Canadian foreign policy. So long as Britain and its perspectives had set Canada's agenda and shaped its likely commitments in world affairs, questions of international relations had tended to divide Canadians. The gradual development of autonomy for the Dominions in external affairs had not eliminated this problem. Especially in Quebec, there had been a perception that international involvement by Canada inevitably meant support for British or imperial ventures. In the rest of Canada, the extent to which

Canadian positions had been defined in relation to British attitudes, and Canadian undertakings had been seen as assistance to the United Kingdom, had often divided public views on international issues. That astute observer, J.W. Dafoe, had identified five major groupings of opinion on international affairs in Canada before the war.[25] So far as national united had been affected by questions of foreign policy, the impact had been negative. There had certainly been no meaningful consensus on external relations in Canada before the Second World War. A contributing factor may have been the preeminence of Britain.

The diminished importance of the United Kingdom after the war made it improbable that Canadian policy would be defined so narrowly. . . . No longer was it axiomatic that an overseas commitment by Canada was determined by the Anglo-Canadian relationship. The projection of Canadian concerns into non-imperial settings also fostered greater public support, as did the dominance of the United States among Western powers after the war. Canada's involvement in world affairs had become less divisive and controversial. For Canadian policymakers, public support for the broad outlines of international engagement was an unaccustomed advantage in asserting a Canadian position.

American ascendance likewise had both advantages and disadvantages for Canada. Quite apart from the obvious dictates of geography and security, which were magnified by the looming prospect of the Soviet–American confrontation, there were many reasons why the continental neighbours had a common outlook in international affairs. However important to Canadians the differences between Canada and the United States may have been from time to time, the similarities and connections have had a more profound impact on foreign policy. Whether one considers flows of investment and trade, migration, popular culture, political and social values, historical traditions, family ties, or any number of other measures, there is no country with which Canada has had more in common than the United States. To the extent, then, that the power of the United States was enhanced in the postwar world and that the United States involved itself more directly and thoroughly in global issues, that trend favoured Canada's positions.

Perhaps predictably, however, that development was not without its negative aspects. As policymakers in Washington lifted their gaze to more distant and ominous points on the globe, there was a tendency to overlook continental matters or to take Canadian consent and cooperation for granted. After the war, doubts and concerns resurfaced about American respect for Canada's sovereignty in the North.[26] Those highlighted a renewed wariness in Canada about the implications of global confrontation for national interests. Anxiety about how American power would affect Canada and about past American stances had prompted Mackenzie King to query various proposals for closer political, military, and economic association with the United States or calls for support of American policy. For others, there was unease about whether the emerging superpower would fulfill its commitments and assume the international role which circumstances demanded. But it would be wrong to allow these uncertainties or hesitations to colour too strongly this brief glance at Canada's postwar perceptions and interests. In fact, the overall reaction in Canada generally and in Ottawa especially was relief and satisfaction that the United States was prepared to take the lead in international affairs. This trend was seen as comparable to the shift in Canadian policy, with participation in the wartime alliance as a factor in both developments.

National self-confidence in Canada had been enhanced by the recent contributions to victory in the Second World War. The Canadian Army, the Royal Canadian Navy, and the Royal Canadian Air Force had all expanded dramatically and their exploits had been celebrated in print, via newsreels and films, and on radio.[27] There had also been widespread publicity for other aspects of the war effort, such as the British Commonwealth Air

Training Plan, the Merchant Marine, Ferry Command, munitions production, food supplies, and financial assistance to Allies and liberated countries.[28] With the defeat and disarmament of the Axis powers and the devastating impact on allies, foes, and neutrals of the battles in Europe, Asia, and Africa, Canada emerged from the war in an unfamiliar position of prominence and relative power. Though its armed forces were dwarfed by those of the United States, the Soviet Union, and the United Kingdom, Canada was ranked next to those countries in several important categories. Of course, that standing was deceptive and temporary, especially as the government was determined to demobilize the armed forces and cut defence expenditures as rapidly as possible.

In other sectors, however, Canada's contribution to postwar reconstruction was expected to equal or exceed its value in wartime. By war's end, Canada was not only a major trading nation but also the second-largest creditor on international accounts, after the United States. Though trade could not be maintained at the artificial levels induced by wartime demands and underwritten by exceptional financial arrangements, the Canadian government was committed to an unprecedented level of exports after the war.[29] Ottawa enacted extraordinary measures to finance its shipments to the United Kingdom and Western Europe, which were seen as vital to Canada's postwar prosperity and as essential to lessen dependence on trade with the United States. Meanwhile, Canada's economic importance and its interests as a dollar country played an increasingly significant part in its reckoning of its capacity and its approach in international affairs. That sense of differentiation from lesser as well as from great powers prompted a preoccupation with categories such as "middle power" among policy makers and scholars in Canada. Whatever the terminology, however, the presumption has been that a commitment to "internationalism" was a consistent element.

That identification was translated into arguments for even greater representation for intermediate or smaller powers, with "functionalism" as a theoretical justification. From its wartime origins as a rationale for representation on some Anglo–American combined boards, the Canadian redefinition of "functionalism" was transformed into a more comprehensive principle for organizing multilateral institutions after the war, according to most Canadian accounts.[30] Whether the new superpowers and the formerly great powers appreciated or even acknowledged its merits, the notion that responsibility or authority among nations should be allocated according to actual or potential contributions to the solution of problems in a sector or region made some sense, especially to a lesser power. There were modest advances for smaller powers in the policies and procedures of the United Nations and its associated agencies. Whether these were triumphs for "functionalism" or trivial sops on peripheral subjects is a moot point. On issues of high policy, the international system had a tendency to revert to form. . . .

Generally, the onset of the cold war made international involvement by Canada more probable and less controversial. Yet it greatly diminished that always elusive and frequently over-valued commodity, freedom of action, for Canada in world affairs. Most questions or issues were assessed in a context in which it was considered essential to maintain at least a semblance of unity in the Western alliance and consequently some support for American policy. From time to time, that seemed to justify Canadian pretensions to act as a "hinge," "linchpin," or "interpreter" between the United Kingdom and the United States.[31] More often, as in the past, no intermediary was necessary. As for that Canadian conceit, the "North Atlantic Triangle," there were vital examples of tripartite cooperation on issues of defence, finance, and trade. But whatever triangular relationship may have been involved was distinctly asymmetrical. That geometric fabrication helped Canadians to identify their interests and values with familiar influences and relationships, but it was fundamentally a restatement of the obvious setting for Canadian decision making. The most important requirement of Canada's international relations had always been Anglo–American harmony and the cardinal principle of its foreign policy after the war, as before, was to help to avoid or to limit clashes between its principal allies. The schism of the cold war affected the interpretation and presentation of Canadian foreign policy, but it did not prompt a critical reconsideration of Canadian values and interests in international affairs. What it did provide was a rhetorical justification for maintenance of Canada's familiar alignments in a divided world. . . .

Before long, the perception of a threat from the Soviet Union became the basis for a more comprehensive response from Britain, the United States, and Canada, in association with other nations. The impetus from the United Kingdom for Western Union, a measure of collective security for Britain, France, and the Benelux countries, was soon broadened into pressure for a commitment from the United States to defend Western Europe. In its eventual form, which Canada helped to shape, the assurance became the key to the North Atlantic Treaty Organization (NATO).[32] Not only did Canadian speakers contribute to the rhetorical context for the deliberations, but Canadian negotiators participated in the initial highly secret talks with British and American representatives. Though there was not yet a price tag on Canada's undertaking, the implications of the decision to formalize the pact were unmistakable. Whatever its limitations and the uncertainties about its consequences for Canada, however, NATO represented a practical response to the cold war, which was consistent with Canada's familiar values and interests, albeit in a "time of fear and hope." Canada's participation in a military alliance in peacetime offered a dramatic contradiction of its avoidance of commitments in the 1930s, but that was true for other signatories of the Washington Treaty as well.[33] Yet there were other manifestations of an apparently fundamental shift in Canada's international relations, as well as of the pervasive impact of the cold war.

Before, during, and after the negotiation of the North Atlantic Treaty, Canada sat as a nonpermanent member of the Security Council. Deadlock in that body had been a significant justification for the mutual defence pact, nominally under the cloak of the UN. Throughout 1948 and 1949, Canadian diplomats at the Security Council participated in discussions of a myriad of issues, most of which split predictably and acrimoniously on East–West lines. In this forum, it was no longer possible for Canada to avoid entanglement in disputes. Instead, Canadian policymakers were often obliged to pursue remedial education on hitherto ignored or neglected parts of the world. In the case of Indonesia's quest for independence from the Netherlands, for example, there was unease in the Department of External Affairs about reliance on British and Dutch reports. That eventually prompted an approach to Australia for information and advice. In that instance, the Canadian government struck an awkward balance between sympathy for Indonesian independence and unwillingness to censure an ally.[34]

The controversy over Britain's decision to quit Palestine and to turn the unresolved problem of relations between Arabs and Jews over to the United Nations inspired even greater anxiety in Ottawa. Initially, that concern centred less on the threat to peace in the Middle East and more on the potential damage to Anglo–American relations, which might stall implementation of the Marshall Plan and consolidation of the Western alliance. Canadian policymakers, including Mackenzie King, tended to sympathize with Britain's predicament and its approach to an intractable problem, while seeking to temper the American response. The United States and the United Kingdom did manage, with difficulty, to prevent this dispute from prejudicing consideration of other matters, but it would be difficult to attribute that to Canadian diplomacy.[35]

The Kashmir dispute between Indian and Pakistan threatened to ensnare Canada more directly, particularly when each party favoured Canada as its nominee for a mediatory panel. The Canadian delegation, inspired by Ottawa, was able to invoke Commonwealth membership as a reason for declining a formal role in a conflict between two other members. However, at the Security Council it was not so easy to avoid entanglement, particularly when the rotating presidency was assumed by Canada's delegate, General A.G.L. McNaughton. In fact, Canada's stint on the Security Council ended with an effort at personal diplomacy by McNaughton, which laid the groundwork for yet another futile mediation later. John Holmes, who was then a member of the Canadian delegation, has commented that the representatives of the Soviet Union were more worried by success in these efforts, as that threatened to turn "the Security Council into a more supple body than they wanted."[36] As a recent study of the Kashmir problem has demonstrated, their anxiety was misplaced.[37]

The United Nations was also a forum for discussion of two events which contributed to the hardening of lines in the global confrontation: the coup in Czechoslovakia in February 1948 and the dispute over access to West Berlin from June 1948 to April 1949. In neither instance was the Security Council or the General Assembly the only, or even the principal, venue at which the clash between East and West was dramatized. Nor was the world body instrumental in resolving either matter. However, Canada's response to these two episodes revealed a great deal about the limitations as well as the implications of the influence of the cold war on Canadian foreign policy. . . .

An occasion when Canada did break ranks was in the government's response to the Berlin crisis. When it became obvious that West Berlin would have to be provisioned by air, the occupying powers, especially Britain, looked to close and distant allies for support. The need for aircrew and aircraft was both symbolic and real, particularly as the matter remained unresolved for weeks and then months. From the outset, the United Kingdom hoped that its associates in the Commonwealth, notably Canada, would assist its efforts to thwart the Soviet blockade of West Berlin. Yet Canada turned a deaf ear to unambiguous informal suggestions from London. Apparently, Britain's appeal for help reminded Mackenzie King of the Chanak crisis of 1922, when a leak to the press had been used by British ministers to try to pressure him into an ill-advised commitment.[38] Whether or not that unpleasant memory was decisive, the Canadian Cabinet supported the line taken by the prime minister and the minister of National Defence, Brooke Claxton, that Canada's air force did not have enough resources to contribute to the Berlin Airlift.

That seemed a curious stance for a country which was negotiating participation in a military alliance which presumably would make much greater demands on its armed forces.[39] Perhaps more pertinent was Mackenzie King's persistent fear that Canada would be directly involved in an incident which might precipitate a third world war. When public pressure mounted for a Canadian contribution, the government sheltered behind the façade that no formal request for assistance had been received. That unhelpful posture was maintained even after South Africa and New Zealand offered aid. Subsequently, more discreet approaches were made from Washington, also without effect. Not until Mackenzie King had retired and Pearson had returned to Ottawa from meetings of the United Nations General Assembly in Paris did the question reappear on the agenda of the Canadian Cabinet. Before a requested survey of aircraft and aircrew was completed, however, the crisis was resolved. What is noteworthy about this failure by Canada to act in support of its allies is not so much the peculiar but familiar influences at work in Ottawa or the arguments deployed to resist entanglement but the fact that it illustrates vividly the limits of the cold war's impact on Canadian policy. After all, the Berlin crisis was the most dramatic and newsworthy confrontation between West and East thus far, yet Canada watched apprehensively from the sidelines.

Generally speaking, however, in this period the influence of the cold war on Canada's international relations was pervasive. To demonstrate that point, let us glance briefly at a few other issues which posed awkward questions for Canadian policymakers. One episode which has received considerable attention was the controversy in the Canadian Cabinet over participation in the United Nations Temporary Commission on Korea (UNTCOK). Within a remarkably short time, Mackenzie King's personal irritation at a supposed slight by his colleagues and his resentment at American presumption had escalated into an absurd farce which threatened to alienate the United States, split the Cabinet, and possibly topple the government. As much diplomatic energy was expended on reconciling Mackenzie King with St. Laurent as on averting a contretemps with Washington. The outcome, a compromise whereby a Canadian member would participate under specified conditions, has been depicted as a defeat for Mackenzie King and evidence for an assertion of interest and leadership by other members of the Cabinet on an important question of foreign policy.[40] That interpretation may be misleading, but that is not what matters here.

There was another reason why Mackenzie King reacted so strongly to the agreement reached in his absence that Canada should accept the American nomination to sit on UNTCOK. By the time he returned to Ottawa, Mackenzie King was convinced that there was a significant risk of another world war. From the British Foreign Secretary, Ernest Bevin, he had learned that the Council of Foreign Ministers (CFM) would likely reach an impasse over the treatment of Germany and the Soviet–American diplomatic confrontation in Moscow could precipitate a military clash, either in Germany or at some other place where the Red Army and the U.S. Army faced each other.[41] Thus, the Korean peninsula was magnified in importance as a potential flashpoint. When Bevin's prediction about the CFM, which was a widely anticipated but still ominous development, came true, Mackenzie King's anxiety increased. Quite apart from eliciting predictable observations about how ignorant his colleagues were about Korea, that fear of an armed conflict helps to explain why Mackenzie King dug in his heels so adamantly on this matter. . . .

In another instance, one cannot attribute the outcome obviously or unambiguously to the influence of the cold war. For nearly two years after the independence of India and Pakistan in August 1947, Commonwealth leaders deliberated about whether India could stay in the Commonwealth after it adopted a republican constitution. The currents and cross-currents which affected this topic would befuddle the most accomplished helmsman. But an examination of the assessments of this problem, particularly those made in Ottawa and London, does suggest that, gradually, there was less preoccupation with the constitutional conundrum and greater attention to India's alignment in world affairs and its implications for the Western alliance. Moreover, when the leaders of the Commonwealth assembled in London in April 1949, Pakistan especially emphasized doubts about India's reliability as an ally in its efforts to embarrass its adversary. But its motives—and those of other members who ultimately decided to lessen the importance of the monarchy to the cohesion of the Commonwealth—were not simple and straightforward.[42]

That suggestion of other influences at work in the assessment as well as the resolution of that issue reminds us to be wary of attributing too much to the impact of one factor, however important it may seem. The onset of the cold war unquestionably swayed public opinion in Canada and it certainly affected the way policymakers in Ottawa viewed and depicted Canada's role in international affairs after the Second World War, especially as the wartime alliance broke down and new alignments displaced it. That reorientation of Canada's position helped to forge an unprecedented national consensus on foreign policy.

The cold war cast its shadow over diverse issues with often decisive results. It also lent unaccustomed coherence to the rhetoric as well as the substance of Canada's international relations. Commitments and stances were frequently justified by reference to the overarching demands of the Western alliance and the need to stand firm against the Soviet threat.[43]

That semblance of a carefully developed and consistent approach to external affairs in Ottawa may itself be misleading. After all, most of the episodes or themes which dominated Canada's international relations in this period involved reactions to events abroad or to proposals articulated by other powers, rather than the application of a predetermined or logically integrated course of action. Certainly, the overall attitude in Canada can be differentiated from earlier periods. In that sense, the perceived ascendance of "internationalism" has not been a misapprehension. But policymaking is rarely an orderly process, especially for a smaller power. For example, the Department of External Affairs devoted considerable attention to analyses of Soviet–American relations in 1947–48. Whether that exercise had any specific impact on the policies pursued by Canada toward either superpower is doubtful.[44] Similarly, the tendency to view events through the prism of the cold war may distort or obscure some motivations for decisions.

There are enough exceptions and qualifications which must be made to any generalization about the impact of the cold war that we must be wary of reading too much into the way in which arguments were adjusted to suit the new context and to provide justification for policies and commitments which may be traced to different origins. The other reasons why Canada played a greater part in world affairs after 1945 should not be downplayed. Moreover, there is ample evidence that the key determinants of Canadian action in this period were firmly rooted in Canada's traditional ties with the United Kingdom and the United States. Especially in external economic policy, Canada sought stability and order at least as much as innovation and exceptional measures.

Arguably the most dramatic manifestation of Canada's new "internationalism" — as well as its dependence on foreign trade for prosperity — was the reconstruction loan of $1.25 billion to Britain in early 1946. That substantial commitment, which greatly exceeded what the country spent on defence in the early days of the cold war, was justified by the Department of Finance and the Bank of Canada principally as an instrument to assure established markets for Canadian goods.[45] For better or worse, another critical measure at that time — the Anglo–Canadian Wheat Agreement — was negotiated by the minister of Agriculture, James Gardiner.[46] These deals were attempts to ease the transition from wartime arrangements to postwar circumstances which bore little relation to the rhetoric of the cold war or to the agenda of the Department of External Affairs, which was only a bit player in the bargaining. In these and other episodes, the files of the foreign ministry can present a false image of Canada's priorities and obligations in international relations. Neither deal was a triumph for "multilateralism," so often seen as the singular expression of "internationalism."

A final cautionary note should be sounded about the relative importance of international questions to Canadians and to their governments in this period. In the aftermath of a global conflict, the principal preoccupations of the Mackenzie King and St. Laurent governments, responding to the views of the electorate, were the reconversion of industry and manpower to peacetime purposes, as well as a demonstration of good faith, but not necessarily good deeds, to fulfill its political pledges on social and economic policy at home. With Canada's dependence on foreign markets for prosperity, policymakers in Ottawa could not ignore the world beyond Canada's borders, but external questions generally did not animate, positively or negatively, the Canadian populace. However frustrating that attitude may have been then to members of the foreign service or subsequently to analysts of Canada's external relations, it was also not exceptional. Budgetary allocations may not be the definitive or most reliable test of the relative priorities assigned to different purposes by governments and peoples, particularly when some of the most important commitments in international affairs have little or no cost immediately attached to them. But they do remind us that international relations were not the exclusive, or necessarily the dominant, focus of attention for ministers and their advisers.[47]

Within the realm of Canada's foreign policy, however, a shift in posture before and after the Second World War is discernible. That the cold war played an increasingly important part in defining context and justifying actions is demonstrable. Whether it was the decisive factor in fostering the growth of "internationalism" in Canada is more problematic. Many of the trends — and some specific developments — in Canada's external relations were well under way before the cold war exerted its pull. Even when the rhetoric of the cold war predominated, traditional values, interests, and doubts still swayed policymakers in Ottawa. But the cold war was vital to broader acceptance of overseas involvement by Canada. That assurance was a critical prop for the elaboration and implementation of "internationalism" by Canada's representatives. There was no "revolution" in Canadian foreign policy, but Canada's international relations certainly evinced a more substantial involvement in world affairs than before.

NOTES

1. James Eayrs, "'A Low Dishonest Decade': Aspects of Canadian External Policy, 1931–1939," in H.L. Keenleyside et al., *The Growth of Canadian Policies in External Affairs* (Durham, NC, 1960), pp. 59–80. Eayrs deals with the subject at greater length in *In Defence of Canada*, vol. 2, *Appeasement and Rearmament* (Toronto, 1965). For assessments of Canadian foreign policy in the interwar years, see Richard Veatch, *Canada and the League of Nations* (Toronto, 1975); C.P. Stacey, *Canada and the Age of Conflict*, vol. 2, *1921–1948, The Mackenzie King Era* (Toronto, 1981); Norman Hillmer and J.L. Granatstein, *Empire to Umpire: Canada and the World to the 1990s* (Toronto, 1994).

2. The most detailed examinations of Canada's international relations in the immediate aftermath of the Second World War are: F.H. Soward, *Canada in World Affairs: From Normandy to Paris, 1944–1946* (Toronto, 1959); James Eayrs, *In Defence of Canada: Peacemaking and Deterrence* (Toronto, 1972); James Eayrs, *In Defence of Canada: Growing Up Allied* (Toronto, 1980); and John Holmes, *The Shaping of Peace: Canada and the Search for World Order, 1943–1957*, 2 vols. (Toronto, 1979 and 1982).

3. John Holmes, "The New Agenda for Canadian Internationalism," in *Canada and the New Internationalism*, ed. John Holmes and John Kirton (Toronto, 1988), pp. 12–23.

4. For a personal interpretation of Canada's postwar foreign policy by a participant, see Arthur Andrew, *The Rise and Fall of a Middle Power: Canadian Diplomacy from King to Mulroney* (Toronto, 1993). The theme of power and responsibility was discussed widely in the 1960s. See especially *Canada's Role as a Middle Power*, ed. J. King Gordon (Toronto, 1966). In that collection, John Holmes noted (pp. 15-16) that "middle power" had acquired a mediatory aspect which went beyond the original connotation of "a power of medium strength." A decade later, Holmes wryly commented on this Canadian obsession by entitling an edition of his essays *Canada: A Middle-Aged Power* (Toronto, 1976). Power in relation to Canada's international relations is ably discussed in the first chapter of Kim Richard Nossal, *The Politics of Canadian Foreign Policy* (Scarborough, 1985).

5. Tom Keating, *Canada and World Order: The Multilateralist Tradition in Canadian Foreign Policy* (Toronto, 1993), especially the introduction. Although there have been studies of Canada's bilateral relationships, particularly with the United States, the "bilateralist tradition" in Canada's international relations has received less attention in examinations of Canada's postwar foreign

policy. For overviews of the Canadian–American relationship, see Robert Bothwell, *Canada and the United States: The Politics of Partnership* (Toronto, 1992); J.L. Granatstein and Norman Hillmer, *For Better or For Worse: Canada and the United States to the 1990s* (Toronto, 1991). An excellent overview of the contradictory impulses in Canada's international trade may be found in Robert Bothwell and John English, "Canadian Trade Policy in the Age of American Dominance and British Decline, 1943–1947," *Canadian Review of American Studies*, 8, 1 (Spring 1977): 54-65.

6. Apart from the general works cited above, see Escott Reid, *On Duty: A Canadian at the Making of the United Nations, 1945–1946* (Toronto, 1983).
7. See especially Denis Smith, *Diplomacy of Fear: Canada and the Cold War 1941–1948* (Toronto, 1988).
8. J.L. Granatstein and Robert Bothwell, "'A Self-Evident National Duty': Canadian Foreign Policy, 1935–1939," *Journal of Imperial and Commonwealth History*, 3, 2 (January 1975): 212–33; Roger Sarty, "Mr. King and the Armed Forces," in *A Country of Limitations: Canada and the World in 1938*, ed. Norman Hillmer, Robert Bothwell, Roger Sarty and Claude Beauregard (Ottawa, 1996), pp. 217–46. Hillmer and Granatstein, *Empire to Umpire*, pp. 143–51. Mackenzie King's biographer regarded the earlier indictments of the prime minister's policies and actions in the 1930s as unduly harsh. "King might have been given credit for a foreign policy which had popular support at home and which revealed a sound awareness of the modest international role which a small North American nation could play. But for most Canadian historians there is the regret that Canada did not adopt a more virtuous or noble pose, though the probably results would have been dissension." H.Blair Neatby, "Mackenzie King and the Historians," in *Mackenzie King: Widening the Debate*, ed. John English and J.O. Stubbs (Toronto, 1977), p. 8.
9. R.J. Sutherland, "Canada's Long Term Strategic Situation," *International Journal*, 17, 3 (Summer, 1962), pp. 199–223.
10. Some of these contributions are recalled in *Canadians and the United Nations*, ed. Clyde Sanger (Ottawa, 1988). See also A.F.W. Plumptre, *Three Decades of Decision: Canada and the World Monetary System, 1944–75* (Toronto, 1977); David MacKenzie, *Canada and International Civil Aviation, 1932–1948* (Toronto, 1989); *Also Present at the Creation: Dana Wilgress and the United Nations Conference on Trade and Employment at Havana*, ed. Michael Hart (Ottawa, [1995]). One exception to the rule in this period later was contradicted by this tendency in Canadian policy: David MacKenzie, "'The World's Greatest Joiner: Canada and the Organization of American States," *British Journal of Canadian Studies*, 6, 1 (1991), pp. 203–20.
11. Escott Reid, "The Revolution in Canadian Foreign Policy," *India Quarterly*, 24 (1958), pp. 188–96, quoted and discussed in Donald Barry, "Continuity and Change in Canadian Foreign Policy: From the Pre-War to the Post-War Experience, 1935–1957" (Ph.D. thesis, Johns Hopkins University, 1977), pp. 152–53. "The 'revolution' in Canadian policy towards international institutions can also be over-dramatized," John Holmes observed in his discussion of Canada's postwar policies. "It was a change more of will than of policy, an enforced adaptation to change in international circumstance. There was much that was traditionally Canadian in the response." *The Shaping of Peace*, vol. 1, p. 4.
12. Notes by author from Robert Bothwell, "Orthodoxy, Revisionism and Post-Revisionism: Canada's Road to the Cold War," presentation at conference of the Organization for the Study of the National History of Canada on "The Canadian State: Successes, Failures, Development," November 1995.
13. Bruce Hutchison, *The Incredible Canadian. A Candid Portrait of Mackenzie King: His Works, His Times, and His Nation* (Toronto, 1952). The titles of the chapters which deal with the postwar period are evocative: "The Wrong World," "The Dwindling Days," "The Heir-Apparent," and "The Pilgrim's Return." For a comprehensive scholarly treatment of Mackenzie King's wartime leadership in domestic and foreign policy, see J.L. Granatstein, *Canada's War: The Politics of the Mackenzie King Government 1939–1945* (Toronto, 1975). J.W. Pickersgill has commented on the irony that "this least military of men should have found only in war the full measure of his capacity for leadership." Pickersgill, "Mackenzie King's Political Attitudes and Public Politics: A Personal Impression," in *Widening the Debate*, ed. English and Stubbs, p. 23.
14. For the text of the Gray Lecture, see *Canadian Foreign Policy 1945–1954: Selected Speeches and Documents*, ed. Robert A. MacKay (Toronto, 1970), pp. 388–99.

15. Escott Reid, "Canadian Foreign Policy, 1967–1977: A Second Golden Decade?" *International Journal*, 22, 2 (Spring 1967): 171–81. Reid identified 1941–1951 as the first "golden decade," though later commentators tend to focus on the postwar (and post-King) era. For example, in his memoirs, George Ignatieff begins the chapter entitled "The Golden Age of Canadian Diplomacy" with Mackenzie King's announcement of his retirement. *The Making of a Peacemonger: The Memoirs of George Ignatieff* (Toronto, 1985). Both Reid and Ignatieff were policy-makers in the Department of External Affairs in the periods they describe. "'Of course,' another golden ager, Charles Ritchie, has observed, 'there never really was a golden age . . . No one wakes up in bed and says here I am in the golden age.' Rather 'there was a feeling that we could make this *contribution*. And there was this famous middle power idea that we could address ourselves to tasks that fitted our capacities and concentrate on them. So there seemed to be some shape to policy.'" Susan Lightstone, "The Observer," *Ottawa Magazine* (March 1991), p. 29, quoted in John Hilliker and Donald Barry, *Canada's Department of External Affairs*, vol. 2, *Coming of Age, 1946–1968* (Montreal/Kingston, 1995), p. 31.

16. "He [St. Laurent] and Pearson established a fruitful working relationship based on mutual trust and admiration." Dale C. Thomson, *Louis St. Laurent, Canadian* (Toronto, 1967), p. 216. John English, *Shadow of Heaven, the Life of Lester Pearson*, vol. 1, *1897–1948* (Toronto, 1989), esp. pp. 314–16 and John English, *The Worldly Years: The Life of Lester Pearson*, vol. 2, *1949–1972* (Toronto, 1992).

17. On Skelton's influence, see especially Norman Hillmer, "O.D. Skelton on War and Peace, 1923–1941: Bureaucracy, Foreign Policy, National Independence," Marston LaFrance Research Fellowship Lecture, Carleton University, 5 March 1996. For Skelton's impact on the institutional development of the Department of External Affairs, see John Hilliker, *Canada's Department of External Affairs*, vol. 1 *The Early Years, 1909–1946* (Montreal/Kingston, 1990), esp. ch. 4 and Part Two.

18. English, *Worldly Years*, ch. 1.

19. There is an excellent assessment of the relationship between Pearson and his advisers in the first chapter of Geoffrey A.H. Pearson, *Seize the Day: Lester B. Pearson and Crisis Diplomacy* (Ottawa, 1993).

20. See Robert Cuff and J.L. Granatstein, "The Rise and Fall of Canadian–American Free Trade, 1947-8," *Canadian Historical Review*, 57, 4 (December 1977): 459–82; Leigh E. Sarty, "The Limits of Internationalism: Canada and the Soviet Blockade of Berlin, 1948–1949," in *Nearly Neighbours, Canada and the Soviet Union: From Cold War to Détente and Beyond*, ed. J.L. Black and Norman Hillmer (Kingston, 1989), pp. 56–74.

21. J.L. Granatstein, *How Britain's Weakness Forced Canada into the Arms of the United States* (Toronto, 1989); B.W. Muirhead, *The Development of Postwar Canadian Trade Policy: The Failure of the Anglo-European Option* (Montreal/Kingston, 1992).

22. J.B. Brebner, *North Atlantic Triangle: The Interplay of Canada, the United States and Great Britain* (New Haven, 1945); Edgar McInnis, *The Atlantic Triangle and the Cold War* (Toronto, 1959); C.P. Stacey, *Mackenzie King and the Atlantic Triangle* (Toronto, 1976); Lawrence Aronsen, "From World War to Cold War: Cooperation and Competition in the North Atlantic Triangle, 1945-1949," in *The North Atlantic Triangle in a Changing World: Anglo-American-Canadian Relations, 1902-1956*, ed. B.J.C. McKercher and Lawrence Aronsen (Toronto, 1996), pp. 181-219.

23. For an excellent assessment of the persistence of British influence on Canadian policy toward Asia, see Steven Hugh Lee, *Outposts of Empire: Korea, Vietnam, and the Origins of the Cold War in Asia, 1949–1954* (Montreal/Kingston, 1995), esp. pp. 23–25. Nearly half the Canadian population in the 1951 census (about 48 percent) identified its origins as "British." *Historical Statistics of Canada*, 2nd ed., ed. F.H. Leacy, M.C. Urquhart and K.A.H. Buckley (Ottawa, 1983), Series A125-163.

24. Hector Mackenzie, "The Path to Temptation: The Negotiation of Canada's Reconstruction Loan to Britain in 1946," *Historical Papers 1982 Communications historiques* (Ottawa, 1982), pp. 196–220; L.S. Pressnell, *External Economic Policy since the War*, vol. 1, *The Post-War Financial Settlement* (London, 1987), ch. 11.

25. J.W. Dafoe, "Canadian Foreign Policy" in *Conference on Canadian–American Affairs*, ed. Reginald G. Trotter, Albert B. Corey, and Walter W. McLaren (Boston, 1937), pp. 220–31 (also discussion by conference participants which follows, pp. 231–46).

26. Shelagh D. Grant, *Sovereignty or Security? Government Policy in the Canadian North 1936–1950* (Vancouver, 1988). See also *Documents on Canadian External Relations [DCER]*, vol. 14, *1948*, ed. Hector Mackenzie (Ottawa, 1994), esp. pp. 1511–28, and *DCER*, vol. 15, *1949*, ed. Hector Mackenzie (Ottawa, 1995), esp. pp. 1471–92.

27. William R. Young, "Building Citizenship: English Canada and Propaganda during the Second World War," *Journal of Canadian Studies*, 16, 3 & 4 (Fall-Winter 1981): 121–32.

28. C.P. Stacey, *Arms, Men and Governments: The War Policies of Canada 1939–1945* (Ottawa, 1970).

29. Hector Mackenzie, "The White Paper on Reconstruction and Canada's Post-War Trade," paper presented at conference of Canadian Committee for the History of the Second World War, Winnipeg, 1995.

30. The best explanations of the functionalist argument as it applied to the combined boards are in Stacey, *Arms, Men and Governments*, pp. 159–80; Granatstein, *Canada's War*, ch. 8; Granatstein, *The Ottawa Men*, pp. 124–33. For a useful assessment of the origins, development, and persistence of "functionalism" as a Canadian creed, see A.J. Miller, "The Functional Principle in Canada's External Relations," *International Journal*, 35, 2 (Spring 1980): 309–28. As Miller points out, what Canadian policymakers advocated and pursued was "functional representation" rather than "functionalism." Most surveys of Canada's international relations, including works cited elsewhere in this article, pay tribute to the triumph of "functionalism," as Canadians understood it.

31. "Since World War II Canada's role as mediator, or linchpin, has displaced the undefended border as the standard Canadian cliché." Blair Fraser, "Canada: Mediator or Busybody?" in *Canada's Role as a Middle Power*, ed. Gordon, pp. 1–12 (quotation from p. 1).

32. For analyses of Canada's participation in the negotiation of the North Atlantic Treaty, see Eayrs, *Growing Up Allied*, pp. 3–128; Escott Reid, *Time of Fear and Hope: The Making of the North Atlantic Treaty 1947–1949* (Toronto, 1977); Hector Mackenzie, "Canada, the Cold War and the Negotiation of the North Atlantic Treaty," in *Diplomatic Documents and Their Users: Proceedings of the Third Conference of Editors of Diplomatic Documents, Ottawa, 11–13 May 1994*, ed. John Hilliker and Mary Halloran (Ottawa, 1995), pp. 145–73. For the documentary record of the negotiations from Canadian sources, see *DCER*, vol. 14, pp. 419–782 and *DCER*, vol. 15, pp. 478–607.

33. Most obviously, this was the case for the United States, which had not been party to a formal alliance in peacetime with a European power since its treaty with France lapsed in the early nineteenth century. The classic American study is by Robert Endicott Osgood, *NATO: The Entangling Alliance* (Chicago, 1962). But NATO was also a significant departure for Belgium, which had begun both world wars as a neutral, and for the United Kingdom, which had resisted the translation of its profound interest in European affairs into a multilateral pact for mutual defence. Michael Howard, *The Continental Commitment: The Dilemma of British Defence Policy in the Era of Two World Wars* (London, 1972).

34. *DCER*, vol. 14, pp. 201–32; *DCER*, vol. 15, 219–301.

35. *DCER*, vol. 14, 247–324; *DCER*, vol. 15, 168–219; Holmes, *The Shaping of Peace*, vol. 2, pp. 63–69.

36. Holmes, *The Shaping of Peace*, vol. 2, p. 73.

37. The best account of the Kashmir issue from a Canadian perspective is E.A. Kelly, "Reluctant Mediator: Canada, the United Nations and the Kashmir Crisis, 1947–1949: (M.A. thesis, Carleton University, 1995).

38. Sarty, "Limits of Internationalism," pp. 56–74.

39. Though it is worth noting that the cost of Canada's commitment to the North Atlantic Treaty was studied after, not before, the treaty was signed. Under considerable prodding from the Department of Finance, the Department of National Defence attempted to assess the impact of participation in the alliance on its budget estimates in successive meetings of the Defence Committee of the Cabinet in the autumn of 1949. *DCER*, vol. 15, pp. 689–91, 1566–69. Though Brooke Claxton, particularly when Acting Secretary of State for External Affairs, was not as

silent in the negotiations which led to NATO as his biographer suggests, the process in Ottawa and Washington was dominated by the Department of External Affairs. David Bercuson, *True Patriot: The Life of Brooke Claxton, 1898–1960* (Toronto, 1993), p. 205.

40. Denis Stairs, *The Diplomacy of Constraint: Canada, the Korean War, and the United States* (Toronto, 1974); Holmes, *The Shaping of Peace*, vol. 2, pp. 65–67.

41. For Mackenzie King's account of the meeting with Bevin (which was attended by Attlee, some members of the British cabinet, and several representatives of the Dominions, including Jan Smuts of South Africa) as well as a subsequent private encounter with Bevin, see *The Mackenzie King Record*, vol. 4, *1947–1948*, ed. J.W. Pickersgill and D.F. Forster (Toronto, 1970), pp. 107–116. Paul Martin suggests that King's attitude was also prompted by his belief "in the state system as it existed; great powers were the ones who determined events and with them decisions should reside." Martin, "King: The View from the Backbench and the Cabinet Table," in English and Stubbs, *Widening the Debate*, p. 36.

42. R.J. Moore, *Making the New Commonwealth* (Oxford, 1987); Hector Mackenzie, "An Old Dominion and the New Commonwealth: Canada and Republican India, 1947–1949," paper presented at Institute of Commonwealth Studies, University of London. In a retrospective introductory chapter to an account of his years as Canada's representative in India, Escott Reid provides an overview of India's importance to Canada in the postwar world. *Envoy to Nehru* (Delhi, 1981), ch. 2.

43. Whitaker and Marcuse, *Cold War Canada*, argue that the Soviet threat to the Western alliance and to Canada's national security (highlighted by the Gouzenko Affair of 1945–46) was also used as the justification for restrictions on domestic freedoms.

44. Don Page and Don Munton, "Canadian Images of the Cold War 1946–7," *International Journal*, 32, 3 (Summer 1977): 577–604; *DCER*, vol. 13, pp. 342–461; *DCER*, vol. 14, pp. 1777–1805.

45. Mackenzie, "Path to Temptation"; Pressnell, *External Economic Policy*, vol. 1, ch. 11.

46. Norman Ward and David Smith, *Jimmy Gardiner: Relentless Liberal* (Toronto, 199), pp. 259, 266–68.

47. A glance at the Cabinet Conclusions for 1948 suggests that more time was devoted to the treatment of oleomargarine under the General Agreement on Tariffs and Trade than to the Czech coup.

Topic Thirteen

Issues in Postwar Canada

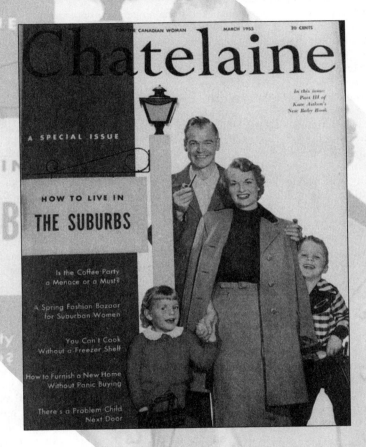

The cover of *Chatelaine* magazine, March 1955.

378

ECONOMIC growth and increased immigration made the 1950s a decade of boom and prosperity. Consequently, the period 1945–60 has tended to be viewed as the "golden years" of Canada's recent past—a period of contentment and happiness for Canadians after a decade of depression and six years of war.

Recently, however, historians have come to challenge such depictions of the postwar era. Were women, for example, universally satisfied with developments in this period? Did the rise of suburbia not marginalize them further, limiting them largely to home-oriented activities? In "Home Dreams: Women and the Suburban Experiment in Canada, 1945–1960," Veronica Strong-Boag explains how suburbs came into existence in postwar Canada, how they differed in nature from their counterparts in the United States, and how they affected the lives of Canadian women.

Also during the postwar period, Canada came to be increasingly influenced—some might even say dominated—by the United States, in both the economic and cultural arenas. Economically, Canada's dependency on its neighbour grew enormously, in terms of both trade—the United States is Canada's major trading partner, taking more than 75 percent of its exports—and direct American investment in Canadian industries, in the form of branch plants. The extent of the latter prompted federal governments in Canada to conduct investigations into Canadian–American economic relations over the course of the three critical decades after World War II, resulting in three influential reports: the Gordon Report, of 1958; the Watkins Report, of 1967; and the Gray Report, of 1972. In the area of culture, many Canadians became alarmed during the postwar years by what they perceived as American assimilation of Canadian culture. In "Canada's Quest for Cultural Sovereignty: Protection, Promotion, and Popular Culture," John Herd Thompson examines this issue and reviews several Canadian governments' responses to the problem over the years, concluding with a discussion of the North American Free Trade Agreement (NAFTA) and its possible implications for cultural sovereignty.

Environmental historians have pointed to increased pollution of Canada's air and water as another problem associated with the boom and prosperity of the 1950s and the 1960s. In " 'Let Us Heed the Voice of Youth': Laundry Detergents, Phosphates, and the Emergence of the Environmental Movement in Ontario," Jennifer Read examines the emergence of environmentalism in Ontario in the post–World War II era over the issue of detergents polluting the Great Lakes basin. It became a battle between Canadian representatives of the detergent multinationals, the Canadian Manufacturers of Chemical Specialties Association, and supporters of environmentalism spearheaded by Pollution Probe. Government was caught in the middle, and in the end, all three levels of government—municipal, provincial, and federal—were involved. Out of the controversy, Read notes, emerged the Ontario Ministry of the Environment in 1972.

General studies of the post–World War II period include Robert Bothwell, Ian Drummond, and John English, *Canada since 1945: Power, Politics, and Provincialism*, rev. ed. (Toronto: University of Toronto Press, 1989); Donald Creighton, *Canada, 1939–1957: The Forked Road* (Toronto: McClelland and Stewart, 1976); J.L. Granatstein, *Canada, 1957–1967: The Years of Uncertainty and Innovation* (Toronto: McClelland and Stewart, 1986); and the relevant chapters in J.L. Granatstein and Norman Hillmer, *For Better or for Worse: Canada and the United States to the 1990s* (Toronto: Copp Clark Pitman, 1991).

Also of interest is Robert Bothwell's *Canada and the United States: The Politics of Partnership* (Toronto: University of Toronto Press, 1992).

On women in the postwar era, see the report of the Royal Commission on the Status of Women in Canada (Ottawa: Information Canada, 1970); Micheline Dumont et al., *Quebec Women: A History* (Toronto: Women's Press, 1987); and Alison Prentice et al., *Canadian Women: A History*, 2nd ed. (Toronto: Harcourt Brace, 1996). Women in Ontario are examined in Joy Parr, ed., *A Diversity of Women: Women in Ontario since 1945* (Toronto: University of Toronto Press, 1995).

Canadian culture during this period can be studied further in the following: the relevant chapters of Bothwell, Drummond, and English, *Canada since 1945* (cited above); the relevant articles in Janice L. Murray, ed., *Canadian Cultural Nationalism* (New York: New York University Press, 1977); and Paul Audley, *Canada's Cultural Industries: Broadcasting, Publishing, Records and Film* (Toronto: James Lorimer, 1983). For a historical perspective, see Maria Tippett, *Making Culture: English-Canadian Institutions and the Arts before the Massey Commission* (Toronto: University of Toronto Press, 1990), and Paul Litt, *The Muses, the Masses, and the Massey Commission* (Toronto: University of Toronto Press, 1992). With regard to television in particular, see Paul Rutherford's *When Television Was Young: Primetime Canada, 1952–1967* (Toronto: University of Toronto Press, 1990), and Richard Collins, *Culture, Communications, and National Identity: The Case of Canadian Television* (Toronto: University of Toronto Press, 1990). On consumer culture see Joy Parr, *Domestic Goods: The Material, the Moral, and the Economic in the Postwar Years* (Toronto: University of Toronto Press, 1999). Doug Owram examines the history of the baby-boom generation in *Born at the Right Time: A History of the Baby-Boom Generation* (Toronto: University of Toronto Press, 1996).

General economic histories of this period include Michael Bliss, *Northern Enterprise: Five Centuries of Canadian Business* (Toronto: McClelland and Stewart, 1987), and Kenneth Norrie and Douglas Owram, *A History of the Canadian Economy*, 2nd ed. (Toronto: Harcourt Brace, 1996). Foreign ownership in the Canadian economy is examined in greater depth in Gordon Laxer, *Open for Business: The Roots of Foreign Ownership in Canada* (Toronto: Oxford University Press, 1989), and Denis Stairs and Gilbert R. Winham, *The Politics of Canada's Economic Relationship with the United States* (Toronto: University of Toronto Press, 1985). See also Bruce Muirhead, "Trials and Tribulations: The Decline of the Anglo-Canadian Trade, 1945–50," *Journal of Canadian Studies* 24, 1 (Spring 1989): 50–65, and his "Perception and Reality: The GATT's Contribution to the Development of a Bilateral North American Relationship, 1947–1951," *American Review of Canadian Studies* 20, 3 (Autumn 1990): 279–301.

On the more recent free-trade debate, see James Laxer, *Leap of Faith: Free Trade and the Future of Canada* (Edmonton: Hurtig, 1986); Laurier LaPierre, ed., *If You Love This Country: Facts and Feelings on Free Trade* (Toronto: McClelland and Stewart, 1987); and Duncan Cameron, ed., *The Free Trade Deal* (Toronto: James Lorimer, 1988). For an overview of Canadian–American relations, see John Herd Thompson and Stephen J. Randall, *Canada and the United States: Ambivalent Allies* (Montreal/Kingston: McGill-Queen's University Press, 1994).

On ecology, see Rowland Lorimer et al., eds., *To See Ourselves/To Save Ourselves: Ecology and Culture in Canada* (Montreal: Association for Canadian Studies, 1991); Monte Hummel, ed., *Endangered Spaces: The Future of Canada's Wilderness* (Toronto: Key Porter, 1989); Candace Savage, *On the Brink: Endangered Species in Canada* (Saskatoon: Western Producer Prairie Books, 1989); J.G. Nelson, "Beyond Parks and Protected Areas: From Public and Private Stewardship to Landscape Planning and Management," *Environments*, 21, 1 (1991): 23–34; and Margaret Johnston, "The Canadian Wilderness Landscape as Culture and Commodity," *International Journal of Canadian Studies* 4 (Fall 1991): 127–44.

On environmental policy, see G. Bruce and Thomas Conway, *The Greening of Canada*: *Federal Institutions and Decisions* (Toronto: University of Toronto Press, 1994); Kathryn Harrison, *Passing the Buck*: *Federalism and Canadian Environmental Policy* (Vancouver: University of British Columbia Press, 1996); and Melody Hessing and Michael Howlett, *Canadian Natural Resources and Environmental Policy*: *Political Economy and Public Policy* (Vancouver: University of British Columbia Press, 1997).

For a historical perspective on ecology, see the essays in *Consuming Canada*: *Readings in Environmental History*, ed. Chad Gaffield and Pam Gaffield (Toronto: Copp Clark, 1995). Janet Foster looks at the awareness of preservation in *Working for Wildlife*: *The Beginning of Preservation in Canada* (Toronto: University of Toronto Press, 1978). On Canada's national parks, see Leslie Bella, *Parks for Profit* (Montreal: Harvest House, 1987), and W.A. Waiser, *Saskatchewan's Playground*: *A History of Prince Albert National Park* (Saskatoon: Fifth House Publishers, 1989). An important study of the Commission of Conservation in the 1920s is Michel F. Girard's *L'écologisme retrouvé* (Ottawa: Les Presses de l'Université d'Ottawa, 1994). A model regional study is Bruce W. Hodgins and Jamie Benidickson, *The Temagami Experience*: *Recreation, Resources and Aboriginal Rights in the Northern Ontario Wilderness* (Toronto: University of Toronto Press, 1989). John Wadland recounts the career of Native writer Ernest Thompson Seton in *Ernest Thompson Seton*: *Man in Nature and the Progressive Era, 1880–1915* (New York: Arno Press, 1978). Donald Smith's *From the Land of Shadows*: *The Making of Grey Owl* (Saskatoon: Western Producer Prairie Books, 1990) tells the story of the transformation of trapper Archie Belaney into conservationist Grey Owl. Farley Mowat reviews the history of wildlife in Atlantic Canada since the Europeans' arrival in his popular work *Sea of Slaughter* (Toronto: McClelland and Stewart, 1984).

Article Twenty-Seven

Home Dreams: Women and the Suburban Experiment in Canada, 1945–1960

Veronica Strong-Boag

In the years after the Second World War in Canada, residential suburbs provided symbolic female counterparts, "bedrooms" as it were, to the male-dominated, market-oriented world of modern cities.[1] Tracts of new housing embodied a separation of the sexes that held women particularly responsible for home and family, and men for economic support and community leadership. Such a gendered landscape was far from new or unusual in Canada. Women and men had long moved in somewhat different worlds, presiding over residential and public space in varying degrees as dictated by custom and, sometimes, by law.[2] After 1945, however, women's, particularly wives', rising labour-force participation might have suggested that spatial segregation on the suburban frontier was ill-timed. Why and how, then, did there occur a massive increase in residential suburbs remote from

Source: "Home Dreams: Women and the Suburban Experiment in Canada, 1945–60," *Canadian Historical Review* 72, 4 (December 1991): 471–504. Reprinted by permission of University of Toronto Press Incorporated.

opportunities for employment, lacking many community resources, and reliant on female labour? What did female residents and contemporary observers make of this investment on the suburban frontier? This article begins to answer these questions by examining the conditions that gave rise to postwar suburbs, the character of housing initiatives, and the nature and meaning of that experience for Canadian women.

Historians of the United States have associated postwar housing development not only with technological improvements, gas and oil discoveries, and a massive increase in the number of private automobiles, but also with political conservatism, racism, and domestic roles for women.[3] While scholars studying Canadian suburbs will find much that is useful in American assessments, particularly in their exploration of suburbia's gendered terrain, Paul-André Linteau's question, "Does the border make a difference?"[4] inevitably arises. Works like Michael A. Goldberg and John Mercer's *The Myth of the North American City: Continentalism Challenged* (1986) and Caroline Andrew and Beth Moore Milroy's *Life Spaces: Gender, Household, Employment* (1988) have offered the beginnings of a reply. In particular, Andrew and Milroy point to safer and more livable cities, a long tradition of resource towns, and "the particular institutional and policy framework that exists in Canada,"[5] all of which distinguish Canadian women's lives. Although comparisons with the United States remain peripheral to the study here, my reading of the Canadian suburban "script" suggests that, for all the proliferation of American influences in the years after 1945, life north of the forty-ninth did indeed differ. In particular, Canada's cities, lacking racial divisions comparable with those in the United States, never lost their attraction for citizens of all classes. And just as flight from urban dangers does not seem as influential in Canada, suburbia does not appear as homogeneous as many American commentators have suggested. Communities composed of war veterans, industrial workers, rural emigrants, newcomers to Canada, and the middle-class native- and urban-born contribute to a picture that, as the sociologist S.D. Clark convincingly demonstrated in *The Suburban Society* (1968), seems every bit as complicated as what was happening downtown. While middle-class WASPs were a major presence, they were never alone on the outskirts of cities. Suburbia's meaning is further complicated by the influence of region. The background of residents and the rate of suburbanization in these years varied from one part of the country to the other, distinguishing the experience of Montreal from Toronto and from Halifax, Winnipeg, Edmonton, and Vancouver. Facing as they did a different set of contingencies, Canadian women were not mere reflections of American suburbanites. The nature of their story is set out below.

The postwar experiment with the promise of a spatial segregation that placed Canadian women in suburban homes and men in employment located elsewhere was fuelled by high rates of fertility. During the Second World War and into the 1950s, couples married at ever younger ages. First and second babies came earlier in these marriages, and increasing numbers of women gave birth to third children (see Table 27.1). Fewer women had no children. Bigger families increased women's home-based responsibilities. Not surprisingly, women were often preoccupied with their roles as wives and mothers. Housing where children could be cared for comfortably and safely was an urgent priority in many women's lives.

Whereas their parents had often had to be crowded and uncomfortable, postwar Canadians aspired to something better. Between 1945 and 1960 nearly continuous prosperity, high employment, the extension of the welfare state, and the presumption of a limitless bank of natural resources generated income and hopes for a better life, and, if possible, the lifestyle of comfortable homes and new products advertised since the 1920s in the continent's popular media.[6] Rising car ownership offered unprecedented numbers

Table 27.1 Age-Specific Fertility Rates for Canadian Women, 1921–1960

	Age Group of Women						
Year	*15–19*	*20–4*	*25–9*	*30–4*	*35–9*	*40–4*	*45–9*
1960	59.8	233.5	224.4	146.2	84.2	28.5	2.4
1940	29.3	130.3	152.6	122.8	81.7	32.7	3.7
1921	38.0	165.4	186.0	154.6	110.0	46.7	6.6

Source: John R. Miron, *Housing in Postwar Canada* (Kingston and Montreal, 1988), from table 3, p. 35.

of citizens the opportunity to search for homes well beyond areas where employment opportunities were concentrated.[7] Many male breadwinners, the most likely both to drive and to control the use of cars,[8] no longer had to rely on walking or public transit to get to work. An increase in the production of oil, gas, and hydroelectric power was available to power both new cars and the central heating characteristic of new homes.[9] Residential suburbs on the periphery were the beneficiaries of these developments.

New housing that enshrined a gendered division of labour also responded to a generation's anxiety about changes in the world about them. The threat of the Cold War and the Korean War encouraged citizens to prize the private consumption and accumulation of products in the nuclear family household as proof of capitalism's success. Stable families, full-time mothers, and the benefits they produced in sound citizenship were to provide the first defence against the "Red Menace," symbolized in Canada by the Gouzenko Affair.[10] Suburban housewives at home in ever larger houses epitomized the promise that prosperity would guarantee both individual happiness and the final triumph over communism.[11]

The inclination to concentrate on private matters and to cling to the faith in women's particular talent and responsibility for family survival was fostered further in the 1940s and 1950s by the highly publicized predicament of many of the world's citizens. The statelessness of the "Displaced Persons," or "DPs," as the 165 000 who had come to Canada by 1953 were commonly known,[12] like the plight of concentration camp survivors, captured especially poignantly what it meant to lose families and homes. The arrival of 48 000 war brides added to Canadians' consciousness of how much the future depended on the establishment of new households and the persistence of marital bonds.[13] The promise of a renewed family life, secured by all the benefits of a revived capitalist economy, became in some ways the *leitmotif* of the second Elizabethan Age. As one typical enthusiast put it, "the Duke and Duchess of Edinborough [*sic*] are young, modern parents who, like many other young people, in an anxious and insecure world, find their deepest happiness and satisfaction in the warm circle of family life."[14] In suburban homes and families, Canadians endeavoured modestly to echo the ideals embodied in the domesticated monarchy of the youthful Elizabeth II.

The popular and academic social sciences of the day sanctioned the inclination to believe that collective happiness and well-being were most likely when women concentrated their energies on the home front. Experts' secular sermons, frequently presented in the guise of a celebration of female nature, stressed women's unique qualities. With some few exceptions, assertions of inferiority were out of fashion. As one Toronto psychiatrist observed, "Today we think of marriage as a partnership of equals."[15] To this end, modern fathers were encouraged to take on some care of children.[16] Yet, while up-to-date advisers flattered their female audiences with claims for equality, even superiority, "true" women had normally to demonstrate their authenticity by pursuing roles centred on the private rather than the public sphere. Women's ability to take on a broad range of duties, so well demonstrated during the years of depression and war, was conveniently dismissed as an aberration. In advising Canadians how to live, experts returned to opinions that were reminiscent of the 1920s.[17]

Lives that were gender-specific lay at the heart of a number of influential texts that enjoyed general circulation across Canada in the years after the Second World War. Among the earliest and most influential was Dr. Benjamin Spock's best-selling *Common Sense Book of Baby and Child Care* (1947).[18] As one Canadian from the suburb of Lachine, Quebec, recalled, "Dr Spock of course was my 'Bible.'"[19] Although most women consulted the good doctor for practical advice on treating childhood ills, his answers reinforced conventions holding women primarily responsible for the emotional and practical functioning of the household. A veteran of suburbs in Cooksville and North York, Ontario, summed up the conclusions of many of her generation: "I felt quite sure in those days that women who chose to have a family should stay home and raise them! I had worked as a social worker for the Children's Aid Society and had seen the emotional devastation in children separated from mothers."[20]

Spock was far from alone in applauding women who mothered. Ashley Montague's best seller *The Natural Superiority of Women* (1953) celebrated women both for their gentler dispositions and for their biological superiority. Not coincidentally, he concluded that "the most important of women's tasks is the making of human beings . . . [and] because mothers are closer to their children than fathers, they must of necessity play a more basic role in the growth and development of their children."[21] A self-proclaimed women's champion, Montague applied his reading of modern science to "undermine the age-old belief in feminine inferiority,"[22] but in the process he reasserted the faith that biology was destiny. The capacity for motherhood was, as with both the older anti-feminist and the maternal feminist tradition, identified as the very source of superiority.

Ashley Montague's fundamentally conservative message appeared in the same year as the publication of *Sexual Behaviour in the Human Female* (1953),[23] the second volume on human sexuality by Alfred Kinsey and his colleagues. In the forefront of the "sexology" of its day, this volume documented women's possession of a powerful libido, the physiological equivalent of male sexual response.[24] Under the influence of such scientific authority, an active sexuality became increasingly accepted as the prerequisite of satisfactory personal and marital life.[25] The result could be higher levels of intimacy and equality between the sexes, but women's erotic potential could easily be incorporated into an updated domestic ideal. Kinsey's support for the female libido and his opposition to guilt and shame about sexual acts were closely tied to marital and social stability. His early work was used to justify Canadians' youthful marriage: only then could sexuality find its proper channels.[26] Ultimately, Kinsey's pioneering studies reinforced the tendency to dedicate women to private life.

The assignment of women to roles as wives and mothers was further legitimated by the popularity of the functionalist school of sociology that dominated the discipline as it established itself throughout Canada. The work of the leading American "father" of this tradition, Talcott Parsons, drew on the "anatomy is destiny" psychiatry of Freud and his followers to argue that women and men naturally had different, albeit compatible and equal, roles within society. Women were responsible for expressive functions of mediating and nurturing; men for instrumental functions of struggle and leadership. The first responsibilities directed women to the private sphere and the second legitimated men's domination of public life. Husbands concentrated on the workplace and its values of "rationality, impersonality, self-interest," while wives guided children in the traditional family values of "love, sharing, cooperation."[27] Domestic life might no longer require long hours of hard physical labour, but the unremitting pressure of modern corporate life on men appeared to make women irreplaceable in the home as psycho-sexual managers.[28] The appropriate division of duties was summed up by Bell Telephone's company magazine, *The Bluebell*, which pointed to wives' appropriate role in a short story entitled "WE Were Promoted."[29] Both capitalist prosperity and humanized relationships were to be guaranteed by the functionalist division of labour. Such conclusions became the stock-in-trade of Canadian sociologists like J.R. Seeley, R.A. Sim, and E.W. Loosley, the authors of one of the foremost North American studies of suburban life, *Crestwood Heights* (1956).

Home-grown authorities like the popular gynecologist Dr. Marion Hilliard of Toronto's Women's College Hospital regularly voiced the conservative conclusions of the contemporary social sciences. Speaking to her own patients and countless others through articles in *Chatelaine*, she spread prevailing medical opinion:

> The burden of creating a happy marriage falls mainly on the wife. A man's life is much more difficult than a woman's, full of the groaning strain of responsibility and the lonely and often fruitless search for pride in himself. A cheerful and contented woman at home, even one who must often pretend gaiety, gives a man enough confidence to believe he can lick the universe. I'm certain that the woman who enriches her husband with her admiration and her ready response gets her reward on earth, from her husband.[30]

Hilliard and most other Canadian "experts" on home and family joined their American colleagues in arguing that women's most basic satisfactions came through service to others in the domestic sphere.

The verdict of professionals was repeatedly echoed in the dominion's mass media. Typical advertisements credited the housewife with "the recipe for good citizenship . . . for a woman's influence extends far beyond the horizons of housekeeping. She guards the family health by her buying standards; she shares in plans for the family welfare; hers is the opportunity of training her children . . . of promoting good character and good citizenship."[31] Companies readily championed a feminine ideal that offered them real benefits. Corporate profits and male careers alike depended on women's concentrated efforts in the private sphere, more especially in new suburban homes, where opportunities for purchases were unsurpassed.

Advertising in these years was only one part of a commercial onslaught hitting Canadians. Newspapers, magazines, radio, films, and, by the 1950s, television entered households with a distinct message about the meaning of the "good life." Radio soap operas such as *Road of Life*, *Big Sister*, *Lucy Linton*, *Life Can Be Beautiful*, and *Ma Perkins* offered women escape from isolation and loneliness in dreams of consumption, romance, and improved family life.[32] Television shows like *The Adventures of Ozzie and Harriet*, *I Love Lucy*, *The Honeymooners*, and *Father Knows Best* made it quite clear that good wives and mothers stayed properly at home, far from the temptations of employment. Just as important, they suggested that women reaped real advantages from this division of duties. Wives may have looked a little foolish in these sitcoms, but audiences were encouraged to join in a conspiracy of good-humoured silence about the real power that they wielded. Housewives, after all, had the freedom to construct their own routines, while spouses were tied to onerous duties as breadwinners.

What the experts and the media largely ignored after World War II was a massive increase in the labour-force participation rate of married women. This increased from 4.5 percent in

1941, to 11.2 percent in 1951, to 22.0 percent in 1961. In the same years, wives rose from 12.7 percent to 30.0 percent to 49.8 percent of all women in paid employment.[33] For all this dramatic change meant in terms of disposable family income and the nature of the labour market, it appears to have done little initially to challenge women's primary identification as labourers in the domestic workplace.[34] Many postwar wives accepted periods of employment before childbirth and, sometimes, after children were in high school, as intervals in a modern life cycle that still saw them as chiefly responsible for home and family. In particular, energetic young wives could take pride in establishing families on a sound economic footing. Such was true of a "white-collar wife" in her early twenties employed by Montreal's CIL. Vivian used her salary to purchase new housing and "other rewards: electrical kitchen appliances, bedroom and living room furniture, a small English car." Her husband, David, paid other expenses. Traditional appearances were maintained when she assumed responsibility for most housework and received an allowance from David. Vivian planned to leave CIL at about the age of 25 to have between two and four children.[35] Many women hoped to do the same. The same assumption underlay the "putting hubby through school" phenomenon that first attracted public attention with the return of war veterans to university.[36] Women's work in the labour market regularly represented an investment in a more domestic future.

Incentives for female citizens to return home as soon as possible always remained considerable. Never missing were unequal opportunity and wages. Resources in support of female workers were meagre.[37] Matters at home were hardly better. Most families could afford only one car, on which the husband had first claim, and few settlements boasted adequate public transportation. Nor was that all. Working wives had to face the "double day of labour." One refugee from a clerical office explained that she had cheerfully given up a schedule that required "twelve hours or more a day, seven days a week."[38] Another clerical worker from North Toronto added:

> As a married woman for fourteen years and a working wife for less than one year . . . the two don't go together. You can't be a success at both. So I decided to quit my job to save my marriage.
>
> You simply can't look after a home and go to the office too. I don't care who you are or how well organized you are, you can't be a good wife and mother, hostess and housekeeper and also do a good job for your employer all at the same time. When you try, someone is bound to get cheated.[39]

Working wives had no right to hope for relief at home. As one writer for the *Star Weekly* insisted: "I don't see how a job gives a woman a legitimate out on housekeeping. She still has the basic responsibility to run a home for the family . . . [and] a man whittles himself down to less of a man by consistently performing woman's work."[40] In the decades after the Second World War, income tax law, the absence of daycare, formal and informal bars to female employment,[41] and school schedules combined with a commercially fuelled celebration of domesticity and maternity and the general reluctance of husbands to assume household responsibilities to confirm the wisdom of staying home, if you had a choice.

Such decisions were applauded by experts who feared the worst. In 1953 a counsellor for Toronto's Family Court and the United Church summed up prevailing opinion, arguing that "where the husband and wife are both working outside the home, very often a dangerous spirit of independence exists. Finally, it is quite impossible to do two jobs well."[42] Women who dismissed such arguments could look forward to being scapegoated for a host of society's problems, blamed for homosexual sons, juvenile delinquents, mental cripples, wandering and alcoholic husbands, and school truants.[43]

When authorities repeatedly insisted that women were needed at home, the corollary often was that men were too weak to have them anywhere else. As the Kinsey reports had documented in detail, sexual orientation was conditional; men were the more vulnerable sex. When men's physical weakness was further disclosed by experts like Ashley Montague,[44] female discontent or competition appeared enormously threatening. A wife's wages might endanger the very core of the fragile male personality.[45] By the same measure, houseworking men challenged the very basis of contemporary masculinity. The Montreal psychiatrist Dr. Alastair MacLeod plaintively summed up modern problems for *Chatelaine*'s readers:

> Father no longer has opportunities for pursuing aggressive competitive goals openly at work. Some of his basic masculine needs remain unmet. Mother no longer feels she has a real man for a husband and becomes openly aggressive and competitive herself, even moving out of the home into industry in her efforts to restore the biological balance.
>
> Faced with an increasingly discontented and dominating wife, father becomes even more passive and retiring. . . . Certain trends in modern industry are theoretically capable of disturbing the biological harmony of family organization. The resulting disharmony can lead to psychological and psychosomatic illnesses.[46]

The message was clear: domestic women guaranteed both their own femininity and their husbands' masculinity.

In the 1940s and 1950s Canadians had many reasons to believe that the gendered division of labour was the most appropriate response to their own and their nation's needs. While some citizens always challenged too narrowly defined roles, many were prepared to accept the fact that women and men had different duties in the family and in society at large. Residential suburbs that enshrined the notion of largely separate spheres for the two sexes proved attractive because most Canadians preferred women at home and out of the labour market.

The recurring housing crisis of the 1940s and 1950s provided the crucial opportunity to fix this preference in space.[47] The dominion entered the postwar years with "a large stock of aging and substandard housing, communities that lacked appropriate municipal services, rural areas that lacked electric power, and with a substantial number of households living in crowded conditions or paying shelter costs they could ill afford."[48] Families with youngsters were particularly hard hit. A boom in babies and immigrants raised the costs of even inferior accommodation.[49] The January 1946 occupation of the old Hotel Vancouver protesting the lack of housing for veterans and their families, like the later seizure of several government buildings in Ottawa by members of the Veterans' Housing League, were only the most visible symptoms of widespread dissatisfaction and rising unrest.[50] The *Star Weekly* summed up popular sentiments: "It must be remembered that the whole situation is charged with an intense emotional desire on the part of veterans and non-veterans alike to have homes of their own. The years of loneliness and being apart, the years of cramped, semi-private living, have created a desire as strong as the migrating instinct in birds to have a home."[51] Not surprisingly, crowded accommodation was regularly cited as contributing to family breakdown and social disarray.[52]

Prime Minister Mackenzie King's postwar government, already alerted by the report of the Advisory Committee on Reconstruction on housing and planning to the magnitude of the housing shortage[53] and fearful of the appeal of the Co-operative Commonwealth Federation, moved to fill the gap. The passage in 1944 of the second *National Housing Act* (NHA) and the creation of the Central Mortgage and Housing Corporation (CMHC) one year later confirmed the significance of housing for peacetime construction.[54] With some few exceptions, strong anti–public housing sentiments and official reluctance to interfere with the "free market" sharply limited the reclamation of urban residential cores.[55] Across the dominion, despite the substantial investment in urban infrastructure — sewers, schools, public transportation, sidewalks, churches, and the like — that cities represented, they did not become the focus of government housing initiatives. Attention focused instead on the construction of new houses in the suburbs.

Despite their neglect by governments, city neighbourhoods continued to attract middle- and working-class Canadians, but many tried to maximize dollars and improve family situations by turning to new residential communities. Not all benefited from state support. In British Columbia's Lower Mainland, poorer citizens made do with little better than squatters' quarters in Bridgeview, a marginal Surrey settlement, without sidewalks and sewers.[56] In Quebec the Montreal working class had to satisfy its land hunger in Ville Jacques Cartier. There the discomfort and distress of life in tarpaper and tin shacks on postage-sized lots bought on the installment plan helped embitter the future separatist Pierre Vallières.[57] In Newfoundland, the city of St. John's was surrounded by "fringe areas . . . characterized by very poor, substandard housing, complete lack of services (piped water and sewer facilities, garbage collection, street-lighting, etc.), poor roads and low family incomes."[58] Few residents in such locations used the provisions of the *National Housing Act*, since borrowers in the years after World War II had to earn steadily higher gross family incomes in order to pay rising down payments and interest rates.[59]

Atlantic Canadians, poorer on average than their contemporaries elsewhere, were particularly unlikely to receive federal mortgage help: between 1954 and 1966 only 23.4 percent of all new "dwelling units" in the Atlantic region were completed with CMHC assistance, compared to 51.9 percent in Ontario in the same period.[60] The variability of financing meant that housewives in different regions sometimes confronted dramatically different working conditions. In 1960 and the first five months of 1961, for example, 38.5 percent of new units located in Atlantic Canada lacked flush toilets and 41.9 percent furnace heating, compared with 8.7 percent and 8.2 percent, respectively, in Ontario.[61] Such distinctions helped ensure that accommodation on the urban periphery varied, often tremendously, from one part of the country to the other. In the Maritimes, suburbia would be neither as extensive nor as prosperous as in many other regions of the country.

In contrast to the plight of the poor, the housing predicament of a broad range of Canadians was addressed by federal enthusiasm for subsidizing the construction of single-family homes and the desire of private developers, contractors, and mortgage lenders to maximize profits. For those who could meet income requirements, mortgage money, at artificially low rates, was made available to build hundreds of thousands of three-bedroom "residential units."[62] While the foremost scholar of Canadian suburbs, S.D. Clark, has concluded that residents were frequently "middle class in terms of income . . . Canadian born, of British origin, and of Protestant religious affiliation,"[63] suburbs always attracted ambitious working-class and immigrant citizens as well. One daughter remembered that "as refugees from Hungary," her parents "could hardly wait to leave" downtown Toronto "for [what was], to them, the lavish splendour of the suburbs," where they settled without regret.[64] In a subdivision of owner-built houses in Cooksville, Ontario, in the 1950s, an English immigrant remembered friendly Italian neighbours whose comfortable homes were constructed by their labouring and small-contractor husbands.[65] The Yugoslav immigrant who began work as a carpenter and plasterer when he arrived after the war and went on to achieve his dream of a suburban bungalow, in his case in Winnipeg's West Kildonan, may not have been in the majority, but he had imitators from one end of the country to the other.[66] The eclectic nature of the suburban community was captured by the comment from a resident who insisted that her modest suburb west of Toronto, whose residents included Olga, Grand Duchess of Russia, was "neither purely WASP nor dull."[67]

Once families moved to suburbia, they often found themselves with people of similar income and in houses of similar price. Neighbours were "all in the same boat."[68] New communities often revealed a distinct class and ethnic character, one that was sometimes legally imposed. Until their overthrow by the Supreme Court in 1951, residential covenants that included race as criteria were commonplace. Drawing on Canadian property law, they were used by land developers to exclude "undesirables" and to set minimum house values.[69] Even after covenants had lost some of their power, homogeneity often survived, a testament to more informal support. In 1957 the new North York suburb of Don Mills, for example, attracted certain occupational groups: 32.1 percent of male homeowners were executives, 23.7 percent professionals, 19.9 percent skilled technicians, 11 percent salesmen, and 3.8 percent teachers and professors, with the remaining 9.5 percent listed as miscellaneous.[70] The hopes of many suburbanites were summed up by one observer in 1945: "It's not just a house, but a way of life that people are seeking . . . Most people wanted to be a part of a community which consisted of congenial people, equality of income—restricted house values."[71] Different suburbs could have distinctive characters, depending on the ability of different groups to afford the cost of houses in their community.

The availability of CMHC mortgages for new homes, relatively low land costs, and builders' incentives, such as that by Saracini Construction in NHA's Glen Park development in Etobicoke in the early 1950s, which gave purchasers the "option of taking a lower priced home and completing part of it at a later date,"[72] made a difference to many Canadians. Despite the continuing decline in the rural population, where ownership was most common, the number of owner-occupied houses in Canada increased from 57 percent in 1941 to 65 percent in 1951 to 66 percent in 1961.[73]

Immediately after the Second World War much new housing was constructed, either individually, often by "do-it-yourselfers," or as part of developments of a few to several hundred houses. Most early construction took place either within older suburbs like East Vancouver or East York in Toronto or in the first ring of surrounding townships or municipalities, such as British Columbia's Burnaby and Ontario's Etobicoke. By the early 1950s, however, high demand plus the enlarged scale of the development industry increasingly directed growth to more remote areas, many without existing municipal services. There, in sites like Halifax's Thornhill Park, Toronto's Don Mills, and Edmonton's Crestwood, appeared the suburban, automobile-dependent sprawl that came to characterize the last half of the twentieth century. Between 1951 and 1961 the population in metropolitan areas around city cores grew far more than that in city centres (see Table 27.2).

These first homes meant a great deal. Coming out of depression and war, couples struggled to become property owners. A team effort was common. As one observer noted of veteran housing: "There is hardly a single case among all these veteran-builders of a wife lounging about. They have been as active in all weathers as their husbands."[74] Such couples had good reason to prize long-awaited houses. Tenants in particular, like one longtime inhabitant of Montreal's Verdun, her husband, and three children, aged five, three, and seven months, were delighted to use CMHC mortgages to move, in their case to Lachine's "Dixie" suburb.[75] Their enthusiasm was matched by the York Township resident in Ontario who remembered being "very poor in the depression—8 people in a 4 room one storey house." She was understandably "really excited—To have a 5 room brick bungalow for the two of us! Such Luxury!!"[76] A Scottish immigrant expressed the same sense of achievement: "We came from a society where houses were scarce, renting was almost

Table 27.2 Percentage Increases in Population for the Central Cities and Remaining Parts of the 1961 Census Metropolitan Areas, Canada and the Regions, 1951–1961

Census Metropolitan Area	Central City	Remainder of Metropolitan Area
Canada	23.8	110.7
Atlantic	11.7	70.6
Quebec	27.9	117.7
Ontario	15.5	116.3
Prairies	50.2	133.0
British Columbia	10.9	90.7

Source: Peter McGahan, *Urban Sociology in Canada* (Toronto, 1986), from table 61.

impossible unless one had the proper connections, and from a country which had spent 6 years at war. So owning a house in the suburbs was a dream for us, a dream we achieved after only 6 years in Canada."[77]

While new suburbs varied in many particulars,[78] all shared a commitment to the gendered division of labour. Purchase of a home—whether in a highly planned community like Etobicoke's Thorncrest Village with its provision of a wide range of urban services expected by upper-middle-class buyers[79] or in a mass-produced subdivision like Scarborough's Wishing Well Acres, where the one millionth new house constructed after VE-Day was officially opened[80]—was part of a child-centred strategy for many Canadians. As a study by Vancouver's Lower Mainland Regional Planning Board discovered, "to a young family without much money, faced with the alternative of a small apartment in the city . . . it is no small thing to be able to look out of the living-room window at one's children playing in relative freedom with fields and woods beyond them."[81] As a mother of two in Toronto's Iondale Heights suburb explained in 1957, "We moved to the suburbs because of the children. We wanted to give them room to romp, where they wouldn't have to worry about street cars and fiend-driven automobiles. True, we have no museums or art galleries. But the children can go outside and see nature as it is."[82] Such commentators took for granted that greater opportunities for children depended ultimately on maternal supervision.

Finally responsible for child care and house maintenance, modern suburban wives were tethered to their communities in ways that few husbands could match. In 1958 one speaker for a Toronto construction company described the suburban home: "A woman is there all the time, she lives there. A man just boards there: he gets his meals there. She is there all day long."[83] A male architect characterized his own experience of gender relations even more vividly: "I spend every day in my Mobile Room [car] going to and from the women at either end [in the office or in his suburban home]."[84] As these remarks suggest, the suburban house remained first of all a workplace for female residents. For husbands, lengthy commutes and long hours at work, not to mention individual preferences, meant that domestic responsibilities were largely subordinated to the demands of waged work.[85] Nor did the suburbs make joint efforts easy. As one husband recalled:

Like most of my fellow male suburbanites I was the sole auto driver. I also drove a lot in my job. Rushing home to take a child to cubs or brownies, to take my wife to a class in the city, to drive to hockey practice or to a game, or to be shopping driver when required was a daily task. Work pressures made this more difficult. There were the open spaces to cut, cultivate and shovel. Social evenings required a driver to pick up the sitter, drive into town, return home and drive the sitter home. The automobile was an itching appendage needing constant scratching.[86]

390

To be sure, some suburban wives always joined their husbands in leaving home for employment. As the expansion of Avon's and other door-to-door sales in these years suggested, earning extra money was never far from many residents' minds.[87] So-called "working" wives shored up families' aspirations to a better standard of living; the husband of a young Bank of Commerce clerk, for instance, was reconciled to her job so she could furnish the house they were building in Saskatoon in 1952.[88] Yet women's ideal primary role remained, especially after babies arrived, in the home. As one resident of a Toronto suburb remembered, her husband "didn't want me to work, and I thought that no one could look after my children as well as I could."[89]

While they may not have remained in the labour market, wives regularly contributed to husbands' careers. Women married to professionals or businessmen often functioned as part of a marital "team," spending hours as unpaid assistants, typing, translating, or entertaining. The wife of a successful academic remembered that "in university circles a wife was expected to entertain—often upwards of 50 people."[90] Another academic spouse found her eyes giving out as she typed the manuscripts that advanced her husband in his profession.[91] Acknowledgement of such contributions forms a regular refrain in scholarly prefaces.

The great majority of wives remained crucially dependent on male wages. Women's financial vulnerability was worsened by the fact that many families purchased suburban homes only by rigorous self-denial. More than one investigator discovered that "Baby sitters were done without, food costs reduced, less spent on clothing, and a hundred and one other small ways discovered to save money. 'I'm not going dancing no more' gave expression certainly to the financial plight of more than one suburban housewife."[92] While such careful juggling of finances was not true of all suburbanites, the strains of budgeting, large or small, were likely to be borne unevenly. Not only did male wage-earners usually have prior right of access to what they commonly held to be "their money,"[93] they frequently had to maintain certain standards as conditions of employment. Women and children could dress, eat, and travel much less well without immediately endangering the family economy.[94]

Suburban houses were the stage on which women explored the meaning of separate spheres. That setting varied greatly depending on income and individual preference, but the introduction of CMHC inspections under the 1954 revision of the *Housing Act* encouraged the giving way of "individual, custom-built homes" to "mass, speculative development" with standardized shapes, sizes, and configurations.[95] In the late 1940s and 1950s master plans and more stringent municipal zoning by-laws across the country, which represented efforts to control errant developers, also contributed to the increasing uniformity of the emerging suburban landscape.[96] CMHC's support of Canadian Small House competitions after the Second World War,[97] like the *Star Weekly*'s sponsorship of the All Canadian Home in 1959,[98] for all their good intentions, had the same effect. In the heady days of easy sales, developers threw up one imitation after another, differing in little but colour and trim. Most models came as Cape Cods, and, increasingly, as bungalows or split levels. Like the split-level winner of the first coast-to-coast architectural contest in 1953,[99] almost all boasted three bedrooms, an L-shaped living–dining-room combination, and, in most areas of the country, a full basement. Increasingly, too, a rumpus or recreation room appeared below level, which, together with the proliferation of televisions, encouraged families to spend leisure time more privately. In these homes, more comfortable than many had ever encountered, women were to forge the moral basis for postwar Canada.

Female residents were expected and urged to bring uniqueness to uniformity through a careful attention to decoration and design. As one commentator insisted, "The bugaboo of uniformity bothers her not at all, because every woman knows she can work out her own individual design for living with colours and furnishings and personal touches."[100] Their choice of furniture, appliances, art, and even clothes was to transform the identical into the distinguishable, in the process confirming housewives' skills and status. No wonder that practically every issue of popular Canadian women's magazines like *Bride's Book, Canadian Home Journal, Canadian Homes and Gardens*, and *Chatelaine*, not to mention their American competitors, offered readers ways, thrifty and otherwise, to personalize suburbia. In a Special Issue in March 1955, for example, *Chatelaine* offered lessons on "How to Live in a Suburb," "A Spring Fashion Bazaar for Suburban Living," and "How to Furnish a New Home without Panic Buying." Subscribers consulted such experts but also prided themselves on developing styles that suited their families best.[101] The mistress of a Rexdale, Ontario, bungalow on "a corner-lot so at least it didn't match everything beside it in either direction, but of course, it matched the house on the corner across the street," spoke for a renovating sisterhood when she reflected that "I almost wrecked it trying to create something unique."[102]

Many women soon found more to concern them in the limitations of the environment at large. Conspicuous in their absence from many new developments in the 1940s and early 1950s, before local governments became more demanding, were public spaces and facilities, such as sidewalks, monuments, parks, and cemeteries. A mother of two children settled in a bungalow on Toronto's outskirts typically remembered that "there were no sidewalks and the road was not paved. The mud and dust were a real pain."[103] For many years developers also counted on the open country that surrounded many subdivisions to provide children with nearby recreational space. In time, as the process of urban sprawl accelerated, this resource disappeared, as it did around Scarborough's Wishing Well Acres subdivision in the 1960s, without any provision for its replacement. For women, the presumed mistresses of suburbia, collective provision was almost always curiously lacking. If landscape was any guide, meeting and play were not part of the female mandate.

The location of most commercial shops and services on the periphery or, more occasionally, in the centre of residential development, either in a strip pattern along major roads or in suburban plazas, showed the same lack of attention to women's needs. Patterns of consumption centred increasingly on shopping centres, which first made their appearance in Canada in 1947 in suburban Winnipeg. By 1951, with the construction of Norgate Plaza in Montreal and Park Royal Plaza in West Vancouver, about 46 shopping centres, all poorly served by public transit and demanding access to a private car,[104] drew buyers from surrounding suburbs.

One Don Mills veteran characterized shopping experiences that were not very different from those of the majority of her contemporaries, especially those whose husbands didn't have the option of commuting by train to work: "Walked and pushed baby carriage to most places. Never had a second car—poor bus service especially with 3 children! Little cooperation, wives did not own car—walked to local shops. Traffic was hazardous on highway & only route to major shopping centre (suburbs were designed for the car & most of us had only one which husband used)."[105] Once visitors got there, new plazas, lacking free public space and cultural amenities, offered them little beyond a community based on a common commitment to purchase. As a self-satisfied Canadian retailer put it, "Suburban living, by its basic structure, generates wants and brings latent desires more sharply into focus. The not-so-subtle effect of competitive living is also a potent influence in creating an environment that encourages liberal spending for better living."[106] The domestic and individualistic orientation of women, families' major purchasers, was readily reaffirmed.

While plazas were increasingly influential, door-to-door sales and deliveries were commonplace in the 1940s and 1950s. Phone orders were taken by butchers, grocers, and department stores, and trucks with milk and bakery goods made their way among suburban homes. Avon ladies, who might be members of a local church, and Hoover, Electrolux, Fuller Brush, and Watkins salesmen were also occasional visitors. The latter were described by a former client as canvassing a Montreal suburb "once or twice per year and I always kept their wonderful salve, 'Good for Man or Beast.' Very strong, didn't burn and helped heal cut knees very quickly. They also had wonderful flavourings and food colourings."[107]

In Metropolitan Toronto, another purchaser implied advantages beyond mere convenience: "We liked to see a vegetable man come along the street. Ice, milk and bread were delivered as were beer and pop. The Avon lady and the Fuller Brush man provided some new faces."[108] Such sentiments were shared by a resident of Clarkson's Corners (Mississauga) who recalled, with affection, a milk man who "always poked his head in to say good morning and took the children on his van for a ride." She observed, "Obviously these services were very important. I realize, however, that my mother had far more people calling than I. (She even had a Hellicks coffee man, Duggan's bakery, etc.)."[109] Although they grew less in time as the private automobile undermined their viability, such deliveries helped knit new communities together in ways that more modern shopping alternatives rarely did.

Suburbia's households were also connected by schools and churches. Although it often happened that housing sprawled well beyond the capacity of religious groups and municipalities to ensure even minimum services, by the 1950s their institutions were normally included in the initial planning of developments. Even then they might well be strained to their limits or inconvenient to reach, as with schools offering shift classes or located across busy intersections. For all such shortcomings, as well as their tendency to deal with female clients almost solely in their roles as mothers and wives, such institutions constituted important collective resources to a community lacking common habits of working together. Parent–teacher associations, or home and school groups, were the most effective in mobilizing women, from room mothers to fund-raisers and executive officers.[110] Auxiliaries and Sunday schools were critical for some residents who kept suburban churches expanding in these years.[111] Work with local institutions offered more activist and sociable suburbanites the chance to combine domestic duties with a manageable level of public involvement.

As they had done in other Canadian settings, women wove the fabric of day-to-day life. As one observer noted, "For most of the day while the men are away at work the women run the community. After the bulldozers have pulled out, the spadework to make a real community out of your particular collection of houses has to be done by . . . the homemakers."[112] Women commonly moved beyond their homes through contacts with children and "in turn, the fathers get to know their neighbours through their own ubiquitous wives."[113] Casual meetings, dismissed by critics as "coffee klatches," or even encounters between Avon "ladies" and their clients, might be followed by both intimate friendships and formal associations. These ties helped women cope with limited resources and new environments. Since children were rarely far from mothers' minds, much cooperative activity centred on them. After the war, women in North Burnaby's new subdivisions established "parent–teacher groups . . . in an endeavour to promote better school conditions and assist in providing hot lunches for the children."[114] In Don Mills, where young children were abundant and teenagers rare, women established baby-sitting co-operatives. In Thornhill, Ontario, mothers formed a community kindergarten and encouraged the fathers, who, "though somewhat apathetic at first . . . to contribute some time and energy in making odds and ends of school equipment."[115] In 1955 mothers at North York's York Mills School, alarmed by sexual attacks on local children, created a Parents' Action League.[116] In Etobicoke's Rexdale development, women protested their lack of public transit to local council and to the Toronto Transit Commission. As they explained, "Nearly all of us have children and they have to be taken to the dentist or doctor occasionally. It takes a full day to make the trip and two days to rest up afterwards."[117] Also in 1955, mothers from North York's Livingstone School fought the Board of Education's transfer of pupils to another school.[118] In Clarkson's Corners a Quebecker prompted her neighbours to create French conversation groups and to fund high school scholarships.

Concerns sometimes broadened beyond children to include a variety of community issues. Thorny questions related to sewers, libraries, and garbage disposal provided lessons in collective action and political lobbying. In North York, residents created the North York Women Electors Association on the model of its Toronto counterpart in September 1954.[119] In Etobicoke, a year later, 22 mothers with children in tow from Goldwood Heights subdivision "stormed" a council meeting, demanding "action — not answers" to the problem created by their developer's failure to finish sidewalks, sodding, and ditching.[120] In effect, such women were transforming suburbs into good neighbourhoods. As volunteers they facilitated the creation of everything from schools, hospitals, and churches to libraries.

For all the evidence of activism, however, the majority of women were rarely visible on the public stage. For many, suburbia constituted a period of deep engagement in the day-to-day running of the family. Very few had assistance with household duties, particularly on weekdays, when most husbands were absent. While a few sometimes found substitutes for their own labour in cooperatives or paid help, others, like a Montreal suburbanite, remembered that "even babysitters were all but unavailable (No Teens, no Grannies)."[121] Questioned about their days as mothers of young children, both happy and unhappy veterans of suburbia remember themselves engrossed in time-consuming duties:

> I had helped my mother in bazaars, tag days, processions, etc. etc., fund-raising, church charitable organizations from the time I was knee high. However, once married, I was apolitical. I guess, basically, because I was so very busy [with nine children].[122]

> I guess there were clubs and political parties but I really didn't have much time or energy with four small children to get involved. I've always been aware of my own limitations in terms of time and energy.[123]

> Not much [leadership from women] in my age group at the time. Too busy at home . . . it was a man's world.[124]

> There was no energy or time to do anything about it [feminism].[125]

> I didn't participate in politics when my children were small, I was too too too busy. None of my neighbours with children seemed to be involved.[126]

Unless they were especially gregarious, such child-rearing women were likely to devote precious free-time moments to private rather than public pursuits.

To the present day, a baleful mythology associated with postwar suburbs and their female residents persists. Suburban women provided a focus for much contemporary debate about the merits of modern life. In particular, in the minds of critics of mass socie-ty who flourished in the years after the Second World War,[127] the suburb emerged as the residential and female expression of the moral bankruptcy they identified in society at large, more particularly in giant corporations, big governments, and the "organization men" who served them.

The most famous indictment from North American feminists was provided by Betty Friedan's *The Feminine Mystique*.[128] This soon-to-be-classic identification of "The Problem That Has No Name" captured the imagination of a generation no longer satisfied with the restricted options of life in suburbia. As one Canadian reader explained:

> I truly considered my genes disturbed until I read Friedan's book. After all, I'd spent my life working to earn, and indeed cherishing, the one compliment that topped them all — "You think like a man."
>
> But I was afraid of that book. I read it in very small snatches, because it stirred me great-ly, and I couldn't see any purpose to that. There I was, a relatively uneducated woman with two small children to raise.[129]

More than anyone else, Friedan helped women challenge the egalitarian claim of North American abundance. Ultimately, she argued, and many readers agreed, the gendered experience of suburbia betrayed women, consigning them to subordination and frustration within society and unhappiness within the family. Limited options for women also meant an immeasurably poorer "Free World," a critical point when winning the cold war was all-important. In Canada, Friedan's dismissal of modern housekeeping as neither sufficiently dignified nor time-consuming to require full-time dedication by wives and mothers was matched by a barrage of popular articles in the 1950s.[130]

Whatever Friedan's insights, her work concentrated on a privileged minority. Her sub-urban women, pushed by the forces of a commercialized culture, appeared to have made the "great refusal" in rejecting purposeful and independent lives in the public sphere. A considerable amount of women-blaming goes on in *The Feminine Mystique*. As with many of her Canadian imitators, Friedan associated suburban women with the evils of modern society — its secularism, superficiality, and materialism. Her feminism, with its support for broader interpretations and expressions of female ability, gave her message special mean-ing, but the message itself, like attacks on suburbia from social critics unconcerned about sexual inequality, finally ignored the complexity of female lives.

Nonfeminist critics of modern society routinely targeted female suburbanites. Marshall McLuhan's *The Mechanical Bride: Folklore of Industrial Man* identified "millions of women who live isolated lives from 8:00 to 6:00 P.M."[131] in suburbia as part of the dilemma of modern men. In 1956 in "You Take the Suburbs, I Don't Want Them," the novelist Hugh Garner, flexing his muscles as a home-grown literary "bad boy," rejected a world in which men could not make the rules.[132] Suburbia's psychological failings were brutally diagnosed by the assistant director of Montreal's Mental Hygiene Institute. In 1958 Dr. Alastair MacLeod warned *Chatelaine*'s readers that "The suburbs give children fresh air, but take away their fathers. They give women efficient kitchens, but are hard on their femininity and gentleness. They give men pride in providing so handsomely, but drive many of them to drink to make up for their watered-down maleness."[133] This psychiatrist damned sub-urbs as "matriarchies, manless territories where women cannot be feminine because expe-diency demands that they control the finances and fix drains and where night-returning men cannot be masculine because their traditional function of ruler and protector has been usurped."[134] While Friedan located suburbia's limitations in the domestic definition of womanhood, few psychiatrists acknowledged that many women needed outlets beyond those provided by purely domestic life.

The indictments of social critics were elaborated most fully in *Crestwood Heights*, a case study of Toronto's Forest Hill, an "inner suburb" built before the Second World War. Dissecting the family lives of an upper-middle-class sample of WASP and Jewish Torontonians, the authors revealed what many critics of mass society feared. Men concentrated on making money, ignoring families' emotional and spiritual needs. Dissatisfied women wielded power in a community in which they were the dominant adults for the daylight hours. Mothers were preoccupied with their offspring, to the detriment of themselves and their children. Both sexes were overly materialistic. The contribution of men and women to the wider society was intrinsically limited. Despite the lack of comparability of this older suburb to what was happening on the periphery of Canadian cities, Crestwood Heights rapidly became the measure by which modern suburbia was judged.[135]

The Royal Architectural Institute of Canada added to the chorus of dismay. Its 1960 *Report* on the design of the residential environment summed up the views of professional architects and representatives of University Women's Clubs and the National Council of Women in its dislike for "the essential identity of houses, the denial of differentiation, built into new suburbs."[136] The *Report* was alert to suburbia's failure to reflect changing Canadian demography. While new buildings took for granted a father in paid employment and a mother at home with two children, many households were very different.[137] The land-eating sprawl of three-bedroom Cape Cods, bungalows, or split levels dependent on private transportation and reflective of a single style of family life was not what all Canadians needed. Preoccupied with aesthetics, however, the *Report* never confronted the problem embodied in the gendered nature of suburban space.

Arguments about the merits of suburban life were not always restricted to polite discourse. Residents of Scarborough's Highland Creek, which their MPP characterized as "a normal Ontario suburban community,"[138] were outraged in 1956 when S.D. Clark, of the University of Toronto, was quoted as accusing them of sexual immorality and hard drinking. The leakage of these observations from a private report to a research group forced him to apologize publicly to Scarborough's residents. Even then there were threats of vigilante justice.[139]

Perhaps chastened by this experience, Clark produced a path-breaking study, *The Suburban Society* (1968), which rejected any simple characterization of suburbia. Dismissing *Crestwood Heights* as unrepresentative in its "culture of a particular urban social class and, in large degree, particular ethnic group,"[140] he championed suburbia's variety and vitality. It was this heterogeneity that Friedan and other critics of modern life, with their focus on middle-class, highly organized communities, had so largely missed. And yet, ironically enough, for all his stress on suburbia's variety, Clark joined critics of mass society in readily sterotyping women. *The Suburban Society* casually dismissed the female resident as "the suburban housewife seeking amusement or instruction in light reading" and the "lone miserable suburban housewife."[141] Making easy generalizations about the "social waste" of women left behind in suburbia,[142] Clark never applied his insight about the complexity of suburban patterns to any consideration of the role of gender. To a significant degree, women continued to be both victims and authors of their own misfortune, keys to the failings of contemporary family life and thus to much of the imperfection of the modern world.

Suburban women, then and today, have their own contributions to make to this debate. In 1959 *Chatelaine*'s readers responded passionately to the attack on suburban women issued by the assistant director of Montreal's Mental Hygiene Institute,

Dr. Alastair MacLeod. In more than 300 letters they captured the complexity of women's lives. In all, 42 percent defended women, men, and suburbia itself, one critic bluntly summing up her rejection of the psychiatrist's misogyny as "Bunk." A further 11 percent of respondents blamed the problems of modern life on something other than suburbia, while 8 percent gave it mixed reviews. The remaining 39 percent agreed, more or less, with MacLeod's criticism of suburban women. Most readers were reluctant to limit women to domestic labour as a solution to the ills of modern society. One woman from Rexdale, Ontario, pointed out that many young wives had more than enough business experience and brains to manage the home and its finances. It didn't make sense to "restrict them to the monotonous unthinking roles of mere cooks and floor waxers."[143] Most suburban women did much more and did it well. A few readers, while admitting something was wrong, refused to blame women. A Regina contributor, for instance, argued that women were feeling frustrated and inadequate because their "opportunity for economic contribution has largely been taken from the four walls of her home."[144] The whole tenor of the published answers to MacLeod's condemnation of suburban womanhood suggested a diversity of opinion and experience.

Suburbia's veterans still remain divided about its meaning. In letters, memos, interviews, and answers to a questionnaire about their experience in the suburbs between 1945 and 1960,[145] women, whose families ranged from the well-to-do to the economically marginal, reflected on what those years had meant. Many, like one Etobicoke, Ontario, resident, offered a blunt calculation of benefits: "Suburban life was fine. We had an auto so we weren't isolated from the Toronto scene. It also enabled us immigrants to make friends. I'd do it over again. Everyone benefited . . . When you live a situation you aren't always analyzing it. The decision was economic. I wasn't buying into an image."[146] Like many others, whose satisfaction seemed grounded in happy marriages, this writer argued that suburban life was vital and fulfilling. Helpmate husbands did much to make suburbia a good place for wives.

Favourable assessments also sprang from a recognition that life in the suburbs was a step up in terms of convenience, comfort, and security. Days spent previously as tenants, in too few rooms and without domestic conveniences, could make even modest bungalows feel very good. While not without flaws, suburbs were a good deal better than the alternatives. The benefits for children were stressed repeatedly, but women, like the two speakers below, were likely to convey a strong sense of their own good fortune as well:

> It was the right choice for us . . . We did not want to raise our kids on city streets, although I realize now they did miss out on many things such as museums, libraries, etc. . . . I think all who chose the life benefited from the freer life, the men for a lot of companionship with neighbours . . . It was a happier time because we no longer worried about friends and acquaintances, schoolmates who were overseas and in danger.[147]

> Those were good years for us. My husband was getting ahead and I saw myself as a helpmate . . . For children suburbia really worked. They always had playmates and they had multiple parenting . . . [but] Suburbia tended to narrow our vision of the outside world. *We* thought we had the ideal life . . . *We* knew little about the world of poverty, culture, crime and ethnic variety. *We* were like a brand new primer, "Dick and Jane."[148]

In reflecting on their suburban lives, women who counted them successful firmly rejected any portrait of themselves as conformists and insisted that the suburbs worked best for the independent and self-motivated. An artist noted that she and her friends "were already in charge of our lives and didn't feel abused."[149] Whether they were gregarious and heavily involved in the community or took pleasure in quiet family pastimes, positive commentators revealed a strong sense of achievement. Happy children, rewarding relationships with spouses, and strong communities were their trophies.

Cheerful accounts contrasted markedly with those who remembered the suburbs as "hell." Days spent largely alone with demanding infants and lack of support from friends, relatives, and sometimes husbands were to be endured. The result could be desperation. One Ontario survivor captured her predicament, and that of others as well, when she wrote: "I began to feel as if I were slowly going out of my mind. Each day was completely filled with child and baby care and keeping the house tidy and preparing meals. I felt under constant pressure."[150] Some women recollected feeling guilty about such unhappiness: If families were more prosperous than ever and husbands doing their jobs, what right did they have to be less than content? When a desperately lonely neighbour hung her three children in the basement, however, one resident of Don Mills put self-doubts aside and set out to create mothers' groups to compensate for the shortcomings of suburban life.[151]

Critics sometimes observed that dissatisfaction extended beyond their sex. Two women explained: "Certainly didn't work for me. I would have been much happier in row housing . . . It seems to me that everyone loses—Women are isolated. Men don't know their families. Children don't know their fathers."[152] And, "I don't think anybody benefited, exactly. You could say men, but they benefited from marriage, suburbs or not . . . And I think a lot of men were miserable trying to play the part imposed upon them in the wasteland."[153] From the perspective of such veterans, women in particular and society as a whole were the poorer because of the investment on the suburban frontier.

Unlike their contemporaries who relished memories of days nurturing children and husbands, critics yearned for lives that offered them more contact with the wider world, more appreciation of their diverse skills, and more financial independence. For them the suburban landscape entailed an unacceptable restriction on options, a source of frustration, anger, and depression. This group often rejected the domestic ideal embodied in suburbia as soon as possible, ridding themselves of unsatisfactory husbands, moving to more congenial settings, and taking paid employment.

Accounts from suburban women rarely match the image presented by Friedan and the critics of mass society. Their experiences were neither homogeneous nor uncomplicated. They were much more than merely the female counterparts of "organization men." Women were both victims and beneficiaries of a nation's experiment with residential enclaves that celebrated the gendered division of labour. Suburban dreams had captured the hopes of a generation shaken by war and depression, but a domestic landscape that presumed that lives could be reduced to a single ideal inevitably failed to meet the needs of all Canadians after 1945. In the 1960s the daughters of the suburbs, examining their parents' lives, would begin to ask for more.

NOTES

1. See Susan Saegert, "Masculine Cities and Feminine Suburbs: Polarized Ideas, Contradictory Realities," *Women and the American City*, ed. C. Stimpson, E. Dixler, M. Nelson, and K. Yatrakis (Chicago, 1981), 106. The appeal of suburbs was not limited to cities. New resource towns, of which 46 appeared between 1945 and 1957, provided numerous instances of what have been termed "suburbs in search of a town," "suburbs in the wilderness," "suburbia in the bush,"

"transplanted suburbia," "experiments in conformity," "displaced southern suburbs," and "suburbs without a metropolis." Cited in Margaret P. Nunn Bray's useful overview, " 'No Life for a Woman': An Examination and Feminist Critique of the Post–World War II Instant Town with Special Reference to Manitouwadge" (MA thesis, Queen's University, 1989), 46. While produced by many of the same forces, the gendered landscape of the resource town is, however, distinctive. This article explores the suburban experience only as it manifested itself around cities.

2. See, for example, the discussion of gendered space in the provocative studies by Joy Parr, *The Gender of Breadwinners: Women, Men, and Change in Two Industrial Towns, 1880–1950* (Toronto, 1990), and Peter DeLottinville, "Joe Beef of Montreal," *Labour/Le Travailleur* 8/9 (Autumn/Spring 1981/2): 9–40 [reprinted in this volume].

3. Among the major studies, see Kenneth Jackson, *Crabgrass Frontier: The Suburbanization of the United States* (New York, 1985); Robert Fishman, *Bourgeois Utopias: The Rise and Fall of Suburbia* (New York, 1987); Elaine Tyler May, *Homeward Bound: American Families in the Cold War Era* (New York, 1988); Margaret Marsh, *Suburban Lives* (New Brunswick and London, 1990); and Dolores Hayden, *Redesigning the American Dream: The Future of Housing, Work and Family Life* (New York and London, 1984).

4. "Canadian Suburbanization in a North American Context: Does the Border Make a Difference?" *Journal of Urban History* 13, 3 (May 1987): 252–74.

5. Caroline Andrew and Beth Moore Milroy, eds., *Life Spaces: Gender, Household, Employment* (Vancouver, 1988), 4.

6. See Veronica Strong-Boag, *The New Day Recalled: Lives of Girls and Women in English Canada, 1919–1939* (Toronto, 1988).

7. The number of passenger automobiles registered in Canada rose from 1 281 190 in 1941 to 2 105 869 in 1951 to 4 325 682 in 1961. Series T147–194, *Historical Statistics of Canada*, 2nd ed. (Ottawa, 1983).

8. See Charles L. Sanford, " 'Woman's Place' in American Car Culture," *The Automobile and American Culture*, ed. David L. Lewis and Laurence Goldstein (Ann Arbor, 1983).

9. See Series Q13–18 to Q75–80, *Historical Statistics of Canada*.

10. See, for example, John Thomas, "How to Stay Married," *Canadian Home Journal* (April 1955): 2–3.

11. For a useful discussion of the impact of the Cold War on sex roles in the United States, see May, *Homeward Bound*.

12. James Lemon, *Toronto since 1918* (Toronto, 1985), 94.

13. See Joyce Hibbert, *The War Brides* (Toronto, 1978), for revealing portraits of the brides who came to Canada.

14. Alice Hooper Beck, "Royal Mother," *Chatelaine* (Jan. 1951): 63. See Hector Bolitho, "The Queen's Conflict: How Can One Woman Fulfill the Dual Role of Monarch and Mother?" ibid. (Feb. 1953): 12–13, 36, 38, 40. See also David Macdonald, "Farewell to the Fifties," *Star Weekly* (2 Jan. 1960): 10–11, 14, who saw the decade as "frantic . . . an age of anxiety," 24.

15. Dr. K.S. Bernhardt, "Happily Ever After," *Bride's Book* (Fall/Winter 1952): 75.

16. See Fred Edge, "Are Fathers Necessary?" *Canadian Home Journal* (Feb. 1953): 24, 63; John Thomas, "Are Fathers Necessary?" ibid., 24, 63–4, and "Father's a Parent, Too," *Canadian Home and Gardens* (April 1952): 29–31.

17. See Strong-Boag, *New Day*.

18. See J. Ronald Oakley, *God's Country: America in the Fifties* (New York, 1986).

19. Mildred Grade Baker, "Canadian Women and the Suburban Experience, 1945–60: Questionnaire for Residents" (henceforth "Questionnaire"), to author (1991), 8. See also note 147 below.

20. Marjorie Bacon, "Questionnaire," 16.

21. A. Montague, *The Natural Superiority of Women* (New York, 1953), 188. See the favourable assessment in Joan Morris, "The Scientific Truth about 'Male Superiority,' " *Canadian Home Journal* (July 1957): 15, 45.

22. Ibid., 25.
23. See the positive, if cautious, review of Kinsey's work by J.R. Seeley and J. Griffin in *Canadian Welfare* (15 Oct. 1948); the optimistic assessment of the utility of early marriage for women, based on Kinsey's findings, in Miriam Chapin, "Can Women Combine the B.A. and the Baby?" *Saturday Night* (21 Feb. 1948): 24; and the positive attitude to the similarity of male and female sexuality in Eleanor Rumming, "Dr. Kinsey and the Human Female," ibid. (15 Aug. 1953): 7–8. See also Gary Kinsman, *The Regulation of Desire: Sexuality in Canada* (Toronto, 1987), 113–15.
24. See Regina Markell Morantz, "The Scientist as Sex Crusader: Alfred C. Kinsey and American Culture," in *Procreation or Pleasure: Sexual Attitudes in American History*, ed. T.L. Altherr (Malabar, 1983).
25. See "Dr. Kinsey Talks about Women to Lotta Dempsey," *Chatelaine* (Aug. 1949): 10–11, 59–60; and Claire Halliday, "A New Approach to the Problem of Frigidity," *Canadian Home Journal* (June 1956): 9, 69.
26. See "The Age for Marriage," *Chatelaine* (May 1948): 2.
27. Jan E. Dizard and Howard Gadlin, "Family Life and the Marketplace: Diversity and Change in the American Family," in *Historical Social Psychology*, ed. K.J. Gergen and M.M. Gergen (Hillsdale and London, 1984), 292.
28. See, for example, Elsieliese Thorpe, "Does He Resent Your Working?" *Star Weekly* (May 1953), who emphasized the husband's right "to have his wife's undivided attentions at times when he needs to unburden himself, the right to have a companion and a friend when he needs one," 7; Charles Cerami, "Are You Jealous of Your Husband's Job?" ibid. (8 Nov. 1958): 30–41; and J.K. Thomas, "If He Lost His Job . . .," *Canadian Home Journal* (Feb. 1957): 10–11.
29. Ken Johnstone, "How Do You Rate with Your Husband's Boss?" *Chatelaine* (March 1953): 70. See also the fierce rejection of the role of business helpmate in Mrs. John Doe, "An Open Letter to My Husband's Boss," *Canadian Home Journal* (May 1954): 10–11, 90, 93.
30. Dr. Marion Hilliard, *A Woman Doctor Looks at Love and Life* (Toronto, 1957), 72–73.
31. Full-page ad for Eaton's, *Saturday Night* (9 Aug. 1949): 19.
32. See the response of 2000 members of *Chatelaine*'s Consumers' Council in Mary Juke, "It Makes Married Life Easier," *Chatelaine* (Sept. 1948): 22–23. On television, see Paul Rutherford, *When Television Was Young: Primetime Canada, 1952–1967* (Toronto, 1990), 200–1, which includes a useful discussion of the sexism of broadcasting in these years.
33. S.J. Wilson, *Women, the Family and the Economy* (Toronto, 1972), 19.
34. For discussion of this phenomenon, see Meg Luxton, Harriet Rosenberg, Sedef Arat-Koe, *Through the Kitchen Window: The Politics of Home and Family*, 2nd ed. (Toronto, 1990).
35. Zoe Bieler, "White-Collar Wife," *Chatelaine* (Aug. 1953): 22–4, 37–40.
36. See, for example, Gwyn Le Capelan, "I Worked My Husband's Way through College," *Chatelaine* (April 1949): 4–5. See also the discussion in National Archives of Canada (NA), MG 31, K8, Mattie Rotenberg Papers, vol. 1, folder 66, radio broadcast "Changing Patterns" (Jan. 1954).
37. See Ruth Roach Pierson, "Gender and the Unemployment Insurance Debates in Canada, 1934–1960," *Labour/Le Travail* 25 (Spring 1990): 77–103.
38. See Anita A. Birt, "Married Women, You're Fools to Take a Job," *Chatelaine* (Jan. 1960): 41.
39. Dorothy Manning, "I Quit My Job to Save My Marriage," ibid. (June 1955): 16.
40. Jean Libman Block, "Husbands Should Not Do Housework!" *Star Weekly* (16 Nov. 1957): 6.
41. See the complaint about discrimination against women in Francis Ecker, "Will Married Women Go to War Again?" *Saturday Night* (30 Jan. 1951): 21–3. For a more extended discussion of the policies of the federal government in this area, see Ruth Roach Pierson, *"They're Still Women after All": The Second World War and Canadian Womanhood* (Toronto, 1986), chap. 2.
42. John G. McCulloch, "How to Be Sure of a Happy Marriage," *Bride's Book* (Spring/Summer 1953): 86. See also John K. Thomas, "How to Stay Married: Can Motherhood and Career Mix?" *Canadian Home Journal* (March 1955): 4, 6. For a contemporary assessment of women's own reservations about paid work, especially for mothers with young children, see Department

of Labour, "Married Women Workers: The Home Situation," in *Canadian Society: Sociological Perspectives*, ed. B.R. Blishen, F.E. Jones, K.D. Naegele, and J. Porter (New York, 1961), 176.

43. See, for example, John Nash, "It's Time Father Got Back in the Family," *Maclean's* (12 May 1956), 28; S.R. Laycock, "Homosexuality — A Mental Hygiene Problem," *Canadian Medical Association Journal* (Sept. 1950): 247, as cited in Kinsman, *Regulation*, 115; Mary Graham, "Mama's Boy," *Canadian Home Journal* (Oct. 1952): 18–19, 37–39; and Hilliard, *Woman Doctor*, passim. The most famous example of "woman-blaming" in these years was Marynia Farnham and Ferdinand Lundberg, *Modern Woman: The Lost Sex* (1947), with its classic Freudian claim that "anatomy is destiny."

44. Montague, as cited in Robert McKeown, "Women Are the Stronger Sex," *Weekend Magazine*, *Vancouver Sun* (22 Jan. 1955): 2. See also Dr. Ashley Montague, "Why Men Fall in Love with You," *Chatelaine* (Oct. 1958): 23, 58, 99; Joan Morris, "The Scientific Truth about 'Male Superiority,'" *Canadian Home Journal* (July 1957): 15, 45; and Florida Scott-Maxwell, "Do Men Fear Women?" *Chatelaine* (Nov. 1959): 39, 50, 54–55.

45. See the argument by the anonymous author of "Careers and Marriage Don't Mix," *Saturday Night* (1 Nov. 1949): 32, who concluded that she had been letting her husband down, despite her higher salary of $10 000 a year, by not keeping up the domestic side of their life.

46. *Chatelaine* (March 1959): 214.

47. See J.N. Harris, "One Vacancy!" *Saturday Night* (15 Nov. 1947), 20; E.L. Chicanot, "Juvenile Immigration Will Help Canada," ibid. (6 Dec. 1947): 24, 37; Benjamin Higgins, "Better Strategy and Tactics to Win the Housing War," ibid. (14 Feb. 1948): 6–7; J. Bhaidlow, "Proper Rentals to Ease Housing Predicament," ibid. (17 April 1948): 17, 32; D. Wilensky, "War's Impact on Family Life," *Canadian Welfare* (15 Oct. 1945): 8–16.

48. Canada Mortgage and Housing, *Housing in Canada, 1945–1986: An Overview and Lessons Learned* (Ottawa, 1987), 6.

49. Ibid., 10.

50. Jill Wade, "'A Palace for the Public': Housing Reform and the 1946 Occupation of the Old Hotel Vancouver," *BC Studies* (Spring/Summer 1986): 288–310; "'Squatter Fever' Spreads to Canada," *The Enterprise* (Lansing, ON), 10 Oct. 1946.

51. John Clare, "Where Are the Houses?" *Star Weekly* (8 June 1946): 5.

52. See Dorothy Livesay and Dorothy Macdonald, "Why B.C. Divorces Soar," *Star Weekly* (15 May 1948): 16; and Marjorie Earl, "Canada's Divorce Headache," ibid. (12 June 1948): Section 2, 2.

53. See Canada, Advisory Committee on Reconstruction, Housing and Community Planning, SubCommittee *Report, No. 4* (Ottawa 1944).

54. For an excellent review of policy, see Albert Rose, *Canadian Housing Policies (1935–1980)* (Toronto, 1980).

55. See John Bacher, "From Study to Reality: The Establishment of Public Housing in Halifax, 1930–1953," *Acadiensis* 18, 1 (Autumn 1988): 120–35; and Albert Rose, *Regent Park: A Study of Slum Clearance* (Toronto, 1958).

56. Graduate Students in Community and Regional Planning, *Bridgeview: A Sub/Urban Renewal Study in Surrey, B.C.* (University of British Columbia, 1965).

57. See his *White Niggers of America* (Toronto, 1971). For an equally unflattering description of Ville Jacques Cartier, see John Gray, "Why Live in the Suburbs?" *Maclean's* (1 Sept. 1954): 7–11, 50–52.

58. See Project Planning Associates Ltd., *City of St. John's Newfoundland: Urban Renewal Study* (Toronto, 1961), 6.

59. See David Bettison, *The Politics of Canadian Urban Development*, vol. 1 (Edmonton, 1975), 110.

60. CMHC mortgage assistance was tied to the earnings of the family head; if earnings were too low, then assistance was denied. In low-income areas such as the Maritimes, CMHC loans were correspondingly fewer. For a discussion of the regional implications of CMHC policy, see Atlantic Development Board, *Urban Centres in the Atlantic Provinces* (Ottawa, 1969), 74.

61. Ibid., 76.

62. For a discussion of the impact of mortgaging by government, see Lawrence B. Smith, *The Postwar Canadian Housing and Residential Mortgage Markets and the Role of Government* (Toronto, 1974), chap. 9, and also Rose, *Canadian Housing Policies*, chap. 3. In 1951 single-family construction made up 77.3 percent of all the dominion's housing starts; in 1955, 71.5 percent and in 1960, 61.7 percent. Smith, *Postwar Canadian Housing*, 22–23.

63. S.D. Clark, *The Suburban Society* (Toronto, 1968), 101.

64. Krisztina Bevilacqua to author, 10 May 1991.

65. Marjorie Bacon, interview with author, 7 June 1991.

66. See John Gray, "A New Life Begins in Winnipeg," *Star Weekly* (9 July 1960): 2–4, 6–7.

67. Lois Strong to author, 29 May 1991.

68. Montreal suburbanite 1, "Questionnaire," 7.

69. See John Weaver, "From Land Assembly to Social Maturity: The Suburban Way of Life of Westdale (Hamilton), Ontario, 1911–1951," *Histoire sociale/Social History* (Nov. 1978): 437.

70. "More Than Half Don Mills Home Owners Professional Men or Executives Survey Shows," *The Enterprise* (Lansing), 26 May 1957.

71. Dottie Walter, "Homes for Tomorrow," *Canadian Home Journal* (June 1945): 30, 33.

72. "Saracinis Will Build 106 Islington Homes," *Etobicoke Press*, 13 April 1950.

73. Rose, *Housing in Postwar Canada*, 168–71.

74. Ronald Hamilton, "You Need a Wife Who Can Saw," *Maclean's* (July 1950): 36.

75. Mildred Grace Baker, "Questionnaire."

76. Helen M. Boneham, "Questionnaire," 5.

77. Catherine Cunningham to author, 14 May 1991.

78. See Clark, *Suburban Society*, 16–18, for his classification of different suburban types. These included "I. The Single-Family Residential Development of the 'Pure' Suburban Type; II. The Semi-Detached Residential Development of the 'Pure' Suburban Type; III. The Single-Family Residential Development in a Built-Up Area; IV. The 'Packaged' or Semi-Packaged Residential Development; V. The Cottage-Type Residential Development; VI. The Residential Development of the 'Pure' Suburban Type, Now Five to Ten Years Old." In the context of this classification, "pure" meant lacking "form and structure" (12) and "packaged" meant growing up "as a result of careful planning and direction" (15).

79. See Collier Stevenson, "City Living in the Country," *Canadian Home Journal* (Nov. 1947): 55–56. For a Scarborough example, see "Guildwood Village on the Move," *The Enterprise* (West Hill) (25 Sept. 1958).

80. "All-Canadian Home Designed from Results of Newspaper Survey," *Canadian Builder* (Jan. 1960): 62, and "Million Mark Reached," ibid. (Oct. 1956): 41. See also "Scarborough Has Canada's Millionth New Home," *The Enterprise* (West Hill) (26 July 1956).

81. The Lower Mainland Regional Planning Board, *The Urban Frontier*, Pt. 2: Technical Report (New Westminster, BC: Oct. 1963): 37.

82. As quoted in William MacEachern, "Suburbia on Trial," *Star Weekly* (18 May 1957): 2. See also, for a continuation of this preoccupation with children, Isabel Dyck, "Integrating Home and Wage Workplace: Women's Daily Lives in a Canadian Suburb," *Canadian Geographer/Le géographie canadien* 33, 4 (1989): 329–41.

83. Mrs. Woods, Saracini Construction, "What the Experts Say about Kitchens," *Canadian Builder* (June 1958): 50.

84. Anthony Adamson, "Where Are the Rooms of Yesteryear?" *Canadian Architect* (June 1958): 74.

85. See, for example, Frank Moritsugu, "Learn How to Relax," *Canadian Homes and Gardens* (Jan. 1955): 7–9, 38–39, 41.

86. Male former resident, Oakridge Acres, London, Ontario, to author, 10 June 1991.

87. See R.D. Magladry, "Door-to-Door Salesmanship Fills the Gap," *Financial Post* 54 (5 March 1960): 13; "Beauty Aid Sales Soar," ibid. (20 Aug. 1960): 1; and J. Schreiner, "Door-to-Door Is a Booming Business," ibid. 55 (30 Dec. 1961): 24.

88. "Wife or Working Girl?" *Bride's Book* (Fall/Winter 1952): 4, 6.

89. Boneham, "Questionnaire," 14.

90. Alaine Barrett Baines, "Questionnaire," 8.

91. Scarborough suburbanite, interview with author, March 1991.

92. Clark, *Suburban Society*, 121.

93. On this male attitude, see Meg Luxton, *More Than a Labour of Love: Three Generations of Women's Work in the Home* (Toronto, 1980), 163–65.

94. On the existence of two standards of living within the family, see the bitter observation in Mrs. John Doe, "An Open Letter to My Husband's Boss."

95. Bettison, *Politics*, 110.

96. As a sign of this interest the Community Planning Association of Canada was created in 1946. See Gerald Hodge, *Planning Canadian Communities* (Toronto and New York, 1986).

97. See the bungalow winner for 1947 in *Etobicoke Press*, 17 March 1947.

98. "First All Canadian Home Completed in Etobicoke," *Star Weekly* (12 Sept. 1959): 14–18.

99. "Home '53," *Canadian Home Journal* (Aug. 1953): 19, 45, 46, 48, 50, 52–53, 58–60.

100. Mary-Ella Macpherson, "Postwar Houses," *Chatelaine* (May 1945): 96.

101. See Betty Alice Marrs Naylor, "Questionnaire."

102. Helen Wallis, "Suburban Experience" (typescript), to author, 3.

103. Boneham, "Questionnaire," 5.

104. John Leaning, "The Distribution of Shopping Centres in Canada," *Canadian Builder* (June 1956): 41–45.

105. Bacon, "Questionnaire," 12.

106. H.J. Barnun, Jr, executive vice-president, Salada-Shirriff-Horsey, Toronto, as cited in "Calls Suburbs Best Place to Develop Retail Sales," *Style Fortnightly* (15 Jan. 1958): 35.

107. Mildred Fox Baker, "Questionnaire," 12.

108. Patricia Margaret Zieman Hughes, "Questionnaire," 12.

109. Alaine Barrett Baines, "Questionnaire," 13.

110. See Eileen Morris, "Your Home-and-School Faces a Crisis," *Chatelaine* (Nov. 1955): 11–13.

111. Between 1947 and 1962, for example, the United Church established 2000 new churches. See Mary Anne MacFarlane, "A Tale of Handmaidens: Deaconesses in the United Church of Canada, 1925 to 1964" (MA thesis, OISE/University of Toronto, 1987), 80.

112. Doris McCubbin, "How to Live in a Suburb," *Chatelaine* (March 1955): 35.

113. See Frank Moritsugu, "The Amazing Don Mills," *Canadian Home and Gardens* (Dec. 1954): 13–19, 55–60, 68.

114. *Vancouver Sun*, 6 Jan. 1951.

115. "Thornhill Women Are Proud of Their Flourishing Nursery School," *The Enterprise* (Lansing), 19 April 1951.

116. "Parents Unite to Catch Man Molesting Children," ibid., 28 April 1955.

117. "1,000 Families Protest Isolation of Rexdale," *Etobicoke Guardian*, 13 Jan. 1955.

118. "Parents Protest Board Moving School Children," *The Enterprise* (Lansing), 2 June 1955.

119. D. Smith, "Don Mills Memo," ibid., 7 Oct. 1954.

120. "Subdivision Problems Cause Angry Mothers to Storm Council Meeting," *Etobicoke Press*, 19 April 1956.

121. Montreal West suburbanite 1, "Questionnaire," 6.

122. Mildred Fox Baker, "Questionnaire," 14.

123. Surrey, BC, suburbanite 1, "Questionnaire," 14.

124. Betty Marrs Naylor, "Questionnaire," 14.

125. Toronto West suburbanite 1, "Questionnaire," 15.

126. Jasper Place, Alberta, suburbanite, "Questionnaire," 14.

127. For one of the few discussions of these critics in Canada, see Rutherford, *When Television Was Young*, esp. chap. 1. For a provocative assessment of the connection between fears about mass society and the maintenance of masculinity, see Barbara Ehrenreich, *The Hearts of Men* (Garden City, NY, 1983).

128. Published in New York in 1963.

129. Wallis, "Suburban Experience," 23.
130. See Richard Roe, "I'm Sending My Wife Back to Work," *Canadian Home Journal* (April 1954): 4–5, 98; Jean Pringle, "How I Broke Out of Solitary Confinement," *Chatelaine* (May 1948): 34; Beverly Gray, "Housewives Are a Sorry Lot," *Chatelaine* (March 1950): 26–27, 37; Isabel T. Dingman, "A Widow Writes an Open Letter to Wives," *Chatelaine* (June 1954): 20–21, 34–35, 37; Dr. Marion Hilliard, "Stop Being Just a Housewife," *Chatelaine* (Sept. 1956): 11, 90; Patricia Clark, "Stop Pitying the Underworked Housewife," *Maclean's* (19 July 1958): 8, 37–38; Jane Hamilton, "Housewives Are Self-Centred Bores," *Star Weekly Magazine* (22 Aug. 1959): 38, 45.
131. Published in New York in 1951. The quote is from page 76.
132. H. Garner, "You Take the Suburbs, I Don't Want Them," *Maclean's* (10 Nov. 1956): 30.
133. Dr. A. MacLeod, "The Sickness of Our Suburbs," *Chatelaine* (Oct. 1958): 23.
134. Ibid., 94–95.
135. See Robert Olson, "What Happened to the Suburb They Called Crestwood Heights?" *Maclean's* (12 Oct. 1957): 24–25, 34–36, 38. The strength of this legacy can be seen in the incorrect identification of Crestwood Heights as Don Mills in McGahan, *Urban Sociology in Canada*, 187.
136. Committee of Inquiry into the Design of the Residential Environment, *Report* (Ottawa 1960), *Journal of the Royal Architectural Institute of Canada* (May 1960): 186.
137. Ibid.
138. "R.E. Sutton Censures Story of 'Carefree' Life at H. Creek," *The Enterprise* (West Hill), 25 Oct. 1956.
139. "There Is No Joy in Highland Creek," *Globe and Mail*, 23 Oct. 1956; "Professor's Report Creates Furor," *The Enterprise* (West Hill), 25 Oct. 1956; and "Letters to the Editor," 1 Nov. 1956.
140. Clark, *Suburban Society*, 6.
141. Ibid., 4.
142. Ibid., 224.
143. Ruth Drysdale, "What Our Readers Say about Suburbia," *Chatelaine* (Jan. 1959): 50.
144. Mrs. J.M. Telford, ibid., 53.
145. Contacts with these women, 32 as of 15 June 1991, are part of an ongoing effort to get in touch with as many women as possible from different types of suburbs in different regions of the country. These women are asked to specify how they wish to be identified, whether anonymously, by community, or by name, and their choice is reflected in the footnotes to this article. After the completion of a manuscript now entitled "Home Dreams: Women and Canadian Suburbs, 1945–60," these research materials, with certain restrictions on their use, will be deposited in a public archive.
146. Etobicoke suburbanite 1, "Questionnaire," 17.
147. Mildred Fox Baker, "Questionnaire," 17.
148. Metro Toronto suburbanite 1, "Questionnaire," 17.
149. London, Ontario, suburbanite 1, "Questionnaire," 17.
150. Niagara-on-the-Lake suburbanite 1 to author, 10 May 1991.
151. Marjorie Bacon to author, 6 April 1991.
152. Toronto West suburbanite 1, "Questionnaire," 17.
153. Wallis, "Suburban Experience," 27.

Article Twenty-Eight

Canada's Quest for Cultural Sovereignty: Protection, Promotion, and Popular Culture

John Herd Thompson

In his polemic *Why We Act Like Canadians*, Pierre Berton lectures Sam, his fictitious American correspondent, on the definition of the enigmatic word "culture":

> As for culture we [Canadians and Americans] don't even speak the same language. You think of culture in terms of opera, ballet, and classical music. To us it covers everything from Stompin' Tom Connors to Hockey Night in Canada. What is merely "industry" to you is culture to us. Books, magazines, movies, radio, television—all culture. Anne Murray is culture. . . . *Maclean's Magazine* is culture. The government subsidizes them all, in one way or another, because all are genuine Canadian artifacts, distinct and unique, something that nobody else has—the ingredients of our national mucilage.[1]

Sam should be forgiven any confusion. Culture, writes Raymond Williams, "is one of the two or three most complicated words in the English language."[2] Nowhere is the word more complicated than in the cultural relationship between Canada and the United States. "Culture" has a number of distinct and incompatible meanings, and those of us who presume to talk about it should define how we are using it. For Berton, his fictitious Sam, and me, the word is not being used in its anthropological sense—meaning "a given people's particular set of preferences, predispositions, attitudes, goals, their particular way of perceiving, feeling, thinking, and reacting to objective reality."[3] Culture in the quotation and in this paper means "the works and practices of intellectual and especially artistic activity."[4] Berton is accusing his character Sam of seeing culture only in terms of *culchah*, the so-called high culture of painting, sculpture, literature, music, opera, and ballet of Europe, adopted by the bourgeoisie of North America to differentiate itself from the masses. What Berton is celebrating as Canada's "national mucilage" is the mass or popular culture that Canadians consume as the product of their subsidized cultural industries.[5] In this context, cultural sovereignty is the power of a sovereign government to control the operation of cultural industries.[6]

Legislating Culture in Canada

For almost a century, Canadian governments have attempted to assert this cultural sovereignty, and to control the allegedly deleterious effects of U.S. newspapers, popular fiction, magazines, comic books, motion pictures (and now videotapes), radio, and eventually television and the associated recording industry. Canadians now routinely use the term "cultural imperialism" to describe these effects; however, an American sociologist has recently suggested that "cultural diffusion" would be more appropriate.[7] However we choose to

Source: *NAFTA in Transition*, ed. Stephen J. Randall and Herman W. Konrad (Calgary: University of Calgary Press, 1995), pp. 393–410. Reprinted by permission.

describe it, no one would deny the widespread presence of U.S. popular culture in Canada. Although every nation-state on the planet is penetrated by U.S. mass media to some degree, Canada's situation has been, and remains, unique. The explanations for this situation are familiar, and may be quickly summarized.

First, Canada's exposure to American mass culture is not mediated by language: 70 percent of its population shares a language with Americans. Second, English Canadians have no long history of national existence upon which to build a national identity: like Americans, they trace their ideological roots back to seventeenth-century Britain. The critical difference is that Canadian exposure to U.S. mass culture is not mediated by distance. Eighty percent of the Canadian population lives within 100 km of the U.S. border, with the result that U.S. print and electronic media are both immediately available.

Canadian cultural nationalists have long had statistics at their fingertips to demonstrate the consequences of this proximity. Rick Salutin's litany in the anti–free-trade anthology *If You Love This Country* can serve to illustrate their case:

> Only 3 to 5 percent of all theatrical screen time in Canada goes to Canadian films; 97 percent of profits from films shown in Canada go out of the country, 95 percent to the U.S.; 95 percent of English-language TV drama is non-Canadian; Canadian-owned publishers have only 20 percent of the book market, although they publish 80 percent of Canadian titles; 77 percent of the magazines sold here are foreign; 85 percent of record and tape sales are non-Canadian. . . . Canadian plays are the *alternative* theatre here.[8]

Allowing for the appearance of new technologies, similar figures could be provided for any decade back to the 1920s. To a Canadian cultural nationalist, these numbers add up to the conclusion that "the overall extent of Canadian cultural domination [by the United States] is effectively unparalleled."[9]

This explains why Canada has been searching for cultural sovereignty for almost as long as the United States has been exporting popular culture. Prodded by a nationalist intelligentsia concerned with creating a Canadian national identity, and by Canadian cultural industries seeking the same sheltered market enjoyed by other Canadian manufacturers, successive governments have groped for policies to cope with U.S. mass culture. The invariable first step has been investigation. From Aird to Massey-Lévesque to Applebaum-Hébert, royal commissions, task forces, and special committees have filled library shelves with weighty reports. The legislation that sometimes followed falls into two broad categories: attempts to *protect* Canadian cultural industries with regulatory or tariff barriers, and attempts to *promote* indigenous Canadian mass culture through subsidies to individual artists, or government-sponsored creation of cultural infrastructures. Policies were not always clear-cut; protectionist and promotional solutions were sometimes applied alternately or even simultaneously.

The most unambiguously protective cultural legislation has been Canada's policy toward U.S. periodicals. The protracted battle between the Canadian government and *Time* is the most intensively studied case,[10] but magazines were first identified as a problem during the 1920s. In 1925, four U.S. magazines had larger circulations than the leading Canadian title, then, as now, *Maclean's*, and *Saturday Evening Post* rubbed salt into the circulatory wounds of its Canadian competitors by (truthfully) billing itself as "Canada's best-selling magazine."

The subsequent campaign against U.S. magazines illustrates the typical alignment of forces behind campaigns for cultural sovereignty. It combined publishing entrepreneurs seeking an advantage against their U.S. competitors with a nationalist intelligentsia that argued that U.S. mass culture was "a menace to Canadian ideals and to the moral development of the youth of this country." It was difficult to accuse *Saturday Evening Post* or *Ladies' Home Journal* of immoral influence, so the target became pulp magazines imported from the United States, with titles like *Black Mask, Dime Detective,* and *Spicy Adventure,* "the off-scourings of the moral sewers of human life . . . a putrid flood of undisguised filth." Aroused Canadians demanded that something be done "to dam this trash flowing over the border." In 1930, Bennett's Conservative government obliged with a tariff that quickly had the desired effect: by the mid-1930s, Canadian circulation rose 65 percent and that of U.S. magazines fell an equal amount.[11]

Legislation to promote alternative Canadian mass cultural industries has been a more typical response than legislating protectionist measures. The first direct subsidy to a mass cultural industry was made in 1903. The Canadian government provided Canadian Associated Press with an annual grant of $60 000 to distribute news from Britain, which had been overlooked by the U.S.-based Associated Press, from whose wires all Canadian dailies received their European news.[12] King's Liberal government evaded demands for a magazine tariff in the 1920s by offering Canadian publishers a tax incentive, a drawback on the import duties they paid on special grades of papers.

But what became the most characteristic Canadian promotional response to the conundrum of cultural sovereignty was the creation of a publicly financed infrastructure, the approach adopted in film-making and broadcasting during the 1930s.[13] After competition from Hollywood suffocated the infant Canadian film industry in its cradle, the Canadian government rejected the quota solution used in Britain and Australia in favour of the Canadian Government Motion Picture Bureau (later, the National Film Board), charged with the production of documentaries, rather than feature films.[14] The Canadian Radio Broadcasting Commission, which became the Canadian Broadcasting Corporation (CBC) in 1936, marks the most visible difference between the cultural industries of Canada and the United States: Canada has a publicly owned and publicly financed radio and television broadcasting system, and the United States does not. The creation of the CBC was an outspoken assertion of cultural sovereignty. "Britannia rules the waves — shall Columbia rule the wavelengths?" was the slogan of the Canadian Radio League, a national lobby group of the early 1930s, which rallied more extensive popular support for public broadcasting than any other cultural sovereignty cause, before or since. As Graham Spry, a League spokesperson, put it to one of those ubiquitous parliamentary committees, "the question is, the State or the United States!"[15] The *Broadcasting Act* of 1968 requires all radio and television stations, public and private, to "safeguard, enrich and strengthen the cultural, political, social and economic framework of Canada" — to be an ingredient, in other words, of Berton's "national mucilage."

Cultural promotion has given Canada cultural industries that are substantially non-market driven, whereas in the United States, for the most part, the market rules. Even with the severe budget cutbacks imposed on the CBC in recent years, Ottawa spends more on culture, broadly defined, than Washington does, to serve a Canadian population one-tenth that of the United States.[16]

Because they do not speak the same language, with regard to culture, Americans have never taken Canadian complaints of U.S. cultural domination seriously. There has never been any conscious government–business conspiracy to push the products of U.S. popular culture northward. Therefore, any cultural influence exerted upon Canada is understood as passive and probably benevolent. Thus, there is no understanding of, let alone sympathy for, Canadian policies to achieve cultural sovereignty. When Parliament first discussed restricting the circulation of U.S. magazines, in 1923, the *New York Times* held up Holland, Switzerland,

and Belgium as small nations that had survived next to large ones: "these examples from Europe ought to convince the Canadians that they are not in danger of cultural extinction."[17]

Americans have also viewed Canada's cultural policies through what Roger Frank Swanson has called a "first amendment optic," the belief that any interference with the free flow of ideas is inherently wrong.[18] "We have learned better," said the same *New York Times* editorial, and "the Canadians, too, may learn that they will gain nothing by giving their own publications virtual freedom from competition." If Canada went ahead with its plan to ban the importation of U.S. magazines, the *Times* suggested "an agreeable form of reciprocity. As Canada bootlegs rum to us, we could bootleg literature to Canada."

Culture and Economic Realities

These American beliefs are not simply rationalizations, but "well entrenched and held largely without cynicism."[19] However, John Meisel has observed "that this ideological position often miraculously coincides with crass self-serving economic interests."[20] The historical and contemporary importance of this economic interest is easily calculated. Although Canada has a much smaller population than the other trading partners of the United States, it has been and remains the most important single export market for U.S. popular culture. These products are not unsaleable surpluses being dumped at fire-sale prices; prices are in fact traditionally "slightly higher in Canada." The most recent figures reflect long-standing trends, again allowing for technological change in the cultural industries. In 1989, Canadians bought 39.9 percent of all the U.S. books and 78 percent of all the U.S. magazines sold abroad—more than U.S.$1.4 billion worth.[21]

Canada is the second-largest absolute consumer of U.S. movies, and by far the largest per capita consumer, returning 1989 rental fees of U.S.$152.5 million.[22] Recorded music sales return about U.S.$80 million, but the Department of Commerce notes that this neglects the "large proportion of pre-recorded music sold [that] is manufactured by subsidiaries of U.S. companies."[23] Sales of television programs earn an estimated $125 million.[24] These are figures for gross earnings from cultural industry exports, but there has traditionally been a very large percentage profit on cultural exports to Canada; once a cultural product has been produced, the cost of exporting it to Canada is minimal, for the linguistic and geographic reasons discussed above. Asked, in 1975, why his magazine was struggling to preserve its Canadian operation, a *Time* executive replied that "they don't call Canada the candy store for nothing."[25]

Neither U.S. cultural industries nor the U.S. government has been prepared to see the so-called candy store close. However, not all of Canada's cultural sovereignty policies are perceived as equally threatening. The pattern of U.S. reactions may be summarized as follows: Canadian cultural protectionism has usually drawn an immediate response, but Canadian attempts to promote domestic, mass, and high culture have usually been ignored, because these attempts have never seriously threatened the profits of U.S. firms exporting cultural products, as with the documentary niche chosen by the National Film Board (NFB). Nor was the demonstration effect of Canada's cultural public enterprise feared by U.S. private business. Corporate America showed a great deal more hostility to Ontario's system of public electric power generation than it did to public film production or broadcasting. Cultural promotion, in its public enterprise form, was not only non-threatening, its effects could even be positive. For example, CBC television has spent millions to buy programs from U.S. networks: in the supreme example of this irony, U.S. football first came to Canadian screens via the CBC![26]

If the general pattern of the U.S. response has been predictable, the precise stratagems employed by business, government, or the two acting in concert, have not. U.S. entertainment companies have not always needed Washington to help them counter Canadian cultural sovereignty policies that threatened their interests. If they had a Canadian subsidiary, U.S. cultural exporters would make their case directly, as *Time* did to dissuade the Diefenbaker government from discriminatory tax changes.[27] Even if they didn't, they could lobby the Canadian government. In 1947, faced with an impending quota law and the possibility that the NFB would begin feature film production, the Motion Picture Association of America sold the Canadian government on the Canadian Co-operation Program, a transparent flim-flam that promised to display Canada to the world through the work of Hollywood studios. Producers were to be encouraged to use Canadian locations whenever appropriate, Canadian news in the newsreels was to be increased, and scriptwriters promised that Canada would be mentioned as frequently as possible in the dialogue of features made in Hollywood! The wonder is not that the plan achieved no results, for Hollywood did not intend it to, but that this bizarre scheme took in such otherwise hard-headed Canadians as C.D. Howe and Donald Gordon.[28]

When the U.S. government intercedes on behalf of a U.S. cultural industry, it is for the same reasons that it acts when any U.S. economic interest is threatened: because the firms concerned are domestically important, and can bring pressure to bear on Washington. This is not calculated subversion on the part of the United States; the goal is to enhance export earnings, just as it would be with any other industry. In addition, as Roger Swanson points out, "Washington is not a monolith." Aggrieved U.S. cultural industries can work through the White House, the legislative branches, or the state or commerce departments.[29] The balance of trade in the products of mass culture industries is so heavily in favour of the United States that it is impossible for them to retaliate by cutting off mass culture imports from Canada. When the Canadian Bill C-58 devastated the advertising income of U.S. border television stations, a proposal to block Canadian exports of film, videotapes, and sound recordings was quickly discarded as useless. Threatened (or actual) retaliation takes place in another trading sector. The twenty-year campaign to defend *Time* and *Reader's Digest* featured alleged threats by the Department of Defence to cancel aircraft purchasing contracts, to block the 1965 Auto Pact, and to impose quotas on oil imports from western Canada.[30]

Canadian Protectionist Policies

The pace and intensity of Canada's action and, thus, of U.S. reaction quickened in the mid-1960s. Standing guard against foreign direct investment and the snares of NATO and NORAD was no longer sufficient, as John Kenneth Galbraith warned the 1968 Couchiching Conference that the critical issues in sovereignty were not economic but cultural. Galbraith urged that it was essential to defend Canadian broadcasting, the publishing industry, and the film industry. "These are the things that count," he added.[31]

Canadian governments accepted Galbraith's advice. There was a flurry of investigation, with findings similar to those of previous investigations. And, when action followed, it became more difficult to distinguish, in policy terms, where promotion left off and protection began. The *Broadcasting Act* of 1968 not only demanded that "programming should be of a high standard," and be "predominantly Canadian in content and character," it also required that the programming be produced "using predominantly Canadian creative and

other resources." The legislative record is too long to describe in detail, but the most important parts must be summarized briefly.

First came quotas for Canadian content on both radio and television, and the creation
of the Canadian Radio-television and Telecommunications Commission (CRTC) to enforce
them. When cable transmission systems were established, Canadian cable companies were
allowed to retransmit U.S. signals without paying royalties to the originating stations. In
the spirit of *Catch-22*, Canadian stations have the privilege of simultaneous substitution;
they can bump from cable distribution U.S. stations that are carrying the same program at
the same time. The government also created the Canadian Film Development Corporation
(now Telefilm), which granted public funds for film (and now, television) production, and,
through a capital cost allowance program, permitted a 100 percent tax credit for investment in a Canadian feature film.

In all cultural industries, Trudeau's Liberal government applied the regulations
restricting foreign investment with particular rigour, but within this already restricted
cultural sector, book publishing companies received special care. Canadian magazines
were protected by tariffs prohibiting the entry of U.S. competitors with more than 5 percent Canadian advertising, and promoted through postal subsidies. The most dramatic of
the new policies, as far as the Canada–United States relationship was concerned, was Bill
C-58, a 1976 amendment to the *Income Tax Act* that denied deductions for advertising
costs to Canadian advertisers who attempted to reach their domestic market via U.S. radio
and television stations or periodicals. It was this Maclean-Hunter monopoly bill that eliminated *Time Canada*, and launched *Maclean's* as English-Canada's newsweekly.

Have these policies worked? Canadian cultural sovereignists grumble that, for radio and
television, "Canadian content . . . continues to be very loosely defined."[32] But, if not strictly defined, the content regulations are strictly enforced, so that in terms of the quantity of
Canadian mass cultural production, the record is uneven, but on the whole impressive.
The most obvious broadcasting failure is English-Canadian television drama, which is
almost nonexistent. The best example of success is recorded music. The combination of a
protective tariff on imported tapes and albums and the promotion of Canadian content
regulations for air play have launched both a domestic industry and a number of individual careers. There is room for skepticism about the quality of the popular culture that government policy is promoting and protecting. Critics sniff haughtily at "filling the airwaves
with undistinguished rock 'n' roll—acceptable as long as it is played by a band from
Sudbury or Winnipeg, but not if it comes from Des Moines."[33] The cultural sovereignist
responses to such comments range from denial to a defensive "sure, it's junk, but at least
it's *our* junk."

Arguing that these policies have established cultural sovereignty would require a leap
of faith that not even a cultural bureaucrat from the Canadian Secretary of State could
make. But the fact that the ultimate goal remains elusive is never accepted by their supporters as a reason for eliminating the policies. As John Hutcheson puts it: "Canadian production holds only a minor share of the market, but what little there is [is] a consequence
of some form of government support, whether subsidy, regulation or tax incentive."[34]

U.S. response to these new cultural policies of the 1970s had evolved a long way from
the bemused paternalism with which the *New York Times* lectured Canada in the 1920s.
As an academic commentator observed in 1976, "there are indications that U.S. tolerance levels are not as high as they were a few years ago."[35] This puts the case in the
mildest terms possible; what are referred to as "irritants" by professional trade negotiators are festering sores to the members of Congress who speak for the U.S. cultural
exporters afflicted by them.

Culture and the Free Trade Agreement

The Canada–United States Free Trade Agreement (FTA) removed few of these irritants. Canada's negotiators claimed that culture had been kept off the negotiating table and had been formally exempted from the final agreement; Canadian critics of the FTA denied both these contentions.[36] In fact, the FTA is ambiguous. Article 2005, paragraph 1, states that "cultural industries are exempt from the provisions of this agreement," with the exception of certain specifically enumerated concessions by Canada: the recording industry is not exempt, and the 11.8 percent Canadian tariff must be eliminated; royalties must be paid to U.S. broadcasters for signals retransmitted on Canadian cable systems. However, this general exemption in paragraph 1 is followed by paragraph 2, which says that "notwithstanding any other provision of the agreement, a Party may take measures of equivalent commercial effect in response to action that would have been inconsistent with this agreement but for paragraph 1." In other words, if Canada's cultural sovereignty legislation is exempted from the FTA, so is the U.S. right to retaliate exempted.

The Canadian government's claim that Canada's cultural legislation has any privileged position in the FTA is specious. The most generous interpretation would be that the FTA restores the cultural *status quo ante bellum*: Canada can keep the policies it already has, but the United States has the power to retaliate against them in any sector it wishes. Testifying before the House Ways and Means Committee in March 1991, U.S. Trade Representative Carla Hills said exactly that: "we didn't give it up in the Canadian agreement. . . . What we did was agree to disagree. We maintain our rights to bring cases against Canada. . . . Canada has maintained its right to disagree with us."[37]

However, after negotiating the FTA, Canada made three significant cultural concessions not formally required by the agreement. When Canadian cultural sovereignists charged that secret undertakings had been reached to water down old policies and shelve proposed new ones, Conservative Secretary of State Flora MacDonald dismissed this as nonsense. "Canada's right to determine its own culture has been respected in every way," she promised in *Quill & Quire*, the trade magazine of the Canadian publishing industry.[38] MacDonald's promises didn't survive the November 1988 federal election—nor did MacDonald, for that matter. Three of the specific promises she made in her *Quill & Quire* article were immediately broken by the Mulroney government: on postal rates for Canadian periodicals, foreign ownership in the publishing industry, and film distribution policy.

A preliminary version of the agreement had called for Canada to equalize postal rates for U.S. magazines. This clause was removed, but the Canadian government in effect carried out what the FTA had not required it to do. A $220 million indirect subsidy was first translated into a vaguely defined $110 million program to begin in March 1991, but the new program was cut by $45 million before it was even introduced.[39]

The second major Conservative culture casualty was the *Film Products Importation Act*, a film distribution policy proposed by Secretary of State Flora MacDonald, a policy that went beyond promoting the *creation* of feature films to require that Canadian companies control the means to disseminate what they created. But, once the legislation had been reworked by Cabinet, it was, in Jeffrey Simpson's words, "lights, camera, *In*action" in Ottawa.[40] "The minister has gone in with a tiger of a policy," wrote Susan Crean, "and come out with kitty litter."[41]

The U.S. lobbying campaign against the bill was carried out by Jack Valenti, president of the Motion Picture Association of America. *Maclean's* columnist Allan Fotheringham described him as "the most important person in the Canadian film industry . . . the rich lobbyist for the Hollywood interests who has R. Reagan's ear . . . through Washington-via-Sussex Drive pressures [he] has emasculated Flora MacDonald's brave but futile attempt to guard Canadian film interests."[42] Valenti appeared on CBC radio, and before the Empire Club, to defend his point of view: if a traditionally cooperative country like Canada challenged the distribution systems of major studios, he argued, it would have what he called a "viral contagion" effect in other countries. A redrafted film distribution bill was described by Daniel Weinzweig of the National Association of Canadian Distributors as "a feeble shadow of what was recommended."[43]

In book publishing, the Mulroney government backed off from its so-called Baie Comeau policy on foreign takeovers, a policy that required that companies up for sale be offered first to Canadian purchasers, and that used the traditional device of state owner-ship of the company as a final alternative to a takeover. The government maintained that the policy remained in force, but "actions speak louder than words," complained publish-er Malcolm Lester after New American Library of Canada vanished into the maw of the Penguin publishing house. "If cultural matters are exempt from the free-trade agreement," Lester asked, "why does the government appear to be caving in to U.S. pressure?"[44]

Fifteen months later, a representative of the Association of Canadian Publishers wrote a requiem on the demise of Lester & Orpen Dennys, Malcolm Lester's publishing house: "The government's so-called Baie Comeau policy to expand Canadian control of the indus-try has been timorously and inconsistently applied."[45]

The government's changes of course on film distribution and book publishing are examples of the sort of dispute-avoidance strategies that have been necessary to make the FTA work. The real significance of the FTA for Canada's cultural industries is that the United States was once indifferent to cultural promotion and, accordingly, left cultural pro-motion activities alone; today, all is negotiable. Canada has conceded the U.S. definition of culture: that culture is a business like any other, and that any action to restrain trade in cultural products calls for retaliation or compensation.

"From here on in, the business definition of culture will prevail in Canada too," argued Susan Crean, and Mulroney's Conservative government made no secret of its distaste for state enterprise in general.[46] The FTA was part of their attempt (similar to that of President Carlos Salinas in Mexico) to make Canada a more market-driven society. The severe cuts in the budget for public broadcasting and the quiet retreat from activist cultural policies were evidence that the Conservatives intended Canada to move toward the market-driv-en model of mass cultural industries that prevails in the United States.

However, this is not to say that the Conservatives used the FTA as a way to deliber-ately sabotage Canada's cultural industries and undermine the nationalist intelligentsia that had so heartily opposed them and their trade policy. Even if they watered down Baie Comeau, Tory policies like that on investment in the book publishing industry still infuriated Americans such as Representative John Dingell, a Michigan Democrat who pressed the administration to "urge the Canadian government to do away with the pol-icy altogether."[47]

Implications of NAFTA for Canadian Cultural Sovereignty

As negotiations to create a trilateral North American Free Trade Agreement (NAFTA) among Canada, the United States, and Mexico began, the Mulroney government stead-fastly insisted that NAFTA would have no effect on Canadian cultural industries. There was no significant cultural industry trade between Mexico and Canada, so "Mexican cultural imperialism is hardly a credible threat," one columnist noted.[48] Even between Mexico and the United States, trade in the products of cultural industries is small, much smaller than that between the United States and Canada.[49]

Thus, if the Canadian negotiators had hoped that Mexico would cooperate with Canada to press the United States for more explicit exemptions for cultural industries, they were disappointed. Although some Mexicans worried about NAFTA's implications for Mexico's cultural sovereignty, most Mexicans neither understood the Canadian point of view on cultural industries nor sympathized with Canada on it.[50] "Canada should be the 51st U.S. state," a young Mexican told a *Globe and Mail* reporter in February 1991: "Canada is so lacking in its own culture that it had to steal hockey and the Stanley Cup from the U.S. to have something to call its own[!]"[51] During his 1990 visit to Ottawa, President Salinas dismissed out of hand the suggestion that cultural issues could be a serious concern for Mexico. On the contrary, increased cultural trade offered Mexican cultural industries the prospect of increased sales in the large Spanish-speaking market in the United States.

NAFTA negotiations in fact threatened to rip the bandages off the festering sores left from the Canada–U.S. FTA. As *Globe and Mail* correspondent Jennifer Lewington put it, "some irritants, especially in the cultural area, are political time bombs with an uncertain fuse."[52] In the Bush administration's successful attempt to persuade the Senate and the House to grant it the "fast track" negotiating authority for NAFTA, one of Carla Hills's most consistently effective sales pitches was the argument that renewed negotiations would mean new opportunities to resolve the question of Canadian cultural sovereignty legislation in favour of the United States.[53] The promise to deal severely with "offensive" Canadian legislation like Bill C-58 was offered to a wary Congress as an inducement to get involved with free trade negotiations with Mexico! Congress also considered, but did not pass, an amendment to the law that implemented NAFTA that would have expedited the process of retaliation against Canadian cultural policies judged injurious to U.S. cultural exporters.[54]

The NAFTA negotiations continued the stalemate on cultural industries. The eventual NAFTA accord left the provisions of the Canada–U.S. FTA — the agreement to disagree about Canada's cultural policies — unchanged. By the time the NAFTA was inaugurated in January 1994, the Republicans and Conservatives who had devised it were both out of office.

In Ottawa, the new Liberal government of Jean Chrétien denounced the "Conservative regime [that] has deliberately undermined our national cultural institutions," and promised "to commit itself to cultural development."[55] Its first year in office, however, offered little evidence that the new Canadian government took these promises seriously. In March 1994, over the protests of the Association of Canadian Publishers, the new government approved the sale of Ginn Publishing Canada to U.S. entertainment conglomerate Paramount Communications Inc., rather than insist that it go to a Canadian buyer.[56]

When Paramount itself was immediately swallowed by still-larger U.S. entertainment conglomerate Viacom Inc., cultural nationalists demanded that Ottawa block the takeover until Viacom agreed to divest some of its Canadian holdings in publishing and film distribution. Despite the protests, the takeover was approved by the Chrétien government without conditions. To sugar-coat the Cabinet's capitulation, Viacom assured that it would reinvest some of its Canadian profits in Canada's cultural industries. In a gesture eerily reminiscent of the "Canadian Co-operation Project" of 1947, Viacom promised that Famous Players, its cinema chain, would "undertake to exhibit more Canadian films," and that its subsidiary, Blockbuster Video, would "promote Canadian films in its U.S. home video stores." Viacom also promised to invest Can.$23.8 million in Canada's Wonderland, an Ontario amusement park.[57] A *Toronto Star* editorialist searched for appropriate denunciations for the Liberal Cabinet: "Cowards? Hypocrites? Or Canadian puppets on American strings?"[58]

Perhaps stung by such reproach, the Chrétien government made sudden nationalist advances on two cultural fronts in January 1995. In April 1993, *Sports Illustrated* had discovered a technological loophole in Canada's restriction on split-run editions of foreign magazines. *Sports Illustrated* simply beamed its U.S. edition to a Canadian printing plant by satellite, added a couple of Canadian stories, and became in the process a "Canadian" magazine in which Canadian advertisers were permitted tax deductions for the cost of their ads.[59] To the cheers of Canadian magazines, Ottawa responded with an 80 percent excise tax.

The second case involved cable television regulation. In 1994, the Canadian Radio-television and Telecommunications Commission had ruled, as Canadian law required it to, that Nashville-based Country Music Television be removed from Canadian cable systems in favour of the New Country Network, a Canadian competitor. In this case Ottawa acted by not acting: the Cabinet refused to override the CRTC's decision. Heritage Minister Michel Dupuy specifically cited the cultural exemption under NAFTA as the basis of Canada's right to protect its cultural industries. "We intend to take a strong line when Canadian cultural interests are threatened," he announced.[60]

Democratic president Bill Clinton, unlike his predecessors, kept silent about these U.S.–Canada cultural differences.[61] But his trade representative, Mickey Kantor, yielded nothing to any Republican in his zealous defence of U.S. cultural exporters. Lampooning the lyrics of country music, *The Financial Post* reported that Kantor was "mighty fussed and he took to making threats about retaliating against a passel of Canadian entertainment industries." Trade war over television regulation was resolved by a merger: Country Music Television absorbed the New Country Network, and suddenly "the hurtin' is over and the lovin' has started between the country music broadcasters."[62] However, the excise tax on split-run magazines remains; the *Sports Illustrated* case may become the first to provoke the United States to exercise its right to retaliate against Canadian cultural protectionism.

Conclusion

No matter how the United States responds to the magazine excise tax, the brief flurry of cultural nationalism directed at Country Music Television and at *Sports Illustrated* cannot obscure the Chrétien Liberal government's continuation of the trend initiated by the Mulroney Conservatives. Canada continues to move toward market-driven, U.S.-style cultural policies.[63] The 1995 Canadian federal budget made substantial cuts to the CBC, the National Film Board, Telefilm, and to subsidy programs for the magazine and book publishing industries. Finance Minister Paul Martin promised further cuts in future budgets. Canada's provincial governments show similar inclinations.[64] This convergence of U.S. and Canadian understandings of "culture" may hold greater peril for Canada's cultural sovereignty than any threatened U.S. retaliation to specific Canadian policies of cultural protection and promotion.

NOTES

1. Pierre Berton, "The Puzzle of Free Trade," in *Why We Act Like Canadians: A Personal Exploration of Our National Character* (Markham, ON: McClelland and Stewart, 1987), p. 9.
2. Raymond Williams, *Keywords: A Vocabulary of Culture and Society* (London: Fontana, 1983), p. 87.
3. Raymond Gagné, "French Canada: The Interrelationship between Culture, Language, and Personality," in *Canadian History since Confederation*, ed. Bruce Hodgins and Robert Page (Georgetown, ON: Irwin-Dorsey, 1972), p. 526.

4. Williams, *Keywords*, p. 90.
5. "Mass" culture is the better descriptive term because, again, as Raymond Williams notes, "popular" culture is not a culture created by the people, and the term itself was not bestowed upon this form of culture "by *the people*, but by others, and it still carries two older senses: inferior kinds of work; and work deliberately setting out to win favour." Williams, *Keywords*, p. 237.

414

6. Given an anthropological definition of culture, cultural sovereignty would be absurd: "a nation doesn't possess a culture as one possesses property, a nation is its culture." Michael Bergman, "Free Trade: Trick-or-Treaty?" *Cinema Canada* 149 (February 1988): 14–15, cited in Barbara Fairbairn, "The Implications of Free Trade for Television Broadcasting in Canada," *Canadian Issues/Thèmes canadiens* 12 (1989): 80.
7. Joel Smith, "Canada's Television, Entertainment, and National Culture Dilemma Reconsidered: Real or Spurious?" (unpublished manuscript).
8. Rick Salutin, "Keep Canadian Culture off the Table — Who's Kidding Who?" in *If You Love This Country*, ed. Laurier LaPierre (Toronto: McClelland and Stewart, 1987), pp. 205–6.
9. Ian Parker, "The Free Trade Challenge," *Canadian Forum* (February–March 1988): 34.
10. See Isaiah A. Litvak and Christopher J. Maule, *Cultural Sovereignty: The "Time" and "Reader's Digest" Case in Canada* (New York, 1974), and "Bill C-58 and the Regulation of Periodicals in Canada," *International Journal* 36 (1980): 70–90; and Roger Frank Swanson, "Canadian Cultural Nationalism and the U.S. Public Interest," in *Canadian Cultural Nationalism*, ed. Janice L. Murray (New York: Council on Foreign Relations, 1977), pp. 54–79.
11. Mary Vipond, "Canadian Nationalism and the Plight of Canadian Magazines in the 1920s," *Canadian Historical Review* 58, 1 (March 1977): 43–63.
12. John A. Schultz, "Whose News: The Struggle for Wire Service Distribution, 1900–1920," *ARCS* 10 (1980): 27–35. The subsidy failed to accomplish its purpose: according to Schultz, "CAP cables consisted mainly of society news and rarely averaged more than 500 or 600 words daily." The experiment was ended in 1910.
13. See Allan Smith, "Canadian Culture, the Canadian State, and the New Continentalism," *Canadian–American Public Policy* 3 (October 1990): 10–20.
14. Peter Morris, *Embattled Shadows: A History of Canadian Cinema, 1895–1939* (Montreal: McGill-Queen's, 1978), pp. 175–95. The governments of Ontario and British Columbia had short-lived and less successful civil service movie companies. British Columbia went so far as to require theatre owners to show these documentaries; however, the government was unable to persuade moviegoers to actually watch them!
15. Plaunt, quoted in Margaret Prang, "The Origins of Public Broadcasting in Canada," *Canadian Historical Review* 46, 1 (1965): 9–31.
16. The budget President Bush presented to Congress for the 1991–92 fiscal year allotted U.S.$833 million to "culture, arts, and humanities." *New York Times* (4 February 1991): 8. Note that U.S. high culture is not governed entirely by market forces, but most patronage comes from private philanthropists, not the state.
17. "Canadian Culture," *New York Times* (7 March 1923): 14.
18. Swanson, "Canadian Cultural Nationalism and the U.S. Public Interest," p. 56.
19. Fairbairn, "Implications of Free Trade for Television Broadcasting in Canada," pp. 80–81.
20. John Meisel, "Escaping Extinction: Cultural Defence of an Undefended Border," in *Southern Exposure: Canadian Perspectives on the United States*, ed. D.H. Flaherty (Toronto: McGraw-Hill Ryerson, 1986), p. 165.
21. U.S. Department of Commerce, International Trade Administration, *U.S. Industrial Outlook*, Articles 26–2; 26–9 (Washington, 1991). The next-largest customer for both is Britain, which purchases 8 percent of U.S. book exports and 5 percent of U.S. magazine exports.
22. Ibid., Article 32–2.
23. Ibid., Article 32–4.
24. Fairbairn, "Implications of Free Trade," p. 76.
25. *Business Week* (20 October 1975): 52.
26. Paul Rutherford, *When Television Was Young: Primetime Canada, 1952–1967* (Toronto: University of Toronto Press, 1990), p. 131.

27. John G. Diefenbaker, *One Canada: Memoirs of the Rt. Hon. John G. Diefenbaker*, vol. 2 (Toronto: Macmillan, 1976), pp. 308–10.
28. The project is described in "Canadian Co-operation, Hollywood Style," chap. 4 of Pierre Berton's *Hollywood's Canada: The Americanization of Our National Image* (Toronto: McClelland and Stewart, 1975), pp. 167–200.
29. Swanson, "Canadian Cultural Nationalism," p. 64.
30. Litvak and Maule, *Cultural Sovereignty*, passim.
31. Galbraith's remarks, reprinted in R.P. Bowles et al., *Canada and the U.S.: Continental Partners or Wary Neighbours?* (Scarborough, ON: Prentice-Hall, 1973), pp. 88–89.
32. Paul Audley, *Canada's Cultural Industries: Broadcasting, Publishing, Records and Film* (Toronto: Canadian Institute for Economic Policy, 1983), p. 257.
33. Dave Chenoweth, "Does the Quantity Equal the Quality?" *Montreal Gazette* (21 March 1980); and Charles Pullen, "Culture, Free Trade, and Two Nations," *Queen's Quarterly* 95, 4 (Winter 1988): 888.
34. John Hutcheson, "Culture and Free Trade," in *The Future on the Table: Canada and the Free Trade Issue*, ed. Michael D. Henderson (Toronto: Masterpress, 1987), pp. 109, 111.
35. Swanson, "Canadian Cultural Nationalism," p. 63.
36. The best-argued example is Susan Crean's "Reading between the Lies: Culture and the Free Trade Agreement," *This Magazine* 22, 2 (May 1988): 29–33.
37. Reuter Transcripts (12 March 1991).
38. Flora MacDonald, *Quill & Quire* 54, 9 (September 1988): 82.
39. Stephen Godfrey, "Is Culture Truly Excluded from Free Trade?" *Globe and Mail* (20 January 1990): C1, C3.
40. Simpson, "Lights, Camera, Inaction," *Globe and Mail* (11 May 1988): A7.
41. Crean, "Reading between the Lies," p. 31.
42. Allan Fotheringham, "The Trouble with Thinking Aloud," *Maclean's* (11 July 1988): 52.
43. Godfrey, "Is Culture Truly Excluded from Free Trade?": C1.
44. Lester, quoted in "Fine Print in Trade Pact Turns Good News to Bad," *Globe and Mail* (16 September 1988).
45. Roy MacSkimming, "Does the Political Will Exist to Save the Publishing Industry?" *Globe and Mail* (16 January 1991): A11.
46. Crean, "Reading between the Lies," p. 31.
47. Dingell speaks for Gulf and Western Inc., which ran afoul of the policy through its acquisition of Ginn & Co. See Jennifer Lewington, "Ottawa Book Policy Target of Attack by Quiet Congress Veteran," *Globe and Mail* (18 March 1989).
48. Jeffrey Simpson, "A Deal Most People Oppose, Offered by an Unpopular Government," *Globe and Mail* (13 August 1993): A16.
49. Using magazines as an (admittedly language- and education-biased) example, Canada takes in 78 percent of U.S. magazine exports and Mexico 3 percent. U.S. Department of Commerce, *Industrial Outlook* (1991), Article 26-6.
50. Katherine Ellison, "Free-Trade Pact Raises Cultural Concerns," *Raleigh News and Observer* (7 April 1991): 22A.
51. Madelaine Drohan, "Here We Go Again," *Globe and Mail* (9 February 1991): p. D1.
52. Jennifer Lewington, "Ottawa Book Policy," *Globe and Mail* (18 March 1989).
53. See her testimony before the Senate Finance Committee, February 21, 1991, and before the House Ways and Means Committee, March 12, 1991.
54. John Saunders, "U.S. Congress Eyes Ways to Hem Canada in on Culture," *Globe and Mail* (21 October 1993): B7.
55. *Creating Opportunity: The Liberal Plan for Canada* (Ottawa: Liberal Party of Canada, 1993) p. 88.
56. Hugh Winsor, "Ginn Fizzle," *Globe and Mail* (19 March 1994): D5.
57. Hugh Winsor and Val Ross, "Viacom Deal to Net Culture $400 Million," *Globe and Mail* (17 December 1994): B1, B7.
58. "The Viacom Mirror," *Toronto Star* (20 December 1994).
59. Val Ross, "Split Decision on Split-Run Invader," *Globe and Mail* (24 September 1994): A20.

415

60. Shawn McCarthy, "New Face-Off Looms with U.S. on Trade," *Toronto Star* (26 June 1995).
61. "Clinton's Tune Was Music to Chrétien," *Montreal Gazette* (25 February 1995).
62. "Back Off, Mickey," *The Financial Post* (27 June 1995).
63. Charlotte Grey, "Donna in the Lion's Den," *Saturday Night* (July/August 1995): 20.
64. Diane Turbide, "Assessing the Damage," *Maclean's* (20 March 1995): 78–79.

Article Twenty-Nine

"Let Us Heed the Voice of Youth": Laundry Detergents, Phosphates, and the Emergence of the Environmental Movement in Ontario

Jennifer Read

You're glumping the pond
Where the humming-fish hummed!
No more can they hum,
for their gills are all gummed.
So I'm sending them off.
Oh, their future is dreary.
They'll walk on their fins
And get woefully weary
In search of some water
That isn't so smeary.
I hear things are just as bad
up in Lake Erie.[1]

Dr. Seuss' timely poem, *The Lorax*, highlighted a number of environmental issues prominent during the late 1960s and early 1970s. The hero of the poem, the Lorax, accuses the exploitative "Once-ler man" of habitat destruction, species extirpation, if not extinction, and air and water pollution. *The Lorax* is still in print today, 25 years later; and the issues retain ongoing significance. Despite the environmental movement's importance in shaping political debate since the 1960s, relatively little has been written about its origins in Ontario.[2] The controversy surrounding detergent pollution in the province, which extended through most of the 1960s, offers an excellent opportunity to examine the shift in attitudes that marked the emergence of environmentalism.

Until the 1960s, conservation concepts influenced natural resource policies. Conservationists emphasized rational decision making based upon scientific principles and technical training to achieve their primary goal—the efficient development of natural resources to ensure strong economic growth. Conservation-minded natural resource managers relied on close cooperation with business for successful programs. During the first five decades of the century, conservation evolved from concentration on forestry and

Source: *Journal of the C.H.A. 1996 Revue de la S.H.C.*, pp. 227–250.

wildlife management strategies prior to the First World War to soil conservation in the "dirty thirties." The federal and provincial governments revived the concept in the immediate postwar era as part of their reconstruction policies, and conservation shifted to focus on river valley development, irrigation, and water pollution control.[3]

The end of the Second World War heralded an unprecedented era of economic expansion in Canada. For the most part, leisure time and real income increased during this period right across the continent, affording people both the time and the affluence to escape the ugly and increasingly polluted urban areas where they lived. They went hiking, canoeing, camping, and for day trips in their cars, all in unprecedented numbers. This forced governments at the state and provincial, as well as national, levels, in both Canada and the United States, to expand their parks systems and accommodate the increasing demand for outdoor recreation opportunities. For instance, the Ontario provincial parks system grew from eight parks at the end of the war to 94 by 1967.[4] Attempting to explain the emergence of the environmental movement in the United States, one historian has suggested that increased exposure to the natural world combined with comparatively higher education levels to produce generally held environmental values among a large segment of the young, and now well-educated, population.[5]

The changing attitudes reflected a growing popular awareness of ecology. Issues raised in the 1950s debate about nuclear fallout — that an unseen pollutant could travel hundreds of miles from its point of origin to endanger human life, were amplified by the appearance of Rachel Carson's book *Silent Spring* in 1962. Carson argued that modern agricultural and forestry practices overused synthetic pesticides, endangering the health of wildlife and humans. Her book helped bring the concept of ecology into general use. The formal science of ecology emphasized the intricate interrelationship between organisms and their physical environment. During the 1960s, the term entered popular vocabulary to represent the complex functioning of the natural world, the impact of human activity upon it, and the need to achieve balance between the two. Several environmental disasters served to drive ecological concepts home. In 1967, for instance, the supertanker *Torrey Canyon* struck a reef off the coast of Cornwall and spilled 117 000 tons of crude oil. Two years later, a Union Oil Company drilling platform off the California coast blew and the well ran freely into the Pacific for two weeks. Later that year, the Cuyahoga River, which empties into Lake Erie at Cleveland, caught fire![6]

Environmentalism emerged out of an intricate and evolving set of values reflecting an understanding of and concern about the human impact on nature as it relates to physical and spiritual human health. It was expressed initially in the efforts of the young, educated, and environmentally aware activists who demanded a decision-making role in areas that traditionally had been within the purview of scientifically trained, expert managers. In the United States environmentalists formed lobby groups which pressed governments at all levels to increase research and adopt the solutions presented by their own scientific experts.[7]

One of the earliest environmental issues to emerge in the Great Lakes basin was the detergent debate, which occurred in two stages during the 1960s. The first stage focused on the problem of excessive foaming, beginning early in 1963. In *Biodegradable: Detergents and the Environment* (1991), William McGucken examined the issue as it played out in the United States. The American industry solved the problem in 1965 by voluntarily changing to a biodegradable, nonfoaming detergent.[8] While similar events occurred on this side of the border they have not yet been examined. Late 1968 marked the beginning of the second stage, when the phosphate content of detergents and its role in degrading water quality, especially in Lake Erie, captured significant media attention. McGucken's article, "The

417

Canadian Federal Government, Cultural Eutrophication, and the Regulation of Detergent Phosphates, 1970" (1989), concentrated on the federal level, briefly touched on a number of environmental groups, but missed the debate's significance at the provincial level, especially the role played by Pollution Probe.[9]

418

Terence Kehoe used both stages of the detergent issue to highlight the shift in American business–government relations which occurred during this period. Traditional cooperation between the public and private sectors disintegrated as public input assumed increased importance in both the political process and business regulation. This was especially significant at the state and local levels. Kehoe stressed growing postwar affluence as a key factor in the change because growing concern about health and "the quality of life led to the creation of an extraordinary number of new laws and agencies charged with regulating the 'social conduct' of business firms."[10] Kehoe's concept of changing government–industry relations applies to the Ontario situation during the same period.

An examination of both phases of the detergent debate as they developed in Ontario will demonstrate the shift in thinking that marked the appearance of environmental values in this province. The first phase was distinguished by traditional business–government problem-solving strategies, which rejected nonexpert input despite a significant outcry from municipal governments across the province. Phase two was markedly different. By 1969, public values had changed significantly, enabling nongovernmental environmental groups, specifically Pollution Probe, to challenge closed-door decision making. A comparison of the effectiveness of the tactics used in both phases will demonstrate the changing milieu created by the emergence of environmental values in the province.

Called "the prosperous years," the 25 years after the Second World War marked a fundamental change in the social and economic composition of Ontario society. The provincial economy grew steadily until the first postwar recession, beginning in 1957; the economy recovered in 1963 to continue expanding into the 1970s. Throughout the period, the unemployment rate rarely rose above 4 percent. Between 1941 and 1961 Ontario's population increased from 3.7 million to over 6 million. The province attracted some 600 000 immigrants during the period, while the baby boom produced an unprecedentedly high annual birth rate of 25–26 per thousand with a high of 28.9 in 1947.[11]

The burgeoning population increasingly concentrated in cities, especially the Toronto-centred area extending along the Lake Ontario shoreline from Niagara in the west to Oshawa in the east, known as the "golden horseshoe." By the 1960s, this region was home to over 50 percent of the province's population. It supported a manufacturing sector which employed roughly 30 percent of the provincial workforce and created significant employment in related industries and services. Here, Ontario firms produced almost half of the nation's manufacturing output and were responsible for over 80 percent in areas as diverse as automobiles, soaps and washing compounds, leather tanning, agricultural implements, and prepared breakfast foods.[12]

The province's lakes and rivers were particularly vulnerable to this postwar industrial surge. Already degraded from depression-era neglect and the considerable industrial measures undertaken during the Second World War, water bore the brunt of the postwar boom.[13] The heavy industrialization of this period ensured the introduction of a wide range of effluents into the Great Lakes; none were as visible as synthetic detergents. Wartime developments in the petroleum sector enabled manufacturers to produce more effective and cheaper synthetic cleaning agents than had previously been possible. This coincided with pent-up consumer demand unleashed by the return to peace. Thousands of new laundry machines and dishwashers readily accommodated the synthetic detergents.

A detergent is any agent that, when added to water, thoroughly saturates accumulated soiling particles such as dirt and oil (wetting), separates the particles from the item (dispersing), then links the particles to water molecules (emulsifying) and carries them away from the item. There are primarily two types of detergents, soaps and synthetics. Soaps are made from animal or vegetable fat and are most useful in soft water, which is low in dissolved minerals such as calcium and magnesium. Both soaps and synthetic detergents have components called surface-active agents, or surfactants, which interface directly with distinct surfaces. Detergents are able to clean because the surfactant inserts itself between dirt and the item being washed and holds the dirt suspended in water.[14] In addition to the surfactant, synthetic detergents also contain a builder, most often a phosphate, which softens hard water by drawing suspended minerals out of the solution. In the early 1960s, surfactants counted for 10–15 percent of synthetic detergents, while the builder made up another 60 percent by weight. The remaining volume was concerned with aesthetic aspects, such as smell.[15] Due to the versatility and new affordability of synthetic detergents, they were favoured by both domestic and industrial cleaning.

A molecule called alkyl benzene sulphonate (ABS) served as the surfactant of the synthetic laundry detergents introduced in the immediate postwar years under names such as Fab, Tide, and Surf. ABS was a long, asymmetrical molecule; one end attracted dirt, and the other attracted water. Between the two ends the molecule branched several times. This structure created two significant and related problems. Because of its design, ABS caused visible and long-lasting foam in concentrations as low as 1 mg per litre in sewage effluent. Other synthetic detergents, such as those used for industrial applications, did not branch and yielded must less foam, which readily broke down in sewage treatment. Detergent manufacturers used the foaming property of ABS as a sales strategy appealing to housewives who, for years, had been encouraged to equate plentiful suds with cleanliness. Ultimately, the excessive sudsing problem was an artificial creation of detergent marketers caught up in a campaign over who had the longest-lasting suds.[16]

The other related problem with ABS was its lack of biodegradability. Easily biodegradable substances can be broken down into harmless materials through the bacterial action of normal biological processes. This is the basis of many sewage treatment plants. Because of its branched construction, ABS was not biodegradable and the long-lasting suds, which so appealed to consumers, piled up along those of the province's fast-running rivers and lake shores receiving treatment plant effluent. University of Toronto professor P.H. Jones noted: "The major hazard created by these foam banks was the break down in public relations between the large soap companies and the customer."[17]

Although complaints about foam in sewage treatment plants and rivers began in the early 1950s, the detergent industry insisted that ABS compounds were only partly responsible for the increasing mess. Surely, they argued, the small concentration of synthetic detergents could not be the primary cause of foaming in plants and in the waters receiving plant effluents.[18] In June 1962, the provincial agency responsible for water quality, the Ontario Water Resources Commission (OWRC), hosted a conference on "Problems in the Use of Detergents," which included representatives of the major detergent manufacturers, Colgate-Palmolive, Lever Brothers, and Procter & Gamble. D.F. Carrothers, representing the Canadian Manufacturers of Chemical Specialities Association, concluded: "While detergent materials can be a contributing factor to some of the problems met in sewage treatment and water pollution, they are by no means the only or necessarily the most important factor. Thus, we consider that much of the publicity blaming detergents specifically is unwarranted."[19] Industry representatives insisted that problems "aggravated" by ABS were restricted to "a few areas in the world and do not yet exist in Canada."[20] Nevertheless, they agreed to cooperate with the OWRC and to look into the Ontario problem.

One area that experienced visible pollution problems was Wentworth County at the head of Lake Ontario. This included the heavily industrialized area surrounding Hamilton Harbour, including the city of Hamilton and, beyond that, Wentworth County. "Sewage, detergents, sludges, chemicals, oil . . . they all pour into the harbour," a Hamilton *Spectator* headline moaned in November 1962. Among the pollution problems explored in the accompanying article, detergents received a significant airing. Detergent residues persisted after sewage and water treatment and, in some American cities, the article noted, "the tap water already comes with a foamy crest." The American and German situations offered examples to be avoided in Canada. The author of the article pointed out that German manufacturers had to be ordered to change the formulation of their detergents in order to address the dilemma there. While the problems in Ontario were not as severe as in Germany, both the local medical officer of health and the director of Hamilton's municipal laboratories predicted that "the probable outcome will be much the same as Germany's, as syndets [synthetic detergents] build up in the water." To emphasise the point, the article featured photographs of an Ontario sewage treatment plant enveloped in foam.[21]

Disturbed by the problem of excessive foam, the Wentworth County Council, consisting of municipal representatives from Stoney Creek, Dundas, Waterdown, and the surrounding Hamilton area townships, unanimously passed a resolution on 18 December 1962 urging the provincial government to ban the use and sale of synthetic detergents. Citing its alarm over the pollution of Ontario waters by laundry detergents, the council noted that

the basic cause of detergent pollution arises from the fact that most detergents marketed in Ontario have a mineral base (i.e. phosphorus) which cannot be broken down and purified by natural or artificial purification methods;

AND . . . the pollution from mineral based detergents does not dissipate but rather has a cumulative effect causing such serious problems as the algae buildup in many lakes and other inland waters with its consequent ill effects;

AND . . . other jurisdictions (i.e. Germany) have solved the detergent pollution problem by prohibiting the use of mineral based detergents;

AND . . . detergents can be produced with equivalent cleansing properties by using an organic base instead of a mineral base (i.e. Germany and some part of the U.S.).[22]

In addition to urging a ban on detergents, the council insisted that the province and the OWRC alert the public to the seriousness of detergent pollution. The council sent a copy of its resolution to every municipal council in Ontario, the chair of the OWRC, the premier, and the leaders of the provincial Liberals and New Democrats.

Thomas Beckett, a Hamilton lawyer who went on to chair the Hamilton Region Conservation Authority as well as to become a member of the Conservation Council of Ontario (CCO), proposed the resolution.[23] The impetus for Beckett's move is unclear. In all likelihood it was a combination of press coverage, similar to the *Spectator* article, and a meeting he had attended that fall at Hamilton's Royal Botanical Gardens with OWRC Secretary, William McDonnell.[24] There, McDonnell had admitted that pollution from detergents was a serious problem of which the public remained unaware. McDonnell pointed out that, unless the public demanded change, the detergent industry would not undertake it voluntarily.[25]

The Wentworth resolution struck a chord with municipal governments across the province and soon letters supporting it flooded the OWRC offices. Some 277 municipalities from all regions of the province endorsed the resolution between January and March 1963. On 11 March, the Ontario Association of Rural Municipalities approved the resolution at its annual meeting.[26]

The OWRC hastened to reassure the municipalities approving the Wentworth resolution that it had the situation in hand. Remedial activity included OWRC meetings with industry representatives and an ongoing Commission investigation into the detergent problem. Although the OWRC admitted that detergent foaming somewhat interfered with the operation of treatment plants, and partially contributed to the growth of algae in rivers and lakes, it maintained that detergents were merely a nuisance.[27] Commission personnel had investigated the assertions in the Wentworth resolution and noted that "the authors of the resolution are mixed up in the causes and effects."[28] In fact the document did confuse phosphorus builders, which readily broke down in sewage treatment plants and provided nutrients to support algae growth, with the ABS surfactant, which did not break down and caused the persistent problems with foaming. To Commission scientists, the Wentworth Council had clearly confused the scientific and technical aspects of the detergent debate and therefore should not be taken seriously. David Caverly, OWRC general manager, believed the Commission's best response to the resolution would be to widely publicize the fact that it remained actively involved in the search for a solution. His attitude was clear: leave problems to the people best able to deliver answers, scientifically trained resource managers.[29]

For the detergent industry, the Wentworth resolution raised the unwelcome spectre of government intervention. The potential for provincial legislation was heightened by European precedents, notably in Germany, and legislation then under consideration in some American states. In the United States, the industry had been searching for a non-foaming substitute for ABS since the 1950s, as pressure from Congress and state legislatures threatened to push detergent manufacturers toward a solution more quickly than they wished. The industry decided to find and introduce alternatives to ABS on its own terms rather than have change dictated by politicians. Detergent manufacturers also recognized that negative publicity had an unfavourable impact on sales. In June 1963, therefore, the American detergent industry announced that it intended to produce more readily biodegradable detergents within two years.[30]

In the meantime, Canadian representatives of the detergent multinationals worked to avert government intervention in Ontario. In May, delegates of the Canadian Manufacturers of Chemical Specialities Association met with the OWRC and reasserted the industry's position that detergent foaming was not yet a serious problem in Canada. They resisted the Commission's demand for expensive research into the problem, arguing that they had access to the extensive work being done in Europe and the United States through their international affiliates. They insisted that coercive legislation would only interfere with their research program and would result in more expensive and inefficient alternatives by rushing the industry to a less than ideal solution. Legislation that emphasized only one aspect of a complex situation, they pointed out, might cloud the real cause of the problem.[31] A few months later, Canadian detergent producers refused outright to implement the detergent formulation changes just announced by the American industry.[32]

By the summer of 1963, the OWRC finally recognized that its cooperation with the industry was not as smooth as had been intimated to the public. The Commission admitted internally that foaming was a problem and that it did not accept the industry's position. Behind closed doors, the OWRC applied pressure for change, but it continued to support detergent manufacturers in public.[33] The OWRC's strategy resembled government–business relations typical of the conservation era. Commission personnel believed that more could be accomplished through dynamic interaction between their experts and business representatives than by offering antagonistic public ultimatums. As long as the technical people were at work on a solution the public did not need to know the details.

Press coverage of the situation generally favoured the industry's stance and ridiculed the Wentworth resolution.[34] Many writers found the industry explanation convincing and echoed the OWRC position that blamed the current confusion on the technical and scientific ignorance of the municipal officials who had drafted the resolution. These comments infuriated Thomas Beckett, the author of the Wentworth resolution, who responded to a particularly scathing article in *The Globe and Mail* by firing off a letter to William McDonnell, Commission Secretary. Beckett accused the OWRC of supporting the detergent industry against the municipalities. Referring to McDonnell's speech at the Royal Botanical Gardens, Beckett reminded Secretary McDonnell that he himself had acknowledged the level of detergent pollution in Ontario waters to be of "'serious proportions.'" All the same, Beckett continued, "it is quite apparent that an attempt is being made to minimize the important [*sic*] of this problem and suggest that the municipalities were badly informed." Beckett was angered that an agency which had been created to meet the needs of Ontarians now acted like "an ally of the soap manufacturers," ignoring "the pleas of several hundred municipalities."[35]

Ultimately, the OWRC continued to ignore the objections of the local governments and allowed the detergent industry to implement its own solution. After a thorough investigation of the matter, the Commission determined that the situation did not require the degree of intervention called for in the Wentworth Resolution. In part, the OWRC based its decision on a 1963 American Water Works Association investigation. The study concluded that U.S. legislators should not address the problem of foam at that time. Various state hearings in the matter had found that the industry was making significant headway toward alleviating the situation. The report also declared that none of the proposed legislation adequately addressed the situation and that forcing a change on the industry, before it was prepared to switch, would only drive up the cost of detergents. The U.S. industry's announcement of a voluntary change reinforced the report's conclusions. The British House of Commons' decision not to regulate the UK detergent industry also offered strength to the OWRCs decision.[36]

The OWRC believed that the American shift to biodegradable detergent, scheduled for 1965, would affect Ontario as well. Given the relatively small number of North American companies manufacturing detergent components, it was unlikely that the material required to produce nondegradable detergents would be available to Canadian manufacturers once U.S. manufacturers had completed the large task of converting to an ABS substitute. "It seems reasonable, therefore, not to insist upon regulation of an industry which is already heavily committed toward regulating itself," David Caverly concluded.[37] Indeed, late in 1963, Canadian manufacturers reversed their initial decision to maintain existing detergent formulations and declared that Canadian detergents would be changed to solve the problem of foam. The new detergents replaced the branched ABS surfactant with an unbranched derivative—linear alkylate sulphonate (LAS). Detergents formulated with LAS surfactants foamed much less and were readily degradable with existing sewage treatment technology.[38] Industry and government newsletters stressed the voluntary nature of the decision and the industry's responsibility in tackling the issue.[39]

By 1965, the issue of foaming appeared to be solved. OWRC attempts to influence the industry had been resisted successfully by the detergent manufacturers and they had been able to address the problem on their own terms. Despite the industry's concern about the Wentworth resolution, concentrated negative reaction to foaming materialized only at the municipal level. The provincial legislature appeared more concerned about declining Great Lakes levels than about pollution problems associated with detergent foaming. The issue was raised during the annual debate on the estimates for the Department of Energy and Resources Management in 1963 but it did not appear to concern Premier John Robarts. In the House of Commons, the possibility of diverting Great Lakes water into the United States dominated federal discussion. In pollution debates, detergent foaming generated little concern.[40]

Oddly, the OWRC did not take the opportunity presented by the Wentworth resolution to use the argument of overwhelming public concern to demand changes in detergent formulas. This stemmed from its reluctance to acknowledge the relevance of the scientifically inaccurate resolution. The press also appeared inclined to trust the scientific experts and to question the credibility of the Wentworth County Council. At this point, the general public demonstrated little interest in environmental issues. For a visible and messy problem, the issue of foaming raised relatively little public complaint in comparison with the later response to pollution problems.

Although the detergent industry had addressed the problem of foaming successfully, another issue associated with detergents soon took its place. The trouble was algae. Whether by accident or design, the Wentworth resolution had addressed the appearance of algae in the province's waters, but had tied it to detergent foaming. However, algal blooms had nothing to do with the ABS surfactant. Phosphate builders were at the root of the new problem.

Algae are rootless water plants that, like all living things, require energy and nutrients to grow. The plants get their energy from sunlight and the nutrient fuel they require from carbon, hydrogen, oxygen, nitrogen, and phosphorus. All these are available naturally to algae, with the exception of phosphorus, which therefore determines the extent of growth and is called the limiting nutrient.[41] When organic matter, including algae, dies in water, it is broken down by aerobic and anaerobic bacteria. The aerobic bacteria require oxygen to convert the material into simpler organic substances, some of which are then used for food. The more organic substance there is to decompose, the faster oxygen is consumed by the bacteria.[42] Thus, a large amount of dying and decaying algae threatens fish and other aquatic life, which require dissolved oxygen to live.

The phosphorus producing the algal blooms entered waterways from three sources: the spring runoff of manure applied to frozen fields during the winter; partially treated sewage effluent rich in the nutrient; and detergents. Sewage treatment plants could remove only the limited amount of phosphorus required in the bacterial treatment process; any amount in excess of that entered the receiving waters with the treated sewage effluent. Even before the introduction of synthetic detergents, sewage contained more of the nutrient than treatment plants could use. After the advent of the new cleaning agents, the phosphate content of sewage more than doubled, causing two to three times the amount to enter North American lakes and rivers than before the Second World War. Scientists called this rapid, human-generated enrichment of water cultural eutrophication to distinguish it from the natural, long-term process.[43]

All this phosphorus created the luxurious blooming of many algae, but particularly one called cladophora which grew in large, filamentous green clumps. In September 1964, some 800 square miles of algal bloom coated the surface of Lake Erie. At the same time, close to 43 miles of shoreline between Toronto and Presqu'ile Point were covered by accumulated cladophora. The following summer, Lake Erie and the southeast section of Lake

Ontario were again subject to extensive bloom. Algal growth interfered with recreational and commercial boating and fishing, affected water intake pipes and treatment plants, and created "obnoxious odours" when it washed up and decayed along the shoreline.[44] Many scientists attributed the growth of cladophora to cultural eutrophication.[45]

In 1964, the Canadian and American federal governments asked the International Joint Commission (IJC) to investigate the pollution of Lakes Ontario and Erie, and the international section of the St. Lawrence River. This was the fourth time the IJC had been asked to assess Great Lakes pollution since its creation under the 1909 Boundary Waters Treaty. Consisting of six commissioners, three each appointed by the federal governments of Canada and the United States, the IJC was assigned investigatory powers under the treaty. The Commission's previous pollution investigations had been limited to the Great Lakes connecting channels — the St. Mary's, Rainy, St. Clair, Detroit, and Niagara rivers.[46]

With increasing instances of algal blooms, fish kills, and oil spills, the two governments asked the IJC to examine pollution in the lakes themselves. For research such as this, the Commission supplemented its staff by seconding federal, provincial, and state civil servants, and occasionally private consultants, to serve on its technical advisory boards. All technical surveys required during the course of the investigation were carried out by government water agencies. The federal departments of Energy, Mines and Resources and of Health as well as the OWRC, contributed both personnel and facilities to the project. This served to tie personnel and research from both levels of government closely together. By December 1965 the IJC had completed its first interim report and sent it to the two governments. The report outlined the eutrophication problem and recommended that both American and Canadian federal authorities cooperate immediately with provincial and state governments to ensure maximum removal of phosphates from municipal and industrial waste being discharged into the lakes and their tributaries.[47]

The IJC report coincided with an outpouring of public concern about the pollution problem in the Great Lakes in general, and about algae in particular. Citing the Commission's findings, in February 1966 *The Globe and Mail* called for swift federal action.[48] When the House of Commons resumed sitting later that month, opposition MPs took up the cry and urged more federal spending on pollution research and control.[49] Growing concern over environmental issues reflected a shift in societal attitudes toward the natural world. By the mid-1960s, Ontarians had come to expect available and abundant outdoor recreation space. Suddenly, Great Lakes beaches, where they had raised their children or grown to adulthood themselves, were a mass of stinking algae and dying fish and no longer the beautiful recreation spots they had once been.

Letters began to flow into the OWRC from a variety of sources over the fall and winter of 1965–66. Among those expressing concern about phosphate pollution were women's groups, the United Auto Workers, and private citizens. One young writer, alarmed by the widely reported death of Lake Erie, wrote: "Why cannot Ontario, which covers half the lake's shoreline, co-operate with other border states to get tough on the sources of this sewage. Our generation will look back either with appreciation to your generation's foresight in this matter, or with disappointment at your inability to deal decisively with this important problem."[50] Such letters reflected the emergence of environmental values in the province, although at this point the concern still lacked focus.

Not surprisingly, Commission personnel reacted defensively to the criticism. OWRC general manager David Caverly scathingly attacked those he called publicity-seeking, scientifically ignorant "Johnny-come-latelies" both inside and outside the government:

They pay no attention to actual figures or to verified statistics. With their pet theories, and their preconceived notions, they belong to that *"my mind is made up, don't confuse me with the facts"* group of people who are a part of any society. The result is that they have stirred up "John Q Citizen" to the point of almost hysteria. The old pollution fighters have been pushed into the background, and our task has been made more difficult.[51]

Caverly's comments echoed the disdain he and his colleagues had shown for the Wentworth County Council. His initial reaction to the new environmental values suggests a continued belief in the superiority of scientific training and expertise. Caverly and his colleagues were also reacting to the growing changes in Ontario society, which encouraged citizens to question government pronouncements rather than quietly accept them.

Detergent manufacturers remained complacent and oblivious to the societal changes occurring around them, relying on the "real spirit of cooperation" which they maintained had developed during the detergent foaming controversy.[52] At the Canadian Council of Resource Ministers conference, "Pollution and Our Environment," held in October 1966, they argued that society would be better served by more effective sewage treatment than by any alteration to their detergent formulas. This technological "fix" would provide the most efficient elimination of nutrients at the lowest cost. It would also ensure that Canadian sanitary standards would remain high, something the industry widely predicted to be in jeopardy if formulas were drastically changed.[53] Clearly the manufacturers expected this phase of the debate to play out much like the detergent foaming stage, with the domination of their agenda and public support from their government "partners." The manufacturers did not count on the changes to Ontario society, which would make the traditional business–government relationship suspect, then impossible, before the decade was over.

As the "baby boom" generation came of age in the late 1960s, the province, along with most of the Western democracies, entered a new moral, intellectual, and political era. The U.S. civil rights movement helped raise questions about the legitimacy of a government that used force to quell peaceful demonstrations on the one hand, while proclaiming itself the protector of democracy and freedom worldwide on the other. Its actions encouraged youth across North America to assume "that if the state was recalcitrant, [peaceful] dissent was insufficient." The civil rights movement also proved the effectiveness of mass protest and gave it legitimacy in the eyes of the media and the public.[54] The protest organizations emerging in Canada during this period originated, for the most part, on university campuses. Here, a minority of radical students encouraged their more moderate cohorts to address issues of social justice, racial equality, and, late in the decade, sexual equality. They reoriented political debate and presented the agendas of the new movements to both the public and the government, in the process shifting the focus of political discourse from the traditional political parties to pressure groups. These organizations were able to rally otherwise nebulous public concern and translate it into demand for government action.[55]

These issues triggered Pollution Probe, an environmental group that emerged at the University of Toronto in February 1969. Concerned with social justice, the students were motivated by a sense of outrage at their voicelessness and by the desire to force patronizing politicians to hear their opinion. Pollution Probe's core came from the university's Department of Zoology and initially organized in response to the controversy surrounding the CBC documentary "The Air of Death." Pollution Probe soon broadened its scope. Its mandate grew to include investigating all environmental pollution, determining its effects on human health and mobilizing public opinion on specific measures.[56] According to a Probe pamphlet, the group represented a "grassroots movement with professional expertise which gives form and strength to the public concern over environmental quality" through research, education and action. "We are fighting not for an antiseptic world, but for a healthy environment. There is a difference."[57]

Several environmental activists, widely recognized as preeminent in their fields, began their work with Probe. For instance, University of Toronto zoology professor Donald Chant chaired the advisory board, which also included professors Ralph Brinkhurst, Henry Regier, John Dales, Phil Jones, and Marshall McLuhan, and broadcaster Stanley Burke. These people lent Probe legitimacy and their expertise when the organization tackled a problem falling within their purview. From the beginning, though, Probe's strength came from its student members, such as Monte Hummel, now head of the World Wildlife Fund (Canada). The students' youthful enthusiasm and idealism propelled the organization. They orchestrated Probe's publicity events, such as the mock funeral held for the "dead" Don River. They canvassed door-to-door and took every opportunity to present their message city-wide, even nationally, through the CBC and Toronto newspapers. It was to this group of energetic and dedicated young people that Chant referred when he urged "Let us heed the voice of youth."[58]

Pollution Probe had been in existence for eight months when the IJC released the *Report to the International Joint Commission on the Pollution of Lake Erie, Lake Ontario and the International Section of the St. Lawrence River* in October 1969.[59] The report recommended comprehensive phosphorus reduction for the lakes, to be achieved by an immediate lowering of the phosphorus content of detergents to the minimum practicable level. In addition, the IJC advocated cutting the nutrient content of municipal and industrial effluent discharged directly into Lake Erie and Lake Ontario by no less than 80 percent. The Commission urged both federal governments to begin research to control agricultural runoff. To avoid further nutrient loading of the already taxed waters of the Great Lakes basin, the IJC also recommended the immediate regulation of all new uses of phosphorus. The report and the possibility of restricting phosphate-based detergents received wide discussion in the press.[60]

Just prior to the release of the IJC report, the federal minister of Energy, Mines and Resources, J.J. Greene, appointed a departmental task force to investigate detergent pollution. When the report came out, the minister directed the task force to consider how to implement the IJC's recommendations on detergents. As part of its investigation, the members of the task force and OWRC representatives visited the Procter & Gamble research facilities in Cincinnati, Ohio, in December 1969. At the meeting, company spokespeople reiterated the position they had taken the month before with the minister. Although they acknowledged concern about the potential for negative publicity in connection with phosphates, they were unwilling to admit that their search for a phosphate substitute had been prompted by the eutrophication problem. Instead, Procter & Gamble spokespeople insisted that their researchers were looking for a substance to enhance product performance.[61] Naturally the government representatives were disappointed with the industry's stance. No doubt the OWRC people experienced a sense of déjà vu. As with the issue of foaming, the detergent producers refused to acknowledge a problem until they had developed their own solution.

On 23 December, the Task Force on Phosphates and Pollution from Detergents submitted its findings to the minister. It advised a multiple-stage solution to curb accelerated eutrophication. The six main recommendations echoed those of the IJC's October report, and included improved sewage treatment to be financed through amendments to the *Canadian Mortgage and Housing Corporation Act*. The task force also advised the government to issue a directive ordering replacements for phosphate builders and urged federal research into possible phosphate substitutes. Finally, the report recommended the development of a water quality plan for the Great Lakes basin which would require federal cooperation with the provinces, the United States, and the chemical industry.[62]

Before the minister could announce federal policy, however, the IJC held public hearings on the October report between 20 January and 6 February 1970. In the Great Lakes states, the Commission met at Toledo, Erie, and Rochester, while in Ontario meetings were convened in London, Hamilton, and Brockville. Many people representing industry, local citizens' groups, various agencies from local, state, provincial, and federal governments, as well as concerned individuals, presented briefs at the hearings.[63] Detergent manufacturers resisted the IJC's recommendation to replace phosphate builders in synthetic detergents. They explained that housewives expected a certain level of cleaning performance and would only use more detergent to achieve the expected results, thereby counteracting the efficacy of the reduction. As no effective phosphate substitute then existed, the best solution was improved sewage treatment facilities.[64] In contrast, Pollution Probe argued that improvements to sewage treatment facilities would take much too long to implement. It urged instead an immediate reduction in the consumption of phosphate-based detergents by the introduction of an immediate ban on their manufacture, sale, and use. To achieve this goal, Probe envisaged a two-part approach—strong consumer demand to convince industry to replace phosphates, combined with public pressure to force governments to legislate a ban on phosphate detergents. "The state of our lakes demands immediate action," Probe asserted.[65]

Probe had already begun its campaign to see both steps carried out. In the early winter, Phil Jones, a University of Toronto Civil Engineering professor, and Pollution Probe volunteers tested samples of all the major detergents and soaps for phosphorus content by weight. When Probe appeared before the IJC, the results were already complete and on 8 February it broke the story on CBC's *Weekend*. Over the next few days, the list and accompanying news release were carried in most Canadian daily newspapers. Probe urged concerned citizens to write to Prime Minister Trudeau and Premier Robarts, the federal and provincial Cabinet ministers responsible for pollution control, and their MPs and MLAs.[66] Brian Kelly, one of Probe's student leaders, appeared on CBC's *Take Thirty* on 13 February and the Larry Solway show on CHUM radio soon after. By March, Probe had received over 7000 requests for the phosphate content list and it had been reprinted and distributed across the country. John Bassett, publisher of the Toronto *Telegram*, helped Probe's campaign by supplying space for free advertisements created by Vickers and Benson, a Toronto advertising agency.[67] Probe's campaign, coinciding with action on the part of both the provincial and federal governments, helped to educate the public and keep enthusiasm high.

On 6 February, the federal minister of Energy, Mines and Resources, J.J. Greene, announced in the House of Commons that the Canada Water Bill, then being considered by a parliamentary committee, would be amended to allow the federal government to regulate the phosphate content of laundry detergents.[68] On 24 March, the coordinators of both the Ottawa and Toronto Probe branches, Phil Reilly and Peter Middleton, along with ecologist Ralph Brinkhurst and limnologist Michael Dickman, appeared before the Commons Committee on National Resources and Public Works. Probe's brief on the Canada Water Bill reflected the organization's belief that its demand for action must be supported by scientific evidence, and thus Reilly, Brinkhurst, and Dickman stressed their expertise as biologists. They emphasized the need for swift federal action on phosphates. Although admitting that more research needed to be done, Dickman and Brinkhurst insisted that the government already possessed enough information to act. They explained that advanced sewage treatment technology existed and should be installed in the Great Lakes basin as soon as possible. Brinkhurst countered industry claims that there was no viable alternative to phosphate builders by reminding the committee that similar objections had been raised over the issue of foam, and it had been resolved responsibly. "I think nothing will work faster than requiring somebody to use their ingenuity," he declared.[69]

On 9 February, the Ontario Department of Energy and Resources Management had announced that the province would introduce legislation to restrict detergent formulations gradually over five years.[70] Concerned that phosphate builders would not be reduced quickly enough, Probe submitted a ten-point brief to Premier Robarts in April. The brief called for provincial legislation limiting the maximum level of phosphorus in detergents to less than 1 percent by January 1971, rather than the graduated plan announced by the province in February.[71] Probe's worry was addressed when, after intense negotiations with the federal government, the provinces agreed that the best approach to the problem would be national phosphate restrictions listed under the *Canada Water Act*.[72] Greene acknowledged the intense federal–provincial consultation that had taken place when he introduced the nutrient loading amendment in the House of Commons. With the difficult aspect of the process over, the *Canada Water Act* quickly passed its third reading and received royal assent by the end of June. The minister announced the phosphate regulations under the act a month later. As of 1 August 1970, the phosphate content of detergents was limited to 20 percent by weight and further reduced to only 5 percent by the end of 1972.[73]

Probe cannot be given sole credit for the new provisions included in the *Canada Water Act* and the first regulations listed under its auspices. As is clear form internal Water Resources Branch memoranda, the minister's advisers had already determined that the federal government should act on the IJC report, and the provincial government had also considered action. Nevertheless, Probe helped to concentrate public concern and kept the issue before the government while the parliamentary committee considered the legislation. Probe's effective use of the news media was perhaps its greatest strength. Certainly the detergent industry felt the impact of Probe's activity. During the first five months of 1970, national sales of synthetic detergent declined by 5 percent while soap flakes and chips rose by 50 percent over the same period of 1969.[74]

In contrast to the issue of foam, the detergent industry was unable to set its own agenda when phosphates became a concern in the late 1960s. This was due, in part, to public receptiveness to the issues, reflecting a dawning wariness of big business and its influence on government, as well as a growing concern about pollution.[75] Probe focused the public debate and suggested actions that the average citizens could undertake, from writing to their MP to buying soap instead of synthetic detergent. Because of its scientific expertise, Probe's recommendations to government were reliable and allowed it to be more than just "another alarmist group." The phosphate issue captured attention in the House of Commons and the provincial legislature so that support, indeed pressure, for government initiatives emanated from that direction as well. Although they did not like criticism levelled by environmental activists, civil servants were less certain that the industry would police itself at this phase of the debate. They joined with citizen groups and urged their political bosses to take coercive, legislative action. In contrast to the detergent foaming phase, the phosphate debate was marked by a convergence of public interest, press, and government pressure, reflecting the new environmental values.

When the Wentworth County Council circulated its resolution urging the provincial government to ban foaming detergents, the issue did not engender substantial public or political support beyond the level of municipal governments. This failure can be attributed partly to the council's lack of scientific credibility, but also to the fact that societal attitudes had not yet shifted to favour environmental issues. The press accepted the assessment of OWRC personnel, which paid little regard to either the resolution or the council. Without significant media promotion, the Wentworth resolution did not garner the public support necessary to influence the provincial government.

In comparison, Pollution Probe's phosphate campaign proved to be much more effective. The group piqued public interest and support by challenging the problem-solving style of the traditional wise-use conservation experts. Pollution Probe's strength lay in its use of scientific expertise to educate the public and offer well-considered alternative solutions to those suggested by the government scientists and manufacturers. This enabled the group to mobilize the public, drawing on emerging environmental concern and focusing on specific issues. Clearly, Probe was more effective than the Wentworth County Council —so much so that the *Financial Post* concluded: "But for the most part, Probe's aims and achievements have become almost as respectable as motherhood, so drastically has public opinion changed [regarding] the need to curb pollution."[76] In fact, it was the OWRC that found itself disconnected from public opinion and unable to adjust to the emerging environmental attitudes. In response to these new values, the provincial government created a Ministry of the Environment, which, in turn, absorbed the Commission in 1972.

NOTES

I wish to thank Leanna Simpson, Sara Morrison, Chris MacLennan, and especially Gerald Killan, whose comments and criticisms helped to strengthen an earlier draft of this paper. I also thank W.J. "Jack" Christie and the anonymous readers of the *Canadian Historical Association Journal* for their input. The University of Western Ontario and the Social Sciences and Humanities Research Council of Canada provided financial support.

1. Adapted by Pollution Probe from Dr. Seuss, *The Lorax* (New York, 1971).
2. Ontario historians have examined the emergence and impact of the Algonquin wildlands League in its efforts to preserve Ontario's remaining wilderness areas. See Gerald Killan and George Warecki, "The Algonquin Wildlands League and the emergence of Environmental Politics in Ontario, 1965–1974," *Environmental History Review* 16 (Winter 1992): 1–27; also Gerald Killan, *Protected Places: A History of Ontario's Provincial Parks System* (Toronto, 1993). Stephen Bocking, "Fishing the Inland Seas: Great Lakes Research, Fisheries Management, and Environmental Policy in Ontario," *Environmental History* 2 (January 1997): 52–73, examines the impact of environmental attitudes on Great Lakes fisheries management policy.
3. Samuel P. Hays, *Conservation and the Gospel of Efficiency: The Progressive Conservation Movement in the United States, 1890–1920* (Cambridge, 1959), remains the classic interpretation of the American conservation movement which influenced its Canadian counterpart. For some of the literature on the early Canadian movement, see Peter Gillis and Thomas Roach, "The American Influence on Conservation in Canada, 1899–1911," *Journal of Forest History* 30 (October 1986): 160–72; Janet Foster, *Working for Wildlife: The Beginning of Preservation in Canada* (Toronto, 1978); Robert Craig Brown, "The Doctrine of Usefulness: Natural Resources and National Park Policy in Canada, 1887–1914," in *Canadian Parks in Perspective*, ed. J.G. Nelson (Montreal, 1970), 46–63; Richard S. Lambert with Paul Pross, *Renewing Nature's Wealth: A Centennial History of the Public Management of Lands, Forests and Wildlife in Ontario, 1763–1967* (Toronto, 1967); Killan, *Protected Places*. Very little has been written on Canadian conservation after the 1920s. In "The Conservation Revival in Southern Ontario: From Flood Control to River Valley Development, Reconstruction Conservation and Emergence of Ontario Conservation Authorities, 1929–1952," unpublished manuscript, University of Western Ontario, 1996, Sara Morrison examines the reemergence of a conservation movement during the Second World War, which she calls recon-

struction conservation. The emphasis of reconstruction conservation on employment is the major difference between it and the earlier progressive conservation. See also Bruce Mitchell and Dan Shrubsole, *Ontario Conservation Authorities: Myth and Reality* (Waterloo, ON, 1992).

4. Killan, *Protected Places*, 74–119.

5. Samuel P. Hays, "From Conservation to Environment: Environmental Politics in the United States since World War II," in *Environmental History: Critical Issues in Comparative Perspective*, ed. Kendall Bailes (New York, 1985), 198–241. Hays explores the topic in greater detail with Barbara Hays, *Beauty, Health and Permanence: Environmental Politics in the United States, 1955–1985* (Cambridge, 1987). In contrast to Hays's emphasis on change and the unique aspects of postwar environmentalism, Robert Gottlieb chooses to focus on continuity by linking the environmental movement to the earlier urban reform movement in *Forcing the Spring: The Transformation of the American Environmental Movement* (Washington, DC, 1993). A comprehensive look at the events that produced the shift in attitudes in North America and Europe is John McCormick, *The Global Environmental Movement: Reclaiming Paradise* (London, 1989).

6. Hays, "From Conservation to Environment," 214–18; Hays and Hays, *Beauty, Health and Permanence*, 21–29; McCormick, *Reclaiming Paradise*, 51–55; Ralph Luts, "Chemical Fallout: Rachel Carson's *Silent Spring*, Radioactive Fallout and the Environmental Movement," *Environmental Review* 9 (Fall 1985): 210–25.

7. Hays and Hays, *Beauty, Health and Permanence*, 531–34. See also Robert Paelke, "Environmentalism," in *Conservation and Environmentalism: An Encyclopedia*, ed. Robert Paelke (New York, 1995), 260–61.

8. William McGucken, *Biodegradable: Detergents and the Environment* (College Station, 1991), 10.

9. William McGucken, "The Canadian Federal Government, Cultural Eutrophication, and the Regulation of Detergent Phosphates, 1970," *Environmental Review* 13 (Fall/Winter 1989): 155–66.

10. Terence Kehoe, "Merchants of Pollution?: The Soap and Detergent Industry and the Fight to Restore Great Lakes Water Quality, 1965–1970," *Environmental History Review* 16 (Fall 1992): 21–46.

11. J.K. Rea, *The Prosperous Years: The Economic History of Ontario, 1930–1975* (Toronto, 1985), 14–15, 193–222. See also Doug Owram, *Born at the Right Time: A History of the Baby-Boom* (Toronto, 1996), 4.

12. Ontario Department of Economics, *Ontario: Economic and Social Aspects Survey* (Toronto, 1961), 143–54; also Rea, *The Prosperous Years*, 14–34. Regional Development Branch, Department of Treasury and Economics, *Design for Development: The Toronto-Centred Region* (Toronto, 1970), 2–4.

13. This account prefaced almost every Ontario Water Resources Commission speech given before groups such as the Ontario Municipal Association, the University Women's Club of Welland, various mining and industrial associations, the Petroleum Association, the Department of Agriculture, the Dairy Branch Field Men's Conference, the London Progress Club, the Consumers' Association, the International Labour Council, the Niagara Regional Development Council, the Engineering Institute of Canada, the Smith Falls Water Commission, the Long point (Norfolk) Ratepayers Association, and various Rotary Clubs. Ontario Archives (AO), RG 84, OWRC, Central Records, "Ontario Municipal Association," and "Public Relations: Speaking, General, 1966–67."

14. McGucken, *Biodegradable*, 12–13; also AO, RG 84, OWRC, Subject Files, "Detergents: Miscellaneous Information," David Caverly to OWRC Management Committee, 29 March 1963. See also the Water Management Committee of the Canadian Manufacturers of Chemical Specialities Association, "Detergents and the Aquatic Environment," *Pollution and Our Environment: Background Papers*, vol. 2 (Ottawa, 1966), 2–3.

15. McGucken, *Biodegradable*, 16–17. See also Tom Davey, "Eutrophication and Detergents: An Interview with P.H. Jones," *Water and Pollution Control* 106 (September 1968): 23.

16. P.H. Jones, "Does LAS Spell 'Pollution Free'?" *Water and Pollution Control* 105 (August 1967), 24; also William Ashworth, *The Late, Great Lakes: An Environmental History* (Toronto, 1986), 134–36; McGucken, *Biodegradable*, 21.

17. Jones, "Does LAS Spell 'Pollution Free'?" 24; also Ashworth, *The Late, Great Lakes*, 136.

18. Water Management Committee of the Canadian Manufacturers of Chemical Specialities Association, "Detergents and the Aquatic Environment," 4–5; McGucken, *Biodegradable*, 22–23.

19. D.F. Carrothers, "Household Detergents in Water and Sewage." AO, RG 84, OWRC, Subject Files, "Algae and Detergents."

20. Ibid., "Detergents: Miscellaneous Information," the Canadian Manufacturers of Chemical Specialities Association, "A Brief to the Ontario Water Resources Commission," 12 June 1963.

21. Hamilton *Spectator*, 8 November 1962.

22. *Wentworth County. Proceedings of the Municipal Council of the County of Wentworth for the Year 1962*, December Session, 18 December 1962 (Dundas, ON, 1962).

23. AO, RG 84, OWRC, Central Records, "Public Relations: 1968, Jan–June, General Information," OWRC memo, 10 April 1968. The Conservation Council of Ontario (CCO) was an umbrella organization founded by Francis (Frank) Kortright in 1952 for groups and individuals with an interest in conservation. It served a lobby/watch dog function. CCO Minutes, 1952–1953, vol. 1, Conservation Council of Ontario Library and Archives.

24. One editorial noted that the Germans had banned nonfoaming detergents by 1965 as well as citing OWRC findings that algal blooms were caused by detergents. *The Globe and Mail*, 3 December 1962.

25. AO, RG 84, OWRC, General Managers' Files, "Detergents: Miscellaneous Information," Thomas Beckett to William McDonnell, 21 June 1963.

26. Ibid., OWRC, Central Records, "Wentworth County Resolutions, 1963." An interesting exception was the Sarnia City Council, which chose not to endorse the resolution after Dr. Duncan Cameron, a researcher at Imperial Oil, warned them that "50 percent of all detergents is used by industries and if it was prohibited this would mean shutting down industry." Cameron suggested that endorsing the resolution would prove embarrassing to the Sarnia council. *London Free Press*, 5 February 1963.

27. One of the inquiries came from the Minister of Transport, James Auld. AO, RG 84, OWRC, Subject Files, "Detergents: Miscellaneous Information," OWRC memo to the Honourable J.A.C. Auld from David Caverly, 13 March 1962. See also ibid., Central Records, "Wentworth County Resolutions, 1963," OWRC press release, 14 December 1962.

28. Ibid., Central Records, "Wentworth County Resolutions, 1963," OWRC memo to David Caverly from F.A. Voege, 27 March 1963; also ibid., Subject Files, "Detergents: Miscellaneous Information," OWRC memo to Management Committee from David Caverly, "Re: Technical Aspects of the Recent Detergent Problem," 29 March 1963. OWRC research into algae growth began during the summer of 1958. In 1963, the Commission's Research Division confirmed phosphorus as the limiting nutrient. OWRC, *Third Annual Report, 1958* (Toronto, 1958), 66–67, and *8th Annual Report, 1963* (Toronto, 1963), 99–100.

29. AO, RG 84, OWRC, Subject Files, "Detergents: Miscellaneous Information," OWRC memo to Management Committee from David Caverly, "Re: Recent Controversy on Detergents," 29 March 1963.

30. McGucken, *Biodegradable*, 66–97. See also Kehoe, "Merchants of Pollution?" 26–27.

31. AO, RG 84, OWRC, Subject Files, "Detergents: Miscellaneous Information," "A Brief to the Ontario Water Resources Commission, Presented by the Canadian Manufacturers of Chemical Specialities Association," May 1963.

32. Ibid., "Meeting with Detergent Industry, August 14th, 1963."

33. Next to the Association's assertion, on the OWRC copy of an industry brief, that "no such situation [similar to Europe] has been created in Canada by the use of synthetic detergents," someone wrote: "We dispute this." See "A Brief to the Ontario Water Resources Commission, Presented by the Canadian Manufacturers of Chemical Specialities Association," May 1963. See also AO, RG 84, OWRC, Subject Files, "Detergents: Miscellaneous Information," "Meeting with Detergent Industry, August 14th, 1963."

34. For sample newspaper items, see *The Financial Post*, 30 March 1963; *The Globe Magazine*, 18 May 1963, reprinted in Conservation Council of Ontario, *Bulletin* 10 (May 1963): 3. Also *The Globe and Mail*, 21 June 1963.

35. AO, RG 84, OWRC, Subject Files, "Detergents: Miscellaneous Information," Beckett to McDonnell, 21 June 1963.

36. Ibid., OWRC, Central Records, "Wentworth County Resolutions, 1963," David Caverly to Wentworth County Council, 21 May 1964.

37. Ibid.

38. Jones, "Does LAS Spell 'Pollution Free'?" 24.

39. Canadian Institute on Pollution Control, *Newsletter* (1964): 19; AO, RG 84, OWRC, Central Records, "Resource Ministers Council, 1962," Pollution and Our Environment newsletter, *Resources* 2 (December 1965). See also "Detergents Made Biodegradable," *Water and Pollution Control* 104 (February 1966): 27; and Water Management Committee of the Canadian Manufacturers of Chemical Specialities Association, "Detergents and the Aquatic Environment," 4–5.

40. For example, see Ontario. Ontario Legislature. *Debates*, 19 December 1962, 473; 11 March 1963, 1576–87; 31 January 1964, 347-58; 24 February 1964, 883; 21 April 1964, 2253–326; 18 March 1965. A good gauge of the pollution debate at the federal level is the annual proposal for an amendment to the *Criminal Code* to make water pollution nuisance punishable under the *Criminal Code*. W.L. Herridge, NDP member for Kootenay West, first proposed the amendment in 1961. He made the proposal annually between 1961 and 1968 while he sat in the House. For sample debates, see Canada. House of Commons. *Debates*, 2 June 1961, 5793–801; 13 February 1962, 822–27; 1 February 1963, 3366–75; 8 July 1964, 1943–50. Select newspaper stories and editorials on general pollution issues: Toronto *Telegram Magazine*, 31 August 1963; Toronto *Telegram*, 6 May 1964; *Simcoe Reformer*, 1 May 1964; *The Globe and Mail*, 5, 6, 12 and 20 May 1964 and *Globe Magazine*, 13 June 1964; *The Montreal Star*, 13 and 22 May 1964; *Windsor Star*, 5 May 1964; and *Toronto Star Weekly*, 13 June 1964.

41. Davey, "Eutrophication and Detergents," 22–25; J.M. Appleton, "'Fertility Pollution': The Rapidly Increasing Problem," *Water and Pollution Control* 106 (June 1968): 26–27 and 44; and Ashworth, *The Late, Great Lakes*, 129–36.

42. Gilbert Masters, *Introduction to Environmental Engineering and Science* (Englewood Cliffs, NJ, 1991), 116–18; also Ashworth, *The Late, Great Lakes*, 126.

43. Davey, "Eutrophication and Detergents," 22–25; Appleton, "'Fertility Pollution,'" 26–27 and 44; also Jones, "Does LAS Spell 'Pollution Free'?" 24–25. See also Masters, *Introduction to Environmental Engineering and Science*, 134–46.

44. International Joint Commission (IJC), *Interim Report of the International Joint Commission United States and Canada on the Pollution of Lake Erie, Lake Ontario and the International Section of the St. Lawrence River* (Ottawa, 1965), 3–5. The OWRC had been investigating the appearance of cladophora since 1958, the year of the first significant bloom after the Commission's creation. See OWRC, *Third Annual Report, 1958*, 66–67, and annual reports through to the 1970s; also OWRC, *A Report on Algae Cladophora* (Toronto, 1958); OWRC, *Cladophora Investigations — 1959 — A Report of Observation on the Nature and Control of Excessive Growth of Cladophora sp. in Lake Ontario* (Toronto, 1959); and Duncan McLarty, *Cladophora Investigations — 1960 — A Report of Observation on the Nature and Control of Excessive Growth of Cladophora sp. in Lake Ontario and Lake Erie* (Toronto, 1960). Until the late 1960s, Commission investigations focused on controlling algae through the application of chemical algicides and through mechanical means of collecting inshore growth.

45. IJC, *Interim Report, 1965*, 6. Eutrophication is a gradual, natural process whereby organic wastes wash into a lake, decompose, and consume oxygen.

46. The IJC also had quasi-judicial powers under the treaty, being the arbiter of boundary water diversion. For its earlier pollution findings, see IJC, *Final Report on the Pollution of Boundary Waters* (Ottawa, 1918); *Final Report on the Pollution of Great Lakes Connecting Channels* (Ottawa, 1951); *Report of the International Joint Commission United States and Canada on the Pollution of Rainy River and the Lake of the Woods* (Ottawa, 1965).

47. IJC, *Interim Report, 1965*, 16. The report also recommended that the construction of combined sanitary and storm sewers be prohibited and that the process of separating combined sewers then in existence be started. During heavy rainfall or spring runoff, combined sewers often outstripped treatment facility capacity and spilled untreated effluent into the lakes and rivers; increasing the phosphorus load and risking bacterial contamination of the receiving waters.

48. *The Globe and Mail*, 3 February 1966. The *Toronto Star* had raised the issue several years previously (3 February 1962).

49. Canada. House of Commons. *Debates*, 8 February 1966, 934–35.

50. AO, RG 84, OWRC, Central Records, "Great Lakes: Public Enquiries, 1964–76," Greg McConnell to Premier John Robarts, 24 January 1966. Other letters in the file include: Ora Patterson, Hamilton Local Council of Women to OWRC, 30 December 1965; Fred Palmer to OWRC, 28 December 1965; George Burt, Canadian Director, Canadian Region, UAW to Prime Minister Lester B. Pearson and Premier John Robarts, 23 February 1966. See also ibid., "Public Relations Information, 1966."

51. D.S. Caverly, "What Are We Doing About Pollution?" *Water and Pollution Control* 104 (September 1966): 50. Emphasised text is Caverly's. For examples, see AO, RG 84, OWRC, Central Records, "Public Relations Information, 1966," OWRC to Pierre Berton and Charles Templeton, 12 May 1966; "Public Relations — Public Speaking, D.S. Caverly," Caverly address to CCO, 16 May 1966; "Public Relations, 1966," OWRC press release, 26 May 1966; "Public Relations, 1967," OWRC press release, 20 March 1967.

52. Water Management Committee of the Canadian Manufacturers of Chemical Specialities Association, "Detergent and the Aquatic Environment," 1–11.

53. Canadian Council of Resource Ministers, *Proceedings: Pollution and Our Environment* (Ottawa, 1966), 151–72.

54. Owram, *Born at the Right Time*, 167. See also A.K. McDougall, *John P. Robarts: His Life and Government* (Toronto, 1986), 205–208. Lutts, "Chemical Fallout," links the American environmental movement to increasing public cynicism and wariness of scientific experts.

55. Owram, *Born at the Right Time*, 216–47. See also A. Paul Pross, *Group Politics and Public Policy*, 2nd ed. (Toronto, 1992), 1–17.

56. Interview with Donald Chant, Toronto, 5 February 1997. Pollution Probe Foundation Library and Archives, "'Air of Death' Pollution Probe Brief to CRTC," 5 March 1969. Also see Donald Chant, "Pollution Probe: Fighting the Polluters with Their Own Weapons," *Science Forum* 14, 3 (April 1970): 19–22; and AO, F1058, Pollution Probe Foundation Papers, MU 7328, "Pollution Probe History," n.d. In response to ongoing complaints about fluoride pollution in Port Maitland and Dunnville, and the CBC program, the provincial government appointed a three-person committee to study the problem. The report criticized the producers of the CBC program for exaggerating, even falsifying, some of the evidence of fluoride poisoning. George E. Hall, W.C. Winegard and Alex McKinney, *Report of the Committee Appointed to Inquire into and Report upon the Pollution of Air, Soil, and Water in the Townships of Dunn, Moulton, and Sherbrooke, Haldimand County* (Toronto, 1968).

57. AO, F1058, Pollution Probe Foundation Papers, MU 7328, "Aims, Objectives, Policies," n.d.

58. Interview with Donald Chant, Toronto, 5 February 1997. Donald Chant, *Pollution Probe* (Toronto, 1970), v; also AO, F1058, Pollution Probe Foundation Papers, MU 7328, "Advisory Board," n.d. For the Don River funeral, see *Toronto Star*, 17 and 18 November 1969; *Toronto Telegram*, 17 November 1969; *The Globe and Mail*, 17 November 1969; University of Toronto *Varsity*, 19 November 1969.

59. The International Lake Erie and Lake Ontario–St. Lawrence River Water Pollution Boards, *Report to the International Joint Commission on the Pollution of Lake Erie, Lake Ontario and the International Section of the St. Lawrence River* (Ottawa, 1969).

60. Ibid., 10–11. Also see Canada. National Archives (NA), RG 89, Water Resources Branch, Vol. 509, File 7875-2, Pt. 1, "Report of the Task Force on Phosphates and Pollution from Detergents," 23 December 1969.

61. Ibid., Memo to A.T. Davidson, ADM (Water) Department of Energy and Resources Management from A.T. Prince, Director, Inland Waters Branch, 10 December 1969. See also McGucken, "The Canadian Federal Government," 160–61.

62. NA, RG 89, Water Resources Branch, Vol. 509, File 7875-2, Pt. 1, "Report of the Task Force on Phosphates and Pollution from Detergents," 23 December 1969.

63. See IJC, Library and Archives, Docket 83-2-4: 1–6. Also see the Hamilton *Spectator*, 3 February 1970.

64. IJC, Library and Archives, Docket 83-2-4: 2, "Briefs: Erie," Dr. Frank H. Healey, 20 January 1970 and W.R. Chase, 20 January 1970; also Docket 83-2-4: 5, "Briefs: Hamilton," Alan Rae, 2 February 1970 and John Dixon, 2 February 1970. The condescending tone of these briefs angered several housewives present, who indicated that they were more interested in the future of the environment than in how white they get their family's laundry. See the Hamilton *Spectator*, 3 February 1970. CCO noted: "Any current emphasis upon 'whiteness' appears to originate from industry-sponsored advertising campaigns, and informed housewives have left no doubt that they would be willing to sacrifice both some cost savings and some 'whiteness' to stem the deterioration of our waters." IJC, Library and Archives, Docket 83-2-4: 5, "Briefs: Hamilton," the Conservation Council of Ontario, 2 February 1970.

65. Ibid., "Briefs: Hamilton," Pollution Probe, 2 February 1970. Other environmental groups that presented briefs at Hamilton included: Bryan Kingdon for CHOP—Clear Hamilton of Pollution; Stewart Hilts for Pollution Probe, London; Committee of a Thousand; and the CCO. These dealt with pollution more broadly.

66. *Toronto Daily Star*, the Toronto *Telegram*, and the Hamilton *Spectator*, 9 February 1970; *The Globe and Mail*, 10 February 1970.

67. AO, F1058, Pollution Probe Foundation Papers, MU 7346, "Probe Newsletter 1969–1972," *Probe Newsletter* 2 (31 March 1970). See Chant, "Pollution Probe," 20–21, and *Business Week*, 8 August 1970. For the press release, see Pollution Probe Foundation Papers, MU 7346, "Press Releases, 1970," Probe press release, 9 February 1970. It is probably no coincidence that Probe's tactics closely mirrored those of the Algonquin Wildlands League, whose leader, Douglas Pimlott was also a biology professor in the Department of Zoology at the University of Toronto. See Killan, *Protected Places*, 155–204.

68. Canada. House of Commons, *Debates*, 6 February 1970, 3293–95.

69. Canada. House of Commons, Committee on National Resources and Public Works, *Standing Committee on National Resources and Public Works, Minutes of Proceedings and Evidence* (Ottawa, 1970), 14:1–14:47.

70. The Toronto *Telegram*, 10 February 1970.

71. AO, F1058, Pollution Probe Foundation Papers, MU 7346, "Probe Newsletter 1969–1972," *Probe Newsletter* 2 (31 March 1970): n. 3, 3–5.

72. OWRC disquiet over the initial provisions of the Canada Water Bill stemmed from concern about duplication of programs, the fight for a limited number of trained water resource personnel and the federal proposal to adopt river basin organization rather than the regional approach favoured by Ontario. These concerns were addressed during the amending process. See AO, RG 84, OWRC, Central Records, "Legal Acts, Canada Water Act, Jan-June, 1970," Minutes of meeting held in Quebec City, 27 January 1970; OWRC memo, 28 January 1970; and OWRC memo, 30 April 1970.

73. NA, RG 89, Water Resources Branch, vol. 52, File 7709-1-2, "Canadian Initiatives Concerning the Eutrophication of the Lower Great Lakes," n.d., 1–2. See also ibid., ACC 88-89/059, Box 24, File 7354-1, Pt. 5, "Phosphorus Concentration Control Regulations"; and AO, F1058, Pollution Probe Foundation Papers, MU 7346, "Probe Newsletter, 1969–1972," *Probe Newsletter* 2, no. 3. See also McGucken, "The Canadian Federal Government," 163.

74. NA, RG 89, Water Resources Branch, ACC 88-89/059, Box 24, File 7354-1, vol. 6. Memo to J.P. Bruce, Dir. Canadian Centre for Inland Waters, from T.R. Lee, 3 September 1970.

75. By March 1970, 91 percent of Ontarians polled had heard about pollution; 78 percent believed the situation was "very serious," while a further 19 percent believed it "fairly serious."

Canadian Institute of Public Opinion, *The Gallup Report: Canada's Only National Opinion Poll with Publicly Recorded Accuracy* (Toronto, 25 March 1970). In December 1970, 65 percent of Canadians polled wished to see the government devote resources to reducing air and water pollution, while the second-place option, reducing unemployment, received the support of 59 percent. Canadian Institute of Public Opinion, *The Gallup Report* (2 December 1970).

76. *Financial Post*, 16 October 1971.

Jean Lesage (centre) in victory pose following his election as
provincial Liberal leader at the Liberal party convention in
Quebec, 1958.

438

THE YEARS 1960–66 represented an era of profound change in Quebec that has come to be known as the Quiet Revolution. The provincial government intervened in the economic, social, and cultural life of the province to a greater extent than ever before. It nationalized the hydroelectric industry, took control of and restructured the educational system, reformed the civil service, and instituted a new labour code. In "The Quiet Revolution: A Turning Point in Quebec History," historian Jacques Rouillard provides an understanding of the roots, nature, and impact of this "turning point in Quebec history." He argues that the roots of the Quiet Revolution lay in the economic changes that Quebec experienced since the turn of the century as it became a predominantly urban and industrial society. Other factors contributing to the change included the impact of the liberation of "oppressed people" following the Second World War, as well as the social and ideological upheaval of the 1950s led by a rising militant middle class. He identifies the changes introduced by the Quebec Liberal government of Jean Lesage after its victory in June 1960, and shows how these fostered a neo-nationalism that challenged Canadian federalism. Ultimately these changes led to the rise and electoral victory of the Parti Québécois, a political party committed to Quebec independence.

The heightened Quebec nationalism led to a series of laws passed by Quebec governments to protect and strengthen the French language in the province. Language has always been a significant and controversial aspect of English-Canadian and French-Canadian relations. But it became an even more pressing issue after the 1960s, as Quebec became a more secular and more urbanized industrial society. Since 1960, a succession of Quebec governments have passed controversial language legislation. Richard Jones discusses these bills and their implications in "Politics and the Reinforcement of the French Language in Canada and Quebec, 1960–1986."

For an overview of Quebec in the last half-century, see Kenneth McRoberts, *Quebec: Social Change and Political Crisis*, 3rd ed. (Toronto: McClelland and Stewart, 1988), and for the current period, his *Misconceiving Canada: The Struggle for National Unity* (Toronto: Oxford University Press, 1997). In French, see Y. Belanger, R. Comeau, and C. Metivier, *La Revolution tranquille, 40 ans plus tard: Un bilan* (Montreal: VCB Éditeur, 2000). For the English-Canadian viewpoint, see J.L. Granatstein and K. McNaught, eds., *English Canada Speaks Out* (Toronto: Doubleday, 1991). Other histories include Susan Mann Trofimenkoff, *The Dream of Nation: A Social and Intellectual History of Quebec* (Toronto: Gage, 1982), chs. 17–20, and Paul-André Linteau, René Durocher, Jean-Claude Robert, and François Ricard, *Histoire du Québec contemporain*, vol. 2, *Le Québec depuis 1930* (Montréal: Boréal, 1986). *Quebec since 1945: Selected Readings*, ed. M. Behiels (Toronto: Copp Clark Pitman, 1987) contains useful articles and documents, as does Hubert Guidon, Roberta Hamilton, and John McMullan, eds., *Tradition, Modernity, and Nationhood: Essays on Quebec Society* (Toronto: University of Toronto Press, 1988). On the important topic of Quebec nationalism, see Ramsay Cook, *Canada, Quebec and the Uses of Nationalism*, 2nd ed. (Toronto: McClelland and Stewart, 1995). Alain-G. Gagnon, ed., *Quebec, State and Society*, 2nd ed. (Scarborough, ON: Nelson, 1993), and Guy LaForest, *Trudeau and the End of a Canadian Dream*, trans. Paul Leduc Browne and Michelle Weinroth (Montreal/Kingston: McGill-Queen's University

Press, 1995) contain valuable essays on Quebec and Canada. For one historian's view after interviews with a number of historians, politicians, and contemporary commentators, see Robert Bothwell, *Canada and Quebec: One Country, Two Histories* (Vancouver: University of British Columbia Press, 1995).

On the Duplessis era, see Conrad Black, *Duplessis* (Toronto: McClelland and Stewart, 1977), and Richard Jones's brief overview in *Duplessis and the Union Nationale Administration*, Canadian Historical Association, Historical Booklet no. 25 (Ottawa: CHA, 1983). The opposition to Premier Maurice Duplessis in the late 1940s and 1950s is analyzed in M. Behiels, *Prelude to Quebec's Quiet Revolution: Liberalism versus Neo-Nationalism, 1945–1960* (Montreal/Kingston: McGill-Queen's University Press, 1985).

For an overview of the Quiet Revolution, see Dale C. Thomson, *Jean Lesage and the Quiet Revolution* (Toronto: Macmillan, 1984), and articles by Ramsay Cook in his collection *Canada, Quebec, and the Uses of Nationalism*, 2nd ed. (cited above). On the Parti Québécois, see Graham Fraser, *PQ: René Lévesque and the Parti Québécois in Power* (Toronto: Macmillan, 1985). Peter Desbarats's *René* (Toronto: McClelland and Stewart, 1976) reviews the life of the founder of the Parti Québécois. See also Lévesque's *Memoirs* (Toronto: McClelland and Stewart, 1986). On Pierre Elliott Trudeau, see Richard Gwyn, *The Northern Magus* (Toronto: McClelland and Stewart, 1980), and Stephen Clarkson and Christina McCall, *Trudeau and Our Times*, vol. 1, *The Magnificent Obsession* (Toronto: McClelland and Stewart, 1990), and vol. 2, *The Heroic Delusion* (Toronto: McClelland and Stewart, 1994). The October Crisis of 1970 is discussed in Francis Simard, *Talking It Out: The October Crisis from Inside*, trans. David Homel (Montreal: Guernica, 1987).

Edward McWhinney analyzes the early stages of the constitutional crisis in *Quebec and the Constitution, 1960–1978* (Toronto: University of Toronto Press, 1979), and in his *Canada and the Constitution, 1979–1982: Patriation and the Charter of Rights* (Toronto: University of Toronto Press, 1982). On the post-1982 period, see Alan Cairns, *Charter versus Federalism: The Dilemmas of Constitutional Reform* (Montreal/Kingston: McGill-Queen's University Press, 1992). The aftermath of the first Quebec referendum and the patriation of the *BNA Act* are discussed in *And No One Cheered: Federalism, Democracy and the Constitution Act*, ed. Keith Banting and Richard Simeon (Toronto: Methuen, 1983). Philosopher Charles Taylor proposes an original analysis of French–English relations in Guy LaForest, ed., *Reconciling the Solitudes: Essays on Canadian Federalism and Nationalism* (Montreal/Kingston: McGill-Queen's University Press, 1993).

Among the many publications bearing on Meech Lake are Michael Behiels, ed., *The Meech Lake Primer: Conflicting Views of the 1987 Constitutional Accord* (Ottawa: University of Ottawa Press, 1989); Andrew Cohen, *A Deal Undone: The Making and Breaking of the Meech Lake Accord* (Vancouver: Douglas and McIntyre, 1990); P. Fournier, *A Meech Lake Post-Mortem: Is Quebec Sovereignty Inevitable?* trans. S. Fischman (Montreal/ Kingston: McGill-Queen's University Press, 1991); and R.L. Watts and D.M. Brown, *Options for a New Canada* (Toronto: University of Toronto Press, 1991). Susan Delcourt's *United We Fall: The Crisis of Democracy in Canada* (Toronto: Viking, 1993) looks at the aftermath of the referendum on the Charlottetown Accord in 1992. John F. Conway's *Debts to Pay: English Canada and Quebec from the Conquest to the Referendum*, 2nd ed. (Toronto: James Lorimer, 1996) includes a chapter on the second Quebec referendum of 1995. Dominique Clift has translated the memoirs of Lucien Bouchard as *Lucien Bouchard, On the Record* (Toronto: Stoddart, 1994).

Analyses of the language question include Eric Waddell, "State, Language and Society: The Vicissitudes of French in Quebec and Canada," in *The Politics of Gender, Ethnicity and*

Language in Canada, ed. Alan Cairns and Cynthia Williams (Toronto: University of Toronto Press, 1986), pp. 67–110; Michel Plourde, *La politique linguistique du Québec, 1977–1987* (Québec: Éditions IQRC, 1988); Marc V. Levine, *The Reconquest of Montreal: Language Policy and Social Change in a Bilingual City* (Philadelphia: Temple University Press, 1990); and Richard Joy, *Canada's Official Languages* (Toronto: University of Toronto Press, 1992).

440

Two recent interpretative articles are Léon Dion, "The Mystery of Quebec," *Daedalus* 117, 4 (Fall 1988): 283–318, and Keith G. Banting, "If Quebec Separates: Restructuring North America," in *The Collapse of Canada?*, ed. R. Kent Weaver (Washington: Brookings Institution, 1992), pp. 159–78.

Article Thirty

The Quiet Revolution: A Turning Point in Quebec History

Jacques Rouillard

In the collective imagination of Quebec francophones, the Quiet Revolution that began with the election of the Quebec Liberal party in 1960 marked a distinct break in the evolution of their society. It is seen as the end of the "great darkness" and the beginning of Quebec's modernization.[1] Francophone society, characterized until then by its conservatism, its basic rural character, and the strong influence of the Catholic Church, thus came to share the values and aspirations of North American urban, industrialized society. The Quebec francophone was thus to be brutally awakened and thrust into the twentieth century later than the surrounding anglophone world. This interpretation, much questioned but still largely dominant,[2] was put forth by a group of intellectuals who fought for the transformation of Quebec society in the 1950s. Their goals, according to them, were finally fulfilled in the 1960s.

The expression "Quiet Revolution" seems to have been used for the first time in an article in the *Montreal Star* or *The Globe and Mail* to characterize the rapid changes taking place in Quebec in the beginning of the 1960s. The political label was exaggerated, but it quickly caught on to identify the period. Led by Jean Lesage, the Liberal party that launched the Quiet Revolution in 1960 succeeded Maurice Duplessis's Union Nationale, which had governed the province since 1936 (except for the period 1939–44). The Liberal party was reelected in 1962, but defeated in 1966 by the Union Nationale.

Historians and political scientists sometimes use the expression "Quiet Revolution" to characterize the transformations of the 1970s as well the 1960s. In its literal sense, however, it applied only to the first years of the 1960s, even if the reforms continued in the same direction in later years—at a slower pace.

There is no doubt that Quebec underwent a rapid and deep evolution during these years. To understand the true meaning of this evolution, this article begins with a brief

Source: "The Quiet Revolution: A Turning Point in Quebec History" by Jacques Rouillard. Printed by permission of the author.

examination of pre-1960 Quebec. Subsequently, I identify the factors that initiated the Quiet Revolution and later on discuss the main changes that took place during these upheavals.

Quebec Society before 1960

Contrary to what the architects of the Quiet Revolution and many academics believed, Quebec before the 1960s was hardly a monolith in either ideological or social terms.[3] From the beginning of the twentieth century, Quebec's conservatism was counterbalanced by a vigorous liberal trend supported by both the French and English business communities, international labour unions, politicians, and the political press. The big Montreal dailies (*La Presse, La Patrie, Le Canada*) and the Quebec *Le Soleil*, all close to the Liberal party, took it upon themselves to spread the liberal ideology. The Liberal party, dominant both federally and provincially on the Quebec political scene from 1896 to 1936, adopted policies in Quebec that were largely similar to those of the governments in other Canadian provinces. Fully at home in the democratic system, the provincial Liberal party worked hard for industrial development and reserved a marginal role for the state.

Unlike most other Canadian provinces, Quebec had to cope with the strong influence of a Catholic Church that was quick to defend its hold on the system of public education and social services (hospitals, hospices, orphanages, and so forth). It was under Church pressure, for example, that the government abolished the Ministry of Education in 1875 and withdrew plans to restore it in 1899 and 1906. It was also to avoid a quarrel with the Church that the government failed to adopt a compulsory education law until 1943, much later than other Canadian provinces. In sum, the reluctance of the Quebec government to adopt social measures and reform the system of education before the 1930s reflected both its liberal ideology (individual responsibility and fear of state intervention) as well as the desire of the Church to safeguard its authority in these sectors.

On the other hand, the Liberal administration, directed by Adelard Godbout, that led the province from 1939 to 1944, adopted a neoliberal posture and initiated a range of measures that required a good deal of state intervention.[4] It created a Council of Economic Orientation to plan postwar reconstruction and nationalized the private electrical utilities companies in Montreal. Scorning clerical opposition, it extended the right to vote to women and ushered in compulsory education (up to fourteen years of age). As well, it agreed to participate in the unemployment insurance and family allowance programs proposed by the federal government. The Liberal government was defeated by the Union Nationale in 1944 as a result of the conscription crisis. Once in opposition, the Liberal party in the 1950s continued nevertheless to stress a neoliberal view of the role of the state.

The Catholic Church represented a considerable social force in Quebec society. In 1961, 88 percent of the Quebec population and 99 percent of francophones were Catholics — the vast majority were practising Catholics. Since the nineteenth century the Church had been able to depend on its vast number of priests, monks, and nuns to establish an imposing network of social control. Not only did it make its influence felt in the educational system and social services, but it was involved as well in the colonization and cooperative movements. To avoid "dechristianization" of the urban masses as had occurred in Europe, the Church, at the beginning of the twentieth century, set up the Catholic Action Movement. These organizations, extremely influential up to the 1950s, were directed by Catholic laity but functioned with the assistance of a chaplain. The range of their activities was vast: students, youth, worker unions, farmers, families, women, leisure activities, among others. To complement such efforts, the Church also published daily newspapers: *L'Action catholique*, founded in Quebec City in 1907, and *Le Droit* in Ottawa/Hull in 1912. *Le Devoir* was also set up in Montreal in 1910 by Henri Bourassa with the same purpose of diffusing the clerical message.

In the publications that it supported and throughout the educational system, the Church spread a very conservative interpretation of the Christian message. We might characterize this message as clerico-conservative, a soft version of the ultramontane ideological current.[5] First, moral and religious values must closely guide the life of both individuals and groups, and the Church felt obliged to specify in detail what these values were. Influenced by French counterrevolutionary thinkers, clerico-conservatism endorsed a social vision based on authority and order. As one might suspect, ideas of individual liberty or social equality were less welcome. Moreover, as its conception of society remained strongly hierarchical, the Church distrusted political systems that made governments dependent on popular sovereignty. The masses, argued *L'Action catholique* in 1917, could not distinguish truth from error; this was the role of the elite.[6] Besides, the Church believed in its superiority over the state because it received its power directly from God; civil society's power was indirect. Its insistence of its priority role over the state in education, health, and welfare is understandable in this light. Lastly, agriculture was valued over industry because it was believed to favour the development of moral qualities. Obviously, these principles fly in the face of liberal ideological trends, which we will analyze later.

The Catholic Church saw in the Great Depression of the 1930s an opportunity to reinforce its influence over society by stressing its hold over the Quebec government.[7] The economic crisis weakened the Liberal party, in power since the end of the nineteenth century. As in many countries touched by the depression, criticisms of economic liberalism and parliamentary democracy became sharper and the population, ravaged by unemployment, was receptive to deeper changes in political direction. In 1933 the clerics and Catholic laity mapped out a program of social reconstruction fuelled by ideological conservatism. Denouncing both communism and the abuses of capitalism, it proposed reforming the social order through rural restoration, corporatism, and the adoption of some social measures by the Quebec government. These ideas inspired the program of a new party, the Union Nationale, born in 1935 and led by Maurice Duplessis. His decisive electoral victory the following year inaugurated a long regime whose policies reflected its conservative origins.

During its nineteen years in power (1936–39, 1944–60), the Union Nationale government emphasized the values of order and respect for authority and the law. Duplessis was authoritarian in his personal style and truly believed in the primordial role of elites in society as well as the importance of the leader.[8] With little regard for democratic principles, he was thus hardly troubled by the extensive practice of electoral patronage during his administration. And not much more concerned by civil liberties, he assented readily, for example, to Cardinal Villeneuve's request to pass the Padlock Law in 1937. The law forbade communist literature and permitted closure of places where communist activities were suspected.

Duplessis's relations with the Catholic bishops were much warmer than those of former Liberal premiers; he strove to live up to episcopal expectations. During his mandates, clerical authority grew at the expense of the state in the realms of health care and public education. In 1945, for example, Duplessis agreed that authority over curriculum and personnel in specialized schools (arts, crafts, engineering, and business), until then under government jurisdiction, should be handed over to the Church. Former Liberal governments had consistently opposed this change.

The Duplessis administration also gave special attention to agriculture — the "basic industry" — which was seen as a source of economic and social stability. It introduced two important measures to help the farmer: low-interest agricultural credit and the extension of rural electrification. These policies significantly increased rural electoral support for the party. The priority given to agriculture did not mean that Duplessis scorned big business. On the contrary, particularly in the postwar era, he sought to develop industry by showing himself friendly to foreign investment. He maintained excellent relations with the francophone and anglophone business communities, who appreciated his social conservatism, his faith in private enterprise, and his desire to minimize the role of the state. Big business was delighted with Duplessis's firm commitment to balanced budgets, a commitment that kept Quebec's per capita debt the lowest of all Canadian provinces during the 1950s.

Duplessis's noninterventionist economic policy pleased businesspeople, while his passivity in education, health, and welfare earned the favour of the Catholic clergy. These two social forces joined to reinforce Duplessis's basic "laissez-faire" orientation. Consequently, Quebec lagged behind the rest of North American society in the process of political modernization. It was this backwardness that the architects of the Quiet Revolution attempted to address, counting on the Quebec government to play a mainspring role.

The Sources of the Quiet Revolution

The profound social changes arising from the Quiet Revolution were not spontaneous. Instead they were part of a long, historical process accelerated by the Second World War. Let us examine several of the factors that combined to speed up this process.

The origins of the Quiet Revolution are often explained by economic factors. Francophone Quebec had changed from a rural to an industrialized and urban society, thanks to the industrial development connected to World War II and the expansion of the 1950s. The clerical-conservative ideology that had suited a rural society became irrelevant in an industrial setting. Contradictions arose between the political and social institutions related to the conservative ideology and the forces emanating from the industrial world. The Quiet Revolution thus consisted of adapting institutions to the necessities of modern life.

However, such an analysis overemphasizes the rural character of the francophone population before the Second World War. Statistics speak for themselves. Since the beginnings of the nineteenth century, the level of urbanization of francophone Quebec has been higher than that of Canada as a whole (towns of 10 000 and over). In 1931, for example, 39 percent of Quebec francophones lived in a city (10 000 people and more), as opposed to 37 percent for other Canadians.[9] In Montreal — until the 1960s, the commercial, industrial, and financial metropolis of Canada — francophones made up more than 60 percent of the population since the end of the nineteenth century. Moreover, the francophone presence made itself strongly felt in the province's manufacturing industries, where they made up 70 percent of the manufacturing industries workforce in 1931.[10] Moving to the cities and joining the working class at a rapid pace, francophones, therefore, were exposed to the influences of the industrial world long before the 1940s and 1950s. Their society, far from being monolithic, was quite diversified in its social stratification and its ideological setting.

443

The trend of francophone urbanization accelerated with the rapid surge of industrialization beginning with the Second World War: the percentage of their population in towns of 10 000 inhabitants and over rose from 40 to 58 between 1941 and 1961.[11] The rise of industries also produced a large expansion of salaried workers among them. Socio-clerical control became more difficult in an urban milieu because of the absence of local community ties. In any case, traditional clerical thought offered only unsuitable solutions to problems coming from an urban-industrialized society: mixed marriages, pressure on married women to join the workforce, exploitation in the work place, school curriculum revision, extension of social services, and so forth.[12] Furthermore, North American influences made themselves felt with greater force through the rise of mass media — daily newspapers, movies, radio, and television. All these factors reversed a trend among religious vocations, which grew less rapidly than the Catholic population in the 1950s. As the clergy started to lack religious personnel to fulfill the needs in education and social services, more and more laypeople were hired, weakening the religious fabric. Among some Catholic intellectuals appeared also an influential trend to reduce the role of the clergy and favour the secularization of social institutions.

Moreover, rapid industrialization also altered the structure of francophone society. The rise of the service economy generated a new social category: a middle class composed of public sector employees (white-collar workers, intellectuals, and administrators) and of middle management working in private enterprises (technicians, professionals, and managers). The first group saw state expansion as a means to increase their control over society, while the second group was frustrated to find their climb to upper levels blocked by anglophones.[13] In addition, organized labour, which saw its membership more than double between 1941 and 1961, became a persistent force of opposition to the Duplessis government. During the 1950s, unions called for state intervention and agitated for reforms that were finally introduced during the Quiet Revolution.[14] The economic slowdown at the end of the 1950s also made French businessmen more receptive to a wider state role. Business associations urged reform of the education system and became receptive to the idea of state economic planning.[15] Thus, dissatisfaction with Duplessis's conservatism and openness to neoliberal reforms marked many social circles.

This brings us to a third, ideologically based, explanation for the Quiet Revolution. The Second World War, in which democratic countries triumphed over authoritarian regimes, reinvigorated Western liberalism and discredited right-wing ideologies (fascism, nazism, corporatism). It reinforced values of liberty, individualism, and materialism and put conservative groups on the defensive. It is significant that during the postwar period many Western countries and the United Nations (1948) adopted charters of individual rights. This international trend influenced a group of young and committed Catholic intellectuals who wanted to reconcile Catholicism and liberalism. Inspired by the French "left-wing Catholics," they diffused their views through the Montreal daily newspaper *Le Devoir* and other influential periodicals (*Cité Libre, L'Action nationale, Vrai, Liberté*). Among them, André Laurendeau, Maurice Lamontagne, Gérard Pelletier, Jacques Hébert, Claude Ryan, and Pierre Elliott Trudeau played important roles in politics in the 1960s and 1970s. Even if they insisted on their devout Catholicism, they rejected all forms of clericalism and stressed the role of laypeople in the Catholic faith. Proclaiming the priority of the human being in society, they hoped to enlarge the spirit of freedom and strengthen democratic values.[16] They also favoured the secularization of public institutions and viewed state intervention positively, especially in education and social services. Their ideas paved the way for the reforms initiated during the Quiet Revolution.

As we will see, a new nationalism flourished in the 1960s, focusing on Quebec's government and territory. It appealed to francophones in part because English Canadians had traditionally resisted linguistic equality outside of Quebec and federal government institutions. Since the beginning of the twentieth century, French Canadians fought for the right to use their own language in Parliament, the courts, and public schools throughout Canada. The abolition of French Catholic schools in the western provinces and in Ontario in the early twentieth century aroused vigorous protest in Quebec. As a result, in the 1920s, French-Canadian nationalism (led by Lionel Groulx) turned more toward the defence of Quebec autonomy, while remaining pan-Canadian and anxious to defend minority francophone rights outside Quebec. The neo-nationalists of the 1960s pushed the separatist cause a step further. The fate of francophone minorities became a minor concern compared with the reinforcement of Quebec government powers. The French-Canadian vision of national identity thus narrowed: Quebec was now seen as the only place where francophones could feel really at home.

Finally, the neo-nationalism of the 1960s was also influenced by international trends, in particular the Third World decolonization movement. More than 60 new countries, mostly former colonies, gained their independence and joined the United Nations between 1946 and 1965. Several Quebec intellectuals saw Quebec's situation as that of a country colonized by Canada since the conquest of New France by Britain in 1760.[17] In Quebec as in Europe, the Algerian struggle for independence at the end of the 1950s reconciled leftist intellectuals with nationalism. Thus they began to argue that it was only normal for Quebeckers to free themselves from their dependence on English Canada.

The Nature of the Quiet Revolution

The Liberal party was elected in June 1960 with a weak majority: 51 seats out of 95, and only 51 percent of the popular vote. Francophone votes were largely split between the two parties, and anglophones voted overwhelmingly Liberal. The Liberals were doubly disappointed at having failed to take further advantage of the weakness of the Union Nationale, which was handicapped by the recent deaths of two of its leaders. Maurice Duplessis died in September 1959, and his successor, Paul Sauvé, passed away three months later. The new UN leader, Antonio Barrette, lacked the charisma of Jean Lesage, a good speaker who surrounded himself with a strong political team.

The Liberal party program advocated a fundamental change in political direction and accordingly adopted the slogan "It's time for change" during the election campaign. Among the principal elements in its platform, it proposed to democratize the political regime, revise the educational system, increase the role of the state in the economy, and adopt several important social measures. The philosophy that inspired its program and the achievements that followed were linked to neoliberalism, a version of liberalism upheld by governments of Western industrialized countries after the Second World War.

This ideology is characterized first and foremost by its strong attachment to fundamental liberal values: individual liberty, the right to private property, and the democratic system of government. It embraced an optimistic and materialistic vision of the world, championing the progress of humanity, mainly through economic development. For liberals, religion was seen as a private affair; the church should refrain from intervening in public life and confine its interests purely to the religious sphere.

In its classic form, liberalism advocated a free-market economy, reserving a minimal role for the state in economic and social matters. But Western countries had revised their belief in such "laissez-faire" postures after the economic crisis of the 1930s. Guided by the policies of the New Deal of Roosevelt in United States and by the ideas of economist John Maynard Keynes, they began to favour limited intervention by the state to stabilize economic cycles. Governments also initiated a variety of social policies, not only to provide better social security, but also to stimulate the consumer economy. Beginning with the Second World War, the Canadian government modelled its economic and social policies on these ideas.

The Liberals, under Jean Lesage, adopted several measures inspired by this neoliberal ideology that clashed sometimes with some important principles of clerical-conservative thought. On the political front, measures were aimed at democratizing political life and promoting the role of the state. The Liberals argued that the state should not be in the service of a ruling political party. Instead, the party must be at the service of the state, seen as an embodiment of the general will. As a first measure, the Liberals tried to eliminate the corruption and patronage that had flourished under the Duplessis regime. They reformed the civil service so that the hiring and promotion of civil servants reflected competence rather than political recommendations or repayment of political favours. To attract the best candidates, they improved working conditions for civil servants and agreed to their unionization in 1964. The following year saw the implementation of their right to negotiate and even to strike.

In a spirit of respect for democracy, the government began to revise electoral laws and the electoral map. To avoid profligate spending during election campaigns, a law was adopted in 1963 limiting the expenditures of political parties and foreseeing partial reimbursement of expenses by the state. As for the electoral map, which overrepresented rural areas at the expense of urban ridings, the Liberals introduced an initial modification in 1965. They increased the number of urban seats. The government also tried to abolish the Legislative Council. Quebec was the only province that had preserved this nonelected body, the equivalent to the federal Senate. It was finally abolished in 1968. Other measures favoured greater citizen participation in political life. These included: the publication of an official record of Chamber debates, the extension of the vote to young people aged eighteen and over, and the willingness to consult the public on important proposed legislation.

Finally, the government worked hard to establish a new balance in its relations with the religious powers. It sought to widen the role of the state in areas that the Church had traditionally reserved for itself. Thus, in 1964, it succeeded where the preceding Liberal governments had failed in restoring the Ministry of Education, giving it broad authority over public school institutions.[18] This department had been abolished in 1875 on the grounds that education was too important to be entrusted to the politicians. The Liberals now insisted that education was so important that authority over it must be moved to the people's elected representatives. As a public institution, the educational system should depend not on religious authority, but on the democratic institutions embodied in Parliament.

The Liberals established a similar state control in the health sector, where more than half of the hospitals remained in the hands of religious communities in 1960. The establishment of the Hospital Insurance Program in 1961 permitted the expansion of state influence. As the sole source of hospital revenues, the state moved to the foreground. In 1962, the government went so far as to reserve only a minor role for religious communities on the hospitals' administrative boards.

Surprisingly, there was little resistance by religious authorities to secularization in educational and health care institutions. They were forced to move aside as urban religiosity declined and the population distanced itself from the teachings of the Church.

Increasingly, the Church was seen as an authoritarian institution whose message was out of touch with modern society. Important signs — among others, the extensive use of the birth-control pill and the rise of civil divorce — illustrated that many Catholics were turning away from Church teachings. Religious dissatisfaction could be found even within the Church itself, as many priests and nuns abandoned their vows and the religious life itself. As we have seen, the individualism and materialism that accompanied industrial growth during and after the Second World War played a leading role in this change. In the 1960s the time had come for the withdrawal of clerical authority and the secularization of francophone society.

This second characteristic of the Quiet Revolution grew out of the changing ideological outlook, as well as nationalist motivations. The Quebec government thus prepared for an important expansion of its authority in the economic, social, and cultural realms.[19] Jean Lesage stated clearly the principles underlying his interventionist policy in a 1961 speech:

> We need powerful tools, not only to meet the inevitable challenges of the coming years, but also to put the French-Canadian people in step with the real world. And the only tool we have, is our state, the state of Quebec. We cannot afford the luxury of not using it . . . If we fail to make use of our state for ourselves, out of fear or prejudice, we will thus deprive ourselves of what is perhaps the only means remaining to us to assure our survival as an ethnic minority and to blossom as a people conscious of the requirements of the modern world in which we are hereafter called upon to live. It is in this perspective that the government of the province of Quebec undertakes all of its activities.[20]

By comparison with the Duplessis years, the economic dimension of government activities during this period took on considerable scope. Two major objectives included the stimulation of Quebec's economic development and increased francophone participation in the economy.[21] The lower level of economic development in Quebec compared with that in Ontario and the underrepresentation of francophones in Quebec big business were particularly resented. The government was ready not only to support private enterprise, but also to play a leading role in economic development. Convinced of the virtues of economic planning, it formed the Conseil d'orientation économique in 1961 to provide advice and plans for the future socioeconomic development of the province. Next, the Société générale de financement was created in 1962 to lend financial support to French-Canadian industrial and commercial enterprises. Two new state corporations were established in 1964 and 1965: Sidbec to set up a steel mill in the province and Soquem to stimulate mining development.

The most important government initiative was the nationalization of the existing private electrical utilities companies in 1963, henceforth incorporated into Hydro-Québec. In the previous year, the Liberal party had won the election mainly on this platform. The objectives of nationalization were to unify the network of electricity distribution, to secure for Quebeckers control of one of their most important resources, and to provide cheap electricity to stimulate industrial progress. Hydro-Québec enforced the use of French as the language of work. Important career openings were thus created for francophone managers and engineers within Quebec. With the construction of large dams, Hydro-Québec became a success symbol for the Québécois. Less spectacular, but still very significant, was the establishment of the Caisse de dépôt et placement in 1965 to administer the funds collected by the Quebec Pension Plan. Many of the funds accumulated went to the purchase of Quebec government and Hydro-Québec bonds; this strategy reduced government dependence on English-Canadian and American financial institutions. During the 1970s, the

Caisse played a more active role in capitalizing Quebec entreprises by purchasing large quantities of their shares.

In the field of education, the Liberal party used the creation of a provincial Ministry of Education in 1964 to undertake a vast reform of the school system. The objective of this reform was to democratize educational institutions, to guarantee access to higher education to all young people who had the necessary talent, and to adapt the education system to the needs of modern society. To expand the educational system, the government in 1961 guaranteed free education and textbooks up to grade eleven while raising mandatory schooling age to fifteen. Important reforms of the structure were also initiated to unify the school system and to facilitate access to university. These reforms continued with the creation in 1967 of a new institution, the postsecondary CEGEP, and in 1968 of a network of Quebec universities (both wholly nonconfessional). Reviews of programs and teaching were sought to ensure respect for individual learning abilities, to increase participation in social, political, and cultural life, and to prepare students more adequately for the labour market. These reforms, which relegated religious instruction to a secondary position, illustrated that public education was no longer in the hands of the Church.

The influence of the state also extended into the fields of health and welfare services. While the Union Nationale government had entrusted clerical institutions with large areas of responsibility in these fields, the Liberal government chose another route. Following the recommendations of the Boucher Commission on Public Assistance in 1961, the provincial government enlarged considerably its role in social security, participating in two important cost-sharing programs set up by the federal government: the Hospital Insurance Program in 1961 and the Canada Assistance Plan in 1966. In becoming the main source of their funding, the government took effective control of hospitals and social institutions. Finally, in 1964, Quebec initiated its own pension plan, administered independently of the Canada Pension Plan. Such actions are testimony to the government's commitment to the welfare state by establishing a social security net to protect its citizens against the risks of poverty, sickness, and old age.

Finally, state intervention spread into cultural activities. Although the Duplessis government had shown no interest in such questions, the Liberal party felt fully justified in intervening to assure the development of French culture. In 1961, a Ministry of Cultural Affairs was set up to coordinate and stimulate cultural activities. It was also at this point that Quebec grew closer to France, the source of French culture. Quebec opened a general delegation in Paris in 1961, and several agreements on cooperation led to a program of cultural exchange over the following years. With the opening of more offices in London, New York, and Milan, and the development of relations with newly independent French African countries, Quebec began to pursue an international policy that soon upset the federal government.

In the 1960s Quebeckers had come to view the state as a powerful instrument to bridge the gap which they believed separated them from other Western societies. The Quebec government's interventionism quickly surpassed that of other provinces due to its powerful mixture of nationalist and reformist agendas.

Toward a Quebec Nationalism

The Quiet Revolution was a major turning point in the definition of francophone Quebeckers' national identity. This transformation weakened Quebeckers' sense of identification with Canada. Such a development was at the source of the constitutional crisis that has troubled relations between Quebec and Canada ever since. Before the 1960s, French Quebeckers identified themselves as French Canadians with common bonds to francophones outside of Quebec. Their nationalism had been based on French language and culture and on the Catholic religion. Their vision, essentially pan-Canadian, had revolved around the idea of complete equality between the two major linguistic groups across Canada.

The Quiet Revolution gradually changed this formulation of their identity. Nothing is more revealing of this change than the gradual shift in self-reference from "French Canadian" to "Québécois." This change illustrated the development of a new nationalism among francophones. As in the past, it expressed fidelity to French language and culture, while abandoning the Catholic religion. There were also other important transformations: nationalism lost much of its pan-Canadian dimension, centring instead on Quebec territory, and it took on a more political tone as the Quebec government was seen as the political expression of the nation. Indeed, the nationalism of this period tended toward the construction of a nation-state for Quebec francophones around the Quebec government. The growing identification of "Franco-Québécois" with their province weakened their attachment to Canada, and their goals began to diverge from those of francophone minorities outside Quebec. Moreover, this new nationalism had as a corollary the wish to strengthen Quebec government power, giving birth to a strong independence movement.

From the beginning of the 1960s, Quebec began to enunciate a new set of goals in its demands to the federal government. The Duplessis government had had a passive attitude in its relations with Ottawa. It defended provincial jurisdictions and denounced the centralization of power in Ottawa. The Lesage government took a more energetic position. It demanded not only the elimination of federal government encroachment in the fields of provincial jurisdictions but also the extension of Quebec legislative powers and the eventual granting of a "special status" for Quebec within the Canadian federation. In support of its claims, the Lesage government began to call for a new principle: Quebec constitutes the government of a "nation" distinct from the rest of Canada. To assure the full development of this "francophone nation," it must, then, have more powers than those of other provinces, more or less a special status. It is revealing that in the early 1960s Lesage began to use the term "Quebec state" instead of "province of Quebec".

According to Lesage, Canadian federalism was nevertheless flexible enough to permit a broadening of Quebec's powers. Indeed, in some domains, Quebec succeeded in securing greater autonomy from the federal government. However, from 1967, with the arrival of a new generation of Quebec politicians in Ottawa (Pierre Elliott Trudeau, Jean Marchand, Gérard Pelletier), the federal government became more rigid in protecting its powers. The Union Nationale government that succeeded the Liberals in 1966 pursued the objectives of greater autonomy for Quebec, demanding an in-depth reform of federalism and a new constitutional status for Quebec. Such reforms were justified on neo-nationalist grounds: "It is in Quebec, where they constitute the majority that French Canadians can fully develop as a nation of French culture. But, because of an antiquated and badly implemented constitution, Quebec does not currently possess all the powers and instruments necessary to function as the nation-state of French Canada."[22]

Some went a step further, demanding that all political power be concentrated in Quebec's hands, thus giving birth to separatist parties. Before the 1960s the idea of independence had appeared periodically in Quebec history, but was confined to small groups of marginal intellectuals. The desire for change stimulated by the Quiet Revolution proved to be a decisive force that launched the idea onto the political scene. Indeed, the *Rassemblement pour l'indépendance nationale*, born in 1960, became a political party three years later and ran candidates in the 1966 election, where it won nearly 6 percent of the vote. But it was really with the creation of the Parti Québécois in 1968, with René Lévesque as its leader, that the idea truly caught on (23 percent of the vote in 1970). For the sovereigntists, anglophones dominated the federal government and the federal regime was paralyzing Quebec development.

The new nationalism accompanying the Quiet Revolution was strongly tied to the penetration of neoliberal values in Quebec. As noted above, neoliberalism includes a materialist dimension in which the possession of wealth becomes an important standard of both individual and collective success. As these values became more important to francophone Quebeckers at the beginning of the 1960s, they came to feel more deeply their economic inferiority. They resented the fact that the economic development of their province eluded them, that their level of income was lower than that of anglophones, and that they had achieved an inferior occupational status. This inferiority, already experienced personally by many francophones, was confirmed by a study sponsored by the Royal Commission on Bilingualism and Biculturalism in the 1960s. In a detailed analysis of 1961 census data, the study revealed that the average income of French Canadians in Quebec was 35 percent lower than that of English Canadians and that francophone salaries were almost at the bottom of the scale if classified according to ethnic origin (only First Nations and Italians were lower).[23] French Canadians were thus performing poorly according to the new values they had adopted.[24]

Determined to rectify this situation, the new political and economic elite in the 1960s found in the Quebec state (an expression that began to replace "province" from 1962) the instrument of economic reconquest. Premier Jean Lesage summed up well this aspiration: "Up to now, the Quebec people believed that its principal wealth — in fact, its only wealth — was found in the cultural values of the French-Canadian nation. But, more recently, we have come to understand that we own the ground on which we live, and that it is up to us and us alone to exploit its immense resources." He added: "All adult peoples have not only the right but the duty to control as much as possible their own economy."[25] The Quebec state, the only government fully controlled by francophones, was thus seen as the lever for their economic and social improvement. This explains the enlargement of the role of the Quebec government in the 1960s, particularly in the economic realm. The nationalization of Hydro-Québec and the creation of state entreprises followed naturally. State control reinforced francophone nationalism and gave it a purely "Quebec" tone.

It remains something of a paradox that "Québécois" nationalism came to challenge Canadian federalism while the sociopolitical values that it embraced were similar to those espoused in English Canada. The initial achievements of the Quiet Revolution were welcomed in English Canada because they were seen as a means by which Quebec could align itself with the rest of North America. English Canadians felt that this would put an end to reactionary nationalism and inaugurate an era of fruitful cooperation between the two communities. However, such was not the case. The new nationalism, born out of the Quiet Revolution, led to the expansion of the independence movement and to demands from the Quebec government to modify the Canadian Constitution and to grant new legislative powers to the province. As previously explained, the sharing of communal values generated a political nationalism that made the "state of Quebec" the instrument through which francophones could catch up with other North American societies.

The reforms undertaken by the Lesage government between 1960 and 1966 did not receive unanimous popular support, and met resistance from the most conservative elements of society. The extension of the state's role into areas traditionally served by the

Church, especially education, aroused resentment, particularly in the rural regions. As well, people worried about tax increases and the rising debt that the Lesage government's "policy of grandeur" would impose on the province. In the 1966 election, the Union Nationale capitalized on this discontent, and to everyone's surprise defeated the Liberals, despite their poorer showing in terms of the popular vote (40.9 percent for the UN versus 47.2 percent for the Liberals). The electoral map, which overrepresented the rural areas, and the presence of a third political party, the *Rassemblement pour l'indépendance nationale*, penalized the Liberals. Nevertheless, these results made it clear that enthusiasm for the achievements of the Quiet Revolution was not shared by the entire population. Nonetheless, the Union Nationale did not look back, but rather continued the objectives set by the Liberals. It reformed the electoral map, abolished the Legislative Council, completed the reforms in education, established a variety of social policies, created state enterprises, and adopted a stronger nationalism than the Liberals.

In other circles, the Quiet Revolution aroused expectations that the Liberals had been unable to satisfy. The affirmation of neo-nationalism gave rise to separatist groups and to the departure of René Lévesque from the Liberal party; he founded the *Mouvement souveraineté-association*, which became the Parti Québécois (PQ) in 1968. The PQ often defined its mandate as carrying the goals of the Quiet Revolution to their final term. The labour movement also underwent a transformation in the mid-1960s, mainly because the reforms of the Quiet Revolution had raised its members' expectations. Labour unions took on a radical stance, resulting in an unprecedented wave of strikes and the adoption of a radical critique of the capitalist system from a Marxist perspective. At the same time, many young intellectuals turned sharply to the left, advocating socialism and Quebec independence.

The direct influence of the Quiet Revolution, promoting both state interventionism and political autonomy for Quebec, lasted to the early 1980s. After the serious recession of 1981–82, however, Quebec began to reduce the role of the state, as did many other Western countries. At the same time, the concept of separation took an important step backwards. It required the failure of the Meech Lake Accord in 1990 to revive the idea of Quebec independence. However, whatever the ups and downs of the sovereigntist cause, francophones have increasingly tended since the Quiet Revolution to define themselves primarily as Quebeckers.[26] This is the legacy of the Quiet Revolution that presents the gravest challenge to Canadian unity.

NOTES

1. For further information on the Quiet Revolution see: Y. Belanger, R. Comeau, and C. Métivier, *La Révolution tranquille, 40 ans plus tard: un bilan* (Montréal: VLB Éditeur, 2000); Dale C. Thompson, *Jean Lesage and the Quiet Revolution* (Toronto: Macmillan, 1984); Kenneth McRoberts, *Quebec: Social Change and Political Crisis* (Toronto: McClelland and Stewart, 1968); W.D. Coleman, *The Independence Movement in Quebec, 1945–1980* (Toronto: University of Toronto Press, 1984); Michael D. Behiels, *Prelude to Quebec's Quiet Revolution. Liberalism versus Neo-nationalism, 1945–1960* (Montreal/Kingston: McGill-Queen's University Press, 1985); Michael D. Behiels, *Quebec since 1945. Selected Readings* (Toronto: Copp Clark Pitman, 1987). In French, see Léon Dion, *La Révolution déroutée 1960–1976* (Montréal: Boréal, 1998); Jacques Rouillard, "La Révolution tranquille: Rupture ou Tournant?" *Journal of Canadian Studies*, 32, 4 (Spring 1997): 23–51.

2. The dominance of this view emerged from a survey conducted among university students. Jocelyn Létourneau, "La production historienne courante portant sur le Québec et ses rapports

avec la construction des figures identitaires d'une communauté communicationnelle," *Recherches sociographiques*, 36, 1 (1995): 30–32.

3. Among recent works questioning the monolithic nature of pre–Quiet Revolution ideology, see Fernande Roy, *Histoire des idéologies au Québec aux XIXe et XXe siècles* (Montreal: Boréal, 1993); Claude Couture, *Le mythe de la modernisation du Québec* (Montreal: Méridien, 1991); Jocelyn Létourneau, "Le 'Québec moderne', un chapitre du grand récit collectif des Québécois," *Revue française de science politique* 42, 5 (October 1992): 765–85; Jacques Rouillard, "La Révolution tranquille." This vision is reflected in the synthesis by Paul-André Linteau, René Durocher, Jean-Claude Robert, and François Ricard, *Quebec since 1930* (Toronto, 1991).

4. See Jean-Guy Genest, *Godbout* (Québec: Septentrion, 1996).

5. Nadia F. Eid describes the ideological base of ninteenth century "ultamontanism" in *Le clergé et le pouvoir politique au Québec* (Montréal: Hurtubise HMH, 1978). The Church softened the tone of its teaching in the twentieth century, but the fundamental values remained the same. See Richard Jones, *L'idéologie de l'Action catholique (1917–1939)* (Québec: Les Presses de l'Université Laval, 1974), or the four books of *Idéologies au Canada français* directed by Fernand Dumont, Jean Hamelin, and Jean-Paul Montminy (Québec: Les Presses de l'Université Laval, 1973–1981).

6. Richard Jones, op. cit., p. 182.

7. This interpretation is developed in my essay "Duplessis: Le Québec vire à droite," in Alain-G. Gagnon et Michel Sarra-Bournet, *Duplessis. Entre la Grande Noirceur et la société libérale* (Montréal: Québec Amérique, [c 1997]), pp. 183–206.

8. For a brief outline of the Duplessis regime, see Richard Jones, *Duplessis and the Union Nationale Administration* (Ottawa: Canadian Historical Association Booklet, 1983).

9. My own calculations based on *Recensement du Canada*, 1931, vol. 3, pp. 258–308, in Jacques Rouillard, "La Révolution tranquille: Rupture ou Tournant?" *Journal of Canadian Studies*, 32, 4 (Spring 1997): 31. As the census definition of an urban area (1000 people and more) is rather low, we redefined it as 10 000 people and more.

10. *Recensement du Canada.*, vol. 7, p. 948.

11. *Recensement du Canada.*, vol. 2, p. 272; 1961, bulletin 1.3-2, table 83.

12. Jean Hamelin, *Histoire du catholicisme québécois. Le XXe siècle*, tome 2, *De 1940 à nos jours* (Montréal: Boréal Express, 1984), pp. 109–89.

13. Marc Renaud, "Quebec's New Middle Class in Search of Social Hegemony: Causes and Political Consequences," in Michael D. Behiels, *Quebec since 1945*, pp. 48–79; Gilles Bourque et Nicole Frenette, "La structure nationale québécoise," *Socialisme québécois* 21–22 (avril 1971): pp. 140–46.

14. Jacques Rouillard, *Histoire du syndicalisme québécois* (Montréal: Boréal, 1989), p. 201.

15. Michel Sara-Bournet, *Entre le corporatisme et le libéralisme: Les groupes d'affaires francophones et l'organisation socio-politique du Québec de 1943 à 1969* (Ph.D. thesis, Ottawa University, 1995), pp. 282–333.

16. Jean Hamelin, *Histoire du catholicisme québécois*, p. 138; Michael D. Behiels, *Prelude of Quebec's Quiet Revolution. Liberalism versus Neo-Nationalism, 1945–1960* (Montreal/Kingston: McGill–Queen's University Press, 1985): Léon Dion, *Québec 1945–2000. tome 2, Les intellectuels et le temps de Duplessis* (Québec: Les Presses de l'Université Laval, 1993), pp. 374–97.

17. Léon Dion, *La révolution déroutée*, pp. 107–69; Michael D. Behiels, "Quebec Social Transformation and Ideological Renewal, 1940–1976," in Michael D. Behiels, *Quebec since 1945*, pp. 35–38.

18. The system, however, remained confessional, and the Catholic and the Protestant committees survived. Still, the power of these committees was limited to religious questions and the representation of bishops was reduced in the Catholic committee.

19. The expansion of the role of the state from 1960 to 1965 increased the number of civil servants by 53 percent as well as government expenses (by 127 percent in constant dollars). Daniel Latouche, "La vrai nature de . . . la révolution tranquille," *Revue canadienne de science politique* 7, 3 (September 1974): pp. 530, 533.

20. Speech given to the Fédération des sociétés Saint Jean-Baptiste in Ottawa in 1961. Jean Lesage, *Un Québec fort dans une nouvelle Confédération* (Québec: Ministère des affaires fédérales provinciales, 1965), p. 18.

21. Account of Roland Parenteau in Robert Comeau, ed., *Jean Lesage et l'éveil d'une nation* (Québec: Les Presses de l'Université du Québec, 1989), p. 190.

22. *Objectifs 1966 de l'Union nationale. Un programme d'action pour une jeune nation. Quebec d'abord*: 4, in Réjean Pelletier, *Partis politiques et société québécois. De Duplessis à Bourassa, 1944–1970* (Montréal: Québec/Amérique, 1989), p. 291.

23. Lysiane Gagnon, "Les conclusions du Rapport B.B.: De Durham à Laurendeau-Dunton: Variations sur le thème de la dualité canadienne," in Robert Comeau, *Économie québécoise* (Montréal: Les Presses de l'Université du Québec, 1969), p. 238.

24. Charles Taylor has pointed out this francophone perception: "They are nagged by a sense of collective inferiority in those fields which they prize." "Nationalism and the Political Intelligentsia," *Queen's Quarterly* 72, 1 (Spring 1965–66): 160.

25. Réjean Pelletier, "La Révolution tranquille," in Gérard Daigle, *Le Québec en jeu. Comprendre les grands défis* (Montreal: Les Presses de l'Université de Montréal, 1992), p. 617.

26. 21% in 1970, 39% in 1985, 59% in 1990, and 63% in 1997. Maurice Pinard, *The Quebec Independence Movement. A Dramatic Reemergence*, Working Papers in Social Behaviour, Department of Sociology, McGill University, 1992, p. 31; Groupe de recherche sur l'américanité (GRA), "L'assurance identitaire se conjugue avec l'ouverture sur le monde," *Le Devoir*, 15 juillet 1998, p. A7.

453

Article Thirty-One

Politics and the Reinforcement of the French Language in Canada and Quebec, 1960–1986

Richard Jones

It is commonplace to affirm that language has been a political issue in Canada ever since 1760, when the British completed their conquest of New France, and the colony's approximately 70 000 French-speaking inhabitants came under British domination. The new masters hoped that time would enable them to transform the French Canadians into good English-speaking members of the Church of England[1] or that British immigration would eventually swamp them. Although the English language rapidly assumed a privileged place in Quebec and in Canada, the French did not disappear; indeed they multiplied prolifically.[2] When Canada assumed Dominion status with a federal form of government in 1867, Quebec, the territory inhabited largely by francophones, became a separate province.[3]

Confederation did not open an era of linguistic harmony in Canada. Indeed, bitter language conflict burst forth frequently as French-speaking minorities outside Quebec saw their few linguistic rights, particularly in the area of education, curtailed or eradicated by English-speaking majorities.[4]

Until 1960, it could be said that the status of the French language in Canada was at best stagnating and that citizens who spoke French or were of French ethnic origin were clearly disadvantaged compared with those who spoke English or were of British ethnic origin.[5] This article seeks to show that, since 1960, the status of the French language in Canada,

Source: *Quebec since 1945: Selected Readings*, ed. Michael Behiels (Toronto: Copp Clark Pitman, 1987), pp. 223–40. Reprinted by permission.

as well as the position of francophones in Canadian society, has, in many ways, improved markedly. Governments, at both the federal and provincial levels, have played a major role in this evolution; they intervened because of powerful political pressures applied by Canada's French-speaking population.[6] Yet many of the changes at the federal level and in the provinces with English-speaking majorities have been cosmetic or at least not very far-reaching. The really significant transformation has occurred in the province of Quebec.

The Federal Government and the English-Speaking Provinces

The Royal Commission on Bilingualism and Biculturalism was established by the federal government in 1963 in response to demands for greater linguistic equality that were being formulated by French Canadians. According to its terms of reference, the Commission was expected to "recommend what steps should be taken to develop the Canadian Confederation on the basis of an equal partnership between the two founding races."[7] During the 1968 federal election campaign, linguistic equality was one of the themes developed by Liberal Prime Minister Pierre Elliott Trudeau. Trudeau was convinced that the federal government had to demonstrate to French Canadians that it was the government of all Canadians, not of English-speaking Canadians alone. Trudeau's concern was that the government of Quebec would succeed in portraying itself as the real representative of French Canadians; this situation could only undermine national unity.[8] The following year, Parliament adopted the *Official Languages Act*, the objective of which was to increase the percentage of French-speaking civil servants, augment the use of French within the civil service, and make French-language services at the federal level available for most French-speaking Canadians.[9] Finally, in 1982, linguistic rights were enshrined in the *Canadian Charter of Rights and Freedoms*,[10] an integral part of the Canadian Constitution.

Fifteen years after its adoption, the *Official Languages Act* had, in the words of Language Commissioner d'Iberville Fortier, produced some remarkable achievements but fallen far short of creating the equality between the two official languages that, after all, was the stated objective of the legislation. In his opinion, Canada had reached a "kind of watershed between the solid accomplishments of the past and new challenges which will take us beyond mere statements of principle."[11]

Since the late 1960s, most of the nine Canadian provinces with English-speaking majorities, and particularly New Brunswick and Ontario, have taken measures to assist their French-language minorities. New Brunswick, approximately one-third of whose population is French-speaking, adopted its own largely symbolic *Official Languages Act* in 1969. Ontario, with nearly half a million citizens of French mother tongue,[12] has also extended French-language rights in areas such as education and the courts, though, probably to avoid a backlash, it has refused to become officially bilingual. Other provinces have also taken initiatives, although, in some important cases, they have acted only under judicial pressure.[13]

This flurry of linguistic activity in Canada has had no effect on the relatively rapid assimilation, into the English-speaking majority, of francophones living in the eight provinces that are massively anglophone. The Task Force on Canadian Unity, created in 1977 with a broad mandate to obtain and publicize the views of Canadians regarding the state of their country, waxed pessimistic in this regard. Attributing the phenomenon to, among other factors, relatively high rates of intermarriage of francophones with anglophones, the Commission concluded: "The rate of linguistic assimilation of French-speaking minorities is quite high, and appears to be accelerating in all English-speaking provinces other than New Brunswick."[14]

The 1981 census figures confirmed this sombre diagnosis, showing that 32.8 percent of Canadians of French mother tongue, living outside Quebec, had shifted to English as the main language of the home. The 1971 figure had been 29.6 percent. Thus, the French mother tongue group now represents only 5.3 percent of Canada's population outside Quebec, and the group for which French is the language spoken in the home constitutes an almost negligible 3.8 percent of the population.[15]

There can be no doubt that, without the presence of the province of Quebec, the situation of the French language in Canada would be bleak indeed.[16] Although the francophone minorities outside Quebec have long been agitating for better treatment, the pressures they could exert on their respective provincial governments as well as on the federal government have been relatively modest. In addition to lacking economic clout, the group has been simply too small, too widely dispersed geographically, and, until recently, too disorganized to wield much weight.

Quebec's presence, then, has been decisive for the French fact in Canada. Four out of five French-speaking Canadians live in that province, Canada's second largest in terms of population. Just as the rest of Canada has become relatively more English-speaking as the francophone minorities retreat, Quebec has, in recent years, become increasingly French-speaking. The 1981 census showed that 82.4 percent of Quebeckers were of French mother tongue and that virtually the same proportion generally spoke French in the home.[17] In other words, languages in Canada seem to be undergoing a territorialization whereby Quebec becomes more French while the rest of Canada registers consistent gains for the English language.[18] Ultimately, this phenomenon could strengthen division within Canada.

The Beginnings of the Language Debate in Quebec

Respecting the reinforcement of the French language in Canada since 1960, Quebec has been a theatre of dramatic activity, and state intervention has been constant and has had measurable impact. The undeniable result has been to strengthen the position of the French language in that province, though the extent of that improvement and particularly its durability remain subjects of rather acrimonious debate.

By the late 1960s, the major political parties in Quebec were all debating the language question and attempting to conceive policies that would not only satisfy their members but also ensure wide support at the polls. The context, as we shall see, favoured the most nationalistic of the three major parties, the Parti Québécois, ideologically committed to a French Quebec. Although after coming to power in 1976 it had to contend with realities that it could neither change nor ignore, it was able to accomplish its objectives in matters of language to a considerable degree.

A series of factors contributed to transforming the issue of language into an increasingly controversial subject in Quebec and finally to forcing the government to legislate. From 1944, the very conservative rural-based Union Nationale had been maintained in power under the firm and, according to his foes, dictatorial hand of Maurice Duplessis.[19] Duplessis died in 1959 and, the following year, the Liberals under Jean Lesage gained power, promising to modernize Quebec. The pace of change became so breathless that a journalist soon baptized the new era the "Quiet Revolution."[20]

The reforms of the Quiet Revolution aimed at modernizing the institutions, developing the economy, and furthering the welfare state. But they also had considerable nationalistic content since they were designed to improve the lot of francophones as well as the position of Quebec in Confederation. The nationalization of the private Anglo-Canadian and American hydroelectric power utilities,[21] Quebec's epic confrontations with the federal government over questions of money and power, and the province's ventures into the domain of international relations, notably with France, were at least partly based on nationalist considerations.

The educational system, revamped at least structurally by the reformers of the Quiet Revolution, began turning out more and more graduates seeking employment. Certainly the expansion of the provincial government during these years created many new jobs for francophones. In other fields, though, Anglo-dominated structures blocked opportunities. The federal civil service as yet offered few possibilities to francophones unwilling to do virtually all their work in English. In addition, private enterprise, particularly the upper echelons, remained an anglophone preserve that French Canadians had great difficulty penetrating. Social scientists have abundantly described the rise of this new francophone middle class.[22] For its members, tangible and intangible objectives of an individual character linked to self-interest, questions of jobs, money, and social status, were not the only motivations. Aspirations of a collective nature were also important. Many francophones were less and less disposed, after the "cultural mutation"[23] of these years, to continue to accept what they perceived as second-class citizenship. This group would be the standard-bearer of the new nationalism.

Nationalists in Quebec were highly sensitive to the nationalist currents that in the early 1960s were sweeping parts of Europe and the newly emancipated states of Africa and Asia. Some Quebeckers saw their province's status as akin to that of a colonized state and they began preaching Quebec's independence.[24] Naturally, an independent Quebec was to be a French state.[25]

The Quiet Revolution can be said to have marked the demise of the traditional Quebec, a Quebec whose identity was based on Catholicism, French language and culture, and ruralism. Of course, since the early twentieth century, the traditional society had been in decline; indeed, by 1921, Quebec's population was half urban. By the mid-1960s, Quebec was rapidly becoming a secular society as the Church withdrew from its temporal preoccupations. What remained to distinguish French Canadians from other North Americans?[26] Language and culture, no doubt, and the nationalists would give the promotion of these traits their full attention.

The preoccupation with language also stemmed from profound feelings of insecurity among francophones. For example, the decline of the birth rate could have potentially disastrous effects on the proportion of the French population in Canada as well as in Quebec. As late as 1947, some observers, like Paul Sauriol, a journalist at the nationalist daily *Le Devoir*, foresaw the day when French-speaking Canadians would form the largest linguistic group in Canada.[27] Traditionally, a high birth rate was seen as a means of counterbalancing the influx of immigrants into Canada, few of whom spoke French or learned that language. But, by the late 1950s and early 1960s, the birth rate began to decline precipitously. In 1954, the rate was still 30.4 per thousand. By 1965, it had dropped to 21.3.[28] The dream of the "revenge of the cradle" was apparently over.

Another worrisome trend was the fact that the great majority of immigrants settling in Quebec chose to send their children to English-language schools[29] and to integrate into the English-speaking minority. For them, English was simply the most "attractive" language. Should they leave Quebec, they would obviously require an excellent knowledge of English. Within Quebec, it did not appear essential for them to learn French, particularly for those living in the Montreal area. Some demographers hypothesized that

Montreal would be close to having an English-speaking majority by the year 2000.[30] Not surprisingly, the increasingly vocal nationalist lobby urged that French be established, to a much greater degree, as the language of work and of education. Only the government could bring about the desired changes.

But the government, regardless of what party was in power, had to be forced to act. The nationalists suspected that, without powerful popular pressure, the parties committed to federalism, specifically the Liberals and the Union Nationale, would not dare adopt the bold pro-French measures that they deemed necessary. But there was another more attractive possibility. Perhaps the nationalists, now more and more favourable to independence for Quebec, could themselves ride to power within a party whose backbone they would form. Then they could write and apply the language legislation. This, precisely, was to come about.

Before studying the ways in which the three major political formations dealt with the language issue, a brief description of each is necessary. The Liberal party, largely urban-based, was the force behind Quebec's modernization in the early 1960s. It was quite willing to promote nationalist causes; still, there were limits beyond which a party committed to maintaining Quebec within Confederation could not go. In addition to widespread backing among francophones, the party enjoyed the support of big enterprise, mostly anglophone, and of the anglophone minority in general.

On the specific issue of language, the Liberals were disposed to taking modest steps to strengthen the position of French. They were, however, unwilling to risk alienating those groups relatively satisfied with the status quo, particularly their English-speaking supporters and the business community. Nor, in the years from 1960 to 1966, when the Liberals held power, was the nationalist lobby sufficiently strong to force it to go further. In their 1960 election program, the Liberals promised to take measures to assist the French language and culture and notably create an Office de la langue française.[31] Few could feel threatened by these proposals. In 1966, the Liberals went somewhat further, declaring themselves willing to make French "the main language of work and of communication in Quebec" in order to "guarantee the vitality of the language and at the same time enable the majority of [Quebec's] population to live in French." Reassuring the hesitant, they declared that this objective was to be accomplished "with full respect for the undeniable rights of the anglophone minority."[32]

The Union Nationale, in power from 1966 until 1970, might have been expected to produce bolder policies than the Liberals. During the Duplessis years, had it not boasted of being the vehicle of nationalism and the ardent defender of Quebec's autonomy?[33] Moreover, it was less beholden to the English-speaking minority, from which it received relatively few votes. Yet it was perhaps more the flag-bearer of an old-style nationalism in which the defence of language through government intervention was not judged necessary. Nor did it desire to rouse English-speaking Canada against it. Thus, in 1966, the party devoted just a single line in a twenty-page program to the subject, vaguely promising to give French the status of "national language."[34] Clearly, the nationalist lobby could not hope for satisfaction from this party!

The impetus for movement on the language question was to come from a new party, established in October 1968, called the Parti Québécois. This left-of-centre political formation was the vehicle of the nationalist aspirations of Quebec's new middle class, the intelligentsia that had come of age during the Quiet Revolution. Teachers, professors, professionals, students, and elements of the working class formed the backbone of the new group.[35] It proposed a modified form of independence for Quebec called "sovereignty-association," a sort of hybrid formula implying political sovereignty for the province coupled with an economic association with the rest of Canada.

The language policy of the Parti Québécois reflected both its orientation toward independence and its middle-class composition. The independentist option meant that it viewed Quebec as a separate entity. The anglophone minority in Quebec was thus not perceived as part of a Canadian majority, a position that, in the eyes of the Liberals and the Union Nationale, justified special status for that group. Rather, Quebec anglophones were simply another minority that would have to learn to participate in the life of a French Quebec. As for the party's middle-class power base, it implied that employers' views risked being given short shrift. Still, it should be noted that the Parti Québécois, mainly because of the powerful influence exerted by its charismatic leader, René Lévesque, did not propose to abolish the English-language school system. Its position on this question would provoke considerable tension within the party.

Language Legislation: From Bill 85 to Bill 22

All three parties ultimately had to wrestle with the language issue, both in opposition and in power. It was during the Union Nationale's mandate from 1966 until 1970 that pressures heated up considerably. In 1968, a local school council in the town of St. Leonard on Montreal Island voted the gradual elimination of schooling in English for the large number of Italian children enrolled in the district. The Italian community protested vehemently while the nationalist camp welcomed the commission's decision. "What we need are ten, twenty, fifty St. Leonards," contended *Le Devoir* editorialist Jean-Marc Léger, echoing the campaign of the group that was spearheading the movement for obligatory French schooling.[36] The English-language community demanded that the government intervene to guarantee by law unimpeded access to English-language schools for any Quebec child. Obviously, anglophones were concerned that this isolated incident could snowball into a powerful and dangerous trend and that the English-language school sector would be deprived of the not inconsiderable reinforcements furnished by the "allophone" community.[37]

The Union Nationale government was thus obliged to come to grips with this very volatile issue. Many of its members in the National Assembly,[38] conservatives from rural districts, had little interest in this question that concerned mainly Montreal and they were primarily concerned with preserving social peace. Pressures from the powerful anglophone community urged legislative action to guarantee what it contended were its rights.[39] But the Union Nationale also counted a few nationalists who were convinced that action was needed to defend the French language. The premier would have to arbitrate these differences.

Daniel Johnson, Quebec's premier from 1966 until September 1968, was assuredly a nationalist. He had frequently criticized the lack of rights of the French-speaking minorities in the other provinces, demanding "Equality or Independence" as well as additional legislative powers for Quebec in the framework of a new constitution.[40] Still, he was a shrewd politician and he found the subject of St. Leonard a slippery banana peel indeed. At a press conference held a few hours before his sudden death, he responded ambiguously to English-speaking journalists who queried him repeatedly on the affair. "We will take all useful measures, not by legislation but by other means, to make non-French-speaking Quebeckers part of Quebec so that they feel at home and learn French, the dominant language of Quebec." But he went on to say that language rights had to be protected and that it was inadmissible that local school commissions have the power to define them.[41] Just like the celebrated Marquess of Plaza-Toro, Johnson seemed to want to mount his horse and ride off in all directions at once. He certainly feared the political consequences of any action his government might take.

Johnson's successor, Jean-Jacques Bertrand, desired a rapid solution. A convinced federalist, he represented a rural district one-quarter of whose population was English-speaking. Perhaps for those reasons he was less given to pushing nationalist themes. In any case, he indicated his intention to legislate "free choice" in respect to the language of instruction, hoping thus, vainly as it turned out, to gain anglophone support in a by-election held to fill a vacancy in the Assembly.[42] Nationalist groups objected strenuously, as did several Union Nationale legislators, and Bertrand decided to withdraw the proposed bill.[43] With the objective of gaining time, he also decided, in the tried and true Canadian manner, to have a study done. He thus set up the Gendron Committee, whose mandate was to "make an inquiry into and submit a report on the position of French as the language of usage in Quebec."[44]

September 1969 brought riots opposing French and Italians in St. Leonard, where the school commission struggled to find a solution acceptable to all sides. The prime minister's office was besieged with letters and telegrams, and the English-language press urged: "Mr. Bertrand must act."[45] In the Assembly, the opposition Liberal party also applied pressure, signifying that, although the Union Nationale appeared divided on the issue, the Liberals would support Bertrand.[46] Disorders in Montreal linked to illegal strikes provoked a veritable panic within the government, forcing it to move to repress the troubles, linguistic and otherwise.[47]

With the support of most of his Cabinet and the elected members of his party, Bertrand decided on what he hoped would be perceived as a middle-of-the-road course. He presented Bill 63, entitled *An Act to Promote the French Language in Quebec*,[48] which proposed to give all new arrivals in Quebec a knowledge of the French language. But the really important part of the new law, the one relevant to the St. Leonard affair, was the clause dealing with the language of instruction: it recognized the right of any Quebecker to enrol his or her child in an English-language school.

In general, English-speaking Quebeckers were satisfied with this new law. The Liberals, with the evident intention of embarrassing the Union Nationale, criticized the bill on the grounds that it did not really make French the "priority language" of Quebec.[49] As for the nationalists, many of whom were already supporting the fledgling Parti Québécois, they were furious at what they perceived as a "linguistic Munich," an ignominious surrender on the part of the Bertrand government, a powerful encouragement to the anglicization of Quebeckers. Immediately, they began urging repeal of the law. Thousands of demonstrators converged upon the National Assembly in Quebec City to express their opposition. Strikes erupted in the colleges and universities. When the next provincial elections were called, in 1970, the Union Nationale was defeated handily by the Liberals, but the two-year-old Parti Québécois managed to garner one-quarter of the vote. It is difficult to judge the role of the language question in the Union Nationale's defeat, but the relative success of the Parti Québécois indicated that nationalist sentiment was rising.[50]

Now it was the turn of the Liberals to open Pandora's box. After the Gendron Commission finally published its report, in 1973, recommending strong measures in favour of French, they could no longer refrain from moving. Fearful of the rapidly improving fortunes of the Parti Québécois (which had obtained nearly one vote in three in the 1973 elections), the Liberals had to make proposals that would conserve the support of at least the less extreme nationalists. The nationalist camp was simply becoming too important to be neglected. Yet the Liberals also represented the non-French-speaking community in Quebec and business had considerable influence in the party. How could the Liberals hope to harmonize the rapidly polarizing positions on the language question?

Bill 22 was the Liberals' attempt to find a solution to the dilemma.[51] It clearly demonstrated their conviction that most French-speaking Quebeckers were now prepared to take strong measures to reinforce the position of the French language. Bill 22 thus proposed a series of measures designed to make French, at least to a greater degree, the language of work and of communication within Quebec. The means to bring this about were persuasive rather than coercive. More radically, though, the bill restricted access to schools in the English sector to anglophones and to allophones who had a sufficient knowledge of English, a level that was to be verified by tests. Moreover, a cap was placed on the size of enrolment in the English-language sector.

This measure showed that the Liberals were now willing to risk provoking the ire of the party's non-French-speaking supporters. Undoubtedly, they calculated that non-francophones, even though unhappy, constituted a captive electorate. After all, they had never backed the Union Nationale in the past and there was certainly no possibility of their supporting the independentist Parti Québécois.

But the Liberals gravely miscalculated the extent of anglophone discontent. A marathon radio program on the English-language station CFCF in Montreal brought 600 000 Quebeckers, mostly anglophones, to sign a telegram-petition to Prime Minister Trudeau urging abolition of the law.[52]

Nationalists bitterly attacked Bill 22 because of numerous loopholes; they insisted that it would do little to bring immigrants into the French-language stream, and the statistics ultimately showed that they were right in this regard. Indeed, in 1976–77, the last year of operation of Bill 22, the percentage of allophone children attending English schools actually increased by 6.4 percent.[53] Still, the anglophone and allophone communities were even more adamant in their opposition to the law, particularly the stipulations regarding the language of education. When, in 1976, the Union Nationale, traditionally the voice of Quebec nationalism, made the sensational promise that, if elected, it would restore free choice of the language of schooling, large numbers of non-francophones rallied to it, deserting the now detested Liberal Party and its despised leader, Robert Bourassa.[54] For numerous other reasons unrelated to this paper, the Liberals lost ground while the Parti Québécois gained sufficient support to win the election and form the next government.

Bill 101: The Charter of the French Language

Contrary to the other two parties, the Parti Québécois had made no secret of its policy on language nor of the priority that it gave that question.[55] After all, the notion of an independent Quebec was predicated on the existence of a Quebec nation, of a separate identity, of a "personality at whose core is the fact that we speak French."[56] An independent Quebec would "make French the country's only official language," the party's 1971 program asserted. French would be the language of governmental institutions, it would be the working language of all enterprises, all new immigrants would be required to pass a French fluency test as a condition for obtaining a permanent visa or Quebec citizenship.[57] Since language was the fundamental value championed by the party, it was only natural that "Péquistes" be intensely concerned with the dangers faced by the French language in Quebec and committed to taking strong corrective measures. As befitted left-of-centre believers in a strongly interventionist government, laws would be adopted to solve linguistic problems.

Parti Québécois adherents were undoubtedly far more united on language policy than were the supporters of the two rival parties. Nevertheless, the Parti Québécois was on several occasions racked by acrimonious disputes concerning what rights or privileges, if any, would be accorded the province's English-speaking community.[58] For example, would there be a publicly financed English-language school sector? Radicals within the party who favoured unilingualism, many of whom had been members of the separatist Rassemblement pour l'indépendance nationale, wanted the demise of English schools; indeed, during the 1971 congress, party president René Lévesque had to threaten to resign in order to have his more moderate position prevail. Again, in February 1973, the party's executive had to take a harder line on public financing of English schools, agreeing to place a permanent ceiling on funding, in order to convince party members to accept simply the principle of the existence of schools for the English minority.[59]

The party program, on language as on all other questions, was defined with impressive democracy by elected delegates during frequent annual or biennial congresses; it certainly reflected the membership's aspirations, though generally tempered by the leadership's more moderate positions. It did not necessarily constitute a shrewd and sound appreciation of the Quebec context in general and of political realities in particular. Thus, after its election in 1976, the Parti Québécois quickly came to realize that designing a general policy was much easier than drawing up specific regulations and applying them to everyday situations. Like the other two parties, the Parti Québécois faced numerous constraints in dealing with language. Specifically, the need to take account of certain pressure made it impossible to build a Quebec as unilingually French as the party had originally intended.

Shortly after its arrival in power, the Parti Québécois government issued a White Paper detailing the language policy that it intended to implement.[60] This policy was soon set out in proposed legislation, the symbolically numbered Bill 1. The bill proposed vigorous measures to make French the language of the workplace and backed these up with threats of fines and other penalties for noncompliance. It also proposed that, generally, only French could appear on signs in public and that hitherto English-language institutions would have to communicate with the government and among themselves in French. The English-speaking school sector was to be maintained but, in most cases, only children with at least one parent who had had his or her primary schooling in Quebec in the English language were eligible. It was clear that the English sector was doomed to atrophy.

Reaction of Quebec's anglophones was uniformly negative, although, contrarily to what they had said of the Liberals, they could not pretend that the Parti Québécois had abandoned them.[61] English-speaking Quebeckers had shown only negligible support for the Parti Québécois, the party of separatism.[62] On language, the party's platform had always been quite clear—and quite unacceptable from the point of view of the English-speaking minority.[63]

In particular, business circles denounced certain aspects of Bill 1 linked to the language of the workplace. Essentially, they maintained that the law's requirements would increase costs and put Quebec enterprises at a comparative disadvantage in relation to firms elsewhere in North America. They also contended that the law gave too much power to workers and unions. Finally, the clauses that severely limited enrolment in English-language schools caused deep concern: would recruiting efforts and transfers from outside the province not be hampered?

Certainly the Parti Québécois numbered few adherents in the business world. Business thus had to make special efforts to make its weight felt once the Parti Québécois came into office. In many respects, its remonstrances were successful in that the modified version of Bill 1, called Bill 101 (in particular, its final version) took heed of business criticism. Of course, the Parti Québécois could not, even had it so wished, have abandoned the key stipulations of its language project; closely surveyed by the party's membership, the government had to remain within bounds. On the other hand, the Parti Québécois could not afford to alienate irreparably the business world. A referendum on sovereignty-association had to be held during its first mandate in office and it was reasonable to assume that if Quebec's economy floundered during this period, the electors would spurn the project.

462

Even with the amendments, anglophone business clearly did not like the law. Many enterprises, particularly head offices, left Quebec, often blaming the language legislation. Sun Life was a noisy and well-publicized example of this exodus. Yet it is very difficult to evaluate the actual causes of these departures. For some, higher Quebec taxes were the important issue. For others, militant unionism made Quebec a difficult place in which to do business. For still others, it was important to be where the action was, and that meant moving west, to Toronto, or to Alberta during the oil boom of the late 1970s.

The Parti Québécois was thus forced to moderate its language legislation and to apply it less rigorously than might otherwise have been the case. For example, head offices and research centres were exempted from the law's provisions. Professionals who had no contact with the public would not have to pass a test of French proficiency.[64] Moreover, it was common knowledge that hundreds of students were illegally enrolled in the English Protestant schools; while denouncing the situation frequently, the government preferred that the law be flouted rather than use force to expel these students.[65]

The courts ultimately constituted an additional constraint. They declared unconstitutional certain sections of the language legislation, thus weakening Bill 101.[66] Since Quebec remains a part of Canada, the Supreme Court of Canada is the court of last appeal, a situation that the Parti Québécois did not foresee or did not want to imagine in the heady days of 1977. In addition, the new Canadian Constitution, adopted without Quebec's consent in 1982, contains certain language guarantees with which Quebec is not in agreement but which nevertheless apply.

One new element that could well have an impact on the language question is the return to power, in December 1985, of the Liberals under their reincarnated leader, Robert Bourassa. The party has again become the advocate of the English-speaking minority, which counts four ministers in the provincial Cabinet. Yet interestingly — and this is surely an indication of the very considerable evolution that Quebec has undergone in matters of language since the early 1970s — the Liberals have indicated that, while they may make certain concessions and adjust Bill 101 to make it more flexible, they will not abrogate the law. Among the modifications envisaged should be mentioned the softening of the requirement that signs be in French only. Public opinion polls show an increasing percentage of Quebeckers willing to accept bilingualism on signs.[67] Still, it is apparent that Quebec has adapted to the law and that the law has changed Quebec. More than half of all allophone children are now enrolled in schools in the French sector.[68] The proportion of workers who say they work in French has increased significantly.[69] Enterprises under French control now furnish more than 60 percent of all jobs in Quebec, up from 47 percent in 1960.[70] Even the English-speaking minority, which has undergone a veritable revolution since 1970, seems able to live with the law.[71] It was inevitable that the changes that occurred in Quebec in the early 1960s would eventually have an impact on language, a highly emotional issue. Within the federal government and the English-speaking provinces, these changes have certainly had some effect. The proportion of French-speakers in the federal civil service has increased and now approaches the proportion of francophones in the total population.[72] French-language services have become more widely available. Bilingualism has become more popular among Canada's English-speaking population.[73] Still, a command of English remains a virtual necessity for francophones outside Quebec, since, with some exceptions, the concentrations of French-speaking population are insufficient to allow daily activities, notably work, to be carried out in French. It is thus not surprising that assimilation takes a large toll among the French-speaking minorities and that even the awakening of the federal government, and at least some provincial governments, to the French fact does not seem to have stemmed linguistic losses.

The Quebec case is very different, since that province has always had a strong French-speaking majority that controls the provincial government. Nevertheless, until very recently, the English-speaking minority in Quebec has wielded enormous economic power (and to a somewhat lesser extent still does)[74] and, in addition, has benefited immensely from the prestige accruing to speakers of Canada's and North America's major language. The Quiet Revolution of the early 1960s made francophones aware of a linguistic disequilibrium that disadvantaged them.[75] But it was inevitable that any attempt to modify fundamentally the balance between the two languages in Quebec would provoke bitter disputes between the majority and the minority.

Three political parties faced the challenge of enhancing the status of the French language within Quebec and of improving opportunities for francophones. Each party's actions in this regard were affected by particular constraints. For the two old parties, the Liberals and the Union Nationale, the language issue caused internecine strife within party ranks as well as considerable harm at the polls. In particular, the Liberals had to deal with the fact that their supporters included virtually the entire non-francophone minority, a group whose conception of Quebec society was markedly different from that of most francophones.

The Parti Québécois, as we have seen, proceeded differently. Far from trying to shy away from the issue and to seek some middle ground that would not alienate important factions, the party placed language reform in the forefront of its program and it hoped that its promise of a strong stand in favour of the French language would generate support among a majority of French-speaking Quebeckers. That hope proved realistic enough, although, once in power, the Parti Québécois could no longer ignore key sectors of opinion that had opposed its language policy.

What does the future bode for the French language in Quebec? The heroic exploits of the knights of language are now fading rapidly into the past. There are many indications that the younger generation of Quebeckers, those who did not fight the battles of the 1960s and 1970s, believe that the question has been permanently resolved and that French is now secure in the province.[76] This phenomenon is perhaps an indication of the relative success of Bill 101 in changing the face of Quebec. Other observers, perhaps more perspicacious, see continued dangers for the French language, regardless of the language legislation. The Conseil de la langue française, charged with advising the government on matters of language, affirms that French has still not become the "normal, habitual language of work, of teaching, of communications, of commerce and business."[77] The English language continues to surround and to penetrate Quebec. Communications, and notably cable television, have made English-language stations more numerous for most subscribers than French-language stations.[78] American culture and cultural practices will undoubtedly have a growing impact on Quebec as an open society. In addition, the tremendous advances of computer science since the late 1970s, a phenomenon entirely unforeseen by the writers of Bill 101, have been largely in English, whether it be manufacturers' manuals or software. Indeed, the three offices concerned with the application of Bill 101 see the francization of this sector as the major challenge of the near future.[79]

Other problems, though having no relation to Bill 101, certainly affect the future of the French language in Quebec. Education critics have decried poor teaching of French in schools.[80] Even business leaders have protested against graduates' insufficient mastery of

464

the French language. Finally, demographic projections for Quebec indicate that the province's population will begin to diminish shortly after the year 2000. Declining births (the Quebec fertility rate now stands at 1.42, considerably below the Canadian average of 1.68), minimal immigration from foreign countries, and, since the mid-1970s, a negative balance in population exchanges with other Canadian provinces explain this phenomenon, the repercussions of which could be dramatic.[81]

Language legislation in Canada, and particularly in Quebec, has undoubtedly had significant effects. Still, it appears certain that legislation alone cannot solve the major challenges that the French language must face if it is to maintain what has been acquired over the past twenty years.

NOTES

1. The secret instructions accompanying the *Quebec Act of 1774* are eloquent in this regard. For historian Hilda Neatby, the act and the instructions taken together signified "gentle but steady and determined anglicization." See her *Quebec: The Revolutionary Age, 1760–1791* (Toronto: McClelland and Stewart, 1966), 139.
2. Historian Fernand Ouellet calculates the birth rate at a very respectable 50 to 55 per thousand during the century following the Conquest. See *Histoire économique et sociale du Québec, 1760–1850* (Montréal: Fides, 1966), 142, 197, 468.
3. In 1851, 75.2 percent of Quebec's population was French-speaking. By 1901, this figure had climbed to 80.3 percent: *Annuaire du Québec, 1968–1969* (Québec: Bureau de la Statistique du Québec, 1968), 179.
4. For a generally good study of English–French relations in the nineteenth century, see A.I. Silver, *The French-Canadian Idea of Confederation, 1864–1900* (Toronto: University of Toronto Press, 1982). On the Manitoba Schools Question, Paul Crunican's *Priests and Politicians: Manitoba Schools and the Election of 1869* (Toronto: University of Toronto Press, 1974) is excellent. As for Ontario's attempts to suppress French-language education, consult Robert Choquette, *Language and Religion: A History of English–French Conflict in Ontario* (Ottawa: University of Ottawa Press, 1975).
5. The Royal Commission on Bilingualism and Biculturalism, in an oft-quoted and abundantly discussed table, showed that French Canadians in Quebec placed twelfth among fourteen ethnic groups by average labour income of male salary- and wage-earners in 1961. Those of British origin placed first, at a level 55 percent higher than that of the French. Even bilingualism did not appear a significant economic asset. Looking specifically at language, unilingual anglophones were at the top of the ladder, well ahead of bilingual francophones: *Report*, Book 3: *The Work World* (Ottawa: Queen's Printer, 1969), 22–24. It should be mentioned, though, that by the 1980s the French had achieved virtual economic parity with the British in Canada: Jac-André Boulet and Laval Lavallée, *L'évolution des disparités linguistiques de revenus de travail au Canada de 1970 à 1980* (Ottawa: Conseil économique du Canada, October 1983).
6. Canadians whose mother tongue (i.e., the first language learned and still understood) was French accounted for 28.1 percent of the population in 1961, and for 25.7 percent in 1981: Statistics Canada, 1961 and 1981 Censuses and tables furnished in *Language and Society* 9 (Spring 1983): 20–21. Also, 24.6 percent of Canadians told government census-takers in 1981 that the language they most often spoke at home was French. This question, more indicative of the actual strength of the French language in Canada, was first asked in 1971.
7. Royal Commission on Bilingualism and Biculturalism, *Report*, Book 1: *The Official Languages* (Ottawa: Queen's Printer, 1967), 173.
8. Daniel Johnson, premier of Quebec from 1966 to 1968, promoted the Two Nations concept. In this regard, he asserted: "French Canadians seek to identify themselves with the State of Quebec, the only state in which they can claim to be masters of their destiny, the only one that

they can utilize to promote the development of their community." On the other hand, English Canadians tend, for their part, to "consider Ottawa as their national state": Daniel Johnson, *Égalité ou indépendance* (Montréal: Éditions Renaissance, 1965), 24, 50.

9. S.C. 1969, c. 54, "An Act respecting the status of the official languages of Canada." The text and comments may be found in Commissioner of Official Languages, *First Annual Report, 1970–1971* (Ottawa: Information Canada, 1971), 105–14 and 1–11.

10. Sections 16 to 23 of the *Constitution Act, 1982,* specify language rights.

11. Commissioner of Official Languages, *Annual Report 1984* (Ottawa: Minister of Supply and Services Canada, 1985), preface.

12. This figure, however, represents a mere 5.5 percent of the total population of Canada's most populous province; francophones tend to be concentrated in the eastern and northern portions of the province.

13. Such is the case of Manitoba, now obliged by the Supreme Court to translate its laws into French. The francophones of that province proposed that, instead of translating thousands of laws, many of them inoperative, the provincial government offer certain services in French. In 1984, after having accepted the proposition, the government yielded to widespread anglophone opposition and backed down from its commitment.

14. Task Force on Canadian Unity, *A Future Together: Observations and Recommendations* (Ottawa: Minister of Supply and Services Canada, 1979), 51.

15. Statistics Canada, 1981 census, and tables furnished in Robert Bourbeau, "Canada's Language Transfer Phenomenon," *Language and Society* 11 (Autumn 1983): 14–22.

16. The most recent Statistics Canada report affirms that the French have maintained their positions, in relative terms, only in Quebec (figures quoted in *La Presse*, 26 janvier 1985).

17. Bourbeau, "Canada's Language Transfer Phenomenon," 15.

18. This phenomenon was first convincingly documented by Richard J. Joy in *Languages in Conflict* (Toronto: McClelland and Stewart, Carleton Library no. 61, 1972). Davidson Dunton, co-chairman of the Royal Commission on Bilingualism and Biculturalism, has remarked on the popularity of the "two unilingualisms" solutions to the Canadian language question: "The Muddy Waters of Bilingualism," *Language and Society* 1 (Autumn 1979): 7.

19. See Richard Jones, *Duplessis and the Union Nationale Administration* (Ottawa: Canadian Historical Association, booklet no. 35, 1983), and reprinted in this volume [*Quebec since 1945: Selected Readings*].

20. This era has recently been chronicled by political scientist Dale C. Thomson in *Jean Lesage and the Quiet Revolution* (Toronto: Macmillan of Canada, 1984).

21. "Masters in our own house" was the theme of the Liberal election campaign in 1962. The major issue of the campaign was the nationalization of the private electrical power companies (*Manifeste du parti libéral du Québec*, 1962, 1).

22. For example, Hubert Guindon, "Social Unrest, Social Class, and Quebec's Bureaucratic Revolution," *Queen's Quarterly* 71, 2 (Summer 1964): 150–62; Roch Denis, *Luttes de classes et question nationale au Québec, 1948–1968* (Montréal: Presses Socialistes Internationales, 1979).

23. The expression is from Université de Montréal sociologist Guy Rocher, *Le Québec en mutation* (Montréal: Éditions Hurtubise-HMH, 1973).

24. The titles of some of the separatist books published in these years are revealing: Raymond Barbeau, *Le Québec est-il une colonie?* (Montréal: Les Éditions de l'Homme, 1962); Raymond Barbeau, *La libération économique du Québec* (Montréal: Les Éditions de l'Homme, 1963); Andrew D'Allemagne, *Le colonialisme au Québec* (Montréal: Les Éditions R-B, 1966).

25. The major independentist group of the early 1960s, the Rassemblement pour l'indépendance nationale, vigorously denounced bilingualism and objected to any legislative recognition of rights for Quebec's English-speaking linguistic minority (*Programme du R.I.N.*, octobre 1962, 2).

26. Université Laval sociologist Fernand Dumont was one of those asking this question. See "Y a-t-il un avenir pour l'homme canadien-français?" in *La vigile du Québec* (Montréal: Éditions Hurtubise-HMH, 1971), 57–76.

27. "Programme d'immigration au service d'une politique raciste," editorial, *Le Devoir*, 7 octobre 1947, 1.

465

28. *Annuaire du Québec* 1968–1969, 255.
29. The percentage of New Canadians enrolled in French schools fell from 52 in 1931–32 to 25 in 1962–63, then to 11 by 1972–73: Gary Caldwell, "Assimilation and the Demographic Future of Quebec," in *Quebec's Language Policies: Background and Response*, ed. John R. Mallea (Québec: Centre international de recherche sur le bilinguisme, Presses de l'Université Laval, 1977), 57.
30. Jacques Henripin saw Montreal as being between 53 and 60 percent French-speaking by 2000, a decline of between 6 and 13 percent, in "Quebec and the Demographic Dilemma of French-Canadian Society," *Quebec's Language Policies*, 43, 48.
31. *Programme politique du Parti libéral du Québec*, 1960, 2.
32. *Québec en marche: Le programme politique du Parti libéral du Québec*, 1966, 5.
33. The best history of the party is Herbert F. Quinn's *The Union Nationale: Quebec Nationalism from Duplessis to Lévesque*, 2nd ed. (Toronto: University of Toronto Press, 1979).
34. *Objectifs 1966 de l'Union Nationale, un programme d'action pour une jeune nation. Québec d'abord*, 3.
35. Of the nearly 90 000 members of the Parti Québécois in 1971, nearly 40 percent belonged to the liberal professions, including a very large number of teachers, nearly 25 percent were white-collar workers, mainly office employees and service workers, and 15 percent were students: *Le Parti québécois en bref* (Montréal: Les Éditions du Parti québécois, 1971), 21.
36. Jean-Marc Léger, "Il faut créer dix, vingt, cinquante St-Léonard," *Le Devoir*, 4 septembre 1968.
37. "Allophone," in the Canadian context, is the term used to describe persons whose mother tongue is neither English nor French.
38. Since 1968, Quebec's unicameral legislature has been called the "National Assembly," an appellation of obvious symbolic value. The other Canadian provinces use the term "Legislative Assembly."
39. From Toronto, a *Globe and Mail* editorial denounced what it saw as "cultural protectionism": "Turning Back the Clock," 2 Sept. 1968.
40. See, for example, Johnson's speech at the first meeting of the Constitutional Conference in Ottawa in February, 1968. Constitutional Conference, First Meeting, *Proceedings* (Ottawa: Queen's Printer, 1968), 53–71.
41. Text of press conference quoted in Paul Gros d'Aillon, *Daniel Johnson, l'égalité avant l'indépendance* (Montréal: Les Éditions internationales Stanké, 1979), 230–34.
42. This was the interpretation of journalists, and even Bertrand admitted that there did seem to be a coincidence ("Des groupes francophones protestent: le bill sur les droits scolaires sera présenté aujourd'hui," *Le Devoir*, 26 novembre 1968). The election theme in the district of Notre-Dame-de-Grâce, an English-speaking constituency in Montreal, was "Remember St. Leonard" (*The Montreal Star*, editorial, 20 Nov. 1968).
43. This is the interpretation of Jérôme Proulx, a Union Nationale deputy, in his book, *Le panier de crabes* (Montréal: Éditions Parti Pris, 1971), 111–24. Journalists agreed ("Le bill sur les droits scolaires: l'opposition du caucus fait reculer Bertrand," *Le Devoir*, 27 novembre 1968, headline; Vincent Prince, "Le bill Bertrand renvoyé à un Comité," editorial, *Le Devoir*, 14 décembre 1968).
44. Order in council no. 3958, 9 Dec. 1968, quoted in Commission of Inquiry on the Position of the French Language and on Language Rights in Quebec, *Report: The Position of the French Language in Quebec; II: Language Rights* (Montréal, 1972), v.
45. Robert J. Macdonald, "In Search of a Language Policy: francophone Reactions to Bill 85 and 63," in *Quebec's Language Policies*, 219–42.
46. Pierre Laporte's speech in *Débats de l'Assemblée nationale du Québec*, 10 octobre 1969, 3152.
47. Proulx, *Le panier de crabes*, 152–53.
48. The bill closely resembled Bill 85, presented a year earlier and withdrawn.
49. Opposition Leader Jean Lesage's speech in *Débats de l'Assemblée nationale du Québec*, 28 octobre 1969, 3376–78.
50. In the opinion of Jérôme Proulx, who resigned as a Union Nationale deputy to vote against Bill 63, the law destroyed the party. See *Le panier de crabes*, 153–54 and 193–94. A poll done for the Quebec City daily, *Le Soleil*, showed that the Union Nationale's stand on the language of education won it no support among anglophones, 71.9 percent of whom proposed to vote for the

Liberals while only 9.4 percent preferred the Union Nationale (*Le Soleil*, 18 avril 1970, 12). Other polling, done by political scientist Peter Regenstreif, showed that at least a small majority of Quebeckers were satisfied with the government's record on language while large majorities were dissatisfied with its record on issues like strikes, taxes, and unemployment. Quoted in Vincent Lemieux, Marcel Gilbert, and André Blais, *Une élection de réalignement: l'élection générale du 29 avril 1970 au Québec* (Montréal: Éditions du Jour, 1970), 86.

51. *Official Language Act*, Statutes of Quebec, 1974, c. 6.

52. William Tetley, "The English and Language Legislation: A Personal History," in *The English of Quebec: From Majority to Minority Status*, ed. Gary Caldwell and Eric Waddell (Québec: Institut québécois de recherche sur la culture, 1982), 381–97. Tetley was an anglophone minister in the Bourassa cabinet that adopted Bill 22. For an informative study of anglophone opinion, see Michael B. Stein, "Bill 22 and the Non-francophone Population in Quebec: A Case Study of Minority Group Attitudes on Language Legislation," in *Quebec's Language Policies*, 243–65.

53. Michel Paillé, "The Impact of Language Policies on Enrolment in Public Schools in Quebec," in *Contribution à la démolinguistique du Québec* (Québec: Conseil de la langue française, avril 1985), 139–40; Claude St. Germain, *La situation linguistique dans les écoles primaires et secondaires, 1971–72 à 1978–79* (Québec: Conseil de la langue française, 1979), 12, 24.

54. Quinn, *The Union Nationale*, 279–80.

55. The party's "political action program," adopted during its third congress in February 1971, specifically promised to mount a campaign to fight for the repeal of Bill 63 (Parti Québécois, *Le programme — l'action politique — les status et règlements, édition 1971*, 35).

56. René Lévesque, *Option Québec* (Montréal: Les Éditions de l'Homme, 1968), 19.

57. Parti Québécois, *Le programme*, 21.

58. For Vera Murray, the Parti Québécois, even while in opposition, was rife with tension on virtually all aspects of its ideology. She sees the battles as pitting a "technocratic" wing, more moderate, emphasizing efficiency and planning, and controlling the party's executive, against a more radical "participationist" wing, representing a minority of the party's members, but very vigorous and noisy in the defence of its left-wing social-democratic positions: *Le Parti Québécois, de la fondation à la prise du pouvoir* (Montréal: Éditions Hurtubise-HMH, 1976), 29–30.

59. *Le Devoir*, 26 février 1973.

60. Camille Laurin, *La politique québécoise de la langue française* (Québec: Éditeur officiel, 1977).

61. Many anglophone organizations and firms testified during government hearings on Bill 1 (Assemblée nationale, Journal des Débats, Commission permanente de l'éducation, des affaires culturelles et des communications, *Délibérations*, juin-juillet 1977). One anglophone pressure group, the Positive Action Committee, sarcastically commented on the bill: "The anglophone collectivity has a place in Quebec on the condition that it is invisible and silent and progressively diminishes in number" (Alison d'Anglejan, "Language Planning in Quebec: An Historical Overview and Future Trends," in *Conflict and Language Planning in Quebec*, ed. Richard Y. Bourhis (Clevedon, England: Multilingual Matters Ltd., 1984), 29–52.

62. Only 9.5 percent of non-francophones proposed to support the Parti Québécois in 1976; 22 percent intended to vote for the Union Nationale and its policy of "free choice"; 40 percent refused to answer, proposed to abstain, or did not know which party they would support (poll figures quoted in André Bernard, *Québec élections 1976* [Montréal: Éditions Hurtubise-HMH, 1976]), 49.

63. Anglophone reactions are analyzed in Nadia Assimopoulous and Michel Laferrière, *Législation et perceptions ethniques: une étude du contenu de la presse anglaise de Montréal au vote de la loi 101* (Montréal: Office de la langue française, 1980).

64. These adaptations are examined in William D. Coleman, "From Bill 22 to Bill 101: The Politics of Language under the Parti Québécois," *Canadian Journal of Political Science* 14, 3 (Sept. 1981): 459–85, and reprinted in this volume [that is, *Quebec since 1945: Selected Readings*]; also in William D. Coleman, "A Comparative Study of Language Policy in Quebec: A Political Economy Approach," in *The Politics of Canadian Public Policy*, ed. Michael M. Atkinson and Marsha A. Chandler (Toronto: University of Toronto Press, 1983), 21–42.

65. Claude Ryan, minister of education in the new Bourassa Liberal government (elected on 2 December 1985), stated that he would prefer to settle the problem of the estimated 1800 "illegals" on a case-by-case basis (*Le Devoir*, 28 et 29 janvier 1986). The government decided nevertheless on a general amnesty, decried by critics because it rewarded those who disobeyed the law.

66. Gilles Rhéaume, president of two nationalist organizations, the Société Saint-Jean Baptiste de Montréal and the Mouvement national des Québécois, declared that the courts had riddled Bill 101 with so many holes that it was beginning to look like a piece of Swiss cheese (*The Gazette*, 5 Jan. 1985).

67. In 1979, fewer than one of three francophone Quebeckers thought that English should be allowed on public signs. A 1981 poll showed that two in three French-speaking Montrealers agreed with bilingualism on signs. By 1984, 80 percent of francophone Quebeckers disagreed with the French unilingualism imposed by the sign stipulation in Bill 101 (Commissioner of Official Languages, *Annual Report 1984*, 37). 1985 polls conducted by the Centre de Recherches sur l'Opinion publique showed similar findings (*La Presse*, 20 janvier and 27 avril 1985).

68. The figure increased from 30 percent in 1976–77 to 57 percent in 1984–85 (Michel Paillé, "Conséquences des politiques linguistiques québécoises sur les effectifs scolaires selon la langue d'enseignement," *Le Devoir*, 29 mai 1985).

69. Numerous surveys have been conducted on this question. The Gendron Commission prepared a lengthy study of the question as it stood in the early 1970s. Sixty-four percent of francophones declared that they worked almost solely in French (Commission d'enquête sur la situation de la langue française et sur les droits linguistiques au Québec, *Rapport*, Livre I: *La langue de travail* (Quebec, décembre 1972, 16–19). According to recent findings, 70 percent of francophones now work only in French, and another 20 percent generally in French ("A Linguistic Scarecrow," editorial, *The Gazette*, 9 Jan. 1985).

70. André Raynauld and François Vaillancourt, *L'appartenance des entreprises: le cas du Québec en 1978* (Montréal: Office de la langue française, 1985).

71. One-half of Quebec's anglophones (two-thirds of those under 30) are bilingual. The population of Anglo-Quebeckers, however, declined by 10 percent during the 1970s because of significant out-migration. Not surprisingly, research has shown that anglophones who left tended to speak only English while anglophones who remained tended to be bilingual (Statistics Canada, *Language in Canada*, quoted in *The Gazette* and *Le Devoir*, 26 Jan. 1985).

72. Commissioner of Official Languages, *Annual Report* 1984, 60. However, over half of all francophone employees are in non-officer positions, including clerks, secretaries, and similar occupations.

73. Fifteen percent of Canadians class themselves as bilingual. Between 1971 and 1981, their number grew at double the rate of population increase. Only 7.6 percent of English Canadians are bilingual as compared with 36.2 percent of French Canadians. Considering only the English-speaking provinces, 5.4 percent of the English speak French while 78.9 percent of the French know English. Quebec boasts by far the highest proportion of bilinguals: Statistics Canada, *Language in Canada* (Ottawa: Supply and Services Canada, Jan. 1985). French immersion programs in the English-speaking provinces have recently become extremely popular (Commissioner of Official Languages, *Annual Report* 1984, 25–29).

74. Sixty-nine percent of managers in Quebec, in the public and private sectors, are now French-speaking. French-speaking managers even have a slight majority in English-Canadian and in foreign firms established in the province. Arnaud Sales, *Décideurs et gestionnaires; étude sur la direction et l'encadrement des secteurs privé et public* (Québec: Éditeur officiel, 1985), 177–202.

75. Language situations in which dominance is not based on demographic supremacy can easily produce social tensions. Such has been the case in Quebec. See Pierre E. Laporte, "Status Language Planning in Quebec: An Evaluation," in *Conflict and Language Planning in Quebec*, 57.

76. Polls conducted by the Conseil de la langue française, one of the organisms created by Bill 101, showed, in the opinion of the Conseil, that the young live "with the peacefulness of security brought about by the French language Charter." (Quoted in *The Gazette*, 22 April 1985.) The

Conseil expressed shock when 40 percent of high school students queried affirmed that "living in French" was not necessary for their personal development! (*La situation linguistique actuelle* [Québec, Conseil de la langue française, janvier 1985], 27.)

77. *La situation linguistique actuelle*, 18.
78. A study commissioned by the Conseil showed that francophones spend about one-third of their television time watching English-language stations. Ibid., 12.
79. Jean-Pierre Proulx, "La question linguistique: la révolution informatique constitue le défi de l'heure," *Le Devoir*, 12 décembre 1985.
80. "Un constat de piètre qualité: l'apprentissage de la langue maternelle à l'école," *Le Soleil*, 17 janvier 1985; "L'apprentissage de la langue maternelle est en crise," *Le Devoir*, 16 janvier 1985.
81. Assemblée nationale du Québec, Commission parlementaire de la culture, *Le Québec à la croisée des chemins démographiques*, septembre 1985; Albert Juneau, "La défaite des berceaux," *Le Devoir*, 7 juin 1985; Jean-Claude Leclerc, "L'effondrement démographique: le réveil risque d'être tardif," *Le Devoir*, 8 novembre 1985; Georges Mathews, "La crise démographique au Québec," *Le Devoir*, 18 and 19 novembre 1985.

Topic Fifteen

Contemporary Canada

The election of Pierre Elliott Trudeau as Liberal party leader at the

Liberal leadership convention in Ottawa, April 1968.

472   **CANADIANS** today face many challenges, some new, others long-standing. One issue is as old as Canadian history itself: to find a means to enable the First Nations, Inuit, and Metis peoples to obtain full participation in Canadian society. The colonization of what is now Canada led to the Native peoples' marginalization by the European newcomers. Only recently have the Aboriginal peoples succeeded in arousing public attention and support in their resistance to assimilation. In "A Note on Canadian Treaties," historian Anthony Hall shows how the Nisga'a Treaty signed in 1998 was "the most recent in a long series of innovations to address one of the world's most pressing and pervasive human rights issues" — Aboriginal and treaty rights. In these modern agreements, he continues, "a major preoccupation of those on the Aboriginal side of these modern-day treaty negotiations has been how to establish a range of new institutions to help liberate indigenous peoples from the weight of an onerous colonial system that has dominated their lives, often for many generations."

A more recent but equally pressing issue that has its roots in Canada's history is the incorporation of ethnic Canadians into Canadian society. Since the immigration of non-English-speaking and non-French-speaking Canadians began, the host society has debated whether they should be accepted, and, if so, how they should be incorporated into mainstream Canadian society. In "The Merits of Multiculturalism," Will Kymlicka analyzes the debate over multiculturalism since its implementation by the Canadian government in the 1988 *Multiculturalism Act*. Contrary to the arguments of opponents of multiculturalism who assert that the policy has promoted a form of ethnic separatism among immigrants, Kymlicka claims that the evidence supports the opposite conclusion, namely that immigrants have chosen to integrate into Canadian society and that the policy of multiculturalism has been a resounding success.

The federal Liberal government of Pierre Elliott Trudeau initiated the policy of multiculturalism, one of a series of policies and controversies that form the legacy of the charismatic leader of the Liberal party and prime minister of Canada from 1968 until 1984 (except for a brief period of Conservative rule under Joe Clark in 1979). At the time of his death in the fall of 2000, an outpouring of emotion for the man, and what he stood for, occurred. It is evident that Trudeau has come to symbolize something greater than the man himself, something that remains after his tenure in office and even after his death. In "Charisma and Contradiction: The Legacy of Pierre Elliott Trudeau," political scientist Stephen Clarkson attempts to understand Trudeau's legacy. In the end, Clarkson concludes that "to make sense of him, we have to make sense of ourselves and the twentieth-century Canada we shared with him."

Recent surveys of the history of Aboriginal Canada include Olive Patricia Dickason, *Canada's First Nations*: *A History of Founding Peoples from Earliest Times*, 2nd ed. (Toronto: Oxford University Press, 1997), and Arthur J. Ray, *I Have Lived Here since the World Began*: *An Illustrated History of Canada's Native People* (Toronto: Key Porter, 1996). Edward S. Rogers and Donald B. Smith, eds., *Aboriginal Ontario* (Toronto: Dundurn Press, 1994), looks at the history of the First Nations in Ontario.

For a review of Canadian Indian policy in the early twentieth century see E. Brian Titley, *A Narrow Vision*: *Duncan Campbell Scott and the Administration of Indian Affairs in Canada* (Vancouver: University of British Columbia Press, 1986). Two important summaries of federal Indian policy are included in Ian A.L. Getty and Antoine S. Lussier, eds., *As Long as the Sun Shines and Water Flows* (Vancouver: University of British Columbia Press, 1983): George F.G. Stanley, "As Long as the Sun Shines and Water Flows: An Historical Comment," pp. 1–26; and John L. Tobias, "Protection, Civilization, Assimilation: An Outlines History of Canada's Indian Policy," pp. 39–55. J.R. Miller provides a complete account in *Skyscrapers Hide the Heavens: A History of Indian-White Relations in Canada*, 3rd ed. (Toronto: University of Toronto Press, 2000); see also Noel Dyck, *What Is the Indian "Problem"? Tutelage and Resistance in Canadian Indian Administration* (St. John's: Institute of Social and Economic Research, Memorial University of Newfoundland, 1991). Still valuable is the early work by the Cree leader Harold Cardinal, *The Unjust Society: The Tragedy of Canada's Indians,* reprint (Vancouver: Douglas and McIntyre, 1999). Two recent contributions by political scientists are C. Cairns, *Citizens Plus: Aboriginal Peoples and the Canadian State* (Vancouver: University of British Columbia Press, 2000), and Tom Flanagan, *First Nations? Second Thoughts* (Montreal/Kingston: McGill-Queen's University Press, 2000).

For First Nations' land claims, see *Delgamuukw: The Supreme Court of Canada Decision on Aboriginal Title,* commentary by Stan Persky (North Devon, England: Greyston Books, 1998). At the provincial level, see: for Saskatchewan, Frank Tough, Jim Miller, and Arthur J. Ray, *Bounty and Benevolence: A Documentary History of Saskatchewan Treaties* (Montreal/Kingston: McGill-Queen's University Press, 2000), and F. Laurie Barron, *Walking in Indian Moccasins: The Native Policies of Tommy Douglas and the CCF* (Vancouver: University of British Columbia Press, 1997); for Ontario, David T. McNab, *Circles of Time: Aboriginal Land Rights and Resistance in Ontario* (Waterloo: Wilfrid Laurier University Press, 1999); for British Columbia, Christopher McKee, *Treaty Talks in British Columbia: Negotiating a Mutually Beneficial Future,* 2nd ed. (Vancouver: University of British Columbia Press, 2000); and Tom Malloy and Donald Ward, *The World Is Our Witness: The Historic Journey of the Nisga'a into Canada* (Calgary: Fifth House, 2000). A good review of Aboriginal issues is David Long and Olive Patricia Dickason, eds., *Visions of the Heart,* 2nd ed. (Toronto: Harcourt Canada, 2000).

A good overview of Canada's immigration policy is Donald H. Avery, *Reluctant Host: Canada's Response to Immigrant Workers, 1896–1994* (Toronto: McClelland and Stewart, 1995). The 1980s in particular are examined in Gerald E. Dirks, *Controversy and Complexity: Canadian Immigration Policy during the 1980s* (Montreal/Kingston: McGill-Queen's University Press, 1995). Another major study of immigration policy is Freda Hawkings, *Canada and Immigration: Public Policy and Public Concern,* 2nd ed. (Montreal/Kingston: McGill-Queen's University Press, 1988). A brief account of Canada's immigration history can be found in Valerie Knowles, *Strangers at Our Gates: Canadian Immigration and Immigration Policy, 1540–1995,* rev. ed. (Toronto: Dundurn Press, 1997). An analysis of the costs and gains of immigration is available in Don J. DeVoretz, ed., *Diminishing Returns: The Economics of Canada's Recent Immigration Policy* (Toronto: C.D. Howe Institute, 1995). Critical studies of Canadian immigration policy include Victor Malarek, *Haven's Gate: Canada's Immigration Fiasco* (Toronto: Macmillan, 1987); Reg Whitaker, *Double Standard: The Secret History of Canadian Immigration* (Toronto: Lester & Orpen Dennys, 1987); and David Matas and Ilana Simon, *Closing the Doors* (Toronto: Summerhill Press, 1989).

Will Kymlicka's defence of Canada's policy of multiculturalism can be found in greater detail in *Finding Our Way: Rethinking Ethnocultural Relations in Canada* (Toronto: Oxford University Press, 1998), from which the excerpt "The Merits of Multiculturalism" is taken. For vigorous criticisms of multiculturalism, see Reginald Bibby, *Mosaic Madness: The Poverty and Potential of Life in Canada* (Toronto: Stoddary, 1990); Neil Bissoondath, *Selling Illusions: The Cult of Multiculturalism in Canada* (Toronto: Penguin, 1994); and Richard Gwyn,

Nationalism without Walls: The Unbearable Lightness of Being Canadian (Toronto: McClelland and Stewart, 1995). An important historiographical work is J.W. Berry and J.A. Lapointe, eds., *Ethnicity and Culture in Canada: The Research Landscape* (Toronto: University of Toronto Press, 1994).

On Pierre Elliott Trudeau and the Trudeau era, see Stephen Clarkson and Christina McCall, *Trudeau and Our Times*, vol. 1, *The Magnificient Obsession*; vol. 2, *The Heroic Delusion* (Toronto: McClelland and Stewart, 1990, 1994); Christina McCall Newman, *Grits: An Intimate Portrait of the Liberal Party* (Toronto: Macmillan, 1982); Andrew Cohen and J.L. Granatstein, eds., *Trudeau's Shadow: The Life and Legacy of Pierre Elliott Trudeau* (Toronto: Random House, 1998); Guy Laforest, *Trudeau and the End of a Canadian Dream* (Montreal/Kingston: McGill-Queen's University Press, 1995). On Trudeau's foreign policy, see J.L. Granatstein and Robert Bothwell, *Pirouette: Pierre Trudeau and Canadian Foreign Policy* (Toronto: University of Toronto Press, 1990). Early biographies of Trudeau include George Radwanski, *Trudeau* (Toronto: Macmillan, 1978), and Richard Gwyn, *The Northern Magus: Pierre Trudeau and Canadians* (Markham, ON: PaperJacks Ltd., 1980). For collections of Trudeau's writings, see Pierre Elliott Trudeau, *Federalism and the French Canadians* (Toronto: Macmillan, 1968); *The Asbestos Strike* (Toronto: James Lewis & Samuel, 1974); *Approaches to Politics* (Toronto: Oxford University Press, 1970); *Conversation with Canadians* (Toronto: University of Toronto Press, n.d.); *Towards a Just Society: The Trudeau Years* (Toronto: Viking, 1990); and *Against the Current: Selected Writings 1939–1996* (Toronto: McClelland and Stewart, 1996).

Article Thirty-Two

A Note on Canadian Treaties

Anthony J. Hall

When a long process of intercultural diplomacy and democracy culminated in the making of the Nisga'a treaty in 1998, the world stopped to take notice. News of the deal made the front page of *The New York Times*. Reports also appeared in Switzerland, Japan, Australia, New Zealand, France, and throughout South America. In Great Britain, the journalists at the BBC and *The Economist* introduced their large global audiences to the Canadian term "First Nation." The latter characterized the tripartite agreement between the people of the Nisga'a First Nation and the governments of Canada and British Columbia as "a historic precedent."[1]

There was some truth in this characterization. For instance, the inclusion of provisions for the Nisga'a Memorial Lava Bed Park devoted to the ideals of cultural renewal and interpretation broke new ground. What the writers at *The Economist* and others failed to appreciate, however, is that the Nisga'a treaty is more about continuity than discontinuity; it is more about elaborating and projecting forward very old traditions of constitutional law than it is about breaking with our heritage in ways that lack precedent.

Source: Tom Molloy with David Ward, *The World Is Our Witness: The Historic Journey of the Nisga'a into Canada* (Calgary: Fifth House Publishers, 2000), pp. 3–10.

The Nisga'a treaty is the most recent in a long series of innovations to address legally one of the world's most pressing and pervasive human rights issues whose origins lie more in the events of 1492 than 1998. Since the beginnings of the Columbian conquests over five centuries ago, the legal minds of one European empire after another have struggled to find rationales for the overseas extension of their sovereigns' territorial claims. While one school of imperial theorists maintained that the rights and titles of the indigenous peoples on the frontiers of Europe's expansionism could be unilaterally extinguished, other voices argued otherwise.

New Spain was the first major laboratory of deliberation on what we today describe in the Canadian Constitution as "existing aboriginal and treaty rights." In this milieu the debate went beyond the question of whether the Aboriginal inhabitants of the colony had any right of ownership and jurisdiction in the soil beneath their feet. The question extended also to whether these Aboriginal peoples could be transformed into property through the institution of slavery. The Vatican weighed into the controversy in 1537 with the *Sublimus Bull.* It stipulated that the Indians of the Americas were indeed fully human. "By no means," directed the Pope, should they be "deprived of their liberty or possession of their property, even though they be outside the Christian faith."[2]

This papal bull extended to the Americas some of the principles already fleshed out by Father Fransisco de Vitoria, a Dominican theology professor at Spain's Salamanaca University. In 1532, in a series of lectures entitled "On the Indians Lately Discovered," Vitoria described the Native Americans as "true owners" of their aboriginal lands with a "true dominion" over themselves.[3] In 1550 the proponents of Aboriginal rights eventually faced in court the advocates of Indian slavery. In seminal litigation Brother Bartolomé de Las Casas made an urgent appeal to stop the murderous letting of so much Indian blood.[4] Its absorption into the soil tragically became a rite of baptism to christen the Born Again New World as an extension of Europe in what David Stannard has termed in his important book of the same name, *The American Holocaust.*[5]

Las Casas's great advocacy of human rights still reverberates across language barriers and generations. Basically he embraced the civilized heritage of First Nations in the Americas as part of humanity's commonwealth of wisdom, invention, and cultural richness. The planet Las Casas sought to enliven with his lofty literature and penetrating legal interventions was one with sufficient checks on Western civilization's expansionary aggressions to afford all indigenous peoples a place of dignity and security.

Las Casas envisaged a world where First Nations could participate in, rather than be engulfed by, the forces of globalization that began in 1492. In an intellectual tradition that would be carried on in the twentieth century by the Shuswap visionary of the Fourth World, namely George Manuel, Las Casas pictured a future where indigenous peoples would have a recognized right to pass onto their progeny the adaptive ingenuity derived from their Aboriginal heritages.[6] He pictured a planet where a regime of respect for Aboriginal and treaty rights would establish the basis for what Richard White has characterized as a "middle ground" of compromise and coexistence between and among distinct peoples. As White would have it, Canada was, in its first incarnation, one of the continent's most important middle grounds of collaborative enterprise between Native and newcomer in the development of the French–Aboriginal fur trade. The Nisga'a treaty can be pictured as yet another effort to find and hold this zone of fruitful cross-fertilization on the middle ground of an expanded, tripartite version of Canadian federalism.[7]

The history of Crown–First Nation treaty making in the English colonies, then in British North America, and then in the Dominion of Canada makes the agreement with the Nisga'a a very recent link in one of the world's oldest and most broad-ranging series of interconnected negotiations on the moving frontier of intercultural relations.[8] The early English colonies were founded in the seventeenth century on legal doctrines of "discovery" that made no provision to incorporate principles of Aboriginal rights such as those articulated by Vitoria and Las Casas.

Little by little, however, some of their ideas entered New England largely by way of Holland. Roger Williams, for instance, led a small group of Protestant dissenters away from the harsh theocracy of Massachusetts. Lacking a land grant from the monarch, Williams turned to the region's Narragansett Indians to authorize a land transfer giving legal sanction to his settlement of Rhode Island. The patriarch of the Quaker colony named after William Penn also went to his Aboriginal neighbours to make purchases from them to gain First Nations sanction for the establishment of Pennsylvania. Hence Williams and Penn are seminal contributors to the constitutional heritage of the tradition of Crown–First Nations treaty making that extended to Nisga'a territory in 1998.

The colonies of New Netherlands and New France provided the British imperial government with evidence that the process of colonizing British North America could be pressed forward in collaboration with First Nations through the medium of the fur trade. The officers of the Dutch colony were especially important in setting examples through their diplomacy with indigenous peoples that treaty making and gift exchanges could be instrumental in helping to extend imperial influence more deeply into Indian Country. The conquest of New Netherlands to create New York colony in 1664 and the conquest of France's colony of Canada a century later laid the groundwork for the expanding importance of imperial recognition of Aboriginal and treaty rights in the expansion of British North America. The culmination of this process was the codification in 1763 of King George III's Royal Proclamation as the constitutional foundation of British imperial Canada, including the new Crown province of Quebec.

The Royal Proclamation of King George III established the constitutional foundation of British imperial Canada after the defeat of the French army in North America during the Seven Years' War. The Proclamation's formulation was hastened in 1763 when news reached the imperial capital that a confederacy of Indian peoples following Pontiac would resist the British colonization of Canada without proper provisions to recognize the collectively held title of First Nations peoples to their ancestral lands.

The Proclamation recognized that title by drawing a westerly boundary for the Anglo-American colonies. The lands to the west of this line were reserved for the Indians as their hunting grounds. The King prohibited private individuals or companies from purchasing any of the reserved land directly from Indian peoples. He stipulated that if non-Aboriginals wanted to colonize this territory in the future only he and his royal heirs had the authority to conduct negotiations with the First Nations to make the appropriate adjustments in land tenure.

By asserting this power the imperial government was attempting to establish its exclusive right to regulate the westward movement of the Anglo-American settlements. Many settlers in the Thirteen Colonies resented this centralized control, and the issue became one of the major grievances of the American Revolution. The other side of the equation in this historical drama was that the Royal Proclamation helped establish a powerful tradition of alliance between First Nations and the imperial government in the interior of North America. The transcontinental fur trade, whose entrepreneurial core was the North West Company of Montreal, helped secure the economic and social basis of that alliance. In 1821 that enterprise merged with the Hudson's Bay Company, which became the Crown's primary instrument in maintaining its claim to the northwestern portion of North America until its titles were purchased by the Dominion of Canada in 1869.

The strong tradition of alliances between the First Nations, the British imperial government, and the fur-trade interests of Canada became the basis of a constitutional heritage that extends to the treaty tradition of the present day. At its most extreme, this tradition was expressed in the military alliance that was integral to the defence of Upper Canada from annexation by the United States in the War of 1812. During this conflict, more than ten thousand Native fighting men rose up in defence of their own country. In return, they expected the imperial government to support the establishment of a sovereign Aboriginal dominion in the heart of North America.

That Crown protectorate was to have been governed by a council of federated Indian nations. Its purpose from the imperial government's perspective was to provide a buffer between the American republic and what remained of British North America. While this outcome was precluded by the martyrdom in 1813 of Tecumseh — the Indian confederacy's great visionary — the Indians' military alliance with the Crown in the War of 1812 was critical in preventing the absorption of Canada into the domain of the Stars and Stripes.

These large geopolitical realities established the atmosphere of friendship and alliance in which the early treaties were negotiated after the establishment of the American republic in 1783. The provisions of the Royal Proclamation were thus applied in the process of opening Upper Canada to non-Aboriginal settlement. Only gradually in the first decades of the nineteenth century did these pre-Confederation treaties with First Nations come to include the establishment of Indian reserves.

In 1850 the tradition of Crown treaty making with the First Nations was extended into the mineral-rich lands north of the Great Lakes. Some of the Anishinabek people in this region, who were mostly veterans of the War of 1812, laid the groundwork for these negotiations by closing down a small mine at Michipicoten. They did so to make the point that the Crown had never properly addressed their land rights. After Governor General Lord Elgin intervened on their behalf, two agreements were negotiated known as the Robinson-Huron and Robinson-Superior treaties. These transactions established 21 new Indian reserves, furthering the entrenchment of this institution into Canada's legal and territorial framework. The Robinson treaties also recognize that First Nations peoples retained hunting and fishing rights on Crown lands.

The tradition of Crown treaties with the First Nations was extended into the vast territories purchased by the Dominion of Canada from the Hudson's Bay Company in 1869. The patriotic assertions by Louis Riel and the Métis of Red River during the winter of 1870 forced dominion officials to recognize that they needed to obtain some kind of sanction from the indigenous peoples for the imposition on their ancestral lands of the new government's jurisdiction. Accordingly, between 1871 and 1929, eleven so-called numbered treaties together with several adhesions were negotiated. Crown officials conducted negotiations with Cree, Oji-Cree, Saulteaux, Dene, Assiniboine, and Blackfoot over a vast area from the western shores of James Bay to the eastern slopes of the Rocky Mountains.

This cycle of treaty making began in 1871, just as Congress passed a law in the United States prohibiting further treaty making with Indian peoples. The persistence of the treaty tradition in Canada has many explanations, some of which go back to the importance of the alliances between First Nations and the imperial government in the era of the American Revolution and the War of 1812. That experience entrenched the legal heritage of the Royal Proclamation into the constitutional and political traditions of Canada. One small manifestation of this heritage are the red jackets of the North-West Mounted Police, a force that was brought into existence largely to conduct treaties and to enforce the reserve system on the Indian peoples of western Canada. The red jackets were to remind the First

Nations of the era when their ancestors had fought side by side with the Crown's Red Coats in defending territory against the American aggressor.

The numbered treaties included promises to Indian peoples such as schools, teachers, and agricultural instructors; reserves calculated at either 160 or 640 acres per family; one-time payments and annuities of five dollars per year for every individual; medicine chests to be maintained on reserves; ploughs, breeding stock, and other agricultural implements; housing; as well as flags, medals, and buggies for the principal men. While some view the legal wording on treaty documents literally, others see these agreements as establishing general principles for relationships between peoples that are to last for as long as the sun shines and the waters flow. They see the truth of these agreements not in specific details but in more general principles that establish a framework of ongoing negotiations that must be made to adapt as Canada changes. Thus the treaty provisions for schooling, health care, economic development, policing, intergovernmental relations, and so forth, must constantly be reworked so that treaty First Nations can contribute effectively in the constructive transformation of the country.

On the Indian side, treaty negotiations were often understood as sacred agreements whose legitimacy was drawn more from the ceremonies that took place in the course of the negotiations than from the signatures at the bottom of legal texts. Most often these ceremonies involved the smoking of special pipes, which gave spiritual significance on the spoken words. This way of viewing these agreements places great emphasis on what was explained by translators to Indian peoples in their own languages in the course of treaty talks. Thus the contemporary interpretation of treaties requires going into the oral traditions kept alive especially by certain accomplished elders whose wisdom and learning are recognized as a primary source of continuity in the maintenance of First Nations heritages.

Except for a few treaties on Vancouver Island, British Columbia entered Confederation in 1871 outside the legal heritage of the Royal Proclamation of 1763. Since the late nineteenth century, First Nations activists in BC repeatedly argued that the provincial government was violating Crown law in opening the province for non-Aboriginal exploitation and ownership without any treaties with the indigenous peoples. Finally, in 1973, some members of the Supreme Court of Canada agreed with this position in an ambivalent ruling to a legal case brought forward by the Nisga'a. The result was that in 1973 the cycle of treaty making going back to the Royal Proclamation was extended to several regions, including Canada's western-most province.

The first of these modern-day treaties was a tripartite agreement in 1975 between the governments of Canada and Quebec as well as the Cree and Inuit east of James and Hudson Bays. In 1983 the Inuvialuit made a similar deal, which became the model for several other agreements in the western Arctic and Yukon. In 1999 Nunavut was established after the federal government and the Inuit of the eastern Arctic arrived at a complex set of compromises about how the terms of the Royal Proclamation should be applied in that vast, sparsely settled part of Canada. The previous year a tripartite agreement with the Nisga'a was formalized.

A major preoccupation of those on the Aboriginal side of these modern-day treaty negotiations has been how to establish a range of new institutions to help liberate indigenous peoples from the weights of an onerous colonial system that has dominated their lives, often for many generations. The core of that colonial system has been the federal *Indian Act*; its primary agents have been the federal Department of Indian Affairs and Northern Development. Thus a key to advancing First Nations self-government is the development of infrastructures capable of generating some degree of economic self-sufficiency for Aboriginal communities. Accordingly, many provisions in modern-day treaties put in place various means and formulas for the sharing and apportioning of natural resources along with the royalties they generate.

Many of the old treaties are sanctioned by Indian peoples with picture signatures representing the animal crests of their clans and confederacies. These pictures signify Aboriginal understandings of the proper balances between society, ecology, and law. It is the juxtaposition of such representations on the same documents with legal texts in European languages that most eloquently embodies the intercultural essence of this genre of agreement between peoples.

The heritage of Crown treaties with First Nations in North America represents in its totality one of the world's oldest and most elaborate experiments in extending democratic principles across boundaries of language, culture, and ethnicity. Certainly there are aspects of this experiment that have proved tragic in the extent of their failure. But these failures are part of a larger set of problems on a planet where too often principles of power outweigh principles of justice in establishing the framework of relationships between peoples.

There is still great capacity for rectifying these inequities in Canada's continued elaboration of the principles of intercultural democracy through the enlightened extension of the Crown's alliances with First Nations through the medium of treaties. The Nisga'a treaty, despite its imperfections, projects forward a very old learning curve about humanity's ceaseless quest to find ways to share, more equitably, the good things the earth has to offer. Accordingly, Molloy's text serves to remind us that whatever lofty theory we might have about what is at issue, in the final analysis Crown–First Nation treaty making comes down to real human beings bargaining face-to-face. Theirs is preeminently the art of the possible in a very complex political environment. Their responsibility has been to seek out workable solutions to problems inherited from history so as to make life a little more harmonious, a little less discordant.

NOTES

1. *The Economist*, August 8, 1998, p. 34.
2. Cited in L.C. Green and Olive P. Dickason, *The Law of Nations and the New World* (Edmonton: University of Alberta Press, 1989), p. 18.
3. Cited in ibid, p. 40.
4. See Lewis Hanke, *The Spanish Struggle for Justice in the Conquest of America* (Boston: Little, Brown, and Co., 1965).
5. David E. Stannard, *American Holocaust: Columbus and the Conquest of the New World* (New York: Oxford University Press, 1992); see also Ward Churchill, *A Little Matter of Genocide: Holocaust Denial in the Americas, 1492 to Present* (Winnipeg: Arbeiter Ring Publishing, 1998); Robert Davis and Mark Zannis, *The Genocide Machine in Canada: The Pacification of the North* (Montreal: Black Rose Books, 1973).
6. George Manuel and Michael Posluns, *The Fourth World: An Indian Reality* (Don Mills, ON: Collier-Macmillan, 1974).
7. Richard White, *The Middle Ground: Indians, Empires, and Republics in the Great Lakes Region, 1650–1815* (Cambridge: Cambridge University Press, 1991).
8. See Anthony Hall, "Indian Treaties," *The Canadian Encyclopedia*, CD-ROM Editions (Toronto: McClelland and Stewart, 2000).

Article Thirty-Three

The Merits of Multiculturalism

Will Kymlicka

In 1971 Canada embarked on a unique experiment by declaring a policy of official "multiculturalism." According to Pierre Trudeau, the prime minister who introduced it in the House of Commons, the policy had four aims: to support the cultural development of ethnocultural groups; to help members of ethnocultural groups overcome barriers to full participation in Canadian society; to promote creative encounters and interchange among all ethnocultural groups; and to assist new Canadians in acquiring at least one of Canada's official languages.[1] This policy was officially enshrined in law in the 1988 *Multiculturalism Act.* Although the multiculturalism policy was first adopted by the federal government, it was explicitly designed as a model for other levels of government, and it has been widely copied. "Multiculturalism programs" can now be found not just in the multiculturalism office in Ottawa, but also at the provincial and municipal levels of government and in a wide range of public and private institutions, including schools and businesses.

Such programs are now under attack, perhaps more so today than at any time since 1971. In particular, they are said to be undermining the historical tendency of immigrant groups to integrate, encouraging ethnic separatism, putting up "cultural walls" around ethnic groups, and thereby eroding our ability to act collectively as citizens. It is understandable that Canadians have had anxieties about multiculturalism, and it would be a mistake to ascribe all of them to xenophobia or prejudice. The process of integrating immigrants from very different backgrounds, including every conceivable race, religion, and language group, who share little in common, is never easy, and historically Canada has been fortunate in having avoided serious ethnic conflict. Canadians have naturally worried that any dramatic change in our approach to integration—such as the adoption of the multiculturalism policy—would change this dynamic, igniting ethnic separatism and conflict.

Thus it is worth having a vigorous discussion about multiculturalism. So far, though, the debate has generated much more heat than light. One reason is that it has been carried on without enough attention to the empirical evidence; as we will see, the critics of multiculturalism are simply uninformed about the consequences of the policy.

But defenders of multiculturalism, including the federal government itself, must also share part of the blame. Virtually every study of the policy in Canada has concluded that it has been "barely explained at all to the Canadian public," and that "no serious effort was made by any senior politician to define multiculturalism in a Canadian context."[2] Insofar as the policy has been defended, the usual approach has been simply to invoke "cultural diversity" and "tolerance," as if these were self-evidently or unqualifiedly good things. In fact, both diversity and tolerance have limits. Diversity is valuable, but only if it operates within the context of certain common norms and institutions; otherwise it can become destabilizing. Similarly, tolerance is a virtue, but only within certain boundaries; otherwise it can threaten principles of equality and individual rights. It is on these questions of the limits or boundaries of multiculturalism that defenders have been strangely inarticulate.

Source: Will Kymlicka, *Finding Our Way: Rethinking Ethnocultural Relations in Canada* (Toronto: Oxford University Press, 1998), pp. 15–24, 187–90.

As a result, the debate over multiculturalism in the last few years has taken on an air of unreality. On the one hand, uninformed critics level unfounded charges of ethnocultural separatism, without regard for the evidence; on the other hand, defenders invoke "diversity" and "tolerance" as a mantra, without explaining the common institutions and principles that define the context within which diversity and tolerance can flourish.

To bring some order to this confusion, I will focus on the evidence regarding the impact of multiculturalism since its adoption in 1971, to show that critics of the policy are indeed misinformed.

The Debate

The debate over multiculturalism has heated up recently, largely because of two best-selling critiques: Neil Bissoondath's *Selling Illusions: The Cult of Multiculturalism in Canada* (1994) and Richard Gwyn's *Nationalism without Walls: The Unbearable Lightness of Being Canadian* (1995).[3] Bissoondath and Gwyn make very similar claims about the results of the policy. In particular, both argue that multiculturalism has promoted a form of ethnic separatism among immigrants. According to Bissoondath, multiculturalism has led to "undeniable ghettoization."[4] Instead of promoting integration, it encourages immigrants to form "self-contained" ghettos "alienated from the mainstream," and this ghettoization is "not an extreme of multiculturalism but its ideal: a way of life transported whole, a little outpost of exoticism preserved and protected." He approvingly quotes Arthur Schlesinger's claim that multiculturalism reflects a "cult of ethnicity" that "exaggerates differences, intensifies resentments and antagonisms, drives even deeper the awful wedges between races and nationalities," producing patters of "self-pity and self-ghettoization" that lead to "cultural and linguistic apartheid."[5] According to Bissoondath, multiculturalism policy does not encourage immigrants to think of themselves as Canadians; even the children of immigrants "continue to see Canada with the eyes of foreigners. Multiculturalism with its emphasis on the importance of holding on to the former or ancestral homeland, with its insistence that *There* is more important than *Here*, encourages such attitudes."

Gwyn makes the same claim, in very similar language. He argues that "official multiculturalism encourages apartheid, or to be a bit less harsh, ghettoism."[6] The longer multiculturalism policy has been in place, "the higher the cultural walls have gone up inside Canada." Multiculturalism encourages ethnic leaders to keep their members "apart from the mainstream," practising "what can best be described as mono-culturalism." In this way the Canadian state "encourages these gatekeepers to maintain what amounts, at worst, to an apartheid form of citizenship."

Bissoondath and Gwyn are hardly alone in these claims; they are repeated endlessly in the media. To take just one example, Robert Fulford recently argued in *The Globe and Mail* that the policy encourages people to maintain a "freeze-dried" identity, reducing intercultural exchange and relationships, and that time will judge it to be one of Canada's greatest "policy failures."[7]

It is important—indeed urgent—to determine whether such claims are true. Surprisingly, however, neither Bissoondath nor Gwyn provides any empirical evidence for his views. In order to assess their claims, therefore, I have collected some statistics that may bear on the question of whether multiculturalism has promoted ethnic separatism, and discouraged or impeded integration. I will start with evidence from within Canada, comparing ethnic groups before and after the adoption of the multiculturalism policy in 1971.

I will then consider evidence from other countries, particularly countries that have rejected the principle of official multiculturalism, to see how Canada compares with them.

The Domestic Evidence

How has the adoption of multiculturalism in 1971 affected the integration of ethnic groups in Canada? To answer this question requires some account of what "integration" involves. It is one of the puzzling features of the Gwyn and Bissoondath critiques that neither defines exactly what he means by integration. However, we can piece together some of the elements they see as crucial: adopting a Canadian identity rather than clinging exclusively to one's ancestral identity; participating in broader Canadian institutions rather than participating solely in ethnic-specific institutions; learning an official language rather than relying solely on one's mother tongue; having inter-ethnic friendships, or even mixed marriages, rather than socializing entirely within one's ethnic group. Such criteria do not form a comprehensive theory of "integration," but they seem to be at the heart of Gwyn's and Bissoondath's concerns about multiculturalism, so they are a good starting point.

Let us begin with the most basic form of integration: the decision of an immigrant to become a Canadian citizen. If the Gwyn/Bissoondath thesis were true, one would expect naturalization rates to have declined since the adoption of multiculturalism. In fact, naturalization rates have increased since 1971.[8] This is particularly relevant because the economic incentives to naturalize have lessened over the last 25 years. Canadian citizenship is not needed in order to enter the labour market in Canada, or to gain access to social benefits. There are virtually no differences between citizens and permanent residents in their civil rights or social benefits; the right to vote is the only major legal benefit gained by naturalization.[9] The primary reason for immigrants to take out citizenship, therefore, is that they identify with Canada; they want to formalize their membership in Canadian society and to participate in the political life of the country.

Moreover, if we examine which groups are most likely to naturalize, we find that it is the "multicultural groups" — immigrants from nontraditional source countries, for whom the multiculturalism policy is most relevant — that have the highest rates of naturalization. By contrast, immigrants from the United States and United Kingdom, who are not seen in popular discourse as "ethnic" or "multicultural" groups, have the lowest rates of naturalization.[10] In other words, those groups that are most directly affected by the multiculturalism policy have shown the greatest desire to become Canadian, while those that fall outside the multiculturalism rubric have shown the least desire to become Canadian.

Let's move now to political participation. If the Gwyn/Bissoondath thesis were true, one would expect the political participation of ethnocultural minorities to have declined since the adoption of multiculturalism in 1971. After all, political participation is a symbolic affirmation of citizenship, and reflects an interest in the political life of the larger society. Yet there is no evidence of decline in such participation.[11] To take one relevant indicator, between Confederation and the 1960s, in the period prior to the adoption of multiculturalism, ethnic groups became increasingly underrepresented in Parliament, but since 1971 the trend has been reversed, so that today they have nearly as many MPs as one would expect, given their percentage of the population.[12]

It is also important to note the way ethnocultural groups participate in Canadian politics. They do not form separate ethnic-based parties, either as individual groups or as coalitions, but participate overwhelmingly within pan-Canadian parties. Indeed, the two parties in Canada that are closest to being ethnic parties were created by and for those of

French or English ancestry: the Parti/Bloc Québécois, whose support comes almost entirely from Quebeckers of French ancestry, and the Confederation of Regions Party, whose support came almost entirely from New Brunswickers of English Loyalist ancestry.[13] Immigrants themselves have shown no inclination to support ethnic-based political parties, and instead vote for the traditional national parties.

This is just one indicator of a more general point: namely, that immigrants are overwhelmingly supportive of, and committed to protecting, the country's basic political structure. We know that, were it not for the "ethnic vote," the 1995 referendum on secession in Quebec would have succeeded. In that referendum, ethnic voters overwhelmingly expressed their commitment to Canada. More generally, all the indicators suggest that immigrants quickly absorb and accept Canada's basic liberal-democratic values and constitutional principles, even if their home countries are illiberal or nondemocratic.[14] As Freda Hawkins put it, "the truth is that there have been no riots, no breakaway political parties, no charismatic immigrant leaders, no real militancy in international causes, no internal political terrorism . . . immigrants recognize a good, stable political system when they see one."[15] If we look at indicators of legal and political integration, then, we see that since the adoption of multiculturalism in 1971 immigrants have been more likely to become Canadians, and more likely to participate politically. And when they participate, they do so through pan-ethnic political parties that uphold Canada's basic liberal-democratic principles.

This sort of political integration is the main aim of a democratic state. Yet from the point of view of individual Canadians, the most important forms of immigrant integration are probably not political, but societal. Immigrants who participate in politics may be good democratic citizens, but if they can't speak English or French, or are socially isolated in self-contained ethnic groups, then Canadians will perceive a failure of integration. So let us shift now to two indicators of societal integration: official language acquisition and intermarriage rates.

If the Gwyn/Bissoondath thesis were true, one would expect to find that the desire of ethnocultural minorities to acquire official language competence has declined since the adoption of multiculturalism. If immigrant groups are being "ghettoized," are "alienated from the mainstream," and are attempting to preserve their original way of life intact from their homeland, then presumably they have less reason than they did before 1971 to learn an official language.

In fact, demand for classes in English and French as second languages (ESL; FSL) has never been higher, and actually exceeds supply in many cities. According to the 1991 Census, 98.6 percent of Canadians report that they can speak one of the official languages.[16] This figure is staggering when one considers how many immigrants are elderly and/or illiterate in their mother tongue, and who therefore find it extremely difficult to learn a new language. It is especially impressive given that the number of immigrants who arrive with knowledge of an official language has declined since 1971.[17] If we set aside the elderly — who make up the majority of the Canadians who cannot speak an official language — the idea that there is a general decrease in immigrants' desire to learn an official language is absurd. The overwhelming majority do learn an official language, and insofar as such skills are lacking, the explanation is the lack of accessible and appropriate ESL/FSL classes, not lack of desire.[18]

Another indicator worth looking at is intermarriage rates. If the Gwyn/Bissoondath thesis were true, one would expect intermarriage to have declined since the adoption of a policy said to have driven "even deeper the awful wedges between races and nationalities" and to have encouraged groups to retreat into "monocultural" ghettoes and hide behind "cultural walls." In fact, intermarriage rates have consistently increased since 1971. There has been an overall decline in endogamy, both for immigrants and for their native-born children. Moreover, and equally important, we see a dramatic increase in social acceptance of mixed marriages.[19] Whereas in 1968 a majority of Canadians (52 percent) disapproved of Black–white marriages, the situation is now completely reversed, so that by 1995 an overwhelming majority (81 percent) approved of such marriages.[20]

Unlike the previous three indicators of integration, intermarriage is not a deliberate goal of government policy; it is not the business of governments either to encourage or to discourage intermarriage. But changes in intermarriage rates are useful as indicators of a broader trend that is a legitimate government concern: namely, the extent to which Canadians feel comfortable living and interacting with members of other ethnic groups. If Canadians feel comfortable living and working with members of other groups, inevitably some people will become friends with, and even lovers of, members of other ethnic groups. The fact that intermarriage rates have gone up is important, therefore, not necessarily in itself, but rather as evidence that Canadians are more accepting of diversity. And we have direct evidence for this more general trend. Canadians today are much more willing to accept members of other ethnic groups as co-workers, neighbours, or friends than they were before 1971.[21]

Other indicators point to the same trends. For example, despite Gwyn's and Bissoondath's rhetoric about the proliferation of ethnic "ghettos" and "enclaves," studies of residential concentration have shown that permanent ethnic enclaves do not exist in Canada. Indeed, "it is scarcely sensible to talk of 'ghettos' in Canadian cities."[22] What little concentration does exist is more likely to be found among older immigrant groups, like the Jews and Italians, whose arrival preceded the multiculturalism policy. Groups that have arrived primarily after 1971, such as Asians and Afro-Caribbeans, exhibit the least residential concentration.[23]

In short, whether we look at naturalization, political participation, official language competence, or intermarriage rates, we see the same story. There is no evidence to support the claim that multiculturalism has decreased the rate of integration of immigrants, or increased the separatism or mutual hostility of ethnic groups. As Orest Kruhlak puts it, "irrespective of which variables one examines, including [citizenship acquisition, ESL, mother-tongue retention, ethnic association participation, intermarriage] or political participation, the scope of economic involvement, or participation in mainstream social or service organizations, none suggest a sense of promoting ethnic separateness."[24]

The Comparative Evidence

We can make the same point another way. If the Bissoondath/Gwyn thesis were correct about the ghettoizing impact of our official multiculturalism policy, we would expect Canada to perform worse on these indicators of integration than other countries that have not adopted such a policy. Both Gwyn and Bissoondath contrast the Canadian approach with the American, which exclusively emphasizes common identities and common values, and refuses to provide public recognition or affirmation of ethnocultural differences. If Canada fared worse than the United States in terms of integrating immigrants, this would provide some indirect support for the Bissoondath/Gwyn theory.

In fact, however, Canada fares better than the United States on virtually any dimension of integration. Its naturalization rates are almost double those of the United States.[25] Canada's rates of political participation and official language acquisition are higher, and its rates of residential segregation are lower.[26] In addition Canadians show much greater approval for intermarriage. In 1988, when 72 percent of Canadians approved of interracial marriages, only 40 percent of Americans approved, and 25 percent felt they should be illegal![27] And ethnicity is less salient as a determinant of friendship in Canada than in the United States.[28]

On every indicator of integration, then, Canada with its multiculturalism policy, fares better than the United States, with its repudiation of multiculturalism. We would find the same story if we compared Canada with other immigrant countries that have rejected multiculturalism in favour of an exclusive emphasis on common identities — such as France.[29] Canada does better than these other countries not only in actual rates of integration, but also in the day-to-day experience of ethnic relations. In a 1997 survey, people in twenty countries were asked whether they agreed that "different ethnic groups get along well here." The percentage of those agreeing was far higher in Canada (75 percent) than in the United States (58 percent) or France (51 percent).[30]

This should not surprise us, since Canada does better than virtually any other country in the world in the integration of immigrants. The only comparable country is Australia, which has its own official multiculturalism policy — one largely inspired by Canada's, although of course it has been adapted to Australia's circumstances.[31] The two countries that lead the world in the integration of immigrants are countries with official multiculturalism policies. They are much more successful than any country that has rejected multiculturalism.

In short, there is no evidence to support the claim that multiculturalism is promoting ethnic separateness or impeding immigrant integration. Whether we examine the trends within Canada since 1971 or compare Canada with other countries, the conclusion is the same: the multiculturalism program is working. It is achieving what it set out to do: helping to ensure that those people who wish to express their ethnic identity are respected and accommodated, while simultaneously increasing the ability of immigrants to integrate into the larger society. Along with our fellow multiculturalists in Australia, Canadians do a better job of respecting ethnic diversity while promoting societal integration than citizens of any other country.

Explaining the Debate

This finding raises a genuine puzzle. Why do so many intelligent and otherwise well-informed commentators agree that multiculturalism policy is impeding integration? Part of the explanation is that many critics have simply not examined the actual policy to see what it involves. For example, both Gwyn and Bissoondath claim that, in effect, multiculturalism tells new Canadians that they should practise "monoculturalism," preserving their inherited way of life intact while avoiding interacting with or learning from the members of other groups, or the larger society.[32] If this were a plausible interpretation of the policy's aims, it would be only natural to assume that ethnocultural separatism is increasing in Canadian society.

In reality, as the government's documents make clear, the main goals of multiculturalism policy (and most of its funding) have been to promote civic participation in the larger society and to increase mutual understanding and cooperation between the members of different ethnic groups. Unfortunately, neither Gwyn nor Bissoondath quotes or cites a single document published by the multiculturalism unit of the federal government — not one of its annual reports, demographic analyses, public education brochures, or program funding guidelines. Their critiques are thus double unreal. They describe a (nonexistent) policy of promoting "monoculturalism" among ethnocultural groups, and then blame it for a (nonexistent) trend toward "apartheid" in Canadian society. They have invented a nonexistent policy to explain a nonexistent trend.

486

But if the Bissoondath and Gwyn accounts are so ill-informed, why have they been so influential? Both books were generally well reviewed, and often praised for their insight into ethnocultural relations in Canada. Why were so many Canadians persuaded by their claims about growing ethnocultural separatism, even though these claims had no empirical support, and indeed are contradicted by the evidence? Why were so many Canadians persuaded by their mistaken characterization of the policy?

Part of the answer, I think, is that defenders of the policy have been strangely inarticulate. The federal government has not clearly explained the aims of the policy, nor has it provided criteria for evaluating its success. Even though the policy has been demonstrably successful, the government itself has made little attempt to demonstrate its success; so far as I can tell, it has never attempted to gather together the various findings on integration discussed in this chapter, or to monitor them systematically so as to measure changes in integration over time.

Collecting and publicizing this sort of information would provide Canadians with the tools to question and deflate the exaggerated claims and misinformed critiques we find in Gwyn and Bissoondath. Yet even if this information were more widely available, it would likely not entirely alleviate public anxiety about multiculturalism. Lack of information cannot, by itself, explain public attitudes. In the absence of information, why do so many Canadians assume that multiculturalism has had negative consequences? Why are they fearful of multiculturalism, rather than confident about it?

Part of the problem may be that Canadians have no clear sense of the limits of multiculturalism. They are not sure that certain "non-negotiable" principles or institutions will be protected and upheld, even if they conflict with the desires or traditions of some immigrant groups. Canadians are not averse to multiculturalism within limits, but they want to know that those limits exist. They value diversity, but they also want to know that this diversity will be expressed within the context of common Canadian institutions, and that it doesn't entail acceptance of ethnic separation. Similarly, Canadians are generally tolerant, but they also believe that some practices, such as clitoridectomy, are intolerable, and they want to know that they won't be asked to "tolerate" the violation of basic human rights.

So long as Canadians feel insecure about the limits of multiculturalism, publicizing statistics about the beneficial effects of multiculturalism will have only limited success in changing public attitudes. The statistics may look good today, but what about tomorrow? Perhaps the policy has worked until now to promote integration, but only because the full "logic" of multiculturalism has not yet been implemented. Perhaps the logic of multiculturalism is to undermine the very idea that there are any principles or institutions that all citizens must respect and adhere to. It is this sort of insecurity that explains, at least in part, the popularity of the Bissoondath/Gwyn account. Until defenders of multiculturalism explain its limits, these sorts of critiques will continue to strike a chord among Canadians, touching deeply felt anxieties about ethnocultural relations.

I think it is possible to address these concerns. In order to do so, however, we need to understand how multiculturalism fits into a larger set of government policies regarding ethnocultural relations in Canada. It is precisely this larger context that is typically ignored in debates about multiculturalism. Both critics and defenders of multiculturalism often talk as if the adoption of the policy in 1971 ushered in an entirely new era in ethnic relations in Canada, overturning the government policies developed over the previous 150 years of immigration. This is a very misleading picture. In many respects, the government policies that encourage the historical integration of immigrants remain firmly in place. After all, multiculturalism is not the only — or even the primary — government policy affecting the place of ethnic groups in Canadian society; it is just one small piece of the pie. Many aspects of public policy affect these groups, including policies relating to naturalization, education, job training and professional accreditation, human rights and anti-discrimination law, civil service employment, health and safety, even national defence. It is these other policies that are the major engines of integration, for they encourage, pressure, even legally force immigrants to take steps toward integrating into Canadian society.

487

The idea that multiculturalism promotes ethnic separateness stems in large part, I think, from a failure to see how multiculturalism fits into this larger context of public policy. When we do situate multiculturalism within this larger context, we see that it is not a rejection of integration, but a renegotiation of the terms of integration — a renegotiation that was in general not merely justified but overdue.

NOTES

1. Trudeau in *House of Commons Debates*, 8 Oct. 1971: 8545–6.
2. Freda Hawkins, *Critical Years in Immigration: Canada and Australia Compared* (Montreal: McGill-Queen's University Press, 1989), p. 221.
3. Neil Bissoondath, *Selling Illusions: The Cult of Multiculturalism in Canada* (Toronto: Penguin, 1994); Richard Gwyn, *Nationalism without Walls: The Unbearable Lightness of Being Canadian* (Toronto: McClelland and Stewart, 1995).
4. The passages quoted in this paragraph can be found on pages 111, 110, 98, and 133 of *Selling Illusions*.
5. Schlesinger, *The Disuniting of America* (New York: Norton, 1992), p. 138. According to his analysis, the United States is witnessing the "fragmentation of the national community into a quarrelsome spatter of enclaves, ghettoes, tribes . . . encouraging and exalting cultural and linguistic apartheid" (137–38). Bissoondath argues that the same process is occurring in Canada.
6. The passages quoted in this paragraph are from pages 274, 8, and 234 of *Nationalism without Walls*.
7. Robert Fulford, "Do Canadians Want Ethnic Heritage Freeze-Dried?," *The Globe and Mail*, 17 Feb. 1997.
8. Citizenship and Immigration Canada, *Citizenship and Immigration Statistics* (Ottawa: Public Works, 1997), Table G2 and Table 1.
9. The remaining differences between citizens and permanent residents relate to (a) minority language rights; (b) protection against deportation; and (c) access to a few sensitive bureaucratic positions, none of which are relevant to most immigrants.
10. The average length of residence before naturalization is 7.61 years, with immigrants from the UK taking the longest (13.95 years); immigrants from China, Vietnam, and the Philippines all take under five years on average (Citizenship Registrar, Multiculturalism and Citizenship Canada, 1992). In 1971, only 5 percent of the Americans eligible to take out citizenship in Canada chose to do so. See Karol Krotki and Colin Reid, "Demography of Canadian Population by Ethnic Group," in *Ethnicity and Culture in Canada: The Research Landscape*, ed. J.W. Berry and Jean Laponce (Toronto: University of Toronto Press, 1994), p. 26.
11. For surveys of the political participation of ethnocultural groups in Canadian politics, see the three research studies in Kathy Megyery, ed., *Ethnocultural Groups and Visible Minorities in Canadian Politics: The Question of Access*, vol. 7 of the Research Studies of the Royal Commission on Electoral Reform and Party Financing (Ottawa: Dundurn Press, 1991); Jean Laponce, "Ethnicity and Voting Studies in Canada: Primary and Secondary Sources 1970–1991" in Berry

and Laponce, eds., *Ethnicity and Culture, pp.* 179–202; and Jerome Black and Aleem Lakhani, "Ethnoracial Diversity in the House of Commons: An Analysis of Numerical Representation in the 35th Parliament," *Canadian Ethnic Studies* 29, 1 (November 1997): 13–33.

12. Daiva Stasiulus and Yasmeen Abu-Laban, "The House the Parties Built: (Re)constructing Ethnic Representation in Canadian Politics" in Megyery, ed., *Ethnocultural Groups,* p. 14; cf. Alain Pelletier, "Politics and Ethnicity: Representation of Ethnic and Visible-Minority Groups in the House of Commons," in ibid., pp. 129–30.

13. Geoffrey Martin, "The COR Party of New Brunswick as an 'Ethnic Party,'" *Canadian Review of Studies in Nationalism* 23, 1 (1996): 1–8.

14. For evidence of the quick absorption of liberal-democratic values by immigrants, see James Frideres, "Edging into the Mainstream: Immigrant Adults and their Children" in *Multiculturalism in North America and Europe: Comparative Perspectives on Interethnic Relations and Social Incorporation in Europe and North America,* ed. S. Isajiw (Toronto: Canadian Scholars' Press, 1997); Jerome Black, "The Practice of Politics in Two Settings: Political Transferability among Recent Immigrants to Canada," *Canadian Journal of Political Science* 20, 4 (1987): 731–53. Studies show that students born outside Canada, as well as students for whom English was not a first or home language, knew and valued their rights as much as their Canadian-born, English-speaking counterparts. See, for example, Charles Ungerleider, "Schooling, Identity and Democracy: Issues in the Social-Psychology of Canadian Classrooms" in *Educational Psychology: Canadian Perspectives,* ed. R. Short et al., (Toronto: Copp Clark, 1991), p. 204–5.

15. Hawkins, *Critical Years,* p. 279.

16. Some 63 percent of immigrants have neither English nor French as their mother tongue, yet only 309 000 residents in the 1991 Census couldn't speak an official language. Most of these were elderly (166 000 were over 55). See Brian Harrison, "Non Parlo né inglese, né francese" (Statistics Canada: Census of Canada Short Article Series, #5, September 1993).

17. Derrick Thomas, "The Social Integration of Immigrants," in *The Immigration Dilemma,* ed. Steven Globerman (Vancouver: Fraser Institute, 1992): 224.

18. Susan Donaldson, "Un-LINC-ing Language and Integration: Future Directions for Federal Settlement Policy" (M.A. thesis, Department of Linguistics and Applied Language Studies, Carleton University, 1995).

19. Morton Weinfeld, "Ethnic Assimilation and the Retention of Ethnic Cultures," in Berry and Laponce, eds., *Ethnicity and Culture,* pp. 244–45.

20. Jeffrey Reitz and Raymond Breton, *The Illusion of Difference: Realities of Ethnicity in Canada and the United States* (Toronto: C.D. Howe Institute, 1994), p. 80; Leo Driedger, *Multi-Ethnic Canada: Identities and Inequalities* (Toronto: Oxford University Press, 1996), p. 277.

21. Driedger, *Multi-Ethnic Canada,* p. 263.

22. John Mercer, "Asian Migrants and Residential Location in Canada," *New Community* 15, 2 (1989): 198.

23. Thomas, "Social Integration," pp. 240, 247.

24. Orest Kruhlak, "Multiculturalism: Myth versus Reality," unpublished paper prepared for the Institute for Research on Public Policy project "Making Canada Work: Towards a New Concept of Citizenship" (1991), p. 10.

25. For example, the naturalization rate of immigrants who arrived in the United States in 1977 is around 37 percent. The comparable rate in Canada is between 70 percent and 80 percent, and is much higher in some multicultural groups (e.g., 95 percent of the Vietnamese refugees have become citizens). For a comparative study of naturalization policies and trends, see Dilek Cinar, "From Aliens to Citizens: A Comparative Analysis of Rules of Transition," in *From Aliens to Citizens: Redefining the Legal Status of Immigrants,* ed. Rainer Baubock (Aldershot: Avebury, 1994), p. 65. For the case of Vietnamese "boat people" in Canada, see Frideres, "Edging into the Mainstream."

26. Krotki and Reid, "Demography", p. 40.

27. Reitz and Breton, *The Illusion of Difference,* pp. 80–81.

28. Ibid., p. 60.

29. See Cinar, "From Aliens to Citizens," p. 65; Stephen Castles and Mark Miller, *The Age of Migration: International Population Movements in the Modern World* (London: Macmillan, 1993), pp. 220–21; Sarah Wayland, "Religious Expression in Public Schools: Kirpans in Canada, Hijab in France," *Ethnic and Racial Studies* 20, 3 (1997): 545–61.

30. Angus Reid, *Canada and the World: An International Perspective on Canada and Canadians.* The polling data is available on the Angus Reid Web site at www.angusreid.com. Australia came second on this question, with 71 percent of respondents agreeing that ethnic groups get along well in Australia.

31. As Freda Hawkins notes, multiculturalism was adopted in both countries in the 1970s "for the same reasons and with the same objectives" (*Critical Years*, p. 214). And they have evolved in similar directions since the 1970s, from an emphasis on cultural maintenance to issues of public participation and institutional accommodation. For a detailed comparison of their origins, see Hawkins, "Multiculturalism in Two Countries: The Canadian and Australian Experience," *Review of Canadian Studies* 17, 1 (1982): 64–80. For a more up-to-date account, see James Jupp, *Explaining Australian Multiculturalism* (Canberra: Centre for Immigration and Multicultural Studies, Australian National University, 1996), and Stephen Castles, "Multicultural Citizenship in Australia," in *Citizenship and Exclusion*, ed. Veit Bader (London: St. Martin's Press, 1997).

32. Similarly, Fulford argues that the multiculturalism policy disapproves of inter-marriage and interethnic friendships ("Do Canadians Want Ethnic Heritage Freeze-Dried?").

489

Article Thirty-Four

Charisma and Contradiction: The Legacy of Pierre Elliott Trudeau

Stephen Clarkson

Pierre Elliott Trudeau's legacy is a subject so distorted by paeans of praise from his acolytes and admirers, so scorched with vituperation by his political and intellectual enemies, so awash in controversy (which he continually provoked by contradicting his critics as well as himself) that making a balanced assessment — even when his agile body and his indomitable spirit have finally been stilled — becomes an extremely delicate task, one made no easier because it can have several meanings. To make sense of him, we have to make sense of ourselves and the twentieth-century Canada we shared with him.

Should our scope be so narrow that we rate him only on those issues in which he was himself personally engaged, such as Quebec nationalism and constitutional reform or, later on, energy and Native rights? Or should our net be cast much more widely? Since his name has become affixed to the whole era from 1968 to 1984, should he not be assessed on *everything* that happened during those dynamic and troubled sixteen years, on the grounds that he was in charge — and so personally responsible for it all?

There is also the tricky question of what has occurred since his retirement. Many blame him for the dramatic adoption of a neoliberal agenda in the Mulroney–Chrétien period, arguing that there would have been no need for the drastic attack on social programs if the

Source: *Queen's Quarterly* 107, 4 (Winter 2000): 591–607.

Trudeauites had not set in train a series of budgetary deficits whose cumulated weight had to be tackled by his successors.

Our understanding of what happened in history often changes, not because *it* has changed but because *we*, the observers, have shifted our positions. The historian Jack Granatstein originally condemned Trudeau's tough action during the October crisis of 1970, but now he applauds it. Right-wingers, who could never bring themselves to vote for such a "socialist" as Trudeau, flocked to support his attack on a distinct society status for Quebec. Those on the left, who excoriated what they saw as his niggardliness toward social policies when he was governing, now wax nostalgic for the golden age of the generous welfare state.

We have to be aware of the extent to which this question of Trudeau's legacy is as much about us as it is about him. In our mourning, are we sloughing off onto him our collective responsibility for what has happened? In our grieving, are we projecting onto him our anger about the lost opportunity to build that independent Canada which no leader could have created under the inexorable pressures of American domination?

The Trudeau Record

This is not the time to do a study of Trudeauology and rank his rankers' assessments of his work, weighing the superlatives of his idolizers and assessing the condemnations of his demonizers. Suffice it to look at Trudeau's record in the light of his own positions, however inconsistent.

Let us start with his first political promise, that of *participatory democracy*. It was a powerful slogan and, as he once acknowledged to me, sprang from both a lack of knowledge of the Liberal party to whose leadership he aspired and his need to induce its activists to support his candidacy. He buttressed the slogan he had pinched from the American Students for a Democratic Society in the 1960s with the thoughts of Jean Jacques Rousseau in the 1760s, whom he paraphrased by telling the public in general, but his Liberal party militants in particular, that they could and should play a direct role in decision making in Ottawa. In this way they could produce the laws by which they would then consent to be governed. Once elected to office he did not weasel out of this promise but continued for a while to hold out the lure to his partisans that they could animate what he suggested would become a mass party and share in deciding policy directions for his government.

Did he fail to make good on this promise? Yes. Was he apologetic? No. Did he explain? Of course. Because he found another rationalization, this time not taken from the populist stream of Western political thought, but from its opposing elitist current. Borrowing from John Locke and Edmund Burke and lifting the ideas of his Harvard University economics history professor, Joseph Schumpeter, he spat back at his astonished supporters that they had no business claiming the right to interfere with the workings of government. Policy was not to be made in the streets by mobs or even students. If they were unhappy with what he was doing, they should shut up and wait for the next election when, if they still had a complaint to make, they could throw him out.

And what about the *Just Society*? This was the great end for which participatory democracy constituted the means, but which Trudeau defined in two different ways. Some of his texts and speeches referred to justice in terms of the liberal notion of equality of opportunity. But he also, and just as clearly, endorsed the thoughts and writings of his covertly Marxist friend at the University of Toronto, Brough Macpherson, to the effect that justice was impossible without social equality—a much higher bar over which to jump.

Depending on which definition of "just" one takes, Trudeau was either a success or a failure. He did improve equality of opportunity by implementing universal medicare and by defending it. He took pride in the steps taken to promote interprovincial equality through regional development programs. But in terms of narrowing the gap between rich and poor, a gap he had brilliantly denounced as part of his 1950s critique of Canadian capitalism, his government achieved very little. Indeed some of the progress made in deepening the welfare state that he had inherited from the much more activist Pearson period, he and his colleagues proceeded to undo by cutting back unemployment benefits and by restraining wages more than prices in both 1975–76 and 1982–83. Social spending actually stayed fairly constant during his period in office. And if our notion of a just society is one where government support systems provide a classless approach to social infrastructure, then the last years of the Trudeau era can be seen to have initiated the move away from universalism to the selected, income-tested targeting of the poorest and neediest that characterizes his successors' neoliberal system. At best, the Trudeau era didn't let material inequality increase.

Trudeau's writings of the 1950s and 1960s were quite clear in their identification of the *unregulated free market* as a source of social inequality. Ironically, what created the mounting deficits and the exponentially rising national debt they produced was not uncontrolled spending on social programs but excessive catering to the business community's agenda.

By appointing John Turner as minister of finance and Simon Reisman as his deputy minister in the early 1970s, Trudeau in effect mandated the most powerful agency of his government to cut back taxes on business and on the upper income strata. Prefiguring Mike Harris and Ernie Eves by a quarter of a century, Turner and Reisman deliberately made the federal government incapable of financing the more generous, guaranteed annual income approach to social welfare whose achievement Trudeau entrusted to his strongest ally, Marc Lalonde, the minister of national health and welfare, assisted by the capable Al Johnson as his deputy. Was this oversight? Was it an accident? It seems more like a perverse application of his much-touted theory of counterweights—blocking the left-leaning thrust of one part of this government with countervailing action by an opposing, right-leaning thrust.

We encounter a similar conundrum when we consider Trudeau's much-mythologized proclivity for *strong central government*. "Who will speak for Canada?" was certainly a legitimate question for the leader of such a decentralized federal system to pose when confronting the baying pack of provincial premiers. Many Canadians supported the view that Canada did indeed need a strong federal government that could provide the universal standards and services they expected a modern state to offer.

By now readers will not be surprised if I point out that, here again, Trudeau's clarity was lavished on both sides of this issue. He had cut his teeth as an intellectual in the 1950s denouncing Liberal Ottawa's centralizing proclivities, when the St. Laurent government pushed grants to universities down the throats of the provinces in defiance of education falling within their constitutional jurisdiction. In office, one of the Trudeau government's most effective—if least understood—actions was to dismantle the fiscal base for federal dominance by abandoning the policy instruments that had made Ottawa's primacy possible in the first place. The Established Program Funding of 1977 washed Ottawa's hands of the conditional grants it had previously made to the provinces in support of specific social programs. In the name of decentralization and provincial autonomy, this new unconditional bloc funding allowed the provinces to do what they wished with the federal tax revenues that were placed in their hands. It prefigured Paul Martin's Canada Health and Social Transfer by almost two decades.

492

When we turn to the neighbouring issue of *national unity*, we come to that policy on which Trudeau first lavished his government's energy. Official bilingualism may have been set in train by Lester Pearson and his bilingualism and biculturalism commissioners, but language rights for francophone minorities outside Quebec and inside the federal government were marketed by Trudeau as the panacea that would mollify the grievances of French-speaking Canadians and, even in Quebec, make the separatists finally feel at home from coast-to-coast-to-coast. By the time the Parti Québécois first won power in 1976, Trudeau himself admitted failure.

But he did not admit error. He could never see that his one-dimensional solution to Quebec's alienation was irrelevant. Insisting it was enough to correct the federal government's past linguistic mistakes, he denied to Quebec nationalists the progressive, interventionalist, muscular state that their vibrant democracy was demanding and that he himself advocated for the federal government. In the end he became an incarnation of that intolerant, overbearing English-Canadian nationalism which he had once decried as the first cause of Quebeckers' defensive nationalism. In this intolerance he reinforced the very separatism that he had entered politics to defeat.

Even his beloved *Charter of Rights and Freedoms* — the product of so much of his political tenacity and the fruit of his Harvard training in individualistic liberal constitutionalism — is lodged in self-contradiction. Trudeau was a child of the modernist generation that came of age during World War II and, armed with Lord Keynes's formulas, committed itself to building a powerful state that could banish unemployment and, harnessing the private sector to public ends, create a social-democratic order for an industrialized society. He preached the virtue of government when run by men of integrity (such as himself) as a necessity for reforming the reactionary society into which he had been born. And he supported the trade union movement to defend the weak against the strong.

But in the *Charter* he created an instrument that weakened parliamentary government. Besides empowering minorities, it gave corporations a greater capacity to defend themselves, by exploiting the new guarantees of individual rights against a state whose mission, in Trudeau's own view, was to defend the interests of the whole. For all its progressive use on behalf of women's rights and those of other beleaguered groups such as gays, lesbians, and handicapped people, the *Charter*'s double-edged blades are sharp enough to enable the forces of the irresponsible free market, which Trudeau understood at one point so clearly, to liberate themselves even further from the balancing effect that democratically elected legislatures might want to impose. For instance, the *Charter* was used to eviscerate the very election expense legislation to increase electoral fairness and contain the corrupting power of corporate cash in politics that the Trudeau government successfully enacted in 1974.

If we turn to Trudeau's foreign policy, especially his handling of Canada's relations with the all-important United States, the same analysis can be replicated. There were daring contradictions between clear views taken on high moral grounds, and clear explanations of low pragmatic performance. Both were equally well justified by his rhetoric, their inconsistency unresolved. Trudeau fought a long, bitter battle to achieve constitutional sovereignty vis-à-vis Great Britain, but it was only late — too late — in his political career that he turned his attention to repatriating some of the country's economic sovereignty from the United States. The same government that stood up to the bullying tactics of Ronald Reagan's administration left Canada vulnerable to an astonishingly disempowering trade agreement with the same president. The inspiring words on developing nations' poverty that Prime Minister Trudeau expressed elegantly and empathetically in a famous speech at London's Mansion House in 1975 made bitter reading for any Third World country expecting them to produce more generous Canadian support for the plight of the clearly oppressed or for those resisting apartheid in South Africa.

Assessed on the basis of the power and contradictions of Trudeau's own printed and spoken words, the prime minister's fifteen years in government raise quite a different question. How can we explain—if reason were our only guide (passion having been banished, as he so famously admonished us)—our interest in this man and his government which was in so many ways a failure?

Most explanations seem circular. *Because* we are interested in Trudeau, therefore he is interesting. *Because* he fascinates us, therefore we find him fascinating. A more sophisticated explanation might suggest that Trudeau has remained a charismatic. But that answer begs a further set of questions. Did the charisma lie in his person? In the Canadian public? Or in their interaction?

The Continuing Charisma

If it takes two to tango, it takes a whole society plus one to charisma. Because charisma is a function of the interplay between the leader and the led, we need to understand the psychology of the connection between the subject (him) and the objects (us). We know that the first burst of Trudeaumania 32 years ago did exhibit the qualities that Max Weber first articulated. A mysterious, somewhat intriguing, powerfully attractive figure and a public with certain psychic and social needs did indeed create the conditions for a charismatic connection. Canadians in 1968 were both full of hope and driven by angst. Pierre Trudeau was perceived as a messiah who could lead them to the greatness that the centennial celebrations in 1967 had made them believe was theirs for the grasping and who could also deal with that threat to this destiny that Québécois separatism presented.

But we also know that, for Weber, charisma cannot last. Once successfully installed in office, the charismatic leader necessarily becomes "routinized" through being drawn into the operations of bureaucratic government. Trudeau governed for a very long period, during which time he alienated almost every group in the public worthy of insult. Unlike the charismatic U.S. President John Kennedy or civil rights leader Martin Luther King, he was not martyred before being discredited. But the charismatic effect continued nonetheless.

Canadians supported his vision in large enough numbers to reelect him prime minister three more times after 1968. They responded personally to his promise of *nirvana-by-Charter* in individual testimonies before the joint committee of Parliament that turned a somewhat timid draft into the more comprehensive document by which so many Canadians swear today. When questioned by opinion pollsters, it turned out that millions felt that the *Charter* had indeed created new rights for them, whether as new Canadians or as ethnic minorities or simply as individuals.

Had this assessment been written on the weekend after his retirement from politics, we probably would have agreed that it was an unusual feat for Trudeau to have retained his charismatic relationship with the Canadian public despite having been routinized with a vengeance in the federal bureaucracy and despite not having been martyred by assassins. Sixteen years later, when Trudeau had been out of office as long as he had been in power, public fascination with him was still such that it could be characterized as charismatic.

Until his terminal illness became public knowledge, focus groups kept reporting that Trudeau was the Canadian most people would prefer to have dinner with—along with Wayne Gretzky. CTV acclaimed him in the final days of 1999 as the most exciting Canadian of the twentieth century.

In a recasting of the gilded legacy, Trudeau is even given credit for the brilliant innovation of the notwithstanding clause, which is correctly lauded for balancing the *Charter* with a legislative counterweight—although he himself had vehemently opposed the device at the time the *Charter* was being negotiated with the premiers. For these enthusiasts, Trudeau's appeal shines on untarnished by time's ravages.

There are, of course, critics like Guy Laforest of Laval University, who see Trudeau as responsible for the "end of the Canadian dream." Because of the prime minister's stubborn insistence on individual rights and bilingualism and thanks to his unrelenting attacks on Quebec nationalists, a core of responsible academic analysts, notably York University's Ken McRoberts, believe he did more than anyone to create Canada's continuing crisis, which could leave the country broken following one more referendum.

In Trudeau's own province there are demonizers in abundance who find his very name a source of apoplexy, who demonstrated outside his house protesting the twentieth anniversary of the *War Measures Act*, and who made his appearance at the last rally of the 1995 referendum campaign a liability for the No side. There is still a feeling of betrayal, a sense that, if he had only been on the other side of the great debate, Quebeckers would by now be independent. The resentment still burns at his stringing rebukes over the bad French they spoke, over their narrowness, their chauvinism.

All these emotions that well up in the Quebec nationalist breast attest to Trudeau's negative power in the Quebec imagination. This demonization does not negate his charismatic appeal; it confirms it: for, if this man is such a source of anger, it is because his magic was feared.

The idolaters I have cited witnessed Trudeau enter the political theatre in the late 1960s. But there is another generation, those who only came to political consciousness in the years when Trudeau was prime minister. These are analysts like Robert Mason Lee, who writes that, if Trudeau could enrage his father the Mountie, he was good enough for the son. Trudeaumania meant love and "Trudeau made me," he wrote. Philosopher Mark Kingwell came to political awareness when Trudeau was already a media icon, a star, a mythical personality whose every move fascinated, whether the "fuddle duddle" in the august parliamentary chamber or the errant wife boogying with the Rolling Stones.

These are Trudeau's children, for whom Canada was great because their prime minister had something special about him. He wasn't just sexy because he was dating Barbra Streisand or Margot Kidder or Liona Boyd; he was completely different from other politicians. His vision shaped much of the Canada in which they were raised. They were sent to be "immersed" in bilingual schools, bearing his example with them in their minds, travelling to the other culture in large numbers, striking up acquaintanceships, making friends and love, all on the altar of the bilingual hope for their collective future. And, like the Quebec separatists, many eager bilingualism recruits came to feel betrayed—because all their linguistic efforts did not prevent the continued national unity crises.

And there is the still younger generation, those who came to political awareness when Trudeau was already history. For them Trudeau is virtual reality, someone seen on the TV screen in news clips or documentary movies, even in textbooks. My students over the past decade, who were toddlers when he left office, have flocked to his book signings.

If you ask today's schoolchildren about Trudeau, you find they have their own ideas about what he means. One high school class in English Canada recently asserted that, for them, he represents "star quality," "being a celebrity," a "lady's man," a "media object," a "wise man"; a politician who "made Quebec angry" but was a "scholar," truly bilingual, who "likes to paddle a canoe," who "has a terrific leather jacket." Equivalent first impressions among Quebec school kids would probably be equally strong but more likely negative rather than positive.

Further up the educational food chain—in university classes where students are given Trudeau's own writings to read alongside works about him—the atmosphere is more critical. In a recent doctoral seminar, I heard the view that, yes, his Constitution and *Charter* may have incorporated the major themes of Trudeau's liberal philosophy—the one-Canada national unity, the equality of provinces, the democratic contract, the individual rights—but they did so too rigidly, too inflexibly to accommodate the country's diversity, too inconsistently with his professed tolerance to allow Quebec to develop within the asymmetrical model it needed. Quebec does need special powers, was the class consensus, and Trudeau violated the respect that was due to provincial jurisdictions, undermining with his dogmatic individualism the communitarian basis on which the Canadian federation had originally been constructed.

In an amnesiac society whose access to its collective memory is blocked by the communications channels kept under Hollywood's control, he symbolizes for many their collective identity by proxy. Standing out in profile, the champion who could face down Ronald Reagan and Margaret Thatcher in debate about how best to deal with the Soviet Union, the man who "branded" Canada as a bilingual and multicultural society, the leader who told us that we could create a just, participatory society through a generous and activist state: he is the idealized model of what Canadians (at least English-speaking Canadians) like to think they are. The point here is the simple affirmation of fact that we the Canadian people—those of us who loved him and those of us who hated him, those who criticized him and those who fantasized about him—responded to his aura and projected it back onto him not just then at the time, but repeatedly afterwards till death has parted him from us, whether the "us" be his fellow travellers, his political children, or his virtual offspring from neoliberal Canada.

In Political Afterlife

The question remains, even if his legacy is remembered, why does he *still* fascinate us? Why, in other words, has there been political life for Pierre Trudeau after the political death that retirement from politics represents for most politicians? Consider that for several years he has been in physical decline, no longer dating the glamorous, sporting an extravagant hat or a cowboy suit. On the rare occasions when he has been photographed recently, he appeared somewhat smaller than life, frail, even reclusive.

The answer lies in something completely unique about the biography of Pierre Trudeau. We know that it was unusual for a man of ideas to go into politics in Canada and be successful. Many an idealistic intellectual has ventured onto the political field only to come to grief. But as a young man Trudeau took until his forties to work out his ideas, clarifying his analysis, writing the script for his own starring role.

Having developed that script, Trudeau entered politics and played the part, considering the camera angles, improvising on occasion, rewriting the lines when they no longer suited his purposes, but dominating the stage, making sure that the play went on and in the direction that he wanted. This was highly unusual, putting him in the ranks of statesmen like Winston Churchill and Charles de Gaulle—those who thought, wrote, and were then able to act in consequence.

But what makes Trudeau unique in modern politics is his political afterlife, his capacity to withdraw from politics while remaining poised to reenter and do battle for the ideas to which he clung, fighting not for votes but for principles, with words that still evoked powerful responses from his public. His interventions during the public debate surrounding the Meech Lake Accord turned the tide that eventually brought Mulroney's first constitutional deal to its knees in 1990. His single speech in an obscure Montreal restaurant two years later on the Charlottetown Accord immediately swayed 20 percent of the vote outside Quebec against the deal.

In Ron Graham's selections from Trudeau's writings, published in 1998, what was interesting was less *The Essential Trudeau*'s conscious modeling on Pascal's *Pensées* (the grandiosity was not new) than the italicized postscripts the former prime minister inserted throughout the text as addenda and errata to his earlier statements. To use a phrase popular among scholars of literature, Trudeau was practising intertextuality: he was dealing with other writings in his text — but the intertextuality was with his own earlier work. He was getting the last word once again, by selecting out the self-contradictory passages we were not meant to remember, expanding on others, and revising lines that he felt needed correcting. His definition of democracy as government by majorities of 50 percent, for instance, got corrected in italics to make exceptions for some decisions (such as the next Quebec referendum?) which should be made by majorities greater than 50 percent plus one vote.

Trudeau may not have been very visible in the daily headlines in the last years of his decline, but he, more than Ron Graham, or his great friend and editor, the late Gérard Pelletier, or his longtime Boswell, Tom Axworthy, was the keeper of his own intellectual heritage. In newsrooms all over the English-speaking world, the obituary writers were kept on edge by his refusal to lie down and let their last draft be the final one.

Charisma *is* circular. We projected onto him our longings and our hope, but he remained the keeper of his faith, the maker of his image, the guardian of his orthodoxy. For sixteen more years he remained charismatic, because he still surprised, he still insisted, he still compelled, he still wielded moral power, he was still the one who defined his Truth.

The Future of Trudeau's Past

The last question to address is why is the present interest in Trudeau's death far more intense than that of any other prime minister? The present tense nostalgia for him may have more to do with the future than the past because of a deep transformation taking place in our political economy, one that is connected both to developments at home and changes abroad.

On the international scene we are experiencing a crisis in the world's political economy. If global financial markets are out of control and the nation-state is scrambling to reassert its authority over its economic frontiers, do we not need some notion of what that state should be? If this is the case, should we not turn back to the era during which the Canadian nation-state reached its highest level of development — that is, to the era that bears Trudeau's name?

Internally, too, there is a sense of crisis in the air, but this time the crisis is in the neoliberal paradigm. The mean state — the one that takes unemployment insurance premiums from workers and uses it to pay off the national debt, the one that cuts education budgets and then blames teachers for the crisis of the school system — is failing. Whether at the federal or provincial levels, the public can contrast neoliberalism rhetoric of progress and prosperity with the reality of emergency room delays and contaminated water systems. If a sullen electorate is reflecting these days with nostalgia on a nobler, more optimistic vision of society, this has something to do with the land mines that Pierre Trudeau and his colleagues had planted in Ottawa's culture and the Canadian psyche. By having defended the *Canada Health Act* to the end, they convinced Canadians that high-quality public medical services were as central to their identity as the canoe and bilingualism.

So we look back from a postmodern, post-sovereign, post-national, post-Keynesian regime — albeit one that is led by a pre-modern prime minister — at a time when globalization has reached a watershed, when neoliberalism has failed to deliver peace, order, and good government, let alone prevent greater disparities and deeper despairs. None of its predictions has proven out, yet the destructive capacities of the market are everywhere evident.

It may be true that Mackenzie King was the one who introduced Keynes to Canadian macroeconomic policy. It may be true that John Diefenbaker was the first to champion the entrenchment of individual rights in the Constitution. It may be true that Lester Pearson did more than all the others to build the welfare state in Canada. But it is Trudeau with whom we identify the state at its apogee. And it is Trudeau who articulated a conceptualization of the state's relationship to society and the individual in coherent, cutting prose which, notwithstanding all its contradictions, still sparkles with lucidity.

Nothing here is fixed. Opinions change. Former critics have become apologists. Old allies have become critics. Different generations select out different parts of his opus for praise or blame. The material is rich, provocative, arresting, and, however contradictory in its multiple versions and realities, we are able to select, turning Pierre Elliott Trudeau in his life, his work, and his writings into a giant set of Rorschach ink blots from which each of us determines the pattern we want to find.

Some maintain that today's Canada is Trudeau's Canada. They cit the familiar list — patriation, the *Charter*, bilingualism, French power in Ottawa, equality of the provinces, multiculturalism, Canada as exemplar to the world.

I beg to differ. Against these markers of the Trudeau era I would put a government constrained from outside by such new trade treaties as NAFTA and the WTO and constrained from inside by its own shift to neoliberal small government. Today's Canada is decreasingly bilingual. Under the Social Union Agreement, Quebec is treated not equally with the other provinces, but distinctly. The Canadian state has been truncated by privatizing the major crown corporations, deregulating transportation, cutting back the cultural agencies, getting out of the business of managing the economy. And it faces the strong possibility of Quebec seceding from the federation.

The issue here is not whether today's Canada is Trudeau's, but whether tomorrow's Canada should be. Some might respond that surely the Trudeau paradigm is passé; it cannot be reestablished by turning back the clock three decades. This objection loses its power once we remember that the paradigm on which neoliberalism is modelled required turning back the clock a whole century.

Those who want to take the "neo-" out of Canadian neoliberalism, now that surpluses have replaced deficits on the public agenda, need to decide which elements of Trudeau's multifaceted and contradictory theory and practice they would resurrect. Of his liberalism, do they want his social, state-centred thrust or his private, individual-rights approach? Of his nationalism, do they feel it is his appeal to patriotic pride on the basis of a bilingual identity that needs reaffirming or is it a nationalism based on achieving some basic economic autonomy? Of his federalism, is it federal leadership or federal passivity? Of his economic management, is it his monetarism or his Keynesianism? Of his leadership model, is it his conservatism that denied that the state could play Santa Claus or his belief in a strong and active state?

The legacy is rich, but for all his attempts to watch over his orthodoxy, there is no consistency. If there are lessons to be culled from the Trudeau past for our future, it is all three generations of people who participated in his charisma who will have to do the hard work.

They will, of course, have to do this without his help. When I had an intense discussion with him not long before his death, it was clear the Pierre Trudeau's views in old age had returned to those more consistently radical positions he had adopted in his younger years. He was dismayed that global capitalism was escaping control by governments, thanks to trade liberalizing agreements like NAFTA. He deplored the social polarization resulting from deficit cutting. If his charisma persists beyond the grave in our consciousness the way he would like it to, it will be as the champion of justice and democracy, of social equality and national integrity.

But it is his survivors who will have to decide. This will not be an easy task. To rework the much-plagiarized opening sentence of the first volume of *Trudeau and Our Times, The Magnificent Obsession*, let me observe by way of warning and conclusion: "He daunts us still."

Contributors

Carl Berger teaches in the Department of History at the University of Toronto.

Nancy B. Bouchier teaches sport history in the faculty of Kinesiology at McMaster University.

Bettina Bradbury teaches in the History Department at York University and in Women's Studies, Glendon College, York University.

Craig Brown teaches Canadian history at the University of Toronto.

Sarah Carter teaches Canadian history at the University of Calgary.

Stephen Clarkson is a professor of political economy at the University of Toronto.

John Dales has retired from the Department of Political Economy at the University of Toronto.

Stephen Davies teaches in the Department of History at the University of Ottawa.

Peter DeLottinville is an archivist at the National Archives of Canada in Ottawa.

René Durocher is the Administrator in the Department of Arts and Science at the Université de Montréal.

James Eayrs has retired from the Political Science Department at Dalhousie University in Halifax.

E.R. Forbes is a professor of history at the University of New Brunswick in Fredericton.

J.L. Granatstein has retired from the Department of History at York University in Toronto.

Sandra Gwyn (1935–2000) taught history at the University of Ottawa.

Anthony Hall teaches in the Department of Native American Studies at the University of Lethbridge.

Richard Jones teaches Canadian history at Université Laval.

Will Kymlicka is visiting professor of philosophy at the University of Ottawa and Carleton University.

David Lee is a historian with Historical Services Branch, National Historic Sites Directorate, Parks Canada, Canadian Heritage in Hull, Quebec.

Joseph Levitt (1920–1995) taught history at the University of Ottawa.

Paul-André Linteau is a professor of history at the Université du Québec à Montréal.

Hector Mackenzie is senior department historian in the Department of Foreign Affairs and International Trade in Ottawa.

J.R. Miller is a professor of Canadian history at the University of Saskatchewan in Saskatoon.

Wendy Mitchinson teaches Canadian history at the University of Waterloo.

Desmond Morton has retired as the Director, McGill Institute for the Study of Canada.

Howard Palmer (1946–1991) taught Canadian history at the University of Calgary.

Jennifer Read is a research associate at the Great Lakes Institute for Environmental Research at the University of Windsor.

Jean-Claude Robert is a professor of history at the Université du Québec à Montréal.

Jacques Rouillard is a professor of history at the Université de Montréal.

Peter H. Russell is retired from the Department of Political Economy at the University of Toronto.

A. Blair Stonechild is Executive Director, Planning and Development, Saskatchewan Indian Federated College, Regina.

Veronica Strong-Boag is the Director of the Centre for Research in Women's Studies and Gender Relations at the University of British Columbia in Vancouver.

James Struthers teaches history and Canadian studies at Trent University in Peterborough, Ontario.

John Herd Thompson is a professor of history at Duke University in Durham, North Carolina.

W. Peter Ward is a professor of history at the University of British Columbia in Vancouver.

Nelson Wiseman teaches political science at Queen's University in Kingston, Ontario.

Photo Credits

Topic One
B.C. Archives/D-01441

Topic Two
National Archives of Canada/C-11583

Topic Three
Saskatchewan Archives Board/R-B714

Topic Four
National Library of Canada/C-050366

Topic Five
National Archives of Canada/C-047042

Topic Six
Archives of Ontario/C 7-3

Topic Seven
McCord Museum, Montreal; Notman
Photographic Archives/N-0000.94.56

Topic Eight
Toronto Reference Library TPL: T 16875

Topic Nine
National Archives of Canada/PA-000568

Topic Ten
National Archives of Canada/PA-036089

Topic Eleven
National Archives of Canada/PA-036089

Topic Twelve
National Archives of Canada/C-018532

Topic Thirteen
Courtesy of Chatelaine magazine © Rogers
Publishing Ltd. Used by permission of the
photographer, Paul Rockett

Topic Fourteen
Southam Inc./Montreal Gazette/ National
Archives of Canada / PA-136677

Topic Fifteen
Duncan Cameron/National Archives of
Canada/PA-111214

Index

health sector in, 446
immigrants in, 456–57, 460
independence of, 449, 456
industrialization in, 444
labour movement in, 444, 451
language legislation in, 458–60
Legislative Council in, 446
liberalism in, 444
Liberal party in, 445–48, 457, 459–60, 462
mass media in, 444
middle class in, 444, 455
nationalism in, 445, 448–51, 456
nationalization of electrical utilities, 447
protectionism and, 37
referendums, 462, 483
residential schools in, 137
secularization of, 444
separation and, 449, 451
social security in, 447
sovereignty-association, 457, 462
state intervention in, 444, 446, 448, 451
as state *vs.* province, 449
Trudeau and, 492, 494
urbanization of, 443
urban population, 156–57, 158 (table)
World War II and, 444
Quebec Act of 1774, 41
Quebec and Lake St. John Railway, 161
Quebec City
ethnic composition, 161
French in, 161
history, 155–56
industry, 160, 161
Irish in, 157, 161
population, 160, 161
railway system, 160–61
transportation systems and, 160–61
Quebec Pension Plan, 447
Quebec Resolutions, 22, 30
Queen's counsel, 23
Quiet Revolution, 440, 443–51, 455–56
Quinn, Jane, 80, 81, 88
Quinn, Thomas, 68, 69, 80
Quinney, Charles and Mrs., 82, 85

Race, 91n.3
Racette, Damase and Rachel, 184
Rae (Indian agent), 66
Railway Brotherhoods, 303
Railways, 9, 37
automobiles and, 172n.16
in the Maritimes, 300–302, 303
Montreal and, 156, 158–59
National policy and, 4–5, 6–7, 16–17n.1
on Prince Edward Island, 304
Quebec City and, 156
subsidies for, 12, 16n.1

tariff and, 9
transcontinental, 36
Western settlement and, 9, 10
Raymond, Maxime, 353
Reciprocity, 5
Reconstruction, postwar, 365, 367, 371
Recorder's Court, 198–99
Red Crow's reserve, 136
Red Pheasant, Chief, 67
Red River carts, 49
Red River Settlement, 78
Reed, Hayter, 73–74, 133
Reformers
in sport, 236–37, 239, 246
on the waterfront area, 205–206, 210
Reform party, 284, 299
Refugees, political, 126
Regina Industrial School, 142
Reid, Escott, 327, 364
Reilly, Phil, 427
Reisman, Simon, 491
Relief, 310–11
camps, 313
federal *vs.* provincial/local responsibility, 312, 313–14, 316, 317–18
immigrants on, 124
projects, 311–12
residency requirements, 312
standard of living on, 316
standards for, 313
unemployment, 310, 311
Western provinces and, 313, 314–15
work ethic and, 318
Religion. *See also* Catholic Church
social-class formation and, 253n.55
Reservation power, 23, 24, 29
Reserves, 477, 478
residential schools' proximity to, 139
Residential schools
attendance, 137–38
competition among, 141
distribution of, 137
funding, 141
Indian control over, 140–41
Indian culture in, 138–39
Indian languages in, 138–39
parents' involvement in, 139, 140, 141, 142
proximity to reserves, 139
recruiting of students, 141–42
runaways from, 139–40
violence at, 141
Responsible government, 4, 22–23
Restrictionism, 118
Rhythm method, of contraception, 226
Riddell, W.A., 352
Riel, Louis, 23, 24, 37, 51–52, 52, 56, 65, 66, 78, 88, 90, 477